GREAT **IRISH** PEOPLE

Overleaf: Sheep Haven, Donegal.

Samuel Beckett Bridge, Dublin.

GREAT
IRISH
PEOPLE

SEAMUS MORAN

LIB
ERT
IES

First published in 2013 by
Liberties Press
140 Terenure Road North | Terenure | Dublin 6W
Tel: +353 (1) 405 5703
www.libertiespress.com | info@libertiespress.com

Trade enquiries to Gill & Macmillan Distribution
Hume Avenue | Park West | Dublin 12
Tel: +353 (1) 500 9534 | Fax: +353 (1) 500 9595
sales@gillmacmillan.ie

Distributed in the UK by
Turnaround Publisher Services
Unit 3 | Olympia Trading Estate | Coburg Road | London N22 6TZ
T: +44 (0) 20 8829 3000 | E: orders@turnaround-uk.com

Distributed in the United States by
Dufour Editions | PO Box 7 | Chester Springs
| Pennsylvania | 19425

Copyright © Seamus Moran, 2013
The author has asserted his moral rights.
ISBN: 978-1-907593-28-4

A CIP record for this title is available from the British Library.
Cover and internal design by www.sinedesign.net
Printed by Nicholson & Bass Ltd.

Previous:
Mother with son enjoying
Slea Head Beach,
Dingle Peninsula.

County Anthems and Populations 2011

Antrim 566,000 'The Green Glens of Antrim'

Armagh 141,585 'The Boys from the County Armagh'

Carlow 54,532 'Follow me up to Carlow'

Cavan 72,874 'Come back Paddy Reilly'

Clare 116,885 'My Lovely Rose of Clare'

Cork 518,128 'Banks of my own Lovely Lee'

Derry 213,035 'The Town I Love so Well'

Donegal 160,927 'Mary from Dungloe'

Down 454,411 'The Star of the County Down'

Dublin 1,270,603 'Molly Malone'

Fermanagh 54,033 'Farewell to Enniskillen'

Galway 250,541 'The Fields of Athenry'

Kerry 145,048 'The Rose of Tralee'

Kildare 209,955 'Curragh of Kildare'

Kilkenny 95,380 'The Rose of Mooncoyn'

Laois 80,458 'Lovely Laois'

Leitrim 31,778 'Lovely Leitrim'

Limerick 191,306 'Limerick you're a Lady'

Longford 38,970 'County Longford'

Louth 122,808 'Turfman from Ardee'

Mayo 130,552 'Moonlight in Mayo'

Meath 184,034 'Beautiful Meath'

Monaghan 60,495 'The Town of Ballybay'

Offaly 76,806 'Offaly Rover'

Roscommon 63,896 'Men of Roscommon'

Sligo 65,270 'Sally Gardens'

Tipperary 158,652 'Slievenamon'

Tyrone 166,516 'O'Neill's March'

Waterford 113,707 'Waterford my Home'

Westmeath 85,961 'Lough Ree, Oh Lough Ree'

Wexford 145,273 'Boolavogue'

Wicklow 136,448 'Among the Wicklow Hills'

During the Irish Civil War in 1922, the Four Courts Buildings in Dublin were destroyed by fire and as a consequence, few records exist for Ireland in respect to population numbers prior to that date. Furthermore, the population in Ireland in 1841, taken from the British Census, cannot be 100 percent accurate, being calculated on the number of baptisms, burials, and marriages. However, it is generally accepted that the population of Ireland in the early 1840s, was in the region of 8,200,000. The arrival in 1845 of the potato blight resulted in one of the worst famines ever seen in the western world. In the five years following, some 1 million people died and a further 1 million emigrated to America. To date, the population of Ireland has never recovered to its original figures and now stands at 4,125,000 for the Republic of Ireland and 1,710,000 for Northern Ireland, making a grand total of 5,835,300.

Two traditional Irish women and the harp of erin. Engraving from 1855, by D Walker.

Foreword

I am honoured to have been asked to write a few words as a foreword to this remarkable book. It is a handsome volume that will not only decorate a coffee table, but provide a fascinating repository of information into which anyone interested in Ireland and its history, but most particularly those of Irish descent, may profitably dip.

It is the handiwork of Seamus Moran who himself has had a most interesting and varied career, which included architecture, building, fast-food businesses and a variety of other jobs. Officially retired, it seems unlikely that he will ever finally do so. It is his relentless curiosity and interest in the byways of life that has driven him to produce this unique volume.

Great Irish People is beautifully illustrated by two talented Argentinian artists who are in fact, a father and son team. Between them, they have provided an astonishing nine hundred portraits to accompany more than a thousand biographical entries and this gives an additional human flavour to the text.

The book, as the name suggests, is about Irish people who made a difference. There is no doubt, based on the evidence of this work, that they certainly did so, affecting change throughout Europe, North and South America and many other parts of the world including their own country. The many-faceted talents of the Irish are very well represented here and would make any patriotic Irish person feel proud of the intellectual and cultural gifts historically revealed. The contribution made by Irish people on a global basis through science, the arts, politics, literature and the environment has been disproportionate to the small size of the island. The fact that the material is arranged on a county-by-county basis, throughout the entire thirty-two counties of Ireland, will probably lead those with particular associations to select first their own county, and they may well be surprised by the colourful characters that have shared their place of origin.

Out of so many entries it would be invidious and parochial to select individual characters for comment. However, one observation must be made and that is the extraordinary number of Irishmen from virtually every county who have been awarded the Victoria Cross — the highest award for gallantry in the British Empire.

This is a book that, in the words of a great Tudor divine, 'One can read, mark, learn and inwardly digest' with considerable profit. It is guaranteed to give many hours of pleasure.

David Norris

A Victoria Cross.

The scales of Repeal. Daniel O'Connell, M.P., (1775-1847),
against Sir Robert Peel,(1788-1880), Arthur Wellesley,
1st Duke of Wellington, (1769-1852), and others.

Introduction

The timescale in producing this county-by-county dictionary of Irish biography spans twenty-five years, although it was not, I might add, a continuous work. A compendium such as this is subject to innumerable stops and starts, and rushes of enthusiasm. It was a curiosity fed, from time to time, by the deeds and actions of Irish men and women, gleaned from various publications, that spurred me on to my end goal with a target of in excess of one thousand characters, and portraits of as many of those as possible.

The catalyst that set me on this venture was a love of history and an admiration for the deeds of my fellow Irish men and women. Prior to commencing in 1982, I contacted Henry Boylan to seek his advice on my idea of a county-by-county dictionary of Irish biography. Boylan, who produced his own excellent *Dictionary of Irish Biography* in 1978, which is now in its third edition and available from Gill and MacMillian, was most helpful and encouraging and he duly emphasised the arduous journey upon which I was preparing to embark. His words have rung true on many occasions down the last quarter of a century or so. At the time of my discussions with Boylan, I decided that only deceased persons would appear in the biography and I requested from him a photograph of himself for entry at some later date down the long road ahead. Henry forwarded to me, a photograph of himself adding, 'As you have to be deceased to qualify for entry, please don't be in any hurry to complete the task.' Henry went to his just reward in 2006 and appears under County Louth in this dictionary of Irish biography. To me, he was most obliging, encouraging and inspirational in my endeavours.

On commencement, two major decisions had to be made; the first, from what date in history to commence, and the second, who to include. The date I chose was from 'The Flight of the Earls' in 1607, a reasonably recent date in historical terms but a most definitive one in the history of Ireland, and indeed the world. This was followed by the plantation of Ulster, and with it perhaps the most dramatic four centuries in the country's history, which culminated in the 1998 Good Friday Agreement, with Irish nationalists and Irish unionists together setting the foundations for a brighter future for all in this 'little island'. In the context of the world, this period witnessed the demise of the colonial powers and the establishment of multiple nations, including the greatest one of all, the United States, with innumerable Irish men and women contributing to their march to nationhood.

The second choice of who to include was a most difficult one, as the 'reservoir' of Irish men and women of merit and achievement is indeed extensive. The decision on it being a county-by-county dictionary of biography brought it to a more local, and thereby a more critical level, where the omission of a character of note in any particular county is more readily noticed. Whilst the entries are my personal choice, I have endeavoured to include the most important, interesting and varied. I acknowledge that there is going to be some important ones that I have omitted, which is inevitable when the research is solely the work of one person. I wish to assure the reader when I am advised of such omissions, as I most definitely will be, they will be noted for entry in future editions. I sincerely hope that the reader from any of the thirty-two counties of Ireland, when first opening the pages of their respective counties, will find the entries interesting and educational, take pride in the achievements of their fellow county men and women and on surveying the overall dictionary of biography, further enhance that pride with the endeavours and achievements of their fellow country men and women.

To the 40 million Irish people living in America and the other millions scattered throughout the globe, *Great Irish People* affords the opportunity for them to survey the achievements of their ancestors and to fully grasp the immensity of Irish contributions, whether spectacular, bizarre or amazing, throughout the world.

Indeed, in light of the immense contributions made by the Irish diaspora, I felt that to omit people such as Éamon de Valera, born in the United States; James Connolly, born in Scotland; Robert Erskin Childers, born in England; Terence O'Neill, born in London, and many others, would be a travesty. Accordingly, I have included a section dedicated to those persons born outside of Ireland to allow for their inclusion.

I decided that portraits of as many of the entrants as possible was a must, as we equate better with the life of a person when we can perceive their image. This addition to *Great Irish People*, whilst seeming simple at the time, added considerable extra work in its compilation and the research taken in acquiring images was vast, particularly at the beginning, prior to the advent of internet search engines, which simplified the effort in later years. The library of images that I gathered from newspapers, periodicals, magazines and more was extensive and has proved invaluable, as it comprises a considerable number of images as yet not available online.

The task of finding an artist capable of producing first class portraits from, in many cases, very poor quality photographs or newspaper and magazine cuttings, was solved when I moved to Spain in 2002 and met art professor Gabriel Enrique Nevarre, and later his son, Diego G. Navarre, two first class portrait artists.

The selection of entrants in this dictionary of biography, while personal, is what I felt would be of interest to the reader, due to the effects the various individuals had on our history and the history of nations throughout the world. In some instances, like Vincent 'Mad Dog' Coll (Donegal), or May Duignan (Longford), their endeavours were ultimately self-serving, but their inclusions certainly add a variant between the ordinary and the extraordinary.

To the question, 'is one Irish man or woman more Irish than the next, or more deserving of entry because he or she was a staunch nationalist, or perhaps less deserving because he or she was a devout unionist?' Such are the cases of George Stuart White, Victoria Cross winner, Knight of the Realm and British field marshal who was born in County Derry, and that of his son, Captain Jack White, DSO, born in County Antrim, co-founder of the Irish Citizen Army with James Connolly, an arch republican, and anarchist. The answer is simply 'no'. The flag that they served under does not matter, to whom they gave their allegience does not matter, for whom the deed was done does not matter. What does matter is that they were all Irish, Irish men and women; whether in politics, battle, the sciences, the literary world, as sportsmen, in the theatre or the arts, their efforts and contributions were indeed immense, and what they accomplished has helped shape the history of Ireland and the world.

> Whilst we may judge the dooer, or the deed
> From a different perspective,
> Judge not the deed or the dooer,
> But the belief, sincerity and effort
> Of the dooer, in achieving the deed
> *Seamus Moran*

Island of Inishfanard, Kenmare. (an emigration incident), by Cole, Charles William., fl. 1880–1905.

Galway Bay.

Author's Biography

Seamus Moran was born in 1936 in Ballinasloe, County Galway. He was educated at St Mary's College in Dundalk, County Louth, and later attended H.S.B. in London, where he studied architecture, before practicing for three years with Sutcliffe, Taylor and Partners of Manchester Square, London. In the early 1960s he entered the commercial side of the building industry, becoming a site surveyor for Terrapin Buildings in Buckinghamshire.

Having returned to Ireland in 1966, he became managing director of Cedarworth Homes (Ireland) Ltd, and in 1972 he formed the Bunratty Construction Company with extensive developments in Limerick. With the downturn in the building industry during the late 1970s and early 1980s, he diverted his interests to fast-food restaurants, under the KFC brand, with outlets in Waterford, Clonmel and Rathmines, Dublin.

In the early 1990s he added to his business portfolio, opening a bar and nightclub in Waterford City and in 2002, with retirement in mind, he went to live in Spain, where he purchased two leisure complexes on the Costa Blanca. With his sons operating the business and a retirement of sorts, Seamus's new found freedom allowed him the opportunity to complete his dictionary of Irish biography. A knowledgeable Irish historian, he has written a film script on the life of Thomas Francis Meagher, and a memoir, *As I Recall It*.

A keen sportman in his day, Seamus played senior rugby with Bohemians Rugby Football Club, Limerick into his thirty-sixth year. He is married to wife Vera (née Gillespie) for fifty-five years, with three sons; Brendan, Paul and Gerald and one daughter, Corinne.

Seamus Moran

Artist's Biography

All portraits and montages in the book are the work of Argentinian artists Gabriel Enrique Navarre and his son Diego G. Navarre. Gabriel Enrique originally studied in Buenos Aires, under world-renowned Argentinian artist, Vincente Puig. He later moved to Alicante, Spain to take up a position as a professor of art at the La Escuela Superior De Bellas Artes. Diego G. Navarre studied at the college under the tutorage of his father, and specialising in portrait painting, they have both exhibited their works extensively throughout Spain, the US and Argentina. An extremely gifted artist, Diego is the third generation of artists in the Navarre family.

Gabriel Enrique Navarre

Diego G. Navarre

Antrim

William Drennan
1754-1820

Patriot William Drennan
gave Ireland the name
'The Emerald Isle'.

THE
EMERALD
ISLE

LET NO FEELING
OF VENGEANCE
PRESUME TO DEFILE
THE CAUSE OF OR MEN OF
THE EMERALD ISLE

William Mulholland
1855-1935

The Mulholland Memorial Fountains in Los
Angeles, California and Mulholland drive
are dedicated to the memory of William
Mulholland, builder of the Los Angeles
water system – a major nineteenth-century
development.

John Joseph Linn
1798-1885

Freedom fighter John Joseph Linn is a significant figure in the history of Texas.

Alexander Turney Stewart
1803-1876

The Marble Palace, 280 Broadway, New York, America's first department store, was built by Alexander Turney Stewart.

Francis Fowke
1823-1865

The National Gallery of Ireland in Dublin, one of Francis Fowke's many designs.

Robert Adrain
Mathematician 1775 – 1843

A self-taught mathematician, Robert Adrain's curiosity led him to the study of algebraic notations. On the death of his parents, he supported his four brothers and sisters by undertaking work as a teacher but was subsequently involved in the Irish Rebellion of 1798. Following its failure, Adrain emigrated with his wife to the United States of America, where he settled in New Jersey. In 1807, he was appointed editor of the Mathematical Correspondent, the first mathematical journal in the US. One of his first papers featured in the publication concerned the steering of a ship and Diophantine algebra (the study of rational solutions to polynomial equations). This was followed by an influential paper on the normal law of errors, published one year before Gauss in 1808, as well as a book in 1818 entitled *Investigation of the Figure of the Earth, and of the Gravity in different Latitudes*. At this time he was considered one of only two mathematicians capable of work of an international standing in the whole of the US, the other being Nathaniel Bowditch. Adrain gained further academic distinction as professor of mathematics at the University of Pennsylvania in 1827.

Thomas Andrews
Chemist 1813 – 1885

Thomas Andrews was born in Belfast, and was educated at the Royal Belfast Academical Institution, following which he entered the University of Glasgow in 1828 to read chemistry. He later studied at Trinity College, Dublin and was awarded a doctorate in medicine at the University of Edinburgh in 1835. Ten years later, Andrews was appointed professor of chemistry at Queen's University, Belfast. An outstanding experimental chemist, he was the first person to show that ozone is a form of oxygen and his experimentation with gases led to the discovery that all gases could be liquefied. An internationally acclaimed scientist, Andrews received a multitude of academic awards and became president of the British Association for the Advancement of Science in 1867. He died on 26 November 1885.

James Brown Armour; Armour of Ballymoney
Presbyterian minister and nationalist
1841 – 1928

Educated at Ballymoney Model School and Queen's University, Belfast, James Brown Armour was appointed minister at Ballymoney in 1869 and was a political radical, representing the extremity of Presbyterian liberalism.

Armour, who condemned landlordism and was a supporter of the Tenant Rights Movement, was also a staunch supporter of British prime minister Gladstone and Home Rule for Ireland. At the Presbyterian church assembly in 1912, when moving an amendment to limit the anti-home rule element in the Presbyterian consensus, he said: 'If you deny the right of private judgment and of free speech, how much do you keep of Protestantism which would be worth keeping? Nothing at all'. An enemy of sectarianism and a partitioned Ireland, Armour's comments at the time placed him in a small minority of Ulster Presbyterians. He retired from his clerical duties in September, 1925, and died on 25 January 1928. A biography, written by his son, W. S. Armour in 1934, is called, *Armour of Ballymoney*.

John Ballance
Premier of New Zealand 1839 – 1893

John Ballance was born in Glenavy, County Antrim and was educated at Glenavy National School and Wilson's Academy, Belfast. He immigrated to New Zealand in 1866, where he became a journalist and editor, founding the Wanganui Herald newspaper. Ballance served in the Māori Wars of 1867, and in 1875 entered parliament, beginning a political career that would eventually lead him to the office of premier of New Zealand in 1891. He was a radical and forward-looking politician, favouring votes for women, land reform, and the introduction of the world's first welfare state. A statue in honour of his memory stands outside the parliamentary library in Wellington, New Zealand. Throughout a distinguished political career, Ballance was described as 'an unassuming, unpretentious, quiet and patient man.'

James M. Bell
Medal of Honour winner 1845 – 1901

Awarded the Congressional Medal of Honour for services he rendered during the Indian Wars, James M. Bell served as a private in Company E, 7th US Infantry, at the Battle of the Little Bighorn on 9 July 1876. His Medal of Honour citation reads: 'He carried dispatches to General Cooke at imminent risk of his life'. Later Bell served as a sergeant in the United States Army. He is buried in Mount Olivet Cemetery in Cooke County, Chicago.

John Stewart Bell
Mathematician 1928 – 1990

John Stewart Bell is considered to have breathed new life into the foundations of quantum theory. He was the originator of Bell's Theorem, one of the most important theorems in quantum physics, which states, 'no physical theory of local hidden variables can ever reproduce all of the predictions of quantum mechanics'. Having studied at the Technical High School, Belfast he gained entry to Queen's University. His subsequent work in the field of quantum theory led to him becoming a fellow of the Royal Society in 1972. Later in life, he was awarded the Hughes Medal of the Royal Society, the Dirac Medal of the Institute of Physics, and the Heineman Prize of the American Physical Society. In 1988 Bell received honorary degrees from both Queen's University, Belfast, and Trinity College, Dublin. He died suddenly on 1 October 1990.

George Best
Footballer 1946 – 2005

A truly legendary footballer, George Best was sometimes referred to as 'the fifth Beatle' due to his long hair and good looks. Best was a phenomenally talented player who played for Manchester United from 1963 until 1973, making some 361 appearances in all. He was capped for Northern Ireland on thirty-seven occasions, becoming European player of the year in 1968 and throughout the world he was renowned for his blistering acceleration and ability to seemingly dance around entire defences. Best, who was undoubtedly one of the greatest footballers the world has ever seen, led an abbreviated career due to his extravagant lifestyle off the playing-field. Sadly, it was this lifestyle that eventually led to his addiction to alcohol, which in turn resulted in him requiring a liver transplant in 2002. Following that serious medical procedure, Best found it increasingly difficult to abstain from alcohol and it eventually led to his death on 25 November 2005. He was just fifty-nine years of age. Approximately half a million people lined the streets of Belfast when the sport star was laid to rest.

23

Francis Joseph Biggar
Lawyer, historian and nationalist
1863 – 1926

The seventh son of a seventh son, Francis Joseph Biggar's home on the Antrim Road became a meeting place for Irish cultural enthusiasts. Educated at the Royal Belfast Academical Institution, he later studied law at Trinity College, Dublin, following which he established a busy legal practice in Belfast. Biggar was the editor of the Ulster Journal of Archaeology and corresponded with scholars from all over the world on all aspects of Irish history and culture. His compilation of writings and letters, held in the Central Library in Belfast, represent one of the most significant local history collections in the library. So endeared was he to all aspects of Irish culture, he spent a considerable amount of his own money restoring castles, churches, crosses and monuments; even having the remains of Henry Joy McCracken reinterred in the McCracken family plot. The most ambitious of Biggar's projects was the renovation in 1910 of Jordan's Tower at Ardglass, which was renamed Castle Shane. An extraordinary man, Biggar was a preserver of all things Irish and is remembered for his extensive contribution to the creative talents and endeavours of Irish poets, artists, musicians, and playwrights. He died in December 1926.

Lilian Bland
The first woman in the world to design, construct and fly a plane
1878 – 1971

The 'tomboy' granddaughter of the dean of Belfast, as a young woman Lilian Bland always wore trousers, smoked cigarettes and tinkered with car engines. In her early twenties she worked as both a sports journalist and a photographer but in 1910, decided to build her own bi-plane, which she named the *Mayfly*, (a play on her belief that it may fly). Initially, the aircraft was built with an under-powered engine but upon securing a 20 horsepower 2-stroke engine, the *Mayfly* finally achieved lift-off from Lord O'Neill's park in Randalstown, County Antrim. It was an event which rendered Bland the first woman in the world to build and fly her own plane but her father, fearing for her safety, brought her aviation career to an end. She emigrated to Canada in 1912 where she married a cousin and became involved in farming. Bland retired to Cornwall, England in 1935, where, in her own words, she lived a life of 'gambling, painting, and gardening'. A historical plaque in her memory is located on the site of Templecorran House, Carnmoney – the place of her birth.

Ernest Blythe
Politician 1889 – 1975

After spending his early years near Lisburn, County Antrim, Ernest Blythe went to Dublin at the age of fifteen where he became a proficient speaker of the Irish language. It is reputed that Seán O'Casey (see page 184) encouraged him to join the Irish Republican Brotherhood and he later enlisted in the Irish Volunteer Movement, which lead to him being imprisoned on multiple occasions for his involvement. In 1918 Blythe was elected to the Dáil where he later served under W. T. Cosgrave as minister for finance. Blythe retired from politics in 1936 and devoted his time thereafter to the revival of the Irish language. He was managing director of the Abbey Theatre from 1939 until 1967, and in 1957 published an autobiographical account of his early life. He died in Dublin on 23 February 1975.

Alexander Brown
Founder of the first invesment bank in the United States 1764 – 1834

Successful in the linen business, Ballymena native Alexander Brown immigrated to the United States in 1800 and settled in Baltimore, where he began importing linen from Ulster. He later expanded his business interests into sterling exchange and international trade in tobacco and cotton, and did so complete with his own fleet of ships. His company became known as Alex Brown and Sons, Inc. and in the early 1820s he established the first investment bank in the United States – Alex Brown and Sons. At the time of his death, Brown was estimated to be worth two million dollars, being one of the first millionaires in the United States. The firm was acquired by Deutsche Bank in 1999.

James Bryce 1st Viscount Bryce
Politician and historian 1838 – 1922

James Bryce was regius professor of civil law in Oxford from 1870 until 1893 and authored a variety of history books, one of which was entitled The American Commonwealth. Published in 1888, the book is considered a classic from a historical and constitutional law perspective. A firm supporter of Gladstone's policy on home rule for Ireland, Bryce was a Liberal Party MP for East London, and in 1905 was appointed Chief Secretary of Ireland. Two years later, he was appointed to the role of British Ambassador to Washington and became a firm friend of Theodore Roosevelt, the US president at that time. Bryce also had a significant hand in the formation of the League of Nations, and was the recipient of the Order of Merit along with honourary degrees from some thirty-one universities. He died on 22 June 1922, in Sidmouth, Devon, England.

Joe Cahill
Irish republican 1920 – 2004

Following his education, West Belfast-born Joe Cahill entered his father's printing business and in 1938 joined the Irish Republican Army in Belfast. In 1942, Cahill was sentenced to death for the killing of a police officer during the Northern Campaign but his sentence was subsequently reduced to life imprisonment and he was released in 1949, having served seven years. Arrested during the Border Campaign of the 1950s, he was once again released, this time taking the decision to distance himself from the IRA due to its left-wing political stance. He was one of the founding figures of the Provisional Irish Republican Army in 1969, becoming its chief of staff in 1972. He was arrested by the Irish Navy the following year for the importation of arms from Libya and served a three-year jail term as a result. Cahill was heavily involved in the IRA Army Council up until the late 1990s, following which he aligned himself with the Sinn Féin political party. He was also a staunch supporter of Gerry Adams and the Good Friday Agreement. He died in July 2004.

Daniel Cambridge
Victoria Cross recipient 1820 – 1882

Born in Carrickfergus, County Antrim, Daniel Cambridge served as a bombardier in the Royal Regiment of Artillery of the British Army. In September 1855, at the assault of Redan at Sebastopol during the Crimean War, he was wounded twice by Russian gunfire but determinedly refused to disengage from the attack until general orders were issued. In a courageous display of disregard for his own safety, he repeatedly returned to the battlefield to carry wounded comrades to safety. However, during one final rescue attempt he was reported to have staggered whilst carrying a fellow infantryman to safety and was subsequently found to have been shot for a third time on the right side of his jaw. For his deeds he was awarded the Victoria Cross.

Joseph Campbell
Poet 1879 – 1944

Poet Joseph Campbell was educated at St Malachy's College before becoming a teacher of English. In collaboration with composer Herbert Hughes, he worked on English-language versions of Irish folk songs, a volume of which was published as *Songs of Uladh* in 1904. Campbell was involved as an intelligence officer in the Easter Rising in 1916, and he took the anti-treaty side in the ensuing Civil War. In 1925 he established the first school of Irish studies in the United States of America, at Fordham University, New York and is also known for the composition of the words of the famed song, 'My Lagan Love'. Campbell settled in Glencree, County Wicklow, and died in June 1944.

Patrick Carlin
Victoria Cross recipient 1832 – 1895

Belfast-born Patrick Carlin served as a private in the First Battalion, 13th Regiment, Light Infantry, British Army. He is best known for his exploits on 6 April 1858 during the Indian Rebellion at Azumgurh, India, where he rescued a fellow soldier of the 4th Madras Rifles who had been wounded on the field of battle. Whilst carrying the wounded soldier to safety on his shoulders, Carlin successfully repelled – using just a sword – the advances

of a mutineer sepoy (Indian soldier) who had opened fire on him. For his bravery, he was subsequently awarded the Victoria Cross. Carlin died in Belfast in May 1895.

Frank Carson
Comedian 1926 – 2012

Renowned for his catch phrase 'It's the way I tell 'em' and 'It's a cracker', winning the talent show *Opportunity Knocks* in the 1960s brought Frank Carson to note in the world of entertainment. The son of a bin man, he started his working life as an electrician, later joining the Parachute Regiment of the British Army. His appearances in shows such as *The Comedians, The Wheeltappers, Shunters Social Club* and children's series *Tiswas* made Carson a household name and he was also knighted by Pope John Paul in 1987 in recognition of his charitable work. Upon meeting Pope Benedict XVI, the pontiff enquired if Carson had ever met Elvis Presley, to which he replied 'no I have not, but it won't be long before I do'. He is remembered as a very funny, generous, and kind-hearted man.

Cardinal William Conway
Cardinal Archbishop of Armagh and Primate of All Ireland
1913 – 1977

Falls Road-born William Conway was educated at St Mary's Christian Brothers School, Queens University, Belfast and St Patrick's College, Maynooth. Ordained in 1937, he was appointed professor of moral theology at Maynooth in 1942, and professor of canon law at that institution, in 1943. Conway was made archbishop of Armagh, and primate of All Ireland on 9 September

1963. He was created cardinal on 22 February 1965, an appointment that coincided with the commencement of the 'troubles' in Northern Ireland. In an oft-recalled quote he stated, 'Who in their sane senses wants to bomb a million Protestants into a united Ireland'. Conway condemned killings on both sides of the conflict, emphasising that all lives were precious in the eyes of God, irrespective of religious orientation. He died on 17 April 1977, and is buried in the grounds of St Patrick's Cathedral in Armagh.

James Craig
First prime minister of Northern Ireland 1871 – 1940

James Craig was born in Sydenham, Belfast and was educated at Merchiston Castle School, Edinburgh. He saw service with the Royal Irish Rifles in the 2nd Boer War, following which he returned to Ireland and became a member of parliament for East Down, and later Mid Down. Craig became leader of the Ulster Unionist Party in February 1921 and in June of that year was appointed the first prime minister of Northern Ireland. A staunch Unionist and a member of the Orange Order, in 1927 he was made first Viscount Craigavon. Craig died at his home in Glencraig, County Down on 24 November 1940.

James Crichton
Victoria Cross recipient 1875 – 1861

James Crichton was born in Carrickfergus, County Antrim. During World War I, at the age of thirty-nine, he became a private in the 2nd Battalion, Auckland Infantry Regiment, New Zealand Expeditionary Forces. His defining moment came in September 1918, when he successfully carried a message to his commanders after his platoon had been forced to retreat. Wounded in the foot and having advanced across difficult canal and river obstacles, he swam a river and traversed an area which was being swept by machinegun fire to ensure safe delivery of the message. Later, he successfully, and single-handedly saved a bridge under fire, removing the fuses and detonators. Crichton would ultimately reach the rank of sergeant before his death in New Zealand in 1961.

Sir William John Crossley
Car manufacturer and philanthropist 1844 – 1911

Though born in Antrim, William John Crossley was educated at the Royal School in Dungannon, County Tyrone. Whilst later working as an apprentice in Sir William Armstrong's works in Newcastle upon Tyne, he developed a steam engine and in 1867, together with his brother Frank, purchased the plant of John M. Dunlop at Great Marlborough Street, Manchester, England. The brothers, who were fiercely committed to their religious faith, refused to sell their products to companies such as breweries and were appropriately teetotal. They went on to develop both petrol and diesel engines, and their introduction of the production line system is said to have impacted upon the great Henry Ford, who visited their manufacturing facility around the turn of the century. The brothers registered Crossley Motors Ltd on 11 April 1906, although their first car was actually built two years earlier, in 1904. With the outbreak of World War II, their factory was commissioned for the production of armaments but following this diversion, Crossley Motors Ltd continued production until 1958, during which time buses were also produced. Unfortunately, the business became unprofitable in the early 1960s and fell into receivership. Both brothers are fondly remembered for their religious integrity and philanthropic contributions.

Sir Josias Cunningham
Politician 1934 – 2000

Josias Cunningham was educated at Fettes College as well as Clare College in Cambridge, England where he read biological science. An Orangeman, Cunningham was elected president of the Ulster Unionist Council in 1991 and played an important role in resolving that party's debate on whether to join a new regional government with Sinn Féin. Cunningham worked quietly and unobtrusively behind the scenes, providing a steadying hand during turbulent times and was knighted in 1999. He tragically died in a car accident at Carryduff, County Down in 2000. The taoiseach of Ireland at that time, Bertie Ahern along with Democratic Unionist Party leader Ian Paisley, John Hulme and David Trimble are amongst those that have paid great tribute to the memory of Sir Josias.

Cahal Brendan Daly
Cardinal 1917 – 2009

Having completed a study in classics at Queen's University, Belfast, Cahal Brendan Daly entered St Patrick's College, Maynooth, County Kildare where he was ordained to the priesthood in 1941, receiving a doctorate in divinity in 1944. The following year, Loughguile native Daly was appointed classics master in St Malachy's College and the year after that, he became lecturer of scholastic philosophy at Queen's University, holding that post until 1967. Later appointed bishop of Ardagh and Clonmacnoise, in 1982 Daly was made bishop of Down and Connor and in 1990, arch-bishop of Armagh and primate of all Ireland. Created a cardinal the following year, Daly was renowned for his firm stance against the IRA and his respectfulness of Protestant rights, but he was roundly criticised for his attitude to the segregation of education between Catholics and Protestants, considered one of the causes of sectarianism in Northern Ireland. The archetypal Catholic, he was also a vigorous opponent of divorce, contraception, abortion and the ordination of women. Daly died on 31 December 2009, aged ninety-two.

Bernard Diamond
Victoria Cross recipient 1827 – 1892

A native of Portglenone, at thirty years of age Bernard Diamond became a sergeant in the Bengal Horse Artillery in the Indian Army. During the Indian Mutiny on 28 September 1857, Diamond, together with fellow soldier Richard Fitzgerald (see page 94), defended a road at Bulandshahr, India. Although all of their comrades were either killed or wounded during the conflict, they continued to operate their machine gun, completely clearing the road of the enemy threat. Diamond was subsequently awarded the Victoria Cross for this feat.

William Drennan
Patriot, radical and poet (The man who gave Ireland the name 'The Emerald Isle') 1754 – 1820

William Drennan was born in the manse of the First Presbyterian Church of Rosemary Street, Belfast and was educated in Glasgow and Edinburgh. A gynaecologist, he was one of the first medical practitioners to advocate for inoculation against smallpox, and the washing of hands to prevent the spread of infection. Together with Wolfe Tone and Thomas Russell, Drennan was a co-founder of the Society of United Irishmen and in 1794 was arrested for seditious libel in connection with pamphlets he had written in support of that movement. He is also famous for his ballad, 'The Wake of William Orr', which is reckoned to have caused more hurt to the government of the day than a lost battle, as well as his poem, 'When Erin first Rose', which contained the first reference to Ireland's universally known title, 'The Emerald Isle'. The poem reads as follows:

> Let no feeling of vengeance
> Presume to defile
> The cause of, or men of,
> The Emerald Isle

Drennan, who was an ardent supporter of Catholic emancipation, died in 1820, but not before issuing funeral instructions to 'let six poor Protestants, and six poor Catholics get a guinea apiece for their carriage of me, and let a priest and a clergyman accompany me to my grave'.

Sammy Duddy
Former commander of the Ulster Defence Association 1945 – 2007

Sammy Duddy was a member of the Ulster Defence Association (UDA) during the most violent period of the troubles on the streets of Belfast. As the organisation's public relations officer he acted as editor of the UDA magazine entitled *Ulster* and also published a book of poetry called *Concrete Whirlpools*. He retired from being an active loyalist in the 1990s following a split in the UDA. Duddy was a charismatic and colourful character and once worked as a drag queen under the moniker 'Samantha'. In later years he pursued a peaceful path for his community but died of a heart attack at the Royal Victoria Hospital aged sixty-two.

Joey Dunlop
Motorcyclist 1952 – 2000

A record-breaking twenty-six-time winner of the Isle of Man TT, in 2005 *Motorcycle News* voted Joey Dunlop as the fifth greatest motorcyclist in history. The winner of the Ulster Grand Prix on twenty-four occasions, Dunlop was awarded the MBE (Member of the Order of the British Empire) in 1986, for his services to sport, and the OBE (Officer of the Order of the British Empire) in 1996, for his humanitarian work, which often saw him loading up his race transport vehicle and delivering food and clothing to the children of Bosnia and Romania. He tragically died whilst leading a race in Tallin, Estonia in 2000. In 2006, Dunlop was posthumously awarded an honourary doctorate from the University of Ulster while his brother Robert, a racing champion himself, was the recipient of a similar honour. Robert also died tragically in a motorcycle accident, during a practice of the North West 200, on 15 May 2008.

Timothy Eaton

Entrepreneur 1834 – 1907

Timothy Eaton was born in the town of Ballymena but left Ireland in 1854 to settle in Ontario, Canada, where he opened his first store in St Mary's. In 1884 he established Canada's first mail-order catalogue service which spawned a colossal retail empire, T. Eaton County Ltd, which at one time employed seventy thousand people in its departmental stores. Eaton's business empire withstood the test of time and existed right up to the 1960s. He died of pneumonia on 31 January 1907 but is immortalised by a life-sized statue that is on display in the Royal Ontario Museum in Toronto.

Sir Samuel Ferguson
Poet and antiquarian 1810 – 1886

Samuel Ferguson was born in High Street, Belfast and was educated at Belfast Academical Insitution and Trinity College, Dublin. He also studied at Lincoln's Inn, London after which he was called to the Irish Bar in 1838, taking Silk in 1859. Ferguson possessed a keen interest in Irish mythology and early Irish history and apart from his poetry, contributed a number of articles on topics of Irish interest to antiquarian journals. A collection of his poems, *Lays of the Western Gael* was published in 1865 and his major work – the long poem, 'Congal' – was published in 1872. Ferguson retired from his legal practice in 1867, becoming the deputy keeper of the Public Records of Ireland office. For his reorganisation of that neglected department, he was knighted in 1878. He died at Howth, County Dublin on 9 August 1886.

Gerry Fitt
Northern Ireland politician 1926 – 2005

Northern Ireland politician Gerry Fitt was born in Belfast and served as a member of the Merchant Navy from 1941 to 1953, before being elected to Belfast City Council in 1958. In 1962 he won a seat at Stormont; taking it from the Ulster Unionist Party, and in the process, becoming the only Irish member of the Labour Party in the Northern Ireland government. In 1966, Fitt won the Belfast West seat in the Westminster parliament but it was in Derry on 5 October 1968 that he came to worldwide prominence when he was seen in television footage being attacked by the Royal Ulster Constabulary in what was supposed to have been a peaceful civil rights march. Fitt was a founder member of the Social Democratic and Labour Party (SDLP) in 1970 and in 1974 was appointed deputy chief executive of the short-lived Northern Ireland Executive. Recognising that a power-sharing agreement between unionists and nationalists was the only solution to the problems in Northern Ireland, he was strongly opposed to violence in pursuit of nationalist interest, a stance which brought him into conflict with northern nationalists and one which resulted in his home being attacked on a number of occasions. He resigned from the SDLP in 1979 but in 1981 protested against the Maze prison hunger strikes and as a result lost his Westminster seat to Sinn Féin's Gerry Adams in June 1983. Later that year he was made baron of Bell's Hill, with a seat in the House of Lords. Fitt, who has always been considered a nationalist politician, would have been better described as a socialist politician, with nationalist interests at heart. He died on 26 August 2005.

Francis Fowke
Architect 1823 – 1865

Francis Fowke was born near Belfast and was educated in Dungannon and later at the Royal Military Academy in Woolwich, England. Commissioned in the Royal Engineers in 1842, he was also an ingenious and extremely inventive architect, engineer, and designer. Fowke designed drawbridges, pontoons, military fire engines and in 1856, patented the folding photographic camera, which became known as the 'Bellows' camera. His architectural works include the Officers' Library in Aldershot, the South Kensington Museum in London, the Museum of Science and Art, Edinburgh and the National Gallery, Dublin. He also designed the Royal Albert Hall in London, which was completed following his untimely death on 4 December 1865. The Fowke Medal, struck in his memory, is awarded annually to young officers who have distinguished themselves in the school of military engineering.

Richard K. Fox
Newspaper publisher 1846 – 1922

Having commenced his journalism career as a young employee of the Presbyterian Church newspaper, the *Banner of Ulster,* Richard K. Fox later joined the staff of the *Belfast News* Letter where he remained for ten years before emigrating to the United States. Despite arriving in New York in September 1874 with just five dollars in his pocket, within two years he had become proprietor and owner of the National Police Gazette, the oldest weekly newspaper in America. Utilising his maxim, 'if they can't read, give them plenty of pictures', he increased circulation of the publication from 50,000 up to 400,000 in a short number of years. Fox was the originator of the banner headline, a century ahead of the tabloid newspapers of today. Upon his death in 1922, his estate was worth in excess of three million dollars, and the premises of the National Police Gazette offices, was considered one of the most prominent buildings in New York City.

Chaim Herzog
President of Israel 1918 – 1997

Chaim Herzog was born at Clifton Park Avenue in Belfast, County Antrim. He obtained a law degree from University College London and having become a barrister at Lincoln's Inn joined the British Army in World War II, during which he witnessed the liberation of several concentration camps while on active service in Germany. Immediately following the allied victory, he went to Palestine and participated in the formation of the new Jewish state. Having fought in the battle for Latrun in the Arab-Israel War in 1948 he served in many political capacities in Israel, and in 1983, was elected the sixth president of that state; a role he served in until 1993. Herzog died on 17 April 1997 and is buried in Jerusalem.

Samuel Hill
Victoria Cross recipient 1826 – 1863

Samuel Hill was born in Glenavy, County Antrim, and was a sergeant in the 90th Regiment of the British Army during the Indian Mutiny. On 16 November 1857, at the age of thirty-one, Hill successfully rescued a captain and two wounded men whilst under heavy fire at Lucknow, India. For this deed he was awarded the Victoria Cross. He was killed in action at Meerut, India, in 1863.

James Hope
United Irishman 1764 – 1847

Influenced by the American Revolution, in 1795, Templepatrick's James Hope joined the Society of United Irishmen where he became a prominent organiser and a close associate of founders Samuel Neilson, Thomas Russell, and Henry Joy McCracken. In the rebellion of 1798 he participated in the Battle of Antrim and following defeat, took refuge in Slemish Mountain where he successfully evaded capture. On the collapse of the general rising, he refused to avail of the terms of an amnesty, stating that to do so would be 'not only a recantation of one's principles, but a tacit acquiescence in the justice of the punishment which has been inflicted on thousands of my unfortunate associates'. Following the rising, he lived for many years on the run and argued against the absentee landlords of the time, opining that those who made no use of land or resources, had no right to it. He is today regarded as the most egalitarian and socialist of all United Irish leadership.

Dennis Ireland
Author 1894 – 1974

Before choosing a career as a writer, Dennis Ireland studied medicine at Queen's University, Belfast. Having later decided to join the Royal Irish Fusiliers in World War I, he was eventually invalided with the rank of captain, at which point he focused his efforts on his writing. Ireland was a Presbyterian with strong nationalist sympathies and he supported the ideal of a united and independent Ireland, maintaining that his political views were in the true tradition of Ulster Presbyterianism. For nearly forty years, he worked as a freelance writer and broadcaster and was nominated to Seanad Éireann in 1948, becoming the first person from Northern Ireland to be bestowed this honour. His books include *The Red Brick City, Patriot Adventurer, The Age of Unreason*, and *Six Counties in Search of a Nation*. He died on 23 September 1974.

Joseph Larmor
Physicist and mathematician
1857 – 1942

Belfast-native Joseph Larmor studied at the Royal Belfast Academical Institution, Queens University, and the University of Cambridge, England. In 1903 he was appointed Lucasian professor of mathematics, at Cambridge and is principally remembered for three extensive papers published in the Philosophical Transactions of the Royal Society during the period spanning 1894 to 1897. Larmor predicted the phenomenon of time dilation for orbiting electrons and was the first to give an explanation of the effects of a magnetic field in splitting the lines of spectrum into multiple lines. He was knighted in 1909 and was Unionist MP for the University of Cambridge from 1911 until 1922. A recipient of many honours, including the Freedom of the City of Belfast, he died at Hollywood, County Down, on 19 May 1942.

Sir John Lavery
Artist 1856 – 1941

Having studied art in Glasgow, London and Paris, in 1888 John Lavery was commissioned to paint a scene depicting the state visit of Queen Victoria to the Glasgow exhibition. Knighted in 1918 following World War I, during which he was an official war artist, many of his works are now exhibited at the Imperial War Museum as well as a number of galleries throughout the world. Lavery, who was later made a free man of both Belfast and Dublin, also painted dramatic pictures of the trial of Sir Roger Casement (see page 159), and the lying-in-state of Terence MacSwiney (see page 101). A portrait of his wife, Hazel, appeared on Irish banknotes from 1928.

William James Lendrim
Victoria Cross recipient
1830 – 1891

From the town of Lisburn, County Antrim, William James Lendrum was a corporal in the Corps of Royal Engineers, British Army, during the Crimean War. On 14 February 1855, during the siege of Sevastopol, he extinguished burning sandbags on an ammunition magazine, whilst under heavy fire from Russian troops. For his bravery he was awarded the Victoria Cross. He later became a sergeant major and died in Surrey, England, in 1891.

Seán Lester
Diplomat 1888 – 1959

A member of a Protestant Unionist family, as a youth, Seán Lester joined the Gaelic League and was adopted into the cause of Irish nationalism before enlisting with Irish Republican Brotherhood. Employed for some years as a journalist in Northern Ireland, in 1919 he became editor of the *Freeman's Journal*. Following the War of Independence in Ireland, Lester was appointed director of publicity and later joined the Department of External Affairs. In 1929 he was appointed to represent Ireland in the League of Nations, a role in which he continuously protested against the German government's persecution of the Jews in the 1930s. Lester was appointed secretary general of the League in 1940, and oversaw its closure in 1946, when he transferred to the United Nations. He retired to the west of Ireland, and died in Galway on 13 June 1959.

Clive Staples Lewis
Writer 1898 – 1963

Born in Belfast and educated at the University of Oxford where he graduated with honours, Charles Staples Lewis was appointed a lecturer at Magdalen College, Oxford. He gained recognition in 1942 as a writer when he published The Screwtape Letters, which focused on the subject of temptation. Most books at the time attempted to convey methods of avoiding a sin such as temptation, however *The Screwtape Letters* emphasised an alternative approach; providing instructions on how to seduce an ordinary person into temptation, sin and eventual eternal damnation. It sold over 1 million copies and is still in print to this day. In 1950 Lewis published *The Lion*, *The Witch and the Wardrobe*, a children's story set in an imaginary world called Narnia. It was an immediate success and was followed by six more books in the series known as *The Chronicles of Narnia*. These stories have been enjoyed by generations of children and have since been adapted for television and motion picture audiences. Though immensely wealthy due to his writing prowess, Lewis was a man of simple needs and enjoyed nothing better than taking walking tours of his native country. In 1954 he was appointed a professor at the University of Cambridge and in 1960 he published *The Four Loves*. Lewis died in November of 1963.

John Joseph Linn
Businessman and freedom fighter 1798 – 1885

John Joseph Linn was born in County Antrim but his father, John Linn, participated in the Irish rebellion of 1798 before escaping to New York with his family in 1800. John Joseph eventually settled in New Orleans, later moving onto Victoria, Texas, where he established a business and resided for over fifty years. A fluent speaker of the Spanish language and amongst the first to oppose General Antonio López de Santa Anna, Linn became quartermaster of the Texas army in 1835, and was heavily involved in Texas' fight for freedom from Mexico. The following year, he was elected to the convention which declared the independence of Texas from Mexico and in 1839, he began a term as mayor of Victoria. Serving on the second and third congress of the republic in 1837 and 1839, in 1865 he began a second term as mayor of Victoria and two years before his death in 1883, published his famous *Reminiscence of Fifty years in Texas*. Linn was a significant figure in the history of Texas and he died on 27 October 1885.

Seán MacEntee
Patriot and political leader
1899 – 1984

Sean MacEntee was born in Belfast and was educated at St Malachy's College. Having initially worked for Great Northern Railways, he later became an engineer for the Dundalk Urban District Council and joined the Irish Volunteers in 1915, taking part in the Easter Rising the following year. Due to be executed upon the failure of that rising, MacEntee's sentence was subsequently commuted and he was later released under the general amnesty of 1918, following which he was elected to Dáil Éireann, under the Sinn Féin banner for County Monaghan. He later opposed the Anglo-Irish Treaty and strenuously argued against the partition of Ireland, recognising what such a decision would mean for Ireland and its people. MacEntee later joined Fianna Fáil and when that political party gained power in 1932, he served in many ministerial positions. Despite these lofty appointments he was not considered to be part of Éamon de Valera's inner circle but was nevertheless seen as an intellectual, honest, biting and sardonic debater. He retired from politics in the 1960s and died in 1974.

Kenneth Mackenzie
Battle of Britain fighter pilot
1916 – 2009

Gifted pilot Kenneth William MacKenzie was educated at the Methodist College, and later Queen's University in Belfast where he studied for an engineering degree. He joined the Royal Air Force as an airman pilot in 1939 and during the Battle of Britain MacKenzie destroyed at least seven enemy fighters, going so far as to ram an aircraft after running out of ammunition. The unorthodox maneuver severed part of his Hurricane wing but despite this, MacKenzie successfully landed in a field near Folkstone, England. For his skill and gallantry he was awarded the Distinguished Flying Cross but MacKenzie had more to give and in September 1941, following an attack on an airfield in France, he ditched in the sea before being captured by the Germans. Having made several attempts to escape, MacKenzie eventually ended up incarcerated at Stalag Luft III, Germany where over a considerable length of time, he feigned madness and developed a severe stammer which eventually led to his repatriation to England in October, 1944. In the following years MacKenzie held various posts in the RAF before being appointed deputy commander of the Zambian air force, a post he held until April 1970. He later became managing director of Air Kenya and worked in this role until his eventual retirement in 1973. He died on 4 June 2009.

Anna MacManus
Writer and nationalist
1866 – 1902

Anna MacManus, perhaps better known by her pen name 'Ethna Carbery', was a significant contributor of articles in *The Nation, United Ireland* and other publications, all of which stimulated the early Sinn Féin movement. Together with Alice Milligan, she founded the newspapers the *Northern Patriot* and later *Shan Van Vocht* (an anglicised translation of 'poor old woman'). In 1902 MacManus published a book of poetry, *The Four Winds of Eirinn*, and in 1903 *The Passionate Hearts*, which was a collection of short stories. Anna MacManus was a strikingly beautiful woman of intense patriotism, who never

Giant's Causeway.

considered herself a literary woman. She died in 1902, and is buried in the little graveyard at Inver, County Donegal.

Eoin MacNeill
Patriot and scholar 1867 – 1945

Eoin MacNeill was born at Glenarm and received his education at St Malachy's College and Queen's College, Belfast. A co-founder of the Gaelic League in 1893, he was appointed professor of early Irish history at University College Dublin in 1908. MacNeill was one of the founder members of the Irish Volunteers, and was later to become its chief of staff. Following the Easter Rising in 1916, he was elected as a Sinn Féin TD and in this role he supported the Anglo-Irish Treaty, becoming the minister for education in the first government of the Irish Free State. MacNeill retired from politics in 1927, publishing a number of Irish history books before he died in Dublin at the age of seventy-eight.

James Joseph Magennis
Victoria Cross recipient 1919 – 1986

James Joseph Magennis served as a clearance diver (frogman) on the HMS *Midget Submarine* XE3 during World War II. On 31 July 1945 he took part in an attack on the Japanese cruiser Atago in the Straits of Johor, Singapore. The attack required Magennis to deploy mines on the hull of the enemy cruiser; however, his attempt at exiting the midget submarine to do so was fraught with difficulty due to the diving hatch being only partly open. Having finally exited the submarine, he had to scrape barnacles off the bottom of the cruiser before attaching his mines. With his breathing apparatus leaking, he returned to the submarine in a state of extreme exhaustion. It was then that his commanding officer noticed that one of the limpet carriers had not jettisoned, which placed the submarine in great jeopardy. Magennis again exited the submarine and after five nerve-racking minutes, using a heavy spanner, he successfully released the limpet carrier. His actions facilitated the submarine's safe return to its mother ship, the HMS *Stygian*. When Magennis returned to his hometown of Belfast, the unionist government refused to honour his great deed, due to the fact that he was a Catholic. Happily, in October 1999, the lord mayor of Belfast, Bob Stoker, unveiled a bronze and stone memorial statue to this very brave man.

Sir Samuel McCaughey
Philanthropist 1835 – 1919

In April 1856, Samuel McCaughey emigrated to Melbourne, Australia where he initially gained work experience as a jackaroo. He eventually went on to operate a sheep station of his own; after which he became known as the 'sheep king' of Australia — due to the fact that at one point in time, he was shearing one million sheep per year. McCaughey would become the wealthiest man in the state of New South Wales, and was knighted in 1905. During World War I, he presented the Australian government with twenty fighter planes. He also extended his generosity to those who most required it, donating vast sums of money to a multitude of charities. Examples of his philanthropy include payments of £600,000 for the training of the children of soldiers killed in combat and £250,000 to the Presbyterian Church, along with considerable sums to many homes and orphanages. He also made contributions to the universities of Queensland and Sydney and a portrait in his honour stands at the latter. McCaughey died on 25 July 1919.

Henry Joy McCracken
United Irishman 1767 – 1798

Henry Joy McCracken was born into a wealthy cotton-manufacturing Presbyterian family and joined the Society of the United Irishmen in 1795. McCracken travelled throughout the island of Ireland, using the cover of his cotton business to establish other United Irish societies. Following the outbreak of the United Irish rebellion in 1798, he was appointed general for Antrim, and formulated a plan to seize small towns throughout the county with the objective of eventually converging on Antrim town itself. His efforts met with initial success but he ultimately failed in the attack on Antrim, after which he was arrested. Though he was offered clemency if he testified against other United Irish leaders, McCracken duly refused. He was court-martialed and hung at Cornmarket in Belfast on 17 June 1798.

Charles McCurry
Victoria Cross recipient 1830 – 1857

Charles McCurry was born in Killeard, County Antrim. As a twenty-five-year-old private in the 57th Regiment of the British Army during the Crimea War at Sebastopol, he threw a live shell over a trench parapet, successfully saving the lives of a number of his fellow soldiers. For this deed McCurry was awarded the Victoria Cross. He died in Malta in 1857.

James McHenry
American statesman 1753 – 1816

James McHenry was born in Ballymena and enjoyed a classical education in Dublin before emigrating to Philadelphia in 1771, where he qualified in medicine under Doctor Benjamin Rush. During the American War of Independence McHenry served as a military surgeon and in 1778 became secretary to George Washington. From 1781 until 1786 he was a member of the Maryland Senate and was a signatory of the United States Constitution from Maryland. Washington appointed him to United States secretary of war in January 1796, a position he also served in under President John Adams. A deeply religious presbyterian, McHenry solicited funds for the first bible society in Baltimore. He died on 3 May 1816.

John Joseph 'Rinty' Monaghan
Undefeated flyweight boxing champion of the world
1920 – 1984

John Joseph 'Rinty' Monaghan took up boxing as a young boy and turned professional in his mid-teens. Navy service interrupted his career during World War II but upon his return in November 1945, he won the Ulster flyweight title and in 1948 defeated Jacky Patterson via knockout at the Kings Hall, Belfast to become the undisputed British Commonwealth and World Flyweight Champion. After defending his world title on two occasions, he was misfortunate to develop a chronic lung condition which forced him to retire undefeated in April 1950, at the age of thirty-two. However, having endeared himself to the boxing public of Northern Ireland by way of the traditional post-fight performance of his trademark song, 'When Irish Eyes are Smiling', Monaghan left behind fond memories and a plaque in his honour is now on display at the Kings Hall in Belfast. He died on 3 March 1984, aged sixty-three.

Brian Moore
Irish novelist 1921 – 1999

Though born into a committed Catholic family, Brian Moore rejected Catholicism in his early life, a fact evidenced by the staunch anti-doctrine and anti-clerical themes prevalent in some of his novels, twenty-five of which were published. A recipient of the James Tait Black Memorial Prize in 1975, Moore's books were short-listed for the Booker Prize on no less than three occasions. Portraying the insight he had into female psychology, the principal character in several of his novels is a woman, and amongst his most acclaimed works are *The Lonely Passion of Judith Hearne*, *The Feast of Lupercal*, *The Emperor of Ice Cream*, *I am Mary Dunne*, and *The Doctor's Wife*. He spent most of his life in Canada, later moving to California where he died in Malibu on 11 January 1999.

St Clair Augustine Mulholland
American Civil War brevet major general and Congressional Medal of Honour recipient 1839 – 1910

A decorated soldier, Lisburn-born St Clair Augustine Mulholland emigrated to Philadelphia as a young boy. At the outbreak of the American Civil War, he was a lieutenant colonel of an infantry unit attached to Thomas Francis Meagher's (see page 393) Irish Brigade but was wounded during the famous 'charge of the Irish Brigade' at the Battle of Fredericksburg. Mulholland was brevetted brigadier general on 13 March 1865 for gallantry at Chancellorsville, a role for which he was also awarded the Congressional Medal of Honour. He was also brevetted major general for gallantry at the Battle of Boydton Plank and Road and is notable for having being seriously wounded on no less than three occasions during the war. Upon his return to civil life he was appointed chief of police in Philadelphia in 1868 and also became active in the Catholic affairs of the city. Mulholland died in Philadelphia on 17 February 1910.

William Mulholland
Engineer 1855 – 1935

Belfast born William Mulholland spent most of his childhood in Dublin before emigrating to New York City where he worked in an assortment of jobs, ranging from lumberjacking to mining. He eventually moved on to Los Angeles to work as a ditch-cleaner for a water supply company and some eight years later, the self-educated engineer was appointed superintendent of the Department of Water and Power, Los Angeles. Mulholland realised that Los Angeles required abundant supplies of water but the only source available was the Owen's River, some two hundred miles away. Together with Fred Eton, a one time Los Angeles mayor, Mulholland, with his vision and dogged determination, created one of the engineering marvels of the age – the Los Angeles Aqueduct. The project was conceived by way of a certain amount of calculated deception and risky tactics, but with millions of dollars to spend from eager investors, the project was completed in 1913. The construction of the aqueduct, which traversed two hundred miles of desert and mountains, created employment for two thousand workers and is still functional today. Mulholland's career ended fifteen years later on 12 March 1928, when the St Francis Dam, which was built on the water route, collapsed and some 450 people, including forty-two school children, lost their lives. Mulholland accepted full responsibility, saying on the occasion, 'The only people I envy in this thing are the dead'. Mulholland died in 1935 and the renowned Mulholland Drive is named in his memory.

Ruby Murray
Singer 1935 – 1996

Making her first television appearance at the age of twelve, it was Ruby Murray's uniquely hoarse voice, the result of a throat operation as a child, that gave her a distinct vocal sound. Her debut single, 'Heartbeat' reached the top five of the UK singles chart in 1954 but she is perhaps best remembered for 'Softly, Softly', which reached number one in 1955 – the same year in which she had five separate singles in the top twenty of the charts – at the same time. During the 1950s, she presented her own television show, performed at the London Palladium with Norman Wisdom and appeared in a Royal Command Performance. Ruby is also fondly remembered for the songs, 'It's the Irish in Me', 'Mister Wonderful' and 'Scarlet Ribbons'. She, who was twice married, died in Torquay, England on 17 December 1996.

William Orr
United Irishman 1766 – 1797

In 1796 William Orr, who was born into a wealthy Presbyterian family, was arrested on a charge of administering a treasonable oath to two soldiers. Later uncovered as a false allegation, he was found guilty of the offence and hanged in Carrickfergus on 14 October 1797 at the age of thirty-one. In a most eloquent speech from the dock, and with reference to his family, he stated: 'May they love their country as I have done, and die for it if needful'. A poem written in his memory by William Drennan, a fellow comrade, became the rallying cry of the United Irishmen thereafter: 'Remember William Orr'.

Cathal O'Shannon
Politician, journalist and trade unionist
1889 – 1969

Cathal O'Shannon was a member of the Irish Republican Brotherhood and was one of the founding members of both the Socialist Party of Ireland, which was led by James Connolly (see page 429), and the Irish Volunteers in Belfast in 1913. Three years later, O'Shannon was responsible for mobilising volunteers at Colisland, County Tyrone, but had to stand down the group when orders from Dublin were not forthcoming. He was later arrested by the British authorities but was released on amnesty in 1917. As a serving member of the Irish Republican Army in 1920 and 1921, he supported the Anglo-Irish Treaty and also served for a time in Dáil Éireann (Irish parliament). O'Shannon was an active participant in the Irish Trade Union Movement for a period of twenty-five years but died in Dublin on 4 October 1969. His son, also named Cathal, was a renowned journalist and broadcaster.

William Paterson
New Jersey statesman and signatory to the US Constitution
1745 – 1806

Whilst still a young boy, William Paterson emigrated with his family to the United States where he was educated at the College of New Jersey (now Princeton University) before being admitted to the Bar in 1768. On the outbreak of the American War of Independence, Paterson joined the New Jersey Patriots and was an outspoken supporter of American independence, representing Somerset County in the first three provincial congresses of New Jersey. As a secretary, he recorded the 1776 New Jersey State Constitution and following independence was appointed the first attorney general of New Jersey. Paterson, who also served as governor of New Jersey and in the New Jersey Senate, was appointed associate justice of the United States Supreme Court in 1790 by George Washington. He died on 9 September 1806 in Albany, New York. Named in his memory are Paterson, New Jersey, and the William Paterson University.

Robert Quigg
Victoria Cross recipient 1885 – 1955

Born near the world-famous Giants Causeway, Robert Quigg was a rifleman in the Royal Irish Rifles 36th Division of the British Army. He fought in the Battle of the Somme on 1 July 1916 and witnessed his unit being driven back by German forces on multiple occasions. When his lieutenant, who was commanding his platoon, was reported missing, Quigg volunteered to enter 'no man's land' under heavy fire, to recover him. Seven times he ventured into the field to locate the missing officer and on every occasion he returned unsuccessful in doing so. What he did accomplish was the retrieval of wounded comrades on each attempt, whom he dragged to safety on a waterproof gun sheet from within yards of enemy lines, until he was forced to call a halt to his exertions due to exhaustion. Quigg was also awarded the Order of Saint George by Russian authorities, which was the highest award made by the Russian Empire to non-commissioned officers. He died in Ballycastle on 14 May 1955.

Bobby Sands
Republican 1954 – 1981

The legendary hunger striker Bobby Sands was born in Rathcoole, Belfast. After his family was forced to flee their home as a result

of loyalist intimidation, he became an active member of the IRA and was subsequently sentenced to five years in prison in April 1973, for the possession of arms. Upon his release he continued his activities with the IRA and in 1977 was once again arrested on a similar charge, this time being handed down a fourteen-year sentence to be served at Long Kesh. While at Long Kesh, commonly referred to as 'The Maze', republican prisoners sought to regain their previous special category status and thus commenced 'blanket' protests, which eventually led to a hunger strike. Whilst taking part in the hunger strike, Sands was chosen to represent the prisoners in the parliamentary elections for the seat of Fermanagh in south Tyrone, which he won with 30,493 votes defeating the Ulster Unionist Party candidate, who gained 29,046 votes. Sands died aged twenty-seven following sixty-six days on hunger strike.

George Shiels
Poet and dramatist 1886 – 1949

Though born in Ballymoney, George Shiels would later emigrate to Canada where in 1913, whilst working on the Canadian Pacific Railway, he was involved in a serious accident which consigned him to a wheelchair for the remainder of his days. As a result of this life-changing event Shiels returned to the town of his birth where along with his brother, he established a shipping company. He also began to write poems and short stories, later progressing to plays, such as *Bedmates* (1921) and *The New Gossoon* (1930). The Abbey Theatre in Dublin regularly showcased Shiels's productions, most notably *The Rugged Path*, which had a record-breaking run in 1940. Such was his success as a playwright, exemplified by the Theatre Players production of several of his plays on Broadway between 1932 and 1937, Shiels was afforded the luxury of ceasing his involvement in his previously established shipping business. He died in September 1949.

Gusty Spence
Leader of the Ulster Volunteer Force (UVF) 1933 – 2011

Born in the staunchly loyalist area of Belfast's Shankill Road, Gusty Spence spent four years in the British Army, rising to the rank of military police sergeant, before retiring due to ill-health. Building a reputation as a 'hard man', he was often involved in street fights with republicans and was expelled from the Orange Order for being involved in a murder. In 1966 Spence was sentenced to life for the murder of a catholic man, a charge he always denied and in 1977 in the Maze Prison, he was recognised as commander of the UVF, a position he resigned from the following year having undergone a dramatic change in his views. Now condemning the use of violence and calling for reconciliation, Spence was released from prison in 1984 upon which time he severed his links with the UVF and chose a political route to peace with the Progressive Unionist Party. Such was his standing within loyalism, he was chosen to announce the immediate ceasefire of the Combined Loyalist Military Command in 1994 and, despite being critical of the established unionist parties whom he accused of not properly representing the working class areas of Northern Ireland, Spence went on to support the peace process, and backed the Good Friday Agreement.

Alexander Turney Stewart
Businessman and philanthropist
1803 – 1876

Alexander Turney Stewart emigrated to the United States when he was fifteen years of age. He returned briefly five years later in 1823, to collect an inheritance that was in the region of five to ten thousand pounds. He used the money to purchase Irish linens and lace and returned to America to open a small store in Lower Manhattan. His mastery of the retail business saw the outlet become one of the largest department stores in the United States. In 1846, during the Great Famine, Stewart sent a boatload of provisions to Ireland and offered to pay for the passage to New York and provide guaranteed employment to any young persons wishing to emigrate who were literate and of good moral character. Some one hundred and fifty young men accepted his life-altering offer. Two years later, in 1848, Stewart built the three-storey Marble Palace on Broadway and such was his prominence in society, he was later offered the position of United States Secretary of the Treasury by President Grant, a potential appointment scuppered by Congress' disapproval. Before his death, Stewart established an extensive mail order business and opened his own mills in the north east. He also invested heavily in New York Central Railroad, and founded Garden City. Upon his death on 10 April 1876, Stewart was the third-richest man in America.

Bartholomew Teeling
United Irishman 1774 – 1798

Coming from a wealthy linen and drapery business-owning family, Bartholomew Teeling received his education in Dublin following which he joined the United

Irishmen in 1792. He travelled to France in 1796 to assist Wolfe Tone in securing support for an invasion of Ireland and along with the French forces, landed back in Killala in 1798. As aide-de-camp to General Humbert, Teeling was captured after the French surrender at Ballinamuck and was subsequently court-martialed in Dublin and sentenced to execution at Arbour Hill on 24 September 1798.

William Thomson (Lord Kelvin)
Physicist 1824 – 1907

William Thomson studied natural philosophy at the University of Glasgow, and was subsequently elected professor of natural philosophy at the university at the age of twenty-two. He established the first physics laboratory in a British university and carried out extensive research in thermodynamics, investigating the inter-relation of heat and mechanical energy. In 1852, together with James Prescott Joule, he discovered what became known as the 'Joule-Thomson Cooling Effect', which causes gases to undergo a fall in temperature, as they expand through a nozzle. He also invented the Thomson mirror-galvanometer, which was used in the first transatlantic telegraph cable linking Ireland with Canada. In 1870, he invented a new and improved compass, which was adopted by the British Navy in 1882. For his outstanding work on the transatlantic telegraph project, Thomson was knighted by Queen Victoria in 1868, and was thereafter referred to as Lord Kelvin.

Jack White
Trade unionist and co-founder of the Irish Citizen Army
1879 – 1946

Son of Victoria Cross recipient Sir George Stuart White (see page 123), Jack was born into a Unionist family at Whitehall in Broughshane, County Antrim. Educated at Winchester College and Sandhurst Military Academy, England, he served with the 1st Gordon Highlanders in the Boer War where he was awarded the Distinguished Service Order. He was one of the first to go 'over the top' at the battle of Doorknop, and on seeing a seventeen-year-old boy shivering with fright in the trenches, was commanded by a senior officer to 'shoot him'. It is reputed that White turned his revolver on the officer and replied, 'do so and I'll shoot you'. He served as aide-de-camp to his father, who was the governor of Gibraltar from 1901 until 1905, but resigned his commission in 1907 and returned to Ireland. In response to the Ulster Volunteers' threat of war against the British government if Ireland was granted any measure of home rule, White organised the first Protestant pro-home rule meeting in Ballymoney, rallying Protestant opinion against what he called, 'bigotry and stagnation'. White was converted to Socialism by James Connolly and in 1913 advocated the formation of a militia to protect picket lines from assault by the Dublin Metropolitan Police, which eventually led to the creation of the Irish Citizen Army. In the late 1930's, he was involved in the support of Spanish anarchists. White died from cancer in 1946 and is buried in the family plot in the First Presbyterian Church in Broughshane. His family, seemingly ashamed of his revolutionary politics, destroyed all of his papers.

Alexander Wright
Victoria Cross recipient 1826 – 1858

Ballymena man Alexander Wright became a private in the 77th Regiment of Foot, British Army at twenty-nine years old and distinguished himself on 22 March 1855, during the Crimean War at Sebastopol, where he almost single-handedly repelled the onslaught of advancing Russian forces. Less than a month later on 19 April, Wright once again displayed outstanding bravery in taking an enemy rifle pit (trench) and he gained further credibility for the encouragement he directed towards his fellow soldiers in holding the pits under severe pressure from Russian fire. Having been wounded in action, he went on to show exemplary bravery throughout the campaign, and died in Calcutta, India in 1858.

Ella Young
Poet, political activist and mystic 1867 – 1956

Though Antrim born, Ella Young grew up in Dublin where she studied Law and Political Science at the Royal University. She became a member of the Theosophy Society and the Hermatic Society, which included such notaries as, W. B. Yeats and George Russell (Æ) and is known for publishing a volume of poetry entitled *Poems* in 1906, as well as volumes of folk tales, *The Coming of Lugh* and *Celtic Wonder Tales* in 1909 and 1910 respectively. Young, a close friend of Maud Gonne, joined Sinn Féin in 1912, and was active in the Easter Rising as a gun smuggler for the republicans. She also opposed the Anglo-Irish Treaty, and was temporarily imprisoned by the Irish Free State government but later emigrated to the United States where she became a lecturer in Celtic Mythology at the University of California, Berkeley. She published many volumes of short stories for children, of which the best remembered is, *The Unicorn with Silver Shoes* (1932).

James Young
Comedian 1918 – 1974

James Young was an amateur actor in his teenage years but later graduated to the professional ranks, sharing in the great success of the Ulster Group Theatre throughout the 1940s and 1950s. He is best remembered as a comedian where he filled the role of characters such as, 'Ernie', 'The Shipyard Worker', and 'Orange Lil'. A talented entertainer, Young appeared in theatres across Ireland, Canada and the United States and sold in excess of a 250,000 records. A blue plaque in his memory, is displayed at his family's home in Ballynafeigh, Belfast.

Armagh

Andrew Trew Wood
1826-1903

The Bank of Hamilton, Ontario, Canada co-founded by Andrew Trew Wood in 1872.

Tomás Ó Fiaich
1923-1990

Cardinal Joseph McRory
1861-1945

St Patrick's Cathedral, Armagh, seat of the Primates of All Ireland.

David Sinton
1808-1900

The home of the pig iron industrialist and philanthropist to the arts and Presbyterian Church, on Pike Street, Cincinnati

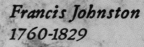

Francis Johnston
1760-1829

The General Post Office on O'Connell Street in Dublin, site of the Easter Rising 1916, was designed by Francis Johnston.

William McCrum
1861-1932

William McCrum introduced the penalty kick into the sport of association football.

James Austin
Entrepreneur 1813 – 1897

Emigrating to Canada with his family in 1829, James Austin became an apprentice in the printing trade and after some time, used his newly acquired skills to found a printing business of his own. Austin, who was a Methodist, established another business with Roman Catholic, Patrick Foy in 1843 and the pair enjoyed much prosperity in their retail and wholesale grocery partnership. Foy later remarked that the success of their business was 'an example of what orange and green might do when working in harmony instead of dissipating their energies against each other.' Displaying extraordinary entrepreneurial skills, which took him from the role of printer's apprentice to bank president, Austin went on to become one of Toronto's leading financiers, founding the Dominion Bank, later to be known as the Toronto-Dominion Bank, in 1871 and becoming president of the Consumer's Gas Company in 1881. In the 1890s, Austin began suffering from increasing deafness which forced him into a reclusive state. He died after an illness of several weeks on 27 February 1897.

Frank Aiken
Politician and IRA commander
1898 – 1983

Camlough's Frank Aiken joined the Irish Volunteers in 1914 and was swiftly appointed commander of the Fourth Northern Division of the Irish Republican Army (IRA), a role in which he was considered extremely proficient. In December, 1920 Aiken led an assault on the Royal Irish Constabulary (RIC) station in Camlough but was the victim of brutal retaliation when the Ulster Special Constabulary burned his home down, taking the lives of ten of his relatives in the process. He took the anti-treaty side in the Irish Civil War, and although he participated in many attacks on pro-treaty forces, he was never enthusiastic about the conflict, and following his appointment as chief of staff of the IRA in March 1923, issued the ceasefire and dump arms order for the cessation of violence. It was this action that effectively ended the Irish Civil War. Aiken was elected Sinn Féin candidate for Louth that same year but later joined Fianna Fáil and was elected at every election until his retirement from politics half a century later. During his political career he held many senior ministerial posts, ranging from minister of finance to minister for external affairs and retired as Tánaiste in 1969. Aiken died in Dublin on 18 May 1983, and was buried with full state honours at the place of his birth.

John Archibald Beckett
Recipient of the George Cross
1906 – 1947

Though born in Lurgan, County Armagh, John Archibald Beckett was educated at St Enoch's School in Belfast. He joined the Royal Air Force in January 1935, and served in Canada, Egypt, and Palestine. Whilst refuelling a Lancaster bomber at Ein Shemer Air Headquarters in Palestine on the night of 28 March 1947, Beckett was engulfed in flames when a fire broke out. In ferocious pain, and realising that the fire could destroy more than twenty aircraft parked nearby, he embarked the refueling vehicle and drove it a safe distance away, averting a catastrophic disaster. The courageous Beckett died of his injuries on 12 April 1947.

Lord William Leslie de la Poer Beresford
Victoria Cross recipient 1847 – 1900

The son of the Marquess of Waterford, Lord William Leslie de la Poer Beresford was born in Mullaghbrack, County Armagh. A captain in the 9th Lancers of the Queen's Royal, British Army during the Zulu War in South Africa, Beresford rescued a non-commissioned officer whose horse had fallen and rolled on top of him. With the enemy advancing quickly and in vast numbers, Beresford, with the help of Edmund O'Toole, freed the young man and subsequently mounted the injured soldier behind him, returning safely to his own lines. For this feat, he was awarded the Victoria Cross, while also recommending O'Toole for the award and would later go on to achieve the rank of lieutenant colonel.

George Dawson
Politician 1961 – 2007

George Dawson was born in Lurgan and educated at Banbridge Academy, County Down. He studied English and modern history at Queen's University, Belfast and became a member of the Democratic Unionist Party (DUP) in 1979. Elected to the Northern Ireland Assembly in the constituency of East Antrim in 2003, he was also the DUP spokesperson on energy and the economy. Dawson managed Sammy Wilson's MP campaign in the 2005 general election and at the time of his death was grand master of the Independent Orange Institution. He was considered one of unionism's most articulate and popular voices and died following a short battle with cancer in 2007.

Field Marshal John Greer Dill
British commander in World War I and World War II
1891 – 1944

A veteran of two world wars, John Greer Dill was born in Lurgan and attended Cheltenham College, England and the Royal Military College at Sandhurst. He served with the Leinster Regiment during the 2nd Boer War in South Africa and was promoted to captain in 1911. During World War I, Dill rose from the rank of brigade major to brigadier general and during the conflict was wounded and mentioned in despatches on eight separate occasions. Dill commanded the British forces in Palestine in 1936 and 1937 but on the outbreak of the World War II saw many junior officers promoted before him; a consequence of his poor standing in the eyes of Winston Churchill. Posted to Washington as Churchill's personal representative in 1941, he was instrumental in the close bond formed between Great Britain and the United States during a difficult period of time. Dill was highly respected by both President Roosevelt and the famously unpleasant Admiral King, whose cooperation he won over for Britain. Dill died in Washington in November 1944, and was buried with full military honours at Arlington National Cemetery.

Francis Johnston
Architect 1760 – 1829

A prominent architect, Francis Johnston's work incorporated both the neoclassical and neogothic styles and is thus considered unique in the world of architecture. Johnston is remembered for the design of the General Post Office on O'Connell Street in Dublin as well as nearby Nelson's Pillar, which was destroyed by the IRA in 1966. Amongst his other works are the Chapel Royal in Dublin Castle and Charleville Forest Castle in Tullamore, County Offaly.

George Lambert
Victoria Cross recipient 1819 – 1860

George Lambert was born in Markethill, County Armagh and was a sergeant major in the 84th Regiment of Foot, British Army. On 29 July 1857, during the Indian Rebellion at Oonao in India, Lambert showed extraordinary bravery in fighting the enemy and over the period from the 16 August to the 25 September 1857, engaged in hand-to-hand combat and bayonet charging on multiple occasions. Such was Lambert's bravery he was awarded the Victoria Cross and later became a lieutenant. He died in Sheffield, England in 1860.

Cecil Lavery
Supreme Court judge and nationalist 1894 – 1967

Judge and Irish nationalist, Cecil Lavery was educated at St Patrick's College, Armagh and later at St Vincent's College, Castleknock, Dublin. One of the first auditors of the UCD Law Society, he was called to the Bar in 1915 and was also a member of the Irish Volunteers, whose first meeting he attended two years prior, in 1913. Joining the volunteer's Armagh division, he was involved in gun running for the IRA into Howth Harbour, Dublin in July 1914 and was later a judge of the republican courts in 1921 and 1922. Lavery took silk in 1927, serving on the bench of the King's Inn, and he was also a member of the Dáil for North County Dublin from 1935 to 1938. In 1948, he was appointed attorney general in the first coalition government and that same year, helped draft the 'Convention of Human Rights' for the Council of Europe as well as the 'Republic of Ireland Bill'. Also a senator, he was appointed to the Supreme Court in 1950 while his keen interest in horse racing led to him being appointed a steward of the Turf Club. He died in Dublin on 16 December 1967.

James Logan
Colonial statesman, scholar and co-founder of Pennsylvania 1674 – 1751

Showing considerable academic prowess from an early age, James Logan gained fluency in Greek, Latin and Hebrew whilst still only a teenager. In 1699, William Penn appointed him as his personal secretary and he accompanied Penn, who was the founder of Pennsylvania, on his second trip to America. Later appointed secretary of the province and clerk of the provisional council of Pennsylvania, Logan held office during the 'Border War' between Maryland and Pennsylvania and was elected mayor of Philadelphia in 1722. In 1731 he was appointed chief justice of the Supreme Court and served in the role until 1739. Also a successful entrepreneur, Logan became one of the wealthiest men in the Colonies after investing in lands and establishing a lucrative business trading with the Native Americans. He retired in 1747, but continued to pursue his academic interests and contributed many scientific articles, one of which was entitled 'Experiments Concerning the Impregnation of the Seeds of Plants'. An area of Philadelphia is named in his memory, and he died on 31 October 1751.

Charles Davis Lucas
Victoria Cross recipient 1834 – 1914

Poyntzpass born Charles Davis served as a junior officer in the Royal Navy during the Crimean War. On 21 June 1854, as the HMS *Hecla* engaged in combat off the Aland Islands in Finland, a shell landed on her upper deck. Lucas, spotting the shell with its fuse still burning, picked it up and with little time to spare, threw it overboard where it exploded before landing in the ocean. He later achieved the rank of rear admiral and died in Maidstone, Kent in 1914.

Joseph MacRory
Cardinal and Archbishop of Armagh 1861 – 1945

Educated at both St Patrick's College, County Armagh, and St Patrick's College in Maynooth, County Kildare, Joseph MacRory was ordained in September 1885 and held a number of teaching posts until 1889 when he was appointed professor of scripture and Oriental languages at the Maynooth institution. In 1915 he became bishop of Down and Connor, and was elevated to Archbishop of Armagh and Primate of All Ireland in 1928, before being created cardinal by Pope Pius XI the following year. MacRory, who laid the foundation stone of Liverpool Cathedral in 1933, was strongly opposed to social injustice, national socialism and the partition of Ireland. He died at his residence in Armagh and is buried in St Patrick's Cathedral Cemetery. The McRory Cup, the GAA's inter-college football tournament in Ulster, is named in his memory.

Tommy Makem
Traditional musician
1932 – 2007

A talented musician, Tommy Makem was born in Keady, County Armagh and later gained international recognition performing with the Clancy Brothers, sparking a huge revival in Irish folk and traditional music. A multi-talented storyteller, actor, songwriter, and poet he joined the Clancy Brothers in New York in 1958 and together they appeared on all the major television networks throughout the US and played to audiences from New York's Carnegie Hall to London's Royal Albert Hall. Makem came from a musical family and his mother, Sarah was a well known traditional singer with a catalogue of over five hundred songs. Along with his distinctive baritone voice, banjo, tin whistle and stagecraft, he is much credited with the worldwide revival of traditional Irish music. He died in August 2007.

Sir Frederick Francis Maude
Victoria Cross recipient 1821 – 1897

Frederick Francis Maude was born in Lisnadill and served as a lieutenant colonel in the 3rd Regiment of Foot, British Army, in the Crimean War. On 5 September 1855, whilst in charge of a covering party of the 2nd Division in the assault on the Redan fortification, he successfully held his position with approximately nine or ten men, and did not retire until all hope of support had disappeared and he himself was seriously wounded. He later became a general and died in Torquay, Devon, in England, in 1897.

Sir Robert McCarrison
Medical scientist 1878 – 1960

A pioneer in the area of modern nutrition, Robert McCarrison was one of the founders of nutritional science and a foremost authority on its application. Joining the Indian Medical Service in 1900, he was the recipient of numerous distinctions, being awarded the Kaiser One Haind gold medal in 1911 for public services in India and the Prix Amussat of the Academy of Medicine, Paris in 1914 for his research on the medical conditions of goiter and cretinism. McCarrison, who was knighted in 1933, served as a regimental medical officer in Chitral, Pakistan and as an agency surgeon in Gilgit, Pakistan. He was also director of the nutrition research laboratory at Coonoor, India, a position he held until he retired in 1935 with the rank of major general. In civilian life McCarrison was the first director of postgraduate studies at Oxford from 1945 until 1953. He died in Oxford on 18 May 1960.

William McCrum
Inventor of the penalty kick in soccer
c. 1861 – 1932

The holder of a special place in the history of the world's most popular sport, McCrum, whose linen-baron father built the model village of Milford, was a keen sportsman and was instrumental in forming the Milford Cricket Club. He played goalkeeper for Milford Football Club and possessed an infectious personality, a brilliant story-telling manner, and was the author of some commendable sketches. In his capacity as a goalkeeper, McCrum was cognisant of the degeneration of the sport of football as a result of cynical foul play and in 1890, as a member of the Irish Football Association, he suggested the idea of a penalty kick in order to prevent this type of behaviour. His idea was not without controversy and caused offence to those who considered football a gentleman's sport, completely devoid of cheating. However, one year later McCrum's proposal was adopted as 'rule number 13' in the 'Laws of the Game'. He died in December 1932 in Armagh and a memorial statute stands in his honour in the town of his birth.

William Frederick McFadzean
Victoria Cross recipient
1895 – 1916

Lurgan native William Frederick McFadzean served as a private in the 14th Battalion, The Royal Irish Rifles, British Army, during World War I. On 1 July 1916, near Thiepval Wood, France, a box of hand grenades slipped down into an occupied trench. Upon seeing that two of the grenades' safety pins had become displaced, McFadzean propelled himself on top of the grenades in a bid to prevent harm to his comrades. The grenades exploded and he was killed instantly, but in the process, prevented injury to all but one soldier. For this brave deed he was awarded the Victoria Cross.

Peter McManus
Victoria Cross recipient 1829 – 1859

Peter McManus was born in Tynan, County Armagh and later became a private in the 1st Battalion, Fifth Regiment of the British Army during the Indian Mutiny. At Lucknow on 26 September 1857, a party of his comrades was besieged in a house in the city. Single-handedly, McManus razed the siege, during which at great risk to his own life, he dashed across the street to the aid of a wounded captain, who he successfully transported to safety. He later became a sergeant and was killed in action at Allahabad, India in 1859.

Bernard McQuirt
Victoria Cross recipient 1829 – 1888

Bernard McQuirt was a private in the 95th Regiment of Foot, British Army during the Indian Mutiny and was awarded the Victoria Cross for his heroics on 6 January 1858 during the capture of the town of Rowa, India. Whilst involved in that conflict, McQuirt was seriously wounded in hand-to-hand fighting with three men. Of those men, he killed one, wounded a second, and captured the third. He died in Erney Street, just off the Shankill Road, Belfast in 1888.

Cardinal Tomás Ó Fiaich
Cardinal and Primate of All Ireland
1923 – 1990

Crossmaglen native Tomás Ó'Fiaich was ordained to the priesthood on 6 July 1948. An academic and noted Irish language scholar, he served as vice-president of St Patrick's College, Maynooth from 1970 until 1974, and as president of that institution until 1977. Ó'Fiaich was appointed archbishop of Armagh in August 1977, a tenure during which he was heavily involved in discussions with the hunger strikers of 1981, and he is widely acknowledged as having significantly helped to end the first of these strikes. Whilst extremely concerned by the treatment of the prisoners, he concurrently condemned the use of violence to advance the cause of Irish nationalism. Ó'Fiaich, who was elevated to cardinal by Pope John Paul II on 30 June 1979, died of a heart attack at the Marian Shrine in Lourdes, France on 8 May 1990.

William Olpherts
Victoria Cross recipient
1822 – 1902

A captain in the Bengal Artillery, Indian Army during the Indian Rebellion of 1857, whilst at the head of the 90th Regiment in Lucknow, William Olpherts charged on horseback and captured two field artillery pieces. He did this in the face of heavy enemy fire and precariously returned to rescue fellow soldiers who had been injured in combat. For this feat, he was awarded the Victoria Cross. He died in London, England in 1902.

Arthur Hunter Palmer
Premier of Queensland
1819 – 1898

Arthur Hunter Palmer was educated at Youghal Grammar School and in 1838, emigrated to Australia. He initially settled in New South Wales before moving on to Queensland where he acquired extensive land and ran a sheep station. In 1866 he was elected for Port Curtis to the Legislative Assembly, and four years later was made colonial secretary and premier of Queensland. He was appointed KCMG (Order of St Michael and St George) in 1881. Palmer died after a long illness on 20 March 1898 in Toowong, Queensland.

George William Russell
Poet and painter 1867 – 1935

Moving to Dublin at the age of eleven, George William Russell initially worked as a draper before later joining the Irish Agricultural Organisation Society (IAOS), a co-operative movement, where he was charged with the task of developing the credit societies and establishing co-operative banks. He was editor of the *Irish Homestead*, the journal of the IAOS from 1905 to 1923, and also editor of the *Irish Statesman* from 1923 to 1930 where he wrote under the pseudonym of 'Æ'. A member of the Irish Nationalist Movement, as well as an accomplished poet and playwright, his works are enjoyed for their mystical tone, their delicate melodious style, and their view of humanities spiritual nature. His *Collected Poems*, comprising one hundred and seventy three works, represents the extent and quality of his productions. Russell, who was also commissioned by the American collector John Quinn, to paint William Butler Yeats in 1902, died on 17 July 1935 in Bournemouth, England.

David Sinton
Pig-iron industrialist 1808 – 1900

David Sinton was born into a Quaker family in County Armagh and in 1811 emigrated with his family to Pittsburg, Pennsylvania. A distinguished businessman, he was primarily concerned with the manufacturing of iron and he was a renowned philanthropist who made significant contributions to the arts and the Presbyterian church. Ohio's richest man at that time, he made his fortune by selling pig-iron at inflated prices during the American Civil War and upon his death on 31 August 1900, left the astronomical sum of 20 million dollars to his daughter. Sinton's former home is now the Taft Museum of Art and the town of Sinton, Texas, as well as the famous Cincinnati hotel, are named in his honor.

Philip Smith
Victoria Cross recipient 1825 – 1906

Phillip Smith was born in Lurgan and was a corporal in the 17th Regiment, British Army, during the Crimean War. On 18 June 1855 at Sebastopol, he repeatedly, under heavy fire, advanced towards the front of enemy trenches in an effort to retrieve several of his comrades and transport them back to safety. For this, he was awarded the Victoria Cross. Smith would go on to achieve the rank of sergeant, and died in Dublin in 1906.

John Stephenson
Builder of the world's first street car 1809 – 1893

John Stephenson was born in County Armagh, but emigrated to the United States with his parents at an early age. When he was nineteen he attained an apprenticeship with carriage maker Andrew Wade and upon completion of this apprenticeship, opened his own business. He designed and built the first omnibus made in New York and also produced cars for the first street railway in the world, the New York and Harlem Railroad. Stephenson, whose company became the largest of its kind, was the originator of the idea of having an entrance at both ends of a coach, a design that allowed for more efficient entry and exit. He died in 1893.

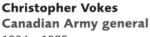

Christopher Vokes
Canadian Army general
1904 – 1985

When his father was appointed to the Royal Military College of Canada in 1910, Christopher Vokes immigrated with his family and later graduated in 1925, from the same institution. After completing his studies at McGill University, Vokes was commissioned into the Royal Canadian Engineers. He rose swiftly through the ranks, leading the 2nd Canadian Infantry Brigade in the Sicily campaign in 1943 as well as the 1st Canadian Division in November of that year. Vokes was successful in driving back German forces as the commander in charge at the brutal Battle of Ortona but later switched to command the 4th Canadian Armoured Division during the bitter Hochwald Forest battle. He was the general officer commanding the Canadian army occupational forces in Europe from 1945 until 1946 and retired from military duty in 1959. Vokes died of cancer in Oakville, Ontario in 1985.

Andrew Trew Wood
Canadian businessman and
parliamentarian 1826 – 1903

Renowned businessman Andrew Trew Wood was born in Mountnorris, County Armagh and was educated in Derrykeighan and Loughgilly before later emigrating to Canada, where he worked in a hardware store. He eventually formed a hardware business of his own in 1856 and after overcoming early setbacks, the business became very profitable, generating revenue in the region of $300,000 per year. Wood later went on to become a director of the Hamilton and Lake Erie Railway Company as well as a founder member of the Bank of Hamilton in 1872. He was also one of the largest shareholders in the Hamilton Iron Forging Company and became a millionaire off the back of his holdings in that firm. Late in life, he served three terms as a member of parliament in the Canadian House of Commons and was elected to the Canadian Senate in January 1901, representing the Senatorial Division of Hamilton, Ontario until his death in 1903.

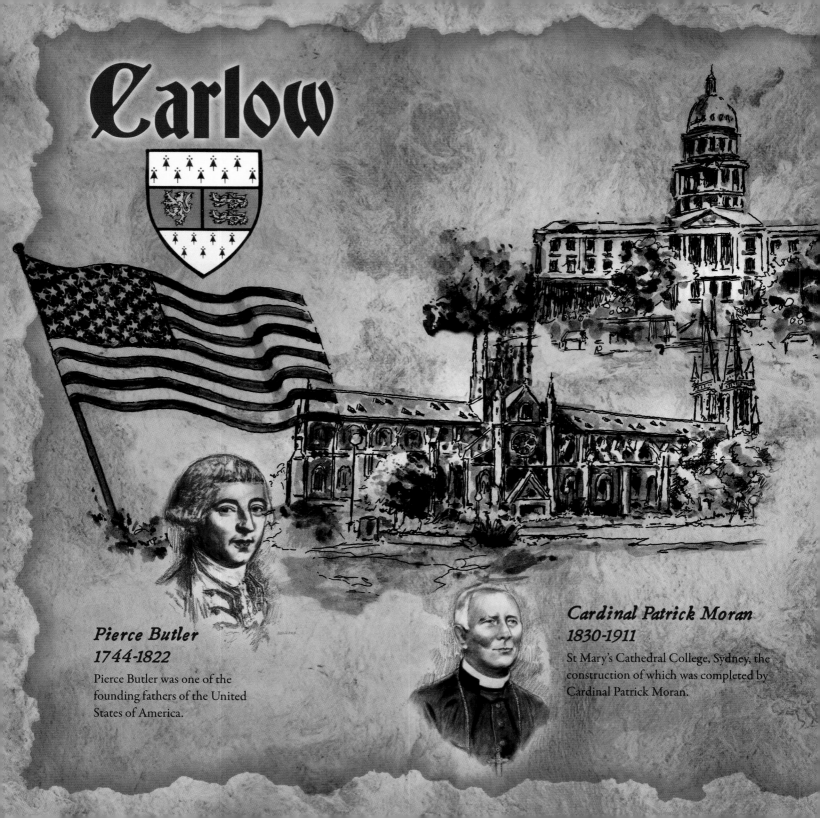

Carlow

Pierce Butler
1744-1822

Pierce Butler was one of the founding fathers of the United States of America.

Cardinal Patrick Moran
1830-1911

St Mary's Cathedral College, Sydney, the construction of which was completed by Cardinal Patrick Moran.

Thomas McDonald Patterson
1839-1916

The Colorado state capitol, where Thomas McDonald Patterson represented Colorado in the Senate.

Peter Fenelon Collier
1849-1909

Collier's Weekly, one of Peter Fenelon Collier's many publications, was one of the largest selling magazines in the United States.

Myles Keogh
1840-1876

The memorial at the site of the Battle of Little Bighorn, Montana, USA, where Myles Keogh was killed in action.

Beauchamp Bagenal

Duellist, hell-raiser and rake 1741 – 1802

Following his inheritance of a huge estate at the age of eleven, Beauchamp Bagenal cultivated a notably lavish lifestyle throughout his life. He embarked upon a grand tour of Europe during which time he visited most of the continent's capital cities and maintained a colourful existence, characterised by some wild adventures. A renowned duellist, many of his contests took place in St Stephen's Green in Dublin, but it is reputed that his favourite battleground of all was a graveyard, where he could lean against a tombstone, due to being lame, whilst firing his pistol. On his aforementioned sojourn to Europe, Bagenal supposedly fought a prince, jilted a princess, carried off a duchess from Madrid, and fought a duel in Paris. For a short period, he also served as a member of parliament for Carlow, significantly proposing that a sum of one hundred pounds be voted to freedom campaigner, Henry Grattan, in respect of the work that he had done for his country. Apart from this he appears to have done little else in public life. He died in 1802.

Pierce Butler

Soldier and statesman 1744 – 1822

Soldier Pierce Butler commenced his army career in the 22nd Regiment of Foot (now the Cheshire Regiment) of the British Army. He travelled with the regiment to the United States in 1758 to participate in the French and Indian War, a conflict which resulted in the capture of Canada from the French. When war broke out between Britain and the Colonies in 1775, Butler defected to the American cause, joining the South Carolina militia to fight against the British forces. Being a former British officer, he became a primary target of British aggression throughout the campaign, but successfully evaded capture. Butler, who represented the South Carolina legislature at the constitutional congress convention in Philadelphia in 1787, served three separate terms in the United States Senate before retiring from politics in 1805. He died in Philadelphia on 15 February 1822. Butler is recognised as one of the United States' Founding Fathers.

Peter Fenelon Collier

Subscription publisher 1849 – 1909

In 1866 Peter Fenelon Collier, a media pioneer and native of Myshall, emigrated to Dayton, Ohio, where he entered St Mary's Seminary in Cincinnati. Lacking in vocation, Collier joined P. J. Kennedy, a publisher of Catholic books, and suggested to the company that sales could be improved by offering the books to consumers on a subscription plan. With P.J. Kennedy failing to see the potential in his concept, Collier established his own subscription service, the first company ever to do so, and in 1888 founded a family magazine, *Collier's Once a Week*, later changing the name to *Collier's Weekly*. Between 1900 and 1910, the company sold over thirty million books and Collier was widely acclaimed as the father of the modern subscription book business. He died in New York, on 24 April 1909.

Samuel Haughton

Scientist 1821 – 1897

Samuel Haughton was born beside the River Burrin Bridge in Carlow Town. Graduating with a degree in mathematics from Trinity College, Dublin, he later became a professor of geology at the college from 1851 to 1881. Haughton, who was a man of prodigious academic talent, communicated papers on widely different subjects ranging from mathematical physics and polarized light to the mineralogy of Ireland and Wales, as well as 'Animal Mechanics' – the study of the mechanical principles of muscular action. At the age of thirty-eight, he decided to study medicine at Trinity College and upon graduating became medical registrar of Trinity Medical School. He is also accredited with the great improvements which were made to the medical facilities in Trinity College during that time. He died at 12 Northbrook Road, Dublin on 31 October 1897 and as his funeral cortege moved through the town of Carlow, all businesses were closed in honor of his memory. He is buried at Killeshin, County Laois.

Myles Keogh
Soldier 1840 – 1876

Leighlinbridge native Myles Keogh is best known for a spectacular military career, which was prematurely cut short after fourteen years. Initially serving as a lieutenant in the battalion of St Patrick in the Papal Army of Pius IX, he received a decoration from the Pope for his distinguished service in defending the port city of Ancona in the war to unite Italy. At the outbreak of the American Civil War, Keogh joined the Federal Army and saw service as a brevet lieutenant-colonel, commanding three thousand cavalry. At the end of the war he joined the peacetime army as a captain in the 7th US Cavalry regiment under General Custer and fought in the Battle of Little Bighorn where he was killed in the summer of 1876. Sioux accounts of that battle indicate great efforts made by Keogh in an attempt to rally his troops and the Sioux chief, Red Horse, said of Keogh that he was the 'bravest he had ever seen'.

John Lucas
Victoria Cross recipient 1827 – 1892

John Lucas was born in Bagenalstown, County Carlow. A colour sergeant in the 40th Regiment, British Army, during the Māori Wars in New Zealand, he was awarded the Victoria Cross for coming to the aid of a fallen lieutenant who lay just thirty yards from enemy lines. He safely conveyed the lieutenant to safety, and defended the position until reinforcements arrived. Lucas died in Dublin on 29 February 1892.

John Lyons
Victoria Cross recipient 1823 – 1867

John Lyons was a private in the 19th Regiment, British Army, during the Crimean War. On 10 June 1855 at Sebastopol in the Crimea, he picked up a live shell that had fallen amongst his fellow soldiers in a trench. Completely disregarding his own safety, he picked up the live shell and hurled it over the parapet of the trench, thereby saving the lives of his fellow soldiers. He died in Naas, County Kildare in 1867.

Bill MacNevin (Val Vousden)
Actor, poet and playwright
1886 – 1951

Born in College Street, Carlow and educated at Mungret College, County Limerick, Bill MacNevin toured Ireland and England with a drama troupe in the early 1900s. Upon the outbreak of World War I in 1914 he joined the British army, eventually reaching the rank of regimental sergeant major. Following the conclusion of the war, MacNevin returned to Newbridge, County Kildare to pursue his acting career and adopted the name Val Vousden as he toured Ireland with a number of theatrical companies. when Radio Éireann was launched,

MacNevin became presenter of the first radio-broadcasted light entertainment show in Ireland and appeared regularly at the Abbey Theatre, Dublin while also featuring in a number of films. His autobiography *Val Vousden's Caravan*, detailed accounts of his touring show experiences, and he also published *Recitations, Monologues, Character Sketches, and Plays*, which was a comprehensive collection of the numerous plays, poems and sketches he produced throughout his career. MacNevin died in Dublin on 6 June 1951.

Cardinal Patrick Francis Moran
Archbishop of Sydney 1830 – 1911

Patrick Francis Moran was born in Leighlinbridge, but left Ireland in 1842 to pursue religious studies at the Pontifical Irish College in Rome. Moran was a brilliant student and extraordinary linguist, speaking Italian, Latin, French, German, Spanish, Irish, and Hebrew fluently. Ordained in 1853, he followed a missionary vocation to Australia and in 1884 was appointed archbishop of Sydney. The following year he achieved the distinction of becoming the first Australian Cardinal. In Sydney, Moran was involved in the building of new schools, churches, and hospitals and he published a dozen books on church history, one of which was entitled *The History of the Catholic Church in Australia*. He died in Manby Palace, Sydney on 16 August 1911.

Michael Nicholas Nolan
American politician 1833 – 1905

Michael Nicholas Nolan emigrated to the US with his family, at the age of ten. Having attended public school in Albany, he went on to study law and was later a director of the National Savings Bank of Albany as well as fire commissioner of Albany from 1869 until 1878. Elected mayor of Albany in 1878, he served in that role until 1883,

River Barrow, Graiguenamanagh, County Carlow.

juggling his duties as an elected Democrat to the 47th Congress from 1881 until 1883. He died on 31 May 1905.

Patrick O'Donoghue
Young Irelander Died 1854

A participant in the Young Irelander Rebellion at Ballingarry, County Tipperary in July 1848, Patrick O'Donoghue was captured and sentenced to death for treason; a judgment later commuted the sentence to transportation for life to Vandiemen's Land (Tasmania), Australia. Upon his arrival in Hobart, Tasmania, he set about producing an Irish newspaper, the *Irish Exile*, which greatly displeased the governor, Sir William Dennison. As a result of this act, O'Donoghue was sentenced to a year of hard labour in a chain gang, but upon his release, immediately set about publishing the newspaper again; this time giving extensive personal accounts of his difficult experiences in the preceding year. Once again vexing the governor with his defiance, O'Donoghue received another sentence of hard labour but was released three months later, and whilst being escorted by guards, escaped to freedom with the assistance of some fellow prisoners. Making his way by ship to Melbourne, he succeeded in gaining passage to San Francisco but died in New York on 22 January 1854, shortly before the arrival of his wife from Ireland. It is thought that the time he spent on the chain gangs contributed to his ill health.

Thomas MacDonald Patterson
Politician and newspaper publisher
1839 – 1916

Born in County Carlow in 1849, Thomas MacDonald Patterson emigrated with his parents to the United States where they settled in New York. There he was educated at a public school following which he worked in a printing office, a jewellers and a watchmakers. During the American Civil War, Patterson enlisted in the 11th Regiment, Indiana Volunteers and following that conflict enrolled at Indiana Asbury University to study Law. Admitted to the Bar in 1867, he became a member of the Democratic National Committee in 1874 and served in the US House of Representatives in the 45th Congress from 1877 until 1879. From there, Patterson moved into media publishing, purchasing the *Rocky Mountain News* in 1890 and later the *Denver Times*. He was an unsuccessful Democratic candidate for governor of Colorado in the early 1890s but atoned for his loss in 1900 when he was elected as a Democrat to the United States Senate, serving a term from 1901 until 1907. He is buried in Fairmount Cemetery in Denver, Colorado.

William Desmond Taylor
Actor and film director
1872 – 1922

Initially known by his birth name, William Cunningham Deane-Tanner, William Desmond Taylor was interested in following in his father's footsteps by pursuing a military career in the British army. However, having failed the cadet's entrance examination, in 1901 he emigrated to America where he married Ethel May Harrison soon after his arrival. Seven years later, for some unknown reason, he disappeared without trace, and with Ethel later divorcing him, it was rumoured that he had a varied and chequered career before finally turning up in Hollywood in 1912. There, he acted in several silent films before turning to directing, upon which time he rose rapidly up the ladder of success. During World War I, in 1918, Taylor enlisted into the Canadian Army but was discharged during the summer of 1919 and returned to film directing with Paramount Pictures. He was president of the Motion Pictures Directors Association on three occasions and among the films he directed were *Davy Crockett, Tom Sawyer, Huckleberry Finn*, and *Anne of Green Gables*. On 1 February 1922, the banner headlines of Hollywood newspapers read, 'Paramount film director, William Desmond Taylor, shot to death in his bungalow.' Rumours abound as to the reason; however his murder was never solved. Taylor's funeral was one of the most impressive ever held in Los Angeles, with every person of prominence in the picture industry attending.

Thomas Traynor
Patriot 1882 – 1921

Tullow patriot Thomas Traynor was a boot maker by trade and was a married family man who had no less than ten children. Fighting alongside Éamon de Valera (see page 431) at the Boland Mills Garrison during the Easter Rising of 1916, he spent some time in prison following that revolt in Wakefield, England. Upon his release he returned to active duty with the IRA and was attached to 'B' Company, 3rd Battalion Dublin Brigade, during the Irish War of Independence. On 14 March 1921, whilst in action against British soldiers and the Black and Tans, he was captured on Pearse Street in Dublin. He was tried and sentenced to death by hanging at Mountjoy Prison on 25 April 1921.

John Tyndall
Inventor and philosopher
1820 – 1893

With his family only able to afford a hedge-school education, Leighlinbridge born John Tyndall did not enter university until he was in his mid-thirties. Despite this obvious disadvantage, Tyndall went on to become one of the most significant scientists of the nineteenth century. A founding father of the science of 'nephelometry', one of Tydall's greatest contributions was the explanation as to why the sky is blue – a phenomenon that is due to the scattering of the sun's rays by molecules in the atmosphere, and which is now known as the 'Tyndall Effect'; while the specific blue colour of the sky is also called 'Tyndall Blue'. In 1853, following a lecture to the Royal Institute of Great Britain, he was elected to the chair of natural philosophy and having invented the 'light-pipe', the forerunner of fibre-optics the following year, he also devised one of the first respirators, which filtered air through a series of mechanisms that allowed air to be exhaled through a separate exhaust valve. It is a system that is used in respirators to this day. An insomniac, Tyndall tragically died whilst experimenting with cures for the condition in 1893 but his contribution to science will never be forgotten.

Cavan

General Philip Sheridan
1831-1888

Philip Sheridan was a brilliant cavalry general during the American Civil War. General Grant, later to become President Grant, stated: 'I rank Sheridan with Napoleon and Frederick'. A Statue to General Sheridan stands near the White House in Washington DC.

General Eric Dorman-Smith
1895-1969

The 7th Armoured Division Thetford Forest Memorial to the Desert Rats. Eric 'Chink' Dorman-Smith, together with General Auchinleck, is often considered the real victor over Field Marshal Erwin Rommel at the First Battle of El Alamein in North Africa.

Andrew Carney
1794-1864

Andrew Carney was the principal benefactor in the construction of Boston College and was also a generous giver of aid to Ireland during the Great Famine.

Margaret Haughery
1813-1882

Known as the 'mother of orphans', Margaret Haughery is held in reverence by the people of New Orleans. Her statue stands in the city's Margaret Place.

Patrick Henry O'Rorke
1837-1863

The Colonel Patrick Henry O'Rorke Memorial Bridge, Rochester, New York is dedicated to one of the Union army's finest commanders during the American Civil War. He died in action at the Battle of Gettysburg.

Thomas Brady

Austrian army field marshal 1752 – 1827

Having originally intended to become a priest, and with this ambition in mind, Thomas Brady set out for Prague, Czech Republic in his mid-twenties. However, he was subsequently advised by his uncle Terence Brady – a physician to Empress Maria Theresa of Austria – that he was more suited to becoming a soldier. A young man of athletic appearance, he was accepted as a cadet in the Austrian army in 1783 and distinguished himself at the battle of Belgrade in 1789. Considered one of the finest swordsmen in the Austrian army, Brady rose rapidly through the ranks to become a general and then a field marshal, and was held in high esteem by the emperors Joseph II, Leopold II and Francis II for his fearless leadership in the field of battle where he sustained innumerous wounds. Brady, who was also reputed to be the lover of Empress Maria Theresa, died in Vienna in October 1827.

Richard Busteed

Union general, American Civil War 1822 – 1898

Having emigrated to Canada with his family when he was a young boy, Richard Busteed later moved to New York City where he studied law and was admitted to the bar in 1846. At the outbreak of the American Civil War, he was appointed brigadier general of volunteers by President Lincoln and served with his brigade near Yorktown, Virginia. His stance on anti-slavery lost him support within sections of the armed forces and he consequently resigned from active service on 10 March 1863. Subsequently appointed to the bench of the US District Court of Alabama, Busteed served there until his resignation in 1874. He later returned to New York City to practise law and he died in that city on 14 September 1898.

Andrew Carney

Merchant and benefactor 1794 – 1864

A native of Ballanagh, Andrew Carney emigrated to America at the age of twenty-two where he arrived virtually penniless. He went on to become a very prosperous tailor and clothing merchant, producing ready-to-wear, off-the-peg clothing and he was also a gracious benefactor to the Catholic Church in Boston. There was no equal to Carney in relation to philanthropic contributions amongst the Catholics of New England of that era: he donated large sums to help in the relief of the Great Famine in Ireland from 1845 to 1849 and he was the principal benefactor in the construction of Carney Hospital, Dorchester and Boston College, Chestnut Hill in Massachusetts, in which Carney Hall is named in his memory. He died in Boston on 3 April 1864.

Marcus Daly

'Copper Mine King of Montana' 1841 – 1900

In 1856, just prior to the Great Famine, Marcus Daly arrived in New York with little money, education or skills, and worked in various odd jobs to sustain himself. Some five years later, he moved to San Francisco where he worked as a ranch hand, a logger, and a railroad worker before once again upping sticks and settling in the silver mines of Virginia City, Nevada where he made friends with George Hearst, a financier who would later become one of his backers. It was in Butte, Montana that Daly finally found his fortune. Butte was the location of the biggest deposit of copper known at the time and with the financial support of Hearst, the father of newspaper magnate William Randolf Hearst, Daly built a smelter to handle the ore and by 1895 had become a millionaire and owner of the Anaconda Copper Mining Company. Next to his mine he founded the town of Anaconda, Montana and a statue to his memory stands at the main entrance of the Montana Tech of the University of Montana in Butte. The Marcus Daly Memorial Hospital in Hamilton, Montana, is also named in his memory.

Major General Eric 'Chink' Dorman-Smith
British army general in the first battle of El Alamein 1895 – 1969

A childhood friend of John Charles McQuaid (page 68), Eric Edward Dorman-Smith emerged from World War I as a major with the Military Cross and in December 1940 was sent as an adviser to Major-General Richard O'Connor and the Western Desert Force in Egypt. In relation to Dorman-Smith's military career, Tim Clayton and Phil Craig wrote in the Daily Mail on 19 October 2002: 'vain, back-stabbing, ruthlessly lying, to destroy his rivals, Field Marshal Montgomery is lionized as the hero of El Alamein, but in fact the desert war was won by two brilliant officers, whose glory he shamelessly stole'. The two officers were General Claude Auchinleck and General Eric 'Chink' Dorman-Smith. It was Chink's ideas for desert warfare that stopped the Germans at the first battle of El Alamein in July 1942 and turned the tide for the British forces in Egypt, thus making Montgomery's later efforts comparatively facile. Disillusioned with his removal from command, and with

Winston Churchill's favoritism of Montgomery, Chink retired to his estate in Ireland and lent his talents to Irish republicanism, becoming an IRA advisor during the 1950s Border Campaign. The renowned German field marshal, Erwin 'The Desert Fox' Rommel, remarked of Auchinleck and 'Chink': 'I was beaten by the best generalship that I met in the entire war.' Auchinleck wrote: 'Chink' was tragically mistreated and betrayed, he was the true hero of El Alamein. Dorman-Smith, later known as O'Gowan due to his change of allegiance, died of cancer on 11 May 1969.

Harold Marcus Ervine-Andrews
Victoria Cross recipient 1911 – 1995

Harold Marcus Ervine-Andrews was born in Keadue, County Cavan. A captain in the East Lancashire Regiment of the British Army during World War II, his defining moment occurred on 31 May 1940, near Dunkirk, France. With his company outnumbered and under severe pressure from German fire, Ervine-Andrews and his men retreated to a barn and using a Bren gun, he successfully killed eleven of the enemy. With the barn catching fire in the exchange, Ervine-Andrews remained with eight of his men, continuing to defend the position until being overwhelmed, upon which time they were forced to retreat by wading in water up to their chins for over a mile. For this deed Ervine-Andrews was awarded the Victoria Cross.

Thomas Fitzpatrick
Explorer, US Indian agent 1799 – 1854

Thomas Fitzpatrick was born in County Cavan but emigrated to the United States at an early age. Having established himself as a trapper, fur trader and guide, his first expedition was up the Missouri River and he spent many of the following years opening up the western frontier of the United States. During his travels, Fitzpatrick discovered the 'South Pass' through the Rocky Mountains which was to become a main passage for settlers into the Oregon territory, and he is believed to have led the first 'emigrant train' to California. In his travels, Fitzpatrick became closely acquainted with the Native Americans and as a result he was appointed as a representative agent, being christened 'Broken Hand' due to the fact that he had two fingers missing from one of his hands. Fitzpatrick was instrumental in organising the Fort Laramie Treaty conference of 1851, where an agreement was achieved with the Cheyenne, Shoshone, and Sioux tribes that established the format for improved relations on the Great Plains. He died of pneumonia while on political duty for the Native American tribes in Washington and is buried in the Congressional Cemetery. 'Broken Hand' has been hailed as the greatest of all frontiersmen of his era.

Matthew Gibney
Catholic Bishop of Perth 1835 – 1925

Matthew Gibney was born in Killeshandra and studied for the priesthood at All Hallows Missionary College in Drumcondra, Dublin. He was ordained as a priest in 1863 and arrived in Perth, Western Australia the same year. A man of great energy and charity, he opened a catholic orphanage for girls in Perth in 1868, and an orphanage for boys in Subiaco.

In 1887 he became Bishop of Perth and during his episcopate, established a number of churches, schools, orphanages, hospitals and a monastery. Gibney, who was horrified at the treatment of the aboriginal people by the white settlers, was one of the first people of his status to strongly defend the indigenous people and in an effort to assist them, he opened a mission at Beagle Bay in 1890. Gibney also identified himself closely with the political and social aspirations of his fellow Irishmen in Australia. He died at his home, in north Perth, on 22 June 1925.

Margaret Haughery
'The Mother of Orphans'
1813 – 1882

A truly great woman, Margaret Haughery is known as 'the mother of the orphans' in New Orleans. Born in County Cavan, she emigrated with her family to the US where they settled in Baltimore, Maryland. Orphaned at an early age, Haughery married in 1835 and settled in New Orleans but experienced tragedy with the death of her husband and an infant child. Following her difficult loss, she embarked upon a career of now-legendary charitable deeds, nursing the sick and dying, regardless of race or creed, during the New Orleans yellow fever epidemic, as well as assuring dying mothers that she would look after their children. She established both a bakery and a dairy in the city and painstakingly delivered milk and bread to the poor for years. A resourceful and energetic businesswoman, her bakery (the first steam bakery in the south) became famous and during the American Civil War, confederate prisoners were the special object of her care. The people of New Orleans held Haughery in reverence and following her death in 1882, the city erected a public monument to her memory. The park in which the monument is erected, is officially named Margaret Place. She died on 9 February 1882, due to an unrecorded illness, but not before receiving a blessing from Pope Pius IX as well as the respects of people from a multitude of classes, races and denominations whose lives she had had a profound impact upon.

Captain James Kelly
Irish army intelligence officer
1929 – 2003

After joining the Irish army in 1949, James Kelly was commissioned as a lieutenant in 1951 and was promoted to captain a decade later. Coming from a long line of Irish nationalists, his father topped the poll for Sinn Féin in the local elections of 1918 and an ancestor of his, Robert Kelly, was a member of the United Irishman. Whilst on holiday in Belfast in 1969, Kelly witnessed the start of the *Troubles*. He reported his findings to his commanding officer, Colonel Hefferon, who in turn advised the then-minister of defence, Jim Gibbons. This communication set in motion a chain of events that culminated in the 1970 trial of a number of government ministers involved in the importation of arms for use in Northern Ireland. Kelly was also tried and, although he was acquitted, his career in the army was in ruins as a result. During the trial, Charles J. Haughey, then a minister who was also involved in the trial, clearly stated, 'with the authority of the government, Captain Kelly had a special job to do'. Maintaining that he was working under government instructions, Kelly spent the remainder of his life endeavouring to clear his name. Although a nationalist at heart, he was a strong proponent of an IRA ceasefire during the 1990s and to this day research into government and army archives continue in an effort to reinstate his reputation. At the time of Kelly's death on 16 July 2003, the taoiseach at that time, Bertie Ahern stated, 'Captain Jim Kelly acted on what he believed to be the proper orders of his superiors. For my part, I never found any reason to doubt his integrity.' Kelly is buried in Glasnevin Cemetery, Dublin.

Richard Charles Mayne
Admiral and explorer 1835 – 1892

As an officer in the Royal Navy, Richard Charles Mayne took part in an expedition to British Columbia and was one of the first surveyors of the two British colonies of British Columbia and Vancouver Island. Mayne authored Four Years in British Columbia and Vancouver Island, an account of the abundant natural resources that lay waiting to be exploited in the north west coast and which is regarded as the classic source of British Columbian history. The son of Sir Richard Mayne, Mayne Island is named in his memory.

John McGovern
Victoria Cross recipient 1825 – 1888

John McGovern was born in Tullyhaw, County Cavan and at thirty-two years old, became a private in the 1st Bengal Fusiliers, Indian Army. On 23 June 1857, during the Indian Rebellion at Delhi, McGovern successfully carried a wounded comrade to the safety of their camp under intense fire and at great risk to his own life. For this deed he was awarded the Victoria Cross. He died in Ontario, Canada in 1888.

T. P. McKenna
Actor 1929 – 2011

One of Ireland's leading stars of stage, screen and radio, Thomas Patrick McKenna was born in Mullagh, and educated at St Patrick's College, Cavan. Upon leaving school in the late 1940s, his first job was with the Ulster Bank in Granard, County Longford but he later commenced an acting career and made his

London West End debut as Cranley in *Stephen D* in 1963. From the mid 1960s McKenna began appearing in such popular television dramas as *The Avengers, The Saint, Jason King, The Sweeney, Dr Who* and *Minder*; and in addition he appeared in films *Ulysses* (1967), *Straw Dogs* (1971), and *Portrait of the Artist as a Young Man* (1977). One of a great generation of Irish actors, with an ability to adapt with ease to the variety of characters he portrayed, McKenna also worked with the Royal Shakespeare Company and the Royal National Theatre Company, directing such productions as *The Playboy of the Western World* and *Shadow of a Gunman*.

John Charles McQuaid
Catholic Archbishop of Dublin
1895 – 1973

John Charles McQuaid was born in Cootehill. He was educated at Cootehill National School, and for a short period, at Blackrock College in Dublin before finishing his secondary school education at Clongowes Wood College, County Kildare. Having joined the religious congregation, The Holy Ghost Fathers, McQuaid became Archbishop of Dublin in 1940 and was also a highly influential political figure who influenced Éamon de Valera in the drafting of the modern Irish constitution. A controversial character in that he condemned the 'Mother and Child Scheme', which provided free access to healthcare for mothers and children, McQuaid engaged in considerable conflict with de Valera due to differing opinions in respect to certain government policies. He died in his private residence in Killiney, County Dublin on 7 April 1973.

Patrick Henry O'Rorke
Union Army officer in the American Civil War 1837 – 1863

Patrick Henry O'Rorke was born in Drumbess. His family emigrated to the United States when he was a child and there they settled in Rochester, New York. O'Rorke graduated from Rochester's public school, in the mid 1850s and entered the West Point US Military Academy as a cadet in 1857, where he graduated first in his class in June 1861. Having distinguished himself in the Civil War as a staff-officer in the engineer corps, he was appointed colonel in the 140th Regiment of New York Volunteers and participated in the Battles of Fredericksburg and Chancellorsville but was killed whilst leading his men in the defence of Little Round Top at the Battle of Gettysburg. Comte de Paris, in his history of the American Civil War, refers to O'Rorke's actions at Little Round Top as 'one of the most striking and dramatic episodes of the battle.' The O'Rorke Bridge in Rochester, New York is named in his memory.

James Owens
Victoria Cross recipient 1829 – 1901

James Owens was born in Killaine Baillieboro, and later became a corporal in the 49th Regiment of the British Army during the Crimean War. In October, 1854, at Sebastopol, Owens displayed exemplary bravery against Russian forces, saving the life of a lieutenant. Awarded the Victorian Cross and later achieving the rank of sergeant, he died in Romford, Essex in 1901.

George Richardson
Victoria Cross recipient 1831 – 1923

At twenty-seven years of age, Killeshandra native George Richardson became a private in the 34th Regiment, British Army. On 27 April 1859, during the Indian Mutiny at Kewane Trans-Gogra, India, he attacked and captured a rebel soldier. Richardson was able to subdue the soldier with the use of just one arm, the other having been incapacitated due to injuries sustained in combat. For his exploits, he was awarded the Victoria Cross and later achieved the rank of sergeant. Richardson died in Canada in 1923.

Mary Anne Sadlier
Irish author 1820 – 1903

Born Mary Anne Madden and originally from Cootehill, Mary Anne Sadlier emigrated to Montreal, Canada in 1844 where she married a publisher, James Sadlier who was also from Ireland. She authored around sixty popular novels with themes pertaining to Ireland including, *The Red Hand of Ulster*

Cavan river Erne.

and *The Old House by the Boyne*, and was a prolific writer whose works included domestic novels, historical romances, and children's catechisms. Awarded the Laetare Medal from the University of Notre Dame, Sadlier was also the recipient of a special blessing from Pope Leo XIII for her services to the church and her impact on Catholic publishing. She died in Canada in 1903.

Colonel Edward Saunderson
Unionist politician 1837 – 1906

Edward Saunderson was born at Castle Saunderson and became a Liberal MP for County Cavan in 1865, filling the same role for North Armagh in 1885 – a seat he held until his death in 1906. Considered the first leader of modern Ulster unionism, in 1886 he became leader of the Irish Unionist Party at Westminster and was an impassioned politician whose speeches were juxtaposed with determination and humour. A statue to his memory stands in Market Street in Portadown, County Armagh.

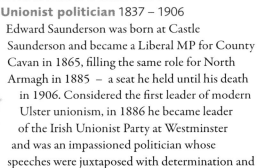

Francis Sheehy-Skeffington
Suffragist, pacifist and writer
1878 – 1916

A native of Bailieborough, Francis Skeffington was an ardent supporter of equal rights for women and took the surname of his wife, Hanna Sheehy, upon their marriage in 1903. In addition to being very active in the development of the Irish Labour Movement, in 1908 Skeffington authored *Michael Davitt, Revolutionary, Agitator and Labour Leader* in honour of the great republican and nationalist (see page 305). Upon the foundation of the Irish Citizens'

Army in 1913, he was elected as one of its vice-chairmen; joining on the strict understanding that it was to defend workers against police, and was not to become a military organisation. In 1915, Skeffington travelled to the United States to campaign for the cause of Irish freedom. Whilst he was a friend of some of the revolutionary leaders of the Easter Rising in 1916, he was very much opposed to military force, preferring instead a pacifist intellectual resistance. On 25 April 1916, Skeffington, who was concerned with the collapse of law and order in the aftermath of the Easter Rising, was arrested whilst trying to prevent citizens from looting and following this incident he was witness to the shooting of an unarmed boy by Captain Bowen-Colthurst of the Royal Irish Rifles. As a result Bowen-Colthurst, who was declared unsound of mind in a subsequent court-martial, had Skeffington shot the next morning. A Royal Commission enquiry on 23 August 1916 resulted in the offer of monetary compensation to his wife, which she refused. A novel Skeffington wrote, *In Dark and Evil Days* was published posthumously.

Philip Sheridan
Union general in the American Civil War 1831 – 1888

A brilliant general in the Union Army during the American Civil War, Phillip Sheridan was born in Killinkere, and was just four months old when he arrived with his family in the United States. He entered the Westpoint Academy in 1848 and graduated in 1853, embarking on one of the most admirable military careers in US history. Sheridan fought in the Indian wars and was promoted from captain to colonel to brigadier general in quick succession. Promoted to commander of cavalry in the Army of the Potomac by General US Grant, Sheridan defeated Confederate forces in the Shenandoah Valley in 1864, and the following year pursued General Robert E. Lee, forcing his surrender at Appomattox. General Grant, who would go on to become President of the United States, said: 'I rank Sheridan with Napoleon and Frederick and the great commanders of history.' The *London Daily News* wrote of Sheridan: 'he was the most brilliant cavalry officer of the American Civil War.' Sheridan died on 5 August 1888, and was buried with full military honours in the National Cemetery at Arlington.

James Somers
Victoria Cross recipient
1884 – 1918

A sergeant in the 1st Battalion, Royal Inniskilling Fusiliers, British Army, James Somers was born in Belturbet, County Cavan. On 1 and 2 July 1915 at Gallipoli in Turkey, he repeatedly ran from his own trench to the those of the attacking Turkish forces and bombarded them with explosives. When the supply of bombs became depleted, Somers returned to his lines where he remained whilst defending with his rifle until reinforcements were deployed and more supplies of bombs were delivered. Previously wounded on the retreat from Mons, Belgium in 1914, Somers died on 7 May 1918 at the age of thirty-three. His headstone bears the simple inscription, 'he stood and defended.'

Sister Dr Mona Tyndall
Religious missionary and doctor 1921 – 2000

Though Cavan born, Mona Tyndall was raised in Glasnevin, Dublin and after graduating with a degree in medicine from University College Dublin, and obtaining further qualifications as an obstetrician and gynaecologist in England, she commenced her African missionary work in Nigeria in 1949. There she became particularly involved in the treatment of the wounded during the Biafran War in 1967, but when Nigerian troops overcame the Biafran resistance, Tyndall and her fellow sisters were imprisoned before eventually attaining release following the intercession of Pope Paul VI. She spent the remainder of her missionary life in Zambia where she endeavoured to reduce the maternal mortality rate by half in the 1990s. With the help of Irish aid, Tyndall established ten maternal health clinics, as well as the country's first ambulance service. A highly dedicated missionary and doctor, she was actively involved in the early fight against HIV/AIDS, and her deep religious integrity enabled her to take on seemingly insurmountable tasks as well as to motivate and inspire others into action. She was a member of the congregation of the Missionary Sisters of the Holy Rosary and retired to Cavan in 1995 where she died in 2000.

Clare

Chartres Brew
1815-1870

Mount Brew in British Columbia is named after Chartres Brew, chief inspector of police in British Columbia.

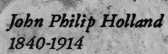

John Philip Holland
1840-1914

The 'Fenian Ram' World War II Class submarine. Its inventor, John Philip Holland was born in Liscannor.

James Bartholomew Blackwell
1763-1820

James B. Blackwell led the successful assault on the Bastille during the French Revolution, 14 July, 1789.

Michael Cusack
1847-1906

The Cusack Stand, Croke Park, Dublin, Michael Cusack was the founder of the GAA.

Patrick Hillery
1923-2008

Áras an Uachtaráin, the Irish president's residence in the Phoenix Park, Dublin where Patrick Hillery served two terms. His contributions as president and as a Fianna Fáil politician were immense.

James Bartholomew Blackwell
Professional soldier and revolutionary
1765 – 1820

Ennis native James Bartholomew Blackwell was educated at the Irish College in Paris, following which he studied medicine. In 1786 he joined the Walsh Regiment as a cadet and was considered highly influential in the successful assault on the Bastille during the French Revolution. In December, 1796, Blackwell set sail for Bantry, County Cork with Wolfe Tone and General Hoche as part of the ill-fated attempt to liberate Ireland. In 1798 he again returned to the country of his birth with fellow revolutionary Napper Tandy to launch another French assisted rebellion. This time Blackwell was captured and he was subsequentally imprisoned at Kilmainham, Dublin. Eventually returning to France in 1802, he joined Napoleon's Irish Legion and became one of its most honoured officers. Blackwell was appointed chef de batallion (lieutenant colonel) by Napoleon but contracted tuberculosis in 1813 and died seven years later following a long battle with the illness.

Chartres Brew
Gold Commissioner, chief constable and judge of British Columbia 1815 – 1870

Chartres Brew served in the Royal Irish Constabulary before being appointed chief inspector of police for the new colony of British Columbia, Canada in 1858. Brew was well respected by his superiors and served as magistrate and acting treasurer, as well as acting chief commissioner of lands and works. He was also appointed a member of the Legislative Council of British Columbia. Two mountain summits in British Columbia, both of which are *Mount Brew* are named in his memory. He died in the Cariboo region of British Columbia in 1870.

Sir Frederick William Burton
Painter 1816 – 1900

Frederick William Burton was born in Corofin and studied drawing in Dublin, where he made a name for himself as a painter of miniatures and watercolour portraits. Having previously spent seven years in Germany studying that country's artistic style, he was appointed director of the National Gallery in London in 1874 and was responsible for the purchase of many important paintings of great value. Knighted in 1884, he died at his home in Kensington, London in March 1900 and is buried in Mount Jerome Cemetery in Dublin.

General Sir Garrett O'Moore Creagh
Victoria Cross recipient 1848 – 1923

Cahirbane born Garrett O'Moore Creagh served as a captain in the Bombay Staff Corps, Indian Army during the Second Afghan War, and with a detachment of 150 men, repelled the onslaught of about 1,500 enemy troops at Kam Dakka. During the successful defence of their position, Creagh's men were reduced to hand-to-hand combat with bayonets until a relief force arrived and the enemy was comprehensively routed. He later became a general and succeeded Lord Kitchener as commander-in-chief of the Indian forces in 1909. He died in London, England in 1923.

Michael Cusack
Founder of the Gaelic Athletic Association 1847 – 1906

A teacher by profession, Michael Cusack taught in some of Ireland's most prestigious schools such as Blackrock College, Clongowes Wood College and Kilkenny College. He eventually settled in Dublin, where he opened the Civil Service Academy on Gardiner Street. At a meeting in Hayes's Hotel in Thurles, County Tipperary on 1 November 1884, Cusack founded the Gaelic Athletic Association (GAA), the governing body of the indigenous Irish sports of Gaelic football and hurling. He later established the *Celtic Times*, a weekly newspaper that focused on native games and Irish culture. Cusack Park stadium, the home of Clare GAA is named in his honour as is the Cusack Stand in Croke Park in Dublin. Cusack died at the age of fifty-nine on 27 November 1906.

Thomas McCarthy Fennell
Fenian 1841 – 1914

Although born four years into the Great Famine, Patriot Thomas McCarthy Fennell received a sound education and was a fluent speaker of the Irish language. Active as a Fenian organiser in Clare in 1863, in March of 1867 he sustained gunshot wounds whilst attempting to commandeer weapons at Kilbaha coast guard station. He was captured a short time later before being tried for treason and sentenced to ten years penal labour in Western Australia. Fennell arrived at Freemantle, Australia on 9 January 1868 but was granted a pardon three years later under an amnesty by British prime minister, William Gladstone, and he later emigrated to the United States. There he became a close associate of John Devoy (see page 239), and it was his suggestions that were ultimately implemented in the Catalpa rescue; a whaling ship that sailed from the United States to Australia to aid in the rescue of six Irish prisoners. Throughout his time in the US, Fennell was involved in fundraising for various Irish causes, including the monument to the Manchester Martyrs in Kilrush, County Clare. He died on 23 February 1914.

Paddy Hannan
Gold prospector 1840 – 1925

Paddy Hannan was born in Quin and emigrated to Australia in 1862. From the moment he arrived in that country he was infected with 'gold fever' and spent thirty years prospecting. In the process, Hannan learned of the need to locate a source of water to increase the chances of success in the pursuit of the precious metal. In June 1893, he discovered gold at Kalgoorlie and thus instigated one of the most sizeable gold finds in Australian history. His find caused the population of Kalgoorlie to soar from zero to twenty five thousand within five years and he retired from gold prospecting at the age of sixty-one, upon which time he was granted a pension of £100 per year by the government of Western Australia. The main street in Kalgoorlie bears Hannan's name and in 1929 a statue was erected on the street in his honour. He died in Brunswick, Melbourne, on 4 November 1925.

The Poulnabrone Dolman Tomb in county Clare.

General Sir Reginal Clare Hart
Victoria Cross recipient
1848 – 1931

A lieutenant in the Corps of Royal Engineers, British Army during the Second Afghan War, Scarriff's Reginald Clare Hart's defining moment occurred on 31 January 1879 when he ran a distance of 1.2 kilometres to rescue a soldier of the 13th Bengal Lancers who was lying wounded and exposed to enemy fire in a river bed. Upon reaching the wounded man, Hart and an accompanying band of soldiers repelled the enemy forces and carried the casualty back to safety. For this deed he was awarded the Victoria Cross. Hart was also a member of The Most Honourable Order of the Bath, The Royal Victorian Order and was a recipient of the Royal Humane Society's Silver Medal.

Patrick J. Hillery
Politician and president of Ireland
1923 – 2008

Studying medicine at University College Dublin, Patrick J. Hillery qualified in 1947 and four years later was elected to Dáil Éireann for the constituency of Clare. He was appointed minister for education in 1959 and subsequently served in a number of ministerial posts. As minister for external affairs in Jack Lynch's (see page 100) government, Hillery created controversy upon the commencement of the troubles in Northern Ireland with his visit to the Catholic Falls Road in Belfast, which the British government declared as 'a serious diplomatic discourtesy'. In rebuttal, Hillery declared that as a minister in the Irish government, he would travel to any part of Ireland that he wished, including Belfast. Following the atrocities of 'Bloody Sunday' in Derry in 1972, Hillery travelled to the United Nations and made an impassioned plea for the deployment of peacekeepers in Northern Ireland, proclaiming that, 'a near neighbour was practicing the arts of war in his country'. Renowned for his loyalty to both his country and to the Fianna Fáil political party, Hillery was appointed vice president of the Commission of the European Communities in 1973, with responsibility for social affairs and he served as European commissioner until 1976 when he was inaugurated as president of Ireland on 3 December of that year. Re-elected to the office again in 1983, Hillery displayed great loyalty and integrity in his service to his country. He died on 12 April 2008.

Austin Hogan
Trade unionist 1907 – 1974

Trade unionist Austin Hogan was educated at North Monastery School in Cork and at the London Institute for Mechanics. In the 1920s he emigrated to the United States where he studied engineering at Columbia University and became acquainted with Michael Quill, the labour leader from Kerry. Together they founded the Transport Workers Union of America but Hogan was later expelled from the union and accused of being a communist. During World War II he served as an engineering captain in the United States army and was severely wounded in the Pacific War. Following this, he took little interest in union affairs due to his injuries and returned to Ireland where he died in Cork, on 26 December 1974.

John Philip Holland
'Father of the Modern Submarine'
1841 – 1914

A prodigious inventor, John Philip Holland was born in Liscannor in 1841. Having joined the Irish Christian Brothers in 1858, he spent fifteen years with that religious order, during which time he became interested in the problems inherent in both flight and submarine navigation. Holland, who built a clockwork model of a submarine in his initial experiment with underwater vessels, emigrated to Boston in 1873 where he joined his family who had previously settled in the city. Five years later and after considerable experimentation, he produced *Holland Boat No 1* and following this, a more workable model known as the *Fenian Ram* was financed by the Fenian Brotherhood in the United States who administered funds with the intention of attacking British ships in Canada. Fortunately for the British, the vessel floundered in the East River. Holland endured many setbacks in the subsequent years and it wasn't until 11 April 1900, the date now celebrated as the birthday of the US Submarine Force, that the United States navy bought the first Holland submarine from the Holland Torpedo Boat Company. Known as the Holland Class and purchased for a sum of $150,000, the submarine was used extensively by the American and British navies during World Wars I and II. Holland eventually died of pneumonia in Newark, New Jersey on 12 August 1914.

General Sir Thomas Kelly-Kenny
British army general 1840 – 1914

Born in Mullagh, Thomas Kelly-Kenny joined the British army in 1858 and was assigned as aide-de-camp to the general officer commanding the Cape of Good Hope in South Africa. Having been promoted to the rank of colonel in 1887, he went on to achieve the rank of adjutant general and was twice mentioned in dispatches during the second Anglo-Boer War from 1899 until 1901. Kenny, who was also awarded the Queen's South Africa Medal with four clasps, was an Irish Catholic and a full time professional soldier, which was a rarity in the officer classes of that time. He served under field marshals Lord Roberts and Kitchener and at the battle of Paardeberg, he conceived a plan to bombard the Boer forces from a distance. Overruled by Kitchener, the resultant and unnecessary sacrifice of hundreds of British soldiers led to the day being known as 'Bloody Sunday'. Kenny retired from the army in 1907 and died in 1914.

James Patrick Mahon, 'The O'Gorman Mahon'
Irish nationalist politician and international mercenary
1800 – 1891

Creating the title 'The O'Gorman Mahon' to convince people that he was the head of the ancient Mahon clan, James Patrick Mahon was born into a prosperous family in Ennis, and was educated at Clongowes Wood College and Trinity College Dublin. Mahon, whose adopted title incorporated the surname of his mother, was elected MP for Clare in 1830 but in 1835 set out to travel the world, taking in the sights of Europe, Africa and South America before returning to Ireland in 1852. Defeated in a general election by thirteen votes, he returned to his foreign travels and took up mercenary pursuits. The Czar of Russia made him lieutenant within his international bodyguards, an appointment which placed him above most of the generals in the Russian army, and he also saw service as a colonel in the French army under Napoleon III. In the 1860s Mahon was a general on the government side of the Uruguayan army in that country's civil war, following which he left for the United States and took part in the American Civil War on the side of the union force. He was a notorious adventurer and duelist and gained a reputation as a 'swashbuckling' Irishman. Well known throughout Berlin, Paris and London, he returned to Ireland in 1871 and joined Parnell's Home Rule Party, being elected for Clare in 1879 and Carlow in 1887. He died in 1891 and is buried in Glasnevin Cemetery, Dublin.

Mick McTigue
Light heavyweight boxing champion of the world,
1892 – 1966

Initially working as a blacksmith before emigrating to the United States, where he worked in New York as a beef handler, Kilnamona's Mark McTigue had his first professional fight in that city in 1909 and thus commenced an illustrious boxing career that spanned a period of twenty-one years. He was a hard hitter and fought some quality fighters such as Harry Greb, Battling Levinsky, Galway man Mick Farrell, and Tommy Loughran. It was a brave Battling Siki that placed his world light heavyweight title on the line at the La Scala Opera House, (later the Rotunda Cinema, and later still, the Ambassador Cinema on O'Connell Street, Dublin) on St Patrick's Day, 1923. Following twenty closely-contested rounds, McTigue was proclaimed the light heavyweight champion of the world – not before breaking his right thumb in the fourth round; an injury which forced him to battle on using his right hand sparingly. McTigue defended the title several times over the next two years, following which his career took an eventual downturn, leading to his retirement in 1930. He died in New York on 12 August 1966 aged seventy-four.

Brian Merriman
Irish-language poet 1747 – 1805

A native of Ennistymon, Brian Merriman was educated at the local hedge school, eventually becoming a hedge school teacher himself in the town land of Kilclaren. Merriman wrote many poems but most notable among them was his long poem, 'Cúirt An Mheádhon Oidhche' (Midnight Court), which he wrote in 1780. This coarse epic mocked sexual morals, celibacy, the clergy and male chauvinism and was translated into English before being banned by the Censorship Board in 1946 due to its sexual content. Within Ireland, no single piece of literature has caused so much controversy and been so dissected and debated upon, as 'The Midnight Court'. Merriman, who has been honoured by the formation of the Merriman Summer and Winter Schools in various locations throughout County Clare, died suddenly on 27 July 1805 and is buried in Feakle churchyard.

William Mulready
Painter 1786 – 1863

William Mulready was born in Ennis but as a young boy, moved with his family to London where he was accepted at the Royal Academy School at the age of fourteen. His talent for depicting the human form earned him a reputation as one of the best draughtsmen of his day and he later became known for his paintings of cottages, rural scenes, and children. His most important works are in the South Kensington Museum and the Tate Gallery. He died in Bayswater, London and is buried in Kensal Green Cemetery.

William Smith O'Brien
Member of Parliament and Young Irelander 1803 – 1864

Patriot William Smith O'Brien was born into a prosperous Protestant family in Dromoland and was educated at Harrow School in Middlesex, England and the University of Cambridge. A conservative member of parliament for Ennis in the 1820s, he also filled that role for Limerick in 1835. O'Brien was an ardent supporter of Catholic Emancipation, joining the Repeal Association in 1843 and becoming a leading member of the Young Irelanders, as well as a co-founder of the Irish Confederation in 1847. O'Brien also took part in the Young Irelanders' rebellion of 1848, following which he was tried for treason and sentenced to death. Though his punishment was later commuted to penal servitude for life in Tasmania, O'Brien obtained an unsolicited pardon following five years imprisonment but was forbidden to ever return to Ireland. It was he, together with Thomas Francis Meagher, who gave Ireland its flag, the tri-colour; green, representing the Catholic south, the orange representing the Protestant north and the white for peace and unity between them. O'Brien eventually returned to Ireland in 1856 and died on 16 June 1864. He is buried in the family vault in Rathronan, County Limerick and a statue in his honour stands on O'Connell Street in Dublin.

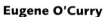

Eugene O'Curry
Irish scholar 1794 – 1862

Although Eugene O'Curry had little formal education, he took an interest in manuscripts from an early age and in 1835, joined the staff of the Ordnance Survey in Dublin where he was principally engaged in the study and interpretation of Irish manuscripts. He transcribed manuscripts for the Royal Irish Academy as well as the library of Trinity College, Dublin and in 1854 he was appointed professor of archaeology and Irish history in the Catholic University of Ireland. O'Curry's most important works were lectures on the manuscript *Materials of Irish History,* as well as *On the Manners and Customs of the Ancient Irish*. He died suddenly in Dublin on 30 July 1862, but his contribution to Irish learning is considered hugely influential to this day.

John O'Donohue
Philosopher and poet 1954 – 2007

A prodigious academic, John O'Donohue studied for the priesthood at St Patrick's College in Maynooth, gaining degrees in philosophy and English literature before attaining a PhD in philosophical theology from the University of Tübingen, Germany. He was a man of deep spiritual beliefs and was the author of the international bestseller *Anam Cara*, which was published in 1997 and was subsequently reprinted six times in its first year. His poetry collections include *Echoes of Memory* (1994) and *Connemara Blues* (2000). O'Donohue lived for a time in Connemara, County Galway but died suddenly near Avignon, France on 3 January 2007.

Bryan O'Loghlen
Premier of the State of Victoria, Australia 1828 – 1905

Educated at Trinity College, Dublin, Bryan O'Loghlen was called to the Irish Bar in 1856 but in 1862, emigrated to Australia where he was appointed crown prosecutor of Victoria. O'Loghlen was the recognised leader of the Irish Catholic community in Victoria and was elected to the Victorian Legislative Assembly for West Melbourne in 1878. He became Premier of Victoria in 1881 and died in 1905 at the age of seventy-seven.

Dr Brendan O'Regan
Businessman 1917 – 2008

Born in the small town of Sixmilebridge, Brendan O'Regan was educated at Blackrock College in Dublin and having studied abroad for a career in hotel management, returned to Ireland in 1938 to manage the Falls Hotel in Ennistymon, County Clare. In 1943 he was appointed catering manager at the Foynes flying boat base by the Irish government and two years later he took up the catering manager's position in Rineanna (now Shannon Airport). O'Regan was instrumental in creating the Shannon Development Company as well as the Shannon College of Hotel Management and the world's first duty-free retail shop at Shannon Airport. An amazingly influential business figure in the midwest region of Ireland, his legacy lives on to this day. He died on 2 February 2008.

Harriet Smithson
Stage actress 1800 – 1854

Harriet Smithson made her first stage appearance at the Cron Street Theatre in Dublin and in 1817, went to London where she appeared at Drury Lane. However, it was as a leading lady in a Paris production of Shakespeare's *Romeo and Juliet* that she really came to prominence with the theatre-going public. The rising young composer, Berlioz was so enchanted by Smithson that he composed *Symphonie Fantastique* in dedication to her and they would eventually marry in Paris in 1833. The composer Litzt was a witness to their marriage. The couple parted ways some ten years later and Smithson sadly developed a paralysis, which left her unable to talk. She died on 3 March 1854, and is buried at Montmartre in Paris.

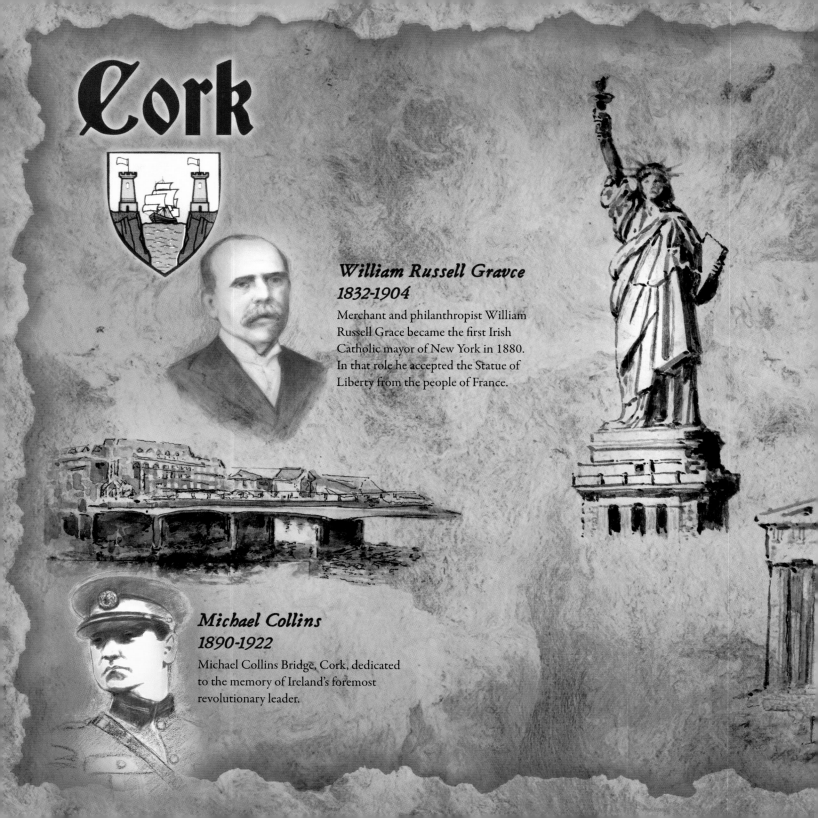

Cork

William Russell Gravce
1832-1904

Merchant and philanthropist William Russell Grace became the first Irish Catholic mayor of New York in 1880. In that role he accepted the Statue of Liberty from the people of France.

Michael Collins
1890-1922

Michael Collins Bridge, Cork, dedicated to the memory of Ireland's foremost revolutionary leader.

Francis Victor Beamish
1903-1942

A Spitfire, as flown by air ace Francis Victor Beamish in the Battle of Britain. He was one of a tiny band of legendary figures known as 'The few'.

Major General
Patrick Cleburne
1828-1864

Cleburne County Courthouse, Heber Springs, Arkansas. From a private soldier to a major general, Patrick Cleburne was one of the finest confederate army generals to serve during the American Civil War. His call for the emancipation of salves was repressed by Confederate president, Jefferson Davis.

General Richard Church
1784-1873

The liberator of Greece, Richard Church led Greek troops in the final definition of Greek territory in 1832.

James William Adams
Victoria Cross recipient 1839 – 1903

At the age of forty, clergyman James William Adams was appointed as a chaplain in the Bengal Ecclesiastical Department, Indian Army during the 2nd Afghan War. On 11 December 1879, at Killa Kazi, Afghanistan. Adams demonstrated a bravery that would later earn him the Victoria Cross. With a number of men of the 9th Lancers having fallen with their horses into a wide and deep ditch, Adams rushed into the waist deep water and dragged the horses off the trapped men while the nearby enemy rained continuous fire down upon them. Having let his own horse go in order to provide more effectual assistance, he was forced to escape on foot but luckily survived the ordeal. He died in England on 24 October 1903.

Mother Mary Aikenhead
Founder of the Sisters of Charity
1787 – 1858

Mary Aikenhead was born into an upper class family on Eason's Hill in Cork city. Though her father was a Protestant and her mother a Catholic, she herself was a Protestant and was deeply touched by her father's work as a doctor amongst the Irish poor, as well as his deathbed conversion to Catholicism. Aikenhead followed suit, becoming a Catholic in 1802; years later she went to Dublin where she was involved in visiting the sick and the poor in their homes. Whilst in the capital, she became a friend of a Father Murray, who later was to be appointed coadjutor-bishop of Dublin. It was through his cooperation that Aikenhead founded the religious congregation of the Sisters of Charity, whose first members took their vows on 1 September 1815. Sister Mary Augustine died in Dublin on 28 July 1858 following a long battle with ill-heath during which she continued to toil in the face of great adversity.

Conel Hugh O'Donel Alexander
Cryptanalyst and chess player
1909 – 1974

Conel Hugh O'Donel Alexander was born in Cork city where his father was an engineering professor at University College Cork. Following his death, the family moved to Birmingham, England, where Alexander attended King Edward's School and became a mathematics student at Kings College, Cambridge in 1928. He later became a mathematics teacher at Winchester and in February 1940 arrived at Bletchley Park, the British code-breaking centre during World War II. Alexander's work entailed breaking the German army and air force enigma messages and in 1944 he was transferred to work on the Japanese JN-25 code. As a chess player he was an Irish international, first winning the British Boys Championships in 1926 before adding two British Senior Championships to his list of honours in 1938 and 1956. Alexander, whose greatest achievement at chess was probably a victory over Soviet grand master David Bronstein in 1954, was a man of razor sharp intelligence and became a legend in the intelligence communities of Britain and the USA. He made an outstanding contribution to Britain and was awarded the OBE in 1946, the CBE in 1955 and the CMG in 1970.

Timothy Anglin

Canadian politician 1822 – 1896

A native of the west Cork coastal town of Clonakilty, Timothy Anglin emigrated to Canada during the Irish potato famine. There he became editor of the newspaper, the *Freeman* and he was elected to the legislative assembly of New Brunswick in 1861.

Having won a seat in the Canadian House of Commons in 1867, he was nominated as speaker of the house in 1874, a position he held until 1878. Anglin later moved to Toronto and became editor of the Toronto Tribune. He died in Toronto on 4 May 1896.

James 'Miranda' Barry

Military surgeon 1795 – 1865

A nephew of the painter James Barry, it was through the influence of his uncle that James 'Miranda' Barry was accepted into high society in London when he moved there in 1812. The following year he was commissioned as a regimental surgeon in the British army and was sent to the Cape of Good Hope in South Africa where, against severe opposition, he organised medical services for the poor and for slaves. Whilst there he set up and supervised a leper colony and also carried out the first caesarean operation on the continent of Africa, which was a success. In 1836 Barry was appointed staff surgeon to the forces in Jamaica where he successfully fought for the improvement of conditions for the soldiers serving there. In 1846 he was appointed principal medical officer to Malta. Six years later, in 1858 he became inspector general of hospitals in Canada, but returned to London two years later due to the deterioration of his own health. Throughout Barry's life, people remarked on his appearance. He possessed no facial hair and the tone of his voice as well as his small hands, made people very curious about him. When he died in London in 1865, the woman who called to lay him out for burial found not only was the body that of a female, but that the female had given birth to at least one child. As it was impossible in his time for women to become professional physicians, Barry may well have adopted the role of a man to allow him to practise his preferred profession.

Leonora Barry, 'Mother Lake'

American labour leader
1849 – 1930

Leonora Barry emigrated to the United States with her family in 1852 and settling in New York, she initially worked as a teacher. She was later widowed when her husband, William E. Barry, died in 1871 leaving two young children whom she supported by working in the clothing industry. Barry was appalled by the working conditions prevalent at the time. In response, she devoted her life to labour reform, becoming the first female labour organiser in United States history. She is considered to have done more for the cause of working women than anyone else in the nineteenth century and, having fought for equal pay and rights for women, as well as racial equality, by the mid-1880s, she was the national women's organiser for the Knights of Labour, a union with approximately 600,000 members. In 1890 she married Obediah R. Lake, and was thereafter referred to as 'Mother Lake' due to her work for women's suffrage. She died in Minooka, Illinois on 15 July 1930.

Vincent Christopher Barry

Scientific miracle worker
1908 – 1975

Little known around the globe, this amazing and unassuming man is responsible for saving the lives of an estimated 15 million people worldwide. Having initially worked in University College Galway, Barry's scientific work led to the establishment of an industry based on seaweeds. He became famous for his work on the degradation of Laminarin, which later became known as 'Barry Degradation' and in 1950 he became director of medical research at Trinity College, Dublin, where he worked on compounds found to be effective against tuberculosis. Barry's work on tuberculosis, together with a team of nine scientists, involved synthesizing a compound called, 'B663' (Clofazimine), which became part of the multi-drug antibiotic therapy used around the world for the treatment of leprosy. A most patriotic man, Barry was proud that Ireland was helping to eradicate leprosy worldwide. He died in Dublin in 1975.

Francis Victor Beamish
Pilot Battle of Britain 1903 – 1942

Qualifying as a flight cadet at Cranwell, England in the autumn of 1921, Francis Victor Beamish cheated death on many occasions as he fought the German Luftwaffe in aerial combat over the English Channel. He is one of the tiny band of legendary figures in the RAF known as 'The Few' and was renowned for always flying missions with his men, despite the fact he was a squadron commander. In March 1942, Beamish's luck ran out when his plane was damaged over Calais, France. His body was never found.

Edward Bransfield
Discoverer of Antarctica 1785 – 1852

Recruited into the Royal Navy as an ordinary seaman at the age of eighteen, Edward Bransfield rose rapidly through the ranks due to his outstanding skills and had obtained his masters certificate by 1812. Having served in the blockade of Brest during the Napoleonic wars, he was appointed navigation officer in 1815 and took part in a naval expedition to the southern region of South America. There, his navigation skills secured him the command of a merchant ship and with instructions to sail south and explore, Bransfield discovered and meticulously charted the South Shetland Islands. In late 1819, he became the first person ever to see the Antarctic continent and during his voyage he claimed King George's Island for Britain and also discovered Elephant Island and Clarence Island. He died in Brighton, England in 1852 at the age of sixty-seven. Bransfield Island, Bransfield Strait, Bransfield Rocks, and Mount Bransfield are all named in his honour.

Robert Cain
Founder of Cain's Brewery, Liverpool 1826 – 1907

Robert Cain was born on Spike Island and spent some time working as a cooper at sea before establishing his brewing operations in Liverpool in 1848, eventually moving to the brewery's present location on Stanhope Street ten years later. Cain became one of Liverpool's most successful businessmen and by the time of his death he was one of Britain's richest men, leaving an estate valued at £400,000 (the equivalent of £30 million today). In Liverpool he became known as the 'King of Toxteth' and the brewery he built exists to this day.

Nellie Cashman
The Angel of Tombstone 1845 – 1925

Born in Cobh, Nellie Cashman emigrated to the United States in the 1860s where she obtained work in a Boston hotel. Following a brief meeting with General Ulysses S. Grant, Cashman was compelled to travel west to seek her fortune and in 1872 found herself in Virginia city, Nevada where she established a restaurant and boarding house for miners who arrived in that city in great numbers following the news of a gold strike. When news broke of another gold strike in the Cassiar Mountains of British Columbia, she once again moved, opening another restaurant and caring facilities for the miners in that remote area of Canada. She stayed in British Columbia for four years and helped in the founding of St Joseph's Hospital in Victoria before heading south to Tuscon, Arizona in 1879 and then on to the legendary gold boom town of Tombstone. There she opened yet another restaurant and rooming house, which gained the reputation of a place where miners, who found themselves in dire straits and without money for a meal, were accommodated. Cashman nursed those who were sick and unable to work and was thus named 'The Angel of Tombstone'. She helped build the first school in Tombstone as well as the town's first Catholic church. Such was the respect held for her by the miners, it was said that not one person failed to repay her what they owed. Some years later, in 1898, she returned to Canada's Yukon Territory and became one of the great figures of the Klondike gold rush, where yet again she established a restaurant and refuge for miners. She finally settled in Victoria, British Columbia in 1923 and died there on 25 January 1925. The inscription on her gravestone bears the title, 'The Miners Angel'.

Sir Richard Church
Greek Army general 1784 – 1873

An army general of note, Richard Church was born into a Quaker family, but was disowned by The Society of Friends at the age of sixteen for leaving home and enlisting in the British army. In July 1800, he was commissioned to the 13th Light Infantry and served in many theatres of war throughout Europe, ranging from Sicily to Malta. In 1809 Church sailed with an expedition sent to occupy the Ionian Islands of Greece and there he formed a British-funded Greek regiment, which comprised many of the men who lead that country in its own war of independence. Church also entered the service of King Ferdinand of Naples and in 1820 he was appointed governor of Palermo, as well as commander-in-chief of troops in Sicily. Awarded a knighthood by King George IV in 1821, Church then took command of the Greek army during the rising against the Turks in 1827. Ill discipline proved to be the Greeks' downfall in an attempt to relieve The Acropolis of Athens and a vicious rout ensued, after which Church turned to partisan warfare in western Greece. There he attained considerable success with frontier lines being drawn favourably to Greece in 1832 and in 1854 he was created general of the Greek army. He died in Athens on 30 March 1873.

Patrick Cleburne
Major general in the Confederate States army 1828 – 1864

The son of a doctor, Ovens born Patrick Cleburne first sought to follow in his father's footsteps but failed his medical entry examination to Trinity College, Dublin. He later enlisted in the 41st Regiment of Foot of the British Army, where he eventually rose to the rank of corporal. Having being demoted for letting Irish prisoners escape from captivity, he later emigrated to the United States where he settled in Helena, Arkansas and worked as a pharmacist. At the commencement of the American Civil War, Cleburne joined a local militia company as a private and was quickly appointed captain. When Arkansas left the union, his company became part of the 1st Arkansas Infantry and he rose to the rank of colonel before being promoted to brigadier-general on 4 March 1862. He served in the Battles of Shiloh and Richmond (Kentucky), and during the campaign of 1863 in Tennessee, he successfully held off a much larger union force with his division, saving the army of Tennessee from complete devastation in the process. For this, he received an official thanks from Confederate Congress. In 1864 Cleburne recognised that the South was losing the war and he called upon the leadership of the army of Tennessee to emancipate slaves and to forgo their enlistment into the Confederate army. The proposal was met with extreme hostility and was suppressed on the order of Confederate President Jefferson Davis. Cleburne, who following this disagreement received no further promotion due to the fact that he was Irish and not a West Point graduate, was killed at the Battle of Franklin on 30 November 1864 during an ill-conceived assault, which he had been opposed to. Several places and geographic features are named in his honour, such as Cleburne County, Alabama, Cleburne County, Arkansas, Cleburne (City), Texas and Lake Pat Cleburne, Texas.

Agnes Mary Clerke
Astronomer and writer 1842 – 1907

Such was the impact of Skibbereen's Agnes Mary Clerke, the lunar crater 'Clerke', which is near to the landing site of Apollo 17, was named in her honour. Taking an interest in astronomy as a teenager, in 1861, at the age of nineteen, she moved to Dublin with her family and later onto to Florence, Italy. Here she further studied the subject at public libraries. Her first important article, 'Copernicus in Italy' was published in 1877 and in 1885 she achieved a worldwide reputation for her exhaustive treatise, *A Popular History of Astronomy in the Nineteenth Century*. In 1892 Clerke became a member of the British Astronomical Association and was awarded one hundred guineas. To this day, her work is considered remarkable in both literary and scientific terms.

William Horace de Vere Cole
Legendary prankster 1881 – 1936

William Horace de Vere Cole was born in Blarney and was educated at Eton and at Trinity College, Cambridge. Although born in Blarney, he was descended from the Hunt family of Asketon, County Limerick and was renowned as a legendary prankster. Cole once masqueraded as the sultan of Zanzibar and together with some fellow students, the complete entourage were wined and dined by the dignitaries of Trinity College. The hoax was only revealed when it was discovered that the real sultan had been in London at the time of the prank. Cole's most outrageous scam took place in 1910 when once again, together with a group of his friends, (including a young Virginia Woolf) he embarked on a full VIP tour of British war ship, the HMS *Dreadnought*. The party were met by a full naval guard of honour and were dressed in costumes with dyed hair and coloured skin having disguised themselves as the emperor of Abyssinia and his entourage. Among Cole's many other pranks was an impersonation of Prime Minister Ramsay McDonald, where he attended a Labour Party meeting and told the members to work more hours for less financial reward. On the occasion of Cole's honeymoon in Italy in 1919, he dropped horse manure on to Venice's Piazza di San Marco, which could only be reached by boat, leaving the inhabitants to wonder how a horse had gained access to the area. On yet another occasion, coming across a group of workmen without a foreman, Cole directed them to Piccadilly Circus, where he had them dig a very large trench, aided by an obliging policeman who re-directed the traffic in order for the works to take place. One whole week passed before public officials had the trench filled in. Cole died on 25 February 1936.

John Coleman
Medal of Honour recipient 1847 – 1897
Recipient of the highest military decoration awarded by the United States government, John Coleman was a United States Marine who served in that country's expedition to Korea in 1871. His citation reads, 'On board the USS Colorado in action at Korea on June 11th, 1871, whilst involved in hand-to-hand fighting with the enemy, he succeeded in saving the life of Alexander McKenzie'. He died on 25 November 1897.

Michael Collins
Revolutionary leader 1890 – 1922
Ireland's foremost revolutionary leader, Michael Collins was born in Sam's Cross near Clonakilty, and was educated at Lisavaird National School. At the age of sixteen, he moved to London where he took up a position in the British Civil Service. Surprisingly, it was there that he was first introduced to the Irish Republican Brotherhood by Sam Maguire (page 101), a Protestant republican from Dunmanway, County Cork. Collins returned to Ireland to take part in the Easter Rising of 1916, where he fought alongside Patrick Pearse (see page 185) at the General Post Office (GPO) in Dublin. Upon the failure of the rising, he narrowly escaped execution and was imprisoned in Frongoch internment camp in Wales.

Following the general release of prisoners, Collins returned to Ireland and represented Sinn Féin in the elections of 1918, being elected an MP for South Cork; however with Sinn Féin refusing to take their seats in London, a new Irish parliament known as Dáil Éireann (Assembly of Ireland) was established in Dublin. In 1919, Collins was appointed director of intelligence of the Irish Republican Army and set up an extremely efficient network of spies throughout Dublin. That same year, President Éamon de Valera (see page 431) appointed him minister of finance and so he set about organising a large bond issue, in the form of a 'national loan', in order to fund the new Irish Republic.

Collins' work load and achievements are impressive; he was in sole control of the IRA while effectively running the newly formed government and as well as arranging arms smuggling operations, he formed a special assassination squad called the 'Twelve Apostles', which effectively eliminated all British agents in Dublin. Through the efforts of Sinn Féin and the IRA, the British government realised that their chances of governing Ireland were dissipating and a truce was called. Much against his wishes, Collins, together with Arthur Griffith (see page 170), led a delegation to London for talks which would eventually lead to the signing of the Anglo-Irish Treaty on 6 December 1921, and to the formation of the new 'Irish Free State', which comprised twenty-six of the thirty-two counties of Ireland. This treaty divided the members of Sinn Féin and although a debate on the matter resulted in a vote of sixty-four to fifty-seven in favour, civil war broke out. Collins took command of the pro-Treaty forces, which were armed and funded by the British. Collins, as commander-in-chief of this new national army, travelled to his native Cork to rouse support for the new state. He made this visit against the wishes of his comrades, including Generals Richard Mulcahy (see page 394) and Eoin O'Duffy (see page 329) and it was whilst travelling through rural Cork, at a place called Béal na mBláth ('the mouth of the flowers') that he was killed in an ambush by anti-treaty forces. Just thirty-one years of age, his body lay in state for three days in St Vincent's Hospital, Dublin, where tens of thousands of mourners filed past to pay their respects. His military funeral at Glasnevin Cemetery was the biggest ever seen in Dublin and was where the 'Big Fellow' as he was affectionately known, was laid to rest. Winston Churchill, in his book, *The World Crisis* described Collins thus: 'he was an Irish patriot, true and fearless, when in future times, the Irish Free State is not only prosperous and happy, but an active and annealing force, regard will be paid by widening circles to his life and death'.

Patrick Andrew Collins
Congressman and mayor of Boston
1844 – 1905

Patrick Andrew Collins was born near Fermoy and emigrated to the United States with his family where they settled in Massachusetts in 1848. Whilst he worked in the upholstery trade, he studied law and became a politician, concurrently nominated to the House of Representatives of Massachusetts in 1867. Collins served two terms in the Massachusetts Senate, in 1870 and 1871, and also qualified in law from Harvard Law School before being admitted to the bar, also in 1871. While practising law in Boston, Collins was elected to the US Congress in 1882 and served three terms up to 1889. He was elected mayor of Boston in 1901 and served in that role until his death in 1905. A bust of Collins stands in the Commonwealth Avenue Mall in Boston.

Joseph Coppinger
Papal officer and Union general in the American Civil War 1834 – 1909

Having joined the Warwickshire Militia in 1857, Joseph Coppinger attained the rank of lieutenant by 1860. Answering the call of Pope Pius IX to defend the Papal States, Coppinger became a captain in the Battalion of St Patrick and was awarded the Papal Medal for bravery before leaving the papal service and joining the United States army, where he was commissioned a captain in the 14th US Infantry. During the battle of Second Bull Run in August 1862, Coppinger was shot through the neck but recovered six months later and went on to see action at Chancellorsville and Gettysburg, before serving in Sheridan's army at Shenandoah and achieving the rank of colonel of the 15th New York Cavalry. He led that unit at Five Forks and Appomattox but was once again wounded in the process. Coppinger's abilities as an officer were described by General Custer as of the highest order and he later served in the Indian war, becoming commissioned as a major in the 10th US Infantry in 1879. Further advancements led to him being promoted to brigadier general in the regular army in April 1895 and he was once again promoted, this time to major general, for his services during the Spanish-American war of 1898. Coppinger, whose marriage to Alice Stanwood Blane at the age of forty-nine was attended by President Chester A. Arthur and his cabinet, died a decorated army veteran, in Washington DC on 4 November 1909.

William Corbet
Soldier 1779 – 1842

While attending Trinity College, Dublin, William Corbet was expelled along with Robert Emmet (see page165) for treasonable activities and later became involved in the 1798 rising as a member of the United Irishmen. Corbet also fought with the French forces under Napper Tandy (see page 195), taking part in the failed expedition to Ireland after which he diverted with the French to Hamburg, where he was arrested and handed over to British authorities. Imprisoned at Kilmainham in Dublin, Corbet escaped in 1803 and returned to France to become a captain in the Irish Legion of the French army. He would go on to lead a formidable military career, distinguishing himself in Massena's Expedition to Portugal, after which he was summoned to Germany where he joined the staff of Marshal Marmont, and served in the battles of Lutzen, Bautzen and Dresden. He was duly promoted to commander of the Legion of Honour and following a successful expedition with French forces to Greece, he was made a member of the Order of Saint Louis and the Greek Order of the Redeemer before being appointed general. In 1831 Corbet was appointed commander-in-chief to the French forces in Greece. He died in Saint Denis, France in 1842.

Daniel Corkery
Writer, teacher and nationalist
1878 – 1964
Daniel Corkery was born in Gardiners Hill in Cork City and was educated at the Presentation Brothers College, following which he trained as a teacher in St Patrick's Training College in Drumcondra, Dublin. Having spent his early years teaching, in 1908 he, along with his friend Terence MacSwiney (see page 101), helped found the Cork Dramatic Society, for which he wrote a number of plays both in the Irish and English languages. In 1930 he became professor of English at University College Cork and he was also a writer of short stories, including the collections, *A Munster Twilight* (1916), *The Hounds of Banba* (1920), *The Stormy Hills* (1929), and *Earth out of Earth* (1939). Corkery also wrote a novel, *The Threshold of Quiet* (1917), and other publications included *The Hidden Ireland* (1924), which promoted strong nationalist feelings. Emphasising both his diversity and versatility, Corkery, who was a proficient watercolour artist, served in the second Dáil for the Sinn Féin political party and went on to become a member of Fianna Fáil in 1926. He served as a senator from 1938 until 1954 and his papers are held in the Boole Library at University College Cork. Corkery died at Passage West, County Cork, on 31 December 1964.

William Cosgrove
Victoria Cross recipient
1888 – 1936
The 'Irish Giant' William Cosgrove served as a corporal in the 1st Battalion of the Royal Ulster Fusiliers, British Army, during World War I and led a company section in an attack on Turkish positions during a beach landing at the Battle of Gallipoli on 29 April 1915. During that attack he happened upon barbed wire on stanchion posts that threatened to halt the company's progress. With casualties falling all around him, Corporal Cosgrove single-handedly pulled the stanchions from the ground in the path of raging gunfire from both sides. His heroic actions would not only earn him the Victoria Cross, but contribute greatly to the successful clearing of the enemy. Cosgrove died in Millbrook in London on 14 July 1936, but his remains were returned to the parish of his birthplace in County Cork and he was buried with full honours complete with a guard of honour.

Thomas William Croke
Archbishop 1824 – 1902
Thomas William Croke was born in Castlecor and was educated at the Irish College in Paris, France. Ordained in 1846, it was claimed by Irish radical William O'Brien that Croke fought on the barricades in Paris during the 1848 revolution. Returning to

Ireland, he was appointed president of St Colman's College in Fermoy in 1858 and became parish priest of Doneraile, County Cork in 1865. Four years later, Croke was appointed second bishop of Auckland, New Zealand and in 1875 he was appointed archbishop of Cashel and Emly. An ardent supporter of Irish nationalism and a member of the temperance movement and the Gaelic League, Croke also strongly supported Parnell's Irish Parliamentary Party. He died on 22 July 1902. Croke Park, the headquarters and national stadium of the GAA, is named in his memory.

John Philpot Curran
Lawyer and orator 1750 – 1817
Educated at Trinity College, Dublin, John Philpot Curran was called to the Irish bar in 1775 and, after overcoming a severe speech impediment, became a skilled orator. Though he was a Protestant, he was a staunch supporter of Catholic emancipation and was renowned for his defence of Catholics in the Protestant courts, earning the nickname 'The Little Jesuit of St Omers'. Curran would also become involved in politics, serving as a member of parliament for Kilbeggan, County Westmeath in 1784; a role in which he opposed the union with Britain. He defended several of the United Irishmen in high treason cases during the 1790s, amongst them, Wolfe Tone (see page 196), Napper Tandy (see page 195), Lord Edward Fitzgerald (see page 240), William Orr (see page 39), and William Drennan (see page 28). Renowned for his quick wit, on one occasion whilst having dinner with notorious 'hanging judge', Justice Toler, Toler enquired, 'is that hung beef?', Curran replied, 'do try it my Lord, and it's sure to be'. On another occasion, a prosecutor having been infuriated by Curran's insults, remarked, 'I could put you in my pocket'. To that, Curran replied, 'if you did so sir, you will have more law in your pocket than you ever had in your head'. On yet another occasion, Curran, once again referring to an opposing prosecutor said, 'his smile is like a silver plate on a coffin'. Curran retired from law practice in 1814 and spent the last years of his life in London before being laid to rest in Paddington Cemetery in 1817. Twenty years later, his remains were removed and transferred to Glasnevin Cemetery in Dublin.

Thomas Osborne Davis
Poet, nationalist and Young Irelander 1814 – 1845
Born in the north Cork town of Mallow, Thomas Osborne Davis was the son of a British army surgeon and was educated at Trinity College, Dublin. He was called to the bar in 1838 and joined Daniel O'Connell's (see page 232) Repeal Association the following year. Davis soon became impatient with O'Connell's constitutional methods and instead joined the Young Irelanders movement. Davis, who was a co-founder of the *Nation* newspaper in 1842, desired that Ireland be free to pursue its own destiny and the ballads he composed such as, 'A Nation Once Again', and 'The West's Asleep' inspired his vision of such a place and still remain popular to this day. He died of tuberculosis in 1845.

Sir Thomas Newenham Deane
Architect 1828 – 1899
Educated in Rugby School, England and Trinity College, Dublin, Thomas Newenham Deane joined his father's architectural practice in 1850, becoming the principal of that practice in 1871. His most prominent architectural works include the National Library and the National Museum in Kildare Street, Dublin and he was knighted at the public opening of these buildings in 1890. He died in Dublin on 8 November 1899.

Jack Doyle, 'The Gorgeous Gael'
Boxer 1913 – 1987

Standing six feet and three inches tall, 'The Gorgeous Gael' Jack Doyle possessed an excellent physique and good looks. He joined the Irish Guards in 1929, upon which time he took up boxing. Having won the British Army Championship with an impressive record of twenty-seven knockouts in twenty-eight fights, Doyle turned professional and had ten victories, all of which took place inside the first two rounds of each bout. In July 1933, he fought Jack Peterson for the British heavyweight title but was disqualified for administering repeated low blows and following that disappointment, he attempted to establish a career in the United States. There he was stopped by Buddy Baer in the first round of a fight that took place amid allegations that Doyle had entered the ring drunk. It was also there that Doyle met, and later married, Movita Castaneda who starred in the 1935 film, Mutiny on the Bounty. He would have a string of affairs with the most glamorous of women, including Delphine Dodge, of the Dodge car family, but he subsequently returned to Ireland with his new wife. Their marriage, however, did not last and Castaneda eventually returned to the US, where she later married legendary actor Marlon Brando. Referred to as 'the Rudolph Valentino' of the ring, seemingly it was Doyle's good looks, generous nature and love of a drink, along with constant attention from the opposite sex that proved to be his ultimate downfall. He died in Paddington, London on 13 December 1978 and is buried in his native Cobh.

John Dunlay
Victoria Cross recipient 1831 – 1863

John Dunlay was born in Douglas. A lance corporal in the 93rd Regiment of Foot, British Army, Dunlay fought in the Indian Rebellion of 1857 and came to prominence at Lucknow, India. Against superior forces he, along with a fellow captain, breached enemy lines at Secundra Bagh and was subsequently awarded the Victoria Cross for his deeds. He died in Cork on 17 October 1863.

Frederick Jeremiah Edwards
Victoria Cross recipient
1894 – 1964

Frederick Jeremiah Edwards was born in Queenstown, (now Cobh) County Cork. Serving as a private in the 12th Battalion, Middlesex Regiment of the British Army in the First World War, the twenty-one-year-old Edwards advanced single-handedly and removed an enemy gun at Thiepval, France on 26 September 1916. With all the officers of his section having been wounded and his line under machine-gun fire, Edwards took great initiative under extreme enemy pressure and his gallant efforts made further advances for his unit possible. For his bravery, he was awarded the Victoria Cross.

Thomas Addis Emmet
Lawyer and politician 1764 – 1827

A graduate of Trinity College Dublin, University College Dublin and the University of Edinburgh, Thomas Addis Emmet was called to the Irish bar in 1790, upon which time he became principal counsel for prisoners charged with political offences. In 1795 he took the oath of the Society of United Irishmen on his understanding that parliamentary reform and Catholic emancipation would not be obtained by constitutional methods, but in 1798 he was arrested for his involvement with the United Irishmen and was imprisoned in Scotland for a period of three years. Following his release, Emmet was in Paris communicating with Napolean Bonaparte when news reached him that a rising that was orchestrated by his brother, Robert Emmet (see page 165), had failed. He subsequently emigrated to the United States where he established a lucrative law practice and in 1812 he was appointed attorney general of New York. Emmet gave invaluable assistance to Irish immigrants arriving in the United States and was also a staunch advocate of the freedom of African-American people from slavery. He died on 14 November 1827 and his grandson, Dr Thomas Addis Emmet, a prominent American practitioner and Irish American activist, had his body interred in Glasnevin Cemetery, Dublin.

William John English
Victoria Cross recipient 1882 – 1941

An eighteen-year-old lieutenant in the 2nd Scottish Horse regiment of the British Army during the Boer War, on 3 July 1901 at Vlakfontein, South Africa, William John English, along with four other soldiers, successfully held a position from enemy attack. Although two of his men were killed and the remaining two wounded, he personally held out under considerable enemy pressure. Short of ammunition, English was necessitated to sprint fifteen yards in open ground under very heavy fire in order to secure supplies from an adjacent company but he returned to single-handedly hold the occupied position and was later awarded the Victoria Cross.

Richard Fitzgerald
Victoria Cross recipient 1831 – 1884

Richard Fitzgerald was born in St Finbar's, Cork City and served as a gunner with the Bengal Horse Artillery, Indian Army during the Indian Mutiny. On 28 September 1857 at Bolandshahr, Fitzgerald, together with Sergeant Bernard Diamond, worked their gun after every other man belonging to it had been either killed or wounded. Both men were under very heavy fire but cleared the road of the enemy and were subsequently awarded the Victoria Cross. It is believed that Richard Fitzgerald died in India.

Gerald Goldberg
Lawyer and politician
1912 – 2003

Educated at the Model School, Presentation Brothers College in Cork, and at a Jewish boarding school in Sussex, England, Gerald Goldberg was qualified with a degree in law and a Master of Arts degree from University College Cork in 1968. He practised law in Cork City for sixty-three years and was considered one of the finest litigation lawyers in Ireland. Goldberg was elected lord mayor of Cork in 1977, the first Jewish person to serve in that role, and he also toured the United States where he was given the freedom of several cities including Philadelphia, New York and Dallas. He died in Cork, on New Year's Eve, 2003 at the age of ninety-one.

William Russell Grace
Philanthropist, merchant and mayor of New York 1832 – 1904

Having travelled to Peru in 1850, Riverstown born William Russell Grace remained in that country following his father's return to Ireland and established a company, W. R. Grace and Co., before leaving South America in 1864 and settling in New York. During the Great Famine in Ireland, his firm contributed one quarter of the provisions sent on the steam ship *Constellation* for his hunger-stricken homeland, and in 1880 he was elected the first Catholic mayor of New York in spite of extensive opposition from bigoted sources. Grace, who was again elected mayor of New York in 1884, accepted the Statue of Liberty from the people of France in 1885 and his aforementioned company is one of the world's largest conglomerates. He also established the Grace Institute for the specific welfare and training of young women in May, 1897 and like his business, it is still in existence today, operating as a non-sectarian institution under the care of the Sisters of Charity. Grace died in 1904.

Tom Hales
IRA volunteer 1892 – 1966

IRA man Tom Hales was born near Bandon and together with his brothers Sean, Bob, and Donal, fought in west Cork during the Anglo-Irish war. Along with Patrick Harte, Hales was captured by the British Army in Cork and was badly beaten and tortured. As a result of this mistreatment, Harte sustained brain damage and the hardship that befell the two men is believed to have inspired similar scenes featured in the motion picture *The Wind that Shakes the Barley* (2006). The principal interrogator was Major Arthur Percival, who during the World War II was responsible for the largest capitulation in British military history, with the surrender of British forces to Japanese in Singapore. During the Irish Civil war, the Hales brothers fought on opposite sides, with Tom commanding the flying column which attacked and killed Michael Collins (page 89) at Béal na Bláth in 1922. In 1933 Hales was elected to Dáil Éireann, and he died in 1966.

Edward Hallaran Bennett
Orthopaedic surgeon
1837 – 1907

Edward Hallaran Bennett graduated in medicine from Trinity College, Dublin where he developed an interest in bone fractures having studied under Professor Robert Smith. He became a fellow of the Royal College of Surgeons in 1863 and a surgeon at St Patrick Dun's Hospital the following year. He is best remembered for 'Bennett's Fracture', which is a fracture of the base of the metacarpal bone of the thumb and he is also accredited with having introduced antisepsis to Dublin hospitals. Bennett served as president of the Royal Academy of Medicine from 1894 until 1897 and died in Dublin on 21 June 1907.

Timothy Charles Harrington
Lawyer, newspaper owner and nationalist 1851 – 1910

Timothy Charles Harrington commenced his working life as a schoolteacher before going on to study law. Called to the bar in 1887, he was the owner of two newspapers, namely, the *Kerry Sentinel*, and *United Ireland*. Harrington was secretary of the Land League in 1882 and he was twice imprisoned under the coercion acts for his activities. He was a member of parliament for Westmeath in 1883 and the Harbour division of Dublin in 1885 and also acted as counsel for Charles Stewart Parnell (see page 423) and many other political prisoners. Harrington supported Parnell after the split in the Irish Party in 1891 and later served under John Redmond (see page 414), following the former's death. He was appointed lord mayor of Dublin from 1901 until 1904 and died in Harcourt Street, Dublin on 12 March 1910.

Anna Haslam (née Fisher)
Suffragist and philanthropist
1829 – 1922

A Quaker, Youghal born Anna Haslam devoted most of her life to the promotion of women's rights, placing particular emphasis on education. She was a founder member of the Dublin Women's Suffrage Association in 1876, and attended a suffrage demonstration in London in 1908 with a view to gaining parliamentary votes for women. Haslam died in 1922, the year that the women of Ireland secured the right to vote on the same basis as men. She is commemorated with a seat in St Stephen's Green in Dublin.

Timothy Michael Healy
Politician and first governor-general of the Irish Free State 1855 – 1931

Born in the west Cork town of Bantry and educated in the east Cork town of Fermoy, Timothy Michael Healy's first position in life was as a railway clerk in Newcastle-upon-Tyne, England. He later moved to London where he became involved with Charles Stewart Parnell (see page 423) and his efforts for Home Rule for Ireland. Healy, who gave Parnell the title of 'the uncrowned king of Ireland', was elected to parliament for Wexford in 1880 and was called to the Irish bar in 1884, also establishing a practice in connection with land reform. He broke ranks with Parnell following the latter's involvement with the O'Shea divorce and instead supported British Prime Minister Gladstone's support for home rule for Ireland, which was conditional on Parnell stepping down from his leadership position in the Irish party. This eventually led to antagonistic camps known as 'the Healyites' and 'the Parnellites' and it was a development which was much to the detriment of Ireland's cause. Following the Anglo-Irish Treaty, the British government appointed Healy as governor-general of the Irish Free State, a position he held until 1928, three years before his death in 1931.

Richard Hennessy
Soldier and distiller
1720 – 1800

Arriving in France in 1740, Richard Hennessy became an officer in Dillon's regiment and fought at Fontenoy in 1745. When he retired from military service, he started a trading business in Cognac, France, on lands which were given to him for services to King Louis XV. There he established a distillery, which produces the world famous Hennessy brandy to this day.

Edward Hincks
Orientalist 1792 – 1866

Educated at Trinity College, Dublin, Edward Hincks, who served as a rector in Killyleagh, County Down, is best remembered for his work in the field of Egyptology. His work in unravelling the mystery of Egypt's fascinating hieroglyphic writings was phenomenal and was firmly put into perspective considering that he never visited Egypt and depended solely on texts and casts of oriental stones which were supplied by the British Museum. In 1848, the Royal Irish Academy awarded Hincks the Cunningham Medal for his research in connection with hieroglyphic and persepolitan writings. He later turned his attention to the Assyrian, Persian, and Babylonian inscriptions and uncovered what was probably the highlight of his career, the discovery of the Persian vowel system. A marble bust of him stands in the Cairo museum. He died on 3 December 1866.

Mary Harris 'Mother' Jones
Labour organiser 1837 – 1930

Better known as 'Mother Jones', Mary Harris moved to the United States in her early twenties where her husband and four children later died during a yellow fever epidemic in Tennessee in 1867. Moving on to Chicago, she endured yet another loss; this time, that of her property in the Great Fire of 1871. Jones sought employment in the labour movement in Chicago and in 1905 she helped found the Industrial Workers of the World, sometimes referred to as the 'Wobblies'. She was involved with the United Mine Workers and the Socialist Party of America and in 1903, organised for children who were working in mills and mines to march to the home of President Theodore Roosevelt, with banners reading 'we want time to play' and 'we want to go to school'. Although the president refused to meet her, the march brought the issue of child labour to the forefront in the United States. Described by the district attorney of West Virginia as 'the most dangerous woman in America', Jones was arrested in 1902 for supporting a miners' strike that disregarded a court injunction which forbade it. A sign of her significant influence, this defiant act led the district attorney to remark, 'she crooks her fingers and twenty-thousand contented men lay down'. In the early 1900s, 'Mother Jones' supported workers in the railroad, steel, copper, brewing, textiles, and the mining industries across the United States. She died on 30 November 1930, and is buried in the Union Miners Cemetery in Illinois.

Paul Kane
Painter 1810 – 1871

An accomplished artist, Mallow born Paul Kane taught himself to paint by copying the European masters he encountered while on study trips to the continent, before emigrating to Canada where he settled in York (now Toronto). In 1845 he travelled throughout the Great Lakes region of Canada, sketching the First Nations people in their homelands and collecting indigenous Canadian legends. In May 1846, Kane travelled to the west of Canada and sketched Mount St Helens and the coastal tribes in the Victoria region. He returned to Toronto having made seven hundred drawings of western scenery and many of the eighty tribes of that region. He then painted canvasses from his sketches, over one hundred of which are on display in the Royal Ontario Museum, and twelve of which are in the National Gallery, Ottawa. Kane published an account of his travels in 1859 which was translated into Danish, French and German. The account paints a distinctly vivid description of the people, the traders and the missionaries in Canada during the 1840s and contributes greatly to his ongoing fame as a result of his depictions of first nations and native American life. He died and is buried in Toronto.

Thomas Kent
Nationalist 1865 – 1916

Thomas Kent was born into a nationalist family who resided at Bawnard House, Castlelyons. Having endeavoured to take part in the Easter Rising of 1916 along with his brothers, Kent stood down when the mobilisation order was cancelled but still engaged in conflict when the Royal Irish

Constabulary was sent to arrest all sympathisers throughout the country. Upon their arrival at the Kent residence, the RIC encountered stout resistance from Thomas and his three brothers, Richard, David and William and following a gunfight that lasted for four hours, during which an RIC officer was killed, the Kents were forced to surrender. Thomas and his brother William were tried by court-martial and whilst William was acquitted, Thomas was sentenced to death and executed by firing squad in Cork on 9 May 1916. Along with Roger Casement (see page 159), Kent was the only other person executed outside of Dublin in connection with the events of the Easter Rising of 1916.

Danny La Rue
Female impersonator and drag queen
1927 – 2009
Danny La Rue was born Daniel Patrick Carroll. Upon the death of his father, his mother brought him to London, England aged just eighteen months. Having later joined the Royal Navy at the age of sixteen, following his demob he entered the theatrical world, becoming one of the most famous drag acts from the mid-1950s until his retirement from show business in 2006. La Rue brought respectability to drag and his originality and professionalism gained him the Variety Club of Great Britain's award for show business personality of the year in 1959. Throughout the sixties he packed variety theatres, breaking box office records, and was a leading personality on television, becoming the highest paid entertainer in Britain in 1970. A much loved performer, La Rue's show business career came to an end when he had a stroke in 2006 and he eventually died from prostate cancer in 2009.

Hugh Lane
Art collector 1875 – 1915
Hugh Lane spent a considerable part of his life in England, where he learned the art of painting and restoration and subsequently became one of London's most successful art dealers. A nephew of Lady Gregory (see page 216), Lane was a regular visitor to her home in Gort, County Galway and was immensely supportive of Irish art and Irish artists. He is perhaps best known for founding the Municipal Gallery of Modern Art in Dublin, which was opened on Harcourt Street in January 1908 and is the first known public gallery of modern art in the world. Lane, who was knighted for his services to art in Ireland, died tragically in 1915 onboard the Lusitania off the coast of Cork.

Thomas Lane
Victoria Cross recipient 1836 – 1889
Thomas Lane served as a private in the 67th (South Hampshire) Regiment of Foot, British Army. At Taku Forts in China he, together with a Lieutenant Burslem, swam the ditches of a fort in order to reach a point where they could facilitate entry by breaching an enlarged opening in the wall. Both men were severely wounded but successfully formed the breach for their column to gain entry to the fort. For their actions, Lane and Burslem were awarded the Victoria Cross. Lane also fought as sergeant in the Zulu Wars and later joined the Kimberley Police in South Africa, where he died in 1889.

Walter Paye Lane
Texas ranger and Confederate general in the American Civil War
1817 – 1892

Future Texas Ranger, Walter Paye Lane emigrated with his family to Ohio when he was four years of age. As a young man he settled in Texas and fought for his adopted state in the Battle of San Jacinto in the Mexican War. Upon the outbreak of the American Civil War, Lane became a Texas cavalry officer and served as a lieutenant colonel, leading his troops in the battles of Wilson's Creek, Missouri and Corinth. Severely wounded as he led the first Texas Partisan Rangers in the Battle of Mansfield in 1864, Lane was promoted to the rank of brigadier general upon his return the following year. After the war he was appointed deputy federal marshal and also shared in the foundation of the Texas Veterans Association. Lane, who never married, died on 28 January 1892 and was buried with full military honours.

Major Samuel Hill Lawrence
Victoria Cross recipient 1831 – 1868

A Lieutenant in the 32nd Regiment of Foot of the British Army during the Indian Mutiny, Samuel Hill obtained a field promotion to captain and on 7 July 1857 successfully captured a house held by a considerable force of enemy troops at Lucknow. Not three months later, Lawrence together with two of his men, successfully charged and captured a nine-pound gun and for these two deeds he was awarded the Victoria Cross.

David Lord
Victoria Cross recipient
1913 – 1944

David Lord was born in St Mary's Avenue in Cork city. During World War II he served as a flight lieutenant in the No. 271 Squadron of the Royal Air Force and on 19 September 1944, at Arnhem, Netherlands, flew his Dakota KG374 through intense anti-aircraft fire in order to drop supplies to the British First Airborne Division on the ground below. With his aircraft having been struck twice and with one engine burning, Lord managed to drop the necessary supplies but discovered at the end of his pass over the area, that there were two containers remaining on board. Disregarding the fact that one of his wings was likely to collapse, he made a second successful run to drop the remaining supplies. Upon realising the plane was about to crash in flames, Lord ordered his crew to disembark while he himself lost his life in the crash. For his bravery, he was posthumously awarded the Victoria Cross.

Eliza Lynch
Mistress to the president of Paraguay 1835 – 1884

In order to escape the Great Famine, Eliza Lynch emigrated with her family to Paris at the age of ten. Whilst there, she met Francisco Solano López, son of the president of Paraguay and she duly accompanied him when he returned home in 1855. Though she never married López, for the next fifteen years Lynch was the most powerful woman in Paraguay and when López became president in 1862, she became de facto first lady. She supported him in what was to become known as the War of Triple Alliance, a disastrous conflict for Paraguay, during which 300,000 Paraguayans lost their lives. Subsequently despised and reviled, she was expelled from the country in 1870 and died in Paris. Around 1971, her status in Paraguay changed and her body was exhumed and brought back to Paraguay where she was proclaimed a national heroine.

Jack Lynch
Politician and taoiseach 1917 – 1999

A gifted athlete in his youth, future taoiseach Jack Lynch was accomplished in many sports, including rugby, soccer, swimming, handball, Gaelic football and hurling. He had the unique distinction of being the captain of the Cork football and hurling Teams in 1939, also winning one All-Ireland football medal, five in hurling and capping it all by being named 'hurling captain of the forties'. Lynch was called to the bar in 1945, following which he set up a private legal practice in Cork. Three years later he was elected to Dáil Éireann as TD for Cork, a seat he held until his retirement in 1981. He served as minister for finance (1965 – 1966), minister for industry and commerce (1959 – 1965), minister for education (1957 – 1959) and minister for the Gaeltacht (1957) and was also leader of the Fianna Fáil party from 1966 to 1979. During his tenure, Lynch was the only Fianna Fáil leader to gain an overall majority of votes in the Dáil and he served as taoiseach from 1966 to 1977 and 1977 to 1979. He died in 1999.

Joe Lynch
Actor and entertainer
1925 – 2001

Actor Joe Lynch graduated with honours in music before turning his hand to acting, prior to which he had engaged in multiple occupations ranging from horse-breaker to tree-feller. Lynch had a wide range of talents within the entertainment industry and could seamlessly juggle the roles of comedian, singer and actor. He appeared in many radio and television productions, including the 1960s comedy *Never Mind The Quality, Feel The Width* and he also appeared in the famous British soap opera, *Coronation Street* in 1979. Irish audiences will best remember him for playing the part of Dinny Byrne in the popular RTÉ soap *Glenroe*. Lynch died in his retirement home in Alicante, Spain on 1 August 2001.

Tomás Mac Curtain
Nationalist leader 1884 – 1920

Irish nationalist Thomas Mac Curtain was born in Ballyknockane, and was educated at North Monastery School, Cork. He joined the Gaelic League in 1901 and Sinn Féin in 1907, also becoming a member of the Volunteers in 1914. He was imprisoned in Wakefield and Reading jails in England for his activities in 1916 and 1917 but was released and became lord mayor of Cork in 1920. Mac Curtain was murdered by the Royal Irish Constabulary in his home on 20 March 1920.

Daniel Maclise
Painter 1806 – 1870

Cork city native Daniel Maclise studied art at the Cork School of Art in 1822, before going on to London in 1828, studying art at the Royal Academy schools and holding his first exhibition at the Royal Academy the following year. One of his greatest works *The Meeting of Wellington and Blücher* was finished in 1861 and adorning the walls of Westminster Palace, opening to the public to outstanding acclaim. Maclise died of pneumonia on 25 April 1870.

Terence MacSwiney
Revolutionary 1879 – 1920

An accountant by trade, University College Cork educated Terence MacSwiney was a founder member of the Cork Dramatic Society, for whom he wrote a number of plays, and was also a founder of the Cork brigade of the Irish Volunteers in 1913. Following the Easter Rising in 1916 he was interned in Reading and Wakefield jails but was elected to represent Mid Cork in Dáil Éireann in the 1918 elections, being appointed lord mayor of Cork two years later. On 16 August 1920, MacSwiney was court-martialed by the British authorities in Dublin for possession of seditious articles and documents and was sentenced to two years in prison at Brixton, where he immediately embarked on a hunger strike that lasted for seventy four days, making it the longest hunger strike in Irish history. This hunger strike, which he died from on 25 October 1920, had such a widespread impact that the United States threatened a boycott of all British goods, four South American countries appealed to the Pope to intervene, and protests were held in Germany and France. MacSwiney's body was returned to Ireland on 1 November 1920 and his burial, which took place at St Finbarr's Cemetery, Cork attracted huge crowds who paid their final respects.

Ambrose Madden
Victoria Cross recipient 1820 – 1863

Sergeant Major Ambrose Madden served in the 41st Regiment, British Army during the Crimean War and, with a small party of men, cut off a section of Russian troops at Little Inkerman. Of the one officer and fourteen privates captured, Madden was personally responsible for the taking of three of the men and for this he was awarded the Victoria Cross. He would late achieve the rank of lieutenant and died in Jamaica in 1863.

John Francis Maguire
Politician and journalist
1815 – 1872

Founder of the *Cork Examiner*, forerunner of the now nationwide *Irish Examiner* newspaper, John Francis Maguire was called to the bar in 1843 and served as a member of parliament for Dungarvan, County Waterford from 1852 until 1865, and for Cork from 1865 until his death in 1872. Maguire became a Knight Commander of St Gregory following the writing of a book on the Pontificate and he produced six publications, one of which was *Irish in America*, showing a record of his travels across the North American continent. He died in Dublin on 1 November 1872 and is buried in Cork.

Sam Maguire
Irish republican 1879 – 1927

A familiar name to those in GAA circles, Sam Maguire was born into a Protestant family near the town of

Dunmanway. He was educated at Ardfield national school, which was also attended by Michael Collins (see page 89). Like Collins after him, Maguire found employment in the British civil service in London and was instrumental in introducing Collins to the Irish Republican Brotherhood in 1909. When Collins returned to Ireland, Maguire became his director of intelligence in Britain and was responsible for the shipment of arms to Ireland. Whilst in London he became chairman of the London county board of the GAA before returning to Ireland to serve in the civil service. However, with failing health he was forced to return to his west Cork home, where he died of tuberculosis on 6 February 1927, at the age of forty-eight. In September 2002, a statue of Maguire was unveiled in the town plaza in Dunmanaway and his name is inextricably linked with the GAA following the naming of the trophy of the All-Ireland Senior Football Championship in his honour in 1928.

Francis Sylvester Mahony (Father Prout)

Humorist and writer 1804 – 1866

Francis Sylvester Mahony was born in Camden Quay, Cork City and was educated at Clongowes Wood College following which he entered the Jesuit College at Amiens in France. He was a brilliant student with an exceptional talent for languages, both ancient and modern. His primary ambition was to become a Jesuit priest but having been rejected by that order on health grounds, he entered the Irish College in Rome under the sponsorship of the bishop of Cork, and was ordained in 1832. During the cholera epidemic in Cork in 1832 and 1833, Mahony was renowned for carrying out his priestly duties and taking care of the poor and destitute during the strife. He left the priesthood around 1934, and for the next thirty years of his life concentrated on more literary pursuits – one of his more well-known poems was 'The

Bells of Shandon'. In his journalistic endeavours, Mahony adopted the pseudonym, 'Father Prout'. He died in Paris, on 18 May 1866.

Daniel Mannix

Archbishop of Melbourne

1864 – 1963

Ordained at St Patrick's College, Maynooth in 1890, Charleville's Daniel Mannix a fierce Irish nationalist who greatly disapproved of violence against the British authorities. He is considered one of the most influential public figures in twentieth-century Australia. Mannix, who was consecrated bishop of Melbourne in 1912, was opposed to the Easter Rising of 1916 but became increasingly radical, and led the funeral cortège through the streets of London following the death of Terence MacSwiney (see page 101) from hunger strike. When he left Australia to visit Rome and the USA in 1920, the British Government refused him permission to visit Ireland or any British cities with large Irish populations; there was even an attempt to prevent him returning to Australia. In that country he strongly supported trade unionism but was bitterly opposed to militancy and the Communist Party of Australia. His legacy is cemented as a result of his forty-seven years as archbishop, during which he established over one hundred parishes and one hundred and fifty schools, which included high schools, and technical and commercial colleges. He died in Melbourne on 6 November 1963.

Edward Corringham 'Mick' Mannock

Victoria Cross recipient 1887 – 1918

Hailing from Ballincollig, west of Cork city, Edward Corringham 'Mick' Mannock was a World War I 'flying ace' by virtue of his prodigious downing of enemy aircraft. He is attributed to have had seventy-three victories and became the leading British pilot in World War I, being awarded the Military Cross and the 'Distinguished Service Order' in recognition of his prowess. Mannock, who amazingly achieved all his accolades with the use of just one eye, initially served in the Royal Engineers and was commissioned as a second lieutenant in June 1915, following which he requested a transfer to the Royal Flying Corps. While waiting for a medical practitioner to arrive for a routine examination, Mannock memorised the letters of an eye testing chart and subsequently passed the test with flying colours. On being congratulated by a friend, who remarked, 'they'll have the red carpet out for you after the war, Mick', Mannock prophetically replied, 'there won't be any after the war for me.' He was shot down on 26 July 1918 having previously been appointed flight commander in March of that year.

John B. McDonald
Builder of the first subway in New York City 1844 – 1911

Fermoy born John B. McDonald emigrated to the United States with his parents in 1847. His father, who he worked for, was a successful New York building contractor with connections in Tammany Hall (Democratic Party Headquarters dominated by Irish-Americans) and he would pass his business onto McDonald upon his death. He went on to become one of the United States' most successful railway contractors and constructed the Baltimore Underground Railroad in the late 1880s, a project which involved digging tunnels under the city for a distance of two miles. Following the completion of that project in 1894, McDonald constructed the Jerome Park Reservoir which was originally the largest reservoir in the world and he also

successfully bid for the New York Subway contract in 1900, with a project estimate of $35 million. Upon his death in 1911, the New York subway was closed for two minutes as a mark of respect for him.

Stephen Moylan
Quartermaster general during the American Revolutionary War 1737 – 1811

Educated in England and France, Stephen Moylan was, for some time, involved in the shipping industry in Portugal but in 1768 moved to Philadelphia, where he became one of the leaders in the movement for the complete independence of the colonies and gave his full support to Washington. In 1776 Moylan took command of a regiment of the American cavalry under General Pulaski, and upon Pulaski's retirement, he took overall command. His cavalry unit became known as 'Moylan's Horse' and saw action at the battles of Brandywine and Germantown. In 1780 the regiment was sent southwards to join Lafayette's forces in Virginia and the following year Moylan commanded his unit at the siege of Yorktown. On 3 November 1783 he was appointed a brigadier-general and following the war, George Washington appointed him commissioner of loans in Philadelphia, a position he occupied until his death on 13 April 1811. Moylan is buried in the grounds of St Mary's Catholic Church, Philadelphia.

Edward Mulhare
Television actor 1923 – 1997

Initially interested in a medical career, Edward Mulhare later opted for acting and following appearances at Dublin's Gate Theatre, he moved to London where he worked with Orson Welles.

Having moved to the United States, Mulhare replaced Rex Harrison as Professor Higgins in the production of the world famous musical *My Fair Lady* from 1957 until 1960, but he is perhaps best known for the television series T*he Ghost and Mrs Muir* (1968-70), in which he played the ghost of a nineteenth-century sea captain. He also acted in such television productions as *Gidget Grows Up* (1969), *The Streets of San Francisco* (1972) and *Knight Rider* (1982 – 86). He died at his home in 1997, following a five month battle with lung cancer.

Dennis J. F. Murphy
Congressional Medal of Honour recipient
1830 – 1901

Dennis J. F. Murphy was born in Cork and was a colour sergeant of the 14th Wisconsin Infantry in the American Civil War. A participant at the Battle of Corinth in Mississippi, on 3 October 1862 his citation reads: 'Although wounded three times, (he) carried the colors throughout the conflict'. For this deed he was awarded the Congressional Medal of Honour.

Tony Murphy
Organiser of the Gay Future horse racing scam 1931 – 1982

A flamboyant and affable racing lover, Tony Murphy had a liking for fine cigars and was a millionaire owner of a golden Rolls Royce. He is infamous for the scam involving Gay Future, the fine racehorse that was brought from Ireland to the stables of Anthony Collins in England, whilst an inferior lookalike was entered in its place at a meet in Cartmel. This replacement horse's performance was such that the real Gay Future received very poor reviews from racing experts and in order to ensure Gay Future held its starting odds of 10 to 1, soap flakes were rubbed into its legs to give the impression that it had been sweating, a move which kept on-track punters from backing it. Collins also entered two other horses in races at the course on that day and Gay Future was backed in doubles and trebles around Great Britain. With the other two horses due to run, they were subsequently pulled from the race at the last moment, meaning that all the bets placed were now transferred to Gay Future, who romped home by fifteen lengths. The scam was only discovered by chance when a reporter learned that the two pulled horses had in fact never left their stables. Murphy subsequently appeared in court in Oxford where a very sympathetic judge fined him just one thousand pounds. Had the scam been successful, the syndicate stood to win £300,000, the rough equivalent of £3 million today (2010). Murphy became a folk hero amongst the racing fraternity and a film called *Murphy's Stroke* starring Pierce Brosnan, with Niall Tóibín playing the part of Tony Murphy, was made in 1979. He died at the age of fifty-one, following a heart attack in October 1982.

James Murray
Victoria Cross recipient 1859 – 1942

James Murray was born in St Michael's Parish in Cork city, and was a lance corporal in the 2nd Battalion, Connaught Rangers, British Army, during the First Boer War. On 16 January 1881 Murray, along with fellow trooper John Danaher, advanced for over five hundred yards under heavy fire at Elandsfontein, near Pretoria in South Africa. In doing so, the two men rescued a severely wounded private who had fallen and they returned the man to safety against an enemy force that numbered around sixty. For this feat, Murray was awarded the Victoria Cross. He died in Dublin in 1942.

Nano Nagle
Founder of the Presentation Sisters 1718 – 1784

The famous Nano Nagle was born in Ballygriffin but was educated in France, due to the fact that at that time, Catholics were denied an education in Ireland unless they converted to the Church of England faith. She entered the Ursuline Convent but in 1749 returned to Ireland where she went about establishing Catholic schools. Despite the fact such activity was deemed illegal, within four years, several hundred girls and boys were attending these schools and by the mid-1770s, she had established the Presentation Sisters who would continue the task of educating young people throughout Ireland. Such was Nagle's generosity, she even went as far as to use inheritance money to build a school which was opened in Cork in 1777. The Presentation Sisters have since spread across the globe and have a significant presence in the United Kingdom, the United States, Australia, and India.

Vincent O'Brien
Racehorse breeder and trainer 1917 – 2009

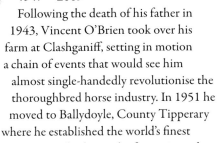

Following the death of his father in 1943, Vincent O'Brien took over his farm at Clashganiff, setting in motion a chain of events that would see him almost single-handedly revolutionise the thoroughbred horse industry. In 1951 he moved to Ballydoyle, County Tipperary where he established the world's finest training centre, also being the first to introduce an all-weather running surface. O'Brien's successes in horse racing were phenomenal and included three Grand Nationals in successive years with three different horses, four Cheltenham Gold Cups, three Cheltenham Hurdles, six Epsom Derby winners, including the Irish Derby, St Leger Stakes and the French Prix de L'Arc de Triomphe, and the Breeders Cup Mile at Belmont Park, New York. It was the bloodline of the Canadian-bred horse, Northern Dancer, that produced probably his greatest horse, Nijinsky, who was just one of O'Brien's greats, the others being Alleged, Roberto, El Gran Senor, Sadler's Wells, Cottage Rake, Sir Ivor, Hatton's Grace, Royal Academy, and Golden Fleece. Lester Piggott, the famed jockey, maintained that O'Brien was the best trainer there ever was and the *Racing Post*, in its 'top one hundred greatest figures in racing', placed the Cork born trainer at number one. He died at his home in Straffan, County Kildare, on 1 June 2009.

William O'Brien
Nationalist 1852 – 1928

William O'Brien was a hardened campaigner for a united Ireland and advocated the peaceful pursuit of such through parliamentary reform. Elected a member of parliament for his native Mallow from 1883 until 1885, in 1887 he was arrested on charges of incitement under the new Coercion Act, for planning a campaign to force landlords to reduce exorbitant rent. His imprisonment caused the notable 'Blood Sunday' riots in London in 1887 and O'Brien continued his protest by refusing to wear a uniform while serving his time. He went on to found the United Irish League in 1898 and was the writer of two novels, *When we were Boys* (1890), and *Queen of Men* (1898). O'Brien, who also represented Cork City in the House of Commons for two stints between 1901 and 1918, died in London on 25 February 1928.

William O'Brien
Trade unionist 1881 – 1968

A close friend of James Connolly (see page 429), William O'Brien became a member of the Irish Socialist Republican Party in 1898, and in 1909 helped establish the Irish Transport and General Workers Union. He ardently fought against conscription during World War I, a stance that resulted in him being interned on several occasions by the Dublin Castle government. O'Brien was elected TD for Dublin South in 1922 and for Tipperary in 1927. He reprised that role for Tipperary in 1937 and continued to be active in politics and the trade union movements into the 1960s. He died on 31 October 1968.

Dr Patrick O'Callaghan
Olympic gold medalist 1905 – 1991

A graduate of Dublin's Royal College of Surgeons, Olympian Patrick O'Callaghan qualified as a doctor in 1926, after which time he served in the Royal Medical Corps of the Royal Air Force for a period of seven years. O'Callaghan came from a prominent sporting family and participated in both Gaelic games and rugby. However, it was in the discipline of track and field that he made his most significant impact. In 1928 at the Olympics in Amsterdam, O'Callaghan won the gold medal for the hammer throwing event, becoming the first Olympic gold medalist in the history of the Irish Republic. He went on to repeat the feat at the Los Angeles games four years later. For a period of sixty years O'Callaghan ran a thriving medical practice in Clonmel, County Tipperary, where he was commonly known as 'Dr Pat'. He retired from the practice in the 1980s and died on 1 December 1991.

Arthur O'Connor
United Irishman and general in Napoleon's army 1763 – 1852

Inspired by the American Revolution, Arthur O'Connor joined the Society of United Irishmen in 1796 and, together with Lord Edward Fitzgerald (see page 240), petitioned France to secure aid for the support of an Irish revolution. Arrested for his involvement in the United Irishmen and imprisoned at Fort George in Scotland, he attained release in 1802 under the condition of banishment, following which he went to France, where Napoleon regarded him as an accredited representative of the United Irishmen.

In 1804, Napoleon appointed him a general of division in the French army and the French minister of war, General Berthier, directed that O'Connor was to join an expeditionary army at Brest, which was preparing for an invasion of Ireland. Unfortunately for O'Connor and Ireland, the plan fell through and he remained in the army for a number of years, before retiring and spending the rest of his life composing literary works on political and social topics. He died on 25 April 1852.

Francis Burdett O'Connor
South American general 1791 – 1871

Francis O'Connor was born in Cork city and was the nephew of the United Irishman, Arthur O'Connor (see above). Setting sail from Dublin in July 1819, he arrived on the island of Margarita, off the coast of Venezuela, as part of the Irish Legion to aid Simón Bolívar's army of independence. However, the fair-skinned Irishmen were unprepared for the tropical climate and with dysentery, typhus and yellow fever decimating the legion, they were forced to reorganise before sailing for the mainland, to attack the city of Riohacha where the Spanish Royal Ensign was hauled down. On 20 March 1820, with a band of just 170 men, O'Connor defeated a Royalist force of 1,700 near Laguna Salada and following that victory Bolivia promoted the young Irish colonel to chief of staff of the United Army of Liberation in Peru. It was O'Connor's strategy under the command of General Antonio Jóse de Sucre, at the battle of Agacucho on 9 December 1824, which led to the final victory over the Spanish and the demise of their rule in South America. Soon after, O'Connor was appointed governor of Tarija. Within that role he issued a proclamation encouraging Irish people to settle in the New Erin of Tarija, 'where the poor of my flesh and blood will be received with open arms'. O'Connor, who was awarded 5000 pesos and the title of 'Liberator' by The Congress of Bolivia, wrote a memoir which was published by his grandson in 1895. It is considered an essential and contemporary account of the South American Wars of Independence.

Frank O'Connor
Author 1903 – 1966

Frank O'Connor was born Michael Francis O'Connor O'Donovan in Cork city. With his childhood having been shaped, in part by the contrasting roles of his saintly mother and his alcoholic father, he joined the Irish Republican Army in 1918 and opposed the Anglo-Irish Treaty of 1921. Having fought on the anti-treaty side in the Civil War, he became an Irish language teacher and librarian and was renowned for his comprehensive and numerous short stories, which he produced between the 1930s and 1960s. His works include, 'Guest of the Nation', 'The First Confession', 'Christmas Morning', 'The Drunkard' and *The Big Fellow* – a biography of Michael Collins (see page 89).

The book *An Only Child*, considered one of O'Connor's best, was a memoir of his early years but was not published until 1961, the same year he suffered a stroke whilst teaching in Stanford University. He later died from a heart attack in Dublin on 10 March 1966. The Frank O'Connor International Short Story Award, now the world's most lucrative short story prize, is sponsored in his memory by O'Flynn Construction.

Seán Ó Faoláin
Short-story writer 1900 – 91

Writer Seán Ó'Faoláin was born John Francis Whelan in Cork city. He was educated at Presentation Brothers College, Cork and fought in the Irish War of Independence, later going on to receive degrees from the National University of Ireland and from Harvard University. He served as director of the Arts Council of Ireland from 1957 to 1959 and wrote numerous books among which are *Midsummer Night Madness and Other Stories* (1932), *Bird Alone* (1936), *Come Back to Erin* (1940) and *The Talking Trees* (1971), as well as biographies of both Daniel O'Connell (1938) and 'The Great O'Neill' (1942). Ó'Faoláin was renowned for his carefully crafted short stories about Ireland's lower and middle classes and he was known for his views on the decline of the nationalist's struggle and the failings of Roman Catholicism.

Hugh O'Flaherty
'The Pimpernel of the Vatican' 1898 – 1963

Hugh O'Flaherty was born in Kiskeam and was educated by the Presentation Brothers and at St Brendan's College, Killarney, and the De La Salle College in Waterford. Ordained in Rome in

1922 and appointed monsignor in 1934, O'Flaherty is accredited with saving the lives of 6,500 allied prisoners of war from the Germans in Rome from 1943 to 1944. Having organised an escape for the prisoners, he gained the title 'The Pimpernel of the Vatican', and his World War II heroism was officially honoured by the governments of Britain, France, Italy and the United States with Britain awarding him the CBE and the United States, the Medal of Freedom. Immortalised in the 1983 film, *The Scarlet and the Black*, O'Flaherty was portrayed by the legendary Gregory Peck. He died at his home in Caherciveen on 30 October 1963.

Standish James O'Grady
Novelist and historian 1846 – 1928
Author, journalist and historian, Standish James O'Grady was born in Castletownbere and was called to the bar when he qualified as a lawyer. However, having been influenced by a chance discovery of a book of Celtic literature, he instead turned to writing and subsequently published *History of Ireland: Heroic Period* (1878) and *Early Bardic Literature of Ireland* (1879). Later, he began writing literary adaptations of Ireland's great legends, producing historical novels such as, *Finn and his Companions* (1891), *The Coming of Cuculain* (1894), *The Chain of Gold* (1895), *Ulrick the Ready* (1896), *The Flight of the Eagle* (1897), and *The Departure of Dermot* (1913).

O'Grady, who became the editor of the *Kilkenny Moderator* in 1898, founded the *All-Ireland Review* in 1900 but immigrated to England due to a bout of ill-health and he died on the Isle of Wight in 1928.

Timothy O'Hea
Victoria Cross recipient 1846 – 68
Timothy O'Hea was born in Schull and served as a private in the 1st Battalion Rifle Brigade of the British Army. On 9 June 1866, while stationed at Danville in Quebec, a fire broke out in a railway carriage, which contained two thousand pounds of ammunition. With the carriage disconnected from the train, O'Hea bravely rushed the car and used water to suppress the fire and was thus awarded the Victoria Cross. He died in Ireland in 1868.

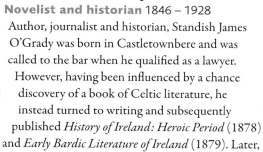

Daniel Florence O'Leary
General in the South American wars of independence 1802 – 1854
Soldier Daniel Florence O'Leary joined the Venezuelan Red Hussars, by way of the British Legion, at the age of sixteen. In 1818 he left with the Hussars to join the forces of Simón Bolívar, who was recognised as the liberator of the northern region of South America and from the outset of his arrival on that continent, O'Leary distinguished himself in numerous battles before later becoming the personal aide to Bolívar, who appointed him brigadier general. Following the death of Bolívar, O'Leary settled in Bogotá, Colombia and served as a diplomatic representative for the government of Venezuela in London for a period of six years. His extensive manuscripts on the South American wars of independence, Memories del General O'Leary, which were edited by his son, Simón Bolívar O'Leary, are divided into thirty-two volumes and are a crucial source of information from that era. He died on 24 February 1854, and his resting place is close to that of Simón Bolívar.

Major Michael O'Leary
Victoria Cross recipient
1890 – 1961
Macroom native Michael O'Leary served as a lance corporal in the Irish Guards, British Army, during World War I. On 1 February 1915, O'Leary single-

handedly stormed an enemy position at Cuinchy, France. Killing all five German occupants. He then charged another enemy position some sixty yards away and captured it, taking three more casualties in the process and retaining a further two as prisoners. At the time of the awarding of his Victoria Cross, the British War Office sought the help of O'Leary's father in recruiting young Irish men to join the army.

This recruitment effort occurred just prior to the Easter Rising in Ireland and so O'Leary's father took the stand and announced to the potential combatants: 'If you don't join the British Army, the Germans will come here, and do to you, what the English have been doing for the last seven hundred years.' Needless to say, his father was not requested to give any further recruitment speeches. O'Leary later achieved the rank of major, and died in London in 1961.

Francis O'Neill
Chicago chief of police and collector of traditional Irish music 1848 – 1936

Francis O'Neill was born near Bantry and became a cabin boy on an English merchant ship at the age of sixteen. Eventually settling in Chicago, he joined the city's police force in 1873 and rose through the ranks to eventually become chief of police from 1901 until 1905. He was a great lover of traditional Irish music and collected tunes from a wide variety of sources. When he retired in 1905 he concentrated his energies on publishing the music he had collected, such as, *O'Neill's Music of Ireland* (1903), which contained 1850 pieces of music, and *The Dance Music of Ireland* (1907), which contained in the region of one thousand tunes. His contribution to traditional Irish music is immense. He died in Chicago on 26 January 1936.

Michael O'Riordan
Founder of the Communist Party of Ireland and member of the International Brigades in the Spanish Civil War 1917 – 2006

Michael O'Riordan was born at No. 37, Pope's Quay in Cork city and joined the Irish Republican Army in his late teens, where he became friends with left-wing republicans such as Peadar O'Donnell (see page 134) and Frank Ryan. He took part in the Spanish Civil War with the XVth International Brigade and was severely injured at the Battle of Ebro, returning to Ireland in 1938 where he continued his involvement with the IRA. Interned in the Curragh Camp by the Irish government from 1939 to 1943, from the mid-1940s he was involved in the Irish Transport and General Workers Union, as well as the Irish Worker's Party from 1962 to 1970. O'Riordan, who was an ardent campaigner on behalf of the Birmingham Six published 'Connelly's Column' in 1979, a story of Irishmen who fought in the Spanish Civil War of 1936 – 1939. His life interest was the establishment of a socialist republic in Ireland and he died at the age of eighty-eight in Dublin. His funeral in Glasnevin Cemetery was attended by over two-thousand mourners including many prominent political leaders, with tributes being paid by president of Ireland, Mary McAleese, then taoiseach Bertie Ahern as well as Gerry Adams of Sinn Féin, and Labour Party leader Ruairi Quinn.

Pádraig Augustine Ó Síocháin
Journalist, author and lawyer 1905 –1995

An author of great repute, Pádraig Augustine Ó Síocháin was born in Kanturk, and educated at Rochestown College and the University of London, where he received a diploma in journalism in 1923. A founder member of the *Irish Press* in 1931, he was also editor of the *Aviation Magazine*, and later the official journal of the Irish police service, the *Garda Review*.

Ó'Síocháin, who qualified in law in 1936 and became senior counsel in 1948, had a deep love of the Irish language which compelled him to change his name from the English edition of 'Sheehan' to the Gaelic version of 'Ó'Síocháin'. He had a number of personal publications, amongst which were *Aran Islands of Legend* (1967), *A Journey into Lost Time* (1983), and *Journey to Freedom* (1990) and he also published a number of books on law. He died in Rathfarnham, Dublin, on 19 December 1995.

Gerald Robert O'Sullivan
Victoria Cross recipient
1888 – 1915

Gerald Robert O'Sullivan was born in Frankfield, Douglas, and was a captain in the 1st Battalion, Royal Inniskilling Fusiliers, British Army, during World War I. In July 1915, O'Sullivan advanced on open ground under heavy enemy fire to throw bombs into an enemy trench at Gallipoli in Turkey. His efforts were rewarded with the eventual capture of the trench but he was wounded in the process and was eventually killed in action in August 1915.

Edel Quinn
Lay missionary 1907 – 1944

Having been educated locally, Edel Quinn, who was born in Kanturk, was sent to a finishing school for girls at Upton Hall in Cheshire, England. Planning to enter the Order of the Poor Clares – she was unable to do so due to tuberculosis – she later joined the Legion of Mary in Dublin and devoted herself to helping the poor in the slums of the city. In 1936,

Quinn became a Legion of Mary envoy and travelled as a missionary to east and central Africa where, despite the fact that she was dying from tuberculosis, she successfully established hundreds of legion branches in the territories known today as Tanzania, Kenya, Uganda, and Malawi. She died in Nairobi, Kenya in 1944 and is buried there in the Missionaries Cemetery. Fifty years after her death, Quinn was declared venerable by Pope John Paul II.

Christy Ring
Hurler 1921 – 1979

Often regarded as the greatest hurler ever, Christy Ring was born in the townland of Kilboy near Cloyne, and was educated at the local national school. His principal occupation was that of a lorry driver, first with CIE and later with Shell Oil, and having played minor hurling for Cork, he made his debut with that county's senior team in 1939. In all, he won eight All-Ireland Senior Hurling Championships, nine Munster Senior Hurling Championships and three National Hurling League medals. But it was perhaps in the 1956 All-Ireland final, that the esteem in which Ring was held, was most explicitly shown when the Wexford players, who had just defeated Cork, carried him shoulder high from the field.

In a career spanning twenty-five years, and with a record-breaking sixty-four championship appearances with the Cork hurling team, Ring's remarkable run came to an end in 1964. A teetotaller, he was a devout Roman Catholic and donated his All-Ireland Championship medals to form part of a special chalice in St Augustines Church, Cork. He died following a heart attack at the age of fifty-eight and his funeral in Cork was attended by sixty thousand people, his coffin draped in the colours of his beloved club, Glen Rovers. A statue in his memory stands opposite the church in Cloyne.

William Randall Roberts
Politician, Fenian, leader and congressman 1830 – 1897

William Randall Roberts was born in Mitchelstown and, at the age of nineteen, left Ireland for New York where he initially worked as a dry goods clerk. He later established his own business, only to come to ruin in the economic downturn of 1857. He bounced back the following year, establishing another business which was so successful that by 1869, he could have retired a millionaire, if he had so desired. He would eventually join the Fenian Brotherhood and was one of the organisers of the planned but aborted invasion of Canada by Irish troops returning from the American Civil War. Following this, he turned to a career in politics in New York City and was elected as a Democrat to the House of Representatives from 1870 until 1874, a term during which he vigorously attacked British policies at every available opportunity. A supporter of Governor Cleveland for the presidency of the United States, Roberts was duly rewarded by Cleveland, and was appointed minister to Chile from 1885 until 1889. He died in New York on 9 August 1897.

Jeremiah O'Donovan Rossa
Irish Fenian leader 1831 – 1915

Jeremiah O'Donovan Rossa was born in Rosscarbery and was one of the founder members of the Irish Republican Brotherhood. Due to his involvement with the Fenians, he was exiled in 1871 and went to the United States. Rossa became infamous in Britain for what became known as the 'Dynamite Campaign', during which English cities were bombarded by Irish republicans. The British Government subsequently demanded his extradition, which was refused by the United States. His actions were condemned in the Irish independence movements but in 1904 he was made a freeman of the city of Cork. Rossa died in St Vincent's Hospital, Staten Island, New York and realising the propaganda value of the old Fenian's death, the Irish Republican Brotherhood had his body returned for burial in Ireland. His funeral cortège to Glasnevin Cemetery drew large crowds and Patrick Pearse (see page 185) administered the graveside oration. There is a statue in St Stephen's Green in Dublin to his memory and a bridge over the River Liffey is named in his honour.

Thomas Russell
United Irishman 1767 – 1803

Thomas Russell was born into an Anglican family in Dromahane and saw service with the British army in India for a period of five years. In 1790, Russell met Theobald Wolfe Tone, (see page 196) who had a powerful influence on his thinking. Russel was arrested in 1796 and spent six years imprisoned without trial in Dublin, denied the opportunity of fighting alongside Wolfe Tone in the rebellion of 1798. Together with Robert Emmet (see page 165), Russell planned the abortive rising of 1803 but was captured following its failure and was tried in Downpatrick, County Down, before being found guilty of treason and executed. To many people of County Down, Russell is referred to as 'The Man from God Knows Where' and as a result he was immortalised in the ballad of the same name by Bangor poet, Florence Mary Wilson.

George Salmon
Mathematician and Anglican theologian 1819 – 1904

At the age of nineteen, George Salmon graduated from Trinity College,

Dublin with exceptionally high honours in mathematics. He became a fellow of the college in 1841 and went on to be appointed professor of divinity in 1866, a role he occupied until 1888. His work *Conic Sections* (1847), was the leading textbook on that subject for over fifty years but in 1866 his career moved in a different direction when he was appointed to the prestigious chair of theology at Trinity College. Though he was awarded the highest honour in British science – the Copley Medal in 1889 – Salmon had become primarily concerned with theology and arguments against Roman Catholicism became an increasingly common theme in his subsequent workings. His book, *Infallibility of the Church* (1889), was widely read and argued against the beliefs of the church in respect of infallibility. Salmon, who also authored books on eternal punishment, miracles and the interpretation of the New Testament, died on 22 January 1904.

Captain Sir Eyre Massey Shaw
Founder of the Metropolitan Fire Brigade (London Fire Brigade) 1830 – 1908

Having served in the North Cork Rifles, a militia regiment of the British army, Eyre Massey Shaw reached the rank of captain, but following parliament's passing of the Metropolitan Fire Brigade Act in 1865, was appointed head of the new brigade. He is noted for his adoption of the famous brass helmet worn by fire-fighters and was an influential thinker on fire fighting, introducing the use of telegraph communications between stations and expanding the use of steam fire engines. Knighted by Queen Victoria on his last day of service with the brigade, he is remembered today as the 'Captain Shaw', to whom the Fairy Queen in Gilbert and Sullivan's comic opera 'Iolanthe' addresses herself. The first fireboat on the River Thames, the *Massey Shaw*, was named after him and it was used in the evacuation of British troops in France in 1940 and has

recently been renovated. His former home, Winchester House in Southwark, London now forms part of the London Fire Brigade Museum.

The Sheares Brothers
United Irishmen
John 1766 – 1798
Henry 1753 – 1798

Born to a father who was a very wealthy banker and a member of parliament, the Sheares brothers were educated at Trinity College, Dublin before both were later called to the Irish bar. They visited France in 1788 and formed revolutionary principles inspired by the French Revolution and so, upon their return to Ireland, they both joined the United Irishmen. Betrayed by a family friend, Captain Armstrong, the two brothers were arrested, tried for high treason and were publicly executed at Newgate Prison in London on 14 July 1798. Being both of the Protestant faith, they are buried in the crypt of St Michan's Church, Dublin.

Patrick Augustine Sheehan
Catholic priest and author
1852 – 1913

Patrick Augustine Sheehan was born at 29 New Street in Mallow and was educated at St Colman's College, Fermoy and St Patrick's College, Maynooth. Ordained in Cork in 1875, he was appointed parish priest of Doneraile in 1895 before being made a canon in 1903, and was thereafter known as, 'Canon Sheehan of Doneraile'. As author of the novel Geoffrey Austin, Student in 1895, and its sequel The Triumph of Failure in 1898, Sheehan dealt with problems of Catholic adolescence and he also wrote numerous other books which had great popularity in Ireland and abroad. He died in Doneraile on 5 October 1913.

Hanna Sheehy-Skeffington
Feminist 1877 – 1946

The wife of Francis Skeffington (see page 70) and a lifelong feminist, following her marriage Hanna retained her maiden name to become Hanna Sheehy-Skeffington. In an effort to secure voting rights for women, she founded the Irish Women's Franchise League but in doing so incurred the wrath of the authorities in 1913, being sentenced to three months imprisonment for protesting outside Dublin Castle. She was released upon the commencement of a hunger strike and in 1917 travelled to the United States to lobby for support for Irish independence. Having met with President Woodrow Wilson, Sheehy, upon her return to Ireland, was once again imprisoned by British authorities but she remained undeterred and went on to oppose the Anglo-Irish Treaty, and also became a founding member of the Fianna Fáil political party in 1926. Her husband Francis was murdered by a deranged British army officer who later pleaded insanity at his trial, and following an enquiry by the British government, Sheehy refused to accept any compensation for her loss. She died on 20 April 1946.

Thomas Alfred Smyth
Union brigadier general in the American Civil War 1832 – 1865

Thomas Alfred Smyth emigrated to Philadelphia, Pennsylvania at the age of twenty-two. In 1861 he enlisted in the Union Army, joining the 24th Pennsylvania, and was later commissioned a major in the 1st Delaware Infantry. Following the battle of Fredericksburg, Smyth was promoted to lieutenant colonel and was made a full colonel at the battle of Gettysburg, where he was injured on the third day of the conflict. Continuing his progression, in 1864 he was promoted to brigadier general during the siege of Petersburg but was fatally wounded in April 1865, when he was shot through the mouth at Farmville, Virginia. Smyth was the last Union general killed in the war, as Confederate General, Robert E. Lee surrendered on the same day. Smyth was promoted posthumously to a brevet major general and was buried in Brandywine Cemetery in Wilmington, Delaware.

John Sullivan
Victoria Cross recipient 1830 – 1884

John Sullivan was born in Bantry and was a boatswain's mate in the Royal Navy during the Crimean War. On 10 April 1855, while serving as captain of one of the guns at Greenhill Battery, he volunteered to place a flagstaff as an aiming point on a mound close to the enemy, which was raining heavy fire on the occupied position at Sebastopol. In carrying out his objective, Sullivan enabled his own guns to open fire on a position that had previously concealed enemy guns. He died in Kinsale, County Cork in 1884.

Timothy Daniel Sullivan
Politician and poet 1827 – 1914

Founder of the National Petition Movement in the 1850s, Bantry born Timothy Daniel Sullivan was a significant contributor of poems to the newspaper, The *Nation* and also composed the Fenian anthem, 'God Save Ireland', following the execution of the group of men known as, the 'Manchester Martyrs' in 1867. He published a volume of poetry, Green Leaves in 1868 and also made strides on the political front, acting as member of parliament for Westmeath in 1880 and mayor of Dublin in 1886. Sullivan, who had earlier been imprisoned in Tullamore in 1880 for his involvement in the Land League, was a supporter of Charles Stewart Parnell (see page 423), but later opposed the parliamentary leader. He published *Recollections of Troubled Times* in Irish Politics in 1905 and died on 31 March 1914.

Thomas William Sweeny
Union general in the American Civil War and Fenian commander
1820 – 1892

Emigrating to the United States, where he settled in New York in 1832, Thomas William Sweeny found employment with a publishing firm. Affectionately known as 'Fighting Tom', he would find his true vocation when he joined Baxter Blues, a local militia group which saw service during the war with Mexico. It was at the Battle of Churubusco that he was severely wounded and had to have his right arm amputated, but this in no way diminished his military career. Following his recuperation, Sweeny embarked on a rapid ascent through the ranks and by the outbreak of the American Civil War he had attained the rank of brigadier general. In August 1861 he was again severely wounded at Wilson's Creek but was back in action within six months, upon which time he commanded a brigade at the Battle of Shiloh. In May 1864, Sweeny, who was now in command of a division, forced the retreat of Confederate General, Joe Johnston. His career took a backward step however, when on 25 July 1864, he was involved in a fight with General Grenville Dodge and Brigadier General John W. Fuller. Sweeny was a regular army officer and had little time for politically appointed generals and though he had the use of just one arm, he apparently defeated both men. Having been cleared by a military court at the war's end, Sweeny still had another fight to undertake, as he was appointed secretary of war by the Fenian Senate. With thousands of Irish Civil War veterans prepared to join him, the possibility of safely crossing the ocean with a sizeable force against the greatest navy in the world, was a very real prospect but never came to fruition. To strike a blow for Irish freedom, Sweeny decided to attack the British in Canada and if successful, use it as a negotiation for the freedom of Ireland. He felt that with only eight thousand regular British troops in Canada, backed up by twenty-eight thousand non-regular troops, the chances of success were good. Sweeny's new army, to be known as the Irish Republican Army, needed the support of the United States Government and in view of the fact that the British supported the Confederates, they were hopeful of receiving it. A successful beginning to their invasion under Colonel John O'Neill took place on 1 June 1866, but President Johnston declared that US neutrality laws were to be upheld and the border was closed by state troops. O'Neill was forced to withdraw and so ended Sweeny's strike for Irish freedom. He thus returned to duty with the United States army before retiring on 11 May 1870. He lived the remainder of his life on Long Island, New York and died there on 10 April 1892.

William Thompson
Philosopher and socialist reformer 1775 – 1833

Although born into a wealthy land-owning family in Rosscarbery, William Thompson was horrified by the social inequalities that existed between tenant farmers and landlords at that time. On his own estate in County Cork, he introduced many agricultural innovations in the interest of improving the welfare of his tenants and the education of their children. A critic of capitalist exploitation, his writings influenced the co-operative and trade union movements and he was referred to by James Connolly (see page 429) as 'the first Irish socialist' and a forerunner to Karl Marx. His major works were *An Enquiry into the Principles of the Distribution of Wealth* (1824), *Appeal of One Half of the Human Race* (1825), *Labour Reward* (1827), and *Practical Directions for the Establishment of Communities* (1830). Thompson, who died on 28 March 1833, left his entire estate to the poor in the hope that it would lessen their plight.

General James Travers
Victoria Cross recipient 1820 – 1884

Thirty-six-year-old James Reavers was serving as a colonel in the 2nd Bengal Native Infantry, Indian Army, during the Indian Rebellion of 1857, when the Presidency at Indore came under intense enemy bombardment. Travers bravely charged the enemy guns with the support of just five other men and drove the gunners away; saving the lives of numerous civilians who had been sheltering in the Presidency. He later achieved the rank of general and died in 1884.

Frederic Herbert Trench
Playwright and poet 1865 – 1923

Frederic Herbert Trench was educated at Haileybury and Keble Colleges, Oxford, and became artistic director at the Theatre Royal in Haymarket in 1909, following which he went to live in Florence. In 1919 his four-act play, *Napoleon* was produced by the Stage Society, and he also produced a list of poems. Trench died in Boulogne-sur-Mer, on 11 June 1923.

Joseph Ward
Victoria Cross recipient 1832 – 1872

Joseph Ward was born in Kinsale, and was a sergeant in the 8th Hussars, British Army, during the Indian Rebellion of 1857. On 17 June 1858 he, together with three others, led a gallant charge through heavy and continuous fire to capture two enemy guns at Gwalior. Later, supported by a division of the Bombay Horse Artillery and the 95th Regiment, they completely routed the enemy. Ward died in Longford in 1872.

James J. Wood
Inventor 1856 – 1928

Born in the picturesque town of Kinsale, James J. Wood arrived in the United States in 1864. At the age of eleven he began a career with a lock company in Bradford, Connecticut and before he was seventeen years of age, he had designed and built a horizontal steam engine. Wood's oil engines provided power for the invention of fellow Irishman, John Philip Holland's (see page 78) submarine, and he also constructed machinery used to make the cables of the Brooklyn Bridge in New York City. In all he possessed more than 240 patents and was one of the first to recognise the business potential of the household refrigerator whilst working for the General Electric Company. Wood was an electrical pioneer and he significantly contributed to the development of electric motors and generators. His impact within the General Electric Company led to it becoming the United States' leading electrical goods manufacturing company and he also installed the first floodlight system at the Statue of Liberty. He died in 1928.

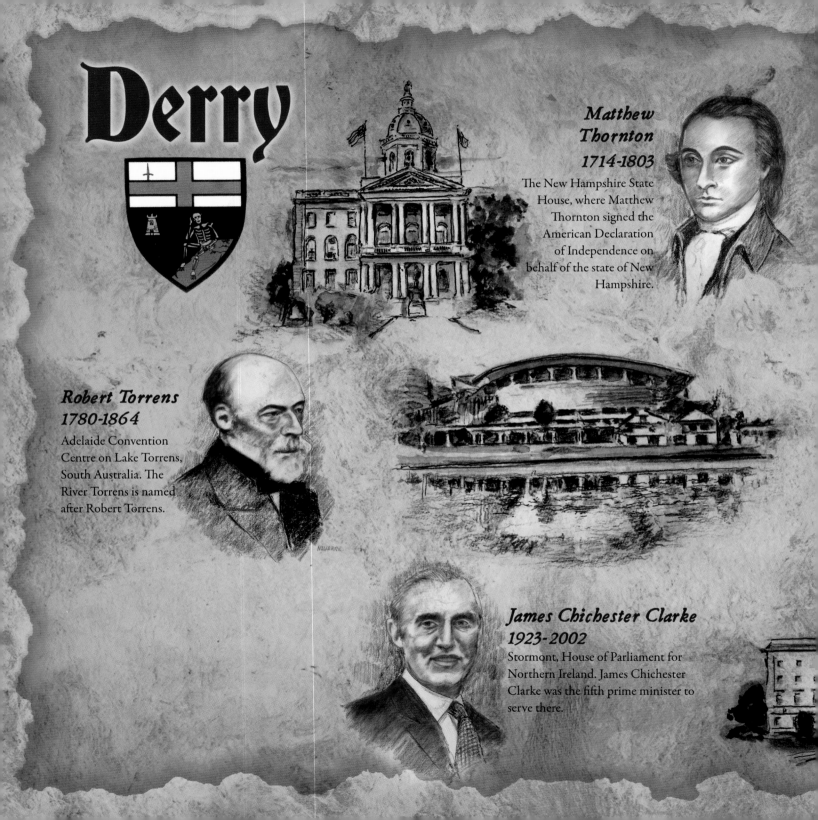

Derry

Matthew Thornton
1714-1803

The New Hampshire State House, where Matthew Thornton signed the American Declaration of Independence on behalf of the state of New Hampshire.

Robert Torrens
1780-1864

Adelaide Convention Centre on Lake Torrens, South Australia. The River Torrens is named after Robert Torrens.

James Chichester Clarke
1923-2002

Stormont, House of Parliament for Northern Ireland. James Chichester Clarke was the fifth prime minister to serve there.

Charles Thomson
1729-1824

The Great Seal of the United States was designed by Charles Thomson.

William Ferguson Massey
1856-1925

Massey University in Auckland, New Zealand is named after William Ferguson Massey, a former president of New Zealand.

William George Aston
Scholar 1841 – 1911

Educated at Queen's University and a fluent Japanese speaker, William George Aston translated many Japanese works into English and compiled two Japanese grammars (1868 and 1872). The doctor of literature was the first person to translate *Nihongi* (the ancient chronicles of Japan) in 1896, and followed this with the translation of *A history of Japanese literature* (1899). He spent most of his life in the research and study of Japanese literature and its translation into English, but also served as consul general of Korea from 1884 until 1886. His collections of some 9,500 Japanese books, including many rare editions, are housed in Cambridge University.

Joyce Cary
Writer 1888 – 1957

Having initially studied art in Edinburgh and Paris, Derry city born Joyce Cary eventually decided on a career as a writer. In 1912, he served as a Red Cross orderly during the Balkan wars and kept a record of his experiences there. Entitled *Memoir of the Bobotes*, it was not published until after his death in 1964. In 1913 Cary joined the Nigerian Political Service and during World War I, served with the Nigerian Regiment fighting Germans in the Cameroon.

An instance during this period was instrumental in him producing the short story, 'Umaru' in 1921. At the end of the war he settled in Oxford, and fourteen years later in 1932, his first novel, *Aissa Saved* became his first success.

In all, he published sixteen novels, including a number of short stories, and two lengthy poems, along with an autobiography that recalled his boyhood years spent in Inishowen, County Donegal. He died in Oxford on 29 March 1957.

James Chichester-Clark
Fifth prime minister of Northern Ireland
1923 – 2002

James Chichester-Clark was born at Moyola Park in Castledawson and was educated in England at Selwyn House in Broadstairs, and later at Eton. Following his schooling, he gained a commission in the Irish Guards and saw action at the Anzio landings in World War II, where he was injured and spent most of that war in hospital. In 1960, Clarke was elected for South Derry in the Northern Ireland parliament and was appointed government chief whip under Terence O'Neill (see page 433) in the 1963 Northern Ireland government. In 1967 he was appointed minister of agriculture and was one of the primary causes of O'Neill's resignation in 1969. Following this, he became leader of the Ulster Unionist Party and prime minister of Northern Ireland. However, due to the forced disbandment of the Ulster Special Constabulary which was brought about by the Hunt Committee report, Clark's tenure was punctuated by civil unrest. In 1971, following the death of three British soldiers, he requested that British prime minister Edward Heath deploy more troops to increase security in Northern Ireland, but with only 1,300 extra men offered, Clark resigned on 20 March of that year – in which he was also created a life peer. Clark was a firm, yet conciliatory unionist and he endorsed the Belfast Agreement in the 1998 referendum. He died on 17 May 2002.

Henry Cooke
Presbyterian leader 1788 – 1868

Ordained a minister in 1808, Henry Cooke is the man most credited with leading Ulster Presbyterianism away from the freethinking radicalism that had become synonymous with the United Irishmen. He was elected moderator in 1841 and again in 1862 and was instrumental in forming an alliance between Presbyterians and the established Church of Ireland, in their defence against the newly-emancipated Catholics. Cooke's statue, which was erected in Belfast in September 1875 and stands in College Square East, is symbolic of the Protestantism of Northern Ireland. Although he was never an orange man, he is portrayed on their banners to this day. He died in Belfast on 13 December 1868.

Robert Greacen
Poet 1920 – 2008

Though Derry born, Robert Greacen grew up in Belfast and spent much of his youth in County Monaghan. Educated at the Methodist College in Belfast, and at Trinity College, Dublin, he spent some time in journalism and adult education in London, before later returning to Dublin where he spent the remainder of his life. A winner of the *Irish Times* literature prize for poetry with *Collected Poems 1944-1994*, his list of poetry is indeed extensive and he once commented on it, 'as a younger man I was a wordy spinner, my later work is less wordy, more compressed'. He was a member of Aosdána due to his outstanding contribution to the arts and he died in Dublin in April 2008.

Robert Hawthorne
Victoria Cross recipient 1822 – 1879

Robert Hawthorn was born in Maghera. Attached to the 52nd Regiment of the British Army during the Indian Mutiny, he distinguished himself on 14 September 1857, at Delhi, India. Whilst on an attack at the Kashmir Gate and under heavy fire, Hawthorn successfully bound the wounds of an officer who had been badly injured before escorting him to safety. For this deed he was awarded the Victoria Cross. He died in Manchester in 1879.

Brian Keenan
Irish republican 1942 – 2008

The son of a Royal Airforce member, Brian Keenan joined the IRA in the early 1970s and became a quartermaster of the Belfast Brigade. Once dubbed 'the single biggest threat' to British rule in Northern Ireland, he was arrested in March 1979 and, accused of organising the IRA's bombing campaign in England, stood trial at the Old Bailey in London in June 1980. Following a sentence of eighteen years in prison, he was released in June of 1993 and supported the Armalite and the Ballot Box strategy, saying 'that both political negotiations and violence were legitimate forms of revolution'. He added, 'the revolution can never be over until we have British Imperialism where it belongs in the dustbin of history.' It was Keenan's turn from a militant to a peace strategist that was most remarkable and he played a key role in the peace process, acting as the IRA's liaison with the Independent International Commission on Decommissioning. Gerry Adams once remarked, 'there would be no peace process if it wasn't for Brian Keenan.' He died of cancer on 21 May 2008.

General Sir Edward Pemberton Leach
Victoria Cross recipient
1847 – 1913

At thirty-one years of age, Edward Pemberton Leach became a captain in the Royal Engineers, British Army during the Second Afghan War. On the 17 March 1879, near Maidanah, Afghanistan, Leach successfully charged a large enemy force along with a small band of his own men, personally killing two or three of the enemy in the process. Although he was wounded in the left arm, his actions saved his whole platoon from annihilation and for that he was awarded the Victoria Cross.

William Ferguson Massey
Prime minister of New Zealand
1856 – 1925

Born in Limavady, William Ferguson Massey emigrated to New Zealand in 1870, having completed his education in Ireland. Initially he worked as a farm hand and in 1877, eventually acquired his own land. However, it was his involvement in Freemasonry and the Orange Order that proved influential in the success of his political career and in 1909, he established the Reform Party, which attained considerable success in the New Zealand elections of 1911. Massey was sworn in as prime minister of New Zealand on 10 July 1912, and served in this position during World War I. A strong believer in the British Empire and New Zealand's links with it, he was forced to relinquish his official duties due to ill health in 1924, and died on 10 May the following year. Massey University, New Zealand, is named in his memory.

Joseph McLaughlin (Josef Locke)
Tenor 1917 – 1999

Performing under the stage name of 'Josef Locke', Joseph McLaughlin was a superstar in Britain and Ireland in the 1940s and 50s. At the age of sixteen, he enlisted in the Irish Guards – having claimed that he was eighteen years old – and he later served with the Palestine Police Force as well as the Royal Ulster Constabulary in the late 1930s. In the early 1940s, he joined impresario Jack Hylton, who was responsible for changing his name from Joseph McLaughlin to Josef Locke, and in 1947 he released, 'Hear my Song' which he was to become forever synonymous with. By this time, Locke was reputed to be earning in the region of two to three thousand pounds per appearance, but he attracted the attention of the British tax authorities following his performance at the Royal Variety Performance in 1958 and subsequently fled to Ireland in order to seek refuge. Having eventually resolved his tax problems, Locke retired to County Kildare and is immortalised by means of his portrayal by Ned Beatty in the Peter Chelsom film *Hear my Song*, which was produced in 1992. A bronze memorial to him which bears the notes of the opening line of 'Hear my Song' was unveiled outside Derry City Hall in 2005.

John Mitchel
Patriot 1815 – 1875

The son of a Presbyterian minister, John Mitchel was educated at Trinity College, Dublin, where he qualified as a lawyer. Seeing the devastation and misery brought on by the Great Famine, Mitchel was convinced that constitutional agitation was useless and so founded the United Irishmen. In 1848 he was arrested, tried for treason and convicted by a packed jury. Having been sentenced to fourteen years imprisonment in Van Diemen's Land (Tasmania), Australia, Mitchel escaped to the United States in 1853 where he published his *Jail Journal* the following year. The book would go on to become a classic in prison literature. Mitchel also partook in the American Civil War, siding with the southern States, where two of his sons were killed in combat. He later returned to Ireland where he was elected MP for Tipperary. He died on 20 March 1875 and is buried in Newry.

Sir James Murray
Inventor of milk of magnesia 1788 – 1871

Culnady native James Murray practised medicine in Belfast. Particularly interested in fluid magnesia, he first published a paper on the topic in 1817. A talented doctor, in 1829 he used fluid magnesia to treat the lord lieutenant of Ireland, the Marquis of Anglesey, following which he was appointed his resident physician and was knighted. Murray was inspector of anatomy at the Royal College of Surgeons and published pioneering works on matters varying from chemical fertilisers to the effects of climatic conditions on health. His lasting claim to fame is his fluid magnesia, which was patented two years after his death, and sold worldwide under the name of 'Milk of Magnesia'. He died in Dublin in 1871.

Michael O'Duffy
Tenor 1928 – 2003

Michael O'Duffy commenced his singing career in his early twenties and appeared in venues worldwide, including Carnegie Hall. His singing has featured in several motion pictures including *The Quiet Man* (1952),

which starred John Wayne, and John Ford's *The Rising of the Moon* (1957). In all, O'Duffy recorded six albums and he also toured the former USSR in the early 1960s. He retired from the entertainment business in his early forties and became a school teacher in England. O'Duffy died on 19 April 2003 in Herefordshire, England.

John Park
Victoria Cross recipient 1835 – 1863

John Park was born in Derry city and at the age of nineteen, became a sergeant in the 77th Regiment of the British Army during the Crimean War. At the Battle of Alma, between 20 September and 5 November 1854, Park was said to have displayed great bravery and he further distinguished himself on 19 April 1855, when he took Russian rifle pits (trenches). He was severely wounded in the process but survived the ordeal before dying at Allahabad in 1863.

Oliver Pollock
Merchant and financier of the American Civil War 1737 – 1823

Originally from Coleraine, Oliver Pollock emigrated to the United States at the age of twenty-three. Settling initially in Philadelphia, Pennsylvania he established a business which traded with the Spanish in Cuba before moving to New Orleans in 1769, where he became involved in considerable land speculation. A staunch supporter of George Washington, in 1777 he was appointed commercial agent of the United States in New Orleans, and with the Spanish in control of Louisiana, he became a wealthy merchant and personal friend of the governor general, Alejandro O'Reilly. Pollock used his vast wealth to finance the American operations in the west, and the successful campaign of General George Rogers Clarke in Illinois in 1778 was largely due to these contributions. Pollock dedicated his complete fortune in support of the Patriots against Britain and was later compensated in part by Washington's

121

government. The dollar sign ($), a capital 'S' with a stroke through it, originates from Pollock using an abbreviation for the Spanish Peso, where his penmanship placed the letter 'P' over the letter 'S'. The town of Pollock, Louisiana is named in his memory and he died on 17 December 1823.

Miles Ryan
Victoria Cross recipient 1826 – 1887

Miles Ryan was a drummer in the 1st Battalion of the European Bengal Fusiliers during the Indian Mutiny. On 14 September 1857, at Delhi, India, he, together with James McGuire (see page 206), saved a large ammunition magazine from exploding. The magazine had been attacked by enemy fire and the two men seized the boxes, which were alight, and threw them over the ramparts of the magazine into a canal, thereby saving many lives of their comrades.

William Sampson
Lawyer, author and patriot 1764 – 1836

William Sampson studied law at Lincoln's Inn in London, before gaining admittance to the Irish bar. After becoming involved in the Reform Movement and the United Irishmen, he was also the subject of a false rumour which placed him as a major general in the French army, and which led to his imprisonment without trial. Sampson was offered release on the condition that he went into exile, and so he travelled to Portugal in 1799 and then to France, before finally settling in New York in 1806. There, he was admitted to the Bar Association of New York, where he became renowned for his eloquence and defence of personal rights. One such example was on the occasion that he defended a Catholic priest who was being compelled to report matters disclosed in the confessional. Amongst his writings was the 1807 work *Memoirs of William Sampson*, which vehemently attacked British policy toward Ireland. He died in New York City on 28 December 1836.

Charles Thomson
Patriot leader during the American Revolution 1729 – 1824

Following the death of his mother in 1739, Maghera's Charles Thomson emigrated with his father to the United States. Sadly his father died on the journey and the young Thomson eventually settled in Pennsylvania where he later became a school teacher. Renowned for being a man of honesty and integrity, the native tribes of Delaware christened him 'Man of Truth', while President John Adams referred to him as 'the life of the cause of liberty'. Thomson was chosen as secretary to the Continental Congress in 1774 and was also one of only two signees of the original declaration of independence, the other being Continental Congress president John Hancock. The document was taken to John Dunlap (see page 380), who then printed the declaration and passed it to members of the congress and the king of England. This original declaration of independence was lost during the fight for freedom. The existing declaration was signed on 2 August 1776 and for some unknown reason, Thomson's signature does not feature. Amongst his accomplishments is the creation of the final design of the Great Seal of the United States, which remains in use to this day. He died in Montgomery County, Pennsylvania on 16 August 1824.

Matthew Thornton
Signatory of the American Declaration of Independence
1714 – 1803

Matthew Thornton emigrated with his parents to the United States when he was a child. They settled in Worcester, Massachusetts, where Thornton became a physician. Appointed surgeon to the New Hampshire troops in 1745, his medical practice was very successful – enabling him to become a large landowner and a leading member of the community of Londonderry, New Hampshire. Thornton eventually became president of the New Hampshire Assembly and drafted a plan of government for the state after the dissolution of the Royal Government. This would become the constitution for the state. He was selected as the first president of the New Hampshire House of Representatives and justice of the Supreme Court under the new constitution and as New Hampshire's representative to the continental congress, he signed the Declaration of Independence on behalf of that state. He died at the age of eighty-nine, whilst on a visit to his daughter in Newburyport, Massachusetts in 1803.

Robert Torrens
British Army officer and political economist 1780 – 1864

A member of a Protestant family from Harvey Hill, Robert Torrens was a strong supporter of Catholic emancipation, as well as being an officer in the British army. He oversaw the defence of the Baltic Island of Anholt, against superior Danish forces in 1811 and was also a forward-looking economist whose writings include an essay on the external corn trade (1815), and an essay on the production of wealth (1821). Torrens was a strong advocate of state-sponsored emigration to relieve population pressure in the United Kingdom and he took a prominent role in the foundation of South Australia as a colony. Lake Torrens and River Torrens, on which Adelaide was built, are named in his memory.

George Stuart White
Victoria Cross recipient
1835 – 1912

George Stuart White served as a second-in-command in the 92nd Regiment of Foot, British Army, during the Afghanistan War. On 6 October 1879, he led an attack on a strongly fortified hill at Charasiah, where the enemy force outnumbered his by around eight-to-one. With his men virtually exhausted, White grabbed a rifle and ran forward on his own in order to shoot down the enemy leader; his decisive action led to the enemy immediately fleeing the scene of the battle. Later, at the battle of Kandahar, White again led a charge against enemy forces and single-handedly captured two of their guns. In addition to his receipt of the Victoria Cross, he was knighted in later life and also became a field marshal. A statue to White is located at Portland Place in London, where he died in Chelsea Hospital in 1912. His son was Jack White (see page 42), the famous Irish republican and anarchist who was also a founder of the Irish Citizens Army with James Connolly (see page 429).

Donegal

Francis Makemie
1658-1708

Makemie Presbyterian Church, Accomack County, Virginia is a memorial to Francis Makemie, founder of Presbyterianism in America and moderator of America's first Presbytery.

Andrew Lewis
1720-1781

In America's fight for independence, George Washington appointed Andrew Lewis a general in the Continental Army. Lewis's statue stands at the base of the George Washington Equestrian Monument in Capitol Square, Richmond, Virginia.

Dave Gallagher
1873-1917

Dave Gallagher was the captain of 'the Originals', the first New Zealand national rugby team to be known as the All Blacks. He later died, alongside two of his brothers, whilst serving in the New Zealand army during World War I.

ALL BLACKS

Red Hugh O'Donnell
1571-1602

Following the defeat of O'Donnell's forces in the Battle of Kinsale in 1601, he sought aid in Spain where he died in 1602 with some believing he was poisoned. Five years later, the Flight of the Earls took place and with it came the demise of the great Gaelic chiefs of Ulster.

Isaac Butt
1813-1879

The Church of Ireland, Stranorlar, burial place of the 'Father of Home Rule', Isaac Butt.

William Allingham
Man of letters and poet 1824 – 1889

Ballyshannon native William Allingham initially worked in the customs house in his hometown and, after working in similar positions in England until 1870, he retired from the service to become sub-editor of *Fraser's Magazine* from 1874 to 1879. He published a volume of poems in 1850 which was followed by *Day and Night Songs* (1855), *Fifty Modern Poems* (1865), *Songs, Poems and Ballads* (1877), *Irish Songs and Poems* (1877), and *Varieties in Prose* (1893).

Interestingly, the opening lines from Allingham's poem 'The Fairies' was quoted by the character of the Tinker in the Mel Stuart film *Willy Wonka and the Chocolate Factory*, and he features in several other works of popular culture. He died in Hampstead, London in 1889 and his ashes were scattered at St Anne's, in his native Ballyshannon.

Sir Alexander Armstrong
Explorer and naval surgeon 1818 – 1899

A talented and professional surgeon, Alexander Armstrong studied medicine in Dublin and at the University of Edinburgh before joining the Royal Navy in 1842. Commended by his superiors for improving naval hygiene, Armstrong was appointed a senior naval surgeon in 1849. The following year Armstrong served as a surgeon on the hazardous and dangerous journey aboard Robert McClure's (see page 413) ship, the *Investigator*, which went in search of the ships of Sir John Franklin who had been missing since 1845. It was during that expedition that the *Investigator* encountered gale-driven pack ice, with McClure eventually completing the trip of the North-West Passage between the Pacific and Atlantic oceans. The crew was forced to endure half-rations for many months and Armstrong's medical capabilities ensured that only six of sixty-six men, who had faced starvation and scurvy, had died during the entire voyage. His personal narrative of the discovery of the North-West Passage was published in 1857 and he was awarded the KCB in 1871. He died on 4 July 1899.

General Sir Andrew Francis Barnard
British Army general 1773 – 1855

Andrew Francis Barnard was born in Fahan. He joined the British army in 1794 and saw service in both Canada and the West Indies, including the Peninsular War. He was wounded at Waterloo, following which he became a general and subsequently, governor of Chelsea Hospital. Barnard would also go on to be knighted.

Neil Blaney
Politician 1922 – 1995

First elected a Fianna Fáil TD for Donegal East on 7 December 1948, Neil Blaney was re-elected on every subsequent general election until his death in 1995. Blaney was minister for post and telegraphs in 1957, as well as minister for local government in 1958 and 1966. Upon the breakout of the troubles in Northern Ireland in 1969 he expressed extremely strong nationalist views, even though this was against his party and government policy. He also became involved in the arms crisis in which he was accused of supporting the importation of weapons into Ireland in support of the nationalist cause. As a consequence, he was dismissed from government along with Charles Haughey (see page 308) but was acquitted in the subsequent trial before being expelled from the Fianna Fáil party in 1971. He stood as an independent Fianna Fáil candidate in all elections thereafter and strongly supported a united Ireland, while canvassing on behalf of IRA hunger striker Bobby Sands in the Fermanagh and South Tyrone by-election in which Sands was elected. Blaney was also elected to the European parliament and served from 1979 to 1984 and again from 1989 to 1994. He died in Dublin on 8 November 1995 at the age of seventy-three.

John McNeill Boyd
Naval officer 1812 – 1861
As a young boy, John McNeill Boyd joined the British navy where he became noted for his hard work and extraordinary courage. He reached the officer ranks rapidly and in 1857, wrote a manual for naval cadets which was published in 1860 and became an official reference of seamanship. In February 1861, whilst in command of a coastguard ship, the HMS *Ajax* off Dun Laoghaire, County Dublin, Boyd saw two sailing colliers which were experiencing difficulties in rough seas and so he launched his ship's lifeboat, in a rescue attempt. When his lifeboat capsized in the seas, Boyd jumped in to retrieve the drowning seamen but unfortunately drowned in the process. His funeral procession in Dublin was estimated to have been six miles long and a memorial to Boyd and his crew of the Ajax, stands on the East Pier of Dun Laoghaire.

Stopford Augustus Brooke
Churchman and writer 1832 – 1916
Born in Letterkenny, Stopford Augustus Brooke was educated at Trinity College, Dublin and was ordained in the Church of England in 1857. Having served as a curate in London and the British Embassy in Berlin, Brooke later became chaplain-in-ordinary to Queen Victoria. In 1880 he seceded from the church and became a Unitarian minister for some years. His *Premier of English Literature*, published in 1876, sold some 500,000 copies and he also published various volumes of sermons and a number of poems. He died in Ewhurst, Surrey on 18 March 1916.

Isaac Butt
Barrister and politician 1813 – 1879
A brilliant barrister, Isaac Butt was known for his opposition to Irish nationalist leader Daniel O'Connell's campaign for the repeal of the act of union with Great Britain. However, with his experience of the Irish famine his views shifted from unionist to nationalist and he became a strong supporter of Home Rule for Ireland. Butt defended many Fenians in the courts, sacrificing lucrative briefs to do so, and he was also a member of parliament for Youghal (1852 – 65) and for Limerick (1871 – 79). In 1870 he founded the Irish Home Government Association, which later became known as the Home Rule League. He died on 5 May 1879 in Clonskeagh and is buried in Stranolar, County Donegal.

Vincent 'Mad Dog' Coll
Mafia gangster 1908 – 1932
Raised in The Bronx borough of New York City, the 1920s saw Gweedore born Vincent Coll develop the risky but lucrative scam of kidnapping gangsters and seeking ransoms for their release. The brazen rogue worked on the principle that his victims would not report the crime to the police, nor would any release monies paid be reported in order to avoid drawing the attention of the IRS. It was the mayor of New York, Jimmy Walker, who christened him 'Mad Dog' following a botched hit in 1931

on Joey Rao, an underling of Dutch Schultz, during which one child was tragically killed and others wounded. On 8 February 1932, Coll finally met his deserved end when he was gunned down by a henchman working for Schultz. Two movies have been made about Coll. Both entitled *Mad Dog Coll*; one was released in 1961 and the other in 1992.

John Connolly
Victoria Cross recipient 1829 – 1888
John Connolly was born in Ballyshannon. A lieutenant in the 49th Regiment of the British Army in the Crimean War, he was awarded the Victoria Cross for repulsing a large Russian attack, which he himself spearheaded from the front, at Sebastopol. Whilst being personally involved in hand-to-hand fighting with a number of Russians, Connolly was seriously wounded but subsequently received the award due to the bravery he displayed.

James Duffy
Victoria Cross recipient 1889 – 1969
A native of Gweedore, James Duffy served as a private in the 6th Battalion, The Royal Inniskilling Fusiliers, British Army during World War I. On 27 December 1917,while acting as a stretcher-bearer at Kereina Peak in Palestine, Duffy attempted to retrieve a wounded man, together with a fellow stretcher-bearer who was also wounded in the rescue operation. Although under considerable pressure from heavy enemy fire, Duffy successfully transported both wounded men back to cover and for this deed he was awarded the Victoria Cross. He died in Letterkenny, County Donegal in 1969.

Paddy 'The Cope' Gallagher
Founder of the cooperative movement in Ireland 1873 – 1964
At the age of ten, Cleendra native Paddy Gallagher was hired out at the Strabane hiring fair and went to Scotland, before moving on to England, where he laboured in the coalmining industry. Returning to Ireland in the early 1900s, Gallagher purchased a farm in Cleendra and began his life's work pioneering the cooperative movement in Ireland. He established the first cooperative in Templecrone, County Donegal in 1906, which became known as 'The Cope', but met with opposition from local merchants. Such was the intensity of this opposition, Gallagher was ultimately forced to buy his own cargo boat to import goods into Donegal. He also organised local knitting and fishing co-operatives where local people could trade their produce for goods in the co-op. Gallagher's movement exists to this day and his autobiography, *My Story* (1939), is an inspirational tale of how local communities combining can challenge the business world.

Rory Gallagher
Irish rock guitarist 1948 – 1995
A world-renowned musician, Rory Gallagher was born in Ballyshannon. In 1966 he formed the legendary band, Taste, which featured himself on vocals, with drummer John Wilson, and bassist Richard McCracken. Gallagher, a legend of blues music, performed with such notaries as Muddy Waters and Jerry Lee Lewis and he sold over 30 million albums worldwide. However, it was his live performances that won him his greatest acclaim. His guitar, a 1961 Stratocaster, was

extensively remodelled by him, giving what some say was his own unique sound, and so great was Gallagher's impact, that the guitar makers, Fender have manufactured reproductions of the instrument. At the home of his birth, there is the Rory Gallagher exhibition which contains details of his life and miscellaneous memorabilia, while a theatre there has been named The Rory Gallagher Theatre. There is also a commemoration to him in Dublin's Temple Bar. He died in London on 14 June 1995.

Dave Gallaher
First captain of the New Zealand All Blacks 1873 – 1917

Born in Ramelton, Dave Gallaher emigrated with his family to New Zealand in 1878, before settling in Auckland in 1890. In a career spanning from 1903 to 1906, Gallaher represented the Auckland province and played thirty-six times for the All Blacks, the highlight being his captaincy in the first ever test played between New Zealand and Australia. A memorial to him in the form of the 'Dave Gallaher Trophy', established in 2000, is contested between the national teams of New Zealand and France, and in 2005, Letterkenny Rugby Football Club named their home ground The David Gallaher Memorial Park. As a volunteer in World War I, he was killed, together with two of his brothers, after being wounded during the attack on Gravenstafel Spur in Belgium on 4 October 1917.

Cahir Healy
Politician 1877 – 1970

Following his education at St Columbus' Hall and Derry Technical School in Cahir, Healy became a journalist with the *Fermanagh News*, and later with the *Roscommon Herald* and the *Sligo Times*. He became a member of Sinn Féin upon its foundation in 1905, but was imprisoned in 1922 for his nationalist activities. Healy was elected to represent Fermanagh and Tyrone as a nationalist MP in the UK general elections of that year; he was also elected to the Northern Ireland House of Commons in 1925 but did not take his seat until 1927 due to the nationalist abstention policy. Later in 1929, he represented South Fermanagh, and in the 1931 by-election he was again re-elected for Fermanagh and Tyrone, standing down in 1935. Interned by the UK government during World War II, in 1950 he was elected to the British House of Commons for a third time but once again did not take his seat until a later date. Standing down in 1955, the remainder of his parliamentary career was restricted to Stormont, where he became 'Father of the House'. Healy also published a volume of verse and a number of short stories on Irish life. A nationalist all his life, his mild personality and sincerity gained him respect both at Stormont and at Westminster. He died on 8 February 1970.

John Kells Ingram
Irish scholar and economist 1823 – 1907

Educated at Trinity College, Dublin, John Kells Ingram was elected a fellow of the college in 1846. Thus began an association that would last for a further fifty-three years, with Ingram serving as a lecturer in English, professor of Oratory, professor of Greek, librarian and finally as vice provost. A prodigious academic, with a deep interest in economics and sociology, his most important work was *A History of Political Economy*, published in 1888 and translated into eight languages. Coming from a strong unionist background, his composition of Ireland's best known patriotic ballad, 'Who Fears to Speak of '98' in 1843, was strange, to say the least and may well be attributed to his association with Thomas Davis (see page 92). Ingram died in Dublin on 18 May 1907.

Sir Robert Johnston
Victoria Cross recipient 1872 – 1970
Robert Johnston joined the British Army in the late 1880s, where he became a captain with the Imperial Light Horse, South African Forces. Whilst involved in the 2nd Boer War on 21 October 1899 at Elandslaagte, Johnston advanced under point-blank fire to rally his men to carry out a successful flanking movement for which he was awarded the Victoria Cross. He later attained the rank of major and he died in Kilkenny on 24 March 1970.

John Pitt Kennedy
Military engineer and agricultural reformer 1796 – 1879
As a young engineering officer, John Pitt Kennedy served Britain in Malta and Corfu, and was superintendent in charge of the construction of a canal at Lefkada (a Greek island in the Ionian Sea). He was also responsible for the construction of the Himalayan highway from the plains of Simla towards Tibet, which bears his name to this day. He later returned to Ireland where he used his engineering experience in endeavouring to help the lamentable conditions of the agricultural classes. Kennedy, whose labours were relentless on behalf of his native land, died in England in 1879.

General Andrew Lewis
Surveyor and soldier 1720 – 1781
At the age of twelve, Andrew Lewis left Ireland with his family for America where he eventually practised the skills of a surveyor.

The family settled in Augusta County, West Virginia and Lewis later became a lieutenant and then a captain of the Augusta County militia, which was involved in the protection against Native American raids. In the French and Indian War, he became a captain in George Washington's regiment, and in 1775, with the creation of the Continental Army, Washington appointed Lewis as a brigadier general, where he oversaw the defence of Virginia. On 9 July 1776 he led the States' forces against loyalist forces under the command of Lord Dunmore and was successful in forcing them from the colony. Due to failing health, Lewis retired from the army in 1777 but was appointed to the council for the state of Virginia by Governor Thomas Jefferson in 1780. He died soon after in Bedford County, Virginia on 26 September 1781. Lewisburg in West Virginia is named in his memory, and in 2001 the General Assembly of Virginia designated a portion of Interstate 81 in his honour, naming it the Andrew Lewis Memorial Highway. His statue in Capital Square in the city of Richmond shows that his adopted state, Virginia, recognised him as one of its most distinguished sons.

Louis Lipsett
Major general, British forces 1874 – 1918
Bundoran's Louis Lipsett was educated at Bedford Grammar School and at Sandhurst Military Academy in England where he was commissioned a 2nd Lieutenant in the Royal Irish Regiment. Initially serving in India, in 1899 his regiment moved to South Africa for service in the 2nd Boer War and he was promoted to captain. Upon the outbreak of World War I, Lipsett was dispatched to British Columbia in Canada and took over command of the 8th Battalion of the Canadian Expeditionary forces, which were later dispatched to France. At the Second Battle of

Ypres, his troops faced the brunt of the German assault where poisoned gas was first used in modern warfare. To counteract the deadly effect, Lipsett ordered his men to urinate on strips of cloth, and tie them to their faces to neutralise the gas. With his battalion holding the line during action, he was made a Companion of the Order of St Michael and St George, and promoted to acting brigadier general. Lipsett also saw action at the Battle of the Somme and was in command for the Canadian victory at the Battle of Vimy Ridge. He was killed in action on 14 October 1918. In the Dictionary of Canadian Biography, Lipsett is remembered as 'arguably the best' Canadian officer of the Great War.

Patrick MacGill
'The Navvy Poet' 1889 – 1963

Patrick MacGill was born in Ardun in the Glen of Glenties and initially worked as a hired labourer before emigrating to Scotland where, at the age of fourteen, he worked in the potato fields. A self-educated man, his literary contributions are considerable. In his books, *Children of the Dead End* and *The Rat-Pit*, he recalls the harshness of life for the Donegal migrant workers in the potato fields of Scotland. In World War I he served with the London Irish Rifles, recording his experiences in *The Great Push* (1916), and also *The Red Horizon*. Each August he is remembered at the Patrick MacGill Summer School in the Glenties.

Francis Makemie
Founder of Presbyterianism in the United States 1658 – 1708

Francis Makemie was born in Ramelton. Educated in Glasgow, due to the fact that Presbyterians were not accepted in Trinity College, Dublin, he was ordained at the Presbytery of the Lagan and emigrated to the United States in 1683, where he was responsible for establishing the Presbyterian faith. Having seen the persecution of Presbyterians and Roman Catholics in Ireland, and having experienced it yet again in New York, he was a distinguished advocate of religious liberty. Makemie laboured for twenty-five years in Maryland and Virginia, as a devout and able preacher, and he died in the latter state during the summer of 1708.

Ray McAnally
Actor 1926 – 1989

Buncrana native Ray McAnally was educated at St Eunan's College and following a brief period in a Catholic seminary, he joined the Abbey Theatre in 1947. Later making his London theatre debut in 1962, he gave an acclaimed performance as George in *Who's Afraid of Virginia Woolf* at the Piccadilly Theatre. McAnally made several television appearances, featuring in such productions as *The Avengers, Man in a Suitcase* and *Strange Report* and he also led a distinguished movie career, his performance alongside Robert De Niro and Jeremy Irons in the Academy award-winning *The Mission* (1986), earning him a BAFTA award. In the latter stages of his life, he gave a stunning portrayal of the father of Christy Brown in the film, *My Left Foot* (1989), which also won an Academy award. The father of the Irish TV presenter and personality, Aongus McAnally, he died of a heart attack in 1989.

131

Seaside resort of Bundoran County Donegal.

Hugh McLaughlin
Publisher and inventor 1918 – 2006

Killygordan born Hugh McLaughlin initially became a barman's apprentice in Gardiner Street, Dublin but later established a tailoring business. In the 1950s he became involved in the printing business and went on to publish such magazines as *Creation, Irish Farmers Journal, Woman's Way, Woman's Choice,* and *Business and Finance.* In 1973 he founded the newspaper, the *Sunday World* and later established another newspaper, the *Sunday Tribune.* In retirement he invented a machine that is used for the removal of water from cricket pitches and golfing greens. He died on 1 January 2006.

Mícheál Ó Cléirigh
Chronicler 1575 – 1643

Mícháel Ó'Cléirigh was born at Kilbarron and although christened Tadhg, he adopted the name Mícheál upon becoming a Franciscan friar. A collector of British manuscripts, Ó'Cléirigh transcribed everything he could find of historical importance in Irish history and was chief author of the *Annals of the Four Masters,* assisted by Fergus O'Mulconry, Peregrine O'Duignan and Peregrine O' Clery. Although referred to as 'The Four Friars', only O'Cléirigh was an actual Franciscan. The Mícheál Ó Cléirigh Institute for the Study of Irish History and Civilisation at University College Dublin is named in his honour. He died in the Franciscan Friary in Leuven, Belgium.

Cardinal Patrick Joseph O'Donnell
Cardinal and Primate of All Ireland
1856 – 1927

Ordained a priest in 1880, Patrick Joseph O'Donnell became bishop of Raphoe in 1888 and was a staunch activist for social justice, taking an active part in the social, political, and economic life of Ireland. He was appointed archbishop of Armagh in 1922 and was raised to cardinal by Pope Pius XI in 1925. He died on 22 October 1927. The St Connell's Museum, in his hometown of Glenties, has a display detailing his life.

Patrick O'Donnell
Member of 'the Invincibles'
1855 – 1883

Patrick O'Donnell was a member of the Invincibles, who were responsible for the Pheonix Park murders in which the permanent under-secretary, Thomas Henry Burke, and the chief secretary of Ireland, Lord Frederick Cavendish, were killed. Six of the Invincibles were captured for the crime, but one, James Carey, struck a deal and turned Queen's evidence while the remaining five were executed. Carey was given free passage to South Africa and travelled on the steamer, Kinfauns Castle, together with his wife and seven children. O'Donnell travelled on the same ship and in Cape Town, he shot and killed Carey. O'Donnell was arrested and sent back to London where he was tried at the Old Bailey. He was executed in December, 1883 at Newgate Prison.

Peadar O'Donnell
Irish republican socialist
1893 – 1986

A native Irish speaker, Peadar O'Donnell attended St Patrick's Teacher Training College in Dublin and taught for some time on Arranmore Island, and later in Scotland. He was from a militant socialist family and in 1919 was a leading organiser for the Irish Transport and General Workers Union.

He also joined the IRA and was active during the Irish War of Independence (1919 – 1921), leading guerilla activities in both Derry and Donegal. Opposing the treaty of 1922, O'Donnell was a member of the IRA unit that took over the Four Courts building in Dublin, an event which helped to spark the outbreak of the civil war. Later captured by Free State soldiers and imprisoned in Mountjoy Jail, O'Donnell undertook a forty-one day hunger strike with other members. He did not see the republican cause solely in Irish nationalist terms but advocated a socialist revolution. O'Donnell was in Barcelona, attending the People's Olympics, when the Spanish war broke out in 1936 and he joined the Spanish republican militia in opposition to the forces of General Franco. He published a number of novels: *Storm* (1925), *Islanders* (1928), *Ardrigoole* (1929), *The Knife* (1930), *On the Edge of the Storm* (1934), *The Big Window* (1955) and finally, *Proud Island* (1975). In addition, his autobiographical works comprised *The Gates Flew Open* (1932), *Salude! An Irishman in Spain* (1937) and *There will be Another Day* (1963).

Red Hugh O'Donnell
Prince of Tyrconnell 1572 – 1602

Imprisoned in Dublin Castle at the age of fifteen by Sir John Perrot, who feared an alliance between the O'Donnell and O'Neill clans, Red Hugh O'Donnell escaped five years later, in the depth of the winter of 1592, and made his way to safety in the Wicklow Mountains. On his return to Ulster, he regained the leadership of the O'Donnell clan in Tirconnell, County Donegal, where he sought military aid from Philip II of Spain. In 1595 O'Donnell declared rebellion against English rule in Ireland and was assisted by Hugh O'Neill, Earl of Tyrone – an alliance which led to what is known in Irish history as the Nine Year War. Spanish aid finally arrived in September 1601, but unfortunately landed at Kinsale, County Cork, forcing O'Donnell to lead his army over three hundred miles in the midst of winter to rendezvous with the Spanish forces. The allies were beaten by Sir Charles Blount (Lord Mountjoy) at the Battle of Kinsale in 1602 and following that defeat, O'Donnell sailed to Spain to seek further aid from King Philip III. He died there at the age of twenty-nine.

Alexander Porter
United States senator 1785 – 1844

Alexander Porter left Ireland at the age of fifteen for America where he settled in Nashville, Tennessee. Porter studied law and was admitted to the bar in 1807, and he was also a delegate to the convention which framed the first Louisiana Constitution in 1812. A member of the lower branch of the Louisiana Legislature from 1816 to 1818, he was elected a judge of the State Supreme Court from 1821 to 1833 and was elected as a member of the Whig party to the US Senate from 1833 to 1837. He died in the Attakapas territory in 1844 and is buried in Franklin, Louisiana.

Patrick Stone
Australian politician 1854 – 1926

Born in the Inishowen Peninsula town of Buncrana, following the emigration of his family to Western Australia, Patrick Stone was educated at the Roman Catholic school at Fremantle. He then settled in Geraldton where he became a prosperous merchant and owner of the Commonwealth Hotel. Between 1888 and 1916, Stone was a member of the Geraldton Municipal Council and on 24 April 1901 he was successfully elected to the Western Australia Legislative Assembly, representing Geraldton. Stone continued to contest elections throughout his life until his death on 23 September 1926.

John Toland
Deist 1670 – 1722

Although born a Catholic, John Toland converted to Protestantism around the age of sixteen before studying theology at the universities of Glasgow and Edinburgh, and at Leiden, Holland. In 1696, his publication *Christianity Not Mysterious* was burned in Dublin by the public hangman and such was the controversy caused as a result, that it led to conflict between deists and orthodox believers. Toland acclaimed that the monarchy had no God-given sanction as a form of government and he challenged the authority of bishops in the established churches. He was the first to advocate full citizenship and equal rights for Jewish people and he also had a belief in the need for perfect equality amongst freeborn citizens. Widely considered a man ahead of his time, it has been argued that Toland was the first 'Marxist'.

Down

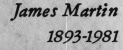

Henry George Ferguson
1884-1960

Inventor Henry George Ferguson revolutionised farming with his Ferguson tractors.

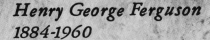

James Martin
1893-1981

Thousands of aviators worldwide owe their lives to James Martin, the inventor of the airplane ejector seat.

Paddy Blair Mayne
1915-1955

Co-founder of the SAS and recipient of four Distinguished Service Orders, Mayne was the most decorated soldier of World War II. His statue stands in his hometown of Newtownards.

Thomas Andrews
1873-1312

Chief designer of the *Titanic*, Andrews was also an exceptionally brave man, giving his life during the sinking of the great vessel in order to save the lives of women and children.

Johnston Blakely
1781-1814

The USS *Wasp*, A US navy sloop of war, was captained by Johnston Blakely, recipient of the Congressional Medal of Honour for service against the British navy during the American war of independence.

John Miller Andrews
Second prime minister of Northern Ireland 1871 – 1956

John Miller Andrews was born in Comber and was educated at the Royal Belfast Academical Institution. The brother of Thomas Andrews (see below), the designer of the *Titanic*, he was a founder member of the Ulster Unionist Labour Association and a Northern Ireland MP from 1921 until 1953. He was elected prime minister of Northern Ireland in 1940, a position he held until 1943, and in 1948 he became grandmaster of the Orange Order. A lifelong member of that order, Andrews was also a member of the Imperial Grand Council of the World from 1949 until 1954 and was a devout member of the non-subscribing Presbyterian Church of Ireland. He died on 5 August 1956.

Thomas Andrews
Chief designer of the *Titanic* 1873 – 1912

Famous for the design of the world's most famous sea-faring vessel, Thomas Andrews was educated in the Belfast Academical Institute and joined shipbuilders Harland and Wolff in 1889. Working as an apprentice, he qualified in 1894 and his progress within the company was rapid before he was appointed head of design in 1903.

Andrews took part in the maiden voyage of the *Titanic* and lost his life when the ship sank on 14 April 1912.

Accounts of the last minutes of his life describe him as a most heroic man, who toiled until exhaustion in order to assist passengers to the lifeboats before going down himself with the ship, thus giving his life to save the women and children of the *Titanic*.

David Bell
Victoria Cross recipient 1845 – 1920

David Bell was a private in the 2nd Battalion, 24th Regiment of Foot in the British Army. He was awarded the Victoria Cross for the bravery he displayed in the process of rescuing many of his fellow soldiers during a tempestuous storm during the Andaman Islands expedition.

Geoffrey Bing
British Labour politician and attorney general of Ghana 1909 – 1977

Banbridge native Geoffrey Bing was a law graduate from the University of Oxford and was called to the bar in 1934. Although from a unionist background, he was a strong supporter of a united Ireland and was also the Labour MP for Hornchurch in north-east London. Bing made an impact in the House of Commons on St Patrick's Day 1952, when he entered wearing a shamrock on his jacket – an act which subjected him to a barrage of abuse from the Conservative benches. During his parliamentary career, he founded the Friends of Ireland Group and represented Hornchurch up to 1955, when he was appointed governor general of Ghana. A fearless man, Bing was indeed a friend of Ireland and never missed an opportunity to speak on behalf of the reunification of the country. He died in London on 24 April 1977.

Edward Barry Stewart Bingham
Victoria Cross recipient 1881 – 1939

Edward Barry Stewart Bingham, who was born in Bangor, was one of the few awarded the Victoria Cross for naval bravery during World War I. As commander of the destroyer HMS *Nestor*, Bingham closed to within 2,800 metres of the opposing battle fleet, thus bringing his torpedoes into range in order to attack enemy destroyers and battle cruisers of the German fleet. As a consequence the HMS *Nestor* was sunk and Bingham was picked up by the Germans, remaining a prisoner of war until the Armistice. He retired from the Royal Navy as a Rear Admiral in 1932.

Sir Henry Blackwood
British naval vice-admiral
1770 – 1832

Entering the British navy as a volunteer in 1781, in 1792 Henry Blackwood travelled to France to learn the French language. Whilst there he was suspected of spying and as a result, was forced to flee the country. In 1795 Blackwood was promoted to the rank of captain and he commanded the Frigates during the Battle of Trafalgar. A witness to the will of his friend Admiral Horatio Nelson, on board the ship *Victory*, Blackwood later went on to become commander-in-chief in the East Indies and a baronet in 1814. He was knighted in 1819 and was appointed vice-admiral three years later. He died in Ballyleidy in 1832.

Johnston Blakeley
Naval officer and Congressional Gold Medal recipient 1781 – 1814

Having emigrated to the United States with his family whilst still a child, Johnston Blakeley graduated from the University of North Carolina and joined the naval service where, in 1814, he was given command of a new ship, the *Wasp*. With orders to disrupt shipping in British waters, Blakeley captained his crew to in excess of fifteen victories and was awarded the Congressional Medal of Honour for capturing the HMS *Reindeer*, which was a far superior vessel to the *Wasp,* weighing in at 382 tonnes and possessing a crew of 118 who had control over twenty-one guns. By contrast, the *Wasp* was a sloop of war with an eighteen-gun armoury. Whilst on another naval mission for the United States, the *Wasp* and her brave commander sailed into oblivion and were presumed lost in a storm in October 1814.

The Reverend Patrick Brontë
Anglican curate and writer
1777 – 1861

Though born in Drumballyroney, Patrick Brontë spent most of his life in England. The father of the famous writers, Charlotte, Emily and Anne Brontë, he studied theology at St John's College, Cambridge in 1802 and was ordained to the priesthood in 1807, before undertaking his priestly duties in parishes throughout England. In 1810, Brontë published his first poem, 'Winter Evening Thoughts', which was followed in 1811 by a collection of moral verse entitled *Cottage Poems*.

He survived all his children and was responsible for the publication of Charlotte's first novel, *The Professor*, in 1857. He died in Yorkshire on 7 June 1861.

John Byrne
Pioneer in electric surgery 1825 – 1902

Born in Kilkeel, John Byrne commenced his medical studies at the Royal Institute in Belfast, and thereafter in Dublin, Glasgow, and Edinburgh, where he obtained his medical degree in 1846. During the Great Famine in Ireland he was appointed medical officer at a hospital in Kilkeel and it was largely due to his advanced sanitary methods that the mortality rate at that hospital was significantly reduced. He emigrated to the United States in 1848 and settled in New York where he studied at the New York Medical College, gaining his American medical degree in 1853.

It was his adoption of the electrocautery knife for use in surgery on malignancies in the uterus that gained him note and his research and technique into its use was published in *Clinical Notes on the Electric Cautery in Uterine Surgery* in 1872. Significantly, that publication showed that Byrne's methods resulted in low mortality rates and excellent final results. He died on 1 October 1902 in Montreux, Switzerland.

Winifred Carney
Socialist, feminist and republican 1887 – 1943

Bangor born Winifred Carney was educated at the Christian Brothers School in Donegal Street, Belfast and later graduated from the Hughes Academy. In 1912 she met James Connolly (see page 429) and became secretary of the Textile Workers Union. She was also involved with the Gaelic League and the suffragette movement, proclaiming that many Belfast mills were 'slaughter houses' for women and 'penitentiaries for children'. Carney joined Connolly upon the formation of the Irish Citizen's Army and was the only woman that took part in the 1916 Easter Rising in the GPO. She later became involved with the Northern Ireland Labour Party and in 1928, surprised many by marrying an Orangeman, George McBride. She died in 1943 and is buried in Milltown Cemetery, Belfast.

Francis Chesney
Soldier and explorer 1789 – 1872

A cadet at the Royal Military Academy in Woolwich, England, Francis Chesney was commissioned in the Royal Artillery in 1805. In 1829 he explored Egypt and Syria and an early report by him showed the feasibility for the construction of what was to later become known as the Suez Canal.

Chesney also explored a new route to India going through Syria and the Persian Gulf and in 1835 he navigated the Euphrates River to the Persian Gulf, charting its exact course. He later chartered the courses of the Tigris and Karum Rivers and published an authoritative book on the subject in 1850 entitled *Expeditions for the Survey of the Euphrates and Tigris*. Chesney retired to his home in Ireland and died on 30 January 1872.

Francis Crozier
British naval officer and explorer 1796 – 1848

Joining the Royal Navy at the young age of thirteen, in 1817 Francis Crozier received his 'Mate's Certificate'. Four years later, he joined Captain William Edward Parry, on board the vessel HMS *Fury*, in an expedition to find the

Northwest Passage. He would return to the Arctic with Parry in 1824, before once again undertaking another expedition with him in 1827. On account of the valuable astronomical and magnetic studies he carried out on the three expeditions, Crozier was elected a fellow of the Royal Astronomical Society and was appointed to the rank of commander in 1837. In 1839 he accompanied James Clarke Ross to explore the Antarctic Continent in two ships, the HMS *Erebus* and HMS *Terror,* which Crozier commanded. During that expedition, they discovered large parts of a continent unknown to that date.

Upon his return from the expedition in 1843, Crozier was elected a fellow of the Royal Society in recognition of his outstanding work on magnetism. In 1845, again as captain of the HMS *Terror*, he joined Sir John Franklin on the Northwest Passage expedition but lost his life along with his whole crew. Crozier's name lives on, with many locations in the Antarctic named in his honour, and a monument stands to him, in his hometown of Banbridge, opposite his birthplace, Avonmore House.

Máire Drumm

Republican activist 1928 – 1976

Born in the city of Newry, Máire Drumm was a member of a staunchly republican family and grew up in the village of Killean, County Armagh. She later became involved in the civil rights movement in the 1960s, also spending some time in an Armagh prison for 'seditious speeches', which included such comments as, 'the only people worthy are those who are prepared to go out and fight for it every day, and die if necessary.' She was shot and killed by loyalist paramilitaries whilst she was a patient at the Mater Hospital in Belfast, on 28 October 1976.

Brian Faulkner, Baron Faulkner of Downpatrick

Prime minister of Northern Ireland 1921 – 1977

Brian Faulkner was born in Helen's Bay. His primary education was attained in Northern Ireland and his secondary at St Columba's College in Rathfarnham, Dublin. He later entered Queen's University, Belfast but due to the outbreak of war, returned to his family's shirt-making business. The first of his family to become involved in unionist politics, Faulkner was elected to the Northern Ireland parliament for East Down in 1949. Ten years later he became minister of home affairs, enhancing his reputation in the eyes of right wing Ulster unionists with his security policies during the IRA campaign of 1956 – 62. In March 1971 he was elected leader of the Unionist Party and prime minister of Northern Ireland. On 9 August that year, he introduced internment with a view to quelling the violence in the northern province. It proved a disastrous move which had the opposite effect, and the infamous Bloody Sunday massacre in Derry in January 1972 signalled the end of Faulkner's government. In 1973 he became chief minister in a power-sharing executive with the SDLP and the Alliance Party, which resulted in the Sunningdale Conference. This caused a rift amongst unionists, resulting in Faulkner's formation of the Unionist Party of Northern Ireland in 1974. That year also saw the fall of the Northern Ireland Assembly as a result of a strike caused by the loyalist paramilitary organisations. Faulkner retired from politics in 1976 and became a life peer in 1977. He died following a riding accident on 3 March 1977.

VISITORS BERTHS

Henry George Ferguson
Inventor 1884 – 1960

At the age of sixteen, Henry George Ferguson joined his brother Joe's car and cycle repair business where he developed a motorcycle and a racing car of his own. In 1909 he designed and built a monoplane, becoming the first man in Ireland to fly. In 1936 he commenced the manufacture of tractors, and entered a partnership with Ford to produce the Ford-Ferguson brand of machinery. A later partnership with Massey-Harris of Toronto gave rise to the world famous Massey-Ferguson Company and in the latter days of his life, Ferguson utilised his creative capabilities in the design of four-wheel drive cars. He died in Stow-on-the-Wold in October 1960.

George Gardiner
Victoria Cross recipient
1821 – 1891

George Gardiner was born in Clonallon, Warrenpoint. At thirty-four years old he served as a sergeant in the 57th Regiment of Foot, British Army during the Crimean War and on the 22 March 1855, he successfully rallied a retreating party of his comrades to face a considerable Russian force at Sebastopol, Crimea. Gardiner successfully dislodged the enemy from its trenches and on 18 June of that year he rallied his fellow soldiers to take cover in holes made by exploded shells, as they continued to fire on the enemy until their ammunition was exhausted and the enemy cleared. For this deed he was awarded the Victoria Cross, and later became a colour sergeant. He died in Lifford, County Donegal in 1891.

Donaghadee harbour, County Down.

Greer Garson
Actress and film star 1904 – 1996

Whilst there are claims that actress Greer Garson was born in London, England she always insisted that she had been born in Ireland. Educated at the University of London, she earned a bachelor's degree in 1926 and while in London, participated in local theatre productions before joining the Birmingham Repertory Company in 1931 where she appeared in small roles in a variety of productions. Garson was noted for her appearance opposite Lawrence Olivier in the play *The Golden Arrow* and she was subsequently brought to the silver screen by MGM mogul, Louis B. Mayer. Elegant and beautiful, Garson exhibited a refined speaking voice, which contributed to her achieving six Academy Award nominations as well as roles in five films that earned best picture nominations. She died on 6 April 1996.

Betsy Gray
Heroine d. 1798

Betsy Gray was a member of the Society of Young Irishmen, which was founded in 1791. Primarily composed of Presbyterians, the society's aims were the unification of all Irishmen under one flag, regardless of their religious persuasions. Gray carried the green flag of the insurgents at the battle of Ballynahinch on 13 June 1798, where she fought beside her brother and her lover, who stayed by her side in the retreat. All three were cut down by the Yeomanry. Gray gave her life in the interest of Irish freedom, and is remembered in both song and verse.

Rev. Hugh Hanna ('Roaring Hanna')
Presbyterian clergyman 1824 – 1892

A former schoolteacher and prominent educationalist, Hugh Hanna was ordained into the Presbyterian Ministry in 1885. In 1872 he built St Enoch's Church, the largest Presbyterian Church in Belfast, and in 1880 he was appointed commissioner of National Education. Hanna was notorious for his controversial sectarian views and also his aggressive, anti-Catholic rhetoric which earned him the sobriquet 'Roaring Hanna', and contributed to the violence against Catholics during the disturbances of 1857.

Robert Hill Hanna
Victoria Cross recipient
1887 – 1967

Originally from Kilkeel, Robert Hill Hanna was a company sergeant major in the 29th Vancouver Battalion, Canadian Expeditionary Forces, during World War I. His defining moment came on 21 August 1917, at Hill 70 in Lens, France when all the officers of his company had become casualties in the conflict. Hanna led a small party of his men against an enemy strongpoint, personally killing four of the opposition, and was successful in capturing their position. He later became a lieutenant and died in Canada in 1967.

Bulmer Hobson
Writer and revolutionary
1883 – 1969

A strong admirer of Wolfe Tone (see page 196), Bulmer Hobson published a work on the legendary revolutionary's life in 1919 and organised a club for boys known as the Protestant National Society, which was used to recruit young Protestants into the nationalist Movement. Hobson was secretary of the first Antrim County Board of the Gaelic Athletic Association and he also founded Na Fianna Éireann, a boys club which he expanded, along with Countess Markievicz, into a militarily trained boy scouts organisation. One of the founders of the Ulster Literary Theatre, for which he wrote poetic drama, in 1907 Hobson was invited to the United States by John Devoy, to introduce the Sinn Féin movement to the Americans. In 1909 he published Defence of Warfare, a handbook for Irish nationalists, and he also became a member of the Irish Republican Brotherhood, for whom he started a newspaper, *Irish Freedom*. Hobson was also a founder member of the Irish Volunteers and published a short history of that organisation. He opposed the Easter Rising, which left him in conflict with the Irish Republican Brotherhood and it was a stance that would lead to his eventual withdrawal from the movement, following its failure in 1916. Hobson then became involved in the Dublin Gate Theatre but upon the establishment of the Irish Free State in 1922, he was appointed chief of the revenue commissioners Stamp Department in Dublin Castle. Some of his later writings include *A National Forest Policy* and *Ireland Yesterday and Tomorrow*.

William David Kenny

Victoria Cross recipient 1899 – 1920

William David Kenny was born in Saintfield and served as a twenty-year-old lieutenant in the 39th Garhwal Rifles, Indian Army. At Kotkai in Pakistan on 2 January 1920, while in command of a small company that was holding an advanced position, he came under repeated attack from superior forces. For over four hours Kenny maintained his position, having to engage in hand-to-hand combat to do so. His gallant leadership resulted in the successful retention of the position, thereby ensuring the safety of troops to the rear. In a subsequent action, he turned back a counter-attack by enemy forces before he and his small column were killed in action. For this deed he was awarded the Victoria Cross.

Henry Newell Martin

Pioneer psychologist 1848 – 1896

Educated principally at home, Henry Newell Martin matriculated at the University of London at the young age of sixteen before earning a scholarship to the University of Cambridge and becoming the first to earn a 'Doctor of Science' degree in physiology. In 1876, Martin was invited to become the first occupant of the Chair of Biology, which had been established in the Johns Hopkins University in Baltimore, Maryland. There he established guidelines for instructions and research in the biological sciences, but his greatest contribution was the discovery of a method to study the isolated heart of mammals and to observe the effect of temperature on the heart. He died in Baltimore in 1896.

Sir James Martin

Inventor 1893 – 1981

In 1924, at the age of twenty-seven, James Martin set up an aircraft company in England with Captain Valentine Baker. Known as the Martin Baker Aircraft Company, it was following the death of Baker in a test flight that Martin commenced work on the ejector seat, which was finally successfully tested in 1945 . Test pilot John Lancaster was the first person ever saved by the invention. At the time of his death in 1981, his invention had already saved the lives of over six thousand aviators.

145

John Martin
Irish nationalist 1812 – 1875

A member of a landed Presbyterian family, John Martin was educated at a private school in Newry and at Trinity College, Dublin. He was a close friend of John Mitchel (see page 120) and so moved was he by the terrible happenings during the famine, he joined Mitchell in the Repeal Association. Martin was a contributor of articles to Mitchell's journal the *United Irishman* and following the latter's arrest in 1848, he produced his own journal, the *Irish Felon*, which led to a warrant for his arrest. He was subsequently tried on 18 August 1848, and sentenced to ten years in Van Diemen's Land (Tasmania), Australia. Pardoned in 1856, Martin returned to Ireland where he became an organiser for the Tenants Rights League and he also opposed the Fenian support for armed struggle, preferring instead the course of diplomacy. In 1871 he was elected to represent County Meath in the British parliament as a Home Rule MP. Commonly referred to as 'Honest John Martin', he strongly supported home rule for Ireland. On his estate in Newry, he was renowned for his generosity towards his tenants, a generosity that left him virtually homeless upon his death in March 1875. His parliamentary seat in Meath was subsequently filled by Charles Stewart Parnell (see page 423).

Lieutenant Colonel Blair 'Paddy' Mayne
Co-founder of the SAS 1915 – 1955

Blair Mayne was born in Newtownards. Standing six feet, three inches tall, he was a supreme athlete and was the Irish universities' heavyweight boxing champion before he played international rugby for Ireland, and the British and Irish Lions. At the outbreak of World War II, he joined the Scottish Commandos but became unimpressed by the condescending nature of some of the British officers, such as Colonel Geoffrey Keyes, who reprimanded Mayne whilst playing a game of chess. Mayne knocked the colonel out with a single punch and was immediately arrested. However, Colonel David Stirling of the Scots Guards, who wanted to establish a no-holds-barred army unit, learned of Mayne's predicament and secured his release in order to become a founder member of the elite SAS unit of the British army. The force transferred to North Africa where Stirling was captured by Rommel's forces, an incident which led to Mayne being promoted to commander of the SAS. It was during that campaign that Mayne obtained his first Distinguished Service Order medal before the unit transferred to Sicily in 1943, where he received his second such distinction for outstanding bravery.

Awarded a third DSO after the D-Day landings in Normandy, it was in Oldenburg, Germany, in April 1945, that he displayed his most extraordinary act of bravery, an act for which he may well have been awarded the Victoria Cross. With a section of the SAS pinned down on the far side of the village and in full view of the Germans posted on either side of the road, Mayne drove his jeep with guns blazing and made three suicidal passes before finally reaching his pinned down comrades. He loaded the wounded onto the jeep and ran the gauntlet of enemy fire to bring them to safety on his return run. Mayne's citation for a Victoria Cross seemingly met with approval at all junctures but was mysteriously downgraded to yet another DSO.

After the war, Major General Sir Robert Laycock, in a letter to Mayne stated, 'congratulations on accomplishing the practically unprecedented task of collecting no less than four DSOs, they should have given you the VC as well'. A motion in the House of Commons in June 2005, supported by over one hundred MPs, recognised the grave injustice incurred by Mayne, which was confirmed by fellow co-founder Stirling, who claimed considerable prejudice existed towards Mayne, and that even King George VI had enquired as to why he had not been awarded the prestigious honour. Mayne was awarded the Legion d'Honneur as well as the Croix de Guerre with palm by the French Government and he also received the African Star. This amazingly brave man, who holds the unique distinction of being the highest decorated soldier in World War II, tragically died in a car crash near his home in County Down on 14 December 1955.

William McWheeney
Victoria Cross recipient 1837 – 1866

William McWheeney, a native of Bangor, served as a sergeant in the 44th Regiment of the British Army during the Crimean War. On two separate occasions, in October and December of 1854, he rescued two of his comrades while under heavy sustained fire and was thus awarded the Victoria Cross. He died in Kent, England in 1866.

Leslie A. Montgomery
Writer and bank manager
1873 – 1961

Born in Downpatrick, Leslie A. Montgomery was educated in Dundalk, County Louth before he joined the Northern Bank in Belfast. He later moved to Skerries in North County Dublin, where he became a manager until his eventual retirement. Under the pseudonym, Lynn C. Doyle, (an adaptation of 'linseed oil'), he wrote in excess of twenty books including the humerous Ballygullion series. Montgomery also wrote a series of short stories, articles, poems and plays and died in Dublin in August 1961.

Samuel Neilson
United Irishman 1761 – 1803

The son of a Presbyterian minister, Samuel Neilson was a prominent and wealthy businessman in the wool and drapery business in Belfast. Inspired by the French Revolution in 1791, he became a founding member of the Society of United Irishmen. Having invested his fortune in founding the newspaper the *Northern Star*, Neilson became a high profile target of the authorities, a status which resulted in him being imprisoned from 1796 to 1798 for seditious writing. Following his release, and with French assistance on the way for the rising of 1798, Neilson attempted to assist in the escape of fellow United Irishman Lord Edward Fitzgerald, who was imprisoned in Kilmainham Jail. Neilson was himself captured in the raid and was imprisoned in Scotland until June 1802. Pardoned on the condition of banishment, he left for New York and whilst there raised funds for another attempt at Ireland's freedom. However, he sadly fell victim to yellow fever and died on 29 August 1803.

Edward John Newell
Informer 1771 – 1798

Edward John Newell was born in Downpatrick but settled in Belfast in his early twenties and commenced work as a miniature portrait painter. He joined the United Irishmen in 1796 but was mistrusted by the leaders, and in response, defected to become an informer. In payment for his treason, Newell was remunerated two thousand pounds by Edward Cooke – the under-secretary in Dublin – for information that led to the arrest of numerous United Irishmen

Having later documented his experiences in *The Life and Confessions of Newell the Informer*, authorities arranged for his departure from Ireland to the United States; it was an escape which never came to pass as Newell was assassinated, as he eloped with the wife of an acquaintance, prior to his departure.

Robert Nugent
Brevet brigadier general in the American Civil War 1824 – 1901

Robert Nugent, who was born in Killkeel, was the last commanding officer of the Fighting 69th Irish Brigade in the American Civil War. He was the colonel in charge of the 69th at the battles of Gettysburg and Fredericksburg as well as the Spotsylvania and Petersburg campaigns. Brevetted brigadier general on 13 March 1865 for his distinguished leadership of the regiment, he proudly led his men in the Washington Victory Parade in May of that year and also to their demobilisation in New York in July 1865. He is buried at Cypress Hill National Cemetery, New York.

Frank Pantridge
Inventor of the defibrillator 1916 – 2004

Frank Pantridge qualified in medicine from Queen's University in 1939, following which he joined the army as a medical officer. Pantridge received the Military Cross for his work in the Battle of Singapore but was taken prisoner by the Japanese and spent much of his incarceration working on the Siam-Burma railway, where he experienced many horrors inflicted by his captors. Liberated in 1945, he worked for a short time in Belfast before going to the United States where he worked on electrocardiography with the renowned Frank N. Wilson. In 1951, Pantridge was appointed consultant physician at the Royal Victoria Hospital in Belfast. From his studies in the United States Pantridge recognised that mortality rates in myocardial infarction (heart attack) were highest in the very early hours of onset. This conclusion led him to the idea of developing the mobile or external defibrillator, which he fitted in a commandeered ambulance. Whilst cumbersome and dependent on a car battery for power, the prototype led to the introduction of the first truly portable defibrillator in 1968. Pantridge's ingenuity has saved innumerable lives and the defilbrillator is now fitted in all ambulances and many workplaces. Pantridge received numerous honours in recognition of his work and was made a Freeman of Lisburn. Pantridge Road in Poleglass, Belfast is also named in his memory. He died on 26 December 2004.

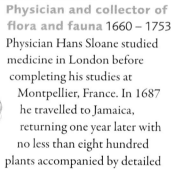

Sir Hans Sloane
Physician and collector of flora and fauna 1660 – 1753

Physician Hans Sloane studied medicine in London before completing his studies at Montpellier, France. In 1687 he travelled to Jamaica, returning one year later with no less than eight hundred plants accompanied by detailed scientific notes of his time on the island. By the mid-1720s, Sloane had become the greatest collector of flora and fauna, books, drawings, maps, medals, coins and paintings ever seen in England and at the time of his death, his treasures comprised some 200,000 items. The collection subsequently became the basis for the establishment of the British Museum and Sloane Square in London is named in his memory. A statue of him stands in his native village of Killyleagh and he died on 11 January 1753. Sloane is buried at Chelsea Old Church, London.

John Smilie
Politician 1741 – 1813

Born near Greyabbey, John Smilie left Ireland for the United States at the age of twenty on 18 May 1762. Surviving a horrific voyage, during which sixty-four passengers died of starvation, he eventually arrived in Pennsylvania and commenced a rapid rise to wealth and influence via the American revolution. He served in both Houses of the State Legislature and represented Pennsylvania in the US House from 1793 until 1795, and again from 1799 until 1812. Smilie was strongly outspoken against the evils of the slave trade and was a strong advocate for the release of those entwined within its rigours, also proposing that slave smugglers face the death penalty. He was elected to the Thirteenth Congress in 1812, but died before it opened in Washington, DC.

Edmund de Wind
Victoria Cross recipient 1883 – 1918

Educated at Campbell College, Belfast, Edmund de Wind served as a 2nd Lieutenant in the 15th Battalion, Royal Irish Rifles, British Army, during World War I. It was whilst fighting at the first Battle of the Somme on 24 March 1918, that de Wind successfully held an important position at the Racecourse Redoubt, near Groagie, France. Though he was twice wounded, he held fast until another unit could be sent to help, and on two occasions during the encounter, left the protection of his trench to face heavy machine-gun and rifle fire in order to clear enemy forces from the trenches. Killing many of them in the process, de Wind continued to repel attack after attack until he was mortally wounded. A housing estate in his hometown of Comber is named in his memory.

John Butler Yeats
Painter 1839 – 1922

John Butler Yeats was born at Tullylish and was educated at Trinity College, Dublin. Having studied law at the King's Inn, he was admitted to the bar in 1866 but chose to become a painter in preference to practising law. He studied art in London and although he secured frequent commissions, Yeats was a poor businessman, and his family was never financially secure. He had four children, all of whom had remarkable literary and artistic talents. William Butler (see page 199), Susan Mary, Elizabeth Corbet, and Jack Butler. Yeats' portrait of his son Jack is one of his most famous works and is held in the Yeats Museum in the National Gallery of Ireland, Dublin; but it is his portrait of John O'Leary (see page 375), painted in 1904, that is considered to be his masterpiece. He emigrated to the United States in 1907 and never returned to Ireland.

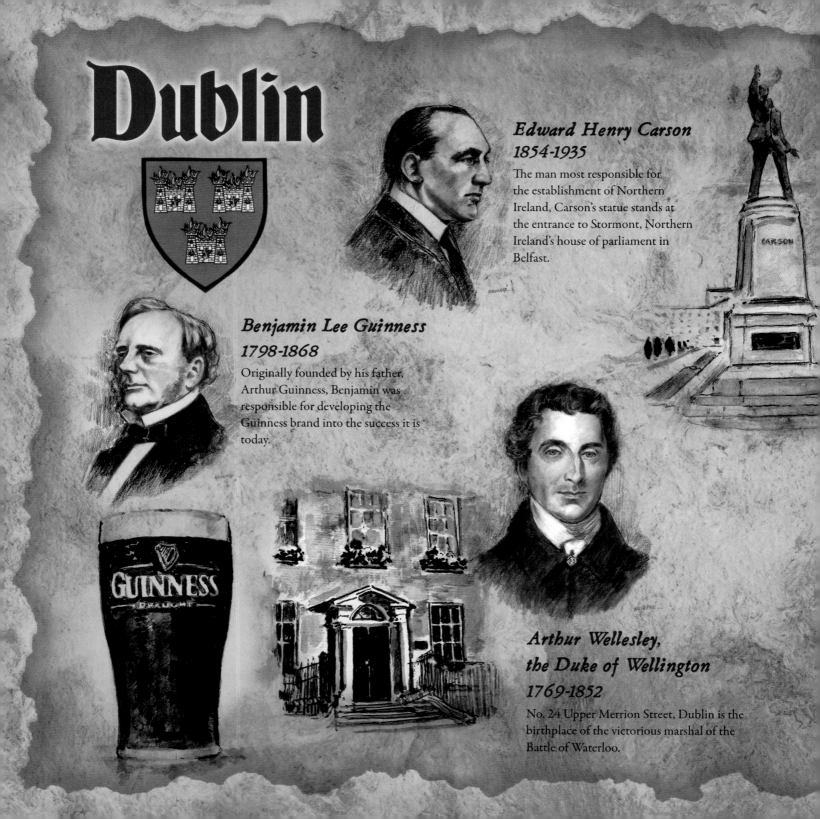

Dublin

Edward Henry Carson
1854-1935
The man most responsible for the establishment of Northern Ireland, Carson's statue stands at the entrance to Stormont, Northern Ireland's house of parliament in Belfast.

Benjamin Lee Guinness
1798-1868
Originally founded by his father, Arthur Guinness, Benjamin was responsible for developing the Guinness brand into the success it is today.

GUINNESS
DRAUGHT

Arthur Wellesley,
the Duke of Wellington
1769-1852
No. 24 Upper Merrion Street, Dublin is the birthplace of the victorious marshal of the Battle of Waterloo.

Oscar Wilde
1854-1900

One of Ireland's foremost playwrights, Wilde lived at No. 1, Merrion Square, Dublin.

Patrick Pearse
1879-1916

Scoil Eanna (St Enda's School), the bilingual school founded by the Irish patriot Patrick Pearse in Ranelagh, Dublin.

Cecil Frances Humphreys Alexander
Hymnwriter and poet
1818 – 1895

A talented songwriter, most of Cecil Frances Humphreys Alexander's hymns are included in the Church of Ireland hymnbook. Her book, *Hymns for Little Children* reached its sixty-ninth edition before the close of the nineteenth century and most famous amongst her works are 'All Things Bright and Beautiful', 'There is a Green Hill Far Away' and 'The Christmas Carol' ('Once in Royal David's City'). Alexander involved herself in many charitable works and money from her publications helped to build the Derry and Raphoe Diocesan Institution for the Deaf and Dumb, which was founded in 1846.

Dave Allen
Comedian 1936 – 2005

David Allen was born David Tynan O'Mahoney in Firhouse and, having been educated at Terenure College, went on to become a journalist with the *Irish Independent* newspaper. His first foray into show business was as a Butlin's Redcoat in Skegness, England and it was there that he adopted the name David Allen. In 1959 he got his first break on a BBC talent show and later toured with legendary musicians, The Beatles. It was an appearance on fellow Irishman Val Doonican's show that brought Allen to prominence and between 1967 and 1994, he had his own shows on both the BBC and ITV television stations, at various times. His comedy sketches, which often included colourful language, caused much controversy and it was his satirical jibes towards the clergy that raised his greatest laughs. Allen was missing the tip of one finger, and when once quizzed if he was 'the Irish comedian with half a finger?' he is reputed to have replied, 'I'm the Irish comedian with nine and a half fingers'. Allen retired from broadcasting in 1999 and died on 12 March 2005.

Eamonn Andrews
Broadcaster and TV presenter 1922 – 1987

Eamonn Andrews began his career as an amateur boxer before going on to be a boxing commentator on Irish radio. In the early 1950s he joined the BBC as a television presenter and hosted a variety of programmes such as *What's my Line?*, *World of Sport*, *Crackerjack* and *This is your Life*. He was married to Grainne Burke of the well-known Dublin theatrical family, making him an uncle-in-law to the broadcaster Gerry Ryan. He died of a heart attack, at the age of sixty-four, in November 1987.

Francis Bacon
Painter 1909 – 1992

Though Dublin born, Francis Bacon had several stints living in both Ireland and England due to his family's nomadic tendencies. As an artist, he is best known for the contorted human forms depicted in his works and he created a sensation in 1945 when he exhibited his *Three Studies for Figures at the Base of a Crucifixion* in the Tate Gallery, London. Bacon, who gained an international reputation for his work in the 1950s, was a technical perfectionist and although his output of art was prolific, he destroyed a great deal of his own work. Even so, some works of his that have remained have been valued at over 16 million euro. Bacon died of heart failure in Madrid on 28 April 1992.

Michael William Balfe
Composer 1808 – 1870

Michael William Balfe was born in Pitt Street, which was later renamed Balfe Street in his honour, although the street no longer exists in modern-day Dublin. He was a proficient violinist, and in 1823 was a member of the Drury Lane Theatre orchestra in London before being commissioned to write the music for the ballet La Perouse by La Scala in Milan. Although he wrote twenty-eight operas, Balfe is best remembered for *The Bohemian Girl* in 1843.

Thomas John Barnardo
Philanthropist 1845 – 1905

The founder of Barnardo's children's charity, Thomas John Barnardo studied medicine in London and Edinburgh before becoming a fellow of the Royal College of Surgeons. Initially it was his intention to become a missionary to China but upon seeing the destitute and homeless state of the young people on the streets of London, Barnardo decided to dedicate his life to their aid. He opened the first of his homes for destitute boys in Stepney, London in 1870 and the mandate of each of these homes dictated that 'no destitute child (would) ever (be) refused admission'. Barnardo was the author of many books dealing with the charitable work to which he devoted his life and he died in London on 19 September 1905.

Kevin Barry
Patriot 1902 – 1920

Kevin Barry studied medicine at University College Dublin before joining the IRA and taking part in a raid on a military lorry in Church Street during which six British soldiers were killed. Barry was captured and court-martialed, following which he was hanged in Mountjoy Prison on 1 November 1920. Just eighteen years of age, his execution was widely condemned and he became an inspiration for young men to join the IRA during the Anglo-Irish War of Independence.

Samuel Beckett
Dramatist, novelist and poet 1906 – 1989

Foxrock-born Samuel Beckett was educated at Portora Royal School in Enniskillen, County Fermanagh and Trinity College, Dublin, where he was a first class cricketer. Upon graduating he became a teacher at Campbell College in Belfast, but later moved to Paris, where he became a friend of the legendary author James Joyce (see page 173). During this period, Beckett produced his first short story, 'Assumption', and he would later return to Trinity College as a lecturer in 1930 before leaving that role the following year, going as far as to celebrate the occasion by composing the poem 'Gnome'.

In 1931, Beckett published *Proust*, his critical study of the French author Marcel Proust and the following year he wrote his first novel, *Dream of Fair to Middling Woman*, which was not published until 1993. That publication served as a source for the 1933 short story collection *More Pricks Than Kicks* and he later published *Murphy* in 1938. Following the outbreak of World War II in 1939, Beckett returned to France where he worked as a courier in the French resistance. He was awarded the Croix de Guerre and the Médal dé la Résistance by the French Government before returning to Dublin in 1945. His dramatic works are considerable, covering theatre, novels, and short stories. Many major twentieth-century composers have created musical works based on Beckett's texts and he is perhaps one of the most widely discussed and highly prized of twentieth-century authors. His real triumph came in 1953 when *Waiting for Godot*, which he wrote in Paris, premiered at the Theatre de Babylon and ran for over four hundred performances. This was followed by a second masterpiece, *Endgame*. He died on 22 December 1989 and is buried in Paris having previously insisted that his headstone was to 'be any colour, so long as it was grey'.

Brendan Behan
Poet, writer, novelist and playwright
1923 – 1964
Having left school at the age of fourteen to pursue his father's trade as a house painter, Brendan Behan later joined the IRA and was arrested in Liverpool in December 1939. Serving three years at a borstal (youth prison), Behan was once again arrested, this time in Dublin, and sentenced to fourteen years penal servitude for shooting at a policeman. While in prison he became a fluent Irish speaker and when released in December 1946, he commenced his career as a writer. Behan's best known works are *The Quare Fellow, Borstal Boy, Confessions of an Irish Rebel, The Hostage* and *Richard Cork Leg*. He died in the Meath Hospital in Dublin on the 20 March 1964 and his funeral was one of the largest ever seen in the city of Dublin. Memorable quotes attributed to Behan being a heavy drinker include, 'I'm a drinker with a writing problem' and 'I only drink on two occasions, when I'm thirsty, and when I'm not'. When once advised

that he had been court-martialed by the IRA and sentenced to death in his absence, Behan humorously remarked that 'they can execute me in my absence as well.'

Harry Boland
Nationalist 1887 – 1922
Active in the GAA in his early life, Harry Boland later joined the Irish Republican Brotherhood and the Irish Volunteers. He took part in the Easter Rising of 1916 before being elected as a Sinn Féin representative for South Roscommon in the 1918 general election. Having refused to take a seat at Westminster, Boland sat in the newly declared Dáil Éireann and was appointed by Éamon de Valera to be principal envoy in a campaign to raise support and finances for the Irish cause in the United States. During the Irish War of Independence, he was a close confidant of Michael Collins (see page 89), but did however, take the republican side after the treaty, which opposed Collins in the Civil War. He was shot by Irish Free State troops at the Skerries Grand Hotel on 31 July 1922 and is buried in Glasnevin Cemetery, Dublin.

John Pius Boland
Olympian, barrister and nationalist 1870 – 1955
Olympian John Pius Boland studied law at various locations before practising in London. Competing at tennis, Boland was the winner of the first two gold medals for Ireland at the inaugural Olympic Games in Athens in 1896, and when

the Union Jack Flag was raised following his victory, he vehemently objected, insisting that it be replaced with a green flag to represent his own country. He was a dynamic parliamentarian and the whip for the Irish Nationalist Party at Westminster. A great admirer of Charles Stewart Parnell (see page 423), Boland was the principal campaigner for the erection of the monument that stands to Parnell in Dublin's O'Connell Street. Boland, who was enthusiastically proud of his Irish nationality, fittingly died on St Patrick's Day, 1955.

Elizabeth Bowen
Novelist 1899 – 1973

Elizabeth Bowen was born in Dublin but moved to England at a young age when her father became ill. She had a great fondness for the country of her birth, as well as her adopted homeland, and this was inherently obvious in her literary works. Bowen's first book was a collection of short stories entitled *Encounters* and in 1927 she wrote *The Hotel*. This was followed by one of her best-known books, *The Last September*, which encompassed the period of the War of Independence in Ireland and the effect that conflict had on upper classes of the time. In 1942 she penned a history of her family but a later novel T*he Heat of the Day*, which she wrote in 1949, is often considered her best. This talented author received many literary awards during her lifetime, and died in London in 1973.

Robert Briscoe
Politician and businessman 1894 – 1969

Robert Briscoe hailed from Lower Beechwood Avenue in Ranelagh and was of Jewish descent. Following the Easter Rising in 1916, he joined Fianna Éireann and was sent by Michael Collins (see page

89) to Germany and the USA in order to obtain funds and arms for the IRA. A founder member of the Fianna Fáil party and a TD for Dublin City South from 1927 to 1965, in 1956 Briscoe was elected the first Jewish lord mayor of Dublin. Three years later, he published his autobiography entitled *For the Life of Me*. Briscoe, who was the subject of a film made for television called *The Fabulous Irishman*, died on 30 May 1969.

Christy Brown
Writer 1932 – 1981

Crumlin born Christy Brown was a sufferer of cerebral palsy and considered disabled until he famously snatched a piece of chalk from his sister with his left foot. Brown's condition caused him great difficulty in communicating with others but his mother, Bridget painstakingly taught him the alphabet and he responded positively, writing each individual letter with a piece of chalk lodged between the toes on his left foot. His autobiography *My Left Foot*, written in 1954, was later expanded into a novel, *Down All The Days*, and later became an international bestseller, translated into fourteen languages. The 1989 motion picture, *My Left Foot*, directed by Jim Sheridan, depicts Brown's life and was the recipient of two Academy Awards as well as three additional Academy Award nominations. Brown, who published a further nine books, was also an accomplished painter and he died in Somerset, England, on 6 September 1981.

Cathal Brugha, (born Charles William St John Burgess)

Revolutionary 1874 – 1922

Forced to leave school due to the failure of his father's business, Cathal Brugha became a clerk with a church supplies company before later founding a company called Lawlor's Ltd, which was involved in the manufacture of candles. In 1899 he joined the Gaelic League and in 1913, became a lieutenant in the Irish Volunteers. While second-in-command to Éamonn Ceannt (see page 212) at the South Dublin Union during the Easter Rising of 1916, Brugha was wounded by a grenade which caused severe injuries to one of his legs, resulting in him having a limp for the rest of his life. In October 1917 he was appointed chief of staff of the Irish Republican Army and the following year was elected to Dáil Éireann as a representative of Waterford. His bitter enmity towards Michael Collins (see page 89) was well known in republican circles and he had also advocated the moving of the front line of war to England, a move Collins was opposed to. Brugha served as minister for defence from 1919 but was replaced by Richard Mulcahy (see page 394) when he voted against the Anglo-Irish Treaty. Brugha died as a result of wounds sustained in a gun-fight with pro-treaty forces in O'Connell Street, on 7 July 1922.

Lucien Bull

Pioneer of high-speed photography and inventor of improved electrocardiography 1876 – 1972

Lucien Bull was born in Dublin but travelled to Paris, France in 1894 to join Etienne-Jules Marey, who was a pioneer in the world of cinematography. It was whilst working in Paris that Bull developed the high-speed cine-camera, with the cine-reel capturing 1,200 images per second. By 1918, Bull had increased this to fifty thousand images per second, and he eclipsed these figures in 1952, recording one million images per second. Marey invented the forerunner of the electrocardiograph and this work was taken over and continued by Bull, whose version was patented in 1908 and was the forerunner of today's ECG. He died in Paris in 1972.

Captain Hugh Talbot Burgoyne

Victoria Cross recipient
1833 – 1870

Hugh Talbot Burgoyne served as a lieutenant in the Royal Navy in the Crimean War. Whilst aboard the HMS *Swallow* in the Sea of Azov, Burgoyne volunteered to land on a beach which was heavily fortified by Russian army units. Together with two accomplices, he set fire to Russian stores and ammunition dumps, successfully destroying a considerable amount of enemy-equipment before returning to the ship. Burgoyne later achieved the rank of captain but lost his life whilst in command of the HMS *Captain*, which capsized in a gale off Cape Finisterre, Spain in September 1870. Burgoyne Bay in British Columbia, Canada was named after him in 1859.

Edmund Burke

Political theorist and philosopher
1729 – 1797

Edmund Burke served as a member of parliament for Bristol, England from 1774 to 1780 and was a strong advocate of conciliation with the American colonies. His best-known and most influential work was *Burke's Reflection on the Revolution in France* and he campaigned vigorously against the persecution of Catholics in Ireland. These political stances were decidedly unpopular with his constituents and led to him losing his seat in Bristol in 1780. Upon the loss of the American colonies, Burke said, 'stupidity has cost us the colonies, stupidity will cost us Ireland'. Another quote attributed to Burke is 'the only thing necessary for the triumph of evil is for good men to do nothing'. A statue to his memory stands in the city of Bristol.

Richard Butler
Army general (American Continental Army) 1743 – 1791

Born in Dublin, where his father owned a gun shop, Richard Butler relocated with his family to Lancaster, Pennsylvania in 1748, where the family continued in the manufacturing of guns. At the onset of the revolution, the Continental Congress appointed Butler a commissioner and briefed him to negotiate with the Native Americans in an effort to secure their support, or at least their neutrality, in the war with Britain. In 1776 he was commissioned a major in the Continental Army and saw action at the battles of Saratoga and Monmouth before being appointed a general by George Washington and given the honour of accepting Cornwallis' sword of surrender at Yorktown, Virginia. Later, Butler served as second-in-command to General Arthur St Clair in the Indian wars but was killed at the Battle of Wabash in what was the biggest defeat the US army ever sustained against Native American forces. Chief Little Turtle and his tribesmen ambushed and killed six hundred people including women and children, but in consideration of Butler's bravery during that battle, the medal he was wearing – the Society of Cincinnati Medal – was returned by the chief to Butler's widow some time later. Butler County, Ohio, Butler County, Kentucky, and Butler County, Pennsylvania are some of the many places named in his memory.

Alfie Byrne
Politician and lord mayor of Dublin 1882 – 1956

Alfred 'Alfie' Byrne was the son of a docker. In his youth he worked as a theatre programme seller and barman, before eventually buying his own pub, 'The Vernon' on Talbot Street in Dublin. He entered politics at the age of twenty-seven, becoming an alderman in the Dublin Corporation and in 1915, he was elected as an Irish Parliamentary Party candidate for Dublin Harbour, later being defeated by Sinn Féin in the 1918 General Election. Following Ireland's independence, Byrne continued his political career, being elected an independent TD for Dublin mid-west in 1922 and he was appointed as a member of Seanad Éireann in 1928. Between 1930 and 1939, Byrne was elected lord mayor of Dublin on nine straight occasions and due to this popularity, was nicknamed 'the shaking hand of Dublin'. A staunch supporter of the poor in the inner-city and dockland areas, whose cause he championed throughout his long and colourful career, Byrne died in March 1956 and his funeral attracted thousands of people.

Thomas Byrne
Victoria Cross recipient 1866 – 1944

Thomas Byrne was born in St Thomas and served as a private in the 21st Lancers of the British Army during the Sudan Campaign, fighting at the Battle of Omdurman. Whilst his unit was in the middle of a charge, Byrne

157

turned back and went to the assistance of a lieutenant of the Royal Horse Guards who had been wounded. Having dismounted, he was immediately attacked by several of the enemy but Byrne fought them off, successfully securing the escape of the officer in the process. He died in Canterbury, England and is buried there.

Martin Cahill
Irish criminal 'The General' 1949 – 1994

Martin Cahill was born on Dublin's north side but moved with his family to Crumlin during the Dublin slum clearances of the 1960s. In 1965, following convictions for burglary, he was sent to an industrial school in County Offaly. Upon his release Cahill recommenced his criminal activities in Hollyfield Buildings, Rathmines, where his family was then living. This led to a further four-year jail sentence in the early 1970s. Cahill had a number of unusual character traits. He was renowned for wearing comic outfits during his numerous appearances in court and he always endeavoured to keep one hand over part of his face in an effort to conceal his identity. Along with his gang, which he ruled with an iron fist, Cahill stole gold and diamonds to the value of two million pounds from O'Connor's jewellers in Harold's Cross, and he was also involved in stealing some of the world's most valuable paintings from Russborough House in County Wicklow. Nicknamed 'The General' because of the military style planning of his crimes, Cahill was shot dead on 18 August 1994, reputedly by the IRA for his alleged involvement with loyalist organisation, the UVF. A book on his life entitled *The General* was published in 1995 and in 1998 a movie of the same name was released, starring Brendan Gleeson in the lead role, supported by John Voight. Due to the lack of images of Cahill in the public domain, the portrait of him shown here was obtained from a very small photograph, taken when he was a member of the Dublin Pigeon Club (source Luke Burke).

James Carey
Fenian and informer 1845 – 1883

James Carey commenced his working life as a bricklayer, later becoming a successful builder. In 1861 he joined the Irish Republican Brotherhood but broke from the organisation in 1861 to form a new group known as 'The Invincibles'. Along with nine members of The Invincibles, Carey took part in what is known as the 'Phoenix Park Murders', during which the under-secretary to the lord lieutenant in Ireland, T.H. Burke, was assassinated along with the newly-appointed chief secretary, Lord Frederick Cavendish. Carey was arrested in 1883, together with sixteen others, but he testified against his compatriots resulting in five of them being condemned to death and executed in public. As a protective measure, the British authorities had him and his family secretly sent to South Africa but it was a move that proved unsuccessful; The Invincibles located Carey and shot him dead on 29 July 1883.

Matthew Carey
US publisher 1760 – 1839

Though his family were originally bakers by trade, Matthew Carey pursued an interest in printing and publishing. His criticism of the British authorities and their attitude towards the ordinary Irish people forced him to emigrate to France, where he gained employment with Benjamin Franklin, the American printer, author and diplomat. Carey also became a friend of the Marquis de Lafayette, the French statesman who fought in the US War of Independence on the side of Washington. Having spent a year in France, Carey returned to Ireland in

1783, but his seditious writings placed him at risk with the authorities in Dublin and he was forced to emigrate to the United States. To ensure a safe passage, he was disguised as a woman and he safely arrived at his destination on 15 November 1784. From 1785 to 1824 Carey established arguably the greatest publishing and book distribution business in the United States, from which he became one of the wealthiest Irishmen in that country. He died in Philadelphia in 1839.

Edward Henry Carson
Lawyer and political leader
1854 – 1935
Edward Henry Carson was born in Dublin and was educated at Trinity College. He was called to the Irish Bar in 1877 and was a solicitor general for Ireland in 1892. Carson was also called to the English Bar in 1893 and made a devastating cross-examination of Oscar Wilde (see page 198) in the latter's libel action against the Marquess of Queensberry. A staunch unionist, when the Home Rule Bill for Ireland was introduced in 1912, Carson took a leading part in the formation of the Ulster unionist in openly defying the bill rather than coming under an Irish Parliament in Dublin. In defiance of the British Government, he advised his unionist compatriots 'don't be afraid of illegalities' and was instrumental in the Ulster Volunteers landing guns in Larne, County Antrim in April 1914. Two years later, following the Easter Rising in Ireland, Carson was assured by Lloyd George that the six northern counties of Ireland would be permanently excluded from becoming part of the United Ireland. It can be safely said that Carson was one of the primary organisers of the statelet of Northern Ireland. Carson took a life peerage as Baron Carson of Duncairn, and died in Kent on 22 October 1935.

Sir Roger Casement
Patriot, diplomat and humanitarian 1864 – 1916
Sandycove born Roger Casement was educated at Ballymena Academy, County Antrim and, having joined the British Colonial Services in 1884, he was commissioned to Africa in 1904, where he reported on the inhuman treatment of native workers in the Belgian Congo. Later promoted to consul general at Rio de Janeiro, Casement further reported on the cruelties practised on the natives by white traders working on the Peruvian rubber plantations. He was knighted for his services in 1911 and retired from the Colonial Services the following year. Recruited by the Irish National Volunteers in 1913, Casement travelled to Berlin in the hope of obtaining German help to win Irish independence and had some degree of success when the German authorities decided to send a ship, the *Aud* to Ireland.

The *Aud* contained a cargo of arms for the Easter Rising and Casement himself returned to Ireland by submarine, landing at Banna Strand in Tralee, County Kerry. He was captured upon his arrival and was taken to England before being tried for treason and sentenced to death by hanging. Casement was executed in Pentonville Prison on 3 August 1916. In 1965, his remains were returned to Ireland where he was honoured with a state funeral.

Austin Clarke
Dramatist, novelist and poet
1896 – 1974
Austin Clarke was born in Manor Street, Dublin and was educated at Belvedere College and Mungret College in County Limerick before entering

University College Dublin. A founder of the Dublin Verse-Speaking Society, he published his first long poem, 'The Vengeance of Fionn' in 1917 and became a lecturer at UCD before travelling to London in 1921 where he wrote reviews for the *Times* and *Observer* newspapers. Clarke produced his first novel, *The Bright Temptation* in 1932, but the publication was banned in Ireland until 1954. He wrote a number of plays, such as *The Viscount of Blarney, As the Crow Flies* and *The Son of Learning* and was also a founder member of the Irish Academy of Letters. Clarke, who was awarded the Gregory Medal by the Academy in 1968, died in Templeogue, Dublin in March 1974.

Harry Clarke
Stained-glass artist and book illustrator 1889 – 1931

Following his education at Belvedere College, Harry Clarke travelled to London where he sought employment as a book illustrator with the London publisher, Harrap. Clarke's stained glass work included many religious windows, such as the Honan Chapel in University College Cork, and The Unhappy Judas in the National Museum in Dublin. His most seen work is the windows of Bewley's Café on Grafton Street and he produced over 130 stained glass windows in all. His work is defined by the finesse of his drawings and use of rich colours and was influenced by the French Symbolist Movement. An artist of great merit, Clarke died of tuberculosis in Switzerland in 1931.

Neville Josiah Aylmer Coghill
Victoria Cross recipient 1852 – 1879

Born in Drumcondra, Neville Josiah Aylmer Coghill was a lieutenant in the First Battalion of the 24th Regiment of Foot of the British Army. In an attempt to save the colours of his regiment during the Zulu Wars, Coghill, together with another officer, crossed the swollen River Buffalo where they were attacked by Zulu warriors. The enemy dislodged Coghill's fellow officer from his horse thus pitching him into great danger, and so Coghill went to the man's aid. The two soldiers were overtaken by the enemy and following a short but gallant struggle, both were killed. For this deed he was awarded the Victoria Cross.

Seán Connolly
Patriot 1883 – 1916

A member of the Gaelic League, Seán Connolly initially worked for Eason's bookshop on Middle Abbey Street before later joining the Dublin Corporation. Connolly was also an actor and he took part in Abbey Theatre productions, playing the lead role in the play, *Under Which Flag* a week before the Easter Rising. The play told the story of an Irishman torn between serving the Irish or the British armies and ended with Connolly raising a green flag and uttering the words 'under this flag only will I serve, under this flag, if need be, will I die.' It was whilst attempting to hoist the Irish flag that he had held in the play onto the dome of City Hall, Dublin, that Connolly was shot and killed – the first casualty of the Easter Rising.

Sir Dominic Corrigan
Physician 1802 – 1880

Dominic Corrigan was born on Thomas Street in a house that stood on the site of the present Augustinian church. Educated in Maynooth College, County Kildare and at Trinity College, Dublin, Corrigan furthered his medical studies in Edinburgh, qualifying in 1825. In 1831 he was appointed physician to the Charitable Infirmary, Jervis Street. The advent of Catholic Emancipation in 1829 made conditions more favourable for young Catholic doctors, and in response, Corrigan established a successful practice at 13 Bachelor's Walk, later joining the staff at the Richmond Hospital. He specialised in diseases of the aorta and his paper on aortic insufficiency (1832) is generally regarded as the classic description of that condition. Conferred with a diploma by the London College of Surgeons in 1842 and an honourary degree from Dublin University in 1849, Corrigan was renowned for his self-sacrifice and devotion during the famine years.

He was also a member of parliament from 1869 until 1874 and was the president of the College of Physicians in Dublin for an unprecedented five years. Later rewarded with a knighthood, it was the French physician Trousseau who proposed that aortic heart disease should be called 'Corrigan's Disease'. He died in Dublin in 1880.

W. T. Cosgrave
Politician 1880 – 1965
William Thomas Cosgrave was born at 174 James's Street and was educated at the Christian Brothers School in Marino. He joined the Irish Volunteers in 1913 and served under Éamonn Ceannt (see page 212) at the South Dublin Union during the Easter Rising but having been captured, Cosgrave received a death sentence which was later commuted and he was released under general amnesty in 1917. He became a member of the first Dáil Éireann and was a supporter of the Anglo-Irish Treaty of 1921.

Appointed chairman of the provisional government, upon the death of Michael Collins (see page 89), Cosgrave took complete control and also served as the first president of the executive council of the Irish Free State from 1922 to 1932. He remained active in Irish politics until 1945 and

died on 16 November 1965. Awarded a state funeral, he was buried at Goldenbridge Cemetery in Inchicore.

John A. Costello
Taoiseach 1891 – 1976
John Aloysius Costello was educated at University College Dublin before eventually graduating in law and being called to the bar in 1914. For the period from 1926 to 1932, he served as attorney general and after being elected to the Dáil in 1933, he went on to become taoiseach of the Inter-Party Government in 1948. It was during this period that the Republic of Ireland was formally inaugurated on Easter Monday, 1949. Costello was again elected taoiseach from 1954 to 1957 and following this appointment he remained in politics until 1969. He died at the age of eighty-four on 5 January 1976.

Major Dr Thomas Joseph Crean
Victoria Cross recipient 1873 – 1923
Thomas Joseph Crean was a surgeon captain in the First Imperial Light Horse, South African Forces, during the Boer War. Crean's defining moment occurred at Tygerkloof Spruit, where he continued to carry out his medical duties, tending to the wounded under heavy fire, despite being wounded himself. With the enemy located within a 150-yard range, Crean only stopped after being hurt for a second time. He would obtain the rank of major before dying in London at the age of forty-nine.

Colonel Dr John Crimmin
Victoria Cross recipient 1859 – 1945

John Crimmin was a surgeon in the Bombay Medical Service of the Indian Army and in January 1889, tended to the injuries of a lieutenant and four of his men under extreme enemy fire at eastern Karen-Ni, Burma. Whilst assisting the men, Crimmin was attacked by several of the enemy but drew his sword and successfully defended the wounded, killing three of the enemy in the process. For his gallant action, he was awarded the Victoria Cross. He was later appointed a colonel and died in Somerset, England in 1945.

Richard Croker
Politician 1843 – 1922

Richard Croker was born in Blackrock, County Dublin, and was taken to the United States by his parents when he was two years of age. Educated in public schools in New York City, he entered politics and became an alderman of New York City from 1868 until 1870 and also held several other prestigious posts. He was the city's fire commissioner from 1883 until 1887 and city chamberlain from 1889 until 1890, later becoming the leader of Tammany Hall – the headquarters of the Democratic Party political machine that played a major role in the control of New York City from the 1790s until the 1960s. Croker, who made graft a fine art by receiving bribe money from brothels, saloons and illegal gambling dens, supported the election of Robert Van Wyck as mayor of Greater New York in 1897 and this gave him the opportunity to completely dominate the government of the city for Van Wyck's period of office.

Upon the election of Seth Low as mayor of New York in 1901, Croker resigned as Tammany leader and returned to Ireland to live a life of leisure, winning the Epsom Derby with his horse, Orby in 1907. He died in Dublin in 1922 and is buried in Glasnevin Cemetery.

Conor Cruise O'Brien
Politician, writer and academic 1917 – 2008

Following his education at Sandford Park School and at Trinity College, Dublin, Conor Cruise O'Brien became a civil servant in the Department of Foreign Affairs. A strong believer in the values of education, O'Brien was a historian, journalist and educator, as well as the writer of numerous academic articles. His fiercely held convictions and opinions vexed and inspired many a reader and he was a man of considerable intellectual ability. As a member of the Department of External Affairs, O'Brien served as a member of the Irish delegation to the United Nations and he spearheaded a peacekeeping mission to the Congolese province of Katanga, on which he later wrote a book, *To Katanga and Back*. He would also become vice-chancellor of the University of Ghana, as well as a member of the Labour Party, becoming Labour minister for post and telegraphs in the Irish coalition government of the mid-1970s. He was also responsible for introducing a ban on Sinn Féin and IRA members being interviewed on radio or television. Having lost his political seat in 1977, O'Brien went on to become editor of the *Observer* newspaper from 1979 until 1981, but his support of Northern unionists and lack of regard for minority nationalists, and later his support for Bob McCartney's UK Ulster Unionists party, lost him much sympathy. O'Brien was an Irish iconoclast and he acheived both domestic and international notoriety in his political and academic careers. He died on 18 December 2008, at the age of ninety-one.

General Sir Alan Cunningham
British Army general 1887 – 1983

Awarded the Military Cross and DSO for his services during World War I, in 1938 Alan Cunningham was promoted to major general and upon the outbreak of World War II, took command of the British East African forces in Kenya. Promoted further to lieutenant general, during the East African campaign Cunningham was commanded to re-take British Somaliland and free Addis Ababa. He successfully entered the Ethiopian capital on 6 April 1941 and his campaign resulted in the capture of fifty thousand Italian prisoners with the comparative loss of just five hundred of his own men. In 1941 he was appointed to command the newly formed 8th Army in North Africa but was relieved of his command for advising that the offensive in that region should be curtailed. At the end of the war in 1945, Cunningham was promoted to general and he died in Tunbridge Wells, England on 13 January 1983.

Mary Frances Cusack
Nun 1832 – 1899

Though Dublin born, Mary Frances Cusack was sent to Devon, England to be privately educated. Following the sudden death of her fiancé, she joined an order of the Anglican nuns but later converted to Catholicism and became a nun in the Order of St Clare. In 1861 she was sent, together with a small group of nuns, to Kenmare, County Kerry, then one of the most destitute parts of Ireland, to establish a convent. In all, Cusack wrote thirty-five books, as well as numerous letters on the Irish causes in the Irish-American and Canadian press. During the famine year of 1871, she raised and distributed fifteen thousand pounds in famine relief funds and she was also an out-spoken patriot, publishing *The Patriot's History of Ireland* in 1869. In 1872, Cusack issued *The Life of Daniel O'Connell,* before later leaving the nunnery in 1881, upon which time she began to establish shelters and vocational schools for female immigrants to the United States. In 1884, with the blessings of Pope Leo XIII, she founded the New Order of the Sisters of Peace, and opened its first house in Nottingham, England before establishing another in New Jersey, the first in the United States. Reverting to her original faith in 1888, Cusack then lectured tirelessly to denounce Catholicism. She died in 1899 in Warwickshire, England.

Emmet Dalton
Revolutionary 1898 – 1978

In 1915, Emmet Dalton enlisted in the British Army where he rose to the rank of major and also won the Military Cross. Upon the conclusion of World War I in 1918, Dalton returned to Ireland where he joined the IRA in 1919, becoming a special advisor to Michael Collins (see page 89). He supported the Anglo-Irish Treaty and was the commander in charge of the artillery attack on the Four Courts in June 1922, as well as the escort in which Collins was killed at Béal na mBláth, County Cork in August 1922. Dalton later carved a career for himself in the film industry in Hollywood and London and his daughter Audrey Dalton was the heroine in the first *Titanic* film.

John Dillon
Nationalist politician 1851 – 1927

The son of John Blake Dillon, (see page 306), the younger Dillon was educated at the Catholic University School and Trinity College, Dublin where he qualified with a degree in medicine. Dillon was one of the primary leaders of the Irish Land League, which provided that tenants should pay rent to the league, rather than the landlords. For his actions he was sentenced to six months imprisonment but was later elected a member of parliament for Tipperary in 1880, before representing East Mayo in 1886. Following the O'Shea divorce (Parnell had had an affair with a married woman, Kitty O'Shea) and the controversy surrounding Charles Stewart Parnell (see page 423), Dillon became chairman of the anti-Parnellite group and strongly criticised the actions of Edward Carson (see page 159) in his opposition to home rule for Ireland during the Ulster crisis of 1913. Following the 1916 rising, Dillon intervened with British Prime Minister David Lloyd George in order to prevent the executions of the Irish revolutionaries, but was unsuccessful in his attempts. He lived to see the atrocities of both the Anglo-Irish War and the Irish Civil War before dying on 4 August 1927 at the age of seventy-six.

Ronnie Drew
Folk musician 1934 – 2008

Born in Dun Laoghaire, Ronnie Drew's unmistakable, gravelly voice made him an icon among folk musicians in Ireland. In the mid-1950s he went to Spain to work as an English teacher and while there, learned flamenco guitar. Upon his return to Dublin, Drew founded the Ronnie Drew Group which later became known as the Dubliners. He was a member of that group from 1962 until 1974, and again from 1979 until 1985, following which he pursued a solo career. With his flowing white beard, he was instantly recognisable everywhere he went; with the Dubliners he spread a love of Irish folk music throughout Europe and the United States. Drew died on 16 August 2008.

Sir Arthur Philip Du Cros
Founder of the Dunlop Rubber Company 1871 – 1955

Having entered the civil service at the age of fifteen, in 1892 Arthur Phillip Du Cros joined his father and brother in a company formed to develop the pneumatic tyre, which was invented by John Boyd Dunlop. In 1901 he founded the Dunlop Rubber Company and Du Cros built Dunlop to become one of the world's leading tyre-producing companies. However, the 1920s depression saw him lose most of his personal fortune. He published the history of the industry, *Wheels of Fortune* in 1938 and died in Hertfordshire, England on 28 October 1955.

Jane Francesca Elgee (Lady Wilde)
Poet 1821 – 1896

Jane Francesca Elgee, later known as Jane Wilde, produced poetic works under the pen name 'Speranza'. Having witnessed the funeral of Thomas Davis (see page 92) in 1845, and having subsequently read his poetry, Elgee produced pro-Irish independence and anti-British writings and poems in the *Nation*, the Irish nationalist newspaper. She became editor of that publication in July 1848, before marrying the eminent eye surgeon, William Wilde (see page 353) three years later.

Together the couple had three children, one of whom was the famous playwright, Oscar Wilde (see page 198). She died in London on 3 February 1896.

Robert Emmet
United Irishman 1778 – 1803

Although distinguishing himself as an outstanding orator during his days at Trinity College, Dublin, Robert Emmet removed himself from education due to an investigation by the college into his membership of the United Irishmen. In 1820 he travelled to France where he held negotiations with Napoleon regarding support for an uprising in Ireland, but he had little faith in Napoleon's interest and returned to Dublin. He pressed ahead with his intended uprising by establishing a number of depots for arms throughout the city. With a possible invasion of England planned by Napoleon in 1803, Emmet intended to time the rising to coincide with this event and in July 1803, he planned attacks on Dublin Castle and other strategic houses and barracks around the city. However, his supporters were most ineffective in their approach and upon leading one hundred of them with the intention of attacking Dublin Castle, Emmet witnessed the undisciplined force attacking and killing Lord Chief Justice Kilwarden and his nephew as they approached in their coach.

Emmet's force disbanded immediately and he fled to the Dublin Mountains before later returning to Harold's Cross to visit his fiancée Sarah Curran. There he was arrested and some weeks later was tried for treason and found guilty, before being hanged at Thomas Street on 20 September 1803. Emmet's speech from the dock prior to sentencing is held in reverence in Ireland to this day: 'Let no man write my epitaph; for as no man who knows my motives dare now vindicate them, let not prejudice or ignorance asperse them. Let them rest in obscurity and peace! Let my memory be left in oblivion, my tomb remain uninscribed until other times and other men can do justice to my character. When my country takes her place among the nations of the earth then, and not till then, let my epitaph be written. I have done!'

John Field
Pianist and composer 1782 – 1837

John Field is best known for being the first composer to write nocturnes. By the age of seventeen, he had premiered his First piano concerto, of which he wrote seven, and in 1806 he moved to Russia where he divided his time between Moscow and St Petersburg. Field is remembered for his eighteen nocturnes: single-movement impromptu compositions for piano that maintain a single mood throughout. He died in Moscow in 1837.

Wing Commander Brendan 'Paddy' Finucane
RAF pilot 1920 – 1942

At twenty-one years of age, Brendan Finucane was the youngest wing commander in Fighter Command of the Royal Airforce during World War II. He was also one of the highest-scoring allied pilots, with thirty-two accredited kills. Finucane was born in Rathmines into a family with strong military ties. His father was a member of the IRA who fought with Éamon de Valera (see page 431) in Boland's Mill during the Easter Rising of 1916, and his brothers, Raymond and Kevin, served in the RAF Bomber Command and the British Army respectively. Educated at Synge Street Christian Brothers School, and later at O'Connell School, Finucane excelled at rugby, Gaelic football, boxing and rowing. He was a deeply religious young man but never fostered his beliefs on others and he was held in high esteem with all ground crews who serviced his aircraft. Although a wing commander (the equivalent of a lieutenant colonel in the army), Finucane would address the crews by their Christian names and requested that they do the same with him. A charismatic character who had a shamrock festooned on the side of his Spitfire, Finucane's age and fantastic achievements in the air, as well as a list of honours that included the DSO and the DFC, had the British and American press clambering for stories.

Referred to by Winston Churchill as the 'amazing young Irish man', Finucane's Spitfire was hit by machine gun fire from the ground at Pointe du Touquet, while returning from a raid over France on 15 July 1942. His final words over the radio were reported to be 'This is it chaps', as his aircraft hit the water. His Spitfire sank instantly, taking him with it. Over 3,500 people attended a commemoration service in Westminster Cathedral in honour of this great young pilot. A memorial, in the form of a painting, is displayed in the Military Hospital in Surrey, and a variety of rose by Sean McCann is named after him. No monument of any form exists to his memory in Great Britain and in his native Ireland, Finucane is virtually unknown.

Barry Fitzgerald (William Joseph Shields)
Academy Award-winning actor
1888 – 1961

Barry Fitzgerald was born William Joseph Shields in Dublin. Initially working as a civil servant, he later joined the Abbey Theatre in Dublin before making his screen debut for Alfred Hitchcock in 1930. Fitzgerald starred in the *The Plough and the Stars*, directed by John Ford, and had a very successful Hollywood career featuring in such films as *The Long Voyage Home, How Green Was My Valley, And Then There Were None*, and *The Quiet Man*. He achieved a feat never before seen in the history of the Academy Awards when he was nominated for an Oscar in both the 'best actor' and 'best supporting actor' categories for the same performance, as Father Fitzgibbon in the film *Going My Way* in 1944. The rules of the Academy have since been changed to prevent this re-occurring. Fitzgerald has two stars on the Hollywood Walk of Fame.

Garret Fitzgerald
Politician 1926 – 2011

Born into a republican family in Dublin, Garret Fitzgerald's parents were both present in the General Post Office during the Easter Rising in 1916. Educated at Belvedere College and University College Dublin, Fitzgerald later worked for national airline Aer Lingus, before studying economics at Trinity College and becoming a lecturer on the subject at UCD. It was the ever-growing death toll in the conflict in Northern Ireland that eventually drew him into politics and he would go on to serve two terms as taoiseach of Ireland from 1981 to 1982, and 1982 to 1987. In that role, Fitzgerald demonstrated how best to respect the people of Northern Ireland and their allegiance, always avoiding claim and counter-claim in respect of territory.

A man of wide vision, he was well read and was considered an intellectual among intellectuals. Fitzgerald guided Ireland carefully during his second tenure as taoiseach, a difficult period of high inflation which was further complicated by north-south tensions. He also endeavoured to impart information to British prime minister Margaret Thatcher on how best to handle the northern population and his efforts led to the signing of the Anglo-Irish Agreement in November 1985. It was the crowning achievement of Fitzgerald's political career and lead eventually to the passing of the Good Friday Agreement some thirteen years later.

George Francis FitzGerald
Mathematician 1851 – 1901

George Francis FitzGerald was born in Kill O' The Grange, Monkstown and was educated at Trinity College. He graduated in 1871 as the best student in both mathematics and experimental science, becoming a tutor and eventually a professor, in 1881. FitzGerald made significant contributions to the development of electromagnetic theory and was the first to suggest a method of producing radio waves that helped to lay the basis for wireless telegraphy. Following his death in 1901, Sir Joseph Larmor (see page 32), cognisant of the value of FitzGerald's work, collected his scientific writings.

Colonel James Fitzmaurice
Aviator 1898 – 1965

James Fitzmaurice was born at 35 Mountjoy Cottages on the North Circular Road, and later moved to Portlaoise, County Laois. He joined an infantry battalion in the British Army in World War I and saw action at the Somme, before enlisting in the Royal Flying Corps (later the RAF) in 1917. Upon the signing of the Anglo-Irish Treaty, Fitzmaurice joined the fledgling Irish Army Air Corps as a lieutenant and together with Baron Von Huenefeld, took part in the first-ever flight from east to west across the Atlantic on 12 April 1928. The men's aircraft was named the Bremen and they carried two copies of the *Irish Times* on the flight, the first newspaper to ever cross the Atlantic by air. Fitzmaurice died on 26 September 1965 in Baggot Street Hospital, Dublin.

George Forrest
Victoria Cross recipient 1800 – 1859

As a fifty-seven-year-old lieutenant in the Bengal Veteran Establishment of the Indian Army during the Indian Mutiny, George Forrest was one of nine men who defended an ammunitions magazine against a large number of rebel mutineers for over five hours. When the rebels finally gained entry, Forrest and his comrades acknowledged that there was no hope of rescue and fired at the magazine.

Five of these gallant men died in the subsequent explosion in which many of the enemy were also killed. Forrest and two of his comrades received the Victoria Cross for their sacrifice.

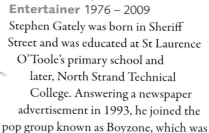

Stephen Gately
Entertainer 1976 – 2009

Stephen Gately was born in Sheriff Street and was educated at St Laurence O'Toole's primary school and later, North Strand Technical College. Answering a newspaper advertisement in 1993, he joined the pop group known as Boyzone, which was under the influence of pop mogul Louis Walsh, and quickly rose to fame, achieving worldwide success with a string of hits such as 'Words' and 'When the Going Gets Tough'. In 2000 the group parted ways, with Gately going on to enjoy a successful career in London's West End, playing the lead role in *Joseph and the Amazing Technicolor Dreamcoat*, before rejoining the group upon its successful reformation in 2008. Noted as a champion of gay rights, in 2003, Gately wed his longtime partner, Andrew Cowles in a ceremony in Las Vegas. With fifteen years at the top of the music profession, his death, from natural causes at the age of thirty-three, was a huge loss to Irish entertainment.

Cedric Gibbons
Film director and designer of the Oscar statuettes 1893 – 1960

Cedric Gibbons was born in Dublin but moved to the United States where he studied art at the Art Students League of New York. He started film work for Edison Studios in 1915 and three years later moved to MGM as an art director, where he was involved for thirty-two years. It has been argued that Gibbons was the most important art director in the history of American cinema and he was the designer of the Academy Awards statuette, proudly collecting eleven of them himself. He died in Hollywood at the age of sixty-seven and is buried in Los Angeles.

Peter Gill
Victoria Cross recipient 18313 – 1868

At twenty-five years of age, Peter Gill served as a sergeant major in the Loodiana Regiment during the Indian Mutiny. On 4 June 1857 at Benares, Gill volunteered, along with two others, to rescue a paymaster and his family from their bungalow. Coming under heavy fire, he successfully saved the family and during the same evening, came to the rescue of a fellow quartermaster sergeant who had just been bayonetted. He is also attributed with saving the life of a major on two occasions during attacks by Sepoys (native Indian soldiers). Gill later became a lieutenant and was killed in action in India on 26 July 1868.

Oliver St John Gogarty
Surgeon, eccentric and writer
1878 – 1957

Educated at Clongowes Wood College and Trinity College, Dublin, in 1907 Oliver St John Gogarty qualified with a degree in medicine before establishing a considerable practice as a nose and throat specialist. He also took part on the side of the Free State in the Civil War and was captured during that conflict before escaping by swimming across the River Liffey. Relieved by his lucky escape, he would later present two swans to that river in a show of gratitude. Gogarty, who was a close friend of James Joyce (see page 173) and Frederic Herbert Trench (see page 115), also published poems and novels as well as a number of volumes of his reminiscences, amongst which were *As I was going down Sackville Street*.

However, he attracted unwanted controversy when he lost a libel action for alleged anti-Semitic remarks about Sinclair in this writing in 1937. Referred to by W. B. Yeats (see page 199) as 'the Arch Poet', Gogarty has a public house named after him in Dublin's Temple Bar area.

Cathal Goulding
Chief of staff of the IRA
1923 – 1998

Born in Dublin's north inner city, Cathal Goulding joined the IRA in 1939. Coming from a family with a staunch republican tradition, his grandfather was a Fenian and his father fought in the 1916 Easter Rising. In 1953 Goulding was imprisoned for eight years for stealing weapons from a British military training base. However, following his release he became quartermaster-general of the IRA, leading the movement to Marxist thinking, rather than military action. This philosophical shift was the catalyst to the formation of the Worker's Party. A strong critic of the Provisional IRA's bombing campaign in Northern Ireland in 1989, Goulding said, 'I believe the only way to have any kind of freedom in Ireland is when Catholics and Protestants are able to unite together for both their rights.' He died in Dublin on 26 December 1998.

Patrick Graham
Victoria Cross recipient 1837 – 1875

Patrick Graham was born in St Michael's Parish, Dublin. A twenty-year-old private in the 90th Regiment of Foot, British Army, his defining moment came to pass at Lucknow, India on 17 November 1857. Under extremely heavy fire, Graham brought a wounded comrade to safety and for this deed he was awarded the Victoria Cross.

Henry Grattan
Orator and patriot 1746 – 1820

The great Henry Grattan was born in Dublin and educated in Trinity College before being called to the Irish Bar in 1772. In 1775 he was elected to the Irish Parliament where he became the spokesman for the patriots within that establishment and his first political success was the repeal of restrictions on Irish trade, where Irish exports to the American Colonies had previously been prohibited. He followed this with a campaign for legislative independence for Ireland, a demand he vigorously pursued, and as a show of gratitude the Irish parliament voted that fifty thousand pounds be advanced to Grattan, who had recognised that the British government's policy was to maintain and widen the divide between Protestants and Catholics thus easily facilitating its continued dominance in Ireland.

He once proclaimed that 'the Irish Protestant will never be free until the Irish Catholic hath ceased to be a slave', in 1782, through the efforts of Grattan, Britain passed the Repeal of the Declaratory Act, thus giving the Irish parliament full legislative power with the king retaining the power of veto. However, this sea change did not represent total independence and in May 1795, Grattan introduced a bill in parliament for Catholic emancipation. With three quarters of the Irish house being of planted stock, the motion was easily and inevitably defeated by 155 votes to 84 and resulted in Grattan becoming disillusioned in his inability to effect the changes he so dearly desired.

He retired from political life in 1797 but returned the following year to vigorously campaign against the Act of Union; he was fighting an uphill battle and was once again unsuccessful. Ill-health forced Grattan to retire once again but with parliamentary power now having transferred back to London, he returned to represent Dublin in the newly formed administration where he tirelessly continued his campaign for Catholic emancipation. Possibly due to his exertions, Grattan's health further deteriorated, leading to his death in London on 4 June 1820.

Robert James Graves
Physician 1796 – 1853

Robert James Graves graduated with honours in medicine, from Trinity College, Dublin in 1818. He had a flair for journalism and languages and his fluency in German was such that on a visit to Austria he was taken for a German spy and imprisoned for a short time as a result. Upon his return to Ireland in 1821, Graves became a physician at the Meath Hospital, Dublin and contributed many essays to the *Dublin Journal of Medical Science*. Renowned for his diagnosis of what is now known as 'Graves Disease' (toxic goitre) he died in Dublin on 20 March 1853.

Bernadette Greevy
Mezzo-soprano 1940 – 2008

Bernadette Greevy was born in the Dublin suburb of Clontarf and was educated at the Holy Faith Convent, and at the Guildhall School of Music and

169

Drama in London. She made her first professional operatic appearance in Dublin's Grand Opera Society production of Verdi's *Rigoletto* and made her Royal Opera House debut in 1982. It was her lack of acting ability that restricted her appearances in many operas, which was indeed a pity, particularly as she had a tremendous voice and was blessed with good looks. Greevy led a very active concert and recital life with engagements in Ireland and overseas, which led to her becoming a household name throughout the country. The recipient of many international awards, she held honourary doctorates from the National University of Ireland and Trinity College, Dublin and her voice was once described by the *Times* as 'full, glowing, rich and firm at the bottom, radiant at the top, and with gloriously expressive phrasing'. Established in 2000, The Anna Livia International Opera Festival was her brainchild and affords many Irish artists the opportunity to work in their own capital city with international colleagues. Greevy died on 26 September 2008.

Arthur Griffith
Political leader 1872 – 1922

Arthur Griffith was, for most of his life, an editor of various newspapers, the best-known of which was the *United Irishman*. He was a strong advocate of passive resistance against English rule in Ireland, as well as the abandonment of Irish politicians at Westminster, and following a legal action against the publication of the *United Irishman* in 1906, Griffith founded a new newspaper, *Sinn Féin*. After the 1916 rising in Dublin, he was initially imprisoned in Richmond Barracks (the barracks was later renamed after him) and was subsequently held at Gloucestershire in England, together with a number of other Irish political activists. In October 1921, Griffith led the Irish delegation that negotiated the agreement that launched the state on its independent course. He died at

the age of fifty-one in the midst of the terrible civil war that was fought over the treaty he had signed with the British authorities.

Sir Richard Griffith
Mining engineer and geologist 1784 – 1878

Richard Griffith was appointed professor of geology and mining engineering to the Royal Dublin Society in 1802. He prepared a geological map of Ireland which is reputed to be one of the most remarkable geological maps ever produced by one man and later, as commissioner of valuation, he carried out a very complete and comprehensive survey of the whole of Ireland. Recognised for his services with a knighthood in 1856, Griffith is often referred to as 'The Father of Irish Geology'.

Sir Howard Grubb
Instrument maker 1844 – 1931

Howard Grubb studied engineering at Trinity College, Dublin before entering his father's instrument-manufacturing business in 1865, where he built astronomical telescopes for observatories around the world. Grubb also constructed gun-sights, rangefinders and submarine periscopes and achieved great international fame, becoming a fellow of the Royal Society in 1864. Knighted in 1887, Grubb's reflecting telescopes can be seen around the world in places such as Australia, India, Saudi Arabia, Spain, the United States, and of course Ireland.

Veronica Guerin
Investigative journalist 1958 – 1996

Having initially studied accountancy and political research, journalist Veronica Guerin founded a public relations company before joining the *Sunday Business Post* and the *Sunday Tribune* in 1990. Four years later she began writing about the activities of criminals and drug dealers in the Dublin area and as a result, received numerous death threats. On 30 January 1995, Guerin sustained a gun-shot wound to her leg having previously been attacked by Dublin criminal John Gilligan, who punched her in the face and later called to her home, threatening to kidnap and harm her son if she was to write anything about him. Guerin was a tenacious reporter who was willing to take any chance to uncover the truth. On June 1996, when Guerin was sitting in her car waiting for the traffic lights to change at Newlands Cross in County Dublin, two men on motorcycles approached her and shot her five times, fatally wounding her in the process. Taoiseach John Bruton referred to her death as 'an attack on democracy' and the aftermath led the Irish Government to establish the Criminal Assets Bureau in order to pursue criminals and the assets gained through their crimes as well as the confiscation of them. The aforementioned Gilligan had his assets confiscated by the bureau in 2008. There are two films based on Guerin's life, *When the Sky Falls* (2000) directed by John Mackenzie, and *Veronica Guerin* (2003) directed by Joel Schumacher.

Sir Benjamin Lee Guinness
Brewer 1798 – 1868

Benjamin Lee Guinness is perhaps the most famous of the Guinness dynasty. In 1855, upon the death of his father, Arthur, he became the sole owner of Guinness breweries and was thus responsible for extending the home market. Guinness built up a large export trade but also diversified himself, becoming the first Lord Mayor of Dublin in 1851. In 1860 he undertook, at his own expense, the restoration of Saint Patrick's Cathedral in Dublin, and personally supervised the work, which cost in the region of £150,000. He died in London, on 19 May 1868.

Sir William Rowan Hamilton
Mathematician and astronomer 1805 – 1865

William Rowan Hamilton was born at 36 Dominick Street, but having been orphaned, he was brought up by his clergyman uncle in Trim, County Meath. Hamilton was a child prodigy, capable of reading Hebrew from the age of four and by the age of fourteen he was fluent in Greek, Hebrew and Latin. By the age of sixteen he was recognised as a mathematical genius and at twenty-one he became a professor of astronomy and was appointed astronomer royal for Ireland, at Dunsink Observatory. Hamilton published a large number of papers on mathematical problems, the most notable of which, 'The Elements of Quaternions', was published following his death in September 1865.

James Hanley
Novelist, playwright and writer 1901 – 1985

James Hanley was born in Holles Street in 1901. He ran away to sea at the age of thirteen and in 1915, during World War I, he jumped ship in Frederick's Town, Canada and enlisted in the Canadian army. Hanley has been compared to D. H.

171

Lawrence and amongst his many writings, perhaps his best known are *The Furys, Another World, Woman in the Sky,* and *The Ocean.* His first novel was rejected by no fewer than seventeen publishers, however his books have now been published extensively by Penguin, with one of his final works, *Against the Stream,* published in 1981. Hanley lived most of his life in Wales, where he spoke the language fluently, and he died there in 1985. In all, he wrote forty-eight books, all of which received wide literary praise on both sides of the Atlantic. Despite this, Hanley remains a relatively unknown author.

Victor Herbert
Composer, cellist and conductor
1859 – 1924

Victor Herbert received his early music training in Stuttgart, Germany where he developed as an outstanding cellist. He then played in the orchestra of Johann Strauss in Vienna before emigrating to the United States in 1886 where he was engaged by the Metropolitan Opera Company. In 1892, Herbert became conductor of the 22nd Regiment Band of the New York National Guard, succeeding the well known Irish conductor, Patrick Gilmore (see page 215), and he also conducted the Pittsburgh Symphony Orchestra from 1898 until 1902. Herbert composed the first of his operas, *Prince Ananias* in 1894, and later *The Wizard of the Nile, The Serenade* and *The Fortune Teller.* His opera, *Natoma* was produced in Philadelphia in 1911 and featured the young Irish tenor, John McCormack (see page 404) in his opera debut. In 1914, Herbert was instrumental in forming the American Society of Composers, Authors and Publishers, an organisation that protects the rights of creative musicians to this day. He died on 26 May 1924.

Seán Heuston
Patriot 1891 – 1916

During the Easter Rising of 1916, Seán Heuston was commander in charge of the volunteers in the Mendicity Institute on Usher's Island where with twenty of his men, Heuston held his position for two days when it was expected that he would only hold out for a mere three or four hours. Following the failure of the rising, Heuston was executed by firing squad in Kilmainham Jail on 8 May 1916. The youngest of the patriots to meet their fate, Heuston Station in Dublin is named in his memory.

Reginald Ingram Montgomery Hitchcock
Film director 1893 – 1950

Reginald Ingram Montgomery Hitchcock, better known as Rex Ingram, was born at 58 Grosvenor Square in Rathmines and was educated at St Columba's College, Rathfarnham. In 1911 he emigrated to the United States where he studied sculpture at Yale University School of Art and two years later he entered the film industry as an actor, before going on to produce, write and direct. Rex Ingram directed some twenty-seven films and is regarded as one of the most important directors in the movie industry in Hollywood during the 1920s. Amongst the better-known films that he directed were, *The Four Horsemen of the Apocalypse* (1921), *The Prisoner of Zenda* (1922), and the hugely successful epic, *Ben Hur* (1925), which he co-directed with Fred Niblo. Hitchcock was awarded honourary life membership of the Directors Guild of America in 1949 and has a star on the Hollywood walk of fame at 1651 Vine Street. He died in 1950 and is buried in Forest Lawn Memorial Park Cemetery in Glendale, California.

James Jackman
Victoria Cross recipient 1916 – 1941

James Jackman served as a captain in the Royal Northumberland Fusiliers of the British Army during World War II. When an assault on El Duda ridge was slowed by fierce enemy fire at Tobruk, Libya on 25 November 1941, Jackman calmly led his company in an attack on the opposition's anti-tank guns. Having succeeded in that task, he then led a truck column into a safe position from where the enemy could be attacked. It is said that his coolness and complete disregard of danger inspired both his own men and the tank crews. Jackman was killed in action the following day but was awarded the Victoria Cross for his bravery.

The Reverend William Jackson
United Irishman 1737 – 1795

In the mid-1740s, William Jackson travelled to London where he became a tutor and took Holy Orders to become Curate of St Mary-Le-Strand church.

A staunch supporter of the American Revolution, Jackson made a reputation as a radical journalist and in 1792 went to France to secure aid for an invasion of Ireland. Returning to London unsuccessful, he made the acquaintance of a Mr Cockayne, the former attorney to the notorious Duchess of Kensington. Cockayne accompanied Jackson to Dublin where he informed the authorities of his involvement in the United Irishmen. Following this, Jackson was arrested and tried for treason, and was found guilty but poisoned himself in the dock on 30 April 1795.

Henry Mitchell Jones
Victoria Cross recipient 1831 – 1916

Henry Mitchell Jones was a captain in the 7th Regiment of the British Army, during the Crimean War at Sebastopol. Jones distinguished himself with extreme gallantry in the taking of quarries, which he defended through the night in a wounded state. He died in Eastbourne, Sussex in 1916.

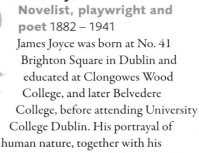

James Joyce
Novelist, playwright and poet 1882 – 1941

James Joyce was born at No. 41 Brighton Square in Dublin and educated at Clongowes Wood College, and later Belvedere College, before attending University College Dublin. His portrayal of human nature, together with his mastery of language, make him possibly Ireland's most influential novelist. His works include the world famous *Ulysses*, which was published in 1922 before being banned in the United States and Great Britain for some years. Bloomsday, which is celebrated annually on 16 June in honour of the life of Joyce, derives its name from the book's protagonist, Leopold Bloom. However, it is *Finnegans Wake* that Joyce considered to be his best work and with good reason – it took him seventeen years to complete. Opinion on the book is divided with many critics having declared the work a masterpiece, while others considered it to be incomprehensible.

Joyce, who was initially rejected by many publishers and attacked by censors and critics, attributed his talent to the Jesuits, although he rejected their religious teachings in later life. He married Nora Barnacle in 1931 and went to live in Trieste, where they had two children. They lived in relative poverty in Italy but despite this, it proved a productive period for Joyce and he wrote most of *Dubliners, A Portrait* of the Artist as a Young Man, as well as completing a large part of *Ulysses* during this time. He returned to Dublin in 1909, where his attempt at cinema ownership failed, and later moved to Zurich. He once proclaimed 'I always write about Dublin, because if I can get to the heart of Dublin, I can get to the heart of all the cities of the world'. Joyce also published a play, *Exiles*, in 1918, and a collection of poems, *Pomes Penyeach*, which was published in Paris in 1927. He died in Zurich on 13 January 1941.

Peadar Kearney
Writer of the Irish national anthem
1833 – 1942
Peadar Kearney was born at Drumcondra Road, Dublin. Joining the Gaelic League in 1901 and the Irish Republican Brotherhood in 1903, he fought at Jacob's biscuit factory during the Easter Rising of 1916 and was lucky to escape before that garrison was captured. Kearney, who took the side of the Pro-Treaty forces in the Civil War which followed, wrote the Irish National Anthem known as 'Amhrán na bhFiann' (The Soldier's Song), but never received any royalties for it. Other songs he composed include, 'Down by the Glenside' and 'Whack for the Diddle'. He died in Inchicore on 23 November 1942.

Lieutenant General Richard Harte Keatinge
Victoria Cross recipient 1825 – 1904
Richard Harte Keatinge served as a major in the Bombay Artillery during the Indian Mutiny. During an assault on Chundairee on 17 March 1858, Keatinge successfully formed a breach in the walls of a fort and led his column into the structure through heavy fire. Wounded in the operation, Keatinge later received the rank of lieutenant general and died in May 1904.

Thomas Kettle
Poet, politician and soldier
1880 – 1916
Artane's Thomas Kettle was educated at the O'Connell Christian Brothers School and Clongowes Wood College. He entered University College Dublin in 1897 and studied law, before being admitted to the Irish Bar in 1903 and qualifying as a barrister in 1905. The following year he was elected an Irish Party MP for East Tyrone, and he was renowned in the House of Commons for advocating a constitutional path to home rule for Ireland. In 1908 Kettle was the first professor of national economics at his alma mater, UCD and he lent his weight in support of the striking workers during the Dublin lockout of 1913, as well as publishing a number of articles revealing the terrible living and working conditions experienced by the poor of the nation's capital. That same year he joined the National Irish Volunteers movement, which was spurned by Ulster unionists who were resistant to home rule and the formation of the militant Ulster Volunteers. It was while in continental Europe on an arms-raising mission on behalf of the Volunteers in 1914 that Kettle witnessed firsthand the outbreak of World War I, and he wrote in the *Daily News* that it was a war of, 'civilisation against barbarians.'

Upon his return to Ireland, having witnessed the atrocities by the Germans in Belgium and with a conviction that Britain would grant home rule for Ireland, he volunteered his services in the British army and served as a captain during the Battle of the Somme, where he was killed in action. The French journal *L'Opinion* wrote, 'He was Ireland! He had fought for all the aspirations of his race, for independence, for home rule, for the Celtic renaissance, for a united Ireland, for the eternal cause of humanity. He died a hero in the uniform of a British soldier.' Kettle penned the poem, 'Reason in Rhyme' which was written in answer to English pleas to forget the past and his political essays are collected in *The Days Burden* (1910), *The Open Secret of Ireland* (1912), and *The Ways of War* (published in 1917, after this death). His poetry was issued as *Poems and Parodies* (1912) and a memorial to him in St Stephen's Green, Dublin is inscribed with the following lines from a sonnet he wrote to his daughter:

> Died not for Flag, nor King, nor Emperor,
> But for a Dream, born in a Herdsman's Hut,
> And for the Secret Scripture of the Poor.

William Knox Leet
Victoria Cross recipient 1833 – 1898

William Knox Leet was born in Dalkey and was a major in the 1st Battalion, 13th Regiment of Foot of the British Army during the Zulu War. At Inhlobana in Zululand on 28 March 1879, Leet bravely rescued a comrade from danger. Upon seeing a lieutenant fall when his horse was shot from under him, Leet charged forward, drove off the Zulus and successfully helped the lieutenant to his feet before riding with him back to safety under heavy enemy fire. For this he was awarded the Victoria Cross. He died in Kent in 1898.

Joseph Sheridan Le Fanu
Novelist 1814 – 1873

Though called to the bar in 1939, John Sheridan Le Fanu never practised law, preferring instead the discipline of journalism. To this end he purchased three Dublin newspapers and amalgamated them to form the *Dublin Evening Mail*. However, Le Fanu is best remembered for his mystery and horror fiction stories – his best tale, 'Carmilla' being a chilling example of his work. Interestingly, it is reputed that 'Carmilla', a tale of a lesbian vampire set in central Europe, greatly influenced Bram Stoker (see page 192) in his writing of *Dracula*. As a writer, the two novels that Le Fanu will best be remembered for are *The House by the Churchyard* (1863), and *Uncle Silas* (1864). He wrote in excess of fifteen novels before his death on 7 February 1873.

Seán Lemass
Taoiseach 1899 – 1971

Seán Lemass joined the Irish Volunteers in 1915, just short of his sixteenth birthday, and took part in the Easter Rising in the General Post Office the following year. After the failure of the rising and due to his age, Lemass was released but he did remain a member of the Volunteers and is reputed to have been one of the 12 Apostles who under the command of Michael Collins (see page 89), took part in the attacks on British agents living in Dublin from 1919 to 1921. Arrested in December 1920 and interned at Ballykinlar, County Down, he was released the following year upon which time he opposed the Anglo-Irish Treaty and took part in the seizure of the Four Courts during the Civil War. Following this, Lemass was once again imprisoned but was released on 18 November 1924 and went on to become a Sinn Féin TD and later a Fianna Fáil TD. A co-founder of the latter political party, he was successfully elected at each election in the following years until his retirement in 1969 and he served in numerous ministerial positions before being elected taoiseach on 23 June 1959, a position he held until 1966. Lemass is regarded as one of the most influential Taoisigh in Irish history and he was a tireless worker in the development of Irish industry, being highly responsible for forging links between the Republic and Northern Ireland.

Often referred to as the architect of modern Ireland, he died in the Mater Hospital in Dublin on 11 May 1971, and was afforded a state funeral.

Hugh Leonard
Playwright 1926 – 2009

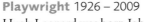

Hugh Leonard was born John Joseph Keyes Byrne, and was adopted shortly after his birth. Growing up in Dalkey, he adopted the surname Leonard to conceal his writings whilst employed by the Irish Civil Service. He published two volumes of autobiographies, *Home Before Night* (1979), and *Out After Dark* (1989), and his plays included *The Big Birthday, A Leap in the Dark, Stephen D, The Poker Session, The Patrick Pearse Motel, The Au Pair Man* and finally, *Da*, which won him a Tony award in 1977 before being later turned into a film starring Martin Sheen. Leonard, whose plays were often provocative, was never afraid to challenge the orthodoxies of the day and he died on 12 February 2009.

Thomas Clarke Luby
Revolutionary, scholar and author 1822 – 1901

The son of a Protestant clergyman, at just eighteen years of age, Thomas Clarke Luby graduated from Trinity College, Dublin and later went on to study law in the Temple, London. He was initially a part of Daniel O'Connell's (see page 232) Repeal Association, which was formed with the aim of repealing the 1802 Act of Union between Great Britain and Ireland, but he was later convinced that the only way to achieve a meaningful measure of freedom in Ireland was by force. Luby subsequently joined the Young Ireland movement and took part in the failed uprising of 1848 and was also a founding member of the Irish Republican Brotherhood a decade later.

Having travelled throughout Ireland organising groups within the movement, in 1863 he went to the United States to establish relationships with the Fenian movement that had been formed by emigrating members of the IRB.

In 1865, together with other IRB members such as John O'Leary (see page 375) and Jeremiah O'Donovan Rossa (see page 111), Luby was arrested by the British authorities in Ireland and charged with treasonable felony before being sentenced to twenty years imprisonment. Having served five years in prison in England, he was released on amnesty in 1870 due to pressure brought by the United States government for the release of American Fenians. Following the men's release, they were invited to a reception hosted by President Grant in the White House in February 1871 and Luby then became active in Clann na nGael and the Irish Confederation and was heavily involved in raising funds and promoting the cause of Irish freedom. He went on to become a lecturer and also published, *The Life and Times of Daniel O'Connell*, as well as *The Life and Times of Illustrious and Representative Irishmen*. Luby died on 1 December 1901, at his home in Oak Street, New Jersey, and is buried in Bay View Cemetery.

Lieutenant General Harry Hammon Lyster
Victoria Cross recipient 1830 – 1922

Harry Hammon Lyster was born in Blackrock and served as a lieutenant in the 72nd Bengal Native Infantry of the Indian Army during the Indian Mutiny. On 23 May 1858, at Calpee, he single-handedly charged, and broke, a skirmish of rebel troops, killing a number of them. He later became a lieutenant general and died in 1922.

John William Mackay
American capitalist 1831 – 1902

John William Mackay arrived in New York in 1840 with his parents at the age of nine. Initially working in a shipyard in New York, he travelled to California in 1851 where he worked in gold mines; the following year he arrived in Virginia City, Nevada, having lost all the money he had made in California. Mackay formed a firm with James G. Fair (see page 381), James C. Flood, and William S. O'Brien and together they discovered the great Bonanza vein in 1873. This firm became known as the Bonanza Firm, with Mackay holding two fifths of the financial interest.

He went on to become one of the United States' wealthiest men and was one of the founder members of the Bank of Nevada in San Francisco. Mackay also funded the first telegraph cable across the Atlantic and founded the first International Communications Corporation. He contributed considerable gifts to the Catholic institutions and to people in need and was a most unassuming man who was held with great respect by the men working in his mine. By the time of his death in London in 1902, it was estimated that Mackay's assets were valued at 100 million dollars, making him one of the richest people in the world. He is commemorated by the Mackay School of Mines building, which is situated at the University of Nevada in Reno.

Leonard MacNally
Barrister and informer 1752 – 1820

Leonard MacNally was called to the Irish bar in 1776 and the English bar in 1783. An original member of the Society of United Irishmen, he defended a number of those men in court, including Lord Edward Fitzgerald (see page 240) and Robert Emmet (see page 165), amongst other leaders. All of MacNally's clients were invariably convicted and it was not until after his death, when his heir claimed continuance of a secret service pension, that it emerged that whilst taking fees for the defence of United Irishmen, he was at the same time betraying them. He died at his home at 22 Harcourt Street on 13 February 1820.

Dr Richard Robert Madden
Doctor, judge, humanitarian and writer 1798 – 1886

Richard Madden was a distinguished scholar who studied the languages and customs of a multitude of nations around the globe. In 1836 he was appointed judge arbitrator in cases involving liberated African slaves in Havana, Cuba – then in Spanish possession. He despised slavery and on one occasion travelled thousands of miles out of his way to defend slaves who had mutinied aboard the *Amistad*, a schooner carrying Africans who had been sold into slavery from Havana and who were being transported to another port in Cuba. Later portrayed in the motion picture *Amistad*, the slaves mutinied with the intention of sailing back home to Africa; with no navigational skills they found themselves on the shores of Long Island, New York. Madden defended the *Amistad* slaves in court and eventually secured their freedom before returning to Ireland to continue his humanitarian and literary works. He wrote the history of the 1798 rising and during his research befriended Anne Devlin, girlfriend of Robert Emmet (see page 165). Devlin was in poor health and Madden cared for her before arranging her burial and erecting a memorial over her grave upon her untimely death.

Tim Mahony
Businessman and philanthropist
1931 – 2008

Tim Mahony was born in Dublin, but at an early age moved to Cork where he was educated at the North Monastery. In sport he had the unique distinction of playing for both Cork and Dublin as a hurler and a footballer and he was also an astute businessman who successfully established the Toyota brand in Ireland. As a philanthropist, his interest in the arts benefited many, including the National Youth Orchestra of Ireland, of which he was a patron, and his generous donations helped to establish the Irish World Music Centre at the University of Limerick and the Helix Centre at Dublin City University. Mahony also set up Toyota sponsorship deals for the GAA and Munster rugby and he was responsible for the development of the world-class Mount Juliet golf course in County Kilkenny. He died on 24 June 2008, and his burial was attended by over 1,500 mourners at Balgriffin Cemetery, County Dublin.

Robert Mallet
Inventor, geologist and civil engineer 1810 – 1881

Robert Mallet graduated from Trinity College at the age of twenty. Thereafter he built the Fastnet Rock Lighthouse at Mizen Head, County Cork, which is the most south-westerly point of Ireland, and was also involved in the construction of the roof to St George's Church in Dublin, which weighed 133 tons. In 1846, he wrote an important thesis on the dynamics of earthquakes, for which he carried out blasting experiments to determine the speed of seismic propagation in sand and solid rock.

In 1859 he was awarded the Telford Medal by the Institute of Civil Engineers. Mallet, who was also responsible for the construction of a number of railway stations and bridges, published two works dealing with the Great Neapolitan Earthquake of 1857. He moved to London in 1861 where he worked as a scientist and a consultant engineer and was also editor of the *Practical Mechanic's Journal*. He died on 5 November 1881.

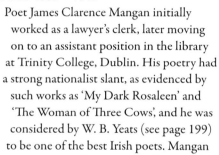

James Clarence Mangan
Poet 1803 – 1849

Poet James Clarence Mangan initially worked as a lawyer's clerk, later moving on to an assistant position in the library at Trinity College, Dublin. His poetry had a strong nationalist slant, as evidenced by such works as 'My Dark Rosaleen' and 'The Woman of Three Cows', and he was considered by W. B. Yeats (see page 199) to be one of the best Irish poets. Mangan had an eccentric appearance and is reputed to have suffered from mood swings. He was also an alcoholic, which led to malnutrition and caused him to sadly succumb to cholera at the age of forty-six. He is buried in Glasnevin Cemetery in Dublin.

William George Nicholas Manley
Victoria Cross recipient 1831 – 1901

William George Nicholas Manley was an assistant surgeon in the Royal Regiment of Artillery of the British Army. He served during the Māori War in New Zealand. During an assault on a rebel position near Tauranga on 29 April 1864, Manley successfully tended to two wounded men whilst accompanying a storming party. He was the last man to leave the scene of the battle and was awarded the Victoria Cross for his actions.

Catherine McAuley
Founder of the Sisters of Mercy 1787 – 1841

Catherine McAuley was orphaned at an early age before being adopted by a Mr and Mrs Callaghan of Coolock House who, on their deaths, left her a large sum of money. At the age of forty-eight, McAuley used her new fortune and purchased a site at Lower Baggot Street in Dublin, where she built a school for poor children called 'The House of Mercy'. She then joined the Presentation Sisters and took religious vows before returning to the House of Mercy where, on 12 December 1831, the Sisters of Mercy were formed. In June 1841 Pope Gregory XVI formally confirmed the order, making them one of the largest religious congregations, with houses established throughout the world. McAuley died on 10 November 1841, and was declared venerable by Pope John Paul II in 1990. Her portrait appeared on the five punt note of the now unused Irish currency.

Sir Frederick McCoy
Professor of natural science and museum director 1817 – 1899

With a passion for natural history, Frederick McCoy published his first scientific paper in his late teens. At the age of twenty-nine his advanced knowledge of fossils gained him an invitation from Adam Sedgwich to arrange the fossil collections at Cambridge's Woodwardian Museum. He subsequently published his first major work, Synopsis of the *British Paleozoic Rocks and Fossils*, before later being appointed professor of natural science at the University of Melbourne in Australia. McCoy built a considerable reputation in the field throughout Australia and later became director of the National Museum, state paleontologist and president of the Royal Society of Victoria. In Australia he assembled one of the finest natural history collections outside Europe and North America but his reputation diminished due to his opposition to Darwin's theories. Awarded the Murchison Medal of the Geological Society of London in 1879, and elected FRS in 1880, he was inducted into the Order of St Michael and St George in 1886 before being knighted in 1891. He died in Melbourne on 16 May 1889.

George McElroy
Fighter pilot 1893 – 1918

Donnybrook born George Edward Henry McElroy was a leading fighter pilot in the Royal Flying Corps during World War I. Upon the outbreak of war he joined the Royal Irish regiment and was wounded by mustard gas in the trenches at Ypres, France. He returned to Dublin to recuperate and was present in the city during the Easter Rising of 1916 when he was called upon to act against his fellow Irishmen. McElroy refused and as a result, was moved south to another garrison, as a form of punishment. He later transferred to the Royal Flying Corps and following flight training, served in Squadron 40 in Bruay, France. A protégé of fellow Irishman, Edward Mannock (see page 102), McElroy achieved forty-seven kills in the space of forty weeks but was lost in action over Laventie on 31 July 1918. He was awarded the Military Cross and the Distinguished Flying Cross.

John McGahern
Writer 1934 – 2006

John McGahern was born in Dublin but spent most of his young life in Ballinamore, County Leitrim. He was educated by the Presentation Brothers and graduated from University College Dublin to begin his career as a schoolteacher. McGahern's first novel, *The Dark* was banned in Ireland for its alleged pornographic content and as a result he was forced to resign his teaching post. His other works include, *That They May Face the Rising Sun*, *The Barracks* and *Amongst Women*, which was nominated for the Booker Prize in 1990.

Joseph McGrath
Revolutionary and founder of the Irish Hospital Sweepstakes and Waterford Crystal 1887 – 1966

Having taken part in the Easter Rising of 1916, Joseph McGrath was arrested and imprisoned in Wormwood Scrubs and Brixton prison in England. After the general amnesty he was elected a Sinn Féin TD for the St James's division of Dublin in 1918 and during his involvement with the IRA in the Irish War of Independence (1919 – 1921), he successfully organised a number of bank robberies for the organisation. McGrath was one of Michael Collins' (see page 89) personal staff and travelled with him to London during the treaty negotiations in October 1921. In the new Irish government he served as minister for labour from January until August of 1922 and minister for industry and commerce from August 1922 until April 1924. He was also a TD for North Mayo but resigned from office in April 1924 due to the government's attitude towards certain army officers, where he felt that original IRA fighters were being overlooked. In 1925 McGrath became the labour advisor to Siemens-Schuckert, the German contractors that built the hydroelectric scheme at Ardnacrusha, County Limerick and in 1930 he founded the Irish Hospital Sweepstakes, which made him a very wealthy man. He also became one of Ireland's most successful racehorse owners and breeders and invested in the fledgling Waterford Crystal, developing it to become a worldwide success before its sad demise in 2009. He died at his home in Cabinteely, County Dublin on 1 March 1966.

Alexander Mitchell
Engineer 1780 – 1868

In 1896 Alexander Mitchell established a brick-building business in Belfast. The company survived for over thirty years and enabled him to indulge in his engineering pursuits, including the building and patenting of brick-making machines. Living by the sea, Mitchell often pondered the trials of shipwrecked men; which set him thinking about how to warn ships of danger on rocky shores and so in 1832, he invented and patented the 'Mitchell Screw Pile and Mooring'. This was a simple method of constructing lighthouses in deep water and on sand banks and it was first utilised in 1838 for the foundations of the Maplin Sand Lighthouse, at the mouth of the River Thames. Mitchell, whose screw-piles system was adopted in the building of viaducts and bridges as far afield as India, was elected an associate of the Institute of Civil Engineers in 1837. He died in Belfast on 25 June 1868.

Richard Montgomery
Major general in the Continental Army during the American Revolutionary War 1738 – 1775

Born in Swords, County Dublin, Richard Montgomery was commissioned to the 17th Foot of the British Army in 1756, serving in both Canada and the Caribbean. In April 1772, he resigned his commission and moved to New York where he bought a farm, in the area that is now known as 'The Bronx'. Three years later Montgomery was elected to the New York Provincial Congress and was also commissioned a brigadier general in the Continental Army. In December 1775 he was appointed major general and led the Continental Army into Canada, where he captured the city of Montreal. He was later killed whilst attempting to capture the city of Quebec during a fierce snowstorm on 31 December 1775. He is buried at St Paul's Chapel, New York City and in all, some seventeen locations are named in his memory ranging from Montgomery in New Jersey, Missouri, Alabama and Minnesota as well as Montgomery County, Kentucky.

Thomas Moore
Poet 1779 – 1852

Poet Thomas Moore lived at 12 Aungier Street and was educated at Trinity College, where he became a friend of Robert Emmet (see page 165). He studied law at the Middle Temple in London, but his primary love was poetry and he published *Odes, Epistles and Other Poems* in 1806. The following year, Moore produced a book of Irish melodies which were published between 1807 and 1834, with the music for them arranged by Sir John Stevenson from traditional Irish tunes. His Irish melodies earned him considerable wealth and he was appointed national lyric poet of Ireland in 1812.

Dermot Morgan
Comedian and television star
1952 – 1998

A legendary comedian, Dermot Morgan was educated at Oatlands College in Stillorgan and at University College Dublin. For a time he worked as a school teacher at St Michael's College on Ailesbury Road in Dublin, but he first came to prominence on Irish television with Mike Murphy on RTÉ's variety show *The Live Mike*. It was the satirical *Scrap Saturday*, produced on radio in the 1980s, which was Morgan's first significant broadcasting success; however, his big break would finally come when he played the role of *Father Ted* in the Channel Four sitcom of the same name. The sometimes controversial but always humourous show had a cult following and won a BAFTA in 1998. Morgan, who also collected a BAFTA, sadly collapsed and died of a heart attack at the age of forty-five on 28 February 1998.

Maria Teresa Mulally
Teacher 1728 – 1803

Maria Teresa Mulally is long considered Ireland's 'Mother Teresa'. Residing in Pill Street (now called Chancery Street), she came from a reasonably prosperous family who fell on hard times. It was a donation made by her aunt in Chester, England, that enabled Mulally to open a milliner business in the parlour of her father's house in Dublin and from resources gained there, she established a school for poor children in Mary's Lane in 1766. With the law declaring that it was a criminal act for Catholics to be educated or to have schools of their own, Mulally had

181

to operate the school under 'covert' conditions, but in a very short period she was educating, clothing and feeding around one hundred girls. She later opened a boarding school for girls in George's Hill and with the assistance of two Presentation nuns, the school was a success. Mulally was the pioneer of free education, and she had the insight to combine learning with religious and technical education. She remained a spinster all her life and died in 1803 at the age of seventy-five.

William Thomas Mulvany
Entrepreneur 1806 – 1885

Businessman William Thomas Mulvany initially qualified as an architectural draughtsman before working for the Irish Surveying Office and the Board of Works, where he supervised the building of a canal to join the River Erne to the River Shannon. In 1854 Mulvany visited the Ruhr district of Germany and, realising that the steel factories of the region required large amounts of coal, he persuaded a group of rich business men to finance the purchase of deep mine machinery from Britain. Thus, the first large mine was appropriately called Hibernia. By 1864, Mulvany and his partners were employing one thousand workers and producing 316,000 tonnes of coal per annum and apart from establishing the German coal industry, he also established a steel works in Duisburg and built three important canals in northern Germany. Mulvany died in Düsseldorf on 30 October 1885. His is considered one of the most successful men in the history of Irish enterprise and he is remembered to this day with streets named after him in Düsseldorf and a number of other cities in the Ruhr district of Germany.

Thomas Murphy
Victoria Cross recipient 1839 – 1900

Thomas Murphy served as a private in the 2nd Battalion, 24th Regiment of Foot, British Army, during the Andaman Islands Expedition. On 7 May 1867, at the island of Little Andaman in the Bay of Bengal, Murphy was awarded the Victoria Cross for bravery at sea, whilst risking his life manning a boat in treacherous waters, in an attempt to save the lives of his stranded comrades. He later moved to the United States where he died in Philadelphia.

James Muspratt
Chemist and industrialist 1793 – 1886

At fourteen, James Muspratt became an apprentice to a wholesale druggist. Following the death of his father, he went to Spain in 1812, where he fought in the Peninsular War, later joining the British navy and taking part in the blockade of Brest, which he later deserted because of its harsh discipline. In 1814 Muspratt returned to Dublin and established a chemical works following the receipt of inheritance money. He later went to Liverpool, England where he established a sulphuric acid factory on the Vauxhall Road. The plant emitted such choking chlorine and sulphur fumes that the area was nicknamed 'Spice Island' and the premises were eventually closed. In response, Muspratt opened plants in Widnes and St Helens in England and founded the United Alkali companies, the biggest of its kind in the world. This paved the way for further mergers, which eventually led to the formation of ICI and in 1848, together with his son, Muspratt established the Liverpool College of Practical Chemistry. He died at Seaforth Hall, England in 1886.

James Sheridan Muspratt
Research chemist 1821 – 71

James Sheridan Muspratt was born in Dublin. The son of James Muspratt, he initially spent time in Philadelphia looking after the business interests of his father, before being sent to Germany to study under Justus von Liebig at the University of Giessen. In 1848, together with his father, Muspratt established the Liverpool College of Practical Chemistry in a disused stable at the back of his house in Canning Street, Liverpool. His most highly recognised publication was his two-volume work, *Chemistry, Theoretical, Practical and Analytical as applied and relating to the Arts and Manufacturers* (1857–1860) and he died at his home in West Derby, Liverpool in 1871.

Dermot Nally
Civil servant 1927 – 2009

Having obtained a science scholarship to University College Dublin, Dermot Nally's academic career was curtailed due to a hiking accident in which he almost lost one of his legs. Nally later graduated from the University of London and was initially employed by the Electricity Supply Board, before transferring to the civil service in 1947. Rising to become the most influential government secretary, he served under five Taoisigh, namely Liam Cosgrove, Jack Lynch (see page 100), Garret FitzGerald, Charles Haughey (see page 308) and Albert Reynolds. Nally, who was highly regarded by the British Establishment for both his mastery of language and his drafting skills, was an enthusiastic advocate of Irish membership of the European Union and as government secretary he led officials in the negotiations leading to the 1985 Anglo-Irish Agreement. Despite retiring in 1993, he remained in office to help draft the Downing Street Declaration and in 1998, was appointed president of the Institute of Public Administration. He died at St Vincent's hospital, Dublin on 30 December 2009.

John Nicholson
British general, East India Company 1822 – 1857

John Nicholson joined the British army circa 1839, eventually becoming an officer in the British East India Company. He is best known for his role in the Sepoy (Indian soldiers) mutiny and leading the storming of Delhi. Referred to as the 'Hero of Delhi', with a foul temper and authoritarian manner, Nicholson had a dislike of the Indians and gained respect from the Afghan tribes for his fairness in his dealings with them. He died at the age of thirty-five and is buried in Delhi.

Claude Joseph Patrick Nunney
Victoria Cross recipient 1892 – 1918

Dubliner Claude Joseph Patrick Nunney was a private in the 38th Battalion of the Canadian Expeditionary Force during World War I. On 1 September 1918, on the Drocourt-Quéant Line in France, his battalion came under intense enemy fire. Taking matters into his own hands, Nunney proceeded to go from post to post, encouraging his fellow soldiers by his fearless example. The enemy was eventually repulsed but not before Nunney was wounded in the process. He died sixteen days later at the age of twenty-five.

Seán O'Casey
Dramatist 1880 – 1964

Seán O'Casey was born at 85 Upper Dorset Street in Dublin – a tenement area in which many of his plays are set. He was a member of the Church of Ireland, an Irish nationalist, a fluent Irish speaker, a member of the Irish Republican Brotherhood and was also involved with the Irish Transport and General Workers Union. O'Casey produced his first play, *The Shadow of a Gunman* at the Abbey Theatre in 1923 and followed it with *Juno and the Paycock* (1924) and *The Plough and the Stars* (1926). He would produce many more plays, none of which had the same dramatic impact as the aforementioned trilogy. Frank O'Connor (see page 107), in *A Short History of Irish Literature, a Backward Look*, says that what unifies these plays, and sets them apart from O'Casey's later works, is 'the bitter recognition that while the men dream, drink, drivel, dress up and go play-acting, some woman, with as much brains and far more industry, sacrifices herself to keep the little spark of human life from going out altogether.' O'Casey died of a heart attack in Torquay, England, at the age of eighty-four.

Kevin Izod O'Doherty
Politician and Young Irelander
1823 – 1905

Kevin Izod O'Doherty studied medicine and joined the Young Irelanders prior to qualification. Following the 1848 rising he was arrested, charged with treason and sentenced to transportation for ten years to Tasmania, where he arrived in 1849. In 1854, O'Doherty was pardoned on the condition that he did not reside in either Great Britain or Ireland, however in 1856 he obtained a full pardon which enabled him to complete his studies in Dublin before graduating as a fellow of the Royal College of Surgeons. In 1862 he returned to Australia, this time to Brisbane, where he became one of the city's leading medical practitioners. O'Doherty also entered politics and was elected a member of the Legislative Assembly in 1867 and was influential in a health act being passed before retiring from politics eighteen years later, upon which time he returned to Ireland. There he became an Irish Parliamentary Party MP for Meath North but he remained for just a short period before again returning to Brisbane where he made an unsuccessful attempt to revive his medical practice. He died on 15 July 1905.

Nuala O'Faolain
Writer and newspaper columnist
1940 – 2008

The outspoken Nuala O'Faolain was educated at University College Dublin as well as the Universities of Hull and Oxford, following which she taught for a while at Morley College in England. Also a producer for the BBC and RTÉ, it was her book, *Are You Somebody?: The Accidental Memoir of a Dublin Woman*, written when she was sixty years of age, which chronicled her upbringing, her own struggle with alcohol and her long lesbian affair with well-known journalist Nell McCafferty. The book had an initial print run of 1,500 copies but went on to become an international bestseller and O'Faolain also wrote a follow-up memoir, *Almost There* (2003), as well as *My Dream of You* (2001), and the biography *The Story of Chicago May* (2005). A regular columnist with the *Irish Times*, it was during a radio interview that she revealed she was dying of cancer and shocked listeners by admitting that she did not believe in heaven or an after-life, adding 'there is nothing much wrong with me, except that I am dying.' She died on 12 May 2008.

Michael O'Hehir
Sports commentator
1920 – 1996
Known as 'the voice of the GAA', Michael O'Hehir exuded great passion and enthusiasm whilst describing Gaelic football and hurling matches. O'Hehir began his career on 14 August 1938, with the broadcast of the Galway vs. Monaghan All-Ireland Senior Football Championship semi-final, played in Mullingar, County Westmeath. Just eighteen years of age, he was an instant hit and thus began a distinguished career in sports commentary which also extended to the sport of horse racing.

Seán T. O'Kelly
Second president of Ireland
1882 – 1966
Seán Thomas O'Kelly was a founder member of the Sinn Féin political party and was a staff captain in the General Post Office during the Easter Rising of 1916. Elected to the first Dáil Éireann in 1918, he rejected the Anglo-Irish Treaty of 1921 and was a founder member of Fianna Fáil, serving in a number of ministerial posts throughout the 1930s. O'Kelly became president of Ireland in 1945 and held the office until 1959. He died on 23 November 1966.

Myles William Patrick O'Reilly
Papal officer and politician 1825 – 1880
Born near Balbriggan in County Dublin, William Patrick O'Reilly was educated in London, where he graduated with a bachelor's degree before going to Rome to study from 1845 until 1847. Returning to Ireland to help the poor during the Great Famine, in 1854 he became a captain of the Louth Rifles. In 1859 O'Reilly offered his services to Pope Pius IX against Garibaldi and was a founder of the Irish Brigade, being appointed major under General Pimodan. He fought in every campaign during that conflict until the final surrender at Spoleto, Italy on 18 September 1860; following that he returned to Ireland where he became a representative for County Longford in the British parliament from 1862 until 1876. In that role, O'Reilly ably supported Catholic interests and was a supporter of Isaac Butt (see page 127) and the home rule movement. He was also a contributor to the *Dublin Review* and other periodicals, writing extensively of the Holy See, and Catholic education. Appointed as assistant commissioner of intermediate education for Ireland in 1879, O'Reilly held that position until his death in 1880.

Patrick Pearse
Patriot and leader of the Easter Rising 1879 – 1916
Patrick Pearse was born at 27 Great Brunswick Street, Dublin (now Pearse Street) and was educated at the Christian Brothers School on Westland Row and at the Royal University of Ireland, following which he was called to the Irish bar. An educationalist with a deep love of the Irish language and its culture, Pearse founded a bilingual school called Scoil Éanna (St Enda's), in Ranelagh, and also became a member of the Irish Republican Brotherhood in 1913, following which he was elected to the Provisional Committee of the newly formed Irish Volunteers. Fiercely patriotic, at the burial of the Irish patriot, Jeremiah O'Donovan Rossa (see page 111) in 1915, he proclaimed that 'Ireland unfree shall never be at peace' and he was one of the signatories of the Proclamation of

the Republic as well as the commander-in-chief during the Easter Rising of 1916. Following that conflict, Pearse agreed to an unconditional surrender but was subsequently court-martialed, sentenced to death and executed in Kilmainham Jail on 3 May 1916.

James Plunkett
Writer 1920 – 2003

James Plunkett was from a working-class background, and drew on his experiences as inspiration for his writings. His best-known work is the novel *Strumpet City* which is set in Dublin in the years leading up to the labour lockout of 1913, and other works include, *Farewell Companions* (1977) and *The Circus Animals* (1990). Plunkett's short story collections include, *The Trusting and the Maimed* and *Collected Short Stories*. He died in Dublin on 28 May 2003.

Joseph Mary Plunkett
Nationalist, poet and journalist 1887 – 1916

A rather frail young man having suffered with tuberculosis, Joseph Mary Plunkett was a member of the Gaelic League and was a close confidant of Thomas MacDonagh (see page 372), joining the Irish Republican Brotherhood in 1915. Plunkett negotiated with Roger Casement (see page 159) and the German government for the shipment of arms to Ireland in order to aid the forthcoming uprising and his training in the officer corps, whilst at Stoneyhurst College, was highly beneficial in his role as a committee member responsible for the planning of the Easter Rising. Days prior to that conflict he undertook a medical procedure for his neck glands and still bandaged, took part in the rising, fighting in the General Post Office under the leadership of Patrick Pearse. Following the failure of the rising, Plunkett was held in Kilmainham Jail, where he was court-martialed and sentenced to execution by firing squad. Hours before his execution, at the age of twenty-eight, he married his sweetheart, Grace Gifford in the prison chapel. The railway station in Waterford City is named in his memory.

Daniel Pollen
Prime minister of New Zealand 1813 – 1896

Daniel Pollen was born in Ringsend and qualified in medicine before moving to New Zealand in the late 1830s. In 1844 he was appointed coroner for Parnell and later became a medical officer for the mining town of Kawau. Elected to the Provincial Council in 1856, Pollen represented Auckland suburbs and later Auckland East before being elected by Prime Minister Vogel to both the Legislative Council and to the Executive. Due to the delayed absence of Vogel on an overseas visit, Pollen served as prime minister of New Zealand in July 1875, but relinquished the premiership upon Vogel's return the following year.

He did however remain in the office of colonial secretary until October 1877 and continued as a member of the Legislative Council for the next nineteen years until he died on 18 May 1896.

James Power
Sculptor 1918 – 2009

James Power attended the National College of Art where he studied under Oliver Sheppard and the painter Sean Keating (see page 281). Working from his father's studio on Berkeley Road in Phibsborough, amongst Power's work is the 1916 Memorial on Sarsfield Bridge, Limerick, depicting the Fenian Thomas Clarke as a young man, armed with a pistol. Other works include a statue of Matt Talbot in Dublin, and former President Erskine Childers (see page 428). Power, who also sculpted the death mask of Brendan Behan (see page 154), was a regular exhibitor at the annual Royal Hibernian Academy and the Oireachtas art exhibitions. He died in the Mater hospital on Monday 13 April 2009.

Major General Hamilton Lyster Reed
Victoria Cross recipient
1869 – 1931

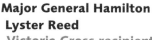

Hamilton Lyster Reed was a captain in the 7th Battery, Royal Field Artillery during the Boer War. At the battle of Colenso in South Africa on 15 December 1899, a significant number of gun carriages were put out of action due to horses being killed. In response, Reed took three teams of horses from his own battery and attempted to save the guns. He did this in the midst of continuous fire and was wounded – along with his horse, which died as a result. Following the incident, he was forced to retire from further action but for his act of bravery was awarded the Victoria Cross. Remaining in the army, Reed later became a major general and died in London in 1931.

Lieutenant Colonel Dr James Henry Reynolds
Victoria Cross recipient
1844 – 1932

Originally from Dun Laoghaire, James Henry Reynolds served as a surgeon major in the British Army during the Zulu War. He was awarded the honour of the Victoria Cross for tending to the wounded under continuous heavy fire. He was also commended for voluntarily carrying ammunition from the stores to the defenders of the hospital, exposing himself to enemy fire whilst doing so. He later achieved the rank of lieutenant colonel and died in Surrey, England in 1932.

Thomas Romney Robinson
Astronomer and physicist
1792 – 1882

Thomas Romney Robinson was educated at the Belfast Royal Academy and at Trinity College, Dublin, where he obtained a fellowship in 1814. In 1823 he was appointed astronomer of the Armagh Observatory where he made considerable contributions to contemporary astronomical research. He also invented the cup-anemometer, a wind measuring device comprising four cups, mounted symmetrically on a rotating vertical axis. Awarded a gold medal for his astronomical work by the Royal Society in 1862, Robinson died suddenly at the Armagh Observatory on 28 February 1882. The Robinson crater on the moon is named after him.

J. C. Kelly Rogers
RAF and airline pilot 1905 – 1981

J. C. Kelly Rogers, who was born in Dun Laoghaire, joined the Royal Air Force in 1927 where he piloted flying boats. In 1935 he joined Imperial Airways (now British Airways) and regularly captained flights on the Egypt-India-Australia routes. Three years later, Rogers made the first in-flight refuelling test, a process which he used in piloting the first British transatlantic airmail flight, and during World War II he was the pilot in charge of Winston Churchill's transatlantic journeys. Following the war he set up the first airline service between London and New York and he later joined Aer Lingus where he became deputy manager in 1952. Rogers, who was a freeman of the city of London and a fellow of the Royal Aeronautical Society, was also one of the founding members of the Irish Aeronautical Museum. He died in Dublin in 1981.

Major General Robert Montresor Rogers
Victoria Cross recipient 1834 – 1895

Robert Montresor Rogers was a twenty-five-year-old lieutenant in the 44th Regiment of Foot during the Second Opium War. On 21 August 1860, Rogers displayed great gallantry in swimming the ditches to gain entry at Taku Forts in China. Together with another lieutenant and a private, he was the first English troop to enter and secure the fort. He later achieved the rank of major general and died in Berkshire, England in 1895.

Stephen C. Rowan
Vice-admiral in the US Navy
1805 – 1890

Stephen Clegg Rowan emigrated with his family to the United States where he would become a midshipman in the US Navy. Rowan served as an executive officer on board the *Cyan* during the capture of Monterey in July 1846, as well as in the occupation of both San Diego and Los Angeles. He was promoted to captain during the Civil War for gallantry and commanded the New Ironsides on blockade duty off Charleston, South Carolina. Following that he assumed command of federal forces in the North Carolina sounds

and he was commissioned rear admiral on 25 July 1866, serving as commander of the Norfolk navy yard until 1867. He was appointed a vice-admiral in August 1870 and died in Washington DC on 31 March 1890.

William Howard Russell
News reporter and war correspondent 1820 – 1907

Originally setting out to study law, Tallaght born William Howard Russell diverted to journalism before joining the *Times* and it was there that he won international renown whilst reporting on the Crimean War. It was during his coverage of the Siege of Sebastopol that Russell coined the phrase, 'the thin red line', which was a reference to British troops holding out against the Russians, and his reports brought attention to the mismanagement of food and medical supplies, as well as the terrible suffering endured by the troops as evidenced by his reference to battlefield surgeons and their human barbarity. Russell's disclosures made him popular with the public, who could read about the reality of warfare for the first time, but they won him little favour with the officer classes.

In 1860 he founded the *Army and Navy Gazette* which he edited himself and he also reported on the American Civil War, and in particular, the First Battle of Bull Run, mentioning in particular, the bravery of the Irish Brigade, 'The Fighting 69th', in later years Russell gave accounts of the Franco-Prussian War as well as the Anglo-Zulu War in South Africa. For his daring work he was knighted in 1895 and he died in London on 11 February 1907. He is buried in Brompton Cemetery, London.

Cornelius Ryan
War correspondent and author
1920 – 1974

Cornelius Ryan became a war correspondent for the *Daily Telegraph* in 1941. Initially covering the air war in Europe, Ryan flew as a correspondent on fourteen bombing missions with the 8th and 9th US air force. Ryan later joined General George Patton's army, and covered his actions during the war in Europe. In 1947 he emigrated to the United States to work for *Time* magazine and in 1956 he began to write perhaps his best-known novel, *The Longest Day*, which he soon followed with *The Last Battle* (1965). *The Longest Day* (1959) tells the story of the D-Day invasion of Normandy and a later book, *A Bridge Too Far* (1974), tells of the ill-fated assault by airborne forces on the Netherlands, concluding at the Battle of Arnhem. Both of these books were made into major motion pictures in 1962 and in 1977 respectively. Ryan died in Connecticut on 23 November 1974.

Gerry Ryan
Broadcaster and TV personality 1956 – 2010

Gerry Ryan was born in Clontarf and educated at St Paul's College in Raheny, followed by Trinity College, Dublin, where he studied law and later qualified as a solicitor. Despite his legal background, Ryan seemed destined for the entertainment business; his mother, Maureen was a member of the well-known Burke family who owned Dublin's Olympia Theatre, whilst his uncle-in-law was Eamonn Andrews, the renowned BBC personality. Having initially become an apprentice solicitor with legal firm Malone and Potter, he got involved with pirate radio station Big D before getting his big break with Radio 2 in 1979, who paid him a weekly wage of £75. At first Ryan worked a night-time spot, but he later switched to his morning show where, with his outspoken and at times controversial opinions, he established a listening audience of over 500,000 people, whilst earning in the region of €550,000 per annum.

Together with his wife, Morah Brennan, he settled in Clontarf where the couple had five children. His death at the age of fifty three, due to a sudden heart attack, was reported around the world, with news of the great presenter's demise reaching countries as far afield as the United States, Australia and New Zealand. Indeed, such was the widespread appeal of this unique broadcasting figure, the *Washington Post* recounted Ryan's illustrious career in a lengthy piece. Having also led a distinguished television career, with shows such as *Secrets, Ryantown, The School Around the Corner, Gerry Ryan's Hitlist, Gerry Ryan Tonight, Operation Transformation* and the recent series *Ryan Confidential*, Ryan was finally laid to rest on 6 May 2010. Tributes were paid to him by President of Ireland Mary McAleese and Taoiseach Brian Cowen.

Dr Francis Rynd
Inventor of the hypodermic needle and syringe 1801 – 1861

It was when treating a woman with severe face pain at the Meath Hospital in Dublin that Francis Rynd decided to use a tube and needle to administer morphine under the skin near the facial nerves. The woman had been ingesting the drug orally to no avail and Rynd's successful use of this technique led to the invention of the hypodermic needle and syringe; hailed as the greatest boon to medical science since the discovery of chloroform.

General Sir Edward Sabine
Soldier and scientist 1788 – 1883

Born in Parnell Street but educated in Woolwich, Edward Sabine devoted his life to his favourite subjects of astronomy, terrestrial magnetism, and ornithology and was appointed astronomer to the Arctic Expeditions of Ross in 1818 and Parry from 1819 to 1822. In 1827 Sabine was given leave of absence from his military duties in order to engage in scientific work. He was instrumental in establishing magnetic observatories on British territories throughout the world and was promoted to General in 1870, retiring from the army in 1877. He died in Richmond on 16 June 1883.

Augustus Saint-Gaudens
Sculptor 1848 – 1907

Augustus Saint-Gaudens was born at 35 Charlemont Street and emigrated as a child to Boston before later moving to New York. Having served an apprenticeship in stone cameo cutting, Saint-Gaudens studied at the Cooper Union Institute and the National Academy of Design and later spent some time in France and Italy, where he studied classical art and architecture. Regarded today as one of the United States' finest sculptors, his rise to fame began in 1867 when he was commissioned to create the war memorial for the American Civil War, which was unveiled in Madison Square Park in New York, in 1881. Arguably, his greatest work is the Robert Gould Shaw Memorial (1897) on Boston Common, which depicts a scene from the Civil War and took fourteen years to complete. Saint-Gaudens' was an artist of prodigious talent and one of his last major commissions was the monument to Charles Stewart Parnell (see page 423) in Dublin. So intense was he in his sculpting of this statue that he built a scale model of the streets of Dublin bordering the site in O'Connell Street where the monument was to stand. He even obtained replicas of the clothes that a firm of Dublin tailors had made for Parnell. The monument arrived in Dublin in 1907 shortly after Saint-Gaudens death.

Patrick Sarsfield
Soldier and patriot
c.1650 – 1693

A member of a Catholic family that supported King James during the Williamite war in Ireland, Lucan-born Patrick Sarsfield was responsible for securing Connacht for the Jacobites and was later promoted to major general by the king. Sarsfield duly distinguished himself as an inspirational leader at the Battle of the Boyne as well as at the Siege of Limerick in 1690 and he successfully captured military stores and artillery at Ballyneety, County Limerick. As a result, the English forces were forced to raise the siege until 1691 and following a sustained attack, with the city refusing to surrender under Sarsfield, an agreement was reached. This agreement, the renowned 'Treaty of Limerick' allowed the Irish forces that defended the city to depart from Ireland and twelve thousand troops subsequently followed Sarsfield to join the Irish Brigade in the services of France. This is historically referred to in Irish history as the 'Flight of the Wild Geese'. Sarsfield was mortally wounded two years later at the Battle of Laden and upon seeing the blood from his wounds he is credited with poignantly proclaiming, 'Oh, that this were for Ireland.'

George Bernard Shaw
Dramatist, literary critic and socialist 1856 – 1950

The legendary George Bernard Shaw was born in Upper Synge Street and was educated at Wesley College, which was then located on St Stephen's Green. During his life he wrote more than sixty plays and was awarded the Nobel Prize in Literature in 1925. He later received an Oscar in 1938 for *Pygmalion*. Shaw was bitterly opposed to schools and teachers; he was a dedicated socialist and a founder member of the Fabian Society, which was set up to promote the gradual spread of socialism. He married Charlotte Payne-Townshend, an Irish heiress, in 1896 and together they moved to a house now called 'Shaw's Corner' in Ayot St Lawrence, a small village in Hertfordshire, England. He was a prodigious writer and most notable amongst his plays are *Fanny's First Play* (1911), and the aforementioned *Pygmalion* (1912), upon which *My Fair Lady* is based. His play, *St Joan* (1923) is generally considered to have been his best; it was an international success and is believed to have led to his Nobel Prize in Literature. In 1914 Shaw's popularity waned when he produced *Common Sense* about the War in relation to World War I, which he was strongly opposed to. His stance ran counter to public opinion and cost him dearly at the box office, but he never compromised on his views.

Additionally, his courageous stance for his native country after the rising in 1916 and his defense of Roger Casement (see page 159), set the public further against him. Upon Shaw's ninetieth year he was made an Honorary Freeman of Dublin City. He died on 2 November 1950 aged ninety-four. By the time of his death he had become a household name in Great Britain and known all over the world.

Richard Brinsley Sheridan
Dramatist 1751 – 1816

Richard Brinsley Sheridan was born at 12 Dorset Street, Dublin and was educated at Harrow School in England. His first play, *The Rivals*, which was produced at Covent Garden in 1775, became hugely popular and immediately established Sheridan's reputation as a quality playwright. This reputation was further enhanced by *The School for Scandal* (1777), which is considered one of the great comedies, as well as *The Critic* (1779) – another success.

Having gained a considerable fortune, Sheridan bought a share in the Theatre Royal on Drury Lane and he was also a Whig politician, entering parliament in 1780. He held the post of receiver general to the Duchy of Cornwall from 1804 to 1807 and treasurer of the navy from 1806 and 1807. His Drury Lane theatre, which was destroyed in a fire in 1809, was the cause of calamitous financial problems and when once asked by creditors to pay at least the interest on the money he owed, the distinguished playwright humorously replied, 'my dear fellow, it is not in my interest to pay the principle, or in my principle to pay the interest'. Sheridan died in poverty on 7 July 1816 and is buried in the Poet's Corner of Westminster Abbey, London.

Lieutenant Colonel Frederick Augustus Smith
Victoria Cross recipient 1826 – 1887

Frederick Augustus Smith served as a captain in the British Army during the Māori War in New Zealand. At Tauranga on 21 June 1864, Smith was severely wounded on an attack of an enemy trench. He had bravely entered the trench and engaged the enemy in hand-to-hand combat, becoming injured in the process. He died in County Meath.

Estella Solomons
Artist and republican 1882 – 1968

Estella Solomons was born into a wealthy Jewish family and in 1898 she entered the Metropolitan School of Art, following which she spent some time studying in Paris, France. Upon her return to Dublin, she set up a studio in Brunswick Street where she painted a variety of portraits of notable people from diverse walks of life including Austin Clarke (see page 159), Arthur Griffith (see page 170), Jack B. Yeats and Padraic Colum (see page 288). In 1917 Solomons joined Cumann na mBan (Women's League), and was involved in the distribution of arms and ammunition to Irish republicans.

She was also involved in the Prisoners Dependent's Fund, where she got family and friends (including the famous painter John Lavery) to donate paintings to raise money for the organisation. Following the Anglo-Irish Treaty, she took the anti-treaty side and as a consequence, became accustomed to having her studio raided by Free State troops searching for republicans. Solomons, who was bitterly disappointed that her hopes of a free and united Ireland had not been realised, fell in love with and married the poet Séamus O'Sullivan (James Starkey) but the relationship was opposed by her parents due to the fact that he was not of the Jewish faith. Solomons painted her last picture, *The Estuary* in 1962; she died in 1968.

William Henry Somers
Orchestra band leader and broadcaster 1890 – 1952

William Henry Somers was born in Dublin and gained his musical expertise at the Royal Irish Academy of Music, before joining the British army as a musician until 1919. Better known as 'Debroy Somers'

in his days as a bandleader, he was a multi-instrumentalist and was a well-built, handsome man. As a musical director, his expertise spanned the spectrum from small ensembles to symphonic-style concert orchestras and he was an innovative musical arranger as well as one of the earliest dance-band leaders. Somers broadcasted on the radio station 2LO, which was a pre-BBC radio station and he also recorded with Columbia Records throughout the 1920s and 1930s. In later years his expertise was in arranging themes from musicals, compressing a ninety-minute score into eight to ten minutes of playing time. His death in 1952 was a significant blow to the music world.

James Stephens
Poet and novelist 1880 – 1950

Not to be confused with the revolutionary of the same name, James Stephens was born in Dublin where he spent some time working as a solicitor's clerk. His storytelling style had a combination of humour and lyricism, based mainly on Irish fairy tales, and he wrote several books, one of which was *The Crock of Gold* and earned him enduring popularity. Stephens, who published his first volume of poems, *Insurrection* in 1909, was a founder member of the Irish Academy of Letters and later in life he became a broadcaster with the BBC, enthralling listeners with his poems and stories. He died on 26 December 1950.

Bram Stoker
Novelist 1847 – 1912

Born at 15 Marino Crescent in Fairview, Bram Stoker was christened Abraham, but was known simply as 'Bram'. Educated at Trinity College, he spent a number of years as a civil servant and also worked as secretary and touring manager of Henry Irving, of whom he wrote a personal reminiscence in 1906. Stoker authored a number of novels and short stories, but he is chiefly remembered for his work *Dracula*, which he wrote in 1897. A tale of vampirism in Romania, it is thought to have been inspired by Vlad The Impaler, a tyrant who lived in Romania and is believed to have feasted amid rows of impaled bodies. Some eleven editions of *Dracula* were produced during his lifetime alone. Stoker married the celebrated beauty, Florence Balcombe, who survived him by twenty-five years and had *Dracula's Guest and Other Weird Stories* published in 1922. He died in London on 20 April 1912, and his ashes, alongside those of his son, rest in Golder's Green Crematorium in London.

Lieutenant Commander Henry Stoker
British Navy commander
1885 – 1966

Although his family had no tradition in seafaring occupations, Henry Stoker requested that he be sent to a school in England, which specialised in preparing boys for entry to the Royal Naval College at Dartmouth. However, Stoker's time at the school was an unhappy one with the teachers and pupils mocking his Irish accent. Despite these early difficulties Stoker entered the naval college at the age of fifteen, following which he joined the Submarine Service and took his first command post in 1914. Setting sail for Australia on 2 March of that year, Stoker undertook an incredible voyage which lasted eighty-three days, sixty of which were spent at sea.

In December 1914, with a crew of English and Australian sailors, he set sail to the war in Europe and took up patrol at the entrance to the Dardanelles at the start of the Gallipoli campaign. It was there that he carried out one of the most daring and extraordinary ventures in World War I, when he brought his AE2 submarine through the thirty-five mile long Straits of the Dardanelles. To do so, Stoker had to sail at periscope depth in order to negotiate the narrow strait, which was littered with mines whose cables the crew could hear scraping the side of the vessel. He successfully navigated the treacherous waters on 25 April 1915, but then had to face an attack from Turkish cruisers and destroyers that attempted to ram him on a number of occasions when he came to periscope depth. On the morning of 26 April 1915, the AE2 entered the Sea of Marmara and Stoker successfully harassed Turkish supply ships. However, four days later the submarine, having surfaced, was attacked by a Turkish motor torpedo boat and was badly damaged. Stoker ordered the vessel to be scuttled and concentrated on saving the lives of his men. His actions gained him the Distinguished Service Order and had a tremendous psychological effect on the troops at Gallipoli when they learned of his achievements. Stoker and his crew were thus proclaimed heroes in both Britain and Australia.

Imprisoned by the Turks, he escaped twice but was to endure numerous hardships in Turkish prisons. Following the war, he took up a career on the stage, and appeared in numerous plays, films, and television dramas. He died on his eighty-first birthday in 1966.

William Stokes
Physician 1804 – 1878

In 1828 William Stokes published his first medical work, *The Application of the Stethoscope*, which was followed in 1837 by *The Diagnosis and Treatment of Diseases of the Chest*. With the latter publication establishing his fame throughout Europe, Stokes was elected a fellow of the College of

Physicians in Ireland in 1839 and also went on to receive honours from the Universities of Oxford and Edinburgh. Awarded the much-coveted Prussian Order of Merit by Emperor William of Germany, Stokes is regarded as one of Ireland's greatest physicians and for fifty years he established one of the finest medical practices ever seen in the country. Though his heyday coincided with a period of considerable religious prejudice in Ireland, Stokes completely disassociated himself with such pointed views. He died in Howth on 7 January 1878.

Jim Stynes
Australia Rules Footballer 1966 – 2012

The Rathfarnham born 'Australian Superstar', whose mode of transport was always distinguishable by his personalised licence plate 'EIRE 32', was a philanthropist, charity worker, and writer. In 1994 the people of Victoria, Australia named Jim Stynes 'Victorian of the Year', for work he had done in co-founding the Reach Foundation and in 2007, he was further honoured with the Medal of the Order of Australia. Educated at the De La Salle College in Churchtown, Dublin, he represented his county at minor level in the All Ireland football championship of 1984, before the offer of an Australian Rules football scholarship brought him down under in November of the same year. In 1987 Stynes made his senior debut for the Melbourne Demons, winning numerous major individual and team awards in the following years and making a total of 264 appearances in the AFL. Such was the esteem in which he was held as a sportsman and in his personal life by the people of Australia, on his death from cancer in 2012; he was awarded the unique honour of a state funeral, which was attended by some 16,000 people.

Darren Sutherland
Olympic bronze medal-winning boxer 1982 – 2009

Commencing his boxing career at St Saviour's club, Darren Sutherland, affectionately known as 'The Dazzler', was Irish Amateur Middleweight Champion for three years from 2006 and also became European Middleweight Champion before going to gain an Olympic Bronze Medal in the 2008 Olympic Games in Beijing. Having turned professional, Sutherland won his first four fights with ease and looked to have a very promising future until his untimely death at the age of twenty-seven. A genuine tragedy for Ireland and the wider world of boxing, Sutherland was viewed as a most accommodating and accessible young man with fixed and determined ideas. Having previously returned to school at the age of twenty to attain his Leaving Certificate of Education, so that he could enter university to train in sports management, he looked to have equipped himself well for life after boxing. On 14 September 2009, Sutherland was found dead by his manager Frank Maloney.

John Sweetman
Politician 1844 – 1936

John Sweetman was a member of the Sweetman family of brewers which was purchased by Guinness in 1891. He was educated at Downside College in Somerset, England and was a prominent Irish nationalist. Sweetman was one of the proposers of Charles Stewart Parnell (see page 423) as president of the Irish Land League and he was the representative of the East Wicklow constituency from

1892 to 1895. An advocate of home rule for Ireland but strongly opposed to armed insurrection, Sweetman was one of the founder members of Sinn Féin and became second president of the party in 1908. He died in Dublin in 1936.

Jonathan Swift
Clerical satirist 1667 – 1745

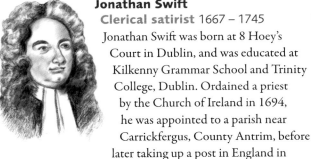

Jonathan Swift was born at 8 Hoey's Court in Dublin, and was educated at Kilkenny Grammar School and Trinity College, Dublin. Ordained a priest by the Church of Ireland in 1694, he was appointed to a parish near Carrickfergus, County Antrim, before later taking up a post in England in 1696, where he wrote *The Battle of the Books,* although it was not published until 1704. Swift received a Doctor of Divinity degree at Trinity College, Dublin in 1702 and was awarded the Deanery of St Patrick's, Dublin in 1713. His best-known book, *Gulliver's Travels* was published in 1726 and would immediately bring him worldwide fame. Seeing the wretched conditions in which the people of Ireland were living, Swift published his first pamphlet on Irish affairs in 1720 and it advocated the boycotting of English fabrics. His other works were *A Modest Proposal, A Journal to Stella, The Drapier's Letters*, and *A Tale of a Tub*. Although less well known for his poetry, Swift did produce a considerable body of poetic work and even wrote his own obituary, 'Verses on the Death of Dr Swift', which was published in 1739. He was buried in St Patrick's Cathedral, Dublin in 1745.

Edmund John Millington Synge
Playwright 1871 – 1909

Although a Protestant, John Millington Synge's writings mainly explored the world of the Roman Catholic peasants of rural Ireland and he spent a number of summer periods on the Aran Islands, off the coast of County Galway, later writing a book entitled *The Aran Islands*. Synge wrote two plays for the National Theatre, *In the Shadow of the Glen* and *Riders to the Sea* based on stories he had heard on the islands, and he was also a co-founder of the Abbey Theatre. His best-known play, *The Playboy of the Western World* (1907) caused riots on the streets of Dublin following its first showing at the Abbey because of its perceived slight on the virtues of Irish womanhood. Synge died in Dublin on 24 March 1909 and is buried at Mount Jerome in Harold's Cross.

James Napper Tandy
United Irishman 1740 – 1803

James Napper Tandy was born in Thomas Street, Dublin and entered politics in 1777, winning a seat on the Dublin corporation where he gained a reputation for his attacks on government and municipal corruption. In 1791, Tandy co-founded the United Irishmen with Theobald Wolfe Tone (see page 196) and Thomas Russell (see page 111), striving for total independence from Britain as the American colonies had previously achieved. However, upon the discovery of his membership in the United Irishmen.

Tandy was forced to flee to the United States but later moved to France where he was appointed a general and sent back to Ireland with a small force which landed at Rutland Island, off the coast of Donegal. When he heard that a larger French force which had earlier landed in Ireland had been defeated, Tandy sailed for Norway but was intercepted in Hamburg, Germany and handed over to the British who sentenced him to death. Napoleon Bonaparte demanded that he be unconditionally released and his wishes were met in 1802 but Tandy was to die in Bordeaux, France, the following year.

His name is held in Irish history in the ballad, 'The Wearing of the Green', wherein it says, 'I met with Napper Tandy and he shook me by the hand, and he said, how's poor old Ireland and how does she stand?' Although he had little success in his efforts to free Ireland, Napper Tandy gained a firm foothold in Irish history.

Richard Todd
Stage and film actor 1919 – 2009

The son of an army doctor who played rugby for Ireland and who also won the military cross for his services during World War I, Richard Todd spent his early years in India where his father was stationed. He eventually returned to England and attended the Royal Military Academy at Sandhurst to train as an army officer. However, upon discovering a love of the theatre, he discontinued his military progression and joined the Italia Conti Stage School, London, making his first professional appearance at Regent's Park open-air theatre in 1936.

At the outbreak of World War II, Todd was commissioned to the parachute regiment and took part in the D-Day landings before later returning to the theatre. He also made his first film appearance in *For Them That Trespass* (1948) and followed this with *The Hasty Heart* (1949), a war story also featuring future United States president Ronald Reagan. This film brought him an Oscar nomination but it was in 1955 that Todd realised his full potential, with his portrayal of Guy Gibson in the film *The Dam Busters*. He later appeared as Major John Howard in *The Longest Day* (1962) but with the decline of his acting career, became a dairy farmer in his latter years. In 1987 Todd published *Caught in the Act,* the first volume of his memoirs, and having suffered from cancer, died on 3 December 2009.

Theobald Wolfe Tone
United Irishman 1763 – 1798

Theobald Wolfe Tone studied at Trinity College, Dublin, where he qualified as a barrister at the age of twenty-six. In 1791 he was one of the co-founders of The Society of United Irishmen, the purpose of which was the unification of Roman Catholics and Protestants in the interest of securing parliamentary reform in Ireland. When it became obvious that this was unattainable by constitutional efforts, the members decided to establish an Irish Republic by armed rebellion.

After the arrest of United Irishmen in 1794, Tone was forced to flee to the United States, following which he went to Paris in 1796 to persuade the French government to send an expedition to invade Ireland. So impressed were the French by Tone's energy, sincerity and ability, they gave him a commission in the French army of adjutant general. He then accompanied a French expedition force to Ireland under General Hoche on 15 December 1796, but upon their arrival in Bantry Bay, County Cork, storms prevented them landing and the expedition had to return to France. A second expedition was also a failure but Tone would take part in a third, which landed at Lough Swilly, County Donegal on 12 October 1798. This landing was intercepted by a British squadron and Tone was arrested and brought to Dublin where he was tried and convicted. He requested that he be shot like a soldier but was denied and he was sentenced to be hanged on 12 November 1798. However, before the sentence could be carried out, Tone took his own life at the age of 35.

His most famous quotation is, 'to unite Protestant, Catholic and dissenter under the common name of Irishmen, in order to break the connection to England, the never failing source of all our political evils, that was my aim.'

Robert Tressell
House painter and writer
1871 – 1911

Robert Noonan saw service with Major John MacBride (see page 310) in the Irish Brigade that fought on the side of the Boers against the English in the Second Boer War. Eventually settling in Hastings, England, he worked as a painter and began using the pseudonym 'Tressell', under which he wrote *The Ragged Trousered Philanthropists*. This book remains hugely popular to this day and is often considered to have been more influential in converting British people to socialism than the writings of Karl Marx. It was also largely responsible for assisting the Labour government in winning the elections of 1945, due to it being distributed among members of the British Army during the war. It was not until 1974, with a book by Fred Ball entitled *One of the Damned* that Tressell's true identity was revealed. In 1911, Noonan decided to emigrate to Canada but died in Liverpool, England and was buried in a pauper's grave. It was his daughter Kathleen who had his book published and to this day he is held in reverence in the town of Hastings – though there is little knowledge of the fact that his real name was Noonan. A statue to his memory stands on the pier head in Liverpool.

Katharine Tynan
Novelist and poet 1861 – 1931

Katharine Tynan was born in Clondalkin and was educated at the Siena Convent School in Drogheda, County Louth. She was a prolific writer and authored many books of poetry. Her novels include *Oh what a plague is love!* (1896), *She Walks in Beauty* (1899), *John-A-Dreams* (1916), and *They Loved Greatly* (1923). She died in Wimbledon, England on the 2 April 1931.

Field Marshal Arthur Wellesley
The Duke of Wellington
1769 – 1852

Arthur Wellesley was born at 24 Upper Merrion Street, Dublin. He entered the army and received his first commission as an ensign in 1787 and, with the help of his brother Lord Mornington, received rapid promotion, becoming aid-de-camp to the lord lieutenant in Ireland from 1787 to 1793. Wellesley, who saw active service in Flanders from 1794 to 1795, gained a high military reputation in India where he spent eight years from 1797. He was knighted in 1804 and in 1809 he was appointed commander-in-chief whilst serving in Spain, where he defeated the French and occupied Toulouse. It was perhaps his defeat of Napolean at the Battle of Waterloo in June 1815 that gained him the most acclaim and following that battle he was heard to declare that the day's bloody and climatic battle was a 'damn near-run thing'. In 1819, Wellesley became the commander-in-chief of the British forces before going on to the office of prime minister in 1828. Together with Robert Peel, he was responsible in seeing through Catholic emancipation in Ireland. As a result, Wellesley went from being the most popular man in England, to the most hated as he was jeered in public, and mobs threw bricks through the windows of 10 Downing Street. However, his popularity was to eventually return. Although he was a fearless and indomitable fighter, Wellseley had a soft side. Upon learning that a godchild of his was being discriminated against by richer children at kindergarten, the Iron Duke (so-called because of the protective iron shutters he had to place on the windows of his house) decided to visit the school and present her with a bunch of flowers. It was an act of great kindness by a man who had many difficult problems of state to deal with. Wellseley died on the 14 September 1852.

Oscar Wilde
Playwright, novelist and poet
1854 – 1900

Oscar Wilde was born at 21 Westland Row, and was christened Oscar Fingal O'Flahertie Wills Wilde. Wilde's father William (see page 353), who later moved the family to 1 Merrion Square, was a leading eye and ear surgeon and a renowned philanthropist, while his mother, Jane (see page 165), was a successful writer and an Irish nationalist who was also known as 'Speranza'. Wilde was educated at Portora Royal School in Enniskillen, County Fermanagh and also studied classics at Trinity College, Dublin where he was awarded the Berkeley Gold Medal. He was subsequently granted a scholarship to Magdalen College, Oxford, where he studied from 1874 to 1878. Whilst there, he had a reputation for being a witty conversationalist, and graduated with first class honours in classics and humanities.

Although Wilde was married and had two sons, in 1891 Wilde developed an intimate relationship with Lord Alfred that his father, the Marquess of Queensberry, was strongly opposed to. Wilde was arrested for homosexual offences and was sentenced to two years hard labour in Reading jail for offences of 'gross indecency'. Wilde's literary career took off in 1888 when he published *The Happy Prince and Other Tales*, a collection of fairy stories, and his only novel *The Picture of Dorian Gray*, was published in 1891. His first comedy play, *Lady Windermere's Fan* (1892), was an instant hit and was followed by three more comedies, *A Woman of No Importance* (1893), *An Ideal Husband* (1895) and *The Importance of Being Ernest* (1895). In 1898 he published 'The Ballad of Reading Goal' based on his experience in prison and he died in Paris on 30 November 1900. Wilde's legacy lives on and many of his legendary quotes have provoked both humour and inward reflection in equal measure. Below are some examples.

'I am not young enough to know everything'.

'Nowadays all the married men live like bachelors and all the bachelors live like married men'.

'One should never trust a woman who tells one her real age. A woman who would tell one that, would tell one anything'.

'Women are meant to be loved, not to be understood'.

'People who count their chickens before they are hatched, act very wisely, because chickens run about so absurdly that it is impossible to count them accurately'.

'The world is a stage, but the play is badly cast'.

Field Marshal Garnet Joseph Wolseley
Soldier 1833 – 1913

Injured in Burma upon having joined the British Army, Garnet Joseph Wolseley also fought in the Crimea, losing his sight in one eye. It was Wolseley's experiences in the Crimean War that led him to believe that an army could be more effectively organised along much stricter and more professional lines, and during the American Civil War, he was sent to Canada where he spent nine years.

There, he was knighted for the defeat of Louis Riel, where he led his men to victory through one thousand miles of unmapped territory, in the process opening up the riches of the Canadian west. Wolseley published *A Soldier's Pocket Book*, the first manual ever devoted to a soldier's tasks in war, and this in turn lead to the eventual *Field Service Regulations Manual*. In Egypt he headed the expedition to relieve General Gordon at Khartoum and was also credited with the development of the Department of Military Intelligence. A remarkable man whose ideas laid the basis of modern army, Wolseley died in Menton, France on 26 March 1913.

William Butler Yeats
Poet and dramatist 1865 – 1939

The world famous William Butler Yeats was born in Sandymount but is strongly affiliated with County Sligo, the birthplace of his mother. Considered to be one of the foremost figures of twentieth-century literature, Yeats was one of the co-founders of the Abbey Theatre and acted as its principal playwright for many years. He was awarded the Nobel Prize in Literature and his work was described by the Nobel committee as giving 'expression to the spirit of the whole nation'. Appointed a senator in the newly established Irish Free State, in recognition of his services to Ireland, Yeats' earliest volume of verse was published in 1887 before his first volume of folk stories, *The Celtic Twilight* in 1893. He fell madly in love with Maud Gonne who was the subject of many of his love poems, but though the love was not reciprocated, it was under her influence that he joined the Irish Republican Brotherhood. Yeats died and was buried in France on 28 January 1939, his remains were later moved aboard an Irish naval service corvette to Drumcliffe, County Sligo, in 1948. His epitaph, taken from 'Under Ben Bulben', one of his final poems, reads 'Cast a cold eye on life, on death. Horseman, pass by'.

Fermanagh

General William Gamble
1818-1866

William Gamble was a cavalry division general in the union army at the Battle of Gettysburg during the American Civil War.

John Mullanphy
1758-1833

The St Louis Hospital (Mullanphy Hospital) in St Louis, Missouri, the first Catholic hospital in the US, was founded by John Mullanphy.

James Gamble
1803-1891

The Procter and Gamble headquarters, Cincinnati, Ohio was co-founded by James Gamble.

Hugh O'Brien
1827-1895

Boston's original city hall. Hugh O'Brien was the first Irish and Catholic mayor of Boston.

Basil McIvor
1928-2004

Lagan College, Belfast, the first integrated school in Northern Ireland. Basil McIvor was its first chairman and he advocated shared Protestant and Catholic education.

Alexander Armstrong
Naval surgeon and explorer
1818 – 1899

Originally from Crahan, Alexander Armstrong was educated at Trinity College, Dublin and at the University of Edinburgh, before joining the British Army in 1842. Under Sir Robert McClure, Armstrong took part in the Arctic Expedition from 1849 to 1854, which went in search of the Sir John Franklin's failed expedition. He also served in the Crimean War, eventually becoming director general of the medical department of the navy before being knighted and elected a fellow of the Royal Society. His journal, *Personal Narrative*, which was published in 1857, outlines the discovery of the Northwest Passage and won him the Gilbert Blane Gold Medal for the best journal kept by a naval surgeon on an expedition. He died on 4 July 1899 at Sutton Bonington in Leicestershire, England.

John Armstrong
American Revolutionary general 1717 – 1795

Having emigrated to the United States, John Armstrong worked as a surveyor for the Penn family who were the founders of the state of Pennsylvania. During the French and Indian War he served as a colonel in charge of militia troops stationed in Cumberland County and when the enemy attacked Fort Granville and captured prisoners, Armstrong led an expedition that destroyed their village and rescued the taken men, before later forcing the French to evacuate Fort Duquesne. A close friend of George Washington, upon the outbreak of the Revolutionary War he served as a brigadier general in the Pennsylvania militia and was later appointed to the same rank in the Continental Army. Having valiantly participated in the battles of Brandywine and Germantown, Armstrong was later elected to the Continental Congress and served from 1877 until 1878. Also a firm supporter of a new United States Constitution, Armstrong County, Pennsylvania is named in his honour. He died at his home in Carlisle, Pennsylvania on 9 March 1795.

Michael Barrett
The last man to be publicly hanged in England
1841 – 1868

Michael Barrett was born in Drumnagreshial and was a member of the Fenians. He was hanged for his supposed part in the Clerkenwell bombing, where in an attempt to enable Fenian prisoners to escape, a bomb was placed outside the wall of Coldbath Fields Prison in England. Some months previously, Barrett had been arrested in Glasgow, Scotland for illegally discharging a firearm and was subsequently arrested and implicated in the Clerkenwell prison explosion. Although he could prove that he was in Glasgow at the time of the event, the court did not accept his alibi and prior to sentence being passed, he delivered a most remarkable speech, eloquently asserting his innocence in which he stated, 'I have never willfully, maliciously, or intentionally injured a human being that I am aware of, not even in character.' Many MPs pressed for clemency and Barrett's mother also appealed to the unionist MP for Fermanagh, Captain Archdale, who was a staunch Orangeman and who predictably rejected her request.

Before a jeering crowd who sang 'Rule Britannia', Barrett was executed outside the walls of Newgate Prison on 26 May 1868. His death highlighted the severity with which the Irish were treated, and the liberal leader Gladstone later proclaimed that it was the Fenian action at Clerkenwell that turned his mind to Irish grievances, and that it was the duty of the British people to remove those grievances. Upon his election as prime minister of Great Britain that year, Gladstone stated, 'my mission is to pacify Ireland.'

Eric N. F. Bell
Victoria Cross recipient
1895 – 1916
At the age of twenty, Eric Norman Frankland Bell served as a temporary captain in the 9th Battalion of the Royal Irish Enniskillen Fusiliers during World War I. Awarded the Victoria Cross for his extreme bravery, having come under intense enemy fire on 1 July 1916 at Thiepval, France, Bell crept forward and shot an enemy machine gunner. On three additional occasions, again under intensive fire, he made solitary advancements using mortar bombs to unsettle the enemy. Upon the exhaustion of his mortar supplies, Bell proceeded to use his rifle to devastating effect and advanced continuously until he was finally killed.

Basil Brooke
First Viscount Brookeborough, Unionist politician 1888 – 1973
Basil Brooke was born on his family's estate at Colebrooke Park, Brookeborough and was educated in France, at Winchester College and at Sandhurst, England. During World War I, as an officer in the 10th Hussars, he was awarded the Military Cross and the Croix de Guerre and following the war, he was elected to the Northern Ireland Senate. Resigning from that position to become commandant of the Ulster Special Constabulary, in 1929 Brooke was elected Ulster Unionist Party MP for the Lisnaskea division of County Fermanagh and in 1933, he was appointed minister for agriculture in the Northern

Ireland parliament. Addressing the Orange Institute on 12 July of that year he said, 'many in this audience employ Catholics, but I have not one about my place. Catholics are just out to destroy Ulster, and if we in Ulster allow Roman Catholics to work on our farms, we are traitors to Ulster. I would appeal to loyalists therefore, wherever possible, to employ good Protestant lads and lasses.' Appointed minister for commerce in 1941 before becoming prime minister of Northern Ireland two years later, in 1952 Brooke was raised to the House of Lords as Viscount Brookeborough and was knighted in 1965. Due to ill health he resigned as prime minister in 1963 and he publicly opposed the liberal policies of his successor, Terence O'Neill, who sought better relationships with the Republic of Ireland. Brooke, who also opposed any grant of civil rights that were demanded by the Northern Ireland Civil Rights Association, served the unionist cause as he thought best and died at his home in Colebrooke on 18 August 1973.

Denis Parsons Burkitt
Surgeon 1911 – 1993
Enniskillen native Denis Parsons Burkitt was educated at Portora Royal School and in 1938, qualified in medicine from the Edinburgh Royal College of Surgeons. During World War I he served with the Royal Army Medical Corps in Africa and following that conflict he moved to Uganda where he settled in Kampala until 1964. It was there that Burkitt noticed children with swellings in the angles of the jaw, which resulted in the discovery of a cancer that had not previously been recognised. This became known as 'Burkitt's Lymphona'. In 1979 he published a book, *Don't Forget Fibre in your Diet*, which was an international bestseller and is as relevant today as it ever was. He died on 23 March 1993 in Gloucester, England.

Arthur Nicholas Whistler Colahan
Medical practitioner 1884 – 1952

Physician Arthur Nicholas Colahan was educated at University College Dublin and University College Galway, where he gained arts and medicine degrees respectively. His medical career commenced in the infirmary in Galway and when World War I broke out he enlisted in the British army Medical Corps. After the war he settled in Leicester, England, where he worked as a neurological specialist in the police and prison services. Colahan wrote the song, 'Galway Bay' in memory of one of his brothers who drowned in the bay and it was subsequently made world-famous by the singer Bing Crosby – it was the best selling song of 1953. The song also was featured in the Academy Award winning film, *The Quiet Man*, which starred John Wayne, Maureen O'Hara, Victor McLaglen and Barry Fitzgerald (see page 166). Colahan died in Leicester on 15 September 1952.

James Gamble
Co-founder of Procter and Gamble
1803 – 1891

In 1819 James Gamble emigrated with his family to the United States, eventually settling in Cincinnati, Ohio where Gamble became an apprentice to a soap maker. Following his apprenticeship he opened his own soap manufacturing business and met William Procter due to the fact that they were brothers-in-law. Procter had a candle-making business and in 1837 the two men decided to pool their resources and form the world renowned Procter and Gamble company. The logo for the company, 'the moon and stars symbol', represents the original thirteen American colonies and has been synonymous with the company ever since.

William Gamble
Union cavalry general in the American Civil War 1818 – 1866

Lisnarrick born William Gamble qualified as a civil engineer before emigrating to the United States in 1838. There he utilised his qualifications in working for the Board of Public Works in Chicago, but upon the outbreak of civil war, served as a lieutenant colonel of the 8th Illinois Cavalry Regiment. He fought in the Peninsula Campaign where he sustained a serious wound to his chest whilst leading a cavalry charge. Following his recovery, on 5 December 1862, Gamble was promoted to colonel and in the spring of the following year he was appointed to command the 1st Brigade of Alfred Pleasonton's Cavalry Division in the Army of the Potomac. It was whilst riding at the head of his brigade, on 30 June 1863, that Gamble and his men spotted elements of the Confederate Army of Northern Virginia and so began the world-famous Battle of Gettysburg. Gamble received a Brevet promotion to brigadier general on 12 December 1864, and full promotion nine months later. He died of cholera in 1866, while en route to California.

William Gorman
Economist and academic
1923 – 2003

Though born in the fishing village of Kesh, William Gorman spent his childhood in Rhodesia (now Zimbabwe) before returning to Ireland following the death of his father. In 1948 he graduated with an economics degree from Trinity College, Dublin and followed this with a mathematics degree the next year. Gorman spent his career in the economics department of some of England's leading universities including Birmingham in the 1950s, Oxford in the 1960s and the London School of Economics in the 1970s. He was elected president of the Economics Society in 1972. Predominantly a theorist, he is recognised for his work on aggregation and the separability of goods and in this context, he developed his famous 'Gorman polar form'. His work has often been considered highly technical and theoretical in nature and deemed at times to be incomprehensible to many of his contemporaries. Gorman was undoubtedly the greatest Irish economist of his generation and amongst his many honours were an honorary fellowship of Trinity College and an honorary doctorate from the National University of Ireland. He died in Oxford on 13 January 2003.

Henry Hartigan
Victoria Cross recipient 1826 – 1886
Henry Hartigan served as a sergeant in the 9th Lancers of the British Army during the Indian Mutiny. On 8 June 1857, during action near Delhi, he went to the rescue of a fellow sergeant who had been wounded and, at great risk to his own life, Hartigan drove off the enemy and carried the casualty back to safety. He was himself injured during the action but would later achieve the rank of lieutenant before dying in Calcutta in 1886.

William Irvine
Physician and brigadier general in the Continental Army 1741 – 1804
Having pursued a degree in classical studies at Trinity College, Dublin, William Irvine later studied medicine before serving as a surgeon on a British Man-of-War. In 1763 Irvine emigrated to the United States where he settled in Carlisle, Pennsylvania, becoming a colonel in the 6th Pennsylvania Regiment in the revolutionary army during the War of Independence. Captured in Canada on 16 June 1776, he remained a prisoner of war for two years. After his release, Irvine was appointed a brigadier general on 12 May 1779, serving until the end of the war. He was also a member of the Continental Congress and undertook two terms; one from 1777 to 1788 and another as an anti-Administration candidate in the 3rd Congress, from 1793 until 1795. He later moved to Philadelphia where he was a superintendant of military stores from 1801 until 1804. He died in Philadelphia on 29 July 1804.

Bobby Kerr
Sprinter 1882 – 1963
Enniskillen's Bobby Kerr emigrated to Canada with his family at the age of five. There he was educated in the Hamilton, Ontario School system and later worked as a fireman. During his spare time he enjoyed taking part in local athletics, becoming the Ontario sprint champion in 1903. The following year Kerr travelled to St Louis, Missouri at his own expense to take part in the 1904 Olympics where he was eliminated in the heats of the 60, 100 and 200 metres sprints. In 1907 he took the Canadian 100 yards title in a time of 9.4 seconds and the 220 yards title in 1908.

It was in 1908 that he travelled to England to take part in the British championships, capturing the 100 and 200 yards titles, and that same year he brought fame to Canada by winning bronze in the 100 metres and gold in the 200 metres at the Olympics in London. His best recorded times were 10.9 seconds and 22.6 seconds for the 100 metres and 200 metres respectively. In 1909, Kerr became Irish champion in both sprint events and upon his retirement he remained involved in both athletics and football. The first person to win Olympic gold for Canada, he died aged eighty-one in Hamilton.

Michael Magner
Victoria Cross recipient 1840 – 1897

Michael Magner was a drummer in the 33rd Regiment of Foot, British Army during the Abyssinia Expedition. In an attack in Magdala, Abyssinia (now Ethiopia) on 13 April 1868, Magner, in the company of some officers and men of the 33rd Regiment, successfully climbed a cliff and forced his way over a wall to defeat the defenders. He was one of the first men to enter Magdala and was awarded the Victoria Cross for the success of the venture. He died in Melbourne, Australia in 1897.

James McGuire
Victoria Cross recipient 1827 – 1862

Enniskillen born James McGuire served as a sergeant in the First Bengal Fusiliers of the Indian Army, during the Indian Rebellion of 1857. Whilst attempting to store ammunition in a small magazine at Delhi on 14 September 1857, three of the boxes were hit by enemy fire and exploded. Recognising the danger, McGuire immediately seized two of the boxes, which were alight, and threw them over the ramparts and into a canal, thereby saving the lives of many of his comrades. For this he was awarded the Victoria Cross.

Basil McIvor
Politician 1928 – 2004

Basil McIvor was born in Tullyhommon, Pettigo and was educated at Queen's University, before being called to the bar in 1950. A unionist MP for Larkfield in the Northern Ireland parliament at Stormont, he is principally renowned for pushing the need for shared schools for Protestant and Catholic pupils in

Monea Castle, County Fermanagh.

order to rid the troubled province of sectarianism. McIvor was the first chairman of Lagan College, the first integrated school in Northern Ireland and to date, there exists some sixty schools that promote integration. McIvor died on 5 November 2004.

Terence Bellew McManus
Revolutionary 1811 – 1860

Terence Bellew MacManus became a successful shipping agent in Liverpool, England during the early 1840s. He later returned to Ireland, joining the Young Ireland Movement, and was involved with Smith O'Brien (see page 80) and John Blake Dillon (see page 306) at the Young Irelander Rebellion of 1848 in Ballingarry, County Tipperary. MacManus escaped following the failure of that rising but was arrested in Cork Harbour while on board a vessel bound for the United States. Sentenced to death for high treason, the penalty was commuted to transportation for life to Van Diemen's Land (now Tasmania), Australia in 1849. Three years later, MacManus, along with Thomas Francis Meagher (see page 393), successfully escaped from Tasmania and settled in San Francisco, California. There he established a business but was unsuccessful and subsequently ended up in poverty before dying in 1860. MacManus' body was returned to Ireland in 1861 and it is estimated that over 100,000 people followed his cortège to Glasnevin Cemetery.

John Mullanphy
Merchant and philanthropist
1758 – 1833

At the age of twenty, John Mullanphy travelled to France to serve in the Irish Brigade, returning following the French Revolution. In 1792 he emigrated to Philadelphia, Pennsylvania with his family but later settled in Baltimore, Maryland until 1799. He left there in 1804 and settled in St Louis, Missouri, where he invested extensively in real estate. He later returned to Baltimore and took part in the defence of that city against the English during the Revolutionary War. Following the war, Mullanphy entered the cotton industry and amassed a great fortune before establishing the St Louis Convent of the Religious of the Sacred Heart in 1827. He later gave a hospital to the Sisters of Charity and upon his death, left twenty-five thousand dollars in his will for the education of the poor.

George Edward Nurse
Victoria Cross recipient
1873 – 1945

George Edward Nurse served as a corporal in the Royal Field Artillery, British Army, during the Boer War. On 15 December 1899, at the Battle of Colenso in South Africa, Nurse, together with three officers, saved the guns of the 66th Battery, Royal Field Artillery. In open ground and under intense fire, the men successfully hooked a team of horses to the guns and lined them up for firing. Nurse himself repeated the exercise with another set of guns and for this he was awarded the Victoria Cross. He later achieved the rank of second lieutenant and died in Liverpool in 1945.

Hugh O'Brien
First Irish born mayor of Boston
1827 – 1895

Hugh O'Brien left Ireland with his family at an early age and settled in Boston where, at the age of twelve, he became an apprentice printer before working as a foreman in his teenage years. He started his own publication,

The Shipping and Commercial List, the success of which led to him becoming a member of the Boston Business Elite. On 10 December 1884, he swept fifteen of Boston's twenty-five wards to become the first Irish born mayor of Boston. In securing the office, O'Brien had to overcome the long domination of Boston politics by the native-born Protestants known as 'Yankees', whose opinion of the Irish Catholic population was one of scorn. This ill-feeling turned into apprehension upon O'Brien's election, with many fearing a vengeful backlash. But with his work ethic and articulate, respectable demeanour, O'Brien defied the Yankee stereotypes of Irishmen, even taking steps towards integration by enlisting Yankee and republican businessmen to serve on various committees and projects. In all, O'Brien served three terms as mayor, during which he cut taxes, widened streets, built the new Boston Public Library in Copley Square and planned the Emerald Necklace Park system. The political foundations layed by O'Brien led to the domination of Boston politics by the Irish, virtually to this day.

Michael Sleavon
Victoria Cross recipient
1826 – 1902

Michael Sleavon was born in Magheraculmoney and was a corporal in the Corps of Royal Engineers during the Indian Mutiny. On 3 April 1858 at Jhansi, India, Sleavon held his position at a strategic point of the Jhansi Fort, for which he was awarded the honour of the Victoria Cross. He died in Sligo in 1902.

Joan Trimble
Composer 1915 – 2000

Educated at the Enniskillen Royal School for Girls before winning a scholarship to Trinity College Dublin, Joan Trimble graduated with a BA in music in 1936. She later attended the Royal College of Music in London, where she studied piano with Arthur Benjamin. She also toured with Count John McCormack (see page 404), playing piano solos and gained recognition as a composer in 1938 with her publication of songs and two-piano music. Two years later she won the Cobbett Prize at the Royal College of Music for her Sonatina and her Phantasy Trio. In 1957, Trimble produced the opera *Blind Rafferty*, commissioned by BBC television. Often appearing with her sister Valerie, who was also an accomplished musician, Joan died in 2000.

Galway

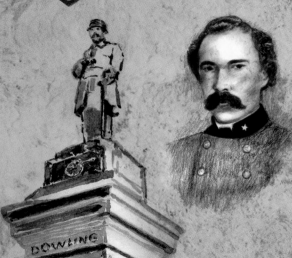

Richard 'Dick' Dowling
1838-1867

The hero of Sabine Pass, commanding a forty-four man confederate army unit, Tuam born Dowling also prevented a five-thousand-strong union navy flotilla from invading Texas. His statue stands in Herman Park, Houston, Texas.

Richard Martin
1754-1834

Known as 'Humanity Dick', Martin was co-founder of the RSPCA.

John K. Mullen
1838-1929

A businessman and philanthropist, Ballinasloe born Mullen donated $500,000 towards the John K. Mullen Memorial Library at the Catholic University of America in Denver, Colorado.

William MacNeven
1763-1841

The New York City Hospital (circa 1808) was where Irish doctor and patriot William MacNeven practised. He is considered the father of American chemistry.

Éamonn Ceannt
1881-1916

Kilmainham Jail, Dublin, where Irish patriot Éamonn Ceannt was executed on 8 May, 1916.

Aedanus Burke
Judge and US representative for South Carolina 1743 – 1802

Initially training for the priesthood in St Omer, France, Aedanus Burke emigrated to the United States and settled in Charleston, South Carolina where he became a lawyer. Named associate judge on the State Court in March 1778, Burke was a member of the South Carolina House of Representatives from 1779 until 1788, and served in the Revolutionary Army from 1780 until 1782, resuming his judicial duties thereafter. He was elected an anti-administration candidate to the First Congress from 1789 until 1791 and was appointed chancellor of the Court of Equity in 1799 where he served until his death in Charleston, on 3 March 1802.

Robert O'Hara Burke
Explorer 1820 – 1861

Robert O'Hara Burke was educated at the Royal Military Academy in England. In 1853 he emigrated to South Eastern Australia, where he became superintendent of police in the colony of Victoria. He was later appointed by the Victorian government to explore a proposed overland telegraph route from the city of Melbourne to the Gulf of Carpentaria. The journey commenced in Melbourne in August 1860 and though Burke's expedition reached their desired destination, their return journey the following year was a nightmare of constant rain and dwindling rations. Burke died en route at the end of June, 1861 with only one member of the expedition surviving.

Thomas Burke
Member of Congress and Governor of North Carolina c. 1747 – 1783

In his early teens, Thomas Burke emigrated to the United States where he settled in Virginia in 1759. Having studied law he was admitted to the bar and commenced practice in Norfolk, Virginia before moving on to Hillsborough, North Carolina in 1771. There his political career flourished and he quickly rose to become a member of Congress, before being appointed governor of his adopted state. Burke rallied opposition to the British invasion of 1781 but he was subsequently arrested for his anti-British activities and was imprisoned in South Carolina. Managing to escape, he resumed his duties as governor of North Carolina in February 1782. He died near Hillsborough, North Carolina on 2 December 1783.

Éamonn Ceannt
Irish nationalist 1881 – 1916

Born in the village of Ballymoe on the Galway and Roscommon border, Éamonn Ceannt was the son of a member of the Royal Irish Constabulary. When his family moved to Dublin in 1892, he became interested in the Irish Ireland movement – a literary association that sought Irish Independence by its writing, and in 1913 he joined the Irish Republican Brotherhood. He was also a founder member of the Irish Volunteers as well as one of the signatories of the Proclamation of the Republic. Ceannt took part in the Easter Rising as commandant of the 4th Battalion of the Volunteers at the South Dublin Union and his unit saw intense fighting before being forced to surrender on the orders of rising leader Patrick Pearse (see page 185). For his participation, Ceannt was held in Kilmainham Jail before being executed by firing squad on 8 May 1916 at the age of thirty-four.

John Joseph Clancy
Nationalist parliamentarian
1847 – 1928

John Joseph Clancy was born in Annaghdown and was educated at the College of the Immaculate Conception in Athlone and later at Queen's College, Galway. From 1885 until 1918, Clancy was the nationalist member of parliament for North County Dublin and was one of the leaders of the Irish home rule movement. He was an ardent promoter of the Housing for the Working Classes (Ireland) Act of 1908, known as the Clancy Act. He died in Dublin on 25 November 1928.

Cornelius Coughlan
Victoria Cross recipient
1828 – 1915

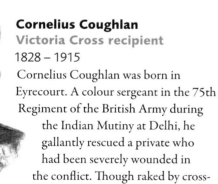

Cornelius Coughlan was born in Eyrecourt. A colour sergeant in the 75th Regiment of the British Army during the Indian Mutiny at Delhi, he gallantly rescued a private who had been severely wounded in the conflict. Though raked by cross-fire, Coughlan led his men against a large contingent of the enemy, killing every one of them, and he later went on to serve in the Connaught Rangers in Ireland, achieving the rank of sergeant major. Coughlan died in Westport, County Mayo in 1915.

John Wilson Croker
British statesman and author
1780 – 1857

Harbouring a great interest in the French Revolution, John Wilson Croker collected a large number of valuable documents that are now housed in the British Museum and in 1804, he wrote a caustic criticism in verse on the management of the Dublin Theatre called 'Familiar Epistles to J. F. Jones, Esquire, on the State of the Irish Stage', which ran to five editions in one year. Croker, who also penned a satire on Dublin society, quickly realised that to achieve a successful political career, he would need to be more English than the English themselves and he thus became a member of parliament from 1807 until 1832 and secretary of the Admiralty from 1810 until 1830. His finest work was his edition of *Boswell's Life of Johnston* (1831) and he died on 10 August 1857 in Hampton, England.

Sir Dominick Daly
Australian governor 1798 – 1868

Dominick Daly was born in Ardfry and was educated in Birmingham, England. Arriving in Canada in 1823, he became secretary to lieutenant governor Sir Francis Nathaniel Burton and in 1827, he was appointed provincial secretary of Lower Canada. Daly was provincial secretary for both Canada East and Canada West in 1844 before returning to England in 1849. In 1852 he was appointed lieutenant governor of Tobago. Continuing his far-flung travels, he was appointed governor of South Australia in 1861 and the town of Daly Waters as well as the Daly River are named after him. He died on 19 February 1868.

Eilís Dillon
Writer 1920 – 1994

Educated at the Ursuline Convent in Sligo, Eilís Dillon was married in 1940 and had three children. Although she was responsible for the running of a busy student hostel for University College Cork, Dillon developed her passion for writing into a highly successful professional career. Initially concentrating on children's books, both in Irish and English, Dillon later began writing novels and detective stories, all of which won her great critical acclaim and a wide readership. Her historical novel about the road to Irish independence, called *Across the Bitter Sea*, was published in 1973 and she later won the Bisto Book of the Year award in 1991 with *The Island of Ghosts*. She died on 19 July 1994 and is buried in Clara, County Offaly.

John Divane
Victoria Cross recipient 1822 – 1888

John Divane was born in Canavane, County Galway and served as a private in the First Batallion, 60th Rifles, in the British Army during the Indian Mutiny. Leading Beeloochee and Sikh troops on foot, Divane led a charge on enemy trenches during which he was shot and seriously wounded. For this action, he was awarded the Victoria Cross and died in Penzance, Cornwall on 1 December 1888.

John Doogan
Victoria Cross recipient 1853 – 1940

John Doogan was born in Aughrim and served as a private in the 1st Dragoon Guards of the British Army during the First Boer War. In a charge of mounted men on 28 January 1881 at Laing's Nek, South Africa, Doogan saw an officer whose horse had been shot. Dismounting, he placed himself in harm's way and although he himself was severely wounded, pressed the officer to take his horse. In his effort to return to his own lines, Doogan was wounded yet again and for this deed he was awarded the Victoria Cross.

Richard William 'Dick' Dowling
Confederate officer and businessman 1838 – 1867

Tuam born Richard William Dowling emigrated with his family to the United States in 1846. Eventually settling in Houston, Texas, he established a chain of saloons, one of which was named 'The Bank of the Bacchus' or just 'The Bank', as it became known. Dowling organised Houston's first city gaslight company and was the first to have it installed in his home and in his public house. At the outbreak of the American Civil War he joined a Texas unit known as 'The Jefferson Davis Guards' and he participated in the Battle of Galveston in 1863. With the rank of lieutenant, together with forty-four men, Dowling was assigned to an artillery post on the Sabine River where he carried out intensive training of his men in artillery targeting, which involved the placing of coloured poles in the river to mark both distance and elevation for the artillery crews. On 8 September 1863, his ingenuity led to the successful halting of a navy flotilla of five thousand Union soldiers who were attempting to invade Texas, and he subsequently won the status of 'Hero of Houston'. A statue to his memory stands in Hermann Park (next to that of Sam Houston) and Dowling Street, Houston is also named in his memory.

Patrick Durack
Australian cattle rancher
1834 – 1893

Following the famine, Patrick Durack emigrated with his parents and siblings to Australia where his father died in an accident soon after the family's arrival in New South Wales. Durack set out to make his fortune on the Ovens river goldfields and together with his brother Michael, he established property in the Kimberley district of Western Australia, amassing some seventeen thousand square miles of land – roughly the size of Belgium. In 1882 he commenced the greatest cattle drive in Australian history, moving in the region of seven thousand cattle and two thousand horses over a distance of three thousand miles. It was an endeavour that took nearly two years and made Durack Australia's richest rancher. He later became involved in mining in the Kimberley goldfields. Durack died on 20 January 1893 in Fremantle, Western Australia.

Patrick Sarsfield Gilmore
Bandmaster and composer 1829 – 1892

Patrick Sarsfield Gilmore was born in Ballygar and settled in Boston, Massachusetts in 1848. As leader of the 'Salem Band' he performed at the inauguration of President James Buchanan in 1857, before founding 'Gilmore's Band' the following year. This band enlisted in the 24th Massachusetts Volunteers and accompanied General Burnside to South Carolina. Appointed bandmaster general by Burnside, in 1872 at the World Peace Jubilee in Boston, Gilmore conducted a concert with an orchestra of two thousand, and a chorus of twenty thousand. He later toured the United States, Canada and parts of Europe with the National Guard Orchestra of New York. Gilmore was also the composer of the civil war song, 'When Johnny Comes Marching Home', having been heavily influenced by the Irish song of the same melody, 'Johnny I Hardly Knew Ye'.

Patrick Glynn
Attorney general of Australia and minister for external affairs
1855 – 1931

Patrick Glynn was born in the south Galway town of Gort and in 1880, emigrated to Australia where he was admitted to the Victorian bar. Later moving to Adelaide where he established his own law firm, Glynn was elected to the South Australian House of Assembly in 1887 and subsequently helped found the South Australian Land Nationalisation Society. A supporter of female suffrage, he served in many positions in the Australian government including attorney general, minister for external affairs and minister for home and territories. Glynn retired from politics in 1919 and died in North Adelaide in 1931.

Thomas Grady
Victoria Cross recipient
1835 – 1891

Thomas Grady was born in Claddagh and served as private in the 4th Regiment of Foot, British Army, in the Crimean War. On 18 October 1854 at Sebastopol, Grady volunteered to repair a sailor's battery under heavy fire and he successfully achieved that feat. Later, on 24 November, he refused to leave his post despite being severely wounded and his example served as inspiration for others to remain and repel considerable enemy onslaught. Grady was awarded the Victoria Cross for his bravery.

Patrick Green
Victoria Cross recipient 1824 – 1889

Patrick Green was born in Ballinasloe and served as a private in the 75th Regiment of Foot during the Indian Mutiny. On 11 September 1857 at Delhi, Green successfully rescued a fellow comrade who had fallen and brought him back to his lines under heavy fire. Wounded himself at the time, Green was awarded the Victoria Cross for his valiance. He later became a colour sergeant and died in Cork in 1889.

Isabella Augusta, Lady Gregory
Dramatist and folklorist 1852 – 1932

Isabella Augusta Persse was born in Roxborough and was educated privately. It was her friendship with William Butler Yeats, formed after their meeting in London in 1898, that led to her interest in collecting Irish folklore and their association led to the formation of the Irish Literary Theatre and the Abbey Theatre. Gregory produced a number of books on Irish mythology as well as short plays for the theatre. Although born into a class closely associated to British rule in Ireland, she became closely associated with Irish nationalism and was a fluent Irish speaker. Her home at Coole Park, served as a meeting place for those interested in the Irish literary revival and led to figures such as Yeats, John Millington Synge (see page 195) and others being frequent visitors. The best known of Gregory's plays were *Spreading the News* (1904), *The Rising of the Moon* (1907) and *The Workhouse Ward* (1908). She died at Coole on 22 May 1932.

James Thomas 'Frank' Harris
Author and adventurer
1856 – 1931

As a young man, James Thomas Harris won a scholarship to the University of Cambridge. However, instead of availing of the opportunity, he took the prize money and emigrated to the United States where he worked in a varied number of jobs from hotel clerk to cowpuncher. Having attended the Kansas State University, he later returned to Europe where in London he commenced his literary career. Harris became the editor of the *London Evening News* in 1880 and later purchased the *Saturday Review*. His writings include, *Elder Conklin* (1894), *The Man Shakespeare* (1909), *The Woman Shakespeare* (1911), and *Contemporary Portraits* (1915). He also wrote a number of plays, with *Mr and Mrs Daventry* the most successful amongst them. He later authored a number of books of famous men whom he had known, as well as the biographies of Oscar Wilde (see page 198) and George Bernard Shaw (see page 191). Harris' own autobiography *The Life and Loves of Frank Harris* was perhaps, the most controversial of all his writings, detailing descriptions of his sexual escapades and exploits. He died in Nice, France on 26 August 1931.

James Lawlor Kiernan
Union general and surgeon
American Civil War 1837 – 1869

James Lawlor Kiernan was born in Galway City and emigrated to the United States where he studied medicine, practised as a doctor and published a number of medical journals. During the American Civil War Kiernan was a surgeon in the Fighting 69th New York

Regiment and saw action at the Battle of the First Bull Run. He was later appointed surgeon to the 6th Missouri Volunteer Regiment but was severely wounded at the Battle of Port Gibson, Mississippi where he was left for dead in a swamp. Having been captured by Confederate troops, Kiernan escaped and was subsequently appointed to brigadier general by President Abraham Lincoln on 1 August 1863, before taking charge of the post at the Battle of Milliken's Bend. On 3 February 1864, Kiernan was forced to resign due to poor health and following the war, he was appointed United States consular to China. He died in 1869 and is buried at Greenwood Cemetery in Brooklyn, New York.

Richard Kirwan
Chemist, mineralogist, meteorologist and geologist 1733 – 1812

Richard Kirwan was educated at the Erasmus Smith School in Galway city. Later, due to the fact that Catholics at that time were excluded from British universities, he was sent to Poitiers in France to complete his education. It was there that he developed an interest in chemistry and in 1754 he returned to Ireland where he studied law for a short period, later changing his religious denomination to become a member of the Church of England and then a Unitarian. It was whilst in London, from 1777 until 1787, that Kirwan established a reputation as a scientist and as a strenuous supporter of the Phlogiston Theory; his essay on the subject was published in 1787 and became his best-known work. He also spent considerable time in the study of meteorology and constructed a table which showed the temperature of all latitudes between the equator and the poles. Appointed president of the Royal Irish Academy in

1799, Kirwan was also reputed to have befriended some of the leading figures of the United Irishmen who were involved in the rebellion of the previous year. He died in 1812 at the age of seventy-nine.

Thomas Laughnan
Victoria Cross recipient 1824 – 1864

Thomas Laughnan was born in Gort and served as a gunner in the Bengal Artillery of the Indian Army, during the Indian Mutiny. In consideration of the gallantry shown by Laughnan throughout November 1857 at Lucknow, he was awarded the Victoria Cross.

Walter Macken
Novelist and dramatist 1915 – 1967

Walter Macken was educated at St Mary's College, Galway and spent some time in London as an insurance salesman before returning to Ireland in 1941. He then joined the Abbey Theatre where his first play, *Mungo's Mansion* (1946) was produced. He went on to publish a number of books of which *Rain on the Wind* (1950), *The Bogman* (1952) and *Seek the Fair Land* (1959) were best known. His most famous play is *Home is the Hero* (1953). He died in Galway in 1967.

William James MacNeven
Medical practitioner and United Irishman 1763 – 1841

In 1775, at the age of twelve, William James MacNeven travelled to Austria in order to join his uncle who was the physician to Empress Mary Theresa. He studied in Vienna, where he obtained a medical degree in 1784, following which he returned to Dublin where Lord Edward Fitzgerald introduced him to the Society of the United Irishmen.

In 1798 MacNeven was arrested with other leaders and imprisoned in Kilmainham Jail and later at Fort George, Scotland, before being released under the Treaty of Amiens in 1802. He subsequently joined the French Army as a captain in the Irish Brigade and endeavoured to persuade Napoleon to invade Ireland; having been unsuccessful in this, MacNeven left France for New York City, arriving on 4 July 1805. He went on to establish an extensive medical practice and in 1808, became professor of obstetrics in the College of Physicians and Surgeons, New York. Despite his successful career MacNeven still harboured a devotion to Irish freedom and he published *Pieces of Irish History* with Thomas Addis Emmet (see page 93) in 1807. MacNeven, whose writings were mainly on medical, scientific, and political subjects, was the founder and president of the Friends of Ireland and he also established an employment agency for Irish immigrants. He died on 12 July 1841.

Dunguaire Castle.

Peter Maher
Boxer 1869 – 1940

In 1888, Tuam native Peter Maher became middleweight champion of Ireland and two years later, heavyweight champion, following which he travelled to the United States where he had a long and successful career. Maher had two weaknesses; one was his lack of refined boxing skills and the other, a weak chin. He did however have a very hard punch and defeated such notables as Frank Slavin, Joe Goddard and Jim Jeffords to name but three. In 1895 he defeated Steve O'Donnell to capture the world heavyweight title but lost it the following year to the great Bob Fitzsimmons.

General Sir Bryan Mahon
British Army general and Irish Free State senator 1862 – 1930

A decorated military man, Bryan Mahon received the DSO for his part in the Dungola campaign in Sudan in 1896 and he also fought at Arbala, Morocco and Omdurman, Sudan. Mahon served as a brigadier general during the Boer war, where he defeated the Boers to relieve Mafeking, the achievement of which was received with great celebration in London. He also served in Egypt and India, being awarded Order of the Bath for middle rank officers as well as a Queen Victoria Military Decoration in 1913. In World War I, Mahon commanded the 10th Irish division at Gallipoli, during which the Irish forces sustained tremendous losses in a campaign that was politically rather than militarily motivated. Mahon served as commander-in-chief in Ireland from 1916 until 1918 and retired from the forces in 1921 before being awarded the Order of the Bath for senior officers in 1922. Nominated to the Irish Free State Senate the same year, he died in Dublin on 24 September 1930.

Richard Martin ('Humanity Dick')
Politician and co-founder of the RSPCA 1754 – 1834

Richard Martin served two separate stints in the Irish Parliament for both Jamestown and Lanesborough between 1776 and 1800. Following the Act of Union he was elected as the County Galway representative at the Westminster Parliament in London and there he continually campaigned for Catholic emancipation, which was finally granted in 1829. Well known for his love of animals, Martin had the first act for the protection of animals passed in Great Britain in 1822 and was a co-founder of the Royal Society for the Prevention of Cruelty to Animals (RSPCA) in 1824. His generosity to his tenants was on a princely scale and would ultimately lead to the demise of his fortune. Dubbed 'Humanity Dick' by George IV, who was a personal friend, Martin died in France on 6 January 1834.

Violet Florence Martin
Author 1862 – 1915

Violet Florence Martin was born at Ross House, Connemara, but moved with her family to Dublin in 1872. Along with her cousin Edith Somerville, Martin formed a literary partnership in 1886 and adopted a pseudonym, 'Martin Ross', which comprised her surname and that of her ancestral home, Ross.

Together the two women became known as, 'Somerville and Ross' under which name they produced such works as, *An Irish Cousin* (1889), and *The Irish R.M.* series which began a decade later. Martin also wrote travel books about the Irish countryside as well as two autobiographical works, *Some Irish Yesterdays* (1906) and *Stray-aways* (1920). She died in Drishane, County Cork in 1915.

Edward Martyn
Playwright 1859 – 1923

Edward Martyn was born in Tullira Castle, Ardrahan and was educated in Beaumont College and at Christ Church in Oxford. In 1899 he founded the Irish Literary Theatre with his friends William Butler Yeats (see page 199) and Lady Gregory (see page 216) and his play, *The Heather Field* was produced by the group. Martyn wrote several more plays including *The Tale of the Town* (1902), *Glencolman* (1912), and *The Dream Physician* (1914). A fierce nationalist, he was strongly opposed to British rule in Ireland and to Irish men joining the British army; he was also active on the political front and one of the co-founders of Sinn Féin with Arthur Griffith (see page 170). Martyn died in 1923 and donated his body to science.

Patrick Theodore Moore
Brigadier general 1821 – 1883

Upon the outbreak of the American Civil War, Patrick Theodore Moore, who had emigrated from Galway and settled in Richmond, Virginia, was appointed a colonel of the 1st Virginia Regiment of 1861. He was wounded at the first Manassas, following which he became aide to General J.E. Johnston in the Peninsula Campaign. Having been promoted to brigadier general in September 1864, Moore returned to Richmond due to his war injuries and there he commanded the local defence troops. Following the war he became an insurance agent and died in Richmond on 19 February 1883.

Lieutenant Colonel Hon. George Henry Morris
British soldier 1872 – 1914

Born in the Irish-speaking village of Spiddal, George Henry Morris was an officer in the Irish Guards of the British Army between 1892 and 1914. As a lieutenant colonel, Morris took command of the 1st Battalion of the Irish Guards in July 1913 and upon the outbreak of World War I, took the battalion to France where he was killed during the retreat from Mons on 1 September 1914. Considered one the British army's finest lecturers, Morris was also an authority on strategy, tactics and military history and was sorely missed following his death.

John Kernan Mullen
Milling magnate and philanthropist 1847 – 1929

Having emigrated with his family in 1856, at the age of fourteen, John Kernan Mullen commenced work in a flour mill in Oriskany Falls, New York. Six years later he moved to Denver, Colorado where he became the manager of the Shackelton and Davis Flour Mill, at 8th Street and Curtis. Within a few years he had established his own mill and by 1911 went on to purchase a number of others before building his first grain elevator – the first in the state of Colorado – and establishing the Colorado Milling and Elevator Company, which operated ninety-one elevators, warehouses and mills throughout Colorado, Kansas, Utah and Oregon. As a philanthropist, Mullen donated vast sums of money to the Catholic Church, the Denver Public Library and the Mullen Home for Boys, in addition to the five hundred thousand dollars he gave to the Catholic University of America in 1924 for the establishment of The John K. Mullen Denver Memorial Library. Knighted by Pope Benedict XV in 1921, Mullen died in Denver in 1929.

Máirtín Ó Cadhain
Novelist 1906 – 1970

Having undertaken a career as a schoolteacher, Máirtín O'Cadhain lost his job due to his involvement with the Irish Republican Army in the 1930s, and during World War II was interned in the Curragh Camp, Kildare by the Irish Government. He published a number of short stories in Irish, the most famous of which is 'Cré na Cille', and he was an official Irish translator of Irish parliamentary debates from 1949. Fluent in eight languages, O'Cadhain was appointed a lecturer in modern Irish at Trinity College, Dublin in 1956 and a professor the year before his death in 1970.

Pádraic Ó Conaire
Irish writer 1881 – 1928

Raised in the dock area of Galway city, Pádraic Ó'Conaire's former home is now a public house bearing his name. A fluent speaker of the Irish language who was very active in the Gaelic League, Ó'Conaire spent a number of years in London before returning to Ireland in 1914. He is best known for his Irish short story collections such as *Nora Mharcuis Bhig agus Sgéalta Eile* (1909) and *An Chéad Chloch* (1914). Many of these stories deal with the theme of Irish immigrants in England around the 1900s. A statue of Ó'Conaire stands in Eyre Square in Galway city and he died whilst on a visit to Dublin in 1928.

Liam O'Flaherty
Irish novelist and short story writer 1896 – 1984

Born on Inishmore, the largest of the Aran Islands, Liam O'Flaherty was educated in Rockwell College, County Tipperary and at University College Dublin. Having joined the Irish Guards regiment of the British army he saw action in World War I, during which he was injured and suffered from shell shock. After the war O'Flaherty moved to the United States where he lived for a time in Hollywood, California. A cousin of the famous film director John Ford, who later turned his novel, *The Informer* into an Academy Award winning movie, O'Flaherty's novel, *Thy Neighbour's Wife* (1923) is considered his best. Apart from his novels, O'Flaherty also wrote a number of notable short stories. He died on 7 September 1984.

Sir George Maurice O'Rorke
Politician, lawyer and and educationalist 1830 – 1916

Born in Moylough, George Maurice O'Rorke studied classics at Trinity College, Dublin in 1852. Emigrating to New Zealand, he settled in the town of Onehunga, Auckland where he obtained a law degree in 1860.

In 1871 O'Rorke was elected chairman of committees for the House of Representatives in Wellington and in 1878 he was appointed chairman of a Royal Commission on the relationships between universities and secondary education.

Under O'Rorke's chair, university colleges were established in Auckland and Wellington and he went on to be elected speaker of the House of Representatives in 1879, before being knighted the following year. A natural linguist, O'Rorke learned Māori to assist him in his public duties and was capable of conversing in classical Greek with the rabbi of Auckland during their regular dinners. Recognised as the father of parliament and one of the co-founders of New Zealand education, he held a seat in the Legislative Council of New Zealand from 1904 until his death in Auckland on 25 August 1916.

Eoghan Ó Tuairisc
(Eugene Watters)
Irish poet and writer 1919 – 1982

Eoghan Ó'Tuairisc was born in Ballinasloe and was educated at Garbally College. Having trained as a teacher in St Patrick's Teacher Training College in 1939, he later obtained an MA from University College Dublin in 1947 before his controversial novel, *Murder in Three Moves* was published in 1960. Also a dramatist and poet, Ó Tuairisc wrote both in Irish and English. He died in August 1982 and is buried in Ballinasloe.

Gideon Ouseley
Methodist itinerant preacher
1762 – 1839

Renowned for his wild ways before converting from the Anglican denomination to become a Methodist; in his youth Gideon Ouseley lost an eye in a tavern brawl but later experienced his emotional religious conversion under the preaching of Methodist soldiers who were stationed in Galway in 1791. Following this, Ouseley travelled throughout Ireland preaching and criticising the doctrines of the Roman Catholic Church, with whom he carried out a vigorous pamphlet war until his death in 1839. A native Irish language speaker, Ouseley had a great understanding of the poor and he became known as the 'Methodist Apostle' to the Irish.

John Purcell
Victoria Cross recipient 1814 – 1857

John Purcell was born in Oughterard and served as a private in the 9th Lancers, British Army during the Indian Mutiny. Despite the fact that his horse had been killed under him, on 19 June 1857 at Delhi, Purcell went to the rescue of a brigadier who was commanding their brigade and who had been severely shot. Lying in open ground, Purcell stayed with the officer until he was dragged to safety. He was later killed in action on 19 September 1857.

Dudley Stagpoole
Victoria Cross recipient 1838 – 1911

Dudley Stagpoole served as a drummer in the 57th Regiment of Foot, British Army, during the New Zealand Land Wars. On the 2 October 1863 at Allan's Hill, Taranaki, Stagpoole was awarded his honour for rescuing a comrade under heavy fire. Lying in open ground, he successfully brought the man back to the safety of his own lines. He was also awarded the Distinguished Conduct Medal for other heroic actions carried out in the same week. Stagpoole died in Herefordshire, England in 1911.

John Sealy Townsend
Mathematical physicist
1868 – 1957

John Sealy Townsend was educated at Trinity College, Dublin and was also a research student at the University of Cambridge. He later became a professor at the University of Oxford and was considered one of the greatest physicists of the twentieth century. Two years previous to his appointment at Oxford, Townsend had been the first to obtain a value for the charge on the electron and to explain how electric discharges pass through gases. Also elected a fellow of the Royal Society, he was awarded the Hughes Medal in 1914 and was knighted in 1941. Townsend died in Oxford in 1957.

Patrick James Whelan
Fenian assassin 1840 – 1869

An apprentice tailor, in 1865 Patrick James Whelan emigrated to Canada where he worked in Quebec City before moving on to Montreal to take up employment with Gibb and Company. Whilst there he apparently became involved with the Fenians and on 7 April 1868, he allegedly shot and killed fellow Irishman, Thomas D'Arcy McGee (see page 300). McGee was an ex-member of the Young Ireland movement who had fled to Canada and was now a member of the Legislative Assembly and an outspoken opponent of the Fenians. Whelan was later convicted of McGee's assassination and hanged at Carleton County jail. Having uttered the words 'they've got to find me guilty yet', his body was buried in an unmarked grave at the aforementioned jail. Decades later, Whelan's guilt was brought into doubt, with some claiming that he was made an unfair scapegoat for the assassination because he was a Fenian sympathiser.

Alexander Young
Victoria Cross recipient 1873 – 1916

A Clarinbridge native, Alexander Young served as a sergeant major in the Cape Police, South African Forces, during the Boer War. At Ruiterskraal, on 13 August 1901, Young, with a handful of men, rushed a small hill being held by about twenty Boers who were then forced to withdraw. On his own, Young then followed the retreating men and shot one of them before capturing their commandant. He was killed in action at the Somme on 19 October 1916.

Kerry

Arthurs Sandes 1793-1832

As commander of the Black Rifles, considered the best regiment in the army of Simon Bolivar, General Arthur Sandes made a major contribution to the liberation of South America.

"WANTS YOU"

Horatio Kitchener 1850-1916

The World War I recruitment poster depicted Horatio Kitchener.

Daniel O'Connell 1775-1847

'The Liberator' Daniel O'Connell's statue stands on O'Connell Street, Dublin.

Tom Crean 1877-1938

The home of Antarctic explorer
Tom Crean at Annascaul,
County Kerry

General Tom Barry 1897-1980

The memorial at Crossbarry commemorating the ambush
that took place on 19 March 1921, following which one
hundred IRA volunteers escaped a 1300-strong
British encirclement

Tom Barry
Commandant general of the IRA
1897 – 1980

Tom Barry was born in Killorglin and was educated at Mungret College, County Limerick. During World War I he enlisted in the British Army, seeing action in Mesopotamia (present-day Iraq) and upon his return to Ireland in 1920, joined the West Cork Brigade of the Irish Republican Army. Barry fought in the War of Independence (1919 – 21) and his involvement with the West Cork Brigade gained him a reputation as a brilliant field commander. On 28 November 1920, he ambushed and killed almost a complete platoon of British auxiliaries at Kilmichael, County Cork and so efficient was the brigade that the British army responded by stationing around 12,500 troops in County Cork during the conflict, completely outnumbering Barry's unit, which never exceeded three hundred men. In the 1940s he served as an intelligence officer in the Irish Army Southern Command and in 1949, published his memoirs of the War of Independence, entitled *Guerilla Days in Ireland*. Barry was supportive of the Provisional IRA campaign, but not supportive of the killing of civilians in England. He died in Cork in 1980.

Helen Blackburn
Suffragette 1842 – 1903

Helen Blackburn was born on Valentia Island and moved to London, England in 1857, where she became involved in the British suffrage movement. Elected secretary of the National Society for Women's Suffrage in 1874, from 1881 until 1890 she served as editor of the *English Woman's Review* and donated her library of books, pamphlets and records to Girton College, Cambridge. Blackburn wrote *Conditions of Working Women and the Factory* (1896), *Women's Suffrage* (*Women's Suffrage: A Record of the Women's Suffrage Movement in the British Isles* (1902)), and *Women under the Factory's Act* (1903). She died in London on 11 January 1903 and is buried in Brompton Cemetery.

Richard Cantillon
Economist 1680 – 1734

Richard Cantillon initially engaged in business in England before moving to Paris, where he opened a banking house. Cantillon was known to some as the father of political economy due to the popularity of one book he wrote whilst in France, *Essai Sur la Nature Du Commerce En Général* (1755). The book is divided into three parts, providing an introduction in political economy, a section dealing with currency and a comprehensive discussion on foreign commerce. On 14 March 1734, Cantillon returned to London where he was murdered, seemingly by his cook, who knew he had large sums of money in his house

Major-General Sir Trevor Chute
British Army general 1816 – 1886

Trevor Chute entered the British army in 1832 and saw service in both Sri Lanka and India, rising rapidly through the service and being promoted to major in 1847, lieutenant colonel in 1849 and full colonel in 1854. In 1861, Chute and his regiment were posted in New Zealand where he became brigadier general and during the

Māori wars, he was described as an effective leader despite being considered ruthless and unsophisticated. Appointed to the Order of the Bath in 1867, the same year that British troops where gradually withdrawn from New Zealand, Chute later returned to England where he was appointed a full general. He died in Reading on 12 March 1886.

Jerome Connor
Sculptor 1874 – 1943

At the age of fourteen, Annascaul born Jerome Connor emigrated with his family to Holyoke, Massachusetts. Two years later, following the death of his father, he moved to New York and commenced work as a sign painter, stone-cutter, bronze founder and machinist. Notable contributions of his include the Civil War Memorial in South Hadley, Massachusetts, and the Fountain of Neptune Bronzes at the Library of Congress in Washington D C In his own studio, Connor did metalwork, castings in plaster and sculpting, and his first big commission was the Marble Memorial to the American poet Walt Whitman. In 1912 he completed the Archbishop Carroll Monument for Georgetown Catholic University and in 1917 a statue of Robert Emmet (see page 165) for the Smithsonian Institution in Washington. A cast of this statue is in St Stephen's Green, Dublin. Connor returned to Ireland in 1925 to work on a memorial in Cobh to those drowned on the *Lusitania* ocean liner, which was torpedoed by a German submarine in 1915. This work occupied him intermittently for the next fourteen years and he died in the Adelaide Hospital, Dublin in August 1943.

Patrick Edward Connor
Union General in the American Civil War 1820 – 1891

At the age of nineteen, Patrick Edward Connor emigrated to the United States where he enlisted in the army and fought under Albert Sidney Johnston in the Mexican-American War. When the American Civil War broke out, Connor took command of the 'Stockton Blues' and bringing it to regimental size, it became the 3rd California Volunteer Infantry before being ordered to the Utah territory to protect overland routes from the enemy and to stop a possible Morman uprising. In 1863, in present day Idaho, Connor was responsible for the annihilation of the Shoshoni tribe at what was called the battle of Bear River. He was then appointed brigadier general and given command of the district of Utah where he routed the Sioux and Cheyenne tribes who were disrupting the Bozeman Trail, which was the overland mail route to the west. In 1865 he defeated the combined Sioux/Arapaho forces at the battle of Tongue River, bringing peace to the territory, but despite his heavy involvement in the war, Connor never saw action against the Confederate forces. He died in Salt Lake City, Utah on 17 December 1891.

John Joseph Connors
Victoria Cross recipient 1830 – 1857

John Joseph Connors was born in Davaugh, Listowel and as a private in the 3rd Regiment of the British Army during the Crimean War, he successfully rescued an officer of the 30th Regiment who was surrounded by Russians. Connors shot one of the enemy and then in hand-to-hand combat he successfully used his bayonet to repel another. For rescuing the officer and for his daring action, he was awarded the Victoria Cross.

Tom Crean
Antarctic explorer and Albert Medal recipient 1877 – 1938

Having joined the Royal Navy at just fifteen years of age, Tom Crean took part in three major Antarctic expeditions: the *Discovery* (1901 – 04), the *Terra-Nova* (1910 – 13), and the *Endurance* (1914 – 16). It was during the *Terra-Nova* expedition, in which Robert Falcon Scott lost his life, 'Tom the Pole', as Crean was known, displayed one of the greatest feats of individual heroism in Antarctic exploration history when he faced the 750 mile journey back to base camp together with Bill Lashly and Lieutenant Teddy Evans. The journey took three months in the harshest of climates but with Evans struck down with scurvy, Crean elected to leave him with Lashly with just thirty five miles to go and strike out alone with only two sticks of chocolate, three biscuits and no sleeping bag or tent. He walked, stumbled and crawled for eighteen hours hours across the treacherous terrain to reach base camp, where a rescue team was sent to retrieve his two compatriots. For this great feat he was awarded the Albert Medal, the highest civilian award for gallantry.

During the 1914 expedition, which was led by the legendary Ernest Shackleton (see page 243), Crean once again displayed amazing courage and endurance when Shackleton was forced to abandon the *Endurance* in the Weddell Sea in October 1915. The expedition was forced to remain until April 1916, when the ship's lifeboats were launched in an effort to reach Elephant Island – about one hundred miles north. Having reached the island suffering from exposure, sea sickness and exhaustion, Shackleton then decided, together with Crean and four others, to attempt a journey of eight hundred miles to South Georgia in an open boat across the most treacherous waters in the world.

Following seventeen days, during which the men endured constant gales, freezing temperatures and enormous seas, the expedition reached its destination. It was then that Shackleton, Crean and Worsley left their compatriots and set out on a thirty-six hour march in atrocious conditions with inadequate clothing and poor equipment. They arrived at a whaling station on the other side of the island on 20 May 1916 and a rescue party was sent out to help their compatriots, while the remainder of the crew left on Elephant Island were rescued by a Chilean ship. Having served in World War I, Crean returned to his home in Kerry, where he opened a pub called the South Pole Inn. He died following a ruptured appendix in 1938.

Frederick Field
British naval officer 1871 – 1945

Killarney born Frederick Field entered the Royal Navy as a cadet in 1884, being promoted to lieutenant in 1893. He served on the HMS *Barfieur* during the Chinese Boxer Rebellion in 1900 and he also received the China Medal and the Relief of Peking Clasp. Promoted to commander in 1902 and captain in 1907, Field's most notable appointment was as captain of the battleship, HMS *King George V* at the Battle of Jutland in May 1916. He was a highly celebrated comabatant, receiving the CB (The Order of the Bath), the CMG (The Order of St Michael and St George), the 2nd Class of Russia Order of St Anne with Swords, the Order of Crown Romania, the Legion d'Honeur and the DSM (Distinguished Service Medal). Field was promoted to the rank of full admiral in 1928 before retiring as 1st Sea Lord in 1933 with the rank of admiral of the fleet. He died on 24 October 1945 in Yorkshire, England.

Christie Hennessy
Irish singer-songwriter 1945 – 2007
Christy Hennessy was born Edward Christopher Ross in Tralee, and left school at the age of eleven being unable to read or write due to dyslexia. Having worked on building sites in London for a time, he toured England as a busker, but his 1972 album *The Green Album* proved unsuccessful. Hennessy continued labouring until 1992 when he won the IRMA award for best newcomer for his album *The Rehearsal*, which went to number one in Ireland, outselling the legendary U2 in the process. Following that success, Hennessy secured a record deal with Warner Music and amongst the many songs he wrote, the two most unforgettable are 'Don't Forget your Shovel' and 'All the Lies That You Told Me.' A down to earth man, Hennessy said of life as a performer, 'It's everyone's dream to live the life of a rock star – but it's not always what it's cracked up to be.' One of Ireland's best-loved entertainers, he died on 11 December 2007.

John B. Keane
Playwright and novelist
1928 – 2002
Born in Listowel, John B. Keane had various jobs throughout his life, commencing as a chemist's assistant and then an antique buyer before later spending four years working in England. Returning to Listowel in 1955, upon which time he became an owner of a public house, Keane also produced in the region of fourteen plays, the most well known being *Sive* (1959) and *The Field* (1965), which was later adapted into a film starring Richard Harris (see page 278), who received an Academy Award nomination for his role as Bull McCabe. Other well known plays of his were *Big Maggie*, and *Moll* and he also wrote five novels, the best known of which are *The Bodhran Makers* and *Letters of a Successful TD*. Keane, whose essays include 'Love Bites' and 'Owl Sandwiches', became an honourary life member of the Royal Dublin Society in 1991 and he was also a founder member of the Society of Irish Playwrights. He died at his home in Listowel in 2002 at the age of seventy-three and a statue to his memory was erected in the town in 2007.

Richard Kelliher
Victoria Cross recipient
1910 – 1963
Tralee-born Richard Kelliher served as a private in the Australian Imperial Force in New Guinea at the Battle of Bunagona. With his platoon having come under heavy attack from a concealed Japanese machine-gun, further advancement was restricted and so Kelliher, on his own initiative, sprinted forward and unleashed two grenades at the Japanese machine-gun defence, knocking it out of action. He then returned to his section and seized a Bren gun before returning to eliminate a considerable section of the enemy force. In addition, Kelliher sought permission to go out and rescue his section leader who was wounded. He undertook these tasks under continuous enemy fire and was thus awarded the Victoria Cross. He died in Melbourne in 1963.

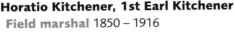

Horatio Kitchener, 1st Earl Kitchener
Field marshal 1850 – 1916

Famous for the World War I recruitment poster that bore his image, Ballylongford born Horatio Kitchener was educated in Switzerland and at the Royal Military Academy in England. Much of his service and accomplishments were achieved in Egypt, where he headed the victorious Anglo-Egyptian army, made up of 8,200 British troops and 17,000 Sudanese and Egyptians, equipped with Lee-Enfield rifles, maxim guns and gunboats, against the Dervish army of 50,000 men equiped with spears and single loading muskets. The Dervish lost 20,000 troops and a further 22,000 were wounded at the Battle, of Omdurman in 1898, compared to Kitchener's 48 dead, and 382 wounded. Following this victory Kitchener was created Baron Kitchener of Khartoum. Churchill, who was present at the battle wrote to his mother in January 1899 'Our victory was disgraced by the inhuman slaughter of the wounded and Kitchener was responsible.' Describing the battle, himself, Kitchener called it 'a good dusting'.

During the Second Boer War (1899 – 1902) in South Africa, Kitchener gained further infamy, together with Lord Roberts (of County Waterford parentage), for their scorched earth policy and the creation of the first ever concentration camps where, for every one thousand persons entering, three hundred and fifty died. He was created commander-in-chief in India from 1902 to 1909, and secretary of state for war at the outbreak of World War I and the famous poster of him, pointing one finger and accompanied by the caption 'your country needs you', was central to recruitment campaigns for the war. He died on the sinking of the HMS *Hampshire* on 5 June 1916.

Thomas MacGreevy
Poet and critic 1893 – 1967

Tarbert native Thomas MacGreevy joined the British Civil Service as a boy clerk at the age of sixteen, but upon the outbreak of World War I, obtained an intelligence post with the admiralty. On completion of his service in the forces, he entered Trinity College, Dublin, graduating with a degree in history and political science. MacGreevy was a close friend of James Joyce (see page 173) and was an executor of his will. He published a book of poems in 1934 and was a significant contributor to the *Times* literary supplement. He was also appointed director of the National Gallery in 1950 and was a devout Catholic whose religious beliefs were a common thread in both his poetry and his professional life.

Fr Malachi Martin
Author 1921 – 1999

Malachi Martin was born in Ballylongford and was educated at Belvedere College, Dublin before joining the Jesuits in 1939. Having had stints studying in Ireland, England, Belgium and Israel, Martin was ordained to the priesthood on 15 August 1954 and from 1958 to 1964, he served in the Vatican where he was professor of the Pontifical Biblical Institute and taught Hebrew, Aramic, paleography and scripture. In his pastoral duties he assisted in several exorcisms, which he dealt with in his book, *Hostage to the Devil*. But in 1965 Pope Paul VI gave Martin a dispensation from all privileges and obligations deriving from his vows as a priest due to a dissatisfaction that emerged because of reforms of the Second Vatican Council. Martin, who was an opponent of the alleged apparitions of the Virgin Mary at Medjugorje, continued to offer Mass privately despite the dispensation from his priestly duties and he exercised his ministry until the day he died, repeatedly affirming his allegiance to the Pope. He produced many best selling fiction and non-fiction literary works, many of which presented a decidedly negative view of the world, invoking dark spirits, conspiracy, betrayal, heresy, widespread sexual perversion and demonic possession, which he proclaimed were rife in the Catholic Church. Martin's book, *The Jesuits* was critical of the Order that he once belonged to, which he claimed deviated from its original characters and mission. In all, he wrote in the region of seventeen books and died in New York in 1999.

William Melville
First chief of the British Secret Service 1850 – 1918

William Melville was born in Sneem and in 1872 joined the London Metropolitan Police. A decade later, he was chosen as a founding member of the Special Irish Branch, established to work against the Fenians and anarchists. A Catholic and a supporter of Gaelic games and Home Rule for Ireland, in 1893 he became superintendent of Scotland Yard's Special Branch and over the next ten years embarked on a large series of well publicised raids against Irish anarchists. Melville, who became head of the British Secret Service in 1903 with the code name 'M', advocated the establishment of a counter-espionage service and he got his wish in October 1909 when the War Office authorised the creation of the Secret Service Bureau with nineteen military intelligence departments. During World War I, Melville served as the chief of the British Secret Service and concentrated his efforts on catching German spies. He died in February 1918.

John Moriarty
Writer and philosopher
1938 – 2007

Educated at University College Dublin, John Moriarty worked as a lecturer in English at the University of Manitoba, Canada from 1965 until 1971 and published a total of eight books over a period of thirteen years. Awarded an honourary doctorate from the National University of Ireland for his contribution to the arts in June 2006, Moriarty's last work, *Serious Sounds*, which was about growing up in Kerry, was published in 2007. He died of cancer later that year.

Maurice Gerard Moynihan
Irish civil servant 1902 – 1999

Having won a scholarship to University College Cork, where he graduated with a first class honours degree in commerce, Maurice Gerard Moynihan joined the Department of Finance in 1925 and was promoted to private secretary to Taoiseach Eamon de Valera (see page 431) in 1932. Moynihan was one of the architects of the 1937 Constitution of Ireland and in 1960 was appointed governor of the Central Bank of Ireland. Following his retirement in 1969, he devoted much of his time to his writings, all of which are now in the custody of University College Dublin. He died at the age of ninety-six in Leeson Park Nursing Home, Dublin and is buried in Clontarf Cemetery.

Daniel O'Connell
'The Liberator' 1775 – 1847

Known as 'The Liberator', Daniel O'Connell was born in Carhen near Cahirsiveen and received his education in France. He was admitted to Lincoln's Inn in 1794 before transferring to Dublin's King's Inn, where he was called to the Irish bar in 1798. A man of peace, O'Connell did not take part in the rebellion of 1798, believing instead that the Irish should assert themselves by political means rather than by force. He vigorously campaigned for Catholic emancipation and the repeal of the Union between Ireland and Great Britain.

In 1828, O'Connell stood for election to the British House of Commons for County Clare, but due to the restrictions on Catholics and Presbyterians, he was not allowed to take his seat. As a result, the British prime minister the Duke of Wellington, fearful of a possible rebellion, convinced King George IV that the Emancipation Bill should be passed and it became law in 1829. O'Connell also supported similar efforts in respect to Jews and the British law 'De Judaismo', which forced Jews to wear certain attire, was repealed in 1846. He became the first Roman Catholic Lord Mayor of Dublin, whose principal street is named in his honour and a magnificent statue to his memory stands at one end. O'Connell died in Rome at the age of seventy-one.

Count Daniel O'Mahony
'The Hero of Cremona' c. 1669 – 1714

Though little is known about his earlier life, Daniel O'Mahony did join the Irish Brigade as an officer in Dillon's regiment of the French army. It was on 31 January 1702, whilst in command of approximately six hundred men, that O'Mahony defended the city of Cremona, Italy against a force of six thousand Austrian soldiers who were under the command of Prince Eugene. With the Austrian troops having entered the city before the Irish regiment was aware of it, the ensuing battle saw 350 Irish troops die but Cremona was saved for the French and in response the King of France rewarded O'Mahony with a brevit as colonel, along with a pension of one thousand livres. He spent the remainder of his life in Spain where King Philip V appointed him a major general, in consideration of his service to the country, and he later became military governor of Cartagena before being promoted to lieutenant general. At the Battle of Almanza, O'Mahony successfully led and Irish regiment of dragoons to victory and was thus made a 'count' or 'castile'. At the Battle of Villaviciosa in late 1710, so impressed was Philip V by the cavalry under O'Mahony's command that he further honoured him by appointing him commander of the military order of St Iago. He died at Ocana, Spain in January 1714.

Michael Joseph O'Rahilly, 'The O'Rahilly'
Irish nationalist 1875 – 1916

Coming from a wealthy family background, Michael Joseph O'Rahilly spent a number of years in the United States before returning to Ireland in 1909, where he aided Arthur Griffith (see page 170), through financial assistance, with running the nationalist newspaper *Sinn Féin*. A supporter of James Connolly (see page 429) and Jim Larkin, and the actions of the 1913 strikers, O'Rahilly showed great sympathy for the oppressed workers at that time. In 1916 he fought at the General Post Office in Dublin during the Easter Rising and was was killed in action. He was the only member of the Provisional Committee of the Irish Volunteers to die fighting and he is buried in the republican plot in Glasnevin Cemetery.

Michael J. Quill
Founder of the Transport and General Workers Union of America 1905 – 1966

Reputed to have been involved with the IRA during the Irish Civil War, following that conflict, Michael Quill emigrated to the United States where he commenced work on the construction of the New York subway, before taking employment with the Interborough Rapid Transit Company. With twelve-hour days, seven days per week the norm, in 1935 Quill began to openly campaign for the formation of a union which would eventually become the Transport and General Workers Union of America. Based on the Irish Transport and General Workers Union, Quill served as its president for over thirty years and is perhaps, best remembered for the 1966 New York transit strike, for which he was jailed. In response to his punishment he proclaimed 'The judge can drop dead in his black robes, I don't care if I rot in jail, I will not call off the strike'. Following thirteen days of the strike

Dunmore Head, County Kerry.

233

a package worth sixty million dollars was awarded by the City of New York. Quill, who died some fourteen days later on 28 January 1966, was honoured by the great Reverend Martin Luther King who paid him the following tribute: 'Mick Quill was a fighter for decent things all his life. Irish independence, labour organisation and racial equality. He spent his life ripping the chains of bondage off his fellow man. This is a man the ages will remember.'

Arthur Sandes
South American soldier 1793 – 1832

Having enlisted in the British army, Arthur Sandes fought at the Battle of Waterloo before leaving the British services in 1815 and sailing for Venezuela. Having seen action at the Battle of Gamarra, Colombia on 27 March 1819, Sandes took command of the 1st Rifles Battalion also known as 'The Black Rifles', and this battalion took part in every theatre of war in South America from 1819 until 1825, eventually becoming known as the best regiment in Simon Bolivar's army. Their finest hour was the defeat of the Spanish on 7 April 1822 at Bomboná and they were later awarded the Order of the Liberators. It was at Corpaguayco on 3 December 1824 that the Black Rifles battalion, under Sandes command, saved the patriot army from defeat, following which, Sandes was promoted to brigadier general. He later fought in the war between Peru and Colombia where he led two Colombian divisions at the battle of Portete de Tarquí on 27 February 1829. With the outcome of that war decided, Sandes retired to settle in Cuenca, Ecuador where he died on 6 September 1832. He is buried in the Carmelite Convent.

Peig Sayers
Author 1873 – 1958

Described as one of the greatest female storytellers of modern times, Peig Sayers spent her early life as a domestic servant and moved to the Great Blasket Island upon her marriage to a fisherman who was a native of that island. Though she was illiterate, Sayers dictated all of her stories and is most famous for her autobiography, *Peig*, which was translated into English by Bryan MacMahon. Peig portrays a simple tale of Irish life, told with sensitivity, about the inhabitants of the Blasket Islands. She left the island in 1953 when it was abandoned due to the declining population and moved to Dingle, where she died in 1958.

Daniel Joseph Sheehan
British pilot 1894 – 1917

An accomplished rugby player, Daniel Joseph Sheehan played two years at inter-provincial level for Munster and was considered one of the finest three-quarter backs in Ireland at the time. Sheehan became a midshipman in the Royal Navy with the intention of training to become a commissioned officer, but upon the outbreak of World War I he obtained his aviator's certificate, before being wounded whilst flying in Belgium. He later transferred to the Royal Flying Corps and met his death on 10 May 1917 when, on a scouting expedition, he encountered a large German force. In the ensuing battle, Sheehan was shot but still managed to land his plane in an open field near Noyelles, France before dying in the cockpit. His commanding officer said of him,

'He was loved by all and was, by nature, absolutely devoid of fear'. Sheehan's brother, Michael Joseph, aged sixteen, was the youngest commissioned officer on the western front during World War I, going on to become brigadier general in World War II.

Austin Stack
Revolutionary 1879 – 1929

A gifted Gaelic footballer, Austin Stack captained the Kerry team to All-Ireland glory in 1904 before joining the Irish Republican Brotherhood in 1908. Stack, who commanded the Kerry Brigade of the Irish Volunteers, is the subject of a certain degree of controversy due to the fact that he could have rescued fellow revolutionary Roger Casement (see page 159) from Ballymullen Barracks in Tralee. He was made aware that a rescue attempt could be easily facilitated by RIC District Inspector Kearney, but despite this information, Stack refused to move. He was arrested following the rising before receiving a death penalty, which was later commuted to penal servitude for life. Released under an amnesty in 1917, Stack opposed the Anglo-Irish Treaty and took part in the subsequent civil war. He was captured by government forces in 1923 and went on hunger strike for forty-one days, before being released in July of the following year. Elected to the third Dáil as an anti-treaty Sinn Féin TD in 1922, he served until 1927 and died in Dublin on 27 April 1929. The GAA stadium in Tralee, Austin Stack Park, is named in his honour.

Maurice Walsh
Writer 1879 – 1964

Maurice Walsh was born in Ballydonoghue and following his education in a local national school, spent two years at St Michael's College in Listowel. He entered the British civil service and spent some twenty years as an excise officer in the Scottish Highlands, but upon the formation of the Irish Free State, he returned to serve in the newly formed Irish civil service. Walsh was a prolific writer of short stories, some of which were so successful he later expanded them into full-length novels, such as *While Rivers Run, The Small Dark Man* and *Blackcock's Feather*. He gained international recognition when the 'The Quiet Man' appeared in the popular American magazine, *The Saturday Evening Post* and was so well received that it was eventually adapted for the big screen. The movie, directed by John Ford and starring John Wayne and Maureen O'Hara, was the recipient of two Academy Awards. Walsh died in 1964 and the archives of his works are stored in the University of Limerick Library.

Kildare

Major General Michael Kelly Lawler
1814-1882

Michael Kelly Lawler was promoted to brevit major-general for his bravery in the union army during the American Civil War.

Ernest Shackleton
1874-1922

Kilkea House, County Kildare is the ancestral home of Ernest Shackleton, the Antarctic explorer.

Charles Fitzclarence
1865-1914

On the Menin Gate Memorial in Ypres, Belguim, the highest ranking officer noted is Brigadier-General Charles Fitzclarence VC.

Lord Edward Fitzgerald
1763-1798

Carton House, circa 1824. The birthplace of United Irishman Lord Edward Fitzgerald.

Cardinal Paul Cullen
1803-1878

One of Ireland's premier hospitals, The Mater in Dublin, was founded by Cardinal Paul Cullen.

Lt Colonel Abraham Boulger
Victoria Cross recipient 1835 – 1900

Abraham Boulger was born in Kilcullen and served as a lance corporal in the 84th Regiment of Foot of the British Army during the Indian Mutiny. In Lucknow, India, Boulger stormed a bridge over a canal to relieve the Residency, knocking out a 68-pound gun that was facing the British troops. He was severely wounded in the defence of the Residency, but went on to become a lieutenant colonel. He died in Ireland in January 1900.

Teresa Brayton
Poet 1868 – 1943

Poet Teresa Brayton was born Teresa Boylan in Kilcock, and emigrated to the United States in 1895, living first in Boston and then in New York where she met her future husband, Richard Brayton. Having been acquainted with the leaders of the 1916 Rising, Brayton promoted their cause with her pen and wrote an extensive number of poems, of which the best known was 'The Old Bog Road' – a song sung by Irish exiles the world over. She returned to Ireland in 1932 and spent her final days near the old Bog Road that she had written about, which leads to the bog at Cappagh. She died there in 1943.

Robert Brooke
Soldier and Governor of St Helena 1744 – 1811

In 1764, at the age of twenty, Prosperous born Robert Brooke entered the services of the East India Company and had a successful military career, reaching the rank of lieutenant colonel in the early 1780s. Following a garrison mutiny run by a civilian governor on the island of St Helena in 1788, it was decided that a military presence would be more appropriate to maintain order. To this end, Brooke was appointed governor of St Helena and held the post for twelve years, until 1800. Whilst on the island he was instrumental in organising a network of pipes for the transportation of fresh water, which enabled extensive farming, and he also built a landing jetty along with defensive positions dispersed around the island to guard against attack. In addition, Brooke introduced rules forbidding the ill-treatment of slaves and he raised a militia to defend the island as well as to provide military support for British-held Cape Town in South Africa. Awarded with a diamond-hilted sword by the East India Company for his work, Brooke died at his home in Bath, England in 1811.

Eamon Broy
Police Commissioner 1887 – 1972

In 1911, Rathangan born Eamon Broy became a member of the Dublin Metropolitan police where he was assigned to the Secret Service arm of the British administration in Ireland. However, Broy's loyalty lay with Irish nationalism and he supplied Michael Collins (see page 89) with much valuable information. Arrested in February 1921 and jailed for six months, he was dismissed from service, but following the Anglo-Irish Treaty and Irish independence, Broy served in the Irish police force before being appointed commissioner in March 1933. He retired in 1938 and died in Dublin on 22 January 1972.

Ambrose Upton Gledstanes Bury
Politician 1869 – 1951

Educated at the High School, Dublin and later at Trinity College, Ambrose Upton Gledstanes Bury was called to the Irish Bar in 1906. In 1912 he emigrated to Edmonton, Canada, where he practiced law and was elected to Edmonton City Council in the Municipal Elections of 1921. Having repeated this feat two years later, Bury was elected to the Canadian House of Commons representing Edmonton East in 1925, and was appointed Mayor of Edmonton the following year, holding that position until 1935, when he chose not to seek re-election. Thereafter serving as a district court judge, Bury retired in 1944 and died in Ottawa on 29 March 1951.

Paul Cullen
Cardinal and Primate of Ireland 1803 – 1878

Paul Cullen was born in Ballitore and was educated at the local Quaker school and at St Patrick's College, Carlow. Ordained in 1829, he became vice-rector and later rector of the Irish National College in Rome and was also an accomplished biblical theologian and scholar of ancient languages. Cullen, who is credited with crafting the formula for papal infallibility at the First Vatican Council, was promoted to the Primatial See of Armagh in 1849 before being elevated to Cardinal in 1866, becoming Ireland's first man to be appointed to that position. He was instrumental in the founding of the Mater Misericordiae Hospital in Dublin and Clonliffe Seminary and died in Dublin on 24 October 1878.

John Devoy
Fenian 1842 – 1928

John Devoy was born near Kill. Upon joining the Fenians, he enlisted in the French Foreign Legion, in 1861 in order to gain soldiering experience. When he returned to Ireland, he was appointed the Fenian organiser for recruitment within the British army. He was arrested for these activities in 1866 and sentenced to fifteen years' penal servitude. Released in 1871 on condition that he left the United Kingdom, Devoy went to the United States and became the principal organiser for Clann na Gael, his objective being to shift American opinion against English rule in Ireland and to raise funds for the Fenians. He was the chairman of the committee that organised the famous rescue of six Fenian prisoners from Fremantle Prison, Australia in 1876, the men escaping aboard the whaler *Catalpa*. Through his Clann na Gael organisation, Devoy raised funds in support of such movements for more than thirty years, taking every possible opportunity to drive a wedge between the United States and Britain. He died in Atlantic City, New Jersey in 1928 and his remains were taken back to Ireland and buried in Glasnevin Cemetery, Dublin. Devoy's *Recollections of an Irish Rebel* was published posthumously in 1929.

Brigadier-General Charles Fitzclarence
Victoria Cross recipient 1865 – 1914

Whilst serving as a captain in the Royal Fusiliers of the British Army during the Boer War, Charles Fitzclarence was noted for his bravery in going to the assistance of an armoured train that was being attacked by superior numbers of Boers. With just a partially trained squadron, Fitzclarence inspired his men to a heavy defeat of the Boers before once again distinguishing when carrying out a daring night attack in which he was severely wounded, on 26 December 1899. He was later promoted to brigadier general but was killed in action whilst commanding the 1st Brigade of the Irish Guards in Belgium in November 1914. Fitzclarence is the highest ranking officer on the memorial in Ypres, Belgium, which commemorates those with no known grave. He was awarded the Victoria Cross for his brave deeds.

Lord Edward FitzGerald
United Irishman 1763 – 98

Born in Carton House, Edward FitzGerald served with the Coldstream Guards regiment of the British Army in the war against the American colonies. Severely wounded at the Battle of Eutaw Springs in 1781, upon leaving the army FitzGerald became a committed revolutionary and headed the military committee of the United Irishmen. In 1796 he accompanied Arthur O'Connor (see page 106) in negotiations with General Hoche for the French military to send aid to Ireland; but with a rising planned for May 1798, British authorities infiltrated the movement with spies in an effort to quell it at its source. Advised that he was about to be arrested, FitzGerald went on the run with a reward of one thousand pounds on his head and he was eventually tracked down and seized by the infamous Major Sirr in a house on Thomas Street, Dublin on 19 May 1798. Following an intense struggle, during which one of the arresting officers, Captain Ryan, was killed and Major Swan was wounded, FitzGerald was shot in the shoulder by Sirr and was beaten unconscious by the accompanying milita. A near successful attempt to rescue FitzGerald was made by a crowd that assembled outside the house but this was thwarted by the arrival of a detachment of cavalry. FitzGerald was taken to Newgate Prison where, due to his wounds, he died on the 4 June 1798. His death was a major blow to the United Irishmen.

Arthur Guinness
Founder of the Guinness Brewery 1725 – 1803

Celbridge born Arthur Guinness was the founder of the world-famous Guinness brand. He had his first experience of brewing in Leixlip, where he brewed ale in 1755. In 1759 he moved to Dublin and bought a brewery on a twenty-four-acre plot of land now known as St James's Gate. Although Guinness, a Protestant, was in favour of Catholic Emancipation, his opposition to the United Irishmen led to the porter he brewed becoming known as 'Guinness Black Protestant Porter'.

The origin of the darkness of Guinness was in the use of roasted barley, which gives it its distinctive colour. This trait proved to be a differentiator for Guinness, who established his brewery in a market dominated by English brewers. This deep, rich beverage eventually ousted all imports from the Irish market and went on to capture a considerable share of the English market. In 1825 Guinness became available in many countries, and by 1838 the Dublin Brewery at St

James's Gate had become the largest in Ireland. Guinness's son Benjamin (see page 171) subsequently brought the beverage to a worldwide market; today it is estimated that 10 million glasses of Guinness are enjoyed daily across the world. Although production has expanded beyond the shores of Ireland to thirty-five countries, the Guinness formula must still contain a flavoured extract brewed only at St James's Gate Brewery.

Gabriel Hayes
Sculptor and coin designer
1909 – 1978

Having originally studied art in Dublin and later in Italy and France, Gabriel Hayes produced artwork in public and religious buildings throughout Ireland. One such example of her work is the sculptured wing-helmeted figure of Lugh, the ancient God of Light, on the Department of Industry and Commerce building in Dublin. Another fine example of Hayes's work is the figures of the Three Graces at the College of Catering on Cathal Brugha Street, but she is perhaps best known for her design of the halfpenny, the penny and the two pence pieces, which were designed for the introduction of decimalisation in Ireland. Hayes died in 1978 and was honoured by the Three Graces being depicted on the 65 cent stamp by the Irish postal service in 2005.

John Vincent Holland
Victoria Cross recipient
1889 – 1975

Born in Athy, John Vincent Holland served as a lieutenant in the 3rd Battalion of the Leinster Regiment of the British Army during World War I. On 3 September 1916, he led twenty-six of his men against heavily fortified dugouts at Guillemont, France. Of the twenty-six soldiers he led out, only five returned, but Holland was successful in capturing fifty enemy prisoners and was subsequently awarded the Victoria Cross.

Molly Keane
Novelist 1904 – 1996

Having written a number of novels under the pseudonym M. J. Farrell, it is believed Molly Keane did so in order to hide her literary leanings from her upper class friends and acquaintances. Having written eleven novels and a multitude of plays, Keane is best known for her 1981 novel, *Good Behaviour*, which was shortlisted for the Booker Prize. She died in Ardmore, County Waterford in 1996.

Jack Kelly (Dempsey)
World middleweight boxing champion 1862 – 1895

Jack Kelly, known as Jack Dempsey, was born near Clane and whilst he was just a young boy, emigrated with his family to the United States where he later became involved in the sport of boxing, adopting the name of Jack Dempsey when a boxer of that name failed to turn up for a bout and he took his place. Such was his capabilities in the boxing ring, he was nicknamed 'Nonpareil' ('without equal') and he went unbeaten in his first fourteen fights. Dempsey became the middleweight champion of America when he knocked out George Fulijames to claim the title and he became undisputed world middleweight champion with his victory over Australian fighter Bill

McCarthy. In 1891 in New Orleans, Dempsey faced the great Bob Fitzsimmons who would later go on to take the heavyweight championship of the world. Dempsey was completely dominated in the fight, which was eventually stopped in the thirteenth round when his second, Jack McAuliffe, threw in the towel. Only McAuliffe knew that Dempsey had contracted tuberculosis and badly needed to support himself and his family. He had placed a bet on Dempsey's behalf laying $1,400 to win $1,000, that Dempsey would last ten rounds. Upon reaching the tenth round, McAuliffe wanted to throw in the towel but Dempsey refused to let him. He finally did so in the thirteenth round. Dempsey died of tuberculosis in 1895. He is not to be confused with Jack Dempsey, the World Heavyweight Champion of the same name.

Michael Kelly Lawler
Union general, American Civil War 1814 – 1882

As a young boy, Michael Kelly Lawler emigrated with his family to the United States where they settled in Gallatin County, near Equality, Illinois. He studied law and was admitted to the bar of Illinois in 1844, before Governor Ford commissioned him a captain in 1846 when he took part in the Mexican War. Upon the outbreak of the American Civil War, Lawler was appointed colonel of the 18th Illinois Regiment and having served in Kentucky and Tennessee in November 1862, he was promoted to brigadier general of volunteers. He also served alongside

Boat house on a river, County Kildare.

with generals John A. Logan and John McClernand, before being appointed a member of the general staff of the Union forces and receiving a brevet promotion to major general on 13 March 1865.

Emily Lawless
Writer 1845 – 1913

An author of note, Emily Lawless wrote nineteen books of fiction, history, nature studies, poetry and a biography. Her novels include: *Hurrish* (1886), *Her Story of Ireland* (1887), *With Essex in Ireland* (1890) and *Grania* (1892). Lawless's best known work is perhaps her volume of poems, *With the Wild Geese,* which was published in 1902. Due to ill-health she moved to the south of England and died in Surrey in 1913.

Kathleen Lonsdale
Scientist 1903 – 1971

Born Kathleen Yardley, in 1908 her family moved to England where she attended the Girls High School at Ilford and studied mathematics at the Bedford College for Women in London. Offered a research position at University College London by the eminent crystallographer, W. H. Bragg, Lonsdale's most important scientific contribution was the studying of hexamethylbenzene crystals. In her studies, she showed that the benzene ring, a most important compound in organic chemistry, is flat; she defined its dimensions accurately. In 1945, she was granted a fellowship of the Royal Society in London, becoming one of the first females to ever receive this distinctive scientific honour, and in 1949 Lonsdale was appointed head of the crystallography at University College London. She was created a Dame Commander of the Order of the British Empire in 1965 and she died in London on 1 April 1971. In her memory, the Lonsdale Prize for Chemistry is awarded annually at NUI Maynooth, County Kildare.

John de Robeck
British Army admiral
1862 – 1928

John de Robeck was born in Naas and entered the British navy in 1875, reaching the rank of rear admiral in 1911. In 1914 he took command of the East-Mediterranean Squadron and was tasked with the Dardanelles expedition, which proved a failure due to the unexpected presence of a Turkish minefield and Turkish troops on high ground around the narrow straits. De Robeck was praised for his role in assisting the evacuation of Gallipoli towards the end of 1915, and the following year was promoted to vice admiral. From 1922 until 1924 he served as commander of the Atlantic fleet and he died in 1928.

Sir Ernest Henry Shackleton
Explorer 1874 – 1922

Ernest Shackleton was educated at Dulwich College London, and, having joined the Merchant Navy in 1890, was commissioned as a lieutenant in the Royal Naval Reserve, where he was part of the 1901 National Antarctic Expedition under Robert Falcon Scott on board the ship *Discovery*. Together with Scott and Doctor Edward Wilson, the expedition trekked toward the South Pole in 1902, but failed to reach it. In 1907, Shackleton organised and led the British Antarctic Expedition on board the *Nimrod*. On this occasion he came within ninety-seven miles of the South Pole, and he was knighted upon his return to England.

Shackleton's most famous expedition was on board the ship *Endurance*, which set out from London on 1 August 1914. In January of the following year, the vessel got locked in ice and was eventually crushed in the Weddell Sea, before finally sinking on 21 November 1915. Shackleton's party then remained on the ice floe for some five months, hoping that the floe would move north, towards to Elephant Island. On 9 April 1916, the crew manned the ship's long boats and finally, after a harrowing journey lasting five days, reached Elephant Island. At this barren outpost, which was around eight hundred miles from the nearest inhabited land, Shackleton left the main party behind and set sail with five of his men through the some of the most treacherous seas in the world. After enduring untold hardships, the men covered the eight hundred mile journey in fifteen days, finally reached South Georgia. Together with Tom Crean (see page 228), Frank Worsley and James Caird, Shackleton traversed mountainous, icy terrain, covering forty miles in thirty-six hours. All members of the crew of *Endurance* were eventually saved. In 1921 Shackleton set out on yet another Antarctic journey but died suddenly in South Georgia on 5 January 1922. He wrote two books on his experiences, *The Heart of the Antarctic* (1909) and *South* (1919).

Barry St Leger
British Army officer 1733 – 1789

Educated at Eton College and the University of Cambridge in England, Barry St Leger joined the British army in 1756 and in subsequent years served at the sieges of Louisbourg and Quebec. Promoted to brigade major in 1760, St Leger served in the campaign against Montreal before being promoted to lieutenant colonel in 1772, seeing service in the Saratoga campaign. In 1777 he was once again promoted, this time to full colonel and he fought in General Burgoyn's failed campaign to capture the state of New York, where St Leger was halted by American militia in Fort Stanwix. Having been forced to retreat to Canada, Burgoyn surrendered to the American forces. For a number of years following that surrender, St Leger served in the British frontier war against the United States and he was commandant of British Forces in Canada in 1784. He retired from military service due to ill health in 1785 and died in Quebec in 1789.

Domhnall Ua Buachalla
Last governor-general of Ireland
1866 – 1963

Domhnall Ua Buachalla was an Irish language activist and member of the Irish Volunteers. Following the Easter Rising, he became a member of Sinn Féin, and served in the 1st Dáil from 1918 to1921. Chosen by Éamon de Valera (see page 431) to become the third and final governor-general of Ireland, he was instructed to keep a very low profile and not to fulfil any public engagements. Ua Buachalla was however, allowed to reside at the governor-general's residence in Dublin's Phoenix Park and it was these tactics that de Valera's used to demean the position of the British representative in Ireland. It is reputed that upon the abolition of the governor-general's office, de Valera called Ua Buachalla on the telephone to inform him, 'You're abolished'. Ua Buachalla, who was hard of hearing, misinterpreted what de Valera had said, and is supposed to have replied, 'You're an even bigger one'. He died in Dublin on 30 October 1963, and was given a state funeral.

George 'Barrington' Waldron
Pickpocket, confidence trickster and author 1755 – 1804

Maynooth native George Waldron was born into a reasonably well-off family but following an incident at school, when he drew a knife on another pupil, he absconded and adopted the name of Barrington in order to escape detection. He later joined a company of strolling players, taking the name George as his acting name, and joined forces with a Mr Price, a well-known pickpocket who was stage manager of the company.

Upon being discovered picking pockets at a racecourse meeting, the two men were captured; with Price sentenced to seven years transportation, Barrington managed to escape to London, where he took rooms in a fashionable Piccadilly hotel. Disguised as a priest, he went to court on the queen's birthday where he picked several pockets and relieved a nobleman of his valuables before escaping without suspicion. However, an attempt to steal jewellery from a Russian prince during a performance at Covent Garden theatre was not so successful and resulted in Barrington serving a period of twelve months on a convict ship on the River Thames.

Following his release, he was again caught picking pockets, this time that of a Henry Hare-Townsend, and once again he was punished, being sentenced to seven years transportation in Botany Bay, Australia. Whilst onboard the convict ship a mutiny took place in which Barrington sided with the ship's crew and for his troubles he was awarded thirty acres of land and one hundred guineas by the governor of Port Jackson, Australia. In 1792 Barrington decided to turn his skills to writing and he published *A History of Australia and Its People,* which became a classic. It was followed by other works such as *A Voyage to Botany Bay* (1801) and *A History of New Holland* (1808). It was around this time that Barrington finally decided to change his conniving ways, ironically becoming superintendent of convicts of Paramatta and also holding the office of high constable. A thoroughly fascinating character, he died in 1821.

Charles Wolfe
Poet 1791 – 1823

Charles Wolfe was born in Blackhall and was educated in Winchester and Trinity College, Dublin. He took Holy Orders in 1817 and served as a curate at both Ballyclog, County Tyrone and Donoughmere, County Down. He is best remembered for one short, but universally known and admired poem, 'The Burial of Sir John Moore', which first appeared anonymously in the *New Telegraph* newspaper in 1817. Amongst the other poems Wolfe wrote were, 'Oh Say not that my Heart is Cold' and 'The Last Rose of Summer'. He died of tuberculosis in Cobh, County Cork.

Kilkenny

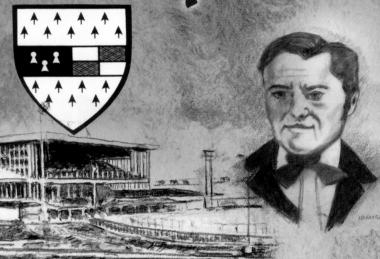

James Butler
1855-1934

James Butler, one of the principal grocery store-owners in the US, built the Yonkers Race Track. He also founded many Catholic charities.

George Berkeley   1685-1753

The South Hall, University of California, Berkeley, named after the philosopher George Berkeley.

Edmund Ignatius Rice
1762-1884

The Callan birthplace of Edmund Ignatius Rice, founder of the Christian and Presentation Brothers.

James Hoban
1762-1831

Carpenter James Hoban, who later qualified as an architect, designed and built the White House in Washington DC.

PATRICK CUDAHY

Patrick Cudahy
1849-1919

Memorial statue to Patrick Cudahy in Sheridan Park, Cudahy City, Wisconsin, USA. The City of Cudahy was founded by the businessman and philanthropist who was a true friend of Ireland.

John Banim
Poet, dramatist and novelist 1798 – 1842

John Banim was educated at Kilkenny College before going to Dublin in 1813 to study art. In 1821 he wrote the tragedy *Damon and Pythias,* which was later played at Covent Garden, London. His later writings, in collaboration with his brother Michael, portrayed the Irish character, customs, and national traits, giving rise to *Tales by the O'Hara Family*, which became immensely popular. He died on 13 August 1842.

John Barry
Victoria Cross recipient 1873 – 1901

John Barry was born in St Mary's Parish and served as a private in the 1st Battalion of the Royal Irish Regiment of the British Army, during the South African war. On the 8 January 1901, at Monument Hill, South Africa, Barry sustained considerable injuries having approached an enemy position during intensive fire on a night attack. Rendering the oppositions maximum gun useless, he carried out this deed with total disregard to his own life, meeting his death in the process. He was posthumously awarded the Victoria Cross.

George Berkeley
Philosopher 1685 – 1753

George Berkeley was born in Dysart Castle, Thomastown and was educated at Kilkenny College and Trinity College, Dublin. Having completed a masters degree there in 1707, he became a tutor and a lecturer in Greek, and he also produced *An Essay Towards a New Theory of Vision*, which was published in 1709 and examined the dynamics of sight and touch. The cause of much controversy, the essay brought Berkeley great notoriety, but over time the theories of the book gained acceptance and are now considered relevant to the theory of optics. His most widely read works are *A Treatise Concerning the Principles of Human Knowledge* (1710) and *Three Dialogues between Hylas and Philonous* (1713). In 1734 Berkeley published *The Analyst*, a critique of the foundation of calculus, and this publication was considered hugely influential in the realm of mathematics. The University of California, Berkeley is named after him and a residential college in Yale University also bears his name. He died on 16 January 1753.

Edward Butler
Politician 1823 – 79

Upon finding that his ambitions to become a lawyer were restricted by the fact that he was Catholic, Edward Butler emigrated to Australia, where he settled in Sydney and studied to become a barrister. His political career commenced with his appointment to the New South Wales Legislative Assembly, in which he served from 1869 until 1877, and he was attorney general from May 1872 until November of the following year. In 1877 Butler was appointed to the Legislative Council for life and he died in Sydney on 9 June 1879.

Hubert Butler
Essayist and translator 1900 –1991

Hubert Butler studied classics at St John's College, Oxford before graduating in 1922. Having travelled extensively in the 1920s and 1930s, Butler wrote about his journeys in the Balkans but was heavily criticised for a radio interview he gave about Yugoslavia in 1946, during which he failed to mention the suffering of Catholics under dictator Tito's regime. Butler countered by referring to the involvement of Catholic clergy with the Ustasa, a Nazi puppet regime in Yugoslavia during World War II, who had waged a genocidal crusade against non-Catholics and he was immediately castigated by the Catholic clergy in Ireland at that time. Butler, who published three collections of essays, *Escape from Anthill* (1985), *The Children of Drancy* (1988), and *Grandmother and Wolfe Tone* (1990), died at the family home at Maidenhall on the banks of the River Nore in 1991.

James Butler
American grocery store and racetrack owner 1855 – 1934

Arriving penniless in the United States at the age of twenty, within ten years James Butler was a millionaire having established one of the nation's largest grocery stores, 'James Butler Grocery County', and a grocery warehouse on Long Island that was the largest of its kind in the world. Having initially commenced business with his landlady's son, Patrick J. O'Connor, together the men opened their first store on Second Avenue, New York. Butler, who eventually bought out his partner, was one of the first to enjoy the benefits of large sales at small profits and he went on to open stores throughout the city of New York. By 1890 his wealth was such that he bought his first racehorse, and he went on to build his own racetrack – the Empire City, at Yonkers. Then living on a three hundred and fifty-acre estate next door to John D. Rockefeller, Butler's business was valued in excess of $15 million and he utilised this wealth in his devotion to Catholic charities, whilst also founding a Catholic girls' school at Tarrytown, New York. Having served as head-waiter at President Cleveland's inaugural dinner twenty-four years earlier, Butler was ironically invited as a guest to President Taft's inauguration and the company he started exists to this day.

John Byrne
Victoria Cross recipient 1832 – 1879

John Byrne was born in Castlecomer and served as a private in the 68th Regiment of the British Army during the Crimean War. With his regiment ordered to retire on 5 November 1854 at the Battle of Inkerman, Byrne, under extreme enemy fire, risked his life to bring back a wounded comrade. He later became a corporal in the 68th Regiment and died in England on the 10 July 1879.

Abraham Colles
Surgeon 1773 – 1843

Abraham Colles was educated at Kilkenny Grammar School before studying medicine at the Royal College of Surgeons in Dublin. A surgeon in Dr Steevens' Hospital from 1799 until 1841, Colles also served as professor of anatomy and surgery at the Royal College of Surgeons from 1804 until 1836. He was a skilled surgeon and his paper 'Fracture of the Carpal Extremity of the Radius' (1814) describes the nature of the injury, which to this day is known as Colles' fracture. He retired in 1841 and died two years later.

Patrick Cudahy
Meat packer and philanthropist
1849 – 1919

As a young boy, Patrick Cudahy emigrated with his family to the United States, where they settled in Milwaukee, Wisconsin.

At the age of fourteen he entered the meat packing industry, becoming superintendent of the Plankinton and Armour meat packing plant in Milwaukee in the early 1880s. He later purchased the company interests with his brother John and renamed it Cudahy Brothers. Cudahy later moved the plant to a large area of land that would become known as the industrial City of Cudahy. He also had other business interests; he was a director of the first Wisconsin National Bank of Milwaukee as well as owning extensive real estate. An active member of the Ancient Order of Hibernians and Friends of Irish Freedom, Cudahy was also a considerable contributor to many charities and donated land to churches and schools. The Cudahy depot, built in 1892, still stands and was designated a Milwaukee County registered landmark in 1983. The Cudahy name still exists in many areas of Milwaukee business to this day.

William Dowling
Victoria Cross recipient 1825 – 1887

Originally from Thomastown, William Dowling was a private in the 32nd Regiment of Foot of the British Army during the Indian Rebellion of 1857. On three separate occasions, Dowling successfully destroyed enemy guns and on each occasion left himself exposed to enemy fire. For these acts of bravery, he was awarded the Victoria Cross. He died in Liverpool in 1887.

City of Kilkenny.

Henry Flood
Statesman and orator 1732 – 1791

Henry Flood was educated at Trinity College, Dublin, and at Christ Church College, Oxford where he became proficient in the classics. A close friend of Henry Grattan (see page 169), who was leader of the Irish Patriot Party, Flood was also a member of parliament for Kilkenny in the Irish House of Commons and was renowned for his oratory skills. One of Flood's principal commitments was the complete legislative independence of the Irish parliament, but upon accepting the government position of vice treasurer of Ireland in 1775, he lost favour with nationalists. Flood's position was further weakened with his opposition to Catholic emancipation and so his place as a leader of Irish nationalists passed to Henry Grattan. In 1783 he served as a representative for Winchester in the British House of Commons but lost his seat in the 1790 elections, before retiring to his home at Farmley, County Kilkenny, where he died on 2 December 1791.

Frederick William Hall
Victoria Cross recipient 1885 – 1915

Frederick William Hall served as a company sergeant major in the 8th Winnipeg Rifles of the Canadian Expeditionary Force during World War I. At the Battle of Ypres on the 23 April 1915, upon discovering a number of his men were missing, Hall brought two wounded comrades back to his lines. Next morning he learned that yet more men were still missing and, despite being under severe pressure from enemy fire, he retrieved an injured soldier before being wounded whilst assisting another.

In Winnipeg, Manitoba there is a street called 'Valour Road', which was so named in view of the fact that three recipients of the Victoria Cross had resided on it. In addition to Hall, the other two men were Leo Clarke and Robert Shankland and a bronze plaque is mounted on a street lamp at the corner of the road to tell the story of these three brave men.

Walter Richard Pollock Hamilton
Victoria Cross recipient 1856 – 79

Born in the village of Inistioge, Walter Richard Pollock Hamilton served as a lieutenant in the Staff Corps of the Indian Army during the second Afghan War. On 2 April 1879, at Futtehabad, Afghanistan, Hamilton led a charge of the guide cavalry against a superior enemy force and when his commanding officer fell, took charge of the regiment and continued to encourage his men forward. During the charge, upon seeing a fellow cavalry man down injured and entangled with his horse, Hamilton rushed to his rescue, killing all three of his attackers and saving the soldier's life. For this he was awarded the Victoria Cross.

James Hoban
Architect who designed the White House 1762 – 1831

James Hoban commenced his working life as a carpenter, before studying architecture at the Royal Dublin Society and emigrating to the United States. He initially established himself as an architect in Philadelphia, Pennsylvania, but later moved to South Carolina, where he won the design for the State Capitol at Columbia, which was completed in 1791. He also won a competition for the design of the president's house in Washington DC, which was later to be called the White House. Hoban, whose design bore striking similarities to Leinster House in Dublin, supervised the White House's construction, during which the corner stone was layed by President George Washington on 13 September 1793. He also designed and built the Grand Hotel Washington and the Little Hotel in 1795 and served as captain in the Washington Artillery. Following the destruction of the White House by the British in 1814, Hoban was retained to rebuild it and he added the State and War Offices to his already impressive portfolio. He died in Washington DC on 8 December 1831, leaving behind an estate of one hundred thousand dollars.

Robert Johnston
Victoria Cross recipient 1872 – 1950
Robert Johnston was educated at King William's College on the Isle of Man. Serving as a captain in the Imperial Light Horse, South African Forces on 21 October 1899 at the Battle of Elandslaagte, Johnston showed great bravery when the momentum of his division was slowed down by very heavy fire at point-blank range. Together with another officer, he rushed forward under heavy fire, relieving the situation and allowing for the advancement of his unit. He was thus awarded the Victoria Cross and later achieved the rank of major before dying in Kilkenny in 1950.

James Mason
Chess player 1849 – 1905
In 1861, James Mason emigrated to the United States with his parents who had adopted him as a child. Although he was highly literate – a rarity for young Irish emigrant at that time – Mason initially worked as a shoe shiner and a news boy, but starting to frequent the chess cafes that were popular at the time. Under the influence of J. Gordon Bennett of the *New York Herald*, who recognised his chess talents, Mason became a journalist and a top flight chess player, going on to become the New York champion. He added the United States title in 1876, winning the Centennial and Fourth National Congress in Philadelphia, and his journalistic prowess led him to an editor's role in the *American Chess Journal*.

In 1878 Mason settled in London, having been enticed by the opportunity to engage with the best chess players in Europe and he defeated the great English champion Joseph Henry Blackburne in 1879. Although wins like this were extremely impressive, Maon's alcoholism proved destructive and the catalyst for losses against players that he was far superior to. In 1894 he published *The Principles of Chess*, which became an immediate bestseller and he followed it with *The Art of Chess*, which was also well received. In his publication on Mason in 2000, Jim Hayes stated that he excelled in the slowly developing attack and in the niceties of pawn play; Hayes considered him a pioneer who greatly contributed towards the making of modern chess. Mason died in Rochford, Essex on 12 January 1905.

Paddy Mullen
Racehorse Trainer 1919 – 2010
'The Family Man' and Irish horse racing legend Paddy Mullins was born in Graignamanagh and commenced his working life painting farm buildings, before later establishing his celebrated racing career of over fifty-two years at Goresbridge, County Kilkenny. His first winner as a trainer was Flash Parade at Punchestown in 1953 and it was his horse, Hurry Harriet, priced at 33-1, that defeated the outstanding French horse Altex in the Champion Stakes at Newmarket in 1973. Mullen felt this to be his own greatest personal achievement but went on to record six

Cheltenham festival winners, four Irish Grand Nationals, and numerous other major prizes in national hunt racing, as well as a considerable number of successes on the flat. He will be best remembered for training the great mare Dawn Run, who won the Champion Hurdle in 1984 and the Gold Cup at Cheltenham in 1986.

John O'Donovan
Scholar 1806 – 1861

Joining the office of the ordnance survey in 1829, John O'Donovan worked mainly on place-name research and he established the correct origin of many of Ireland's sixty-three thousand town land names. He wrote *A Grammar of the Irish Language* (1845) and *Leabhar na gCeart* (1847), and also carried out the translations of the *Annals of the Four Masters* in six volumes from 1846 to 1851. O'Donovan also transcribed and translated nine volumes of legal manuscripts and is considered to have made a very significant contribution to Irish literature and history. He died on 10 December 1861.

Tony O'Malley
Painter 1913 – 2003

Tony O'Malley was born in Callan and worked as a bank official until he developed tuberculosis in the 1940s. It was during this time he began painting and exhibiting his work. O'Malley, who emerged as one of Ireland's major contemporary artists, moved to Cornwall, England in 1960 and remained there for almost thirty years of his life. Much of his work maintains a strong spiritual theme and it also holds specific reverence to landscapes, such as those of Ireland, Cornwall and the Bahamas. O'Malley returned to Ireland in 1990 and in 1993 he was conferred by President Mary Robinson with the Aosdána title of Saoi, an honour bestowed on only five living artists. He died in 2003.

Edmund Ignatius Rice
Missionary and Educationalist 1762 – 1844

Despite his family's wealth, Edmund Ignatius Rice was initially educated at hedge schools, due to the Popery Act of 1709 which forbade teachers giving instructions in the Catholic faith. Following this rural instruction, he spent a further two years being schooled in Kilkenny. Rice married and had a successful career in business, but following a tragic accident in which his wife was killed and his daughter was left disabled, he devoted his life to the education and service of the poor. The founder of two religious orders, the Congregation of Christian Brothers and the Presentation Brothers, Rice died on 29 August 1844 at Mount Sion in Waterford. He was beatified in October 1996 and has become known as 'Blessed Edmund Ignatious Rice'. His feast day is 5 May.

John Ryan
Victoria Cross recipient 1823 – 1858

A private in the 1st Madras Fusiliers during the Indian Mutiny, whilst sheltering in a house that was being heavily besieged on 26 September 1857, at Lucknow, India, John Ryan rushed out into the street to the aid of a wounded captain, carrying him back to the safety of the house. Later in the day, he devoted himself to rescuing other wounded soldiers in the neighbourhood and for his great bravery, he was awarded the Victoria Cross before being promoted to the rank of sergeant. Ryan was killed in action in Cawnpore, India in 1858.

Richard Lalor Sheil
Politician, Dramatist and Orator
1791 – 1851

Richard Lalor Sheil was born at Drumdowney, Slieverue and was educated at Stoneyhurst College in Lancashire, England and at Trinity College, Dublin. Admitted to the Irish Bar in 1814, he initially supplemented his legal earnings by writing plays such as *Adelaide, or The Emigrants*, which was performed at Covent Garden in 1816, and *The Apostate*, which announced his true arrival as an accomplished dramatist. Sheil was one of the co-founders of the Catholic Association with Daniel O'Connell in 1823 and he was a strong supporter of Catholic emancipation, also winning admiration in the House of Commons for his brilliant oratory skills. He died in Florence, Italy on 23 May 1851.

James Stephens
Irish nationalist 1825 – 1901

A Protestant railway engineer, James Stephens participated, along with Smith O'Brien (see page 80), in the abortive rising of 1848, following which he escaped to France. Having returned to Ireland in 1856, Stephens founded the Irish Republican Brotherhood and in Fenian circles, earned the code name 'An Shabhac' ('The Hawk'). Referred to by London politicians, who had no knowledge of the Irish language, as 'The Shooks', Stephens planned a rising for the 20 September 1865, but was arrested on 15 September, before escaping from Richmond Bridewell Prison and fleeing to the United States. Whilst there, Stephens had a dispute with the American Fenians and so returned to France where he spent a number of years as a journalist and teacher. He returned to Ireland in 1868 and died at his home in Blackrock, County Dublin in April 1901.

Laois

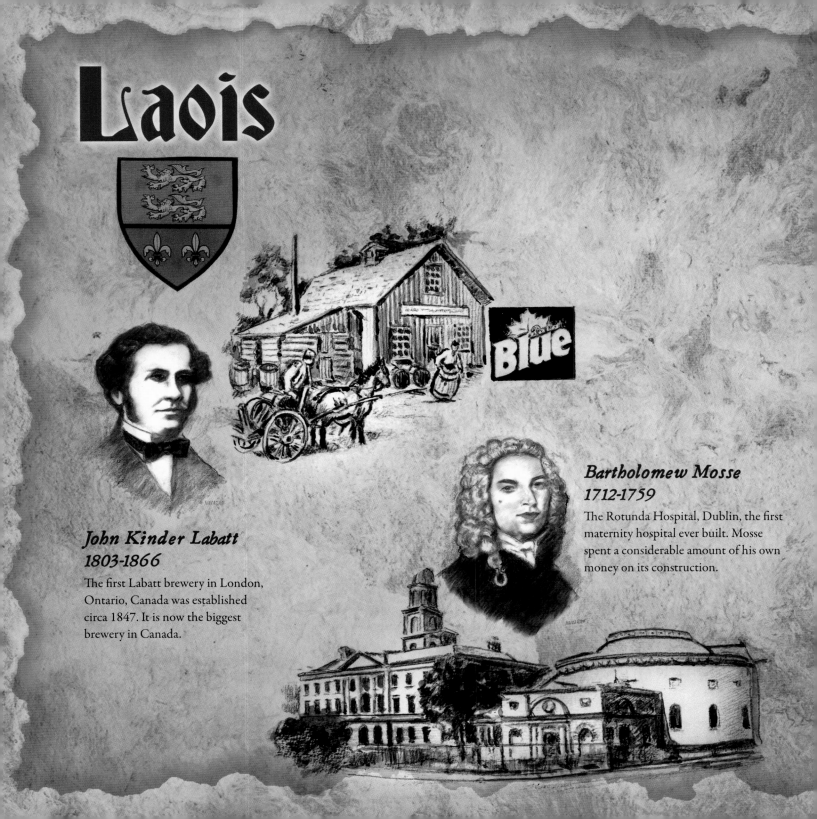

John Kinder Labatt
1803-1866

The first Labatt brewery in London, Ontario, Canada was established circa 1847. It is now the biggest brewery in Canada.

Bartholomew Mosse
1712-1759

The Rotunda Hospital, Dublin, the first maternity hospital ever built. Mosse spent a considerable amount of his own money on its construction.

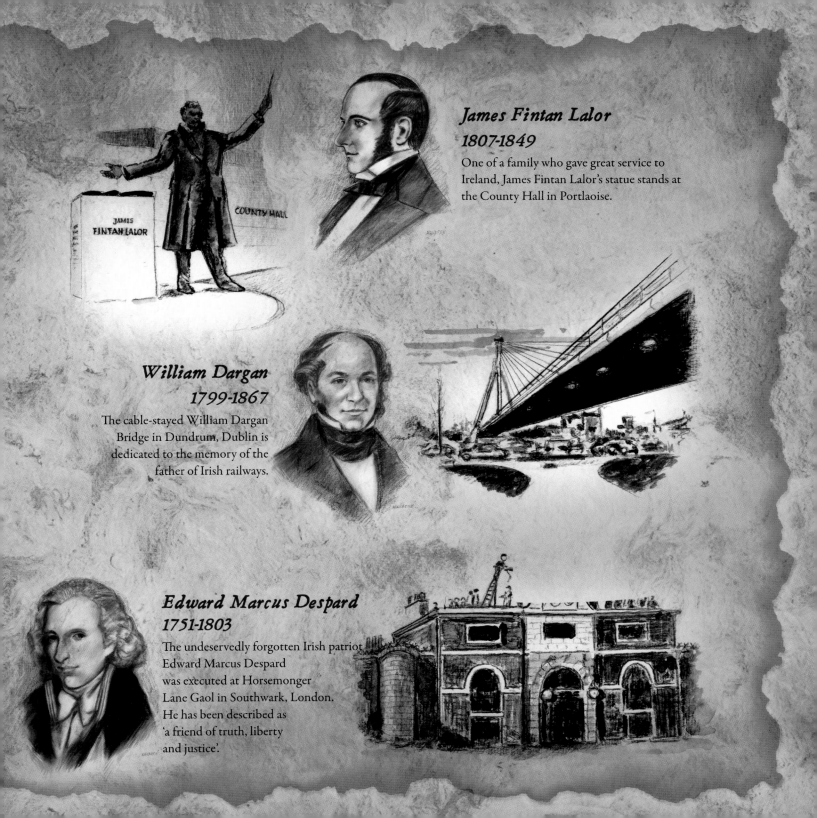

James Fintan Lalor
1807-1849

One of a family who gave great service to Ireland, James Fintan Lalor's statue stands at the County Hall in Portlaoise.

William Dargan
1799-1867

The cable-stayed William Dargan Bridge in Dundrum, Dublin is dedicated to the memory of the father of Irish railways.

Edward Marcus Despard
1751-1803

The undeservedly forgotten Irish patriot Edward Marcus Despard was executed at Horsemonger Lane Gaol in Southwark, London. He has been described as 'a friend of truth, liberty and justice'.

John Barrett
Antiquary and biblical scholar 1753 – 1821
Educated at Trinity College, Dublin, where he became professor of Oriental languages, John Barrett served as a don at his alma mater for most of his career. Barret was an eccentric and his publications include *An Enquiry into the Origin of the Constellations that form the Zodiac*. He also wrote an essay on the early life of Dean Swift and his two passions were reading and the hoarding of money. Whilst he spoke Latin and Greek fluently, Barrett had great difficulty in expressing himself in English. He was renowned for his frugal existence in the fifty years he spent living in Trinity and upon his death, left a legacy of eighty thousand pounds for the poor. The trustees of his will ensured that his poverty-stricken brothers and sisters also benefited.

James Bergin
Victoria Cross recipient 1845 – 1880
James Bergin was a private in the 33rd Regiment of Foot (Duke of Wellington's Regiment), British Army during the Abyssinian Expedition. Together with a number of his comrades, Bergin scaled a cliff and a high wall to attack and wipe out the defenders of a gateway, thus enabling his regiment to advance. He died at Poona, India in December, 1880.

Mike Cleary
Boxer 1858 – 1893
In the 1870s, Mike Cleary emigrated with his family to the United States where they settled in New York. A boxer during the era of bare-knuckle fighting, in only his second fight Cleary broke his wrist whilst facing Jack Langdon. He was renowned as a hard hitter and between 1875 and 1882, he had a successive run of six knockouts in ten fights. In 1882 Cleary fought George Rooke for the Middleweight Championship of America and successfully stopped him in the third round. He also fought fellow Irishman Jack Dempsey (see page 241) in New York on 10 April 1886 and took on such notables as Jack Kilrain and the great 'Gentleman' Jim Corbett, who described Cleary as one of the hardest hitters he had ever met. In 1893 Cleary suffered an accident which required the amputation of one foot, and he later developed tuberculosis before dying in Belfast, New York on 5 September 1893.

Sir William Cosby
Governor of New York
1690 – 1736
William Cosby was born in Stradbally Hall and enlisted in the British army as a teenager in the early 1700s. By 1717 he had reached the rank of colonel of the Royal Regiment of Ireland and was transferred to Minorca, Spain the following year. Cosby became Governor of the island but was later transferred to New York, where he was appointed governor by King George II of Britain. Whilst serving in that role, he established a reputation for oppression and amassed a large but questionably-attained fortune, having been accused of stealing collected taxes and misappropriating Native American lands. He died of tuberculosis on 10 March 1736.

William Dargan
Engineer 1799 – 1867

Considered the father of Irish railways, William Dargan constructed Ireland's first railway line from Dublin to Dun Laoghaire in 1833. Indeed, he is responsible for the construction of nearly eight hundred miles of railway throughout the country. The National Gallery was built to commemorate his services and a statue to him stands on the lawn. A cable-stayed bridge over the Luas tramline at Dundrum is named in his honour.

Cecil Day-Lewis
Poet and critic 1904 – 1972

The father of Academy Award-winning actor Daniel Day-Lewis, Cecil Day-Lewis was born in Ballintubbert, Stradbally and was educated at Sherborne and Wadham Colleges, Oxford. Lewis had an illustrious career both as an academic and as a literary figure and he produced many collections of poetry, critical works, translations and novels. Under the pen name Nicholas Blake, he wrote many successful murder mysteries, and he also served as poet laureate from 1968 until his death in 1972. He died in Hertfordshire, England on 22 May 1972.

Edward Marcus Despard
Revolutionary 1751 – 1803

Edward Marcus Despard was born in Mountrath and served as an officer in the British Navy in the West Indies, where he was superintendent of the Bay of Honduras. He was subsequently recalled to Britain in order to answer trivial and unfounded charges that he supported the poorer inhabitants of that settlement, to the great annoyance of the local oligarchs. He was thus dismissed from the British navy, but Britain's loss would be Ireland's gain and one year after joining the Society of United Englishmen, Despard was a guiding spirit in the campaign to assist the United Irishmen in their struggle for independence in 1797.

In 1802 Despard was named as a member of a conspiracy to seize the Tower of London and the Bank of England and to assassinate King George III. Horatio Nelson acted as a character witness at his trial but despite flimsy evidence, Despard was found guilty and sentenced to be hung, drawn and quartered, the last of such sentences to be carried out in England. Interestingly, the 20,000 people that attended his execution remained silent throughout as a mark of respect, and a memorial on the grave of his wife, Charlotte Despard in Glasnevin Cemetery bears an inscription, which was part of an oration he made to that crowd prior to his hanging: 'a friend to truth, liberty and justice'. A man undeservedly forgotten in Irish history, he was hanged in London on 21 February 1803.

Joseph Dobbs
Diplomat 1915 – 2002

Due to his father's bankruptcy, Abbeyleix born Joseph Dobbs financed his own way through school and subsequently won university scholarships. At Trinity Hall, Cambridge he read modern languages and was fluent in Spanish, French, Italian and Russian. Dobbs was also an eloquent and witty speaker and he was fiercely proud of his Irish origins. He was Britain's leading Kremlinologist during the Cold War and several successive British prime ministers sought his advice in dealing with Soviet leaders, ranging from Stalin to Brezhnev. He also served in the British embassy in Moscow for fourteen years and was awarded the MBE for services during the war in Italy. Dobbs was further appointed an OBE in 1957 and a CMG in 1972. He died on 28 September 1989.

Patrick J. Dowling
Businessman and Irish historian
1904 –19 98

Patrick J. Dowling was born in Camross and began his working life as a messenger and labourer. Seeing no future in Ireland, in 1926 he emigrated to the United States where he settled in San Francisco, California. Dowling was a man of sharp intelligence and having attended night school, he became manager of a large branch of a national food chain within five years.

He later founded his own business, which afforded him the time to follow his great passion for tracing the history of Irish immigrants in California. He was one of the co-founders of the Irish Cultural Centre of California, where the Patrick J. Dowling library, containing more than three thousand titles on a variety of Irish topics, is open to descendants of immigrants seeking information on their roots and heritage. Today it is one of the largest depositories of Irish Americana.

Denis Dynon
Victoria Cross recipient 1822 – 1863

Denis Dynon was born in Kilmallon and served as a sergeant in the 53rd Regiment of Foot of the British Army during the Indian Mutiny. At Chota Behar, together with Lieutenant Daunt, he displayed extreme gallantry during the capture of two guns whilst under heavy enemy fire in open ground, and for this deed he was awarded the Victoria Cross.

Samuel Jacob Jackson
Politician 1848 – 1942

Following his family's emigration to Canada, Samuel Jacob Jackson was educated at Brantford, Ontario. A farmer by trade, he was elected to the Manitoba Legislature in 1883 and acted as speaker of the Legislative Assembly of Manitoba from 1891 until 1895. In 1904 he won a seat in the Canadian House of Commons, and he also served as an alderman in the Winnipeg City Council in 1877, 1878 and 1880. He retired from politics in 1908 and died on 29 May 1942.

Arthur Jacob
Surgeon and opthalmologist 1790 – 1874

Arthur Jacob studied medicine at Stephen's Hospital, Dublin and having also studied in Paris, Edinburgh and London, he was appointed demonstrator of anatomy at Trinity College, Dublin, where he discovered a previously unknown membrane of the eye that has since been known as Membrana Jacobi. In 1826 Jacob was elected professor of anatomy at the Royal College of Surgeons in Dublin, and he held that chair until 1869. He was also a founder member of the Irish Medical Association and apart from his discovery of Membrana Jacobi, he described Jacob's ulcer and revived cataract surgery through the cornea with a curved needle. His principle publications were *A Treatise on the Information of the Eyeball* (1849) and *On Cataract and the Operation of its Removal by Absorption* (1851). He died in Barrow-on-Furness, England on 21 September 1874.

Anne Jellicoe (née Mullin)
Educationalist 1823 – 1880

A member of a Quaker family, upon her marriage to John Jellicoe, Anne Jellicoe moved to County Offaly and established an embroidery and lace school to provide employment for young girls. In 1858 she moved to Dublin where she established a school for poor children that was run by the Quakers but accommodated all denominations. A woman of immense vision, in 1861 Jellicoe founded the The Queen's Institute, which was the first society for the employment of women in Ireland, and in 1866 she founded Alexandra College – the first college in Ireland to offer a university-type education for women.

John Kinder Labatt
Founder of the Labatt Brewing Company 1803 – 1866

John Kinder Labatt was born in Mountmellick and emigrated to Canada in 1833. He began work as a farmer but some thirteen years after arriving in Canada, he invested in a small London brewery. From an initial production of four thousand barrels per year, Labatt built the brewery into a giant enterprise that has served as a distinctive strand of Canadian commerce since the mid-nineteenth century. Labatt's Brewery of London in Ontario is now Canada's second-largest brewery and is a public company involved in extensive interests, from entertainment to sports networks. Labbatt died on 26 October 1866.

James Fintan Lalor
Revolutionary and journalist
1807 – 1849

Despite suffering from a growth defect due to a spinal injury during his childhood, James Fintan Lalor was a lively and dedicated activist and reformer, who wrote many stirring and controversial letters and articles to newspapers such as the *Felon* and the *Nation*. An outspoken critic of the British government's policy of exporting grain to Britain, whilst Irish peasants starved during the Great Famine, following a failed attack on a RIC Barracks in Cappoquin, County Waterford, Lalor was jailed and later died in prison. Twenty-five thousand people attended his funeral at Glasnevin Cemetery and in 2007, the Laois County Council erected a monument to his memory. Designed by Mayo-based artist, Rory Breslin, it stands outside the council chambers, facing James Fintan Lalor Avenue in Portlaoise.

Peter Lalor
Eureka Stockade leader and politician 1827 – 1889

A brother of James Fintan Lalor (see above), Peter Lalor was educated at Carlow College and in Dublin before he became a civil engineer. Lalor emigrated with his brother Richard to Melbourne, Australia in 1852 and in 1854 he moved to Ballarat, Victoria, where he staked a claim in the Eureka mines. Later elected by the miners to lead them against the incompetent and often brutal administration of the mines, during a skirmish with the authorities Lalor received a wound, which eventually led to the amputation of his arm. Governor Hotham offered a reward for the capture of Lalor for treasonable acts and inciting men to take up arms against the queen. Despite this, Lalor was never tried; instead, enormous political change after the Eureka stockade saw him appointed to the Victorian Legislative Assembly in 1855. He served as postmaster general in 1875 and minister for trade and customs from 1877 until 1880. Lalor was speaker of the Legislative Assembly of Victoria from 1880 to 1887 until his retirement due to ill health, and he died on 9 February 1889. The Melbourne suburb of Lalor is named in his memory.

Bartholomew Mosse
Surgeon and founder of the Rotunda Hospital, Dublin
1712 – 1759

Bartholomew Mosse was born in Portlaoise and worked as an apprentice barber surgeon with John Stone from 1729 until 1733, following which he passed examination by the surgeon general. In 1738 he was appointed surgeon in charge of troops in Minorca, Spain, but he later decided to focus his interests on midwifery, spending some time in Paris to further his education on the subject. Mosse was shocked by the number of mother and infant deaths during childbirth and he returned to Ireland determined to raise money for a purpose-built maternity hospital. He achieved this through subscriptions and the hospital now known as the Rotunda Hospital in Parnell Street, Dublin was opened in 1745. Apart from achieving his aims by subscriptions, Mosse spent a considerable amount of his personal fortune on the venture. The hospital was the first maternity hospital ever built and a deep debt of gratitude is owed to the memory of this man for achieving it.

John Moyney
Victoria Cross recipient 1895 – 1980

At the age of twenty-two, Rathdowney born John Moyney served as lance sergeant in the 2nd Battalion, Irish Guards of the British Army during World War I. On 13 September 1917, at Broembeek, Belgium, whilst commanding fifteen men who were surrounded by the enemy, Moyney held out for ninety-six hours with sparse rations of food and water. After five days of continuous enemy onslaught, he counter-attacked with great effect and successfully led a charge through enemy lines, before reaching a stream, where together with a Private Thomas Woodcock, he covered his party whilst they crossed unscathed. Moyney died in Roscrea, County Tipperary in 1980.

Myles Poore O'Connor
Lawyer, businessman and philanthropist 1823 – 1909

Myles Poore O'Connor emigrated with his family to England in 1825, before moving on to the United States where they settled in St Louis, Missouri in 1838. There O'Connor studied law and he graduated in 1846. In 1848, at the advent of the Gold Rush in California, he travelled west, settling in San Francisco, where he quickly established a legal business predominately centred on the mining industry. Such was his success that, in a very short period, O'Connor was in a position to buy a palatial home in downtown San Francisco and in 1863, he struck riches beyond his wildest dreams with the development of the Idaho Mine, which produced $4.5 million worth of precious metal. He also entered into politics and in 1869 became a democratic senator for the state of California. However, it is perhaps as a philanthropist that O'Connor deserves most recall. On a site of eight thousand acres near Steven's Creek and

Meridian Road, San Jose, he built the O'Connor Sanitarium and the O'Connor Hospital, as it is now known, exists to this day. O'Connor, whose contributions to the Catholic Church and charitable organisations were immense, died On 9 June 1909. His funeral cortege was one of the most impressive in Santa Clara County's history.

Kevin O'Higgins
Statesman 1892 – 1927

Educated at Clongowes Wood College and University College Dublin, Kevin O'Higgins was a member of the Sinn Féin political party. Despite his imprisonment in 1918, he was elected a member of parliament for Laois and supported the Anglo-Irish Treaty of 1921, which brought the Irish Free State into existence. In the new government, O'Higgins was appointed minister for justice and was also on the committee that drafted the Constitution of the Irish Free State. He was also primarily responsible for the establishment of the new Civic Guard. In 1927 he became minister for external affairs, but on 10 July of the same year, he was assassinated on Booterstown Avenue, Blackrock in revenge for his part in the execution of IRA men during the Civil War. O'Higgins was awarded a state funeral and is buried in Glasnevin Cemetery.

James Pearson
Victoria Cross recipient 1822 – 1900

Born in Rathdowney, James Pearson served as a private in the 86th Regiment of Foot of the British Army during the Indian Mutiny. Despite being wounded by rebels at Jhansi, Pearson successfully killed one enemy and bayoneted two others, and was thus awarded the Victoria Cross. He later achieved the rank of sergeant and died in India in 1900.

James D. Phelan
Mayor of San Francisco and US Senator for California 1861 – 1930

Having emigrated to the United States with his family at the age of five, James Phelan's education was cut short at an early age when he was forced to leave school due to family circumstances. He thus commenced work as a grocery clerk, but as a young man with considerable entrepreneurial skills, by 1846 he was running his own profitable dry goods business in Cincinnati, Ohio. With the arrival of the gold rush in California, Phelan sensed an opportunity to supply dry goods such as nails, cooking utensils and tools to the miners, and he purchased an extensive stock which he consigned to San Francisco. Phelan reinvested his profits into the city's booming real estate, as well as the banking and insurance sectors. By 1883 he had sufficient finances to construct the Phelan Building at the intersection of O'Farrell and Market Street in San Francisco, and he later became mayor of that city, serving from 1897 until 1902. Phelan was also the democratic senator for California from March 1915 until March 1921 and following his time in the senate, he returned to banking and collecting art. He died on his country estate, 'Villa Montalvo' in Saratoga, California in 1930. In his memory, the town of Phelan, California, as well as Phelan Avenue in San Francisco, are named after him.

Walter Shanly
Civil engineer and politician 1817 – 1899

Walter Shanley was born in Stradbally and in 1836 emigrated to London, Ontario in Canada where he gained practical engineering experience working on the

Beauharnois Canal in Montreal. He later engaged in engineering work on the Welland Canal in the Niagara Falls area and in 1848 he moved to Boston, Massachusetts to work on drafting plans for a railway line from Ogdensburg, New York to Boston. In 1851 Shanly became the chief engineer of Bytown and Prescott and was in charge of a trunk railway connecting Quebec City, Montreal, Toronto and Sarnia. He became increasingly famous as a consultant engineer and advised on many major engineering works. Shanley even branched into the world of politics, and was elected to the Legislative Assembly of the Province of Canada in 1863, and to the House of Commons in 1867. He died on 17 December 1899.

John Shaw
Captain in the US Navy 1773 – 1823
Mountmellick born John Shaw moved to the United States in 1790, settling in Philadelphia, Pennsylvania. Having initially served in the Merchant Navy, he became a lieutenant in the United States navy in 1798 and was given command of the schooner Enterprise in 1799. Within a year, he had captured seven armed French vessels and recaptured a number of American merchant men, making the Enterprise one of the most famous ships in the United States navy. Shaw, who has had a number of ships named in his honour, died in Philadelphia on 17 September 1823.

Launt Thompson
Sculptor 1833 – 1894
During the famine of 1847, Launt Thompson emigrated to the United States with his mother, settling in Albany, New York. An Abbeyleix native, Thompson studied anatomy with a physician, Doctor Armsby, and he also spent nine years in the studio of sculptor E. D. Palmer. He opened his first studio in New York in 1857 and for inspiration visited Rome on two occasions

in the mid-1860s and 70s. Thompson, who also lived for a time in Florence, produced several notable works, such as Napoleon I, which is held in the Metropolitan Museum, New York, an equestrian statue of General A.E. Burnside as well as a statue of General Winfield Scott. Amongst his patrons were wealthy New Yorkers, city and state governments and the United States Congress. In 1862 Thompson was elected an academician at the National Academy and his work is considered a valuable component of the art produced in his adopted homeland. He died at Middletown, New York on 26 September 1894.

Kivas Tully
Architect 1820 – 1905
Kivas Tully was born in Garrarucam and trained as an architect at the Royal Naval School in Camberwell, England. Later returning to Ireland, where he trained under W.H. Owen Architects and Civil Engineers in Limerick, he emigrated to Canada in 1844. There, in his first year of practice, Tully secured two prestigious commissions: the Bank of Montreal Building and the Customs House in Toronto. In 1851 he secured further commissions for Trinity College, Toronto, and the Welland County Courthouse at Merrittville, Ontario. The following year Tully received a commission for Cobourg Town Hall. All three buildings have Classical and Gothic revival styles. In 1868 he joined the New Ontario Department of Public Works where he was appointed architect engineer and chief officer, and he held this position until his retirement in 1896. Tully, who was also one of the founder members of the Canadian Society of Civil Engineers, died on 24 April 1905.

Mary Frances Xavier Warde
Religious leader and educator
1810 – 1884

Mary Frances Xavier Warde was born in Bellbrook House, Mountrath. Having lost both her parents as a young girl, in her early twenties, Warde offered her services to the founder of the Congregation of the Sisters of Mercy, Catherine McAuley (see page 179). She joined the newly formed Sisters of Mercy in 1831 and was appointed superior of St Leo's Convent, County Carlow in 1837. Warde later travelled to the United States on behalf of the order and there she founded one hundred institutions of Mercy. Her amazing work there ranged from caring for wounded soldiers of both the Union and Confederate armies, as well as tending to Native American women and the poor and destitute. The institutions that she founded were multi-faceted and served as places of education, orphanages, hospitals and homes for the aged. Warde contracted pneumonia in March 1884 and she died on 17 September of that year.

Leitrim

Robert Strawbridge
c.1734-1781

The Strawbridge home in Frederick County, Maryland. In 1776, Strawbridge left Ireland and settled in Sam's Creek, Maryland, where he founded some of first Methodist societies in the US.

John Robert Godley
1814-1861

The region of Canterbury, New Zealand was established by John Robert Godley, whose statue stands in Cathedral Square, Christchurch.

William 'Bill' Riley
1917-1942

A World War II biplane, as flown by fighter ace William Riley.

Seán MacDermott
1883-1916

The birthplace of Kiltyclogher patriot Seán MacDermott who was executed on 12 May 1916 following the Easter Rising.

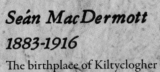

John Willoughby Crawford
1817-1875

The Royal Canadian Bank (circa 1850) was founded by John Willoughby Crawford, lieutenant governor of Ontario, Canada.

John Willoughby Crawford

Businessman, lawyer and lieutenant governor of Ontario 1817 – 1875

Born in Manorhamilton, John Willoughby Crawford left Ireland with his family at an early age and settled in Brockville, Ontario. Educated at York , Toronto, Crawford was called to the bar in 1839 and although he was a lawyer, he was more active in business, serving at one time as president of the Royal Canadian Bank. Crawford was also president of the Toronto and Nipissing Railway, in addition to being a director of several other companies. The Roman Catholic Education Rights, entrenched in Ontario's constitution under Section 93 of the British North American Act, were enacted by his support, despite the fact he himself was a Protestant. Crawford was a member of the Legislative Assembly of the Province of Canada, representing for East Toronto from 1861 to 1863 and he was also a member of parliament from 1867 to 1873. Later appointed lieutenant governor of Ontario, he died in office in 1875.

William Henry Drummond

Canadian poet 1854 – 1907

William Henry Drummond was born in Mohill and emigrated with his family to Canada as a young boy. Settling near Montreal, Drummond attended high school and later enrolled at McGill University and Bishop's College, where he graduated in medicine in 1884. In 1898 he published *The Habitant and Other French-Canadian Poems*, which brought him substantial income in royalties, and he followed this with *Johnnie Courteau And Other Poems* in 1901. Continuing his occupation as a medical professor, Drummond was elected a fellow of the Royal Society for Literature in England, as well as the Royal Society of Canada. He died on 6 April 1907.

Patrick Duigenan

Lawyer and politician
1735 – 1816

The son of a Catholic farmer, a local Protestant clergyman gave Patrick Duigenan tuition at a young age, which resulted in him gaining a scholarship to Trinity College, Dublin in 1756. Called to the Irish Bar in 1767, following which he established a very wealthy practice, Duigenan was totally opposed to Henry Grattan (see page 169) and the Irish parliament, and he was a strong supporter of the Union. He violently contested Catholic emancipation and upon the formation of the Union, was elected a member for Armagh, becoming a well-known character at Westminster where he died on 11 April 1816.

Colonel Anthony William Durnford

Soldier 1830 – 1879

William Anthony Durnford entered the Royal Military Academy, Woolwich in 1846 before he was commissioned in the Royal Engineers in 1848. Between 1851 and 1856 he served in Ceylon where he was stationed in Trincomalee. There he assisted in the designing of the harbour and he later saw service in Malta before being promoted to captain and returning to England in 1864. On 23 January

1872, Durnford was transferred to Cape Town, South Africa where he disapproved of the policy of the colonial government towards the natives, by whom he was highly regarded. A brevetted colonel, he was involved in the British army's defeat by the Zulus at the Battle of Isandlwana, where he was killed with all his men on 22 January 1879.

Phillip Fitzpatrick
New York policeman and songwriter 1892 – 1947

A New York policeman, Aughavas born Phillip Fitzpatrick left Ireland in the early 1930s but was shot and killed having responded to a robbery on 26 May 1947. The song below was written by him and has since become the anthem of County Leitrim. The final lines of the song entitled 'Lovely Leitrim' are as follows:

> *Last night I had a pleasant dream*
> *I woke up with a smile*
> *I dreamed that I was back again*
> *In my dear old Erin's Isle*
> *I thought I saw Lough Allen's Banks*
> *In the valley down below*
> *It was my lovely Leitrim*
> *Where the Shannon waters' flow...*
> *...And if ever I return again*
> *The place that I will go*
> *Will be to lovely Leitrim*
> *Where the Shannon waters flow*

Unfortunately, Fitzpatrick never lived to fulfil the wish in his song.

John Robert Godley
Founder of the province of Canterbury, New Zealand
1814 – 1861

A member of a landed gentry family who also had a home at 33 Merrion Square, Dublin, John Robert Godley was educated at a preparatory school in Buckinghamshire, England and later at Harrow. Following this, he enrolled on a scholarship at the University of Oxford, before touring Europe in 1837 and returning to Ireland where he was called to the bar in 1839. Godley was appointed high sheriff of County Leitrim in 1843 and in 1849 he travelled to New Zealand as the representative of the Canterbury Association, which was formed to establish an Anglican Church settlement at Christchurch. Desiring that the colony be self-governing and not ruled by the association, he later returned to London and died on 17 November 1861. The people of Christchurch erected a statue in his honour in Cathedral Square that year.

Jim Gralton
Communist 1886 – 1945

Having deserted his post in the British Army, Jim Gralton worked for a time on the Liverpool docks and in the coalfields of Wales before emigrating to New York in 1909. There he established a James Connolly Club, but in 1922 he returned to Ireland and was instrumental in the re-building of the Pearse Connolly Hall in his hometown. Having returned to New York in the late 1920s, Gralton once again left for Ireland in 1932 and this time joined the Revolutionary Workers Group, which was later to become the Communist Party of Ireland. He re-established the Pearse-Connolly Hall, which became a venue for meetings of the Revolutionary Workers Group, and this resulted in him becoming the focus of an anti-Communist witch-hunt. With pressure from the Catholic Church, the Éamon de Valera (see page 431) led government deported Gralton to the United States in 1933. Considered an 'undesireable alien', he became the first Irish person to be deported from his own country. In the United States he became an active member of the Communist Party for the remainder of his life and died there in 1945.

269

Lough Rynn Castle, County Leitrim.

Charles Irwin
Victoria Cross recipient
1824 – 1873

Manorhamilton born Charles Irwin served as a private in the 53rd Regiment of Foot of the British Army during the Indian Mutiny at Lucknow. Irwin was awarded the Victoria Cross for displaying extreme bravery under heavy fire whilst assaulting the Secundra Bagh and although severely wounded in the right shoulder, he was the first to enter the building, which was eventually secured for the British Forces. He died in Newtownbutler, County Fermanagh on 27 March 1873.

Seán MacDiarmada
Patriot 1883 – 1916

A member of the Irish Republican Brotherhood and the Gaelic League, Seán MacDiarmada moved to Dublin in 1908 and became a close friend of Tom Clarke (see page 429). MacDiarmada developed poliomyelitis and as a result of that illness he walked with a cane. One of the founding members of the Irish Volunteers in 1913, his disability did not prevent him from taking part in the Easter Rising at the General Post Office, Dublin in 1916, but following the failure of that rising he was court-martialed on 9 May and executed by firing squad on 12 May. It was Daniel Hoey who identified MacDiarmada for the court-martial but he himself was shot by Michael Collins' (see page 89) squad in Spetember 1916. The British officer Lee-Wilson, who ordered MacDiarmada's death was also killed on Collins'

order. Seán McDermott Street in Dublin is named in his honour, as is the railway station in Sligo and the GAA stadium in Carrick-on-Shannon, County Leitrim.

James McCombs
New Zealand politician
1873 – 1933

Having emigrated to New Zealand with his family in 1876, James McCombs was educated at Sydenham and Christchurch East, following which he became a draper's assistant. His political career began with involvement in the Progressive Liberal Association and he was later appointed an MP for the Social Democratic Party. Elected the first President of the newly-founded Labour Party in 1916, McCombs represented Lyttelton in the New Zealand Parliament from 1913 until 1933 and he was a staunch supporter of women's rights, including their right to be elected to parliament. Noted for his debating skills, McCombs was a conscientious, hard-working politician who spent all of his twenty years in parliament on the benches of the opposition. He died in Christchurch on 2 August 1933.

John Joe McGirl
Republican 1921 – 1988

John Joe McGirl was born in Ballinamore and became involved with the IRA in the 1940s. Due to his participation in the IRA Border Campaign in 1957, he was convicted at Ballinamore Court House and jailed in Mountjoy Prison, but during his incarceration he was elected a Sinn Féin TD for Sligo Leitrim. Losing his seat in the 1961 elections, McGirl sided with the Provisionals in the IRA split of 1969 between the Officials and the Provisionals, but having supported the continuance of their campaign against British rule in Northern Ireland, he was interned in 1974. He remained supportive of the policies of Gerry Adams and Martin McGuinness and the methods they were undertaking to solve the issues in Northern Ireland by political means, and was later elected a Sinn Féin councillor for Leitrim County Council. He served in that role until his death and a monument to his memory stands in his native town of Ballinamore.

Susan Mitchell
Poet and editor 1866 – 1926
Susan Mitchell was born in Carrick-on-Shannon but was brought up in Dublin by her unionist aunts. Rebelling against the privileged society and the Protestant church in which she was raised, Mitchell was an accomplished poet who was noted for her parodies and witty verse. She became part of a circle of noted Irish poets and writers, whilst also working as an editor for the *Irish Homestead* and the *Irish Statesman*. A beautiful woman with flame-red hair, she was highly regarded in the literary world, as evidenced by the admiration she received from W. B. Yeats (see page 199).

Anthony Mulvey
Nationalist politician 1882 – 1957
Anthony Mulvey initially worked as editor of the *Ulster Herald* before he was elected to the British House of Commons representing Fermanagh and Tyrone in 1935. A Nationalist Party member, Mulvey adopted an abstentionist policy with regard to the British House of Commons, but following the election of a Labour government in 1945, he decided to take a seat and in his opening address to the British Parliament stated, 'Now that Britian has elected a more enlightened government, my people have released me. Before peace can be established, justice must be done to Ireland.' In the 1950 general election, Mulvey moved to represent Mid-Ulster but retired from politics the following year. He died on 11 January 1957.

Thomas Heazle Parke
Surgeon and explorer
1857 – 1893
Educated at the Royal College of Surgeons in Dublin, Thomas Heazle Parke joined the British Army and saw service in Egypt as part of the rescue columns that were sent to assist General Gordon in 1887. He also volunteered to join Welsh explorer Henry Morton Stanley in the relief of Emin Pasha, Governor of Equatoria. That relief expedition travelled more than one thousand miles up the Congo River, through the vast Congo Forest, and Stanley said that 'without Parke, the expedition would have been a failure'. Upon his return to England, Parke received numerous honours from the army and learned societies, and he was awarded the gold medals of the British Medical Association and the Royal Geographical Society of London. He died in Argyll and is buried in Kilmessen, County Leitrim. A statue to his memory stands on the lawn of Leinster House, home of the Irish Parliament.

William 'Bill' Riley
Biplane fighter ace
1917 – 1942

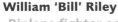

William Riley joined the Royal Air Force on a short service commission in 1935, before becoming acting pilot officer in October of that year. Promoted to pilot officer in August 1936, in 1939 Riley became a Spitfire fighter pilot with 610 Squadron. Having converted to Gladiators, flying off the HMS *Furious* to their base in Norway, he later transferred to the Polish Squadron 302 as a flight commander and saw action over Bridlington and the Thames Estuary, where he destroyed three German aircraft between 21 August and 15 October 1940. Riley later served in Malta and was promoted to squadron leader in June 1941. He was awarded the Distinguished Flying Cross that same year and in all, he was accredited with nine kills during his service in Norway, England and the Mediterranean. Riley was killed as his squadron took off from an Egyptian airbase on 16 July 1942. His aircraft collided with another and he was lost at sea.

Gordon Wilson
Peace campaigner 1927 – 1995

A member of the Methodist faith for most of his life, Gordon Wilson was involved in his family's drapery business on High Street, Enniskillen. It was the Enniskillen Rememberance Day bombing, carried out by the Provisional IRA in 1987, as Wilson held his daughter, Marie as she lay dying after the atrocity, that demonstrated his strong Christian faith. In a television interview broadcast on BBC on the evening of his daughter's death, he described his last conversation with her and went on in part to say, 'I will pray for these men tonight, and every night, I bear no ill will, I bear no grudge.' Wilson's words had a powerful and emotional impact on people both north and south of the border. In 1993, at the invitation of the taoiseach Albert Reynolds, Gordan Wilson became an Irish senator. He died of a heart attack on 27 June 1995.

Robert Strawbridge
Co-founder of Methodism in
America c. 1734 – 1781

A Methodist, Robert Strawbridge was converted by founder John Wesley, who frequently visited Ireland on evangelical excursions. In 1776 Strawbridge left Ireland, settling in Sam's Creek, Maryland and it was there that he founded some of the first Methodist societies in America. He is also credited with establishing Methodist classes in many other locations throughout the country and is said to have preached the first Methodist sermon ever heard in the state of Maryland.

Limerick

Liam Lynch
1893-1923

The sixty-foot high Lynch Tower in the Knockmealdown Mountains is dedicated to the patriot Liam Lynch. It is the site on which he was shot during the Civil War, 10 April 1923.

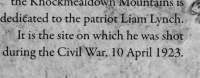

Mary O'Connell
1814-1897

Sister Mary O'Connell was known as 'the Angel of the Battlefield', and as the Florence Nightingale of the American Civil War. In appreciation of her work, two businessmen purchased the US Marine Hospital for the Sisters of Charity and it is now known as the Good Samaritan Hospital, Cincinnati, USA.

Field Marshal Peter Lacy
1678-1751

Peter Lacy took part in the Flight of the Wild Geese following the Treaty of Limerick, and joined the services of the Tsar Peter the Great of Russia, eventually attaining the rank of field marshal.

Donogh O'Malley
1921-1968

St John's Castle, Limerick was a site familiar to Donogh O'Malley as he crossed Sarsfield Bridge from his home on the North Circular Road. His introduction of free secondary education in 1966, as minister for education, was a major contribution to the later success of Ireland.

Michael O'Shaughnessy
1864-1934

The O'Shaughnessy Dam at Hetch Hetchy Valley, California is dedicated to San Francisco's extraordinary engineer, who also constructed that city's water and streetcar system.

Timothy Joseph Ahearne
Olympic Gold Medal Winner 1885 – 1968

From an early age, Timothy Joseph Ahearne was a prolific performer in the long jump and triple jump at sporting events throughout Ireland. Whilst representing Great Britain and Ireland at the London Olympics in 1908, he successfully won the gold medal with his final jump and until Lynn Davies won the long jump event fifty six years later, Ahearne was the only man representing Great Britain and Ireland to take gold in a field event. His brother Dan was also an accomplished athlete and together the brothers held the unique distinction of holding both the world and Olympic records for the triple jump between them, before their records were beaten by Anthony Winter of Australia at the 1928 games. Ahearne died in New York in December 1968.

Joseph Bradshaw
Victoria Cross recipient 1835 – 1893

Joseph Bradshaw was born in Dromkeen and served as a private during the Crimean War. He distinguished himself when, together with another soldier, he attacked and captured a Russian rifle pit, the taking and subsequent destruction of which was of immense importance to an engagement that was being undertaken by his brigade. For this he was awarded the Victoria Cross.

George Browne, Count de Browne
Russian Army field marshal 1698 – 1792

Excluded from a military appointment in Ireland due to his status as a Catholic, Camas born George Browne entered the service of the Elector Palatine, Germany in 1725. In 1730 he joined the Russian army, where he distinguished himself in the Polish, French and Turkish wars before being made a general with the command of over thirty thousand troops. Captured by the Turks, who sold him as a slave, Browne obtained his freedom through French ambassador Villeneuve. However, following his release Browne elected to remain incognito in Constantinople in order to discover important state secrets, which he relayed back to the Russian authorities. In recognition of his services, he was raised to the rank of major general and in this capacity he accompanied his fellow county man, General Peter Lacey on his first expedition to Finland. There Browne gave distinguished service in the Seven Years' War, being raised to the rank of field marshal by Peter III. He was appointed governor of Livonia by Catherine II and he ruled that province for thirty years, where he was renowned for his ability and fairness. Browne died on 18 February 1792.

Nathaniel Burlem
Victoria Cross recipient 1838 – 1865

Nathaniel Burslem was a soldier who served with the 67th Regiment of the British Army during the third China War at Taku Forts in August 1860. He displayed great bravery when, together with another recipient of the Victoria Cross, he swam the ditches of the North Taku Fort and breeched an opening in its wall, thus enabling entry. Burslem and his companion were severely wounded in the process. He later became a captain and died in New Zealand in 1865.

William Coffey
Victoria Cross recipient 1829 – 1875

William Coffey served as a private in the 34th Regiment during the Crimean War. Whilst engaged in action in the trenches during the war, a live shell landed within close proximity of his comrades. Coffey immediately dived, retrieved the shell and threw it over the parapet of the trench, thereby saving the lives of his fellow soldiers. He later became a sergeant and was buried in an unmarked grave in Chesterfield, England in July 1875. In 1970 a commemoration stone was placed on his grave in respect of his service.

Cornelius Colbert
Revolutionary 1888 – 1916

Born in Athea, Cornelius Colbert was educated at Richmond Street Christian Brothers School in Dublin. Later working in Kennedy's bakery on Parnell Street, Colbert became involved in the movement for Irish independence and he was a fluent Irish speaker who joined Na Fianna Éireann (Irish Warriors) in 1909. He later enrolled in the Irish Republican Brotherhood and the Irish Volunteers, serving during the Easter Rising of 1916 where he commanded the volunteer garrison in Watkin's bakery, Ardee Street, before moving to the Jameson's distillery as the fighting intensified. Colbert was recognised as a person of high esteem, to such a degree that the British soldier who was ordered to pinion him requested the privilege of shaking his hand. He was executed on 8 May 1916 in Kilmainham Jail. Colbert railway station in Limerick City and Con Colbert Road, Dublin are both named in his memory.

John Creaghe
Physician and Anarchist 1841 – 1920

John Creaghe qualified as a doctor at The Royal College of Surgeons in Dublin before establishing a medical practice in Mitchelstown, County Cork, which he operated until 1874. He later emigrated to Buenos Aires, Argentina where he became a follower of anarchism, but by 1890 Creaghe had relocated to Sheffield, England and co-founded the *Sheffield Anarchist* newspaper. In 1892 he returned to Argentina where he established *La Protesta* in 1903; a publication that exists to this day. Although continuing to work as a doctor, Creagh invested a considerable amount of his time, energy, and money into propagandist ventures, one of which resulted in the formation of the Regional Workers Federation of Argentina (FORA) and in 1911 he moved to the USA, settling in Los Angeles, California. There he became associated with Mexican anarchists and produced another influential anarchist newspaper, *La Regeneración*. During his life, Creagh helped pioneer a movement of great significance to labour history in Argentina and Latin America in general, and he died whilst imprisoned for anarchist activities, on 19 February 1920 in Washington DC.

Edward Daly
Patriot 1891 – 1916

Edward Daly was the younger brother of Kathleen Clarke, wife of Tom Clarke (see page 429), who was a signatory to the Irish Declaration of Independence. Stationed as commandant of the 1st Battalion of the Irish Volunteers during the Easter Rising in the Four Courts, Daly was involved in the most intense fighting of the rising. He was forced to surrender his battalion on 29 April 1916, and was subsequently tried by court-martial and executed by firing squad on 4 May 1916. He was just twenty-five years old.

John Danagher
Victoria Cross recipient 1860 – 1919

John Danagher was awarded the Victoria Cross when he served as a twenty-year-old trooper in the Transvaal Horse of the South African Forces during the First Boer War, stationed at Elandsfontein, near Pretoria in South Africa. Danagher, together with a corporal from the Connaught Rangers, advanced five hundred yards towards the enemy lines and under extremely heavy fire, successfully brought back a private who had been severely wounded. He later achieved the rank of sergeant, and died in Portsmouth, England in 1919.

Philip Embury
Co-founder of Methodism in the United States 1728 – 1773

Phillip Embury was born in Ballingarrane and was educated at the village school before becoming a carpenter's apprentice. On 9 June 1760, he set sail from Customs House Quay in Limerick for New York, where he arrived on 10 August. Having settled, he commenced his missionary work and in 1768, utilising his carpentry skills, he helped build the first John Street Methodist Church in Manhattan, New York. Along with his cousin Barbara Heck, as well as Robert Strawbridge (see page 273), Embury is considered to be have been a co-founder of Methodism in the United States.

Marie Dolores Eliza Rosanna Gilbert (Lola Montez)
Uncrowed queen of Bavaria 1818 – 1861

Once described by music composer Wilhelm Richard Wagner as 'a common Irish hussy with a brass neck and a personality that men found irresistible', Marie Dolores Eliza Rosanna Gilbert fraudulently adopted the name Lola Montez and was married on many occasions. She enjoyed some success as an exotic dancer and had liaisons with a number of famous men, amongst them the Tsar of Russia, Nicholas I, the French novelists Balzac and Dumas, as well as the composer Franz Liszt. Around 1845, sixty-year-old King Ludwig of Bavaria, who was smitten by Gilbert's charms, bestowed upon her the titles of 'Countess of Lansfeld' and 'Baroness Rosenthal' and he spared no expense in granting her anything and everything she desired. This meant that, for a not inconsiderable amount of time, Gilbert was the de facto ruler of Bavaria. However, due to the many rash acts she carried out, she was eventually banished from the kingdom, with the king being forced to abdicate in favour of his son, Maximilian II. Gilbert eventually travelled to the United States where a play on her life, *Lola Montez in Bavaria*, was successfully staged. In the final years of her life she engaged in many charitable activities before she died in New York in 1861.

Richard Harris
Actor 1930 – 2002

The great thespian Richard Harris was born in Limerick city and was educated at Crescent College. A talented and passionate rugby

Adare Manor, County Limerick.

player, he played for the famous Garryowen club before his sporting career was cut short due to tuberculosis. Following that illness Harris decided to go to London with the intention of becoming an acting director. There he enrolled in the London Academy of Music and Dramatic Arts and made his film debut in *Alive and Kicking* (1958). Harris had a long and distinguished career, appearing in such films as *The Guns of Navarone* (1961), *This Sporting Life* (1963), *Camelot* (1967) and *The Molly Maguires* (1970). But he is perhaps best remembered for his stirring portrayal of Bull McCabe in Jim Sheridan's *The Field* (1990). One of his final roles was as Albus Dumbledore in the first of the popular Harry Potter movies. Harris was a member of the Knights of Malta, despite having been divorced twice, and he was also knighted by Denmark in 1985. His list of honours includes two Academy Awards, one BAFTA, one Golden Globe and an Emmy nomination. He died of Hodgkin's disease in 2002 at the age of seventy-two.

Catherine Hayes
Opera singer 1818 – 1861

Catherine Hayes was born in Patrick Street, Limerick city and coming from a poor background, worked for a while at the home of Lord Limerick in Henry Street. There, Church of Ireland bishop, Doctor Edmund Knox heard her singing as she worked and was so impressed by the quality of her voice, he arranged for her to study under Antonio Sapio in Dublin. At the age of nineteen, Hayes gave her first performance and she went on to become a prima donna at La Scala, Milan. In 1849 she gave a command performance to Queen Victoria with the Royal Italian Opera Company, and made a triumphant return to Limerick the following year to appear at the Theatre Royal. She gained world renown as an opera singer, touring extensively throughout Europe, Australia and the United States, where there is a street in San Francisco named after her. Throughout her life, Hayes was a generous benefactor to many charitable organisations and she helped in the restoration of St Mary's cathedral in Limerick. She died from a stroke in London, England at the age of forty-three and is buried in Kensal Green Cemetery, London.

Lady Heath
Aviatrix 1896 – 1939

Sophia Theresa Catherine Mary Pierce-Evans was born in Knockaderry House, Newcastle West, and was raised by two aunts from infancy after her father brutally murdered her mother. Educated in Dublin, she was a keen athlete and was the first Irish woman to compete in the Olympics. Heath, who was also a founder of the Women's Amateur Athletics Association of Great Britain, spent two years as a dispatch rider based in England and France during World War I and it was whilst in France that she had her portrait painted by Sir John Lavery (see page 32).

She took up flying lessons in 1925 and became the first woman to hold a commercial flying licence in Britain the following year. Heath was also the first woman to parachute from an airplane and she made her name as an aviator, being the first female to fly a small open cockpit airplane from Cape Town to London, England. Married three times, it was her marriage to Sir James Heath, some forty years her senior, that bestowed on her the title of 'Lady' and which also financed her flying ambitions. She became the first female pilot with Dutch airline KLM but unfortuntaley suffered a serious accident when she crashed her plane into a factory roof during the National Air Races in Cleveland, Ohio in 1929. Heath had a metal plate inserted into her skull as a result of the accident, and it had a detrimental effect on her health for the remainder of her life. She died destitute, following a fall from a tramcar, in London in 1939.

Sean Keating
Portrait and figure painter
1889 – 1977
Sean Keating was educated at St Munchin's College where, by his own admission, he spent his time 'as a dreamer and an idler'. However, this did not prevent him gaining a scholarship to the Dublin Metropolitan School of Art in 1911 and he went on to win the Taylor Scholarship with Appeals for Mercy in 1914. Sometimes referred to as an Irish nationalist painter, Keating executed several iconic images of the Irish Civil War era, one of which was *Men of the South* (1921), depicting a group of IRA men about to stage a military ambush. In 1920 he was commissioned to record the building of the hydro-electric power station at Ardnacrusha, and he also exhibited extensively in London and New York. Appointed professor of art at the National College of Art in 1934, he served as president of the Royal Hibernian Academy from 1949 until 1962, exhibiting nearly three hundred works throughout the period. Keating painted in excess of one hundred portraits, but his best known work is perhaps *Men of Aran* (1925), a landscape painting inspired by his many visits to the Aran Islands on the west coast of Ireland.

Count Peter Lacy
Russian field marshal
1678 – 1751
A lieutenant for the Jacobites during their defence of Limerick whilst under siege from the Williamites in 1690, Peter Lacy later took part in the 'Flight of the Wild Geese' and, together with his father and brother, joined the Irish Brigade in France. However, following the loss of his relatives fighting for Louis XIV, he served with the Austrian army for two years before joining the Russian army where the Czar, Peter the Great of Russia, placed him in command of a company of Grand Musketeers. Lacy later distinguished himself in the war against Sweden in 1708 and he served his adopted country in many campaigns against the Swedes, the Danes and the Turks. As the head of thirty thousand men, he entered Poland in 1733 and his triumphant entry to Warsaw in 1735 resulted in him being created a field marshal. Lacy, who was involved in many other campaigns for Russia, died there on 11 May 1751.

Liam Lynch
Patriot 1893 – 1923
A distinguished military man, Liam Lynch initially commanded the Cork No. 2 Brigade of the IRA during the Black and Tan War and, by the time the Treaty with Britain was signed in December 1921, he had risen to command the 1st Southern Division. Like many IRA men, Lynch refused to accept the terms of the Treaty, which led to the Civil War. In April 1923 he and six of his fellow soldiers were cut off by state troops in the Knockmealdown Mountains on the Waterford/Tipperary

border and in the ensuing encounter, Lynch was critically wounded, later dying as a result of his wounds in Clonmel on 10 April 1923. Fifteen thousand people attended the dedication ceremony in memory of this patriot and in 1935 he was honoured by his comrades, who erected a sixty-foot high round tower on the spot where he was shot.

Patrick Henry McCarthy
Labour Leader and Mayor of San Francisco 1863 – 1933

Patrick Henry McCarthy was born near Newcastle West and studied law before foregoing that career in favour of carpentry. In 1880 he emigrated to the United States where he became an active member in the National Union of Carpenters, and in 1886 he moved to San Francisco, California where he joined Local 22, the oldest carpentry union in the city. Eventually becoming that union's president, McCarthy was best known for his dominance of the Building Trade Council of San Francisco, where he secured an eight-hour working day for the building trade workers. However, with the owners of the large mills refusing to comply with the new regulation, McCarthy used union funds to build a mill of his own, which he had operating to full capacity within six months, thereby forcing the mill owners of San Francisco to concede defeat. A strong leader, he was renowned for discouraging ill-timed and badly conceived strikes, as well as unrealistic demands and, having served as mayor of San Francisco from 1910 to 1912, his term in office saw the establishment of a requirement that all city employees were to become union members. McCarthy, who also raised the minimum wage for city employees from two dollars to three dollars per day, died in San Francisco on 1 July 1933.

Seán Moylan
Soldier and politician 1888 – 1957

Coming from a strong republican background, Kilmallock born Seán Moylan was a member of the Gaelic League and the Gaelic Athletic Association and, having qualified as a carpenter, he established a business in Newmarket, County Cork where he also joined the local Volunteers. Moylan rose to the rank of commander of the Cork No. 2 Battalion of the Irish Republican Army and led an active service unit in north Cork in 1920 before he was captured and interned at Spike Island in May 1921. It was whilst in prison that Moylan was elected a Sinn Féin TD and so began a long and distinguished political career. He was opposed to the Anglo-Irish Treaty of 1921, fighting on the republican side during the Civil War and in 1926 joined the Fianna Fáil political party, being elected a TD for North Cork. He was appointed parliamentary secretary in 1937, minister for lands in 1940 and he also served as minister for education from 1951 to 1954. Moylan later lost his seat but he was elected to Seanad Éireann (the Irish Senate) in 1957, before later being appointed cabinet minister for agriculture, which made him the first senator to be appointed as a government minister. He died on 16 November 1957.

William Nash
Victoria Cross recipient 1824 – 1875

Newcastle born William Nash served as a corporal in the 2nd Battalion of the Rifle Brigade of the British Army during the Indian Rebellion of 1857. On the 11 March 1858 at Ironbridge, Lucknow, whilst in the company of five comrades, he was surrounded and attacked by a considerable number of enemy soldiers. Under intense fire, Nash carried one of his fellow soldiers to safety. He was subsequently awarded the Victoria Cross. He died in Middlesex, England in 1875.

Kate O'Brien
Writer 1897 – 1974

Kate O'Brien was educated at Laurel Hill Convent, Limerick and University College Dublin, following which she joined the *Manchester Guardian* newspaper. In 1926 she wrote a play, *Distinguished Villa*, but despite its great success, she decided instead to dedicate herself to writing novels. Her books include: *Without My Cloak* (1931), *The Ante-Room* (1934), *Mary Lavelle* (1936), *The Land of Spices* (1941), *The Last of Summer* (1943) and *That Lady* (1946). O'Brien, whose novels often featured lesbian characters and relationships, had the unique distinction of having books banned in Ireland (*Mary Lavelle* and *The Land of Spices*) and in Spain (*Farewell Spain*). Awarded the James Tait Black Memorial Prize and the Hawthornden Prize for *Without my Cloak*, O'Brien was an author who wrote with great authority and subtlety about women. She died in Kent, England in 1974.

Mary O'Connell
Roman Catholic nun, 'The Angel of the Battlefield' 1814 – 1897

At a young age, Mary O'Connell emigrated to the United States with her parents, settling in Boston, Massachusetts. She entered the Order of the American Sisters of Charity at Emmitsburg, Maryland in 1835 and was instrumental in founding an orphanage in Cincinnati, Ohio in 1839. At the outbreak of the Civil War, she worked as a nurse in riverboat hospitals, thus earning the sobriquet 'The Florence Nightingale of America', and in appreciation for O'Connell's service during the war, two non-Catholic benefactors purchased the United States Marine Hospital for her order. It was to be used as a maternity hospital, the first of its kind in Cincinnati. O'Connell, or Sister Anthony as she was known, died on 8 December 1897.

Sylvester O'Halloran
Surgeon and historian
1728 – 1807

Sylvester O'Halloran studied surgery in England, the Netherlands and France, before returning to Limerick in 1749 to practice opthalmic medicine. He founded the infirmary there in 1760 and wrote many important medical texts dealing with glaucoma and cataracts. O'Halloran, whose criticism of Irish surgery was considered to have been influential in the foundation of the Irish College of Surgeons in 1784, also held a deep interest in Irish history and archaeology and he published major studies of Irish antiquities in 1770 and Irish history in 1774. He died and is buried at St Munchin's cemetery, Killeely near Limerick. The annual Sylvester O'Halloran meeting, named in his honour, commenced in 1992.

John O'Mahony
Young Irelander and founder of the Fenian Brotherhood in America 1816 – 1877

John O'Mahony attended Trinity College, Dublin where he studied Sanskrit, Hebrew and Irish. As a member of the Young Irelanders, he took part in the failed rebellion of 1848, following which he fled to France, later joining his comrade, John Mitchel (see page 120), in New York. There O'Mahony became active in Irish exile groups devoted to the promotion of Irish freedom and he organised the foundation of the Fenian Brotherhood in 1858. Upon the outbreak of the American Civil War he joined the Union Army where he rose to the rank of colonel and following that conflict, he was involved with the Fenian's attempt to capture Campo Bello Island in New Brunswick, Canada in April 1866. O'Mahony would continue to support the Fenian movement in the United States before he died in New York on 7 February 1877. His body was brought home to Ireland and he was buried in Glasnevin Cemetery.

Donogh O'Malley
Politician 1921 – 1968

Donogh O'Malley was educated at Clongowes Wood College and at University College Galway, where he qualified in engineering. In his youth O'Malley was an outstanding sportsman and rather uniquely, he played representative rugby for three provinces: Leinster, Munster, and Connaught. As a TD he represented the East Limerick constituency from 1954 until 1958 and served as both minister for health from 1965 until 1966 and minister for education from 1966 until 1968. His son Daragh in the book, *Unfulfilled Promise* by P.J. Browne, stated, 'My father's three main passions in life were politics, gambling, and alcohol, not necessarily in that order, or even in any order.' At times considered a wild playboy, O'Malley was, despite that reputation, highly influential in laying the foundation for the 'Celtic Tiger' economical success and his lasting legacy was the introduction of free education for all in 1966. A charismatic man with an endless appetite for work, O'Malley is considered to have done more for the people of Ireland than all the ministers of education that came before or after him. Married to the strikingly beautiful Doctor Hilda Moriarty, for whom the poet Patrick Kavanagh (see page 328) wrote the famous poem, 'On Raglan Road', O'Malley died suddenly at the age of forty-seven in Sixmilebridge, County Clare in 1968.

Seán Ó Riada
Musician and Composer
1931 – 1971

Adare native Seán Ó Riada was educated at the Christian Brothers School, Adare and later at University College Cork. Having received a Bachelor of Music degree, he is perhaps best known for his pioneering work in traditional Irish music, as well as the music he wrote for the documentary film *Mise Éire*. An assistant music director at Radio Éireann between 1954 and 1955, he spent a short time studying in France and Italy before being appointed music director of the Abbey Theatre from 1955 until 1962. Ó Riada was also a lecturer of music at University College Cork from 1963 until 1971. He was treated for cirrhosis at King's Hospital, London and died there on 3 October 1971. He is buried in Ballyvourney, County Cork.

Michael James O'Rourke
Victoria Cross recipient
1878 – 1957

Michael James O'Rourke served as a private in the 7th Battalion of the Canadian Expeditionary Force during World War I. In August 1917, at Hill 70 near Lens, France, O'Rourke, who was a stretcher bearer, worked nonstop for three days and nights by retrieving the wounded and looking after them. The area in which he worked was continuously swept by heavy machine gun fire and on a number of occasions he was knocked down and partially buried by enemy shells. In spite of exhaustion, O'Rourke worked incessantly during that period and saved the lives of many officers and men. He died in Vancouver in 1957.

Michael O'Shaughnessy
Engineer 1864 – 1934

Michael O'Shaughnessy was born in Jointer and was educated at University College Galway. Having emigrated to San Francisco in March 1885, where he was involved in many major civil engineering projects, he later travelled to Hawaii where he engaged in the design and construction of several major water supply projects.

O'Shaughnessy later returned to the mainland where he was involved in the Morena Dam project in San Diego, California and in 1912 he was appointed city engineer for San Francisco. In that role he undertook the building of new infrastructures for the city following the disastrous earthquake of 1906 and he was instrumental in the construction of the Twin Peaks Tunnel, the famous Seashore Wall, the San Francisco streetcar (tramway) system, and the greatest of all, the San Francisco water supply and electric power project, which incorporated dams, power houses and one hundred and sixty miles of transmission towers, pipelines and tunnels that reached the city via 'The O'Shaughnessy Dam' in the Sierra Nevada mountains.

The Hetch-Hetchy project, as it is sometimes called, is numbered amongst the great engineering projects of the twentieth century. O'Shaughnessy was also responsible for the concept of the Golden Gate Bridge and partially financed its development. However, he never lived to see its completion and he died in San Francisco at the age of seventy.

Ada Rehan
Actress 1860 – 1916

Actress Ada Rehan's correct name was actually Ada Delia Crehan, but a printer's error on a programme displayed her name as Ada Rehan and she retained this name thereafter. Having joined John Drew's Philadelphia troupe as a leading lady, she performed with the Augustin Daly Stock Company in New York and was very popular for her comedy roles. She moved to London, England in 1884 and there she received great acclaim for her Shakespearian roles, in particular for her portrayal of Katherine in *The Taming of the Shrew*. Admired and complimented during her lifetime by George Bernard Shaw (see page 191), among others, Rehan died on 9 January 1916.

Eithne Strong
Writer and poet 1923 – 1999

A writer of poetry and short stories in both English and Irish, Eithne Strong's poetry collections include: *Songs of Living* (1961), *Sarah, in Passing* (1974), and *Flesh – The Greatest Sin* (1980). Her short stories include the collection *Patterns* (1981) and her novels are *Degrees of Kindred* (1979) and *The Love Riddle* (1993). She won the Kilkenny Design Award for *Flesh – The Greatest Sin* in 1991 and died in Monkstown, County Dublin in 1999.

Longford

Oliver Goldsmith
1728-1774

The writer of *She Stoops to Conquer*, Oliver Goldsmith was a writer, poet, physician and gambler. His statue stands in Trinity College, Dublin.

John Henry Patterson
1867-1947

John Henry Patterson was a major figure in Zionism and in World War I he commanded the Zion Mule Corps, which later formed the basis for the Israel Defence Forces. He actively supported the establishment of the Jewish state.

Patrick Egan
1841-191

Patrick Egan was the founder of the Irish National League of America. A supporter of Charles Stewart Parnell, He was also a member of the Irish Republican Brotherhood (IRB).

Kitty Kiernan
1892-1945

The Grenville Arms Hotel, Granard was the home of Kitty Kiernan, the love of Irish patriot Michael Collins.

Seán MacEoin
1893-1973

Ballinalee, the village Seán MacEoin (The Blacksmith of Ballinalee) held against superior British forces in the War of Independence in February 1921.

Patrick Belton
Irish politician and anti-communist 1885 – 1945

Patrick Belton was born near Lanesborough and was educated at the local national school before winning a scholarship to King's College, London. He later entered the British civil service and was also involved in the Gaelic Athletic Association in London, becoming secretary of the London County Board in 1909. The following year Belton transferred to the Irish Land Commission in Dublin and became involved in the Easter Rising in 1916. As a result he temporarily lost his job in the Land Commission but was later reinstated before being elected a Fianna Fáil TD for County Dublin in 1927. However, after refusing to take the oath of allegiance to the British crown, Belton was expelled and in 1936 he became president of the Irish Christian Front, which was formed to support pro-Franco Spanish citizens in their war effort. He held many pro-Catholic and anti-communist rallies, sometimes drawing estimated crowds of thirty thousand. Throughout this time, Belton was also a Cumann na nGael TD for Dublin City North, but he lost his seat in the 1937 general election. He died in Killiney, County Dublin on 30 January 1945.

Padraic Colum
Writer and poet 1881 – 1972

A member of the Gaelic League, Padraic Colum worked for a short period with Irish Rail but left to concentrate on his writing. He was also a militant nationalist, who was involved in the Howth gun-running in 1914. Around 1910 Colum wrote perhaps his best-known lyrics, 'She Moved Through the Fair' and 'A Cradle Song'. He has left a great record of the lives of famous Irishmen, as well as children's stories and a number of plays, and he was considered a literary ambassador of Ireland. Colum died in the United States in 1972 and is buried in Dublin.

George Edward Dobson
Zoologist and surgeon 1848 – 1895

George Edward Dobson was educated at Portora Royal School in Enniskillen, County Fermanagh before qualifying in medicine and chemistry from Trinity College, Dublin. Having entered the British Army Medical Corp in 1868, Dobson's principle posting was to India where he served until his retirement in 1888. He also served for a period in the Andaman Islands, where he made a number of anthropological photographs of the natives. Whilst in India, his background in anatomy enabled him to make a careful study of the bats of that country and he also carried out important work on the form and classification of the Insectivora group of mammals. Dobson, who was a member of several scientific societies, including the Royal Society and the Zoological Society of London, retired from the army with the rank of surgeon major and died in Kent, England on 25 November 1895.

James Dooley
Politician 1877 – 1950

At the age of eight, James Dooley left Ireland for Australia with his family. There he attended state school and later worked as an apprentice tailor, before attending evening classes with a view to furthering his career prospects. Around 1900 Dooley joined the Australian Labour Party and in 1907 he was elected to the Legislative Assembly in New South Wales. In 1920 he became colonial secretary and the following year he was appointed premier of the state of New South Wales.

May Duignan ('Chicago May')
Prostitute and blackmailer
1871 – 1929

At the age of nineteen, May Duignan was reputed to have stolen her family's life savings in order to dress herself in the latest fashion. An attractive woman with typically Irish red hair, Duignan also purchased a ticket to the United States where she settled in Chicago, Illinois, earning the nickname 'Chicago May'. There she attained a questionable reputation, getting involved in dubious activities ranging from prostitution, blackmailing, swindling, assault, pick-pocketing and even attempted murder. Her life story is portrayed by Nuala O'Faolain (see page 184) in her book, *The Story of Chicago May* (2005).

Francis Edgeworth
Mathematician 1845 – 1926

Francis Edgeworth was born in Edgeworthstown and was educated privately until reaching university age. Having studied ancient and modern languages at Trinity College, Dublin and at Balliol College, Oxford, he qualified as a barrister in London in 1877 but did not practice. A self-taught mathematician and economist, Edgeworth was appointed to the chair in economics at King's College, London in 1888 and at the University of Oxford in 1891, having previously published his most famous book, *Mathematical Psychics* (1881). A leader in the development of mathematical economics, Edgeworth's contribution to that field was significant in its detail and innovation. He was, perhaps, one of the most outstanding intellectuals of the nineteenth and twentieth centuries, whose contribution to mathematics and economics paved the way for those that succeeded him.

Patrick Egan
Patriot and politician 1841 – 1919

In his early teens, Ballymahon native Patrick Egan joined the North City Milling Company in Dublin as a junior clerk, eventually rising to the role of managing director. He also joined the Irish Republican Brotherhood and was a staunch supporter of home rule for Ireland. Elected treasurer of the Irish Land League in 1879, Egan was a close confidant of Michael Davitt (see page 305) and Charles Stuart Parnell (see page 423) and following the latter's arrest, he fled to Paris with the funds of the league in order to prevent their confiscation by the British Authorities. Whilst there, Egan was twice nominated for election to parliament in Ireland but on both occasions declined to take his seat as he was not prepared to swear the oath of allegiance to Britain. At the beginning of the 1880s he fled to the United States, settling in Lincoln, Nebraska, where he established a successful grain milling company. Whilst there, Egan continued to support the Irish Land League and formed the Irish National League of America. When the British government and the *London Times* entered a conspiracy to destroy Charles Stewart Parnell based on letters forged by a man named Richard Pigott (see page 322), it was Egan who secured the proof that the letters were a forgery via facts known to him combined with comparisons of Piggott's handwriting. The case against Parnell was dismissed amid the derision of the world. Following the election of Benjamin Harrison as President of the United States, Egan was appointed by Harrison as minister to Chile, where he served from 1889 until 1893. He died in New York in 1919.

Oliver Goldsmith

Writer, poet and physician 1730 – 1774

Born in Pallas near Ballymahon, Oliver Goldsmith was educated at Trinity College, Dublin where he studied theology and law and obtained a bachelor of arts degree in 1749. He then studied medicine at the University of Edinburgh and the University of Leiden in the Netherlands, thereafter touring Europe. Forever in debt, due to his addiction to gambling, Goldsmith had a massive output as a hack writer for publishers in London and is best known for his novel *The Vicar of Wakefield* (1766), as well as his plays *The Good Natured Man* (1768) and *She Stoops to Conquer* (1771). He also is generally believed to have written *The History of Little Goody Two Shoes* (1765). Goldsmith misdiagnosed himself with a kidney infection and as a result, he died in 1774. A statue to his memory stands in the centre of Ballymahon and Goldsmith Hall in Trinity College is named in his honour.

Kitty Kiernan

Fiancee of Michael Collins 1892 – 1945

Kitty Kiernan was born in Granard and was educated at the Loreto Convent, County Wicklow. Born into a wealthy merchant family who owned the Greville Arms Hotel in Mullingar, it was there that Kiernan met future husband Michael Collins (see page 89) and his compatriot Harry Boland (see page 154). Both men were smitten with her charms but it was Collins who won her heart and the two became engaged. Collins would become a regular visitor to Granard from 1917 until his assassination in 1922, after which Kiernan married Felix Cronan, quartermaster general of the National Army, in 1925. Together they had two sons, the second of whom they called Michael Collins Cronan. Portrayed by Julia Roberts in Neil Jordan's film *Michael Collins*, Kiernan died on 24 July 1945. She is buried in Glasnevin Cemetery, Dublin.

Seán MacEoin

Soldier and politician 1893 – 1973

Seán MacEoin was born at Bunlahy, Granard and began his working life as a blacksmith in his father's forge. Serving as leader of the North Longford Flying Column during the War of Independence, after holding the village of Ballinalee against superior British forces in February 1921, MacEoin was nicknamed 'The Blacksmith of Ballinalee'. He was captured one month later and was sentenced to death but was released upon the signing of the truce. MacEoin took the treaty side in the War of Independence, joining the new Free State Army as a senior officer, and he served as chief of staff in 1928 before resigning the following year to take a seat in the Dáil as a deputy representing Sligo/Leitrim. He later represented Longford/Westmeath and served as minister for justice in the first coalition government from 1948 to 1951, as well as minister for defence from 1954 to 1957. He died in Dublin on 7 July 1973.

Frank McCoppin

First Irish-born mayor of San Francisco 1834 – 1897

Frank McCoppin was born in Longford Town and emigrated to the United States at the age of eighteen, first settling in New York City, and later moving to Illinois where he studied engineering. He moved on to California in 1857, settling in San Francisco where he became a district engineer and also became involved in politics. With San Francisco dominated by the republicans, McCoppin chose the Democratic Party, who realised that he would win the all-important Irish vote and so chose him to stand for the mayoral office. McCoppin, who was an articulate man with good looks, secured the position of mayor of San Fransisco on 2 December 1867 and although he served just one term as mayor, his selection set in motion an Irish political surge in California that lasted for over a century. During his term, he obtained approval for the Golden Gate Park and he later went on to serve two terms for the California State Senate. In 1894, President Grover Cleveland appointed him as post master for San Francisco and he served in that role until his death on 26 May 1897. McCoppin Square in the Parkside district of San Francisco is named in his memory.

Joseph McGuinness
Republican and Sinn Féin politician
1875 – 1922

A member of a well-established family who had a business on Main Street, Longford Joseph McGuinness's family home was threatened by the Black and Tans during the War of Independence and he himself was imprisoned. It was whilst in prison that McGuinness was elected a Sinn Féin member of parliament for South Longford and following this success he was re-elected in the general election of 1918. With a slogan used by those canvassing for him of, 'vote him in to get him out', upon his election, McGuinness did not take his seat in the British House of Commons, sitting instead as a TD in the new Dáil, the newly-formed independent Irish government. Elected again in the 1921 general election, this time for the Longford-Westmeath constituency, McGuinness was a confidant of Michael Collins (see page 89) and voted in favour of the Anglo-Irish Treaty. He died on 31 May 1922.

George Monro
British Army officer 1700 – 1757

George Monro was born in Clonfin and joined the 35th Regiment of Foot of the British army in 1718, eventually reaching the rank of lieutenant colonel by 1750. With the renewal of hostilities between Britain and France during 1757, he sailed for the colonies and took command of some two thousand troops at Fort William Henry on the shores of Lake George, New York. Monro was the central figure in the James Fenimore Cooper's classic, *The Last of the Mohicans*, in which Fort William Henry is attacked by the French and their Native American allies, the Mohicans. With the combined force numbering eight thousand men, Monro was cut off from the main British force, under the command of General Daniel Webb, and stood little chance against the siege which commenced on 3 August 1757. He and his men carried out a spirited defence but were forced to surrender under insurmountable pressure. In the subsequent negotiations, Monro agreed with the French that his troops would be allowed safe passage to Fort Edward, twenty miles away, but as he led them from the fort, the native tribe ambushed them. Though Monro survived the attack, a number of his men were not so lucky. He died suddenly three months later on 3 November 1757.

James Bronterre O'Brien
Chartist 1805 – 1864

Granard born James Bronterre O'Brien graduated with honours from Trinity College in 1825, before studying law at King's Inn, Dublin where he again graduated with honours in 1829. Instead of pursuing a legal career, O'Brien decided to enter the field of journalism and he became editor of the *Midland Representative* and the *Birmingham Herald*, a radical weekly. A staunch supporter of radical causes, including Chartism (possibly the first working class labour movement in Britain and Ireland), he was considered to be a most charismatic and popular leader and was seen as a dangerous man by the British government of the time. O'Brien, who was imprisoned in April 1840 and released in September 1841, was initially an advocate of 'physical force within the movement' but he later renounced that strategy. He was to leave an indelible imprint on the British labour and socialist movement and later made his living lecturing at the John Street Institute and the Eclectic Institute of Soho, London. He died in London on 23 December 1864.

John Henry Patterson
Author, soldier, hunter and Zionist
1867 – 1947

John Henry Patterson joined the British army in 1884 and rose speedily through the ranks to attain the position of lieutenant colonel.

Patterson was commissioned by the British East Africa Company to supervise the building of a railway at Tsavo, Kenya, but during the construction over one hundred people were attacked and killed by rogue lions. With the local population and workforce in a terrified state, Patterson took it upon himself to personally rectify the situation and following months of hunting and several narrow escapes, he eliminated the two lions after which the work on the railway and bridge at Tsavo was completed. He thus became a local hero and was presented with a silver bowl by the natives as a token of their appreciation.

In 1907, he published his first book, *The Man-eaters of Tsavo*, which inspired the making of three films, *Bwana Devil* (1953), *Killers of Kilimanjaro* (1959), and *The Ghost and the Darkness* (1996). In 1909 he wrote his second book, *Grip of Nyika*, which details his experiences as the chief game warden in the East Africa Protectorate. Patterson was also a fierce soldier and he served in both the Boer War and

World War I and although he was a Protestant, became a major figure in Zionism. He served as commander of both the Zion Mule Corps and the 38th Battalion of the Royal Fusiliers, a Jewish legion of the British Army in World War I, and it was this legion that served as the foundation of the Israeli Defence Forces. Patterson's final two books, *Zionists at Gallipoli* (1916) and *Judeans in Palestine* (1922), are based on his experiences during these times. He continued supporting Zionism, advocating the establishment of a Jewish state, which became a reality when Israel was founded in 1948. He died in San Diego, California on 18 June 1947. His ashes were returned to present-day Israel.

Thomas Quinn
Nationalist MP and London builder 1838 – 1897

Thomas Quinn was born in Longford Town and was educated locally, following which time he became a carpenter. Moving on to London at an early age, he established a large building contract business and was one of the pioneers of the building of flats and apartments. In 1883 Quinn served as treasurer of the National League and the Land League of Great Britain and as a member of the Irish Parliamentary Party he was selected to represent Kilkenny City in 1886. When that party split over the question of Charles Stewart Parnell's (see page 423) leadership in 1890, Quinn supported Parnell before later turning and joining the anti-Parnellite Parliamentary Party. In 1892 he retired from politics due to ill-health and died at his home in Kensington, London on 3 November 1897.

Henry Hughes Wilson
British field marshal 1864 – 1922

Born in the village of Ballinalee, Henry Hughes Wilson was educated at Marlborough College in Wiltshire, England. Having failed to gain entry to both Woolwich and Sandhurst military academies, he attained a backdoor route to a military career by joining the Longford Militia and later saw service during the Second Boer War from 1899 to 1902. During the campaign he became military secretary to Lord Roberts and was awarded the Distinguished Service Order; he was promoted to brigadier general in 1907.

Due to injuries received whilst on active service in Burma, Wilson walked with a stick but nevertheless took command of the IV Corps during World War I. However, his fledgling reputation as a battle commander was to take a severe knock due to the loss of a significant number of his men at Vimy Ridge, France. Wilson's friendship with British prime minister David Lloyd George led to him being appointed chief of the Imperial General Staff in February 1918 and following the war, he was promoted to field marshal on 3 July 1919. The recipient of many awards during his army career, as he was returning to his house at 36 Eton Place, London, on 22 June 1922, Wilson was killed by two Irish Republican Army activists. The two men, Reginald Dunne and Joseph O'Sullivan, were convicted and hanged for his murder.

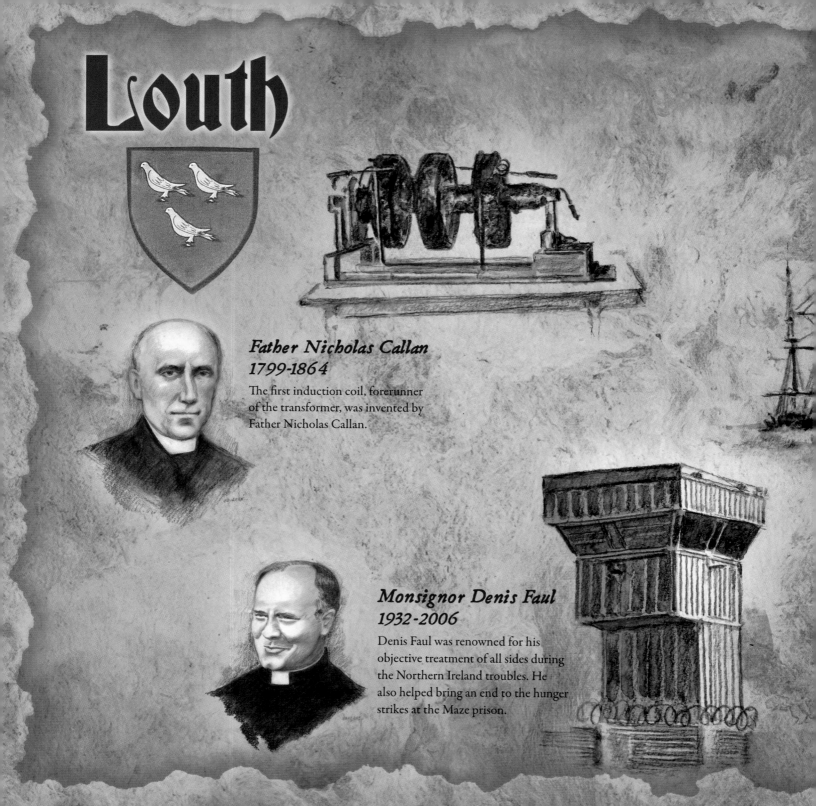

Louth

Father Nicholas Callan
1799-1864

The first induction coil, forerunner
of the transformer, was invented by
Father Nicholas Callan.

Monsignor Denis Faul
1932-2006

Denis Faul was renowned for his
objective treatment of all sides during
the Northern Ireland troubles. He
also helped bring an end to the hunger
strikes at the Maze prison.

John Ignatius Kilmartin
1913-?

A Hurricane fighter, as flown by the Dundalk-born squadron leader during the Battle of Britain. Kilmartin was credited with bringing down thirteen enemy planes and was a recipient of the Distinguished Flying Cross.

Francis Leopold McClintock
1819-1907

Explorer Francis Leopold McClintock was commander of the *Intrepid* expedition in 1852. It is seen here, icebound, with the *Resolute* in the Antarctic.

Thomas Charles James Wright
1799-1868

The Guayaquil Navy Headquarters, Ecuador. The country's navy was established by Thomas Charles James Wright.

Henry Boylan
Public servant and biographer
1912 – 2007

Henry Boylan was born in Drogheda and was educated at the local Christian Brothers school and at Trinity College, Dublin. Married to Patricia Clancy in 1941, Boylan was a public servant who was active in the Gaelic language movement. His *Dictionary of Irish Biography* was first published in 1978 and contained 1,500 entries, requiring many arduous hours spent compiling its content. An educational, interesting, and readable scholarly work, a third edition of the book was published in 1998. Boylan also published other works such as a biography of Wolfe Tone (1981) and studies of Gaelic writers as well as a memoir entitled *A Voyage Round My Life* (2002). He died on 24 May 2007.

William Boyle
Writer and civil servant 1853 – 1923

William Boyle was educated at St Mary's College, Dundalk, following which he joined the civil service in 1874. A writer, Boyle's first publication was, *A Kish of Brogues* (1899), which was a description of Irish country life, and he was one of the first to write plays for the Abbey Theatre. Amongst his dramatic productions were: *The Building Fund* (1905), *The Tale of a Town* (1906), and *The Mineral Worker* (1906). He died in London in 1923.

John Elliott Cairnes
Economist 1823 – 1875

Following his education at Trinity College, Dublin, John Elliott Cairnes worked in an engineer's office in Galway where he became acquainted with William Nesbitt, a professor at Queen's College, Galway. It was he that persuaded Cairnes to compete for the Whately Professorship at Trinity College and he subsequently became the sixth incumbent of the chair in 1856. Cairnes, who published his lectures under the title *The Character and Logical Method of Political Economy*, was appointed to the chair of jurisprudence and political economy at Queen's College, Galway in 1859, and in 1862 he published *The Slave Power*, a defence on the position of the northern states in the American Civil War. This considerably enhanced his reputation and in 1866 he was appointed professor of political economy at University College London. Cairnes died on 7 July 1875 at Blackheath, London.

Fr Nicholas Joseph Callan
Inventor 1799 – 1864

Nicholas Callan enrolled at St Patrick's College, Maynooth in 1816. There he developed an interest in electricity and magnetism before being ordained in 1823. Following three years in Rome, Callan returned to St Patrick's where he was appointed to the chair of natural philosophy and he established a scientific laboratory in the basement of the college. In that laboratory, he made a major breakthrough in 1836 with the invention of the induction coil, which served as the forerunner of today's transformers, revolutionising the phenomenon of electricity. Callan's primary purpose in life was his devotion to his faith and and to his fellow man and so all monetary profits from his inventions were donated to the starving poor during the famine in Ireland. In 1853 he patented the process whereby iron is galvanized and in the following years he invented the Maynooth battery and the single fluid cell battery. Callan, who also built electric motors, died in Maynooth on the 10 January 1864.

Paul Vincent Carroll
Dramatist 1900 – 1968

In 1921, Dundalk native Paul Vincent Carroll emigrated to Scotland where he worked as a teacher in Glasgow. He also began writing plays, the first of which was *The Watched Pot* (1930). This was followed by *Things that are Ceasar's* (1932). Carroll's most significant work was *Shadow and Substance* (1937), which was produced at the Abbey Theatre, Dublin and also in New York where it won the Drama Critics' Circle award for best foreign play in 1938. It also received the Casement Award from the Irish Academy of Letters. Carroll's play, *The White Steed* (1939), rejected by the Abbey Theatre on the grounds that it was anti-clerical, won him a second Circle Award in New York in 1939. He settled in England in 1941 and died there in 1968.

James Samuel Emerson
Victoria Cross recipient 1895 – 1917

James Samuel Emerson was born in Collon, Drogheda and served as second lieutenant in the 9th Battalion of the the Royal Inniskilling Fusiliers of the British Army during World War I. On 6 December 1917 at the Hindenburg Line, north of La Vacquerie, France, Emerson led his company in an attack that cleared the enemy from four hundred yards of trench. Though wounded in the inevitable counter-attack, he faced eight men head on, taking six prisoners and with all other officers in his attachment becoming casualties, Emerson refused to leave his lines. He continued to repel enemy attacks before he was mortally wounded and for his brave deeds he was awarded the Victoria Cross.

Monsignor Denis Faul
Roman Catholic priest and pacifist 1932 – 2006

Denis Faul was educated at St Patrick's College, Armagh. Having studied for the priesthood in Maynooth, he was ordained in 1956 and is perhaps best remembered for his involvement in the troubles in Northern Ireland. Renowned for his even-handed criticism of all sides during that bloody conflict, Faul protested vigorously against civil rights abuses by the British army and the Royal Ulster Constabulary, but also continuously condemned the killings perpetrated by the Provisional IRA. He was also the first to recognise the innocence of the Birmingham Six and the Guildford Four and campaigned strongly for their release. In 1981 Faul served as chaplain at the infamous Maze Prison and he played a decisive role in ending the hunger strike. A BBC report in 2006 defined him as follows: 'His whole life was an eloquent testimony that justice requires consistent courage and that peace must be underpinned by morality at all times.' Faul died in Dublin on 21 June 2006.

Monasterboice High Cross and tower, County Louth.

Percy Hetherington Fitzgerald
Author, sculptor and painter 1834 – 1925

Percy Hetherington Fitzgerald was born in Slane Valley and was educated at Stoneyhurst College in Lancashire, England and at Trinity College, Dublin. Later called to the bar, he acted as crown prosecutor on the north east circuit before settling as a man of letters in London. In all, Fitzgerald published over one hundred titles, which are listed in the National Library, and as a sculptor he executed a bust of his friend Charles Dickens, the statue of Samuel Johnson that stands outside St Clement Danes church in London, as well as Boswell's statue in Lichfield. Fitzgerald died in London and is buried in Glasnevin Cemetery, Dublin.

John Foster
First Baron Oriel and last speaker of the Irish House of Commons 1740 – 1828

Elected a member of parliament to the Irish House of Commons in 1761, John Foster was appointed chancellor of the exchequer in 1784 and it was his law-giving bounties on the exportation of corn, together with the imposition of heavy taxes on its importation, that were responsible for making Ireland an arable country. Appointed speaker of the Irish House of Commons in 1785, Foster opposed the union with Britain and upon its adoption, refused to surrender the speakers' mace which was kept by his family. He became a member of the parliament of the United Kingdom for County Louth and in 1804 was appointed Irish chancellor of the exchequer under William Pitt. He was created a peer of the United Kingdom as Baron Oriel of Serrard in County Louth and died on 23 August 1828.

Sir Gordon Morgan Holmes
Neurologist 1876 – 1965

Castlebellingham neurologist Gordon Morgan Holmes was educated at Trinity College, Dublin, graduating in 1897. He also studied at the National Hospital for Nervous Diseases in London and during World War I, served in France as a consultant neurologist to the British Army. There, Holmes was highly influential in the management of shellshock cases and he masterminded a radical change in clinical practice. He, more than any other individual, was responsible for the form of neurological examination as it is now performed and following the war, he became the leading neurologist at the aforementioned National Hospital for Nervous Diseases. A brilliant and formidable neurologist, Holmes died on 29 December 1965.

John Ignatius Kilmartin
RAF squadron leader 1913 – ?

Dundalk born pilot John Ignatius Kilmartin pursued a career as a cattle ranch worker in Australia in the late 1920s and later became a professional jockey in Singapore before joining the Royal Air Force in 1937. At the start of World War II, Kilmartin went to France with No. 1 Squadron and whilst there he brought down eleven German planes in combat. Later returning to Britain where he flew with No. 43 Hurricane Squadron during the Battle of Britain, Kilmartin brought down two further enemy planes in September 1940. He was fortunate to be amongst the few that survived the war.

Dorothy MacArdle
Historian, novelist and republican
1889 – 1958

Born into a wealthy brewing family, Dorothy MacArdle was educated at Alexandra College and University College Dublin. A member of Cumann na mBan (Women's League) during the War of Independence, she became a teacher at her alma mater but lost her position due to her anti-treaty leanings following the Civil War. During that conflict, MacArdle was imprisoned in both Mountjoy and Kilmainham jails and she recounted her experiences in *Earthbound: Nine Stories of Ireland* (1924). She later became a playwright, using the pseudonym 'Margaret Callan', and she was renowned for her extreme political views as expressed in her book *The Irish Republic* (1937). MacArdle was also an advocate of women's working rights and was most vociferous of the Employment Bill (1935), which sought to limit such rights. In 1951 she served as president of the Irish Association of Civil Liberties and she died of cancer in Drogheda on 23 December 1958.

Admiral Sir Francis Leopold McClintock
Explorer and British naval officer
1819 – 1907

Francis Leopold McClintock joined the British navy when he was just twelve years of age, and in 1848 experienced his first arctic voyage, aboard the *Enterprise*. He later commanded the *Intrepid* on another arctic expedition in 1852. A man of considerable endurance, he set out from Melville Island on a sled journey of 1,210 miles, a journey which took 105 days to complete. During this expedition he mapped the unchartered islands of Prince Patrick and Island's Eye, in effect discovering 768 square miles of previously unknown land. Aboard the *Fox* in 1857, McLintock undertook the search for the Sir John Franklin's expedition, at the request of his wife, and upon his return to London, he advised the woman that there were no survivors. McClintock, who received a knighthood, recorded his adventure in a book entitled *The Voyage of the Fox in the Arctic Seas*. He finished his naval services as a rear admiral and died in London in November 1907.

Thomas D'Arcy McGee
Politician 1825 – 1868

At the age of seventeen, Thomas D'Arcy McGee emigrated to the United States where he became editor of the *Boston Pilot*, a Catholic newspaper. In 1846 he returned to Ireland and became one of the leaders of the Young Ireland rebellion, but upon coming to the notice of the law, McGee fled back to the United States. He later moved to Montreal, Canada where he founded the newspaper *New Era* and was elected to the Legislative Assembly of the province of Canada in 1858. In that role he became quite vocal in his opposition to the Fenians and as a result, he was shot and killed as he returned to his home in Sparks Street on 7 April 1868. The Fenian Patrick Whelan (see page 223), was eventually hanged for the murder and McGee was given a state funeral and was buried in Montreal.

Arthur Thomas Moore
Victoria Cross recipient 1830 – 1913

Carlingford born Arthur Thomas Moore was a lieutenant in the 3rd Bombay Light Cavalry of the Indian Army during the Persian War. At the Battle of Khoosh-ab on 8 February 1857, Moore charged five hundred Persians and jumped his horse over the bayonets of the oncoming enemy. His brave actions were an inspiration to his fellow cavalrymen and he subsequently won the Victoria Cross. Moore later attained the rank of major general and died in Dublin in 1913.

Hans Garrett Moore
Victoria Cross recipient 1830 – 89

Hans Garrett Moore was born in Carlingford and was a major in the 88th Regiment of the British Army during the Ninth Cape Frontier War. On the 29 December 1877, near Komgha, South Africa, he gallantly attempted to save the life of a private in the Frontier Mounted Police. The man, who had been knocked from his horse, was lying defenseless on the ground but Moore put himself in harm's way in an effort to save his life. Unsuccessful in his attempt, Moore was seriously injured and for this he was awarded the Victoria Cross. He later achieved the rank of colonel and died in Lough Derg, County Tipperary in 1889.

Dermot O'Brien
Musician, singer and sportsman
1932 – 2007

Dermot O'Brien was born in Ardee and had the distinction of captaining the last Louth team to win the All-Ireland Senior Football Championship in 1957. As an entertainer, he was known nationwide for his singing and his mastery of the accordion, and he was also a fluent Irish speaker. O'Brien was a great ambassador for Ireland in the United States, where he performed with Bing Crosby and appeared on the Ed Sullivan show. O'Brien, whose best-known record was 'The Merry Ploughboy', died of cancer on 22 May 2007.

Thomas Charles James Wright
Officer in Simón Bólivar's army and founder of the Ecuadorian Navy 1799 – 1868

Thomas Charles James Wright was born in Drogheda and was trained in the British Naval College at Portsmouth, England. As a commissioned officer he served on the HMS *Newcastle*, which was engaged in blockading the Atlantic coast off the United States. While on home leave in 1817, Wright developed republican ideals and thus enlisted as an officer in the British Legion of Simón Bolívar. Together with two hundred men and thirty two officers who supported Bolívar's cause, Wright landed in Venezuela on 3 April 1818 and his first action was at Trapiche de Gamarra in March of the following year. His success there inspired Bolívar to undertake his audacious New Granda campaign, which required a march across the Andes, and Wright was to become his close confidant, seeing action by his side in many battles.

Later appointed commodore of the patriot naval forces, Wright was asked to organise a patrol of the Pacific coast and in a major sea battle at Callao, Peru he prevented the Spanish from obtaining reinforcements. As a result he is attributed with a final overthrow of Spanish power in South America. As commander of the brigantine Chimborazo, Wright took Bolívar to Chile, where he witnessed the Chilean independent struggle, and he later returned to Ecuador in 1826, settling in Guayaquil before joining fellow Irishman Daniel Florence O'Leary (see page 108) in battle against Peru. In 1830 the Ecuadorian government commissioned Wright to form the new state's navy and the nautical school which he founded in Guayaquil still functions to this day.

Mayo

Admiral William Brown
1777 -1857

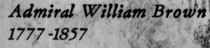

Plaza de Mayo, Buenos Aires, Argentina
is dedicated to the
memory of Admiral William Brown, the
founder of the Argentine navy
and the man most responsible for ending
Spanish rule in Argentina.

Charles J. Haughey
1925-2006

During his term as taoiseach,
Charles Haughey organised
the establishment of the
International Financial Services
Centre in Dublin.

Monsignor James Horan
1911-1986

Founder of the famous Tooreen Ballroom in County Mayo, the entrepreneurial James Horan also established the Marian Shrine at Knock, in addition to Knock Airport.

Louis Brennan
1852-1932

Among the many inventions of Louis Brennan were the gyroscopically-balanced monorail locomotive, the steerable torpedo and a helicopter for the Air Ministry in England.

Paul O'Dwyer
1907-1998

The New York City Hall where Paul O'Dwyer, politician and lawyer, advocated the rights of African-Americans, Irish nationalism, the state of Israel and an end to the Vietnam War.

Louis Brennan
Inventor 1852 – 1932

Louis Brennan was born in Castlebar and immigrated with his family to Australia in 1861. Trained as a civil and mechanical engineer by Alexander Kennedy Smith in 1874, Brennan conceived the idea of a dirigible torpedo, having observed that if a thread is pulled on a reel, the reel will move away. This gave him the idea for his invention and the government of Victoria granted him seven hundred pounds towards the development of the torpedo. Some two years later Brennan went to England where he had the pleasure of selling his invention to the British government for one hundred thousand pounds. Having also developed a monorail locomotive that was kept erect by a gyrostat, he also spent a considerable number of years on the invention of a helicopter for the British Air Ministry. However, in 1926 he was disappointed when the government decided not to continue with the work. Brennan died following a car accident in Switzerland in January 1932.

William Brown
Founder of the Argentinian Navy
1777 – 1857

William Brown, or Guillermo Brown in Argentina, was born in Foxford and aged nineteen was press-ganged into the British Navy, in which he served for a number of years. In 1809 he secured the command of a merchant ship trading between New York and Buenos Aires, but later procured two ships of his own and began trading relations between Sacramento, California and Buenos Aires.

Following the Argentinean uprising against Spanish rule in 1813, the Spanish captured Brown's ships during the blockade of Buenos Aires. However, he was to gain retaliation by taking a Spanish frigate. He then wrote a letter to General Vigodet, the Spanish Governor of Montevideo, Uruguay, requesting the release of both his ships and their respective crews. Vigodet remained defiant and he informed Brown, in no uncertain terms, that he would suffer the same fate as his men should they cross paths. Having harboured no initial intention to partake in the uprising, Brown felt compelled to join the patriots and he thus took command of a small fleet of ships in March 1814, before breaching the Spanish blockade of Montevideo and capturing Vigodet. Rather than harming him, Brown released him back to Spain with the sum of one hundred gold crowns, a gratuity which was later returned by the Spanish authorities, along with a message that complimented Brown on his leniency. In 1816 Brown blockaded the Peruvian port of Callao for three weeks and this action proved the catalyst to the end of Spanish rule in South America. He retired in 1819 and the Plaza de Mayo, in the main square of Buenos Aires, is named after his birthplace. Numerous other locations in Argentina are also named in his honour and to this day, he is held in great reverence in that country.

William Montague Browne
Confederate general in the American Civil War 1823 – 1883

William Montague Brown was educated at Rugby School, England and Trinity College, Dublin. Having seen service in the Crimean War, Brown later joined the British Diplomatic Service before moving to New York in 1851.

He eventually settled in Athens, Georgia, where he became a friend and confidant to Confederate President Jefferson Davis. He was subsequently appointed his aide-de-camp with the rank of colonel. In 1864 Brown was appointed brigadier general and was assigned an infantry brigade in Georgia, where he saw action opposing the advance of the Union general, William Tecumseh Sherman. Following the war, he studied law at the University of Georgia and was later appointed professor of law, history and political science at that institution. He died on 28 April 1883.

Margaret Burke-Sheridan
Opera singer 1889 – 1958

Regarded as Ireland's first prima donna, Margaret Sheridan was affectionately known as 'Maggie from Mayo' and following her success at the Feis Ceoil, she studied at the Royal Academy in London where the Italian inventor Guglielmo Marconi heard her sing. So captivated was he by her voice, that he informed her, 'yours is the voice I've been waiting to hear all my life', and he subsequently brought her to Italy where she began work as a mezzo soprano. Though Sheridan was in her late twenties and was considered too old to succeed, extensive practice and determination saw her become a soprano and it was not long before she was offered lead roles, with Giacomo Puccini describing her portrayal of Madama Butterfly as 'full of charismatic intensity and childlike appeal.' Puccini also coached her to star in his opera *Manon Lescaut*, and numerous other operatic appearances followed, including the title role of La Wally for her appearance at La Scala in 1920. Sheridan later returned to London to appear at the Royal Opera House, where she fell in love with the married managing director of that establishment. Whilst singing on the BBC,

Sheridan cracked on a high note, which signalled the end of her career. She later returned to Dublin where she died of cancer in relative obscurity on 16 April 1958.

John Francis D'Alton
Cardinal and Primate of All Ireland 1882 – 1963

Born in Claremorris, John Francis was educated at Blackrock College, the Holy Cross College, Drumcondra and the Royal University, Dublin. Having obtained a Bachelor of Arts Degree in mental and moral science, he later studied in Rome and spent some time at the universities of Oxford and Cambridge. D'Alton was a lecturer in classics at Maynooth College and for a time served as president of that institution. In 1943 he was appointed bishop of Meath before later being made archbishop of Armagh. Elevated to cardinal by Pope Pius XII in 1952, D'Alton died in Dublin on 2 February 1963 and is buried in the grounds of St Patrick's Cathedral, Armagh.

Michael Davitt
Nationalist and founder of the Land League 1846 – 1906

Michael Davitt was born in the village of Straide, near Castlebar, but following the Great Famine his family were evicted from their home and forced to emigrate to Lancashire, England. Davitt, who had his arm amputated following an accident while working at a cotton mill, studied Irish history at the Mechanics Institute, and joined the Fenian Movement in England. He was arrested in 1870 for arms smuggling and was subsequently sentenced to fifteen years penal servitude, of which he served seven. Having being released on 19 December 1877, he returned to a hero's welcome in Ireland where he vigorously campaigned for the ownership of the land to be in the hands of those who had cultivated it. He thus travelled to the United States, promoting the rights of Irish people to own their own land and on 16 August 1879, the Land League was founded in Castlebar. The league was to receive active support from Charles Stewart Parnell (see page 423), and it organised resistance to evictions while denouncing any form of violence in the pursuit of its aims, instead campaigning for the ostracism of landlords who treated their tenants unfairly. It was during one such campaign against Captain George Boycott, that the word 'boycott' eventually entered the English language. Davitt was a man of immense humanity and he highlighted the plight of the underprivileged, not only in Ireland but in other countries too, such as the Boers in South Africa, the Māori in New Zealand, the Aborigines in Australia and the Jews in Russia. He was also the author of six books and was a patron of the Gaelic Athletic Association. The church where Davitt was christened is now the Michael Davitt Museum. He died on 30 May 1906.

Edward Delaney
Sculptor 1930 – 2009

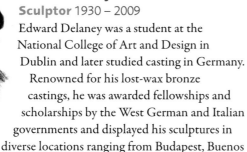

Edward Delaney was a student at the National College of Art and Design in Dublin and later studied casting in Germany. Renowned for his lost-wax bronze castings, he was awarded fellowships and scholarships by the West German and Italian governments and displayed his sculptures in diverse locations ranging from Budapest, Buenos Aires and Tokyo. Delaney's best known works were commissions for the Irish government and they include the Famine Memorial and the statue of Wolfe Tone (see page 196) at St Stephen's Green and a statue of Thomas Davies on College Green in Dublin. A winner of the Arts Council Prize for Sculpture in 1962, he was also the recipient of the Royal Hibernian Academy award for Sculpture of Distinction in Bronze in 1991. His works are displayed in many institutes throughout Ireland, also appearing in the First National Bank of Chicago, the First City National Bank of New York, KLM Airlines headquarters in New York and the Abbey Theatre, Dublin. Delaney, who was also a member of Aosdána, did not live to see two of his pieces, *King* and *Queen* being sold for €190,000, smashing the Irish record for a sculpture by over €100,000. He also designed the front covers for some of The Chieftains' records. He died on 23 September 2009.

John Blake Dillon
Nationalist 1816 – 1866

Called to the Irish bar in 1841, together with Thomas Davis (see page 92) and Gavan Duffy (see page 326), John Blake Dillon founded *The Nation* newspaper in 1842. Following the failed Young Ireland rebellion in 1848, Dillon was sentenced to death for high treason, but with the sentence being commuted to transportation for life to Tasmania, Dillon escaped to France before he was sent south. He duly made his way to the United States, where he served in the New York bar, but the amnesty in Ireland afforded him the opportunity to return to his homeland where he became a member of parliament for Tipperary in 1865. Dillon died suddenly of cholera in Killarney on 15 September 1866.

Thomas J. Flatley
Builder, donor, visionary
1931 – 2008

Born on a twenty-five-acre farm in County Mayo, Thomas J. Flatley arrived in New York City in 1950 with only thirty-two dollars to his name. Serving two years in the United States military, he later trained as a plumber and an electrician and went into business in the construction industry. Over the next forty years, he would become one of the richest men in the United States, amassing a property portfolio that by 1996 included twelve shopping centres, fifty-six office buildings, fifteen hotels, seven nursing homes and fourteen apartment complexes. A devout Catholic, Flatley attended Mass daily and was a most generous philanthropist, donating millions to homeless shelters. He raised 2 million dollars to build the landmark Boston Irish Famine Memorial and was also a founder member of the Ireland Fund, which donated massive aid to cultural and peace initiatives in Northern Ireland and in the republic. Flatley, who was instrumental in the setting up of the Morrison and Donnelly visas, which enabled many young Irish to gain access to the United States, was a very grounded individual and once stated, 'When I leave this world, I don't take anything with me, I wind up with thirty-six square feet.' He died on 17 May 2008.

Colonel Sir James Gildea
Soldier and philanthropist
1838 – 1920

James Gildea was born in Kilmaine and was educated at St Columba's College, Dublin and Pembroke College, Cambridge. Having served with the National Society for Aid to the Sick and Wounded in War, during the Franco-Prussian War, he later raised funds for those killed in the Zulu War of 1879 and the second Afghan war of 1880. Five years later Gildea founded the Soldiers' and Sailors' Families Association, which later became known as the Soldiers', Sailors' and Airmen's Families Association, and in 1890 he became commander of the 6th Militia Battalion of the Royal Warwickshire Regiment. Later appointed a companion of the Order of the Bath, Gildea was also one of the founders of the St John Ambulance Association. Knighted in 1902, he died in London on 6 November 1928.

John Gray
Doctor, journalist and politician 1815 – 1875

John Gray was born in Claremorris and was educated at Trinity College, Dublin and the University of Glasgow where he qualified with a degree in medicine in 1839. In 1841 Gray became joint proprietor of the *Freeman's Journal*, a publication he went on to own in 1850 and as a Protestant nationalist, he was a strong supporter of the repeal movement led by Daniel O'Connell (see page 232). Later elected to the Dublin Corporation, he was knighted in 1863 for his promotion of the Dartry Water Supply Scheme, which supplies water to the city of Dublin. Gray, who was also a strong advocate of tenants' rights and the home rule movement, was elected as a Home Rule League member of parliament for Kilkenny in the general election of 1874, and he held this seat until his death in Bath, England on 9 April 1875. His remains were returned to Ireland and he was honoured with a public funeral at Glasnevin Cemetery and a statue in his memory was erected in O'Connell Street, Dublin in 1879. It was dedicated to the 'appreciation of his many services to his country.'

Charles J. Haughey
Politician and taoiseach
1925 – 2006

Born in the town of Castlebar, Charles James Haughey was educated at the Christian Brothers School in Fairview, Dublin and at University College Dublin, where he studied accountancy. Later qualifying as a barrister, following which he set up an accountant's firm, Haughey was first elected to the Dáil in 1957 and held his seat until 1992. As a member of the Fianna Fáil political party, he served in numerous ministerial positions and, as minister for finance in 1966, he introduced free travel and subsidised electricity for senior citizens. Controversy struck in 1970 when he was accused, along with Neil Blaney (see page 126), of using one hundred thousand pounds to support the importation of arms for the IRA during the northern troubles, but in the following trial, Haughey was found not guilty.

In 1979 he was appointed leader of Fianna Fáil, as well as taoiseach, which was a role he was to serve in for three non-consecutive terms. In 1987 Haughey established the highly successful International Financial Services Centre (IFSC) in the centre of Dublin and he retired as leader of Fianna Fáil on 30 January 1992. He was, perhaps, the most controversial Irish political leader of the twentieth century and quoting Shakespeare's *Othello* in his closing speech he said, 'I have done the state some service and they know it, no more of that'. Haughey died on 13 June 2006.

Monsignor James Horan
Entrepreneurial priest 1911 – 1986

Ordained a priest in 1936, in 1944 James Horan was appointed curate in Tooreen, where he built the famous Tooreen Ballroom. In 1963 he was appointed parish priest of Knock and with a reputation for getting things done, he was instrumental in the building of the new cathedral, Our Lady of Knock, Queen of Ireland Basilica, which is large enough to accommodate ten thousand people. Horan was also the driving force behind Knock airport and it was through his foresight and bravery that it was developed, with the first flight departing for Rome in 1985. On 1 August 1986, just two months after the opening of the airport, Horan died while on a pilgrimage to Lourdes.

Edward Jennings
Victoria Cross recipient
1820 – 1889

Edward Jennings was born in Ballinrobe and was a member of the Bengal Artillery of the British Indian Army during the Indian Rebellion of 1857. For the bravery displayed dring the struggles at Lucknow, India in November 1857, Jennings was awarded the Victoria Cross.

John King
Two-time recipient of the Medal of Honor 1865 – 1938

One of just nineteen recipients of two Medal of Honor awards, Ballinrobe born John King displayed extraordinary heroism on two occasions involving accidents to boilers aboard ships he was serving on. The first of these incidents occurred aboard the USS *Vicksburg* during the Philippine-American War and the second on the USS *Salem* on 13 September 1909. Discharged from naval service in 1916, King was recalled during World War 1 in 1918 and served in New York. A statue to his memory was unveiled in Ballinrobe by Irish Minister for Defence Tony Killeen on 4 September 2010, and the American guided missile destroyer the USS *John King* is also named in his memory. He died on 20 May 1938.

Fr Patrick Lavelle
The parish priest of partry 1825 – 1886

Follwing his ordination, Patrick Lavelle spent some time in Paris and he was later appointed a curate in Mayo Abbey, as well as parish priest of Ballyovey in 1858. He is renowned for his battles against the Protestant Bishop Plunkett, who tried to force Catholic tenants to send their children to Church of Ireland schools under threat of eviction if they refused to comply. Lavelle highlighted Plunkett's threats on the world stage, so much so that the *Times*, a newspaper not known for its love of Catholic Irish, was forced to condemn Plunkett in its columns. Lavelle thus forced Plunkett to leave Mayo and take up residence in Tuam, County Galway. The dispute is often referred to as 'The War of Partry'. Continuing to court controversy, Lavelle preached at the funeral of revolutionary Terence Bellew McManus (see page 208), much to the disdain of Cardinal Cullen of Dublin, who was renowned for his hatred of the Fenians. The cardinal duly reported him to the Catholic authorities in Rome, but Lavelle had the support of his bishop, John MacHale, and he visited Rome himself in his own defence. There, the priest often known as 'the clerical combatant', was completely absolved. He died in Cong, County Mayo on 17 November 1886.

Henry Blosse Lynch
Explorer 1807 – 1873

Henry Blosse Lynch was born at Partry House, Ballinrobe and grew up on the family estate of 1,500 acres. In 1823 he became a midshipman in the Indian navy and served in the Persian Gulf, during which time he learned the Arabic and Persian languages. After being shipwrecked in the Red Sea in 1832, Lynch crossed the Nubian Desert and descended the Nile to Egypt, before accompanying Francis Chesney on his exploration of the Euphrates river two years later. His most famous expedition was in 1837, when he mapped the course of the Tigris from its source in Armenia to Baghdad, Iraq, and for this feat he was made a member of The Order of the Lion and The Sun of Persia. Lynch, who later commanded a squadron of the Indian navy during the 2nd Burmese War, retired in 1856, settling in Paris where he died in 1873.

Kathleen Florence Lynn
Patriot, doctor and humanitarian 1874 – 1955

Kathleen Florence Lynn was born into a Protestant family in Killala and was the first woman to achieve a medicine degree in Ireland. She was also a close friend of James Connolly (see page 429), who appointed her captain and chief medical officer in the Irish Citizens Army. She was subsequently jailed in Kilmainham for her involvement in the rising of 1916. Following the signing of the Anglo-Irish Treaty, Lynn took the side of the republicans in the Civil War. Elected Sinn Féin TD to the Dáil for Dublin North, she refused to take her seat because it involved taking an oath to the British crown and in 1919, she founded St Ultan's infant hospital, the first hospital to specifically care for children. She also became vice-president of 'Save the German Children', an organisation which helped to find homes for German children during World War II, and her services to Ireland as a patriot, doctor and humanitarian are considered immense. She is buried in Deansgrange Cemetery, County Dublin.

Major John MacBride
Irish republican 1865 – 1916

Having initially begun studying medicine, John MacBride left university to become a chemist's assistant in Dublin and joined the Irish Republican Brotherhood. A close personal friend of Arthur Griffith (see page 170), in 1893 MacBride was considered by the British government to be a 'dangerous nationalist' and so he emigrated to South Africa where he joined an Irish Brigade, which was formed to fight the British. Having risen to become second in command, with the rank of major, following the war MacBride went to Paris and married the Irish nationalist Maud Gonne. The following year their son, Sean MacBride (see page 432), was born but the marriage failed and MacBride returned to Dublin where he took part in the Easter Rising of 1916. Fighting at Jacob's factory, he was captured by British forces and executed at Kilmainham on 5 May 1916.

Sir Antony Patrick MacDonnell
Politician 1844 – 1925

Swinford's Anthony Patrick MacDonnell was educated at Summerhill College and University College Galway, where he studied modern languages. Entering the Indian civil service, he arrived in Calcutta in 1865, rising rapidly through the ranks, holding senior positions in that administration. MacDonnell was also a member of the Indian Council in 1902 but he retired from the administration late that year and was appointed permanent under-secretary for Ireland. He was a supporter of home rule for Ireland and gave his support to the 1903 Land Act, which allowed tenants to buy their smallholdings from the landlords through a system of state provided loans. MacDonnell's sympathy for home rule enraged Ulster unionists and this friction eventually led to his resignation. Knighted in 1903, he was elevated to the House of Lords five years later and given the heredity title, 1st Baron MacDonnell of Swinford, County Mayo. A statue to his memory stands in Lucknow, India and he died on 9 June 1925.

Patrick McHale
Victoria Cross recipient 1826 – 1866

Patrick McHale was born in Killala and served as a private in the 1st Batallion of the Fifth Regiment of the British Army during the Indian Mutiny. At Lucknow, India, McHale successfully and single-handedly captured two enemy guns and on numerous occasions was the first man to meet the enemy attack. Such was his determination that he proved a great inspiration to those around him and he was instrumental in increasing the morale of his comrades. A brave soldier, McHale died in Kent, England in 1866.

George Moore
Novelist 1852 – 1933

Born into a landed gentry family, George Moore was educated at Oscott College in Birmingham, England, following which he moved to France to study painting. Moore inherited an estate of twelve thousand acres upon the death of his father in 1870, but with his painting career in France having met with little success, he took up writing and duly published a book of verse, *Flowers of Passion* (1878). He later moved to London, where he published additional poems and a number of novels including *A Modern Lover* (1883), *A Mummer's Wife* (1885) and the successful novel *Esther Waters* (1894). In 1899 Moore returned to Ireland where he became involved in the development of the Irish National Theatre and he also continued to write, publishing two collections of short stories. The final twenty years of his life were spent in London and, having produced more than sixty titles, Moore died there in 1933.

John Moore
Rebel leader and president of Connacht
1763 – 1799

During the Irish Rebellion of 1798, French forces, under the command of General Humbert, landed in Killala where John Moore, who was from a prosperous land owning family, joined them, along with a number of his tenants. This combined Irish and French force saw success at the Battle of Castlebar on 27 August 1798, following which Humbert issued a decree appointing Moore as president in the government of the province of Connacht. However, the allies were defeated at the Battle of Ballinamuck in September 1798 and Moore was captured by the British who sentenced him to transportation. While en route to England, it is believed that Moore died in the Royal Oak Inn, just off Broad Street, Waterford and was buried in Ballygunner Cemetery just outside that city. In recent times his remains have been returned to his native Mayo, where they were interred beside the 1798 memorial in Castlebar. The inscription on the memorial reads, 'The first President of Ireland.'

Delia Murphy
Singer 1902 – 1971

Coming from a reasonably wealthy family, Claremorris-born Delia Murphy was educated at the Presentation Convent in Tuam, County Galway, the Dominican College, Dublin and at University College Galway. Having married Tom Kiernan, who was a member of the Irish Diplomatic Service, in 1939 Murphy recorded three songs on the HMV label, 'If I were a Blackbird', 'The Spinning Wheel', and 'Three Lovely Lasses', all of which became international hits. During World War II, her husband was posted to Rome, where Murphy became associated with Father Hugh O'Flaherty (see page 107) and she helped him to hide British, American and Italian troops, as well as protecting Jews from the Nazis. In all, Murphy recorded some four hundred ballads and she died of a heart attack on 11 February 1971.

Patrick Mylott
Victoria Cross recipient 1820 – 1878

Patrick Mylott was born in Hollymount, Claremorris and was a private in the 84th Regiment of Foot of the British Army during the Indian Rebellion of 1857. Awarded the Victoria Cross for extreme gallantry throughout that campaign, it was one act in particular that would prove to be his defining moment. Under intense fire, Mylott crossed a road and single-handedly captured an enemy enclosure. He later achieved the rank of sergeant and died in Liverpool in 1878.

Paul O'Dwyer
American politician and lawyer 1907 – 1998

Paul O'Dwyer was born in Bohola and emigrated to the United States where he grew up in Brooklyn, New York. Having qualified as a lawyer, he established a practice in Lower Manhattan and earned a reputation as a supporter of striking workers and a staunch supporter of African-

Americans and their struggle for civil rights. He was also a supporter of both constitutional and physical force in relation to Irish nationalism, and was instrumental in protecting several Irish Republican Army members from deportation from the United States. O'Dwyer, who was in favour of the creation of Israel, as well as an end to the Vietnam War, was highly active in New York politics and was elected president of the New York City Council. He died just before his ninety-first birthday in 1998.

William O'Dwyer
Lawyer and mayor of New York
1890 – 1964

William O'Dwyer was born in Bohola and was educated at St Nathy's College, Ballaghaderreen, following which time he studied for the priesthood in Salamanca, Spain. Deciding that he did not have a vocation, he left for the United States, arriving in New York in 1910, and there he worked in an assortment of menial jobs before enlisting in the New York police force in 1917. O'Dwyer, who was the brother of Paul O'Dwyer (see page 311), also attended night school to study law at Fordham University, graduating in 1923, and he was subsequently appointed a magistrate in Brooklyn, New York. Later serving as a county judge, in 1939 O'Dwyer was district attorney in Kings County, Brooklyn and there he carved out a reputation as a vigorous prosecutor, determined to quell organised crime. He was eventually elected mayor of New York in 1945, following which President Truman appointed him ambassador to Mexico. Better known as 'Bill', O'Dwyer died in New York on 24 November 1964, and is buried in Arlington National Cemetery, Virginia.

Ernie O'Malley
Nationalist and writer
1897 – 1957

Writer Ernie O'Malley was born in Castlebar but later moved with his family to Dublin, where he was educated at O'Connell School and studied medicine at University College Dublin. Having taken part in the Easter Rising and fought at the General Post Office, in February 1920, along with Eoin O'Duffy (see page 329), O'Malley captured the Royal Irish Constabulary Barracks in Ballytrain, County Monaghan. This was the first capture of such a barracks in the War of Independence and he was later responsible for the capture of the British Army barracks in Mallow, County Cork. O'Malley, who was wounded several times during the War of Independence, was jailed in Kilmainham, from which he escaped with the aid of a sympathetic British soldier. Referred to by the British authorities as a notorious rebel, they expressed great determination in their efforts to capture him. O'Malley took the anti-treaty side during the Civil War and was present at the Four Courts bombardment but escaped before being captured by Free State troops in Ballsbridge, on 4 November 1922. Sustaining twenty bullet wounds in that particular struggle, during the imprisonment that followed, O'Malley went on hunger strike for forty-one days but following the cessation of hostilities, he was released. His writings include *On Another Man's Wound* and *The Singing Flame* and he also produced a large volume of poetry. He died in 1957 and was awarded a State funeral. A sculpture, donated by O'Malley's family, stands in the Mall in Castlebar.

Fr Patrick Peyton
The Rosary Priest 1909 – 1992

As a young man, Patrick Peyton hoped to become a priest. However, unable to afford an education in Ireland, in 1928 he emigrated to the Unites States with his brother and there he studied for the priesthood. During the final year of his studies, Peyton developed tuberculosis and was given little hope of survival. He made a surprising recovery and was ordained in 1941, upon which time he gained permission from his superiors to commence a prayer crusade in thanks of his recuperation. This crusade took Peyton all over the world, preaching to tens of thousands of people; he appeared on hundreds of radio and television programmes and became known as the founder of the 'family rosary'. Peyton, whose famous slogan was 'the family that prays together, stays together', died on 3 June 1992. A memorial centre in his name has been constructed in his home village and on 10 October 1998, it was officially opened and dedicated.

Martin Sheridan
Athlete 1881 – 1918

Born in Bohola, at the age of sixteen Martin Sheridan emigrated to the United States where he became a policeman in New York. He was also an accomplished athlete, taking the gold medal at the St Louis Olympics whilst representing his adopted country in the discus event. He was also a talented sprinter, jumper and pole-vaulter, becoming all-round champion of the world in 1905, 1907 and 1909. In the London Olympics of 1908, Sheridan again won honours and in commemoration of his exploits, the New York Police Department established the Martin J. Sheridan award for Valour. Also honoured by Greece, the home of the Olympic Games, a statue of a discus thrower was erected in Athens. Upon his death from pneumonia in 1918, the *New York Herald Tribune* proclaimed that 'the greatest all-round athlete ever known has passed away.'

Michael Joseph Staines
First commissioner of An Garda Síochána 1885 – 1955

Michael Joseph Staines served in the Gaelic League and Sinn Féin, as well as being a member of the Irish Volunteers. A quartermaster general in the General Post Office during the 1916 rising, Staines was interred in Frongoch Internment Camp in Wales, but upon the formation of the new provisional government in 1922, he was appointed the first commissioner of the newly named Civil Guard on 10 March of that year. In that role he relied heavily on former Royal Irish Constabulary senior officers, in particular District Inspector Patrick Walsh, who was appointed deputy commissioner. With anti-treaty supporters within the Civil Guard issuing an ultimatum demanding the expulsion of Walsh and other former RIC officers, Stains called out the names of the ringleaders of this uprising as he paraded his new force on 15 May 1922. However, he was immediately shouted down and in view of this protest, chose the only honorable option available to him and resigned. In 1923, he was appointed to the Irish senate by W. T. Cosgrave and later went into business as a manufacturer's agent. He died in 1955.

Meath

Richard Farrelly
1916-1990

Richard Farrelly was a songwriter, policeman and poet who composed the famous song 'The Isle of Inisfree'.

Charles Yelverton O'Connor
1843-1902

Engineer Charles Yelverton O'Connor is responsible for the contruction of Freemantle Harbour and the Goldfields Pipeline, a major engineering feat in Australia. His statue stands in Freemantle Port.

Francis Ledwidge
1887-1917

The Slane birth home of the love poet Francis Ledwidge. Though an Irish nationalist, he gave his life in the service of Britain in World War I.

Richard C. Kerens
1842-1916

A chief mule driver, pony express contractor, railroad magnate and lumber and mining stockholder, Kilberry born Kerens also served as US Ambassador to Austria and Hungary, having previously served in the union army.

John Boyle O'Reilly
1844-1890

Escaping from Freemantle Gaol, Australia on the 18 February 1869, John Boyle O'Reilly fled to Boston. There he raised funds to purchase the whaler *Catalpa*, which took part in the rescue of six fellow Fenians from Freemantle on 28 March 1876.

Sir Francis Beaufort
Admiral and inventor 1774 – 1857

Born to a father who was a well-known geography and topography expert, Francis Beaufort commenced his nautical career as a cabin boy in the British Navy at the age of thirteen. Rising through the ranks, he attained command of the naval ship HMS *Woolwich*, and as commander of that ship he carried out a hydrographic survey in South America. Beaufort was renowned for writing meteorological journals on weather conditions during his years at sea and in 1829 he was appointed hydrographer to the admiralty. It was at this time that he developed the Beaufort scale of wind force, which was officially adopted for use in the British navy in 1838. Later appointed a rear admiral, he was bestowed with the title Knight Commander of the Order of the Bath in 1848, and retired from naval service in 1855. Beaufort died some two years later.

Colonel Thomas Blood
Adventurer 1618 – 1680

The son of a prosperous blacksmith, in 1642 Thomas Blood travelled to England in order to fight for Charles I. However, it was soon apparent to him that Oliver Cromwell was going to win in his battle with the Royalists and that the monarchy would be abolished. He promptly changed sides and joined the Roundheads but in 1660, returned to Ireland when Charles II became king and, with the support of disgruntled Cromwellians, attempted to sieze Dublin Castle and capture Lord Ormond. The plot failed and Blood fled to the Netherlands before brazenly returning to England a decade later to practice medicine, despite being a wanted man. Dressed as a clergyman, he became friendly with the keeper of the Crown Jewels, Talbot Edwards, and later aided by two companions, stole the priceless paraphernalia. Blood was arrested when he attempted to flee, but safe in the knowledge that King Charles II had a liking for scoundrels, he asked to be taken before the king, where he reckoned that his considerable Irish charm would save his neck. It did and Blood was subsequently awarded Irish lands worth £500 per annum, becoming a familiar figure in royal circles in the process. He died at his house in Bowling Alley, Westminster on 24 August 1680.

Thomas Brennan
Co-founder of the Irish National Land League 1853 – 1912

Though born in County Meath, as a youth Thomas Brennan lived in Dublin where he found employment in the North City Milling Company. He went on to become the first secretary of the Land League when it's offices were opened in Abbey Street. In his days as a promoter of the Land League with Michael Davitt (see page 305), Brennan was renowned for the eloquence of his speeches and was thus compared to Thomas Francis Meagher (see page 393), who was also talented in this regard. Brennan was later arrested for his involvement in the Land League and imprisoned in Kilkenny Jail. Upon his release he left Ireland for the United States, settling in Omaha, Nebraska where he opened a prosperous investment and insurance brokerage. Having previously played a pivotal role in the regeneration of the country of his birth, Brennan's company became one of the leading concerns in the region and displayed his significant contribution to United States' commerce. He died in Omaha on 19 December 1912.

Turlough O'Carolan
Harpist and composer 1670 – 1738

The musically gifted Turlough O'Carolan was born near Nobber, but in his mid-teens, moved to County Roscommon where he received his education. Having developed smallpox in his late teens O'Carolan was left blind but this did not stop him spending almost fifty years of his life travelling the length and breadth of Ireland, composing and performing music. His compositions were distinctively Irish yet retained an international flavour and they can be found in the repertories of a great number of modern Celtic bands. O'Carolan is honoured by a plaque in St Patrick's Cathedral, Dublin, which refers to him as 'The Last of the Irish Bards.'

John Cassidy
Sculptor 1860 – 1939

John Cassidy was born in Littlewood, Slane and served an apprenticeship as a barman in the White Horse Hotel, Drogheda. In 1880 he went to Dublin and attended night classes in art school, where he gained a scholarship to study in Milan. Finally settling in Manchester, England, where he spent the remainder of his life, Cassidy established a studio in Barton Arcade in the city centre and his reputation grew rapidly. He subsequently exhibited his works at the Royal Academy, the Hibernian Academy and in Manchester City Art Gallery. Many of his sculptures can be found at various sites throughout Britain but his greatest works are in the John Rylands Library, Manchester, where his white marble statues of John Rylands and his wife, Enriqueta, are located in the reading room. Cassidy's best-known work in

Ireland is the full-length figure of Queen Victoria in Belfast, County Antrim. He died on 19 July 1939 and is buried in Southern Cemetery, Manchester.

Jim Connell
Writer of 'The Red Flag'
1852 – 1929

Born in Kilskyre, near Kells, Jim Connell joined the Irish Republican Brotherhood as a teenager, later becoming a worker on Dublin's docks. Having moved to London in 1875 he became a member of the Social Democratic Federation, led by Henry Hyndman, and this organisation was a strong supporter of the cause of Irish land reform and self-determination. In the 1890s Connell joined the Independent Labour Party of Great Britain and it was after attending a meeting during the London docker's strike of 1889 that he wrote the socialist anthem 'The Red Flag', which has been sung at Labour conferences ever since, and has become the anthem of oppressed workers all over the world. Connell died in Lewisham in February 1929 and a bronze bust in Crossakiel, near Kells, exists to his memory.

Eamonn Duggan
Lawyer and Nationalist 1874 – 1936

The son of a Royal Irish Constabulary officer from County Armagh, Eamonn Duggan qualified as a solicitor in 1914. He established a successful legal practice and became a supporter of Sinn Féin, fighting in the Easter Rising of 1916. Due to his involvement, Duggan was court-martialed and sentenced to three years penal servitude before being released under a general amnesty the following year. For a time he served as director of intelligence in the Irish Republican Army and was also elected to the first Dáil Éireann for South Meath in 1918. Re-arrested in 1920, Duggan was once again released following the truce in July 1921, upon which time he was re-elected for South Meath. Later that year he was appointed as one of the five envoys to negotiate and conclude a peace treaty with the British government, which he signed at 22 Hans Place, London. In the new provisional government, Duggan served as minister for home affairs and later became parliamentary secretary to the minister for defence as well as the Executive Council. He was elected to the Senate in 1933 but died suddenly in Dun Laoghaire, County Dublin on 6 July 1936.

Richard Farrelly
Song-writing policeman 1916 – 1990

Richard Farrelly was born in Kells where, as a young boy, he learned to play the piano. He joined An Garda Síochána (Irish police force) in 1939. It was the song 'The Isle of Innisfree', recorded by Bing Crosby in the early 1950s, that made Farrelly one of Ireland's most famous songwriters and it would go on to become a worldwide hit, used by John Ford in his epic movie, *The Quiet Man*, starring John Wayne and Barry Fitzgerald (see page 166). Farrelly, or 'Dick' as he was commonly known, was a prolific songwriter and had other hits such as, 'The Cottage by the Lee', 'If You Ever Fall in Love Again', 'The Gypsy Maiden' and 'We Dreamed our Dreams'. He died in 1990 and as a tribute, his daughter-in-law, Sinead Stone, and his son, Gerald Farrelly, recorded an album of his songs entitled *Legacy of a Quiet Man* (2002).

Alice Stopford Green
Historian and nationalist
1847 – 1929

A member of a Protestant family in Kells where her father was a rector before the family moved to London in 1874, Alice married the historian John Richard Green, who later died in 1883. Green wrote her first volume of history, *Henry II* in 1888 but she later directed her attentions to early Irish history and Irish nationalism. A supporter of the Anglo-Irish Treaty, which gave Ireland its independence in 1921, she also published *The Making of Ireland and Its Undoing* (1908) and *Irish Nationality* (1911). Following the Easter Rising of 1916, Green returned to Ireland, where she resided at 90 St Stephen's Green, Dublin. In 1918 she published a pamphlet, 'Ourselves Alone in Ulster', which attacked Edward Carson's policies north of the border. She was nominated to the Irish Senate in 1922 and published her last work, *A History of the Irish State to 1014* in 1925. Green died in Dublin on 28 May 1929.

Charles Graham Halpine
Journalist, soldier, politician
1829 – 1868

Originally attending Trinity College, Dublin to study medicine before later turning his interests to journalism, Charles Graham Halpine emigrated to the United States in 1851 and went on to become associate editor of the *New York Times*. Upon the outbreak of the American Civil War, he joined the 69th New York Regiment (Irish Brigade) and proved himself a formidable soldier, being promoted several ranks. However, Halpine's greatest contribution to the conflict was as a writer and satirist and he penned numerous biting letters criticising northerners who did not support the war effort. Written in character, under the pseudonym of an ignorant Irish private named 'Miles O'Riley', the accounts were compiled into two best-selling books entitled *The Life and Adventures of Private Miles O'Riley* (1864), and *Baked Meats of the Funeral* (1866). Following the war, Halpine returned to journalism, becoming editor of the *New York Citizen*, and he also championed the rights of the Fenian Brotherhood to win Irish independence. Halpine, who was elected registrar of the county and city of New York in 1866, suffered from insomnia, alcoholism and depression, and committed suicide on 3 August 1868.

Frederick Maurice Watson Harvey
Victoria Cross recipient
1888 – 1980

Frederick Maurice Watson Harvey was born in Athboy and served as a lieutenant in the Royal Canadian Horse of the Canadian Army during World War I. His defining moment occurred when he happened upon a wired trench containing a machine gun, whilst leading a troop of his command at Guyencourt, France. Harvey immediately swung from his saddle and made straight for the trench, scaling the wire and shooting the gunners in the trench before capturing the gun itself. He was awarded the Victoria Cross and later became a brigadier before dying in Alberta, Canada in 1980.

Guy Johnson
Crown military officer during the american revolutionary war
1740 – 1788

At the age of sixteen, Dunshaughlin native Guy Johnson emigrated to the United States where he settled in New York. A military man, in 1774 he became superintendent of Indian Affairs and served in the French and Indian War. During the American Revolution, Johnson helped to keep the majority of the Iroquois tribe loyal to the British and he also established a headquarters in Niagara, New York where he directed loyalist raids against the patriot frontier settlements. He was suspended from his position for exaggerating accounts of his escapades in Canada, and died whilst on a visit to London, England, which he undertook in order to defend the accusations made against him, on 5 March 1788.

Sir William Johnson, 1st Baronet
Pioneer and army officer
1715 – 1774

Having emigrated to the United States in 1738, William Johnson originally intended to take up a legal career. He instead became a trader and for a period, took up residence with the Mohawk tribe from whom he purchased extensive lands. Having been appointed superintendent of Indian affairs, Johnson later became a major general in the British forces during the French and Indian wars, defeating Baron Dieskau at the Battle of Lake George and becoming a baronet in the process. He was also involved in the siege of Fort Niagra in the summer of 1759, and the capture of Montreal in 1760, before later founding the city of Johnstown. Johnson had extensive business interests in the New York area, where the Native Americans dubbed him 'Warragghivagey' (he who does much business). He died in Johnstown in 1774.

Kate Kennedy
Founder of America's first union of schoolteachers 1827 – 1890

Kate Kennedy was born in Gaskinstown but due to the famine and the death of her father, she emigrated to the United States in 1849. Together with her sister Alice and her younger brother, she initially settled in New York before moving on to San Francisco, California in 1857. In 1859 Kennedy excelled in the examination for principal schoolteachers and this won her an appointment as principal of the North Cosmopolitan Grammar School. She also won awards for being the best teacher in the city but despite the fact that she was principal of a senior school, she was still only paid the salary of a primary school principal. This was simply because she was a female. She thus founded a teachers' union and with great determination, pursued the rights of female teachers, which resulted in the passing of a law in 1847 stating that, 'females employed as teachers in public schools in the state of California shall, in all cases, receive the same compensation as allowed to male teachers for like service, when holding the same grade of certificate.' The Kate Kennedy elementary school in San Francisco's Mission district is named in her memory.

Richard C. Kerens
Railroad builder and politician 1842 – 1916

Richard C. Kerens was born in Killberry but later emigrated to the United States, settling in Iowa with his family when he was just an infant. Kerens joined the United States Army at the age of nineteen and became chief mule driver for the Army of the Potomac, as well as chief of transportation in 1863. Following the Civil War he became the proprietor of a livery stable, contracting with the Pony Express system for carrying mail. Kerens soon realised that railroad construction would be a profitable venture and so he moved to St Louis, Missouri where he became involved in the construction of some of the southern states' most prominent railroad lines. He also became a stockholder and director of some of the major systems and his wealth was substantially increased by his involvement in the development of lumber and mining industries in West Virginia. Kerens, who was also vociferous in Missouri politics, was a major contributor to the Republican Party funds and in 1909 was honoured by President William Howard Taft who appointed him United States ambassador to Austria-Hungary. A devout Catholic, he was awarded the Laetare Medal from the University of Notre Dame in 1904 and he died on 4 September 1916.

Francis Ledwidge
Poet 1887 – 1917

Slane born Francis Ledwidge finished school at the age of fifteen, upon which time he found work as an apprentice grocer in Rathfarnham, Dublin. Suffering extreme homesickness, it was there that Ledwidge wrote his first poem,

'Behind the Closed Eye', and in the following years he would work as a farmhand, a road worker and a miner. Another poem, 'Spring Love', reflects the relationship he had with a young girl named Ellie Vaughey and in response to the quality of Ledwidge's work, Lord Dunsany became his patron, ensuring that the poetry would reach a wider audience. Ledwidge was also a founder member of the Slane Corps of the Irish Volunteers in 1913, and though a convinced nationalist, he enlisted in the Royal Inniskillen Fusiliers of the British Army at Richmond Barracks in Dublin. His collection of poetry, *Songs of the Fields*, was published in 1916 and was followed by *The Complete Poems* in 1919. He was killed whilst serving in Belgium on the 31 July 1917.

Charles Yelverton O'Connor
Engineer 1843 – 1902

Charles Yelverton O'Connor was born at Gravelmount House, Castletown and was educated at the Bishop Foy's School in Waterford. Having apprenticed as a railway engineer in 1859, the following year he emigrated to New Zealand where he was appointed assistant engineer of the Canterbury Province. There, he supervised construction of railways through the Southern Alps before being appointed inspector of engineering for the entire South Island of New Zealand in 1880. O'Connor, who was later made marine engineer for the entire colony, accepted the position of engineer-in-chief of Western Australia in 1891 and was involved in two enormous projects over the following years; the building of the harbour for the city of Perth at Freemantle, as well as the construction of a pipeline from the Helena River to the Goldrush district of Coolgardie. This project spanned a distance of 328 miles and is regarded as one of the greatest engineering

feats of the time. Due to the immense pressure of work on the scheme, and unfounded allegations made against him, O'Connor took his own life on 10 March 1902. A bronze statue to his memory stands in front of the Freemantle Port Authority Buildings, and the beach where he died has also been named after him.

Brian O'Higgins
Patriot and writer 1882 – 1963

Born near Kells, Brian O'Higgins played an active part in the cause of Irish freedom and the promotion of the Irish language. An active member of the Gaelic League, O'Higgins was a member of the garrison at the General Post Office during the Easter Rising of 1916, following which he was imprisoned at Frongoch in Wales. O'Higgins opposition to the Anglo-Irish Treaty resulted in him being imprisoned at the Curragh, County Kildare, where he went on hunger strike for twenty-five days, following which he was released. In 1925 he published *The Soldier's Story of Easter Week, and in 1926, Ten Golden Years*. Writing under the name of Brian na Banban, he was a prolific writer of patriotic ballads and was also widely known for his greeting cards, which contained a verse set in a Celtic design. O'Higgins carried out his literary pursuits until his death in 1963.

Alexander 'Alejandro' O'Reilly
Spanish field marshal and governor of Madrid
1722 – 1794

Alexander O'Reilly was born in Beltrasna and left Ireland, along with tens of thousands of other Irish men in what is known as 'The Flight of the Wild Geese', to serve as soldiers in continental armies. Initially a colonel in the Austrian army, O'Reilly later moved to Spain and swore his allegiance to that country. Rising to the rank of field marshal in 1765, he was sent to assist in the defence and military reorganisation of Puerto Rico and later, in 1769, he was appointed captain-general of Louisiana, where he re-established Spanish control of that territory. Returning to Spain, he led forces on the assault of Algiers in 1775, but failed in this endeavour. O'Reilly, who was also made a count, held many senior positions in Spain in addition to being a field marshal. He was governor of Madrid, captain general of Andalusia as well as governor of Cadiz. He died in Cadiz in 1794 and is buried in the parish church in Bonete, Spain. A street in Cadiz is named in his honour.

John Boyle O'Reilly
Fenian and novelist 1844 – 1890

Having served some time as an apprentice in a local Drogheda newspaper, John Boyle O'Reilly went to Preston, England where he became a reporter for the *Guardian* newspaper. Returning to Dublin in 1863, he became a member of the Irish Republican Brotherhood but enlisted in the 10th Hussars of the British Army with the sole intention of recruiting members to join the Fenians. However, authorities gained knowledge of his persuasive actions and he was arrested and sentenced to death, before having his punishment commuted to twenty years penal servitude in Western Australia. Escaping from Freemantle Gaol, on 18 February 1896, John Boyle O'Reilly fled to Boston, where he later organised fundraising that would finance the famed *Catalpa* rescue of six fellow Fenians from Australia on 28 March 1876. He also wrote a considerable number of poems and a novel, *Moondyne* (1879), which was based on his experiences whilst incarcerated at Freemantle. Strongly opposed to anti-Semitism and racism, O'Reilly died on 9 August 1890. The song, 'Van Diemen's Land', sung by Irish rock band U2, is dedicated to him.

Edward Lovett Pearce
Architect 1699 – 1733

Described as the father of Irish Palladian architecture and Georgian Dublin, Edward Lovett Pearce studied under his cousin, Sir John Vanbrugh, and his principal works include the original Irish Houses of Parliament, now the Bank of Ireland in Dame Street, Dublin. Pearce, who also designed Bellamont House in Coote Hill, County Cavan, was appointed surveyor general of Ireland in 1730 and was knighted two years later. Awarded the freedom of the city of Dublin in 1733, he died of septicemia at his home in Stillorgan, County Dublin at the age of thirty-four.

Richard Pigott
Journalist and forger
c.1828 – 1889

Richard Pigott commenced his working life as an errand boy in the office of *The Nation* newspaper and later obtained a position as a clerk in the Belfast newspaper, the *Ulster Man*. He returned to Dublin in 1858 when the owner of that publication changed its name to the *Irish Man* and relocated to the capital.

In 1865, Pigott became the owner and he subsequently founded a weekly magazine, the *Shamrock*, which was followed by another magazine, the *Flag of Ireland*. All three publications propagated extreme nationalism and Pigott was imprisoned for publishing seditious matter. In the early 1880s he sold the newspapers to the Land League, of which Charles Stewart Parnell (see page 423) was president, but for some unknown reason, he turned against his nationalist-inclined associates and began selling information on them to their political opponents, who included the Irish Loyal and Patriotic Union, an anti-home rule organisation.

In 1886 Piggott sold information to the aforementioned group regarding Charles Stewart Parnell's supposed complicity in the Phoenix Park murders, which were later published by the *Times* under 'Parnellism and Crime'. On 18 April 1887, the *Times* published a letter from Pigott's collection, which was supposedly signed by Parnell, condoning those murders and in August of the following year a special commission was established to investigate the validity of the allegations. Pigott was called as a witness but during the enquiry, which took place on 21 February 1889, he broke down during cross-examination, confessing his guilt and immediately fleeing the country. He made it to Madrid, Spain but was later traced there and when police entered his hotel on 1 March 1889, Pigott shot himself dead.

Sir Oliver Plunkett
Roman Catholic archbishop of Armagh 1629 – 1681

Born in Loughcrew, Oliver Plunkett entered the Irish college in Rome where he was ordained in 1654. The Cromwellian conquest of Ireland from 1649 to 1653 resulted in the practice of Roman Catholicism being banned throughout the country and with clergy being executed, Plunkett chose not to return to Ireland until 1669 when he was appointed archbishop of Armagh. It was the enactment of the Test Act (a religious test that imposed various civil disabilities on Roman Catholics) in 1673 that brought him into conflict with the authorities and his defiance of the act, together with an accusation that he was plotting to bring French troops into Ireland in order to commence an uprising, led to his arrest. In the knowledge that Plunkett would never be convicted in Ireland, he was moved to Newgate Prison, London, where a first trial found him not guilty. However, a second trial under Sir Francis Pemberton, which was claimed to be a 'kangaroo court', found him guilty of treason and promoting the Roman Catholic faith. Lord Campbell, writing about the judge, claimed that the trial was a disgrace to both the judge and his country. On 1 July 1681, Plunkett was hanged, drawn and quartered at Tyburn – the last Roman Catholic martyr to die in England. His head is enshrined in St Peter's Church in Drogheda, County Louth. Plunkett, who was beatified in 1920 and canonised in 1975, was adopted as the patron saint for peace and reconciliation in Ireland in 1997.

Richard Kirby Ridgeway
Victoria Cross recipient 1848 – 1924

Richard Kirby Ridgeway served as a captain in the Bengal Staff Corps of the Indian Army during the Basuto War. During an assault on Konona, India on 22 November 1879, Ridgeway, facing continuous enemy fire, rushed a barricade and attempted to tear it down in an effort to gain entry to an enemy position. Whilst doing so, he was severely wounded in the right shoulder but was awarded the Victoria Cross for his great bravery. He later achieved the rank of colonel and died in Yorkshire, England in 1924.

Monaghan

Lady Mary Bailey
1890-1960

The de Havilland Cirrus Moth aircraft, flown by Lady Mary Bailey in her epic flight from London to Cape Town in 1928.

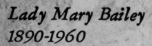

Colonel John O'Neill
1834-1878

The uniform of the Fenian soldiers under the command of Colonel John O'Neill, who invaded Canada in 1866. He did so with the intention of capturing it and exchanging it for Ireland with the British authorities.

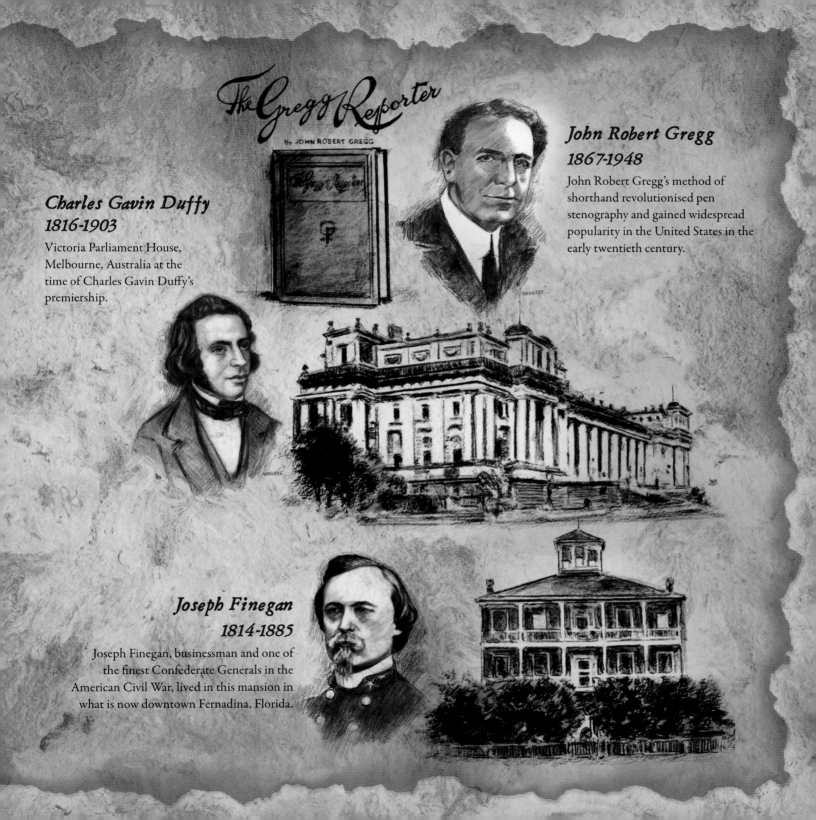

The Gregg Reporter
By JOHN ROBERT GREGG

John Robert Gregg
1867-1948

John Robert Gregg's method of shorthand revolutionised pen stenography and gained widespread popularity in the United States in the early twentieth century.

Charles Gavin Duffy
1816-1903

Victoria Parliament House, Melbourne, Australia at the time of Charles Gavin Duffy's premiership.

Joseph Finegan
1814-1885

Joseph Finegan, businessman and one of the finest Confederate Generals in the American Civil War, lived in this mansion in what is now downtown Fernadina, Florida.

Māori Land, were published in 1890 and he died in Dunedin, New Zealand on 16 February 1898.

Mary Bailey
Aviatrix 1890 – 1960

Mary Bailey was born Mary Westenra at Rossmore Castle, and lived a life of hunting, shooting and fishing with little formal education, before marrying Sir Abe Bailey, a South African millionaire. Having begun flying lessons in secret, rapidly became one of the world's most celebrated aviators and, upon receiving her pilot's licence in 1927, Bailey became the first woman to fly across the Irish Sea. The following year she made an epic, solo return flight from Croydon, London to Cape Town, South Africa in a de Havilland Cirrus Moth. She was later awarded the Britannia Trophy. Bailey, who was created a DBE in 1930, died in 1960.

Thomas Bracken
Poet and writer of the national anthem of New Zealand 1843 – 1898

At the age of twelve, Clones born Thomas Bracken left for Australia, settling with an uncle in Geelong, Victoria. Having moved to New Zealand in 1869, he won the Otago Caledonian Society's prize for poetry and subsequently entered journalism, becoming an editor of the *Saturday Advertiser*. It was in this paper he published 'God Defend New Zealand', which was widely admired and was thus adopted as the nation's national anthem. Bracken, who championed sovereignty for the native Māori people, also had a brief political career and he showed great support for the Roman Catholic desire to obtain public support for church schools, even converting to that faith in 1896. His collected poems, *Musings in*

John Bagnell Bury
Irish historian and scholar
1861 – 1927

Born in Clontibret, John Bagnell Bury was educated at Trinity College, Dublin where he became a fellow in 1885. In 1902 he was elected regius professor of modern history at the University of Cambridge and amongst his greatest writings are: *A History of Greece to the Death of Alexander the Great, A History of the Later Roman Empire, A History of the Roman Empire 27BC – 180AD* and *The Life of St Patrick and his Place in History*. For his work, Bury received many honours including degrees from the Universities of Oxford, Edinburgh, Glasgow, Aberdeen and Durham. He died on 1 June 1927.

Charles Gavan Duffy
Nationalist and prime minister of Victoria, Australia
1816 – 1903

A dedicated nationalist, the failure of the repeal movement along with the horrors of the famine and the death of Daniel O'Connell (see page 232) weakened Charles Gavan Duffy's faith in the power of constitutional action to secure Irish freedom, and so he instead advocated revolutionary measures. Along with Thomas Davis (see page 92) and John Dillon (see page 164), Duffy was a cofounder of *The Nation* newspaper, but this publication was suppressed by the authorities and as a consequence, he was arrested in July 1848 but discharged the following year. Elected a member of parliament for New Ross in 1852, Duffy agitated for land reform, but seeing his desires continually blocked by the House of Lords, he despairingly decided to emigrate to Australia. There he continued his political career, becoming prime minister for Victoria in 1871 before he was knighted for his services to the colony in 1873. He died on 9 February 1903 and is buried in Glasnevin Cemetery, Dublin.

Joseph Finegan
Confederate general 1814 – 1885

Joseph Finegan was born in the border region town of Clones and emigrated to the United States, settling in Florida in 1830. There he studied law before establishing a sawmill, becoming involved in railroad construction and purchasing extensive lands in what is now downtown Fernadina. When the American Civil War broke out, Finegan was appointed to the position of brigadier general and in February 1864, he stopped the federal advance from Jacksonville, as well as the capture of Tallahassee, by defeating the Union Army at the battle of Olustee. Later ordered to lead the newly formed 'Florida Brigade' with the army of Northern Virginia, following the war Finegan returned to Fernadina where he had lost most of his property. He decided to move to Savannah, Georgia, where he worked as a cotton broker, regaining some of his wealth and he died at Rutledge, Florida on 29 October 1885.

Francis Fitzpatrick
Victoria Cross recipient 1859 – 1933

Francis Fitzpatrick was born in Tullycorbet and served as a private in the 94th Regiment (later the Connaught Rangers) of the British Army during the Basuto War. On 28 November 1879, at Sekukuni's Town, South Africa, Fitzpatrick, along with another private and six native soldiers, served under the command of a young lieutenant of the 1st Dragoon Guards. With the lieutenant badly wounded in combat, the native soldiers immediately fled leaving the two privates to face an enemy that numbered approximately thirty soldiers. Fitzpatrick's co-private carried the lieutenant to safety whilst he himself covered the retreat, thereby saving the man's life. For this deed he was awarded the Victoria Cross.

John Robert Gregg
Inventor of Gregg Shorthand 1867 – 1948

John Robert Gregg was born at Rockcorry and was educated in Glasgow, Scotland, studying the theory and practice of many systems of stenography. At the age of twenty-six he emigrated to the United States where he first published *Gregg Shorthand Manual*. He later settled in Chicago, establishing the Gregg Publishing Company. He died in New York on 23 February 1948.

Thomas Hughes
Victoria Cross recipient 1885 – 1942

Thomas Hughes was born in Castleblayney and served as a private in the 6th Battalion, Connaught Rangers of the British Army during World War I. On 3 September 1916 at Guillemont, France, Hughes was wounded in the midst of heavy fire. Despite his injury, he charged a machine gun point and killed the gunner before capturing three of his comrades. For this deed Hughes was awarded the Victoria Cross and he died in County Monaghan in 1942.

327

Patrick Kavanagh
Poet 1904 – 1967

Legendary poet Patrick Kavanagh commenced his working life as shoemaker and small farmer. Born in Inniskeen, he was educated locally and his first book, *The Ploughman and Other Poems*, was published in 1936. *The Green Foot*, described by him as a stage Irish autobiography, was published in 1938 and the following year he sought a precarious living as a literary journalist in Dublin, submitting articles and poems to various publications. In 1942 Kavanagh published 'The Great Hunger', an extensive poem on the difficulties of Irish rural life that stirred much controversy by attacking the sexual and religious oppression of the Catholic Church. He published a collection of poems, *A Soul for Sale*, in 1947, and the following year, a novel entitled *Tarry Flynn*. It was perhaps his *Collected Poems* (1964) that solidified Kavanagh's standing among the literary greats and gained him extensive recognition outside of his homeland. He is one of the most significant of Irish poets, the lyrical quality of his work enhancing his reputation, and a statue to him stands on the banks of the Grand Canal in the place he loved most – Dublin. He died on 30 November 1967; his grave in Inniskeen is near the Patrick Kavanagh Centre, dedicated to his memory.

Shane Leslie (Sir John Randolph Leslie, 3rd Baronet)
Diplomat and writer 1885 – 1971

Initally educated at the Ludgrove School, Eton College, it was whilst attending King's College, Cambridge that Shane Leslie converted to the Roman Catholic faith and also became a home rule-favouring Irish nationalist, even adopting the anglicised Irish variant of his name, 'Shane'. Glaslough born, Leslie's first publication was a collection of verse, but he later turned to prose work on religious and philosophical themes, writing biographical studies of Dean Swift, George Lee Ford and Cardinal Manning among others. His family owned an estate of 49,000 acres in County Monaghan and for a short time Leslie was the primary operator. He did, however, find this work very boring and later transferred it to his eldest son, John Norman Leslie, who became the 4th Baronet. Interestingly, Leslie was the first cousin of Winston Churchill and as such, he acted in the periphery of the negotiations of the Anglo-Irish Treaty of 1921. Pope Pius XI honoured Leslie by making him a privy chamberlain and he was also acknowledged by the University of Notre Dame for presenting an ancient Irish script to that institution. Leslie, who also transferred St Patrick's Purgatory on Lough Derg to the Catholic Bishop of Clogher, died in Hove, England on 13 August 1971.

John MacKenna
General in the Chilean War of Independence 1771 – 1814

Born at Willville House, near Monaghan town, John MacKenna left Ireland at the age of eleven to be educated at the Military College in Barcelona, Spain. There he studied military engineering and he later entered the Spanish military as a cadet in the Regiment Irlanda (The Irish Regiment). Following participation in the War of the Pyrenees against the French, in 1795 MacKenna was promoted to captain and left Spain for South America, arriving in Chile, where he utilised his engineering skills in the reconstruction of the city of Osorno, which had been destroyed by the indigenous Huilliche people in October 1602. He was subsequently appointed governor of the city by fellow Irishman, Sligo born Ambrose O'Higgins (see page 360) and on the death of O'Higgins, he joined the rebel forces of his son Bernardo O'Higgins, in which he was appointed commandant general. At the Battle of Membrillar in 1814, MacKenna defeated a much superior Spanish force in a victory which brought an end to Spanish rule in Chile. Mackenna died in a duel the same year as his famous victory but he is not forgotten; on 28 October 2010, An Post, the Irish postal service, issued a stamp in his honour.

Michael McLaverty
Short-story writer 1904 – 1992

Michael McLaverty was born in Carrickmacross and was educated at St Malachy's College and at Queen's University, Belfast, graduating in 1927. One of Ireland's finest exponents of the art of short story writing, in 1929 McLaverty became a teacher of maths and physics in St John's PES, West Belfast and he also authored eight novels, which include *Call My Brother Back, Lost Fields, In This Thy Day* and *The Three Brothers*. Retiring from teaching in 1964, his last novel, *The Brightening Day* was published the following year. He died in 1992.

Anew McMaster
Actor 1894 – 1962

Anew McMaster first appeared on stage in 1911 in *The Scarlet Pimpernel* by the Fred Terry Company. Having toured Australia in 1921, upon his return to Ireland he formed a touring company to present productions by William Shakespeare and he managed, acted and directed most of these shows himself. In 1933 McMaster appeared as Hamlet in the Memorial Theatre, Stratford-upon-Avon and, having toured the Irish provinces for a number of years, he once again ventured to Australia where he wowed crowds in 1950. Married to a sister of actor Michael MacLiammóir, McMaster died in Dublin on 24 August 1962.

David Nelson
Victoria Cross recipient 1886 – 1918

David Nelson was born in Stradnode and served as a sergeant in the Royal Artillery during World War I. On 1 September 1914 at Nery, France, Nelson was awarded his honour for keeping his guns in action during intense enemy fire, despite the fact that he was severely wounded. Nelson remained at his guns until his ammunition ran out, even though he had been ordered to retreat to cover. He later achieved the rank of major, and was killed in action at Lillers, France in 1918.

Eoin O'Duffy
Commissioner of An Garda Síochána irish police force
1892 – 1944

Eoin O'Duffy was born in Castleblayney and apprenticed as an engineer in County Wexford before later working as an architect. Having joined the Irish Republican Army in 1917, he took part in the War of Independence, during which he was imprisoned on several occasions and was also appointed director of the army in 1921. A supporter of the Anglo-Irish Treaty, the following year O'Duffy became chief of staff of the IRA, replacing General Richard

Mulcahy (see page 394) and at the age of thirty he was appointed commissioner of the new police force, An Garda Síochána. However, as head of the new Fianna Fáil government, Éamon de Valera (see page 431) dismissed O'Duffy from office on the grounds that he was likely to display bias due to his past political affiliations. He was subsequently offered an alternative but similarly salaried position in the civil service but declined to accept.

That same year O'Duffy was appointed leader of the Army Comrades Association, whose name he immediately changed to the 'National Guard', no longer an organisation interested in the welfare of former soldiers, but a political entity which, due to its adoption of the colour blue, became known as 'The Blueshirts'. In 1933, the organisation was proclaimed illegal by government order following attempts to hold parades in commemoration of Arthur Griffith (see page 170), Michael Collins (see page 89) and Kevin O' Higgins (see page 263). Later devolving to form the Fine Gael political party, O'Duffy became its first president before retiring from office in 1934.

Due to his interest in the fascist movements in Europe in 1935, he would later found the National Corporate Party and he also organised an Irish Brigade of seven hundred men, to support General Franco in the Spanish Civil War. Returning to Ireland in 1937, O'Duffy's health was deteriorating and he retired from politics before eventually dying on 30 November 1944. He was afforded a state funeral and is buried in Glasnevin Cemetery, Dublin.

John O'Neill
Commander of the Fenian invasion of Canada 1834 – 1878

A native of Clontibret, John O'Neill emigrated to the United States at the age of fourteen in order to join his mother who had gone there in 1840.

During the American Civil War he served with the 5th Indiana Cavalry where his pursuit of John Hunt Morgan's Confederate Cavalry gained him a reputation as a formidable soldier and leader. Following the end of that war, O'Neill became colonel of the 'Fenian Army', which was made up of battle-hardened Irish troops who had taken part in the civil war. This 'army' was in the overall control of Cork man, Brigadier General Thomas William Sweeny and on 1 June 1866, O'Neill, with approximately eight hundred men, crossed the Canadian border and took control of Fort Erie and the small town of Ridgeway, where his troops succeeded in defeating several Canadian units, including the Queen's Own Regiment. Despite success in battle, O'Neill's Irish Republican Army, as it was called for the first time, needed the tacit support of the United States government because it was not an official army and was operating from US territory. Initially hopeful of receiving that support due to the fact that the British sided with the Confederate Army in the American Civil War, Fenian troops amassed on the border in support of O'Neill. However, not wishing to be seen to allow an act of war, the United States government moved to close the border and without the support needed, O'Neill was left with no alternative but to withdraw. He spent the remaining days of his life promoting Irish migration to Nebraska O'Neill Town, Nebraska, is named in his memory. He died on 7 January 1876.

Thomas Devin Reilly
Irish revolutionary and journalist 1823 – 1854

An espouser of the republican beliefs of Theobald Wolfe Tone during the potato famine, Thomas Devin Reilly was a member of the Irish Confederation where he advocated the breaking up of bridges and tearing up of railway lines in order to prevent food being brought from Ireland to England during those lean times. He was also involved in the Young Ireland Rebellion of 1848, following which he was forced to flee to the United States where he became active as a journalist and was a pioneer of American labour journalism. Reilly died suddenly at the age of thirty and is buried in Mount Oliver, Washington DC.

Thomas Taggart
Businessman, banker and senator 1856 – 1929

Thomas Taggart left Ireland with his parents in 1861, settling in Ohio where he initially found work at the lunch counter of a railroad depot. Later employed as manager of a restaurant and hotel in Garrett, Indiana, in 1877 Taggart moved to Indianapolis where he became active in local politics and was appointed mayor of the city from 1895 until 1901. In 1916 Governor Samuel M. Ralston appointed him to the United States Senate but beyond his career in politics, Taggart successfully managed such business ventures as the operation of the Grand and Deninson Hotels in Indianapolis and he also had interests in the mining and banking fields, serving as chairman of the board of directors at Fletcher-American National Bank. He died on 6 March 1929.

Lt. Colonel William Temple
Victoria Cross recipient 1833 – 1919

Born in Monaghan town, William Temple served as an assistant surgeon in the Royal Regiment of Artillery during the Māori Wars, New Zealand. On 20 November 1863 at Rangiriri, New Zealand together with another officer, Temple crossed in front of enemy lines to assist wounded soldiers. The men did so under continuous deadly fire and his courage was rewarded when he was later given the Victoria Cross. He died at Tunbridge Wells in Kent, England on 13 February 1919.

331

Offaly

Thomas Cass
1821-1862

Commander of the 9th Massachusetts Infantry at the capture of Richmond during the American Civil War, Thomas Cass's statue stands in Boston's Public Garden.

THOMAS CASS

John Kerans
1915-1985

HMS *Amethyst*, commanded by John Kerans during the Yangtze River incident in China in 1949.

Cornelius Heeney
1754-1848

Cornelus Heeney was the first Irish Catholic to hold public office in New York. He served on the State Assembly from 1818 until 1822 and he also founded the Brooklyn Benevolent Society for poor children. A memorial to him stands to the front of the New York State Supreme Court in New York City, USA.

Major General Edward Hand
1744-1802

Rock Ford, Lancaster, Pennsylvania was the home of medical doctor Edward Hand who was a Continental Army general in the American War of Independence.

Kate Shelley
1865-1912

The Des Moines River Bridge, Iowa, USA, over which Kate Shelley crawled in darkness and during a storm to warn an oncoming Chicago Express of the collapse of a second bridge over the river. In doing so she saved the lives of over two hundred people.

Thomas Armstrong
Banker and railway promotor
1797 – 1875

In 1817 Thomas Armstrong was sent by his wealthy father to Buenos Aires, Argentina, where he established a company called Armstrong and Co. Over the years, Armstrong became one of the most influential businessmen in Argentina. He was most supportive of the Irish community in that country, on one occasion offering lifetime accommodation, free of charge, to Father Anthony Fahy, a Catholic priest who had arrived in Argentina from Ireland. Armstrong, who was a co-founder of the Buenos Aires stock exchange, helped to establish the Provincial Bank, which later became the Central Bank of Argentina, and he also served as director and substantial investor in the major rail companies. He died in Buenos Aires on 9 June 1875 and a village and railway station in Santa Fe are named in his memory

William Bulfin
Writer 1864 – 1910

Having emigrated to Argentina in 1884, William Bulfin spent a number of years working as a gaucho on the Pampas before moving on to Buenos Aires, where he became editor and proprietor of the *Southern Cross* newspaper. Bulfin, who was a vigorous defender of the rights of Irish immigrants in Argentina, published writings and sketches of his travels around Ireland and these works also appeared in the the *United Irishmen* and the *New York Daily News*. Adapted to book form as *Rambles in Eirinn* in 1907, Bulfin also published *Tales of the Pampas* and he went on to become a knight of St Gregory for his work

on behalf of the Irish community in Argentina. He had strong republican links and returned to Ireland in 1909 before travelling to the United States with Michael Joseph O'Rahilly (see page 232) in order to seek funds for the Sinn Féin newspaper. His son, Eamon Bulfin, was present at the GPO during the Easter Rising of 1916.

John Caffrey
Victoria Cross recipient
1891 – 1953

John Caffrey was born in Birr and at twenty-four years of age, served as a private in the 2nd Battalion of the York and Lancaster Regiment during World War I. At La Brique, France in November 1915, with one of his comrades badly wounded and lying about 350 yards from enemy lines, Caffrey and a corporal in his regiment attempted to retrieve the injured man whilst under heavy fire. Though initially driven back by the enemy onslaught, a second attempt proved successful. However, whilst bandaging the man's wounds, the accompanying corporal was wounded with a shot to the head. Caffrey thus turned his attention to the corporal and helped him back to safety before returning to retrieve his other wounded comrade. For these acts he was awarded the Victoria Cross, before later being appointed a lance corporal. He died in February 1953.

Colonel Thomas Cass
Merchant and Soldier 1821 – 1862

Thomas Cass was born in Farmsley and was brought to United States by his parents as an infant. He was educated in Boston, Massachusetts, before entering the world of business and becoming the owner of several ships trading out of Boston Harbour. Having served as a captain of the Boston-Irish Militia, at the outbreak of the American Civil War Governor John A. Andrew appointed Cass to lead a newly formed Irish regiment from Boston, namely the 9th Massachusetts Volunteer Infantry.

In the spring of 1862, the new regiment, forming part of the Army of the Potomac, were successful in capturing Richmond, Virginia but during the battle for Malvern Hill, Cass was shot in the mouth and also received an exit wound through his ear. He returned to Boston to recuperate but succumbed to his wounds on 12 July 1862. A statue to his memory stands in the public garden in Boston.

Henry D'Esterre Darby
British admiral 1750 – 1823

Born in Leap Castle, Henry D'Esterre Darby joined the Royal Navy in his early teens and was promoted to captain in 1783. Commanding the HMS *Bellerophon* at the Battle of the Nile in 1798, he served under Horatio Nelson before being appointed vice admiral in 1811. Darby was knighted in 1820 and died on 30 March 1823. He is buried in Aghancon Graveyard, near Leap.

Patrick Bernard Delany
Electrician and inventor 1845 – 1924

Arriving in the United States in his early teens, Patrick Bernard Delany became a telegraph operator in Hartford, Connecticut. His inventions include more than 150 patents, ranging from anti-induction cables to a system whereby six messages could be sent simultaneously over one telegraph wire. Delany also invented the Vox Humana talking machine, as well as a device for submarine detection. Amongst his many awards was the John Scott medal of the Franklin Institute, and he served as president of the American Institute of Electrical Engineers from 1893 until 1895.

John Doyle
Soldier and survivor of the Charge of the Light Brigade 1828 – 1892

Having enlisted in the British Cavalry in Newbridge, County Kildare in 1850, Birr born John Doyle served as a cavalry soldier in the Charge of the Light Brigade at Balaclava, Crimea. Slightly wounded during that conflict, Doyle went on to serve in four major battles during the Crimean War at Alma, Balaclava, Inkerman, and Sebastopol, and following his retirement from the service, he published a memoir entitled *A Descriptive Account of the Famous Charge of the Light Brigade at Balaclava* (1877). He died in Liverpool, England in August 1892.

Frederic Charles Dreyer
British Admiral 1878 – 1956

Frederic Charles Dreyer was born near Birr and was educated at the Royal School, Armagh, following which he joined the Royal Navy. In 1902 he served as gunnery officer on the cruiser HMS *Scylla*, and the following year he undertook the same role aboard the newly commissioned battleship, HMS *Exmouth*. Following service on a number of other battleships, Dreyer was given command of the scout cruiser, HMS *Amphion* in 1913 and three years later, he was appointed flag captain on the HMS *Iron Duke*, seeing action at the Battle of Jutland. An expert in naval gunnery, he developed a fire control system for British warships and in late 1923 he was promoted to rear admiral before becoming vice admiral and full admiral in 1929 and 1933 respectively. Knighted in 1936, Dreyer died on 12 December 1956.

Baron Winston Joseph Dugan
British army officer 1876 – 1951

Enlisting in the British Army in 1896, Winston Joseph Dugan was commissioned to the Lincolnshire Regiment in 1900 and saw active service in South Africa. Born in Parsonstown, Dugan served with gallantry on the western front during World War I and was later awarded the Distinguished Service Order. He was seriously wounded whilst in command of the 184th Infantry Brigade in September 1916, before later being appointed aide-de-camp to King George V. He was awarded the CB (Companion of the Order of the Bath) in 1929 before being promoted to major general the following year. In 1934 Dugan was appointed governor of South Australia and proved a popular leader. He was knighted in 1935 and elevated to GCMG (Grand Cross of St Michael and St George) in 1944, before being made a baron in 1949. A deeply religious Anglican, he died on 17 August 1951 at Marlybone in London.

Edward Hand
Physician and Soldier 1744 – 1802

A surgeon in the 18th Royal Irish Regiment of Foot of the British Army, Trinity College graduate Edward Hand sailed to the United States, arriving in Philadelphia on 11 July 1767, where he served until he resigned his commission in 1774. He later moved to Lancaster, Pennsylvania and set up a medical practice. Upon the outbreak of the revolutionary War of Independence, Hand joined the Continental Army as a lieutenant colonel, later promoted to brigadier general, serving as the commander of Fort Pitt. He subsequently served as a brigade commander in Major General Lafayette's division and during the siege of Yorktown, was appointed adjutant general. In view of Hand's long and distinguished service to the American cause, he was promoted to major general in September 1783, but he resigned from the army two months later and saw out the rest of his life in the medical practice at the family estate in Lancaster. He later died of cholera and is buried in St James's Cemetery in Lancaster, Pennsylvania.

Cornelius Heeney
Merchant and philanthropist 1754 – 1848

In 1784, Cornelius Heeney emigrated to the United States where he gained employment in a New York fur-dealing store. Some years later his employer retired and left the business to Heeney and John Jacob Astor. Together, the two men prospered for a number of years before separating. Heeney continued in the same line of business and amassed a considerable fortune, which he used to promote religious and charitable works. One of the first Catholics to hold public office in New York, he served five terms in the State Assembly from 1818 until 1822. A bachelor, Heeney left his estate for the benefit of the poor and orphaned and to this day, that estate is administered by the Brooklyn Benevolent Society on behalf of the poor Catholic children and widows of Brooklyn, to whom yearly presents of shoes, clothing and fuel are given. A memorial to Heeney, in black granite and bronze, is located at the front of the New York State Supreme Court building at Montague and Court Streets.

Sir Herbert Samuel Holt
Civil engineer, banker and businessman
1856 – 1941

At the age of nineteen, Herbert Samuel Holt emigrated to Canada where he worked as an engineer and contractor on railway construction projects. He also became a pioneer developer of energy businesses in the province of Quebec, where he established the Montreal Gas Company. That company later merged with the Royal Electric Company to become the Montreal Light, Heat and Power Company and in 1915, it was nationalised, making Holt a very wealthy man in the process. He later served as president of the Royal Bank of Canada from 1908 until 1934 and was chairman of that bank from 1934 until his death, having been knighted by King George V in 1915. Holt's contribution to the Canadian economy was immense and was recognised as such when he was elected to the Canadian Business Hall of Fame. He died on 29 September 1941 and is buried in Mount Royal Cemetery, Montreal.

Charles Jervas
Portrait painter 1675 – 1739

Charles Jervas was born in Shinrone and, having studied painting under Sir Godfrey Kneller in London, he visited Rome where he learned to draw by copying antiques. Later returning to London, Jervas established a studio at Bridgewater House in Cleveland Court and he soon distinguished himself as a proficient painter of portraits, with Alexander Pope, Joseph Addison, and Jonathan Swift (see page 196) some of the better known personalities to sit for him. Jervas was appointed principle painter under George I in 1723 and he retained that post under George II. He died in London on 2 November 1739.

Dr Jasper Robert Joly
Book collector 1819 – 1892

Jasper Robert Joly was born in Clonbullogue. An avid collector of books, sheet music, maps, prints and manuscripts, Joly initially studied law and was called to the bar but never practiced. In 1863 he presented 23,000 printed volumes and unbound papers to the Royal Dublin Society with the stipulation that they be held in trust for a national library. They later formed the basis of the National Library of Ireland.

John Joly
Scientist 1857 – 1933

John Joly was born in Holywood House, Bracknagh and graduated from Trinity College, Dublin with an engineering degree in 1882. Thereafter he worked in that institution's engineering department before becoming a professor of geology, a post he held from 1897 until 1933. Previous to this, Joly had patented his method for colour photography and he went on to write in excess of 270 scientific papers, as well as a number of books. He is possibly most famous for his development of radiotherapy in the treatment of cancer and he also developed a method to estimate the age of a geological period, a technique based on the radioactive elements present in minerals. He died in Dublin on 8 December 1933.

Baron John Keane
General in the british army 1781 – 1844

John Keane was born in Belmont and joined the British army as an eleven-year-old ensign in 1792. Rising through the ranks to command a brigade in the Peninsular War, he was promoted to major general and commanded the 3rd Brigade at the Battle of New Orleans where he was wounded twice. Keane later served as commander-in-chief in the West Indies and was government administrator of Jamaica before later moving on to India, where he was commander of the combined British and Indian armies during the First Afghan War. Keane was victorious at the Battle of Ghazni in July 1839 and following this he was elevated to the peerage as Baron Keane. He died in Hampshire, England on 24 August 1844.

John Kerans
Hero of the Yangtse River incident of 1949 1915 – 1985

Born in Birr, John Kerans was the central character in the book *The Last Action Hero of the British Empire* by Nigel Farndale. An officer in the British navy, he was known for his fierce temper and this, along with his fondness for alcohol, resulted in him being posted to a mundane job in Nanking, China. In April 1949, a Royal Navy frigate the HMS *Amethyst* was fired upon by the Chinese in the Yangtse River and with no captain on board, Kerans was the only officer available as a replacement. The authorities were left with no option but to place him in command of the ship. The attack provoked outrage in Britain where the Communist red flag was burned while members of the British Communist Party were attacked. Meanwhile on the Yangtse River, Kerans spectacularly rose to the occasion and following one hundred days in captivity on the river, he decided to make a dramatic dash for the sea.

With 150 miles of river ahead of him and with only half a crew who were manning a shell-damaged ship, he raised anchor at night and without lights, a pilot or adequate charts, set sail past the treacherous range of enemy guns. In an extraordinary display of seamanship, the Amethyst eventually reached the open seas and Kerans was hailed a hero on par with Admiral Francis Drake and Sir Walter Raleigh. Humorously, it is reputed that Keran's cousin sent him a message which read, 'I should have realised that the supplies of gin would be getting low, and it would take all the devils of hell to stand between you and fresh supplies.'

Alfie Lambe
Member of the Legion of Mary 1932 – 1959

Having spent a period of his youth as a novitiate of the Irish Christian Brothers, Tullamore born Alfie Lambe was forced to leave that religious order due to poor health. He did, however, find his vocation in the Legion of Mary, and later left for Colombia where he assisted in the promotion of the legion in that country, as well as in Argentina, Ecuador, Uruguay, and Brazil. He had a passionate devotion to the Blessed Virgin and during his years in South America he set up a number of branches of the Legion of Mary before dying in Buenos Aires on 21 January 1959. Lambe is buried in the vault of the Irish Christian Brothers, in the Recoleta Cemetery in Buenos Aires.

Birr Castle County Offaly.

Hugh Mahon
Journalist and politician 1857 – 1931

Born near Tullamore, in 1867 Hugh Mahon emigrated with his family to United States, where he found employment in the printing trade. Returning to Ireland in the early 1880s, Mahon worked as a reporter for a newspaper in New Ross, County Wexford. A member of the Irish National Land League, he was imprisoned in Kilmainham Jail, Dublin and following his release he went to London and later, in 1882, to Australia, where he managed fundraising tours as a paid agent on behalf of the league. In 1895 Mahon became editor of a paper in Coolgardie, Western Australia and he also won a political seat as a labour candidate for Coolgardie in 1901. He held a number of government ministerial posts and used his authoritative position to voice his opinions, as was the case following the death of Cork's Lord Mayor Terence McSwiney (see page 101), who had gone on hunger strike. Mahon savagely attacked the policies of the British Empire, referring to its 'bloody and accursed despotism' and due to this and other outbursts, he was expelled from the house in a procedure unique in the history of the Commonwealth parliament. However, such was his popularity that he successfully contested the following by-election, regaining his seat. He later died on 28 August 1931 at Ringwood, Victoria in Australia.

Dick (Pat) McRedmond
Heavyweight boxing champion 1906 - ?

Dick McRedmond was born at the Curragh, Cadamstown and was educated at the Albert Agricultural College in Glasnevin, Dublin. Having emigrated to Australia in 1925, he worked in a variety of jobs ranging from sheep shearing to foundry work. He started boxing after joining the St Joseph's club in Sydney. A magnificently built, all-round athlete, whilst still a teenager McRedmond stood six-feet three-inches tall and weighed in excess of 200lbs, a physical advantage that enabled him to enter the professional ranks almost immediately, where he changed his name to Pat McRedmond. With his great punching power, McRedmond made quick progress through the heavyweight division in Australia, culminating in a bout with Australian heavyweight title-holder Dom McLeoid, who halted his rise by stopping the Irishman in the seventh round of the championship fight. McRedmond bounced back to have a number of very successful fights before once again receiving a title shot, this time proving victorious against Joe Brogan. He later faced Primo Carnera in a losing attempt to capture the world heavyweight title, before later returning to Ireland where he settled in County Limerick. He died there whilst still a young man.

John Meredith
Medical doctor and brigadier general in the Australian Army 1864 – 1942

Doctor and military man John Meredith was born at Derrylough and studied medicine in Dublin, qualifying as a licentiate of the Royal College of Surgeons and Physicians, Edinburgh in 1888. Meredith later emigrated to Australia where he purchased a practice at Raymond Terrace, New South Wales but in 1899, he volunteered to serve with the Australian forces in South Africa. He later served in England and Ireland before returning to Australia in 1910 where two years later, he was promoted to lieutenant colonel of the 6th Light Horse Regiment. Meredith served in this position for the 1st Light Horse Regiment in the first Australian Imperial Force at Gallipoli during World War I and was also in command of the 1st Light Horse Brigade at the Battle of Romani in August 1916. Awarded the Distinguished Service Order for his strong performance, he lead his brigade once again at the second Battle of Gaza and went on to command the second cavalry brigade from 1921 until 1923 when he retired with the rank of honourary brigadier general. He died at Maitland, New South Wales on 1 January 1942.

James Lynam Molloy
Poet, author and song composer
1837 – 1909
Clara native James Lynam Molloy attended St Edmund's College, Hertfordshire in England and the Catholic University, Dublin, graduating in 1858. Called to the bar in 1863, Molloy elected not to pursue a legal career and instead concentrated his efforts on writing and publishing songs such as 'The Kerry Dance', 'Old Cottage Clock' and 'Bantry Bay', which became popular in the concert halls of his day. Having also written a book, *Our Autumn Holiday on the French Rivers* (1874), his most successful song was 'Love's Old Sweet Song', which he composed in 1894. Molloy died on 4 February 1909.

Maura Murphy
Writer 1928 – 2005
Enduring the hardships of rural Ireland in the late 1930s and 40s, Maura Murphy married in 1953, and had five children before emigrating to Birmingham, England where the family eventually grew to nine children. In 1989 Murphy, who was born near Edenderry, returned to Ireland in what was supposed to be full retirement but at the age of seventy, discovered she had lung cancer and moved back to England while her husband, who suffered with alcoholism, remained in County Offaly. It was then that she decided to write about the hardships she had endured throughout her life and her memoirs were subsequently published as a book entitled *Wake Me at Doyle's,* which became a bestseller around the world. Happily, Murphy was reconciled with her husband shortly before her death on 5 October 2005.

John Murray
Victoria Cross recipient 1837 – 1911
John Murray was born in Birr and served as a sergeant in the 68th Regiment of the British Army during the Māori War in New Zealand. At Tauranga on 21 June 1864, Murray ran to a rifle pit (trench) containing eight to ten of the enemy and single-handedly wounded or killed all of them by shot and bayonet, a deed for which he was awarded the Victoria Cross. He died in Derrinlogh in 1911.

Joseph Prosser
Victoria Cross recipient
1828 – 1867
John Prosser was born in Monegal. A private in the 2nd Battalion, First Regiment of the British Army during the Crimean War, he was awarded the Victoria Cross in respect of two deeds: one was the prevention of a fellow soldier attempting to desert to the enemy who he pursued and apprehended, and the other occurred on 11 August 1855. Whilst under heavy fire, Prosser left his trench position to rescue a soldier of the 95th Regiment who was unable to move, and brought him back to the safety of his own lines. He died in 1969 and is buried in Liverpool, England.

Kate Shelley
Railway heroine and schoolteacher
1865 – 1912

As a child, Kate Shelley emigrated to the United States with her family, where they settled in Moingona, Iowa. It was during a fierce storm in that district that Shelley performed an extraordinary deed of bravery. Realising that one of two bridges over the Des Moines River had collapsed in the storm, and with only a lantern to guide her in the darkness, Shelley struggled over the one remaining bridge, which was fifty feet above the raging river torrents below. With the transrails of the bridge spaced at one yard apart, she had to crawl on hands and knees to the next station down the line, where she successfully warned and stopped the midnight express train bound for Chicago, Illinois. Shelley saved the lives of around two hundred people that night and for her actions she was granted a scholarship to Simpson College, Indianola, where she eventually graduated as a teacher. She died on 21 January 1912 and a train, the Kate Shelley Express, was named in her memory. In addition, a bridge over the Des Moines River is named the Kate Shelley High Bridge.

George Johnstone Stoney
Irish physicist 1826 – 1911

Scientist George Johnstone Stoney was born in Oakley Park and was educated at Trinity College, Dublin. A man with terrific scientific vision, his most important scientific work was the conception and calculation of the magnitude of the atom, or particle of electricity, for which he coined the term, 'electron'. In addition, Stoney made significant contributions to cosmic physics, and to the theory of gases. He died on 5 July 1911 and his ashes were buried in Dundrum, County Dublin.

Mary Ward
Microscopist, artist, entomologist and author
1827 – 1869

A member of an aristocratic family, Mary Ward was educated at home, where she took an interest in plants and animals from an early age. A keen microscope user, she created beautiful drawings of the plants and animals that she studied but as women were not accepted into the scientific societies at the time, Ward had great difficulty publishing her book, *Sketches with a Microscope*. Finally in 1858, it was released under the name *The World of Wonders as Revealed by the Microscope,* and such was the book's success, it went through eight re-prints over the following twenty-two years. In 1859 Ward published *Telescope Teachings*, in addition to a number of journal articles of her findings, and she also had her name added to the Royal Astronomical Society's mailing list, one of only three women to have enjoyed such a privilege, the others being Queen Victoria and Mary Sommerville of the University of Oxford.

Ward received international recognition when two of her books were selected for display at the international exhibition held at the Crystal Palace, London in 1862 and this highlighted her position as one of the nineteenth century's best-known writers on the use of the microscope. She died tragically on 31 August 1869, when she fell from a steam carriage (invented by her cousin William Parsons), becoming one of the world's first victims of an automobile accident.

William Telford Webb
Farmer and politician 1842 – 1911

William Telford Webb was born in Tullamore and emigrated with his family to Melbourne, Australia in 1859. In 1863 he went to the Dunstan gold fields in New Zealand where he was moderately successful, but he later returned to Australia, purchasing a farm near Rochester. Elected a farming representative to the Rochester council, Webb served for a number of years and became president for two years from 1877. In 1883 he represented Rodney in the Legislative Assembly, where he became a powerful advocate of farming and irrigation interests and he later became minister for agriculture and vice president of the Board of Lands and Works. Webb later retired from farming and politics, and established businesses in grain-purchasing, milling and butchery. He also founded the Yeomanry Stores in Mackie Street, Victoria. He had further involvement as a shareholder in fresh foods and a frozen storage company, all of which made him a wealthy man, and he died on 17 January 1911.

Roscommon

John B. Bannon
1829-1913

Saint John's Church, St Louis, Missouri was co-founded by Father John Bannon, a Confederate chaplain. General Sterling Price of the Confederate Army referred to him during the American Civil War as 'the greatest soldier I ever saw'.

George Arthur French
1841-1921

The Royal Canadian Mounted Police were founded by George Arthur French on 1 December, 1873.

Doctor Douglas Hyde
1860-1949

Áras an Uachtaráin, the residence of the President of Ireland, was occupied by Douglas Hyde, the first person to be appointed to that role. As a protestant man, he was chosen, by all parties, to represent the non-sectarian stand of the newly established Irish Free State.

Edward Joseph Flanagan
1886-1948

'He ain't heavy, father, he's m'brother' is the caption at the entrance to Boys Town in Omaha, Nebraska. It was founded by Father Flanagan in 1917.

John Gately Downey
1827-1894

The home of *Apollo*, the city of Downey was founded by John Gately Downey, the first Irish born governor of California, USA.

John B. Bannon

Confederate chaplain during the
American Civil War 1829 – 1913

Born in the village of Roosky on the banks of the River Shannon, John B. Bannon was ordained a priest at St Patrick's College, Maynooth in County Kildare. In May 1853 he emigrated to the missions in the United States, where he settled in St Louis, Missouri, and in November 1860 he joined Captain Kelly's Washington Blues as a chaplain. The following year Bannon became a member of the 'Patriot Army of Missouri' under the command of General Sterling Price, and during the Civil War he routinely accompanied the troops into battle in what was a typically uncommon action of the chaplains of the time. It was not unusual to see Bannon in the thick of the fighting, kneeling beside men, consoling them and administering the last rites, regardless of their religious leanings. General Price later described him as 'the greatest soldier I ever saw' and in a letter sent home to Ireland, Bannon displayed this great spirit in proclaiming, 'I am doing God's work and He has no use for cowards.' In 1863 he was chosen by President Jefferson Davis to travel to the Vatican City in an effort to seek papal support for the Confederate states and their cause. Also at the request of Davis, he returned to Ireland to beseech Irishmen going to United States not to support the Union cause. Bannon never returned to the United States, instead remaining in Ireland, where he joined the Society of Jesus religious order. Although he is little known stateside, his legacy lives on in St John's Church of which he was a founder, and which continues to serve the people in downtown St Louis. He died on 14 July 1913.

Jim 'The Roscommon Giant' Coffey

European heavyweight
champion 1891 – 1959

Jim Coffey was born in Tully and emigrated to the United States in 1910, settling first in Boston, Massachusetts and later in New York. One day, as he passed a group of policemen, Coffey heard disparaging remarks being made about his Irish parentage; a fight ensued and he subsequently overcame the offenders, details of which reached the New York Polo Club, where he was appointed a sparring partner, earning fifteen dollars per week. Standing six feet three inches tall and weighing in at 210lbs, Coffey had an eighty-two inch reach and a knockout punch in either hand, all of which earned him the title of 'The Roscommon Giant'.

He had his first professional fight on 11 August 1911, a winning effort against Young Bernard, who he knocked out in the second round, and in a professional career that spanned ten years, Coffey had in excess of eighty fights – losing only six. Having defeated Otto Flint in Hamburg, Germany on 12 July 1919, Coffey became the European Heavyweight Champion and also fought such notables as 'Battling Levinsky' and the great Frenchman Georges Carpentier, who he defeated in his defence of his title. In 1922 he married schoolteacher Kate Kenny at Gorthaganny, County Roscommon and it was she who persuaded him to retire from boxing on a permanent basis. One of a long line of accomplished Irish boxers, the great Coffey died on 20 December 1959.

Margaret Cousins
Champion of women's rights
1878 – 1954

In 1908, Margaret Cousins established the Irish Women's Franchise League, the aim of which was to persuade the government to extend the right to vote to women. Around this time she went to England to support the women's suffrage movement but was jailed for one month for taking part in a riot outside the prime minister's home in Downing Street. She subsequently returned to Ireland, where once again she was jailed for her activities in fighting for women's rights before. Released after going on hunger strike, in 1913 Cousins emigrated to India where she set up the Indian Women's Association before being appointed that country's first woman magistrate in 1922. However, controversy was never far away and she once again served jail time after protesting against the lack of freedom of speech in India. A supporter of Mahatma Gandhi, Cousins formed the Children's Aid Society and was elected president of the All India Women's Conference in 1938. She died in Madras, India on 11 March 1954.

Laurence Dermott
Freemason 1720 – 1791

Having travelled to London in the late 1740s, Laurence Dermott was appointed the first grand secretary, and afterwards, deputy grand master of the 'Antient Masons'. He also published *The Book of Constitutions of this Grand Lodge*, under the title of *Ahiman Rezon* (1756). This was a remarkable book, which set out the laws of masonry and explained its origins. Dermott died in London in 1791.

John Gately Downey
Governor of California
1827 – 1894

At the age of fourteen, John Gately Downey emigrated to the United States with his family. Settling first in Maryland, where he apprenticed as an apothecary (a predecessor to the modern pharmacist). In 1846 Downey moved to Cincinnati, Ohio, becoming a partner in a drug store. Three years later he travelled to California where he found similar work in San Francisco and uprooting once again, this time to Los Angeles, Downey established successful businesses in cattle ranching, real estate and banking. As a democrat he made a move into politics, being elected to the California State Assembly in 1856. Following that appointment he was elected as lieutenant governor, and then governor, to the state of California and he served in that role during the first half of the American Civil War. The first ever foreign-born governor of California, at thirty-two years of age, Downey was also the youngest and although the majority of his fellow Democrats were secessionists, his leadership kept California in the Union ranks. The principle organiser of the Los Angeles City Water Company, he also donated a tract of land for the establishment of the University of Southern California and was the funder of the City of Downey, which is now best known as the birthplace of the *Apollo* space programme. Downey died at his home in Los Angeles on 1 March 1894 and is buried at Holy Cross Cemetery, Colma.

McDermotts Castle. Lough Key, Roscommon.

Fr Edward Joseph Flanagan
Samaritan and founder of Boys Town 1886 – 1948

Edward Joseph Flanagan was born in Leabeg and left Ireland for the United States in the summer of 1904. Two years later, he entered St Joseph's Seminary in New York and as part of his parochial studies, he attended the Gregorian University in Rome, as well as the University of Innsbruck, Austria where he was ordained in 1912. Flanagan commenced his priestly duties in Omaha, Nebraska and in 1916 opened a working man's hostel, which served the homeless and jobless men of that city. The following year he opened the first of Father Flanagan's boys' homes, which became known as 'Boys Town', adopting the slogan 'He ain't heavy, Father, he's m'brother' as it's motto . He ran that institution with a student government and an elected mayor. Boys Town was very well regarded, so much so that MGM produced the movie *Boys Town* in 1938. In 1947 at the invitation of the war department, Flanagan toured Japan and Korea to investigate the needs for aid to war orphans and there he met with General Douglas MacArthur. Upon his return from Asia, he presented his findings to President Harry S. Truman at the White House but soon after suffered a fatal heart attack. His body is entombed at Boys Town and in 1986, one hundred years after Flanagan's birth, the US Postal Service issued a four-cent stamp in commemoration of his life.

Roderick Flanagan
Historian and anthropologist 1828 – 1862

Roderick Flanagan emigrated as a boy to Australia, where he was educated at the Ryder School, Sydney before commencing work at the *Daily News* in Melbourne in 1849. Flanagan's contribution to Australian history was considerable and his understanding of its indigenous people was extensive. He composed poems and prose about his adopted land and also wrote a major history of New South Wales, which is considered the main reference work on the early European presence in Australia. Upon its publication, Flanagan received considerable praise from the *Sydney Morning Herald* but his life was soon cut short when he died from tuberculosis on 13 March 1862. His brother Edward saw that Flanagan's essays, *The Aborigines of Australia* were published, and it was this small book that demonstrated his great understanding of the plight of the native Australian people.

George Arthur French
Founder of the Royal Canadian Mounted Police 1841 – 1921

Born near Castlerea, George Arthur French was educated at the Sandhurst and Woolwich military academies in England before being commissioned to the Royal Artillery in 1860. In 1871, at the request of the Canadian government, French was sent to Canada as a military inspector and it was there that Canadian prime minister, John McDonald, requested him to establish a mounted police force in order to offset the problem of American whiskey peddlers, and also to protect the building of a railway that traversed Canada from east to west. French was subsequently appointed the first commissioner of the North West Mounted Police, now known as the Royal Canadian Mounted Police, on 1 December 1873 and under his control, the new force established a reputation for honesty, justice and fairness. He resigned in 1876, returning to duty with the British army, where he attained the rank of major general. His military impact was significant and with the organisational skills he developed in Canada, he helped establish police forces in India and Australia. He was knighted in 1902 and died in London in 1921.

Percy French
Songwriter and entertainer 1854 – 1920

Elphin born Percy French penned his first successful song, 'Abdulla Bulbul Ameer', as a student of Trinity College, Dublin, in 1877. He later graduated from that institution as a civil engineer before working in Cavan as an inspector of drains. Following the death of his wife in 1891, French toured Ireland performing a one-man show where he sang many of the songs he had composed. Though born William he adopted the name Percy as a stage name before later moving to London, where he performed on stage until his death in 1920. Amongst his best-known songs are, 'Are Ye Right There, Michael', 'Come Back Paddy Reilly', 'Phil the Fluter's Ball', 'Slattery's Mounted Fut' and 'The Mountains of Mourne'.

Colonel Henry George Gore-Browne
Victoria Cross recipient 1830 – 1912

Henry George Gore-Browne was born in Newtown and served as a captain in the 32nd Regiment of Foot of the British Army during the Indian Mutiny. During the siege of Residency at Lucknow, Browne led a number of his force to attack two heavily-fortified guns, which were supposedly impenetrably positioned. He successfully entered the fortification and destroyed the guns whilst killing up to one hundred of the enemy in the process. For this deed he was awarded the Victoria Cross.

William Griffiths
Victoria Cross recipient 1841 – 1879

William Griffiths served as a private in the 2nd Battalion, 24th Regiment of Foot during the Andaman Islands Expedition. Whilst manning a small boat with five comrades at Little Andaman in the Bay of Bengal on 7 May 1867, Griffiths negotiated treacherous surf in order to rescue fellow soldiers who had been marooned on the island. He was later killed in action in the Battle of Isandhlwana, Zululand.

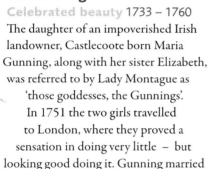

Maria Gunning
Celebrated beauty 1733 – 1760

The daughter of an impoverished Irish landowner, Castlecoote born Maria Gunning, along with her sister Elizabeth, was referred to by Lady Montague as 'those goddesses, the Gunnings'. In 1751 the two girls travelled to London, where they proved a sensation in doing very little – but looking good doing it. Gunning married the Earl of Coventry and had five children before dying at the age of twenty-seven when she was poisoned by the lead and arsenic in her cosmetics. Her sister had three children by her first husband, the Duke of Hamilton, and five by her second, the Duke of Argyll. She died in London on 20 May 1790.

Douglas Hyde
First president of Ireland 1860 – 1949

Douglas Hyde was born at Longford House, Castlerea and spent his formative years in County Sligo where his father was a Church of Ireland rector. Later enrolling at Trinity College, Dublin, he became a fluent speaker of French, Latin, German, Greek and Hebrew, as well as retaining a passion for his native tongue. Hyde was a co-founder of Connradh na Gaedhilge (Gaelic League) and in 1905 he travelled to the United States in order to collect funds for that organisation. Upon his return, he was presented with the freedom of Dublin and Cork cities and he also made strides in the literary sphere, authoring a number of works including *A Literary History of Ireland* (1899) and *Love Songs of Connacht* (1894). Hyde, who was greatly admired by Taoiseach Éamon de Valera (see page 431) and opposition leader W. T. Cosgrave, was chosen as the first president of Ireland in a move that emphasised the non-sectarian standing of the newly established free state. Hyde was inaugurated in June 1938 and he finally retired from office on 25 June 1945. He died on 12 July 1949 and was accorded a full state funeral, before being laid to rest in his native County Roscommon. It is notable that Hyde is the only leader of independent Ireland to appear on the currency of the state, his portrait featuring on the fifty-pound note of the now-retired currency.

John Leydon
Public servant 1895 – 1979

Having joined the British civil service in 1915, Arigna born John Leydon transferred to the new Irish established civil service following the passing of the Anglo-Irish Treaty, rising rapidly through its ranks. In 1932 Seán Lemass (see page 175) appointed Leydon secretary of the Department of Industry and Commerce and in that capacity he proved one of the driving forces in the establishment of companies such as Aer Lingus, Bord na Móna, Irish Shipping and later the Insurance Corporation of Ireland. Described by Lemass as one of the ablest men he had ever met, Leydon retired from the service in 1955, following which he was appointed chairman of the National Bank. He was also made a Knight Commander of St Gregory. He died on 2 August 1979.

Owen Edward Pennefather Lloyd
Victoria Cross recipient 1854 – 1941

Owen Edward Pennefather Lloyd served as a surgeon major in the Army Medical Service of the British Army in Burma. Whilst under heavy fire at Fort Sima, on 6 January 1893, Lloyd went to the assistance of his commanding officer who was lying wounded on open ground. With the enemy located no more than forty metres away, the surgeon tended to the officer's wounds and with the aid of another soldier, carried the officer back to the fort. Wounded in the process, Lloyd was later to become a major general and he died in Sussex, England in 1941.

Major General Sir Luke O'Connor
First recipient of the Victoria Cross
1831 – 1915

Though the Victoria Cross did not exist at the time of his deed, so memorable were the actions of Elphin born Luke O'Connor, he was awarded that great honour upon its introduction, thereby becoming the first recipient of the Victoria Cross. Serving as a twenty-three-year-old sergeant in the 23rd Regiment of the British Army during the Crimean War, on 20 September 1854, whilst carrying the company colours at the Battle of Alma, O'Connor was shot. Despite his wounding he continued to carry out his duties until end of the action, refusing to retreat on account of his injuries. Once again wounded at the assault of Redan on 8 September 1855, O'Connor later achieved the rank of major general and died in London, England in 1915.

Fr Michael O'Flanagan
The rebel priest 1876 – 1942

Michael O'Flanagan was born near Castlerea and was educated at Summerhill College, County Sligo and St Patrick's College, Maynooth before being ordained for the Diocese of Elphin in 1900. In 1914 he was appointed to the north Sligo Parish of Ahamlish and there he became involved in a remarkable incident when he took on the establishment by leading the local people in cutting turf on a bog that had been reserved for British army and Royal Irish Constabulary members only. O'Flanagan, who was vice president of Sinn Féin, was a supporter and publicist for the Irish Republican Army, a role for which he was suspended from his clerical duties in 1927. One of the few Catholic priests who defended the Spanish Republic during that country's civil war, O'Flanagan was conferred with the freedom of Sligo in June 1918. He also remained a diligent scholar throughout his life and wrote a series of county histories for the Department of Education before dying in Dublin on 7 August 1942.

James O'Moran
General in the French Army 1739 – 1794

The son of a shoemaker, Elphin born James O'Moran travelled to France at an early age and enlisted as a private in Dillon's Regiment of the Irish Brigade, rising through the ranks to become a major general in 1784. He is famous for his performance at the defence of Dunkirk, France in 1793 when, along with three thousand French troops, he resisted an assault by an English force that outnumbered them by more than ten to one. O'Moran later fell foul of some of the agitators in the French Revolution and his high position as a major general proved ineffective in protecting him as he was seized and put to death on the guillotine, due to the fact he was an aristocrat, in 1794.

Maureen O'Sullivan
Actress 1911 – 1998

Maureen O'Sullivan was born in Boyle and was educated in Dublin and also at the Convent of the Sacred Heart at Roehampton in London. Having attended finishing school in France, she returned to Dublin to begin working with the poor. It was film director Frank Borzage who first suggested she take a screen test, following which she had a small role in a film starring Irish tenor, John McCormack (see page 404). O'Sullivan, who subsequently moved to Hollywood, California where she was contracted to MGM, is perhaps best known for her part as Jane in the *Tarzan* films, where she acted opposite Johnny Weissmuller, and she also appeared in *The Thin Man* and *Pride and Prejudice*. Married to John Farrow, who died in 1963, the couple had seven children, one of whom was actress Mia Farrow. O'Sullivan was a widow for twenty years before marrying James Cushing and she died in Scottsdale Arizona, at the age of eighty-seven.

Patrick Roddy
Victoria Cross recipient 1827 – 1895

Born in Elphin, Patrick Roddy was an ensign in the Indian Army during the Indian Mutiny. Whilst returning from Kuthirga on 27 September 1858, Roddy became aware of a sniper who was covering his cavalry unit. He boldly charged forward and although his horse was shot from under him, he seized and killed the sniper with his sword. He later achieved the rank of colonel and died in Jersey in 1895.

Sir William Robert Wills Wilde
Antiquarian and surgeon
1815 – 1876

William Wilde was born at Kilkeevin and was educated at the Elphin Diocesan College and at the Royal College of Surgeons, Dublin. An internationally renowned eye and ear surgeon, medical historian, statistician, and archeologist, in 1844 Wilde established St Mark's Eye and Ear Hospital in Dublin, which later became known as The Royal Victoria Eye and Ear Hospital. In 1864 he was knighted for his medical contributions and his involvement with the Irish census of 1851, and he was also a well travelled man who wrote detailed accounts of his excursions to the eastern Mediterranean and Austria. Wilde, who also published archeological studies of the Boyne River and Lough Corrib areas, married Jane Francesca Agnes Elgee (see page 165) in 1851 and together they had several children, one of whom was Oscar Wilde (see page 198).

Sligo

William Bourke Cockran
1854-1923

Saint Peter of Alcantara Roman Catholic Church, Port Washington, New York. Its site was donated by statesman, lawyer and orator William Bourke Cockran, on condition that the structure replicated a castle he recalled from his boyhood days in Ireland.

General Michael Corcoran
1827-1863

Memorial to the union army general Michael Corcoran, who commanded the 69th New York Militia in the American Civil War. The structure stands at Ballymore, County Sligo.

Andrew Kerins
(Brother Walfrid)
1840-1915

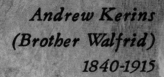

The Celtic Football Club, Glasgow
was founded by Marist Brother
Walfrid on 6 November 1887.

Eva Gore-Booth
1870-1926

Lissadell House, the birthplace
of poet Eva Gore-Booth who
was the sister of the
Countess Markievicz.

Harold J. C. Swan
1922-2005

The Cedars-Sinai Medical
Centre, Los Angeles, where
Harold Swan developed the
Pulmonary Artery Catheter.

Sir John Benson
Architect and engineer 1812 – 1874

John Benson was born in Collooney and was educated at the Dublin Society's School of Architectural Drawing, having been sent there by his patron, Edward Cooper of Markree Castle, County Sligo. In 1851 he was appointed surveyor to Cork city and county and the following year he designed the buildings for the Irish Industrial Exhibition in Dublin. Knighted on that exhibition's opening, Benson designed the Athenaeum in Cork, which later became Cork's Opera House, and he also adapted and extended the Cork Corn Exchange to serve as a National Exhibition Building in 1852.

William Bourke Cockran
Statesman, lawyer and orator
1854 – 1923

Educated in Ireland and France and, having emigrated to the United States when he was seventeen years of age, William Bourke Cockran studied law and was admitted to the bar in 1876. Practicing in Mount Vernon, New York he became a prominent politician and a democratic member of Congress, serving two terms from 1887 until 1889 and again from 1891 until 1895. Cockran, who also campaigned for the election of William McKinley for president, was a brilliant orator with a bellowing voice and he had a significant impact on a youthful Winston Churchill, whom he met on a visit to the United States. Churchill referred to him as 'a remarkable man, on whom I have based my oratorical style,' and also claimed, 'I learned from William Cockran, how to hold thousands enthralled.'

Cockran died in Washington DC on 1 March 1923 and is buried in the Gate of Heaven Cemetery, New York.

Mary Colum (Mary Catherine Gunning Maguire)
Literary critic and writer
1885 – 1957

Born Mary Catherine Gunning Maguire in Ballisodare, Colum was educated at St Louis Convent, County Monaghan and at the Royal University, Dublin (later the National University of Ireland). Working as a teacher in St Ita's, Dublin, Colum was a friend of Thomas MacDonagh (see page 372) and William Butler Yeats (see page 199), who encouraged her to specialise in French literary criticism and to translate the works of French poet Claudel. She later married Padraic Colum (see page 288) and moved with him to New York, where she established herself as a literary generalist in American journalism. Colum was a progressive literary critic with a great appreciation of modernist literature. She wrote several books, including *These Roots* (1937), which traced the early influences that led to the development of modern writing, as well as *Life and the Dream* (1947), which was an autobiography that took a romantic view of literary revival. Her last publication, published posthumously, was *Our Friend James Joyce* (1958), which she wrote with her husband. It recounts the couple's friendship with James Joyce (see page 173). Colum, once referred to as the best female critic in the United States, died in New York in 1957.

Michael Corcoran
Union Army general in the American Civil War 1827 – 1863

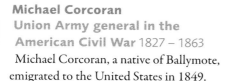

Michael Corcoran, a native of Ballymote, emigrated to the United States in 1849. A decade later he became colonel of the 69th New York Militia, but was temporarily suspended the following year when he refused to parade the regiment before the Prince of Wales, who was visiting New York. Corcoran, who became a hero at the First Battle of Bull Run, was later captured by Confederate forces and subsequently spent a number of years in custody before being released in August 1862, upon which time he was commissioned a brigadier general and was invited to have dinner with President Abraham Lincoln. He later raised and took command of what was called the Corcoran Legion (also called the Irish Legion), which was sent to Fairfax, Virginia. While stationed there he had an accident, falling suddenly from his horse and suffering a brain hemorrhage from which he died on 22 December 1863. His body was embalmed, returned to New York, and was laid in state whilst the flags of the city flew at half mast in honour of his memory.

Pauline Flanagan
Actress 1925 – 2003

Educated at the Ursuline Convent, Sligo, Pauline Flanagan initially worked as a teacher but had a long-held desire to become an actress. Along with her friend Aileen Harte, she placed an advertisement stating that 'two young ladies with extensive amateur dramatic experience, wish to join an exclusive repertory company for the summer season.' This led to the two girls joining the Garry Owen Players Company in Bundoran, County Donegal and it proved the catalyst for Flanagan's acting career, which would eventually span five decades. She often appeared at off-Broadway's Irish Repertory Theatre, in plays such as *Philadelphia, Here I Come* and *Grandchild of Kings* and in her home country she performed with the O'Casey Theatre Company in *The Shadow of a Gunman*, *Three Shouts from a Hill* and *Tarry Flynn* at the Abbey Theatre, Dublin. Flanagan, who also appeared in the 1960 television version of the Irish classic *Juno and the Paycock*, was born into a politically-active family with both of her parents serving as Lord Mayor of Sligo. Her brother also served with the anti-treaty forces during the Civil War. In 2001 Flanagan won the Olivier Award for her performance in *Dolly West's Kitchen*, and she died one day before her seventy-eighth birthday on 28 June 2003.

Eva Gore-Booth
Poet 1870 – 1926

Eva Gore-Booth was born at Lissadell. Her father was a good landlord during the famine, providing free food for his tenants, and it was undoubtedly his good example that gave his daughters Eva and Constance (see page 432) a deep concern for the poor. Between 1904 and 1918, Gore published ten volumes of poetry and verse dramas including *Unseen Kings* (1904) and *Death of Fionavar* (1916). For a time she lived in Manchester, England, where she became active in the National Union of Women's Suffrage Societies, and she died in Hampstead on 30 June 1926.

Sir Henry William Gore-Booth
Arctic explorer and landowner
1843 – 1900

Henry Gore-Booth was born on his family's 32,000-acre Lissadell estate, which he later inherited, and on which he was viewed as a most benevolent and progressive landlord who was interested in the development and welfare of his tenants. Booth was also a prolific writer on a variety of topics, including arctic exploration, yachting, whaling, polar bear hunting and shark fishing; interests which no doubt stemmed from his arctic expedition and from hunting game in Africa. His daughter, Countess Constance Markievicz (see page 432), is the renowned Irish patriot.

Bryan Higgins
Chemist and physician 1741 – 1818

Born in Collooney, Bryan Higgins qualified in medicine at Leiden University in the Netherlands. Having opened a school of practical chemistry at 13 Greek Street in Soho, London, in 1789 Higgins obtained a patent for cheap durable cement. In 1797 he was hired by a public committee, established by the Jamaican House of Assembly for the improvement in the manufacture of muscovado sugar and rum and he resided in Jamaica until 1799. The results of his work were published in 1880 and he died at his estate in Staffordshire, England.

William Higgins
Chemist 1763 – 1825

As a young man William Higgins worked in London with his uncle Bryan Higgins (see above), who was a chemist. He later studied at the University of Oxford, returning to Ireland in 1795 to become a chemist and librarian to the Royal Dublin Society. Higgins is best remembered for his contribution to the new atomic theory and his work,

Parke's Castle, Lough Gill, Co. Sligo.

A Comparative View of the Phlogistic and Antiphlogistic Theories with Inductions (1789), is claimed to have anticipated the findings of English scientist John Dalton. In his book, he suggested the existence of atoms and the attraction between them, which refuted the current phlogiston theory. Higgins, who spent his life trying to introduce new chemical technology into Ireland, was chemist to the Irish Linen Board from 1795 until 1822, and he also published 'An Essay on the Theory and Practice of Bleaching', in connection with the linen industry in 1799. He died at 71 Grafton Street, Dublin in June 1825.

Andrew Kerins (Brother Walfrid)
Founder of Glasgow Celtic FC
1840 – 1915

Born in Ballymote, Andrew Kerins became a Marist brother in 1864. Adopting the name 'Walfrid' in his religious life, in 1870 he moved to Scotland where he took up a teaching post in St Mary's School in Carlton, Glasgow. It was whilst in St Mary's church hall, on 6 November 1887, that Walfrid founded Glasgow Celtic Football Club, the purpose of which is stated in the official club records as 'to alleviate poverty in Glasgow's East End parishes.' Walfrid's own suggestion of the name 'Celtic' was intended to reflect the club's Irish and Scottish roots, and whilst the commonly known nickname of the club is 'The Bhoys', it was then known as 'The Bold Bhoys' or 'The Bould Bhoys'. The addition of a 'h' to the word 'bhoys' was to reflect the Irish accent. Celtic quickly established themselves as one of the strongest sides in Scotland when they won the Scottish Cup in 1892. Walfrid, who also founded St Joseph's College in Dumfries, later moved to Bethnell Green and Bow in London, where he continued his work in organising football matches for the bare foot children of the district. He died on 17 April 1915.

Martin Joseph Moffat
Victoria Cross recipient 1882 – 1946

Martin Moffat was born in County Sligo and served as a private in the 2nd Battalion of the The Prince of Wales Leinster Regiment during World War I. At Ledeghem, Belgium, on 14 October 1918, he was advancing towards a heavily defended house across open ground with five other comrades. Moffat dashed towards the house under heavy fire, throwing grenades, before charging the door and killing two and capturing thirty of the enemy. For this he was awarded the Victoria Cross and died in Sligo in 1946.

Ambrose O'Higgins
Spanish statesman
1720 – 1801

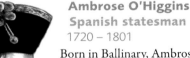

Born in Ballinary, Ambrose O'Higgins intially settled with his family in County Meath, before heading for Spain where he lived for a short period, in the southwestern city of Cádiz. He enrolled in the Spanish Imperial Service and later served in present-day Argentina, after which he moved to Chile. Rising in the services of Spain to become governor of that country, O'Higgins was instrumental in the construction of a road between the capital, Santiago and the port of Valparaiso, and he was also heavily involved in the building of the Palacio de la Moneda (Mint Palace) in Santiago. He later established the first overland postal service between Argentina and Chile, before being appointed viceroy of Peru in 1796, a position which presided over an area comprising present-day Peru, Chile, Bolivia and parts of Argentina and Brazil, and this made O'Higgins one of Spain's most prominent and powerful overseas representatives. His son, Bernardo O'Higgins, would later become Chile's independence leader, and the family name lives on in modern day Chile with the

O'Higgins region and Club Deportivo O'Higgins – a soccer team that competes in the first division of Chile's national league.

Sir George Gabriel Stokes, 1st Baronet
Physicist and mathematician
1819 – 1903

A native of Screen, scientist George Gabriel Stokes was educated in Dublin and in Bristol, England. Having entered Pembroke College, Cambridge, he became a fellow in 1841 and Lucasian professor of mathematics in 1849. His honours include the Rumford Medal in 1852, which he received in recognition of his inquiries into the wavelength of light, and in 1889 he was conferred with a baronetcy having carried out important work in the fields of hydrodynamics, elasticity and the diffraction of light. In hydrodynamics he devised the formula now known as 'Stoke's Law', giving the force-resisting motion of a spherical body through viscous fluid. Stokes, who received numerous honorary degrees from many universities, was also awarded the Codley Medal in 1893 and he held his chair at Cambridge until his death on 1 February 1903.

Dr Harold J. C. Swan
World-renowned cardiologist
1922 – 2005

Following in the footsteps of his parents, Harold J. C. Swan studied medicine at St Thomas' Hospital, London and became a member of the Royal College of Physicians. In 1951 he received his doctorate, before commencing work in the Mayo Clinic of Rochester, Minnesota, where his work led to his appointment as professor of medicine at the University of California in 1965. Swan also became director of cardiology at the Cedars-Sinai Medical Centre, Los Angeles. During his term there, he made a breakthrough in using catheterization in the treatment of acute myocardial infarction – having conceived the idea of putting a flotation balloon on the end of a flexible catheter in order to ease its passage to the pulmonary artery. Swan received many awards for his ground-breaking work; having earlier taken the Walter Dixon Memorial Award from the British Medical Association, he was afforded the prestigious honour of being named a master of the American College of Physicians in 1985. He also received the James B. Herrick Award of the American Heart Association. A prodigious and committed scientist, he left a legacy of more than one hundred peer-reviewed articles including the classic, 'Pulmonary Hypertension in Congenital Heart Disease' (1954). Having served for a short period with the Royal Air Force in Iraq, Swan died on 7 February 2005.

Nicholas Taaffe
Field marshal in the Austrian Army c. 1685 – 1769

Nicholas Taaffe was born at O'Crean's Castle and was educated in Lorraine, France. Having joined the Austrian army, he saw service against France in 1734 and 1735, and again in the Turkish wars from 1736 to 1739. Promoted to major general in 1739, Taaffe's estates in Ireland were sold to a Protestant claimant under the reign of Queen Anne and he received only one third the value. He is also reputed to have introduced the potato to Silesia in 1763.

Tipperary

David McKinley
1913-2002

A World War II twin-engine Catalina, the type of which was flown by air vice-marshal David McKinley in June 1942. He took part in one of the most daring flights of that conflict when he safely transported an American envoy to Russia.

Peter Campbell
1780-1832

Guerilla leader under José Artigas and liberator of Uruguay, Peter Campbell went on to establish that country's navy.

Tony Ryan
1936-2007

From a clerk in Aer Lingus to billionaire, Tony Ryan brought affordable flights to the masses with Ryanair.

Edward Stephen (Fogarty) Fegen
1891-1940

In November 1940, whilst commanding the converted cruise ship HMS *Jervis Bay*, Captain Fegen was escorting thirty-seven merchant ships in the north Atlantic. Taking on the mighty German battleship *Admiral Scheer*, he facilitated the escape of thirty-one of the fleet before later going valiantly down with his ship. For his bravery he was awarded the Victoria Cross.

Seán Treacy
1895-1920

The house at Soloheadbeg where Irish republican Seán Treacy was born.

Daisy Bates (née O'Dwyer)
Journalist and 'Protector of Aborigines'
1863 – 1951

Born at Ashberry House, Caraig Hill, Daisy Bates was a well-educated young lady who, due to health reasons, emigrated to Australia in 1880. There she married John Bates, and together the couple had one son. Whilst on a visit to England in 1899, Bates read an article in the *Times* about the mistreatment of the Aborigines in Western Australia. She subsequently offered her investigative services to that newspaper, and so began her life living amongst the indigenous Australians. During her thirty-five years with those people, Bates studied their customs, languages, rites and legends, all of which she recorded in her book, *The Passing of the Aborigines*. Because of the care and interest she took in Aborigines, she was given the name of 'Kabbarli', meaning 'grandmotherly person', and in 1933, for her services to the Aborigine people, Bates was created a Commander of the Order of the British Empire by King George V. She died in Adelaide, Australia in 1951.

John Desmond Bernal
Scientist 1901 – 1971

John Desmond Bernal was born in Nenagh and was educated at the University of Cambridge in England. Considered one of the most influential scientists of his generation, due to his brilliance his peers nicknamed him 'Sage'. Bernal is recognised for his studies of the atomic structure of solid compounds, through which he made major contributions to x-ray crystallography, and in 1924 he determined the structure of graphite. He was also the co-inventor of the Mulberry Harbour, used in the D-Day landings during World War II. A member of the Communist Party of Great Britain, Bernal was awarded the Lenin Peace Prize in 1953.

Marguerite Blessington, Countess of Blessington
Novelist 1789 – 1849

Having had a rather unhappy childhood, at the age of fifteen, Marguerite Blessington was forced to marry Captain St. Leger Farmer, from whom she fled after three months. Moving to Hampshire, England, she met Charles John Gardiner, 1st Earl of Blessington, and was married to him on 16 February 1818. Blessington, who was renowned for her beauty, charm and wit, spent most of the 1820s in continental Europe with her husband, who died in Paris, France in 1829. She returned to London, where she took to writing, and published her first novel, *Grace Cassidy; or, The Repealers: A Novel* (1843), which was a great success. She followed this with *Conversations with Lord Byron* (1834), *The Idler in Italy* (1839) and *The Idler in France* (1841), all of which, though well-received and financially rewarding, were not sufficient to maintain Blessington's lavish lifestyle. With her financial difficulties coming to a head in 1849, she fled to Paris where she died suddenly three months later.

Brendan Bracken
Publisher, politician and confidante of Winston Churchill
1901 – 1958

Brendan Bracken's father was a member of the Fenian Brotherhood and one of the co-founders of the Gaelic Athletic Association. Born in Templemore and educated at Mungret College, County Limerick until he ran away from school at the age of fifteen, Bracken's mother sent him to Australia to be looked after by his clergyman cousin. In 1920, having returned from Australia and through a certain amount of deception, Bracken gained a teaching job at Liverpool College, England, claiming he was a graduate of the University of Sydney. His rise from then was phenomenal. He founded the *Financial Times* newspaper empire in London, where he mixed in high society circles and became Winston Churchill's wartime minister of information. Bracken is credited with having composed many of the famous leader's legendary speeches, a contribution recognised by Danny Conlon, writing in the *News of the World* in 2003: 'Brendan Bracken sustained and guided the great wartime leader Churchill safely through a decision-making minefield few mortal minds could cope with.' He later became Viscount Bracken but was forced to retire from politics due to ill health and he died in London in 1958.

William Bradshaw
Victoria Cross recipient 1830 – 1861

William Bradshaw was born in Thurles and was an assistant surgeon in the 90th Regiment of the Cameroonians, British Army. At Lucknow, India on 26 September 1857, he was ordered to remove wounded men from the battlefield who had been left behind following a troop withdrawal. Notwithstanding the close proximity of the enemy, Bradshaw was successful in securing the safety of a considerable number of the injured parties. He died on 9 March 1861 and is buried in St Mary's Church in Thurles.

Dan Breen
Irish republican 1894 – 1969

Having joined the Irish Volunteers in 1914, on 21 January 1919, together with Séan Treacy (see page 377) and Séamus Robinson, Dan Breen carried out an ambush for explosives during which two Royal Irish Constabulary policemen were killed at Soloheadbeg, County Tipperary. The attack proved a catalyst for the Irish War of Independence and earned Breen a bounty on his head of £10,000. He subsequently went on the run, moving on to Dublin where, following a shoot-out at Drumcondra in which he was accompanied by Treacy, he sustained twenty-two bullet wounds before miraculously escaping. Breen, who opposed the Anglo-Irish Treaty of 1921, was involved on the republican side in the Irish Civil War and in 1923 was arrested by the Irish Free State Army, before being imprisoned in Limerick and Mountjoy jails. Released the following year, he served as a Sinn Féin TD after the civil war and he later emigrated to the United States before returning to Ireland in 1932. Joining the Fianna Fáil party, he was elected a deputy for Tipperary in the general election of that year and he held his seat until his retirement in 1965. Breen, who authored the book *My Fight for Irish Freedom*, died on 27 December 1969. He is buried at Donohill, near the place of his birth.

William Francis Butler
British army general 1838 – 1910

William Francis Butler was born at Ballyslateen, Suirville, near Golden, and was educated at St Stanislaus College in Tullabeg, County Offaly. Joining the British Army as a junior lieutenant in 1858, Butler took part with distinction in the Red River Expedition from 1870 to 1871, and he also served under General Wolseley in the Zulu war. Appointed colonel in 1885 and brigadier general the following year, he was also made a KCB, before being promoted to major general in 1892. Butler continued his rise to become lieutenant general in 1900 and remained in that position until his retirement in 1905, when he returned to Bansha Castle, County Tipperary. He died there on 7 June 1910.

Peter Campbell
Founder of the Uruguayan Navy 1780 – 1832

An apprentice tanner before enlisting in the 71st Highland Regiment of the British Army, Peter Campbell was present when those troops invaded Buenos Aires, Argentina in 1806. Following the withdrawal of that regiment, he remained and joined the Argentine patriot ranks as a guerrilla leader, rising to prominence and serving under liberator, José Artigas. Considered a superb guerrilla fighter, he established and led a regiment of Tape indigenous people that proved to be a much feared cavalry and infantry force. In 1818 Campbell put together a squadron of river vessels to support Artigas and on 21 August of that year, he was appointed first naval commander of the Patriot fleet. In achieving this, he is thus acknowledged as the founder of the Uruguayan navy. He died in 1832 and was buried with full military honours in Villa del Piler, Paraguay, before his remains were handed over to Uruguay for re-internment in that country's capital, Montevideo.

Liam Clancy
Folk singer and entertainer 1935 – 2009

Liam Clancy was born in Carrick-on-Suir and was the youngest and last surviving member of folk group, the Clancy Brothers. Having met his lifelong friend and musical collaborator, Tommy Makem (see page 49) in 1955, the following year the two emigrated to the United States where they formed a popular folk duo in the nightspots of Greenwich Village, New York. Later joined by his brothers Paddy, Tom and Bobby, the Clancy Brothers gained international fame with their appearance on the *Ed Sullivan Show*, on St Patrick's Day 1961, and they followed that appearance with performances at Carnegie Hall and the Royal Albert Hall in London. Donning traditional Aran sweaters on stage, the rural style was to become the brothers' trademark.

In 1973, Clancy embarked on a solo career, settling in Calgary, Alberta, Canada and hosting his own television show. In 1984 the group reformed with a tour of Ireland and a sell-out appearance at New York's Lincoln Centre, but a serious rift with his brother Paddy during the 1990s prevented the group performing on a permanent basis. Despite this, they did reform for a farewell tour in 1996. Referred to by Bob Dylan as the best ballad singer he had ever heard, Clancy, later retired to Ring, County Waterford and gave his final performance at the National Concert

Hall in Dublin, during which he recited Dylan Thomas' poem, 'And Death Shall Have No Dominion', perhaps in the knowledge that he himself was close to his own death. He died of pulmonary fibrosis on 4 December 2009.

Edward Joseph Conway
Biochemist 1894 – 1968

Edward Joseph Conway was born in Nenagh and educated at University College Dublin where he graduated in medicine and science.

In 1932 he was appointed professor of biochemistry and pharmacology at UCD and he subsequently developed a method of analysing the constituents in tiny quantities of body fluids, to work on cellular chemistry and the source of acid in the stomach. In 1947 Conway was elected a fellow of the Royal Society and was made a member of the Pontifical Academy of Sciences in 1961. An extraordinary, investigative biochemist, ten of Conway's former students attained the status of professor during his tenure, and he was one of the first Irish biologists to carve out an international reputation.

John Cunningham
Victoria Cross recipient 1890 – 1917

Thurles native John Cunningham served as a corporal in the 2nd Battalion of the Prince of Wales's Leinster Regiment during World War I. Whilst manning a Lewis gun at Barlin, France, Cunningham's section came under heavy attack and although severely wounded in the exchange, he took control of his firearm and exhausted its ammunition against twenty counter-attacking Germans. When Cunningham's gun jammed he began using bombs and continued to fight single-handedly to repel the enemy, before making his way back to the main British lines with a fractured arm and other wounds. He was awarded the Victoria Cross for his efforts.

Maurice Davin
Cofounder and first president of the GAA 1842 – 1927

Maurice Davin was born in Deerpark, Carrick-on-Suir and was educated at O'Shea's Academy, Castle Street. An athlete of considerable accomplishment, he competed in a variety of sports, including athletics, wrestling, hurling and gaelic football. Appropriately, Davin was elected president of the newly formed Gaelic Athletic Association at Hayes Hotel, Thurles on 1 November 1884.

Michael Doheny
Writer and Young Irelander 1805 – 1863

Having mastered the Greek and Latin languages, Michael Doheney attended a school in Thurles, following which he went to London to study law. In 1835 Doheney returned to Ireland, where he enrolled as a student of the King's Inn and in 1838 was called to the bar. He subsequently established a successful legal practice in Tipperary and joined Daniel O'Connell's (see page 232) Repeal Association. However, realising that the British government had no intention of dissolving the union, he, together with a number of other Young Irelanders, formed the Irish Confederation. Upon seeing the British government's apathy towards the famine of 1845 and the resultant and widespread death, destruction and eviction

Rock of Cashel, County Tipperary.

of tenants, the Young Irelanders decided to commence a rebellion in 1848. Marshal law was subsequently declared and due to a spy in their midst, most of the Young Irelanders were arrested. However, Doheney together with James Stephens (see page 255) escaped and travelled by foot over 150 miles to Dunmanway, County Cork before eventually crossing the Atlantic to the United States, where Doheney proved instrumental in the formation of the Fenian Brotherhood. He later returned to Ireland to accompany the remains of fellow Fenian Terence Bellew McManus (see page 208), and received a rapturous welcome in his native Tipperary. He returned to the United State on 6 December 1861, where he had established a very substantial legal practice, but less than two years later he died suddenly. Doheney's funeral was a significant public occasion and was led by the Irish military regiments of the United States army.

Patrick Donohoe
Victoria Cross recipient 1820 – 1876

Patrick Donohoe was born in Nenagh and served as a private in the Ninth Lancers of the British Army during the Indian rebellion of 1857. On 28 September 1857 at Bolandshahr, India, Donohoe went to the assistance of a lieutenant who had been seriously wounded. He successfully brought the lieutenant to safety through a large body of enemy cavalry, and for this deed he was awarded the Victoria Cross.

Edward Stephen Fogarty Fegen
Naval captain and Victoria Cross recipient 1891 – 1940

Edward Stephen Fogarty Fegen served as acting captain of the converted cruise liner *Jervis Bay* which in November 1940, was protecting thirty-seven merchant ships en route from

Canada to Britain. During the course of the crossing, the German pocket-battleship, the *Admiral Sheer*, equipped with six 11-inch guns and eight 5.9-inch guns, was spotted on the horizon. Fegen ordered the merchant ships to scatter whilst he engaged the battleship; outgunned and outmaneuvered, the *Jervis Bay* lasted two and a half hours in battle, enabling thirty-one of the thirty-seven strong merchant fleet to escape. Near the end of the conflict, with his ship sinking, Fegan ordered his crew to abandon ship whilst he himself remained on board. He was awarded the Victoria Cross and Winston Churchill, in his famous broadcast speech of 13 May 1945, which mentioned Irish Victoria Cross winners and included Fegen, said, 'they had defended Ireland's honour.'

Stephen Garvin
Victoria Cross recipient 1826 – 74

Stephen Garvin was born in Cashel and was a thirty colour sergeant in the 1st Battalion of the 60th Rifles during the Indian Mutiny. At Delhi, India, on 23 June 1857, Garvin successfully led a small party of men, under heavy fire, to dislodge a considerable number of enemy forces in the Sammy House. He was further commended for his gallantry throughout the operations in Delhi and was awarded the Victoria Cross. Garvin died in Oxfordshire, England in 1874.

Patrick Robert Guiney
American Civil War soldier
1835 – 1877

Patrick Guiney was born in Parkstown but emigrated with his family to the United States when he was just a boy. Settling in Maine, he was educated at Holy Cross College of Worcester, Massachusetts and then studied law before being called to the bar in 1856. When the American Civil War erupted, Guiney joined an Irish regiment, the 9th Massachusetts, under the command of Offaly man, Colonel Thomas Cass (see page 334). Guiney quickly rose through the ranks to become lieutenant colonel. Following the capture of Richmond, Virginia, during which Cass was shot and injured, command was relinquished to Guiney who presided over a depleted 'Fighting Ninth' that lost 421 men on the southern advance.

On 5 May 1864, Guiney, who had now been promoted to colonel following the death of Cass, was himself shot through the eye and forced to return to Boston. During his service he wrote a considerable number of letters to his wife, which give details of the conflict and the suffering of Irish soldiers in the service of the Union Army. On 26 May 1866, President Andrew Johnson signed a brevet promotion making Guiney a brigadier general, 'for gallant and meritorious service during the war.' In Boston Guiney returned to his law practice, where he vigorously fought for the emancipation of black slaves; but on 21 March 1877, whilst crossing to his home in Franklin Square, he collapsed and died as a result of injuries sustained during the war. He was forty-two years of age.

Thomas Bernard Hackett
Victoria Cross recipient
1836 – 1880

A native of Riverstown, Bernard Hackett was twenty-one when he served as a lieutenant in the 23rd Regiment of Foot, British Army during the Indian Mutiny. On 18 November 1857, Hackett successfully rescued a corporal who was lying wounded in a very exposed area at Secundra Bagh, near Lucknow, India. He was later promoted to the rank of lieutenant colonel and died in County Offaly in 1880.

Bartholomew Hayden
Officer in the Brazilian Navy
1792 – 1857

Having joined the armed forces of King George III of Great Britain, Bartholomew Hayden saw service as a midshipman during the Napoleonic wars. In 1821 he sailed for Peru on the HMS *Conway* and there, in order to pursue a career as a trader, he resigned his commission before purchasing a brig called the *Colonel Allen*. With the Brazilian war of independence against Portugal in progress, Hayden offered his assistance to the government of Brazil, who purchased his ship and converted it to a man-of-war, renamed Bahia. He was subsequently appointed to the rank of commander and saw action when the principle Portuguese base at *Bahia* in Brazil was captured in 1823 and the Portuguese were removed from the country. Hayden also served against Argentina, whose naval forces were led by fellow Irishman Commodore William Brown (see page 304) and upon the termination of the war, he was appointed commander of the Brazilian naval division of the east, taking part in the suppression of the slave trade in that area. In 1849 he was promoted to commander of the Brazilian navy but with his health failing, he died on 19 September 1857.

Major General Sir William Bernard Hickie
British Army general and Irish senator 1865 – 1950

William Bernard Hickie was born in Borrisokane and was educated in England at Oscort College in Birmingham and at the Royal Military Academy, Sandhurst. Commissioned to the Royal Fusiliers in 1885, he rose through the ranks and in 1899 was appointed a staff captain, serving in the Second Boer War. In 1907 Hickie returned to Ireland, where he was appointed to the staff of the 8th Infantry Division, Cork. Upon the outbreak of World War I, he was promoted to brigadier general with the British Expeditionary Forces in France and, having taken part in many major engagements during that conflict, including the Third Battle of Ypres, he was knighted for his distinguished services in 1918. Being an Irish Catholic officer, Hickie was a rare breed in the British army of the time, but he was also a strong supporter of home rule for Ireland and was outspoken in condemning the activities of the Black and Tans and their involvement during the Irish War of Independence. On his retirement from the army, he was elected with a record number of votes as a member of the Irish Senate in 1925 and he died in Dublin on 3 November 1950. He is buried in Terryglass, County Tipperary.

Henry Kellett
Vice admiral and explorer
1806 – 1875

Henry Kellett joined the British Navy in 1822, spending five years in the West Indies and later some time in the East Indies, where he served in the Opium War with China. Kellett was involved in the search for Sir John Franklin's expedition in 1848 and the following year he became the first European to sight and chart Wrangel Island, north of Eastern Siberia. In 1852 he commanded the HMS *Resolute* and went to the aid of Robert McClure (see page 413) whose vessel *Investigator* was trapped in the Antarctic, and two years later Kellett became a rear admiral and was later knighted. Cape Kellett, which is located in the easternmost point of Banks Island, Canada, is named in his memory.

Seán Kenny
Architect and stage designer 1932 – 1973

Having studied architecture in the US under Frank Lloyd Wright, Seán Kenny moved to London in 1963. There he was involved in the re-design of the Old Vic Theatre and in 1967 he designed the Gyrotron rollercoaster for Canada's exposition, a piece of work that brought him great renown outside of theatre design. His most famous work was the moveable lanes, bridges and houses for the stage in Lionel Bart's *Oliver!*, but his most lavish was the Casino de Paris in Las Vegas, Nevada, where he designed a complex system of hydraulics and electronics, in order to transform the scenery in full view of the watching audience. Kenny, who also designed an underwater glass restaurant in the Bahamas, died at the age of forty in 1973.

Charles Joseph Kickham
Patriot, novelist and poet 1828 – 1882

When he was just thirteen years of age, Mullinahone's Charles Kickham was involved in a gunpowder accident that affected both his sight and hearing. This did not, however, prevent him from making his mark in the literary world and he was a significant contributor of articles to the *Irish People*, before later becoming its editor. Arrested in 1865 for writing 'treasonous' articles, Kickham was tried and convicted before being sentenced to fourteen years in penal servitude. He wrote his first novel, *Sally Kavanagh* (1869) whilst in prison in England and due to poor health, he was released in 1870, publishing a volume of collected poems and stories that same year. Having returned to Ireland, Kickham resided in Blackrock, County Dublin and his novel *Knocknagow* or *The Homes of Tipperary*, which he published in 1879, was a phenomenal success. Coming from a reasonably wealthy Protestant family, he was convinced that parliamentary politics was 'a harmful waste of time' and his aspiration was for a completely independent Ireland. He died on 22 August 1882 and his funeral was attended by almost ten thousand mourners.

Captain John Lonergan
Congressional Medal of Honour recipient 1839 – 1902

At the beginning of the famine in 1845, John Lonergan emigrated with his family to the United States. Settling in Burlington, Vermont, he worked with his father as a cooper and on occasions, in a grocery business. When the American Civil War broke out in 1861, Lonergan quickly enlisted and was commissioned a captain, leading Company A, 13th Regiment of the Vermont Volunteers, who were also known as 'Emmet's Guards', in honour of Robert Emmet (see page 165). The unit distinguished itself at the Battles of Wilderness and Gettysburg, and it was for his actions at the latter that Lonergan received the Congressional Medal of Honour. His citation reads, 'gallantry in the re-capture of four guns and the capture of two additional guns from the enemy' and 'also the capture of a number of prisoners.' He is buried in the St Joseph's Cemetery at Burlington, Vermont.

Thomas MacDonagh
Nationalist, poet and dramatist 1878 – 1916

Like his parents before him, Thomas MacDonagh became a schoolteacher, where his interest in the Irish language led him to join the Gaelic League. It was whilst on a visit to the Aran Islands, off the coast of County Galway, that he first met Patrick Pearse (see page 185), and he subsequently joined the teaching staff of Pearse's St Enda's School in Dublin. MacDonagh was the founder of the Association of Secondary Teachers in Ireland and having obtained a master's degree in art, he was appointed a professor of English at University College Dublin. In 1913 he was appointed to the Provisional Committee of the Irish Volunteers, which led him to the position of commandant of the Dublin Brigade, and he was also a signatory of the Proclamation of the Republic. During the Easter Rising, MacDonagh's battalion was stationed at the Jacob's Biscuits factory, but saw little fighting as the British Army surrounded the structure with a large force. MacDonagh was left with little option but to surrender on 30 April 1916. Following the surrender, he was court-martialed and executed by firing squad on 3 May 1916. Described as a 'wit' and a family man, one English officer, when talking of the rising, commented that 'they all died well, but MacDonagh died like a prince'.

Fr Theobald Mathew
Temperance advocate
1790 – 1856

Theobald Mathew was born at Thomastown Castle, Cashel and was ordained into the Capuchins order in Dublin in 1814. Having spent the next quarter of a century in Cork City where he helped the poor and deprived, in 1838 he formed the temperance movement – the result of which saw a large reduction in the duty on spirits and a subsequent fall in crime. Mathew's temperance association spread to Britain and the United States and in consideration of his efforts, the Vatican proposed to make him a bishop. However, ill health prevented Mathew from accepting this honour and he died in Cobh, County Cork on 8 December 1856.

David McKinley
Air vice-marshal 1913 – 2002

A master pilot and navigator, in 1941 Cashel born David McKinley was given the responsibility of escorting Harry Hopkins, President Theodore Roosevelt's special envoy, to the Soviet Union. In a marathon flight of two thousand miles, McKinley safely transported the dignitary in twenty-two hours, having had to avoid German fighters, the heavily fortified Norwegian coast en route. On his return journey he was harassed by more German fighters and as well as having to avoid friendly fire from Russian anti-aircraft gunners on land and sea. Exhausted, McKinley landed at Scapa Flow, Scotland twenty hours later. His mission would eventually lead to the United States provision of aid to the Soviet Union. He was also awarded the Distinguished Flying Cross for defending the western approaches in 1942, and two years later he completed the first Royal Air Force circumnavigation of the globe in a Lancaster aircraft. Significantly, McKinley was the first to fly over the Magnetic North Pole and to calculate its exact position. He was appointed a CBE in 1957 and he died on 23 April 2002.

John Morrissey
Gambler, congressman and boxing champion
1831 – 1878

A native of Templemore, in 1833 John Morrissey emigrated with his family to Troy, New York where as a teenager, he became involved with New York street gangs, gaining a reputation as a tough brawler. Appointed a 'shoulder hitter' (political enforcer) by Tammany Hall politician Isaiah Rynders, Morrissey was nicknamed 'Old Smoke', a moniker he gained after being knocked over a stove during a brawl, before continuing the fight and overcoming his adversaries with his back smoldering. In 1851 he journeyed to the gold rush in California, where he made a considerable fortune by gambling, before pursuing a professional prize-fighting career, following which he became 'Champion of America' in 1853. Morrissey later became the owner of a number of successful saloons and gambling houses, and also invested his money in real estate and the Saratoga Springs racing track in New York. He later turned his efforts to politics and was elected as a Democrat, serving two terms in Congress before being elected to the New York State Senate in 1875 and again in 1877. He served in that role until his death in May 1878.

Michael Murphy
Victoria Cross recipient 1831 – 93
Michael Murphy was born in Cahir and served with the 17th Lancers at the relief of Lucknow, India. Severely wounded whilst attempting to defend the injured Lieutenant Hamilton, Murphy was unsuccessful in doing so but was awarded the Victoria Cross for his bravery in attempting to save his comrade's life.

Edward Thomas O'Dwyer
The battling Bishop of Limerick 1842 – 1917
Ordained at Maynooth College, County Kildare in 1867, Edward Thomas O'Dwyer served in many parishes in the diocese of Limerick and was a campaigner for temperance who showed great concern for the poor, forcing

the local merchants and wealthy landowners to provide hundreds of homes for the underprivileged. At the age of forty-five he became the first curate to be elevated to the position of bishop of Limerick and in that role, one of his primary aims was to secure a good education for Catholics. Completely fearless, O'Dwyer was, for a time, condemned by nationalists including Michael Davitt (see page 305) and John Dillon (see page 164). This changed dramatically when the British general Sir John Maxwell wrote a letter seeking O'Dwyer's support in having removed certain priests who had spoken out against conscription to the British Army during World War I. O'Dwyer's reply, which he made public, was carefully worded and he condemned the British general for the execution of the leaders of the Easter Rising, contrasting it with Maxwell's own involvement in an attempted and illegal insurrection against the Boer government in 1895. He went on to highlight, 'you took care that no pleas for mercy should interpose on behalf of the poor young fellows who surrendered to you in Dublin, and who had been shot in cold blood. I regard your actions with horror, and I believe that it has outraged the conscience of the country.' O'Dwyer died in 1917 and did not live to see the eventual outcome of the rising of 1916.

Michael O'Dwyer
Lieutenant governor of the Punjab 1864 – 1940
A member of a wealthy farming family, Michael O'Dwyer was educated at St Stanislaus College in Tullamore, County Offaly, before he completed the exams for the Indian Civil Service in 1884. Joining that service the following year, he served in many roles including that of revenue commissioner in the North West Frontier Province and eventually became lieutenant governor of the Punjab, a position he held from

1912 until 1919. It was during O'Dwyer's tenure that the infamous Amritsar Massacre took place, which occurred when some twenty-thousand demonstrators supporting Indian independence gathered in an enclosed public square called Jallianwala Bagh, and Brigadier General Reginald E.H. Dyer, along with a company of Gurkha troops, was dispatched to restore order. Dyer, who was born in India of Irish parents, assembled fifty soldiers at the square's only exit, and ordered them to fire without warning. During a fifteen minute period, some 1,600 rounds of ammunition were fired, resulting in the deaths of an estimated 380 protesters and the wounding of a further 1,200. O'Dwyer, who gave his full support to the massacre, was condemned at the British Labour Party conference in Scarborough, England on 24 June 1920 where his actions were described as 'cruel and barbarous'. O'Dwyer later returned to England where he was shot dead on 13 March 1940 by Udham Singh, an Indian nationalist whose brother had been killed in the massacre. Singh was subsequently hanged for the murder.

John O'Leary
Irish poet and Fenian 1830 – 1907

Associated with the Young Irelander movement, Tipperary native John O'Leary was briefly imprisoned in 1848 having travelled to the United States to seek support for the Fenians. Joint-editor of the *Irish People* newspaper, together with Charles Kickham (see page 372), he opposed clerical interference in politics and following further imprisonment, from 1865 until 1874, he lived in exile in Paris, France before returning to Ireland, where he became an important figure within cultural and nationalist circles. O'Leary was immortalised in Yeats's poem, 'September 1913', where his passing is lamented with the lines: 'Romantic Ireland's dead and gone,/ It's with O'Leary in the grave.' He died on 16 March 1907.

Martin O'Meara
Victoria Cross recipient
1882 – 1935

Martin O'Meara was born at Sharragh and served as a private in the Australian Imperial Force during World War I. Embarking for France in December 1915, over a four-day period in August of the following year O'Meara entered 'no man's land' at Pozieres and continuously retrieved wounded officers and men from the battlefield, whilst under intense artillery and machine-gun fire. In addition, he volunteered to bring ammunition to trenches that were under heavy bombardment and he was wounded three times during the war, before returning to Australia in 1918. He later achieved the rank of sergeant and died in Australia in 1935.

Frank Patterson
Ireland's golden tenor
1938 – 2000

Having begun his working life in his mother's printing business, Clonmel born Frank Patterson relocated to Dublin in 1961. There he studied vocal techniques, which eventually led to him signing a contract with Phillips Records. Thereafter, Patterson went on to become one of Ireland's foremost concert tenors, appearing at some of the world's most prestigious venues including the Royal Albert Hall, Carnegie Hall and Radio City Music Hall. Patterson, whose principle accompanist was his wife, Eily O'Grady, performed for Pope John Paul II on three occasions and also for presidents Reagan and Clinton. He died of a brain tumour in New York on 10 June 2000.

George Rowland Patrick Roupell
Victoria Cross recipient 1892 – 1974

A twenty-three-year-old lieutenant, George Rowland Patrick Roupell served in the British Army as a member of the 1st Battalion, East Surrey Regiment during World War I. Whilst in command of a company that was under continuous bombardment at Hill 60, Belgium on 20 April 1915, Roupell, although wounded several times, remained at his post and successfully repelled strong German attacks. During a lull in the fighting he had his wounds dressed and immediately returned to the trenches, continuing to hold his position until relieved the next morning. He later achieved the rank of brigadier and died in Surrey, England, in 1974.

John Ryan
Victoria Cross recipient 1839 – 1863

John Ryan was born in Barnalisheen and served as a lance corporal in the 65th Regiment of Foot of the British Army during the Māori War in New Zealand. With the aid of two privates, Ryan successfully removed the body of a captain from the field of action during a period of heavy fire near Cameron Town on 7 September 1863. Surrounded by the enemy, he remained with the injured man in the bush but was unable to prevent him dying. Ryan was drowned whilst trying to rescue a comrade in December of the same year and he was buried in New Zealand in 1863.

Tony Ryan
Aviation entrepreneur 1936 – 2007

A native of Thurles, Tony Ryan commenced his career as a clerk for Aer Lingus, eventually rising to the position of director of aircraft leasing. In conjunction with Aer Lingus, he set up Guinness Peat Aviation in 1975 and it was from this venture that he gained his initial fortune. The company became the largest aircraft-leasing operation in the world and although it had a disastrous flotation on the stock market, Ryan received an estimated $55 million from its sale in 2000. In 1985, with a single fifteen-seat plane operating from Waterford to London, he established Ryanair and today the airline employs around five thousand personnel, operating nearly six hundred routes in twenty-six countries, and carries more than 50 million people annually. Ryan completely changed the face of European civil aviation, bringing affordable prices to the masses and making his the largest airline in Europe. A true entrepreneurial genius, he amassed a fortune of €1.5 billion before his death on 4 October 2007.

Laurence Sterne
Novelist 1713 – 1768

A native of the town of Clonmel, Laurence Sterne was educated at Hipperholme Grammar School in Halifax, England and Jesus College, Cambridge, which he entered in 1733. There he obtained a Bachelor of Arts degree in 1737, before taking Holy Orders the following year. In 1759 Sterne wrote *The History of a Good Warm Watch Coat*, which was published posthumously and in 1760 he wrote the opening two volumes of *The Life and Opinions of Tristram Shandy, Gentleman*, which brought him overnight success in the literary world. He published his second novel, *A Sentimental Journey through France and Italy* in 1768, before contracting tuberculosis and dying at Old Bond Street, London on 18 March 1768.

George Thomas
Adventurer, Soldier and Rajah
1756 – 1802

Born in Roscrea, George Thomas joined the British Navy at Youghal, County Cork before deserting his position at Madras, India in 1781. Later, in Delhi, Thomas entered the service of the Begum Samru of Sardhana who appointed him commander of her army. He went on to capture and hold the territory of Hariana in 1798 – an area of over three thousand square miles – and established himself as the Rajah of Hariana, even going so far as to mint his own coins. Thomas held that territory until he was forced out by combined Sikh and French forces three years later, and with intentions of returning to Ireland in 1902, he died of a fever aged forty-six.

John Toler (Lord Nobury)
Chief justice 1745 – 1831

Known as 'The Hanging Judge', John Toler was educated at Trinity College, Dublin and called to the bar in 1770. His support for the government of the time resulted in his appointment as solicitor general in 1789, and it is reputed that through bribery and deception, he was appointed a judge. Though lacking in legal skills, Toler used his power to intimidate lawyers and defendants and his most famous trial was that of Robert Emmet (see page 165), in which he continually interrupted and abused the defendant before sentencing him to death. Toler, who was despised by Daniel O'Connell (see page 232), was eventually removed from the bench in 1827. He died at 3 Great Denmark Street, Dublin on 27 July 1831.

Seán Treacy
Republican 1895 – 1920

At the age of fourteen, Seán Treacy left school to commence work as a farmer. A member of the Irish Volunteers, Tracy was imprisoned for two years following the Easter Rising, Embarking on hunger strike on a number of occasions, he was released in 1918. On 21 January the following year, together with Dan Breen (see page 365), Seán Hogan, Séamus Robinson and five others, he virtually ignited the Irish War of Independence when the group ambushed a Royal Irish Constabulary (RIC) contingent who were transporting gelignite explosives at Soloheadbeg, County Tipperary. Two British constables were killed in the exchange and as a result, south Tipperary was placed under martial law. Seán Hogan was later arrested on 12 May 1919. The next day, whilst Hogan was being transported by train from Thurles to Cork, Treacy and a contingent of IRA men boarded the train at Knocklong, County Limerick and during a shoot-out in which both Treacy and Breen were seriously injured and two policemen were killed, Hogan was rescued.

Treacy later spent some time as a member of Michael Collins' (see page 89) 'assassination squad' in Dublin, where he was involved in the attempted killing of British general Sir John French in December 1919. He later returned to Tipperary and carried out a number of attacks on the RIC Barracks before returning to the capital where, on 11 October 1920, he and Breen were almost captured in a safe house in Drumcondra. Following another shoot-out, the two men escaped but not before the owner of the house, Doctor Carolan, was killed. Three days later, Treacy was recognised by a police detective on Talbot Street and in the ensuing gunfight he was killed. Despite a significant presence of British military personnel, he was buried with full military honours, in Kilfeacle, County Tipperary.

Tyrone

Archbishop John Joseph Hughes
1797-1864

Archbishop John Joseph Hughes was responsible for the construction of St Patrick's Cathedral, New York City and was also the founder of Fordham University.

John Dunlap
1747-1812

Independence Hall, Philadelphia is where the Declaration of Independence was adopted. John Dunlap printed two hundred copies of it on 4 July, 1776.

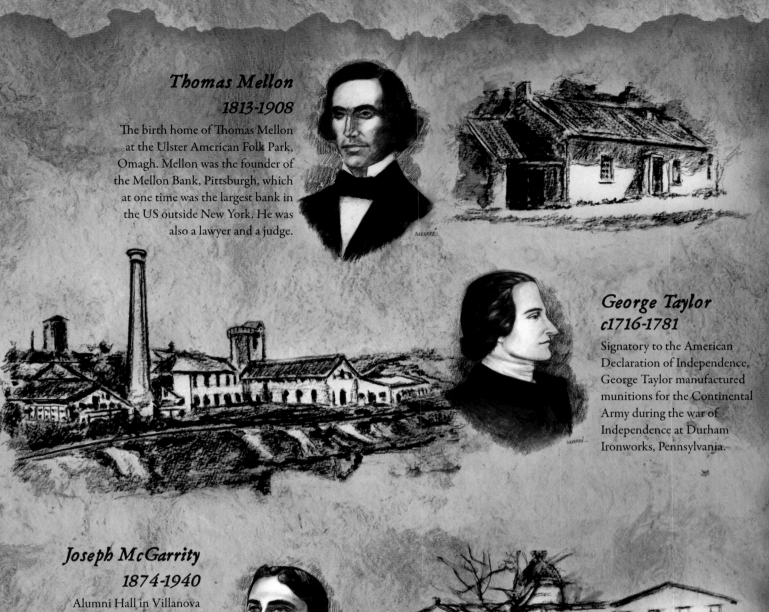

Thomas Mellon
1813-1908

The birth home of Thomas Mellon at the Ulster American Folk Park, Omagh. Mellon was the founder of the Mellon Bank, Pittsburgh, which at one time was the largest bank in the US outside New York. He was also a lawyer and a judge.

George Taylor
c1716-1781

Signatory to the American Declaration of Independence, George Taylor manufactured munitions for the Continental Army during the war of Independence at Durham Ironworks, Pennsylvania.

Joseph McGarrity
1874-1940

Alumni Hall in Villanova University is where Joseph McGarrity donated over ten thousand volumes of Irish and American literature. He also financed arms for the Easter Rising of 1916 and gave $100,000 of his own money in support of Irish freedom.

Harold Rupert Leofric George Alexander

British army field marshal 1891 – 1969

Having served with the Irish Guards in France in World War I, Harold Rupert Leofric George Alexander was wounded twice and was awarded the Military Cross, Légion d'Honneur and the Russian Order of St Anne. He later served in Burma, the Middle East, North Africa and Italy during World War II, becoming Allied commander in the Mediterranean where he achieved the rank of field marshal. Alexander, who was appointed first governor general of Canada in 1954, also served as minister for defence in the government of Winston Churchill and he received the Order of Merit in 1959, being raised to the peerage as Earl Alexander of Tunis and Errigal. He died in London, England on 16 June 1969.

Guy Carleton

Soldier and governor of Canada 1724 – 1808

Considered one of the most significant historical figures of the eighteenth century, Strabane's Guy Carleton joined the British Army at the age of eighteen and served as a lieutenant colonel, seeing action at the siege of Louisborg in Nova Scotia, Canada. In 1758 Carleton fought at the Battle of Quebec, but four years later he was wounded at the siege of Havana, Cuba. In a distinguished military career, he was appointed governor of Quebec in 1772 and defended that province against the American invaders in December 1775.

Carleton also commanded the army that invaded New York the following year and a decade later, he would become governor-in-chief of British North America. Raised to the peerage in August 1786, he returned to England in 1791 and took a seat in the House of Lords. He died in Hampshire, England on 10 November 1808. Carleton University, Ottawa and Carleton County, Ontario are named in his honour.

William Carleton

Novelist 1794 – 1869

Author William Carleton was born near Clogher and was educated in the local hedge schools. Although his family encouraged him to join the priesthood, Carleton resisted and even became a Protestant later in life. His literary reputation was established with the publication of *Traits and Stories of the Irish Peasantry* (1830), and his novels include, *The Black Prophet* (1847), *The Emigrants of Ahadarra* (1848), *The Tithe Proctor* (1848) and *The Squanders of Castle Squander* (1852). Carleton's writings were a representation of Irish life and were highly praised by Maria Edgeworth and William Butler Yeats (see page 199). He died in Dublin in 1870.

John Dunlap

Printer of the American Declaration of Independence 1747 – 1812

As a young boy, Strabane born John Dunlap emigrated to the United States where he joined his uncle William Dunlap – a printer and publisher – in Philadelphia, Pennsylvania. There he founded the *Philadelphia Packet*, the first daily newspaper in the United States and with the wording of the Declaration of Independence being agreed on 4 July 1776, that same evening Dunlap printed two hundred copies of the historical document. He was also the founder and officer in the first troop of the Pennsylvanian cavalry, which became the unit to protect George Washington at the battles of Trenton and Princeton. He died in Philadelphia in 1812.

James Graham Fair
United States senator and entrepreneur 1831 – 1894

James Graham Fair was born in Clogher and at the age of twelve went to the United States, where he grew up on a farm in Illinois and received an extensive education in business. Moving on to California in the 1850s, Fair obtained work as a mine superintendent and later formed a company with three fellow Irishmen, which became popularly known as 'The Bonanza Firm'. Having made a large fortune, Fair invested most of his money in railroads, San Francisco real estate and the formation of the Nevada Bank of San Francisco, which at the time was the largest bank in the nation. In 1881 he was appointed to the United States Senate by the Nevada legislature and upon his death in 1894, he left in excess of 40 million dollars in his will.

John Joseph Hughes
Archbishop of New York 1797 – 1864

In the early 1800s, John Joseph Hughes emigrated with his parents to the United States. In order to pay for the cost of his education, Hughes worked as a gardener at Mount St Mary's College in Emmitsburg, Maryland, where he was eventually ordained a priest in 1826. In 1838 he was made a bishop and in 1850 he became archbishop of New York. Having actively campaigned on behalf of Irish immigrants, Hughes was instrumental in founding an independent Catholic school system throughout New York and he was also the founder of St John's College, which is now Fordham University. Hughes was also responsible for the construction of the renowned St Patrick's Cathedral, New York and he is buried beneath its altar.

Jimmy Kennedy
Songwriter and lyricist 1902 – 1984

In a career spanning fifty years, Trinity College graduate Jimmy Kennedy wrote some two thousand songs, and until the arrival of the Beatles, had more hits in the United States than any other artist. As a captain in the British Army, Kennedy wrote the wartime hit, 'We're Going to Hang out the Washing on the Siegfried Line', and he was also awarded the Ivor Novello Award for his contribution to music. Appointed an OBE in 1983, amongst his hits were: 'Red Sails in the Sunset', 'South of the Border', 'The Isle of Capri', 'My Prayer', 'Teddy Bear's Picnic', and 'Hokey Cokey'. Having died in Cheltenham, England on 6 April 1984, Kennedy was posthumously inducted into the Songwriters Hall of Fame in 1997.

Benedict Kiely
Author 1919 – 2007

Writer Benedict Kiely was born near Dromore and grew up in Omagh. A prolific author, most significant amongst his works are *Land Without Stars* (1945), *The Cards of the Gambler*

381

(1953) and *Nothing Happens in Carmincross* (1985). Kiely, whose elaborate prose explored and celebrated humanity in its great complexity, had a highly distinctive speaking voice and he regularly featured on Irish radio broadcasts. He also published a number of children's stories and his non-fiction work includes *Counties of Contention: A Study of the Origins and Implications of the Partition of Ireland* (1945). Having lived most of his life in Dublin, he died on 9 February 2007.

Joseph McGarrity
Republican, business man and
revolutionary financer 1874 – 1940

Joseph McGarrity was born in Carrickmore and emigrated to United States in 1892. Settling in Philadelphia, Pennsylvania, he established substantial business interests in the wine and spirits trade. Having joined Clan na Gael (Family of the Gaels) in 1893, he generously contributed to the cause of Irish freedom and was responsible for financing the importation of arms from Germany prior to the Easter Rising. McGarrity, who helped raise in the region of $8.5 million for the Irish struggle, was also a poet and collector of Irish and Irish-American books and he donated over ten thousand volumes to the University of Villanova. His passion for Ireland's freedom was unequalled, but on his last trip home to Carrickmore in 1939, he was served with an expulsion order by the British government. He died on 5 August 1940.

Thomas Mellon
Entrepreneur, lawyer, judge and founder of
Mellon bank 1813 – 1908

Born in Cappagh, Thomas Mellonemigrated to the United States with his family at the age of five. Settling in Pennsylvania, he graduated from the University of Pittsburgh with a law degree in 1837 and was admitted to the bar the following year. Mellon was financially savvy and he invested the proceeds from his legal career, purchasing extensive real estate in downtown Pittsburgh. In 1870 he opened the T. Mellon and Sons bank, which became the foundation of a financial and industrial empire and by the end of the nineteenth century, it was the largest banking institution in the United States outside of New York. He died at his home in East Liberty on 3 February 1908, but not before he had a chance to return to his boyhood home some sixty-four years after he left it. Central to the Ulster American Folk Park just outside Omagh, County Tyrone, Mellon remarked that 'it is as I had seen it when a child and still remember it.'

Alice Milligan
Writer and nationalist
1865 – 1953

Born in Omagh and educated at the Methodist College, Belfast and at King's College, London, Alice Milligan settled in Dublin for a period, to learn Irish and became enthusiastically involved in the political independence of Ireland. She wrote several plays for the Irish Literary Theatre and together with Ethna Carbery, founded the nationalist newspaper the *Northern Patriot* in 1890, and later the *Shan Van Vocht*. Her father was the writer Seaton Milligan, and her friends included O'Donovan Rossa (see page 111), Douglas Hyde (see page 351) and Roger Casement (see page 159). A member of a small Protestant group of nationalists and one of the most politically aware Irish women of the twentieth century, Milligan died in 1953 and is buried at Drumragh Old Graveyard, outside Omagh.

Robert Morrow
Victoria Cross recipient 1891 – 1915

Robert Morrow was born in Dungannon, County Tyrone and served in the British Army during World War I as a private in the 1st Battalion of the Royal Irish Fusiliers. On 12 April 1915, near Messines, Belgium, he successfully rescued several men who had been buried in a trench that had been devastated by a shell. Morrow carried out this brave deed under continuous enemy fire, and was thus awarded the Victoria Cross. He was killed in action at St Jan, Ypres in Belgium in 1915.

Eoghan Rua Ó Néill
Spanish army commander and Irish army general
c. 1590 – 1649

The nephew of 'The Great Earl' Hugh O'Neill, in 1607 Eoghan Rua O'Neill left Ireland with his uncle in what was known as the Flight of the Earls. After attending the University of Salamanca in northern Spain, O'Neill joined the Spanish army, rising through its ranks to become a commander of forces in the Spanish Netherlands, (now Belgium, Holland and northern France). With two thousand soldiers he defended Arras against a French force numbering in excess of thirty thousand, successfully holding out for two months in 1640. Reputed to be a great tactical general, O'Neill returned to Ireland in 1642, landing on the coast of County Donegal with a considerable supply of arms and ammunition, as well as three hundred seasoned Irish soldiers from the Spanish army.

He was immediately appointed commander-in-chief of Irish rebel forces in Ulster but given that these forces were untrained, O'Neill actively avoided confrontations with the enemy, which comprised twelve thousand battle-hardened English and Scottish soldiers. However, try as he might, he was reluctantly forced into battle at Clones, County Monaghan where he was defeated, but not before withdrawing with much of his force intact. Some four years later and with a better trained army, O'Neill faced General Munro at the Battle of Benburb, and although considerably outnumbered and lacking the artillery that Munro had at his disposal, he scored an epic victory, killing and capturing in the region of three thousand Scottish soldiers and their arms. Due to animosity amongst the Catholic leaders at the time, O'Neill's success was not capitalised upon and it was not until the arrival of Oliver Cromwell in 1649 that the acrimony was settled. However, O'Neill fell ill before dying in County Cavan on 6 November 1649 and Ireland thus lost the only general who stood a chance against Cromwell and his considerable forces.

Earl Hugh O'Neill
Irish rebel leader 1550 – 1616

Though born in County Tyrone, Hugh O'Neill grew up in London, England, where he was a supporter of English rule in Ireland. However, following assistance given by him to survivors of the Spanish Armada in 1588, suspicions were aroused in relation to his loyalty to the crown and in 1591 he engineered the escape from Dublin Castle of Red Hugh O'Donnell, which led to the latter being inaugurated as chief of the O'Donnells the following year. In 1595 O'Neill took arms against the English, defeating Sir John Norris in the Battle of Clontibret, but then followed a period in which O'Neill, O'Donnell and other chiefs parleyed with the English whilst opening secret negotiations with the Spanish. Following three years of fruitless talks, O'Neill re-opened hostilities, securing an important victory at the battle of Yellowford, which sparked general revolt throughout Ireland.

With Spanish troops under the command of Don Juan del Aguila arriving in Kinsale in September 1601, English General Lord Mountjoy laid siege upon them whilst O'Neill and O'Donnell marched south from their base in Tyrone and Tyrconnell (Donegal), three hundred miles north, in the depth of winter. Their armies were decimated during the long march and having faced bitter weather, occasional skirmishes and a shortage of food, upon arrival in Kinsale, O'Neill decided it would be best to avoid direct assault on the English forces. However, apparently overruled by O'Donnell and del Aguila, who both believed their combined forces were stronger than the English, they attacked on 24 December 1601 but were defeated. This lead to the eventual Flight of the Earls, which saw O'Neill and O'Donnell leaving for continental Europe and the subsequent demise of the great Irish chieftains. O'Neill later died in Rome, Italy.

Sir Phelim O'Neill
Leader of the Rising of 1641
c.1605 – 1653

Phelim O'Neill was a member of the famous O'Neill clan, who retained lands in Ulster following the Flight of the Earls. However, having become disenchanted with the Protestant English government of Ireland, the exclusion from public office of Catholics and the continued confiscation of Catholic-owned land, O'Neill took a leading part in the rising of 1641. Chosen as commander-in-chief of the Irish forces in the north, he issued a forged commission from Charles I that legalised his position of command, but with the rebellion initially faltering at Lisburn, County Antrim, O'Neill was forced to break off a siege of Drogheda, County Louth. Upon the arrival of Eoghan Rua O'Neill in

August 1642, he lost command of the Ulster forces before later fleeing to an island hideout in County Tyrone where he was betrayed by a kinsman in February 1653. At his trial before the Cromwellian judges, O'Neill admitted the forgery of the commission from Charles I, thereby forfeiting any chance of escaping death. He was executed as a traitor on 10 March 1653.

Brian O'Nolan (Flann O'Brien and Myles na gCopaleen)
novelist and satirist
1911 – 1966

Born in Strabane, Brian O'Nolan was educated at University College Dublin, where he graduated with a degree in Celtic Languages in 1932. Following his graduation, he joined the Irish civil service and published his first book, *At Swim-Two-Birds* (1939). O'Nolan, who produced most of his works under the pseudonym of Flann O'Brien, published a book written in Irish, *An Béal Bocht* in 1941. He also wrote a satirical column in the *Irish Times*, but used name of Myles na gCopaleen, due to the fact that as a civil servant, he was not permitted to explicitly express political views. Amongst O'Nolan's best-known works are: *Dalky Archive* (1964), *When the Saints Go Cycling* (1964) and *The Third Policeman* (1967), which was published posthumously. A much-loved writer, his mastery of comedic prose made him one of the greatest comic writers in the English language.

James Shields
United States general and senator 1806 – 1879

James Shields was born in Altmore and later emigrated to the United States, where he initially settled in Kaskaskia, Illinois. There he became a lawyer and in 1835 he was elected to the State Legislature. In the United States' war with Mexico, Shields was commissioned a brigadier general of the Illinois Volunteers and during that campaign, in which he was seriously wounded twice, he was amongst the first to enter Mexico City when it fell. Having returned to Illinois a hero, Shields was elected a senator, but he lost his seat in 1855 and went west to the Minnesota territories where he attempted to establish Irish colonies. Upon the outbreak of the American Civil War he returned to his military duties and fought against the Confederates and 'Stonewall' Jackson in the Valley of Virginia. Wounded at the battle of Kernstown on 22 March 1862, Shields' troops inflicted Jackson's only tactial defeat during the campaign, and he was subsequently promoted to major general. He left the army in 1863, spending the latter days of his life in Missouri and he died in Ottumwa, Iowa, on 1 June 1879. In United States politics, Shields holds the unique distinction of being a senator of three states.

George Taylor
Signatory of the American Declaration of Independence
1716 – 1781

Around 1738, George Taylor emigrated to the United States and commenced work in a forge, where he was given a clerical position. In 1764 he was elected to the Pennsylvania Provincial Assembly and a decade later he purchased the lease of the Durham Ironworks in Upper Bucks County, Pennsylvania. His company later became the first supplier of munitions to the Continental Army in the American War of Independence. The following year Taylor was appointed a delegate to the Continental Congress, where he replaced a Pennsylvanian delegate who refused to support independence. On 2 August 1776 he became a signatory of the United States Declaration of Independence. Having served on the supreme council of Pennsylvania for only six weeks, Taylor was forced to retire due to ill health in 1777. He is buried in Easton Cemetery, Pennsylvania.

Waterford

Robert Boyle
1627-1691

The 'Father of Chemistry', Robert Boyle was born at Lismore Castle.

Thomas Francis Meagher
1823-1867

The statue of Irish revolutionary and Union Army general Thomas Francis Meagher stands outside the Montana State Capitol in Helena, Montana. A similar statue stands in his native Waterford City.

William Hobson
1792-1842

The Treaty of Waitangi secured New Zealand for the British Crown and it was Governor William Hobson who influenced the Māori people to sign the treaty.

Ernest T. S. Walton
1903-1995

Ernest Walton, in partnership with John Cockroft, split the nucleus of the atom. For this feat, both men were awarded the Nobel Prize in 1951.

ELECTRON

PROTON

NEUTRON

Margaret Louisa Aylward
Founder of the Sisters of the Holy Faith
1810 – 1889

Born into an extremely wealthy family who were close associates of Daniel O'Connell (see page 232) and the family of the Thomas Francis Meagher (see page 393), one of Margaret Louisa Aylward's most prized possessions was a signed portrait of Meagher, inscribed 'to my dear friend and respected fellow citizen.' Aylward was an exceptionally skilled business woman and having left the convent in Thurles at the age of twenty, she became a teacher at the Waterford Presentation Convent where she remained for four years. In 1834 she joined the Irish Sisters of Charity in Dublin, but later returned to Waterford to join the Ursuline Sisters. Active in Dublin during the famine years, she took great care of destitute women and children and also founded St Brigid's Orphanage and the Sisters of the Holy Faith with the support of Cardinal Paul Cullen (see page 239). She died on 11 October 1889 and her funeral procession to Glasnevin Cemetery was followed by hundreds of the poor of Dublin.

Francis Barker
Physician 1773 – 1859

Francis Barker was educated at Trinity College, Dublin and at Edinburgh Medical School in Scotland where he qualified as a physician. Having later returned to Waterford, Barker opened the first fever hospital in Ireland, on John's Hill in the city, and he spent five years there before returning to Dublin where he was appointed senior physician at Cork Street Hospital. Appointed professor of chemistry at Trinity College in 1808, Barker established the first Irish medical journal and was also editor of the *Dublin Pharmacopoeia*. He died in Dublin in 1859.

Maurice Patrick Barrett
Catholic brother and religious leader 1900 – 1990

Maurice Patrick Barrett was born on the Upper Yellow Road, Waterford City and was educated at De La Salle on Stephen Street. Having initially commenced his working life as a carpenter, he later entered the Order of St John of God in Dublin but retired in 1950 before moving to Albuquerque, New Mexico where he established a new order, The Little Brothers of the Good Shepherd. Renowned for dedicating his life to the poor, Archbishop Robert Sanchez of Sante Fe, New Mexico recommended Barrett for the Lumen Christi Award for his outstanding work, and he was also made the 23rd Freeman of his native city of Waterford. The Little Brothers of the Good Shepherd has now over thirty houses in the United States and also has one location in Kilkenny. He died in 1990.

Edward Barron
Bishop and missionary 1801 – 1854

Educated at St Edmund's College in Hertfordshire, England and later in France, Edward Barron returned to Ireland to read law at Trinity College, Dublin. Having spent three years there, he decided to enter the seminary at St John's College in Waterford in order to study for the priesthood. In 1824, he was sent to study at the Propaganda College in Rome. Barron was ordained in 1829 and later that year he returned to St John's where he taught French, Hebrew and Philosophy until 1836, when he transferred to the United States to take up an appointment as vicar general and pastor of St Mary's Church in Philadelphia. In 1840, following the Holy See request for American bishops to care for Catholics in Liberia, Barron took up the challenge and became one of the first missionaries from the United States. He was later appointed bishop of Liberia and following his consecration in Rome on 22 January 1842, he continued his labours until 1845, when he was forced to return to the United States due to ill health. In his missionary work in Liberia, Barron spent the inheritance he received from his family on large amounts of food, medicine, seeds and equipment for the needy. He died of yellow fever whilst caring for victims of a plague in Savannah, Georgia on 12 September 1854 and is buried next to the cathedral in Savannah.

Robert Boyle
Philosopher, chemist, physicist and inventor 1627 – 1691

A fluent speaker of French, Italian, Hebrew, Greek and Syriac, Robert Boyle's experiments on the properties of air were first published in 1660. In physics, Boyle's work included the discovery of air's influence on the transmission of sound, as well as investigations into specific gravities, reflective powers, crystals, electricity and colour. Born in Lismore Castle, he is perhaps best known for 'Boyle's Law', which states that the volume of gas is inversely proportional to its pressure at constant temperature. A deeply religious man, Boyle was responsible for Bedell's Bible being translated into Irish. The 'father of chemistry' died in London, England on 31 December 1691.

Noel Browne
Politician and doctor 1915 – 1997

Qualifying as a doctor from Trinity College, Dublin, Noel Browne was a controversial public representative who served as a TD for five different political parties. Whilst still a student, he developed tuberculosis and as a result, as minister for health from 1948 to 1951, he instigated a programme for the eradication of that disease in Ireland. His proposed 'Mother and Child' scheme, which would have provided free prenatal and post-natal medical services, brought him into conflict with the Catholic Church, who considered his actions to be 'rampant socialism' and as a result, Browne's controversial scheme eventually resulted in the downfall of the first inter-party government in 1951. Whilst a member of the Labour Party from 1969 to 1973, he introduced the first Family Planning Bill, and he later detailed these events in his autobiography, *Against the Tide*. A man of great ideas, Browne died in County Galway on 21 May 1997.

Denis B. Cashman
Irish patriot 1842 – 1897

As a teenager, Denis B. Cashman became a member of the Irish Republican Brotherhood. Arrested for holding membership of the Fenians in 1867, he was sentenced to seven years penal servitude in Fremantle, Australia. While en route there, on board the *Hougoumont*, he formed a close relationship with fellow Irishman John Boyle O'Reilly (see page 322). Having been pardoned in 1869, Cashman made his way to the United States where he settled in Boston, Massachusetts. Boyle was reunited with O'Reilly, who had escaped from Autralia, and in the early 1870s the two men helped plan the rescue of Fenian military prisoners still remaining in Fremantle. To this end, the whaling ship *Catalpa*, was sent from the United States to Australia in order to help in the rescue. With the successful return of the *Catalpa* to New York, Cashman spent his time thereafter writing poetry and articles for the *Pilot* and the *Boston Herald*. He also wrote *The Life of*

Michael Davitt: With a History of the Rise and Development of the Irish National Land League (1881) and he died in Boston in 1897.

Major Redmond Cunningham
Military Cross recipient 1916 – 1999

Educated by the Christian Brothers at Stephen's Street, Waterford, Major Redmond Christopher Archer Cunningham, who was named after his godfather John Redmond (see page 414), later became an architectural draughtsman for a local firm of architects. In 1942 he relocated to Omagh, County Tyrone where he was employed as a civilian clerk-of-works by the British Army and the following year, he was gazetted as a second lieutenant in the Royal Engineers, transferring to Scotland where training operations were underway for the invasion of Normandy.

On D-Day, 6 June 1944, as part of the 79th Armoured Division, he commanded a troop that landed on Queen Red Beach (Ouistreham) where with his own tank being disabled, he commandeered another and cleared a path for the 2nd Battalion Royal Ulster Rifles, before holding the position until the arrival of relieving infantry the next day. For these actions he was awarded the Military Cross – the only Irishman to receive this award on D-Day. Cunningham was also awarded the Croix de Guerre by the Belgian government for his part in evacuating the dead and wounded from Antwerp and he later crossed the Rhine to lead an assault on a heavily fortified German position, capturing two hundred prisoners in the process. Following the war he became well known in racing circles and also resumed his architectural career, establishing a successful practice with his brother Willie. Cunningham was a family man and was married with three daughters and two sons, one of whom is the acknowledged Irish writer Peter Cunningham.

Teresa Deevy
Playwright 1894 – 1963

Teresa Deevy was born on the Passage Road, Waterford City and was educated at the Ursuline Convent. It was whilst training to be a teacher that she lost her hearing through Ménières disease and in 1914 she went to London, England to learn lip-reading, also joining Cumann na mBan (Women's League). In 1930 her first play, *Reapers* was produced at the Abbey Theatre, Dublin and she also wrote *A Disciple, Temporal Powers, The King of Spain's Daughter,* and *The Wild Goose*. Deevy, who was elected to the Irish Academy of Letters in 1954, died in Waterford in 1963 and is buried in Ballygunner Cemetery, Waterford.

Seán Dunne
Poet and author 1956 – 1995

Seán Dunne was born in St John's Park, Waterford City and was educated at Mount Sion CBS and University College Cork. A freelance writer and broadcaster, he published a bestselling biographical memoir of his childhood in Waterford, which he called *In my Father's House* (1991), and he also wrote a number of spiritual-based works such as *The Road to Silence* (1994) and *Something Understood* (1995). Dunne, whose first poem ran to several pages and was about the Vietnam War, contributed over three hundred various articles to books and journals, a prolific output for such a young writer. Always the observer, another poem described a young girl who took his eye on his way to school at Mount Sion. He died on 3 August 1995 and the following year the Seán Dunne Writers' Festival was inaugurated by the Waterford City Council in his honour. It is now Ireland's largest festival for writers of all categories.

Thomas Esmonde
Victoria Cross recipient 1829 – 1873

Thomas Esmonde was born in Butlerstown and served in the British Army as a captain in the 18th Regiment of Foot, during the Crimean War. Following an engagement on the Redan at Sebastopol, Crimea on 18 June 1855, Pembroke rescued many wounded men under heavy fire and whilst in command of a covering party two days later, he extinguished a fireball that had landed close to his position, thus saving many of his men from injury. Later achieving the rank of lieutenant colonel, he died in Belgium in 1873.

William Henry Grattan Flood
Organist and music writer
1857 – 1928

An organist at Thurles Cathedral, Belfast Pro-Cathedral and Enniscorthy Cathedral, Lismore-born William Henry Grattan Flood was also professor of music at Clongowes Wood College in Kildare, as well as Cotton College, Staffordshire, England and St Kieran's College, Kilkenny. Created a Knight of St Gregory's in 1922, he was a prolific music writer and his works include *The Story of the Harp, The Story of the Bagpipe, The History of Enniscorthy, The History of Ferns,* and *A History of Irish Music.* Flood also edited Thomas Moore's (see page 181) *Irish Melodies and Selected Airs of O'Carolan.* He died in Enniscorthy, County Wexford in 1928.

Edmund John Fowler
Victoria Cross recipient 1861 – 1926

Edmund John Fowler served as a private in the 2nd Battalion of the Cameroonians, British Army during the Zulu War. At Zlobane Mountain, South Africa Fowler, together with a captain and a lieutenant, was ordered to dislodge a considerable number of enemy forces that had positioned in the caves above. The path the men had to progress along was so narrow that they could only advance in single file. Though the captain was shot and killed, Fowler and the lieutenant continued on and successfully removed the opposition from their stronghold. For this feat he was awarded the Victoria Cross.

Dan Fraher
Irish language and GAA promoter
1852 – 1929

Dan Fraher was born near Touraneena and took up a position as a draper's assistance in Dungarvan in 1868. An Irish language enthusiast with republican ideals, he had an immense interest in the Gaelic Athletic Association and became an active organiser and administrator of the sport. Fraher was a distinguished referee and he was also chairman of the Waterford County Board and a member of the Munster Council. In 1885, he leased a portion of land from Captain Richard Curran at Shandon, County Waterford, and on it he developed a sports ground that became known as Shandon Park and later as Fraher Field, in memory of its founder. With the exception of Croke Park, Fraher Field has been the venue of more all-Ireland senior hurling finals than any other in the country, hosting the 1903, 1905, 1907 and 1911 finals. Fraher died in 1929 and is buried at Knockboy.

Frank Gillespie
Ireland's greatest alto-sax player
1929 – 1967

Frank Gillespie was born in John Street, Waterford City and was educated at the Manor School and at Mount Sion. A musical prodigy, he was the first boy soprano to broadcast

391

with Radio Éireann and as a twelve-year-old, he toured with Jack Doyle and Movita, playing a 124 base-accordion, which he played on rollers due to his diminutive size. At seventeen Gillespie joined the Number One Band of the Royal Air Force, later gaining a degree in music. Upon leaving the RAF at the age of twenty, he was appointed lead alto with the Ken McIntosh orchestra and went on to appear with such well-known bands as Ted Heath and Joe Loss. He was the only instrumentalist ever named by Joe Loss on his records, with the record 'Zambezi', on which he is principally featured, entering the British charts in the late 1950s. In 1960 Gillespie was rated by *Melody Maker* as being in the top thirteen best alto-saxophone players in the world, and he was also rated number two in Europe to Johnny Dankworth. His sisters, Vera and Angela were the Gillespie Sisters, with Vera writing the Waterford anthem, 'Waterford My Home'. Gillespie died in London, England in 1967.

William Hobson
Naval officer and first governor of New Zealand 1792 – 1842

William Hobson joined the British naval service at an early age, going on to serve in the Napoleonic wars. Rising through the ranks, he reached the position of commander by the early 1820s and his distinguished service earned him the command of the frigate *Rattlesnake*, which sailed for the East Indies in 1835, and onward to Australia and New Zealand. In New Zealand, Hobson's leadership qualities and knowledge of the area obtained him an appointment as governor of that country, and he was highly influential in the Māori people ceding their lands to Queen Victoria in the Treaty of Waitangi. Although he influenced the native New Zealanders to hand over their homeland to the British Empire, Hobson was revered by

them and was recognised for his fair and just rule. He died on 10 September 1842 and is buried at Symonds Street Cemetery in Auckland, New Zealand.

John Hogan
Sculptor 1800 – 1858

A native of Tallow, near the border between Counties Waterford and Cork, John Hogan initially set out as a lawyer's clerk, before becoming an apprentice to architect Sir Thomas Deane, who helped develop his talents for drawing and carving. Hogan later studied in Rome, at the School of St Luke and the Galleries of the Vatican, and his best-known works are three versions of *The Statue of the Dead Christ*. Created in Carrara marble, he produced the first statue in 1829 and it is located in St Thérèse's Church in Dublin. The second one, which he created in 1833, is in St Finbarr's, Cork, and the third version (1854) is in the Basilica of St John the Baptist, Newfoundland, Canada. Considered to be Ireland's greatest sculptor, Hogan's international reputation was assured with his creation of *The Dead Christ*.

Rosamund Jacob
Feminist, nationalist and writer 1888 – 1960

Born into a Quaker family, Rosamund Jacob was educated at Newtown School in Waterford City. One of the early members of Sinn Féin, she was against the Anglo-Irish treaty and was also a militant suffragette. From 1920 Jacob lived in Dublin where she was the lover of the IRA chief of staff, Frank Ryan and amongst her writings are *The Rise of the United Irishmen* and *The Rebel's Wife*, which was based on the life of Henry Joy McCracken's (see page 37) wife. In the promotion of her feminist commitment, Jacob was a member of such organisations as the Women's League for Peace and Freedom, the Women's Social and

Progressive League and the Irish Housewife's Association. Other historical novels she wrote were *Callaghan* (1921), *The Troubled House* (1928) and children's story, *The Raven's Glen* (1960). She died in Dublin in 1960.

Dorothy Jordan
Actress and mistress of King William IV of England
1761 – 1816

Dorothy Jordan, née Bland, first appeared as an actress in Dublin in 1777. Having mothered an illegitimate child by her manager, Richard Daly, she apparently changed her name to Jordan in an attempt to salvage respectability. Appearing at Drury Lane in 1785, Jordan was a witty, intelligent and attractive woman who became the mistress of the Duke of Clarence in the late 1780s. She bore him at least ten illegitimate children, all of whom took the surname 'Fitzclarence', but when the duke became King William IV, he decided to 'tidy' his extra marital affairs and sent her a note, advising her that he was reducing her annuity of one thousand pounds down to five hundred pounds. In response to the king's note Jordan allegedly returned the stub of a theatre ticket, which stated 'no money refunded once the curtain has been raised.' She died on 3 July 1816 and is buried at St Cloud, France.

Daniel J. Kiely
Papal army commander 1829 – 1867

In March 1860, Daniel J. Kiely answered the call of Pope Pius IX for young men of Ireland to help preserve the sovereignty of the Papal States. In response, Kiely, together with Myles Keogh (see page 57), John Joseph Coppinger (see page 90) and some 1,400 other Irish men, formed the Battalion of St Patrick and in that battalion, Kiely served as a commander and brevet brigadier general. However, the army was defeated in the Battle of Castelfidardo on 29 September 1860 and following a brief incarceration in Genoa, Italy, Kiely, Keogh and forty-five other Irish comrades were appointed to the Papal Guard. Later learning that the US Secretary of State, William H. Seward, was seeking experienced European officers to serve the Union cause in the American Civil War, the men resigned their commissions in the Battalion of St Patrick in March 1862. The following month Kiely was appointed a captain in the Union Army but was severely wounded at the Battle of Port Republic. He never fully recovered, and died of Yellow Fever in Louisiana five years later.

Patrick Mahoney
Victoria Cross recipient 1827 – 1857

Patrick Mahoney was a sergeant in the 1st Madras Fusiliers of the Indian Army during the Indian Rebellion of 1857. On 21 September of that year at Mungulwar, India, he, together with a company of volunteers, successfully captured the regimental colours of the First Regiment Native Infantry. For this deed he was awarded the Victoria Cross. He was killed in action at Lucknow.

Thomas Francis Meagher
Revolutionary and brigadier-general 1823 – 1867

Thomas Francis Meagher was born at 19 The Mall, Waterford City and was educated at Clongowes Wood College, County Kildare and at Stoneyhurst College, England. A founder member of the Young Ireland Group, it was a fiery speech by him supporting armed insurrection as the only means of obtaining Irish independence that earned him the title 'Meagher of the Sword'. Together with William Smith O'Brien (see page 80) he produced the design for the new Irish flag, which he based on the French equivalent following an investigative trip to that country. Commenting on the flag, Meagher stated, 'the white in the centre signifies a lasting truce between the orange and the green, and I trust that beneath its folds, the hands of the Irish Protestant and the Irish Catholic may be clasped in generous and heroic brotherhood.' Following the Young Ireland Rebellion of 1848, Meagher was captured and sentenced to death by hanging. However, this sentence was commuted to transportation to Van Dieman's Land (now Tasmania) in 1849. Having escaped in 1852, Meagher arrived in New York and he took part in the the American Civil War, where he became a brigadier-general noted for his bravery, and his leading of the Union Army's famous 69th Regiment. Following the Civil War, he was appointed acting governor for the territory of Montana but he tragically drowned in the Missouri river in the summer of 1867. A statue to his memory stands in front of government buildings in Helena, Montana, and also in the centre of his native city of Waterford.

David Patrick Moran
Journalist 1869 – 1936

Having worked for a time as a journalist in London, David Patrick Moran returned to Ireland to promote cultural and economic nationalism. He founded the *Leader* newspaper in 1900 and was renowned for his powerful vocabulary of disparagement, introducing such terms as 'shoneen', 'west-brit', and even going so far as to describe Protestant unionists as 'sour faces'. Moran highlighted the anti-Catholic discrimination by Protestant employers and advocated cultural nationalism based on Catholic and Gaelic values. Although the *Leader* declined in later years,

Moran continued to publish essays, such as 'The Philosophy of Irish Ireland', and a novel entitled *Tom O'Kelly*. He died in County Dublin in 1936.

Richard Mulcahy
Army general and politician
1886 – 1971

Having initially joined the postal service, Richard Mulcahy worked in Thurles, Bantry and finally Dublin, where he joined the Irish Volunteers upon its formation in 1913. During the Easter Rising he was second in command to Thomas Ashe at Ashbourne, County Meath, but was arrested and interned at Frongoch, Wales. Released in the amnesty of 1917, Mulcahy returned to the Irish Republican Army and was appointed chief of staff. He was subsequently elected as a Sinn Féin member of parliament for Clontarf in 1918.

A staunch supporter of Michael Collins (see page 89) as well as the Anglo-Irish Treaty of 1921, he was appointed the commanding officer of military forces of the provisional government during the Civil War. Following that conflict, he held a number of ministerial positions. In 1944 Mulcahy became leader of the Fine Gael party and served as minister for education in the first coalition government from 1948 until 1951. He resigned the leadership of Fine Gael in 1959, left politics the following year and died in Dublin on 16 December 1971.

Richard Thomas O'Brien (Richard Garrick)
Film director and actor
1878 – 1962

Born in the village of Portlaw, Richard Thomas O'Brien emigrated to the United States with his family in 1882. He enlisted in the United States Army and following three years of service, he pursued an acting career in New York. Working under the stage name of 'Richard Garrick', he later moved to Los Angeles, California where he entered into the film industry, working in silent movies both as a director and an actor. In 1916 O'Brien was appointed director general of Gaumont's Florida Studios, but he later left the position in order to establish his own venture in Jacksonville, Florida. When that enterprise failed due to the lack of interest in film-making in the area, O'Brien spent some years directing films in France and the United Kingdom, before returning to the United States where in 1947, he appeared in the stage show *A Street Car Named Desire* alongside Marlon Brando. He also played a role in the film version of the show in 1951. Throughout his illustrious career, O'Brien performed with some of the industry's biggest names, including Charles Laughton, Vivien Leigh, Victor Mature, Marilyn Monroe and Richard Widmark to name but a few. His credits include *A Street Car Named Desire* (1951), *Desirée* (1954), *East of Eden* (1955) and *High Society* (1956). He died in Los Angeles on 21 August 1962 and is buried as a United States veteran at Fort Rosecrans National Cemetery, San Diego, California.

John Palliser
Geographer and explorer
1817 – 1887
From 1839 until 1863, John Palliser served in the Waterford Militia. Also sheriff of Waterford, whilst on a hunting expedition to North America in 1847 he wrote *Solitary Rambles and Adventures of a Hunter in the Prairies,* which was first published in 1853. Palliser returned to North America in 1857, embarking on an expedition financed by the British Colonial Office and the Royal Geographical Society, during which he made a topographical delimitation of the boundary between Canada and the United States from Lake Superior to the Pacific Ocean. Warning that an area of Canada in South Eastern Alberta and South Western Saskatchewan was too arid for farming, today this area is known as 'Palliser's Triangle'. He was awarded the Royal Geographical Society Victoria Gold Medal and was also made a fellow of the society. Palliser died at his home at Comeragh House on 12 August 1887.

William Palliser
Politician and inventor
1830 – 1882
Brother of explorer John Palliser (see above), William Palliser was educated at Trinity College, Dublin and at the Cambridge University in England. He patented some fourteen ordnance-related inventions, one of which was the development of small bores into rifled guns, and his expertise in field led to him receiving a knighthood from Queen Victoria in 1873. Palliser was also a member of parliament, representing Taunton, Somerset from 1880 until his death in London in 1882. He is buried in Brompton Cemetery, London.

Hal Roach
Comedian 1927 – 2012
Hal Roach is best remembered for his world record twenty-six year run as resident comedian at Dublin's Jurys Hotel. With his catchphrase 'Write it down, it's a good one', Roach was renowned for his wholesome humour, as highlighted by *USA Today*, which observed that his act comprised 'nearly two

hours of humour and not one off-colour joke'. Educated at the Manor School, Waterford, as a talented eleven-year-old soprano, Roach won a talent show which resulted in a trip to New Zealand and he later gained the name Hal – his real name was John – for his likeness to a character in the *Our Gang* movie series. A devout family man, he had four children, one of whom, John, was born with Down Syndrome. Inspired by his son, Roach gave much of his time and money to establishing the Hal Roach School for Exceptional Children.

John Roberts
Architect and builder 1712 – 1796

The son of a building contractor, as a young man John Roberts spent some time in London, England, returning to Ireland to later become involved in the design and construction of some of the finest buildings in Waterford City. These include the Catholic Cathedral of the Most Holy Trinity (1779), Newtown School (1786) and Waterford City Hall (1788). He was also involved in the construction of the city's Christ Church Cathedral and the Chamber of Commerce building. John Roberts Square in the centre of Waterford is named in his memory.

Thomas Sexton
Politician 1848 – 1932

Thomas Sexton's childhood home was located at the corner of Newgate Street and Mayor's Walk in Waterford City, and he was educated at Mount Sion. Later employed by the Waterford and Limerick Railway Company, following this Sexton moved to Dublin where he took up journalism and joined the staff of the *Nation*, where he was an outspoken advocate of nationalist principles. In the late 1870s he joined the Land League and following representations that he made on that organisation's behalf in County Sligo, he was elected a member of parliament for the Sligo constituency from 1880 until 1885. Following support for the non-payment of rent by Land League members in October 1881 Sexton was imprisoned, along with Charles Stewart Parnell (see page 423) in Kilmainham Jail, but was later released due to ill health. A brilliant public speaker, he gained the nickname 'Silver-Tongued Sexton', and later used these skills when serving as Lord Mayor of Dublin in 1888 and representing North Kerry from 1892 until 1896. Sexton left politics soon after the Parnellite split and took charge of the *Freeman's Journal* until 1912. He died in Dublin on 1 November 1932 and Sexton Street, Waterford City is named in his memory.

William Vincent Wallace
Composer 1812 – 1865

William Vincent Wallace was born in Colbeck Street, Waterford City. Displaying remarkable musical talent from an early age, with tuition from his bandmaster father, Wallace went on to study with noted Waterford tutor Otto Hamilton, as well as John Ringwood, who was the organist at the Waterford Cathedral. At the age of twelve he was a clarinettist in his father's band and having married in the early 1830s, he converted to Catholicism and added 'Vincent' to his name in honour of his new sister-in-law, a nun in Thurles, County Tipperary. In 1835 Wallace emigrated to Australia, following which he travelled to many locations around the world, at one stage becoming a director of music at the Italian Theatre in Mexico. Following his excursions, Wallace returned to Europe and eventually to England where he immersed himself in the composition of music for operas, eventually composing his famed opera *Maritana* in 1845. He died in 1865 and is buried in Kensal Green Cemetery, London, England.

Ernest T.S. Walton
Nobel prize-winning physicist and first man to split the atom
1903 – 1995

Ernest T.S. Walton was born in Abbeyside, Dungarvan and in 1922 entered Trinity College, Dublin on a scholarship. There he studied mathematics and experimental science, specialising in physics and having graduated with first class honours in 1926, he was awarded a research scholarship the following year, going to the University of Cambridge to work in the Cavendish Laboratory under scientific leader Lord Ernest Rutherford. Whilst there, Walton worked on experiments with his colleague John Cockcroft in a partnership that led to the development of the theory of wave equation and a new era of accelerated-based experimental nuclear physics. Walton, who along with Cockcroft had split the nucleus of the atom by artificial means, returned to Ireland in 1934. He became a fellow of his Dublin alma mater and was appointed Erasmus Smith's professor of natural and experimental philosophy in 1946. On 16 November 1951, Walton and Cockcroft were awarded the Nobel Prize for their work on splitting the atom.

Thomas Wyse
Educator and diplomat
1791 – 1862

Thomas Wyse was born at St John's in Waterford and was educated at the Jesuit College in Stoneyhurst, Lancashire, and Trinity College, Dublin. On a tour of Europe, he met and married Laetitia Bonaparte, niece of Napoleon, and although they had two sons together, the pair parted in 1828. Wyse returned to Ireland, where he vigorously fought for Catholic emancipation and his progress proved the catalyst for Daniel O'Connell (see page 232) to successfully contest the County Clare by-election in 1828, becoming the first Irish Catholic to be elected to parliament since the late-seventeenth century. Wyse himself was elected a member of parliament for Tipperary in 1829 and also served for Waterford City from 1835 until 1847. Later appointed ambassador to Greece by Lord Palmerston, he made great efforts to secure Greek neutrality during the Crimean War (1854 – 1856) and these actions secured him a knighthood in 1856. A progressive politician, many reforms were introduced in the education system as a result of his advocacy. Wyse died in Athens on 16 April 1862 and was afforded a state funeral by the king and queen of Greece.

Thomas 'Bullocks' Wyse
Businessman and prankster
1701 – 1770

Thomas Wyse was born at the Manor of St John, outside Waterford, and as a child, lived in Newtown House, now Newtown School, which was built by architect John Roberts (see page 396). His family lost its land to the Cromwellians but regained them again after the restoration of the monarchy in 1660. Wyse gained the nickname 'Bullocks' due to a penal law which forbade any Catholic from owning a horse worth more than five pounds, and if a Protestant offered a Catholic that sum for a horse, the Catholic was obliged to sell. In response to this law, 'Bullocks' harnessed a team of bullocks to draw his carriage through the streets of Waterford City. Despite his many escapades, Wyse was a forward-thinking businessman who established a copper smelter near the city in 1747. He was also involved in copper mining and established a hardware factory in Waterford, where he strove for the repeal of the penal laws. Wyse, who died in 1770, was the grandfather of the famous Sir Thomas Wyse (see above).

Westmeath

Thomas Power O'Connor
1848-1929

The bust of journalist and Irish nationalist MP. Thomas Power O'Connor in Fleet Street, London The inscription reads: 'His pen could lay bare the bones of a book or the soul of a statesman in a few vivid lines.'

George Wade
1673-1748

Field Marshal George Wade cemented the union in Scotland by founding the Union Watches to control the Scottish. The regiment later became known as the Black Watch. Wade is mentioned in the last verse of the British national anthem.

John McCormack
1884-1945

A Papal Count, John McCormack was one of the finest tenors of the twentieth century and was knighted for his performance at the Eucharistic Congress in 1932. The congressional seal was based on the Cross of Cong.

John Fitzpatrick
1871-1946

A great friend of Ireland, the Chicago labour leader John Fitzpatrick, who fought for the rights of Slavic immigrants, black workers and the rights of women, secured an eight-hour working day for Chicago steel workers.

John Keegan Casey
Poet 1846 – 1870

Born in the midst of the famine of 1846, in his teen years John Keegan Casey wrote 'The Rising of the Moon', a popular song commemorating the 1798 Rebellion. In the early 1860s he moved to Dublin where he became active in the Fenian Movement and in 1866, he produced a collection of poems entitled *A Wreath of Shamrocks*. Following the Fenian Rising of 1867, Casey was imprisoned without trial in Mountjoy jail and died some three years later as a result of the brutal treatment he received there. The prison doctor, Robert McDonnell, reported on his injuries, and the government was forced to hold a commission of enquiry. He died on St Patrick's Day 1870 and is buried in Glasnevin Cemetery. The newspapers of the time reported that between fifty and one hundred thousand mourners attended his funeral.

George Arthur Boyd-Rochfort
Victoria Cross recipient 1880 – 1940

George Arthur Boyd-Rochfort served as a 2nd Lieutenant in the Scots Guards of the British Army during World War I. Near La Bassee, France on 3 August 1915, a German mortar landed on top of Rochfort's communications trench, but instead of moving to safety he shouted to his men to take cover before picking up the bomb and hurling it away where it exploded immediately. Having saved the lives of his comrades, Rochfort later became a captain and he died in Dublin in 1940.

John L. Broderick
Writer 1924 – 1989

John L. Broderick was born in Athlone and was educated at Summerhill College, County Sligo and Garbally College in Ballinasloe. A distinguished author and critic, his works offer a bleak portrait of embittered lives in the midlands, with his first novel, *The Pilgrimage* (1961) exploring the themes of marital infidelity and religious devotion, eventually being banned by the Irish Censorship Board. Other publications by Broderick include: *The Fugitives* (1962), *The Waking of Willie Ryan* (1965), *An Apology for Roses* (1973), *The Pride of Summer* (1976), *London Irish* (1979), *The Trial of Father Dillingham* (1982) and *The Irish Magdalen* (1991). He died in Bath, England in 1989 and his memory is commemorated by a street being named after him in his native Athlone.

Eugene Casserly
Lawyer and Californian senator 1822 – 1883

Politician Eugene Casserly was born in Mullingar and while still a child, he emigrated to the United States with his parents. As his father was a teacher, Casserly received an excellent education and went on to study in Georgetown College in Washington, later entering a law office in New York. Admitted to the bar in 1844, he practiced as a corporation attorney before moving to San Francisco, California where he set up a substantial legal practice and took an active part in both local and national politics. Joining the Democratic Party, in 1869 Casserly was elected a United States senator for California but was forced to retire from duty in 1873 due to ill health. He later resurrected his legal practice, which he worked in until his death on 14 June 1883.

James Daly
Connaught Rangers mutineer
1899 – 1920

Born in Tyrrellspass, James Daly was the last soldier in the British Army to be executed for the crime of mutiny. A private in the Connaught Rangers serving in India, when news from home told of the atrocities being committed by British soldiers and the Black and Tans, Daly led a mutiny of seventy men in protest against events in Ireland. However, the mutiny was suppressed and twenty-one-year-old Daly was tried by court-martial, found guilty and shot by firing squad in Dagshai Prison, India on 2 November 1920 (Incidentally, the sentencing judge was Major General Sydney Lawford, father of actor and Rat Pack member, Peter Lawford). In 1970 Daly's remains were returned to Ireland where he was given a full military funeral.

Maurice Dease
Victoria Cross recipient 1889 – 1914

Maurice Dease was born in Gaulstown and was educated in England at Stoneyhurst College and the Royal Military College at Sandhurst. A lieutanant in the Royal Fusiliers during World War I, whilst defending Nimy Bridge at Mons, Belgium on 21 August 1914, Dease continued to fire his machine gun in a valiant effort to protect the retreat of his comrades. When his injuries became too severe to continue, he had to be carried away and he eventually died of his wounds aged twenty-four. An only son, the lineage of the Dease family, which had survived for three centuries in County Westmeath, also died that day. A cenotaph to his memory stands in the grounds of the Parish Church in Coole.

Joe Dolan
Singer and entertainer 1939 – 2007

The much-loved Joe Dolan was born in Mullingar and initially worked as a compositor with the *Westmeath Examiner*. He and his brother joined the Drifters in the early 1960s, signalling the start a phenomenal entertainment career that spanned over forty years. Dolan's first big hit was 'Make Me An Island', which was number one in fourteen countries, as well as reaching number three in the UK singles chart in 1969, as well as reaching number three in the UK singles chart in 1969. Dolan later travelled the world, appearing in Las Vegas, Nevada on a number of occasions, and also became the first western pop singer to perform in the Soviet Union in 1978. 1997's 'Good Looking Woman' was another chart-topper for Dolan, who sadly died of a brain hemorrhage on 26 December 2007.

Thomas Duffy
Victoria Cross recipient 1806 – 1868

Athlone native Thomas Duffy served as a private in the 1st Madras Fusiliers (later the Royal Dublin Fusiliers) at Lucknow, India. There, on 26 September 1857, a twenty-four pounder gun had been left in an exposed position from action the previous day. With all efforts to retrieve it unsuccessful, Duffy, under heavy enemy fire, successfully fastened a rope to the weapon so that it could be pulled back to his own lines. For this deed he was awarded the Victoria Cross. He died in Dublin on 23 December 1858.

401

Kenneth Edgeworth
Astronomer, economist and engineer
1880 – 1972

At the age of fourteen, Kenneth Edgeworth won a scholarship to Marlborough College in Wiltshire, England, following which he attended the Royal Military Academy at Woolwich. During World War I Edgeworth served as an officer in the Royal Engineers, where he was awarded the Distinguished Service Order and a Military Cross and was mentioned in dispatches three times. He was later promoted to the rank of lieutenant colonel before retiring from active service in 1926. He returned to Ireland to study international economics, publishing four books on the depression of the 1920s. Through his uncle, Edgeworth became interested in astronomy and in that field he is best known for proposing the existence of a disc of icy bodies beyond the orbit of Neptune. He died on 10 October 1972 and the asteroid '3487 Edgeworth' is named in his honour.

John Fitzpatrick
Chicago Labour leader 1871 – 1946

Born in Athlone, John Fitzpatrick was orphaned at the age of ten, before being taken to Chicago, Illinois to live with an uncle. Later serving as an apprentice to a horseshoe-trader, he became a member of the Horseshoers Union and rose rapidly through its ranks to be elected president of the Chicago Federation of Labour. With the exception of one intervening year, Fitzpatrick led that organisation from 1899 until his death in 1946, becoming a revered figure in the trade union movement. Together with union official William Foster, he secured an eight-hour working day and higher wages for the Chicago area meat packers, and he later fought on behalf of the steel workers, successfully negotiating similar conditions for them in 1918. Fitzpatrick, who was renowned for his work on behalf of Slavic immigrants, black workers, and the rights of women in the workforce, never forgot the land of his birth and he ensured that the Chicago Federation of Labor's publications always carried news of developments in Ireland, as well as criticism of the British government. He also gave aid to Éamon de Valera (see page 431) when the Irish president visited the United States in order to seek support for the Irish War of Independence in 1919. A friend of Irish labour leader James Larkin, Fitzpatrick died in Chicago in 1946.

Thomas Flinn
Youngest-ever recipient of the Victoria Cross 1842 – 1892

At fifteen years of age, Thomas Flinn served as a drummer boy in the 64th Regiment of the British Army during the Indian Rebellion in 1857. Whilst taking part in a charge on enemy guns on 28 November 1857, Flinn was severely wounded, yet he still engaged in hand-to-hand fighting with two of the rebel artillerymen. Having secured the enemy guns along with his comrades, he was awarded the Victoria Cross, thus becoming the youngest recipient of the prestigious award. He died in Athlone on 10 August 1892.

Josephine Hart
Author 1942 – 2011

Josephine Hart was born in Mullingar and educated at the Convent School in Carrickmacross, County Monaghan where she developed her love of poetry. In 1964 she moved to London where she worked in telesales and studied drama at night, before moving to Haymarket Press and becoming the firm's only woman director. A founder of the Gallery Poets and West End Poetry Hour, Hart produced several West End plays and her first novel, *Damage*, which was later made into a film, sold over one million copies and was translated into over 30 languages. Her death, from a rare form of ovarian cancer, reflected the characteristics of her novels in being dramatic and shocking; she concealed her sickness from her friends to her very last days.

Richard Henry Jackson
Union army general In the American Civil War 1830 – 1892
In 1851, Kinnegad native Richard Henry Jackson emigrated to the United States, where he enlisted as a private in the United States Army. Following service in Florida, he was commissioned a second lieutenant, later becoming a first lieutenant in the 4th US Artillery, before once again being promoted, this time to lieutenant colonel at the Siege of Charleston. Jackson also fought at the Battle of Petersburg and by November 1865, he had reached the rank of major general. Following the war he continued his service in the army and he died on 28 November 1892. He is buried in the United States Military Academy Post Cemetery at Westpoint, Orange County, New York.

Patrick Henry Jones
Union army brigadier general In the American Civil War 1830 – 1900
Having moved with his family to New York, Patrick Henry Jones studied law in Ellicottville and was later called to the bar. Upon the outbreak of the American Civil War, he enlisted in the 37th New York Volunteers Infantry Regiment, known as the Irish Rifles, and was commissioned second lieutenant on 7 July 1861. At the First Battle of Bull Run he was promoted to first lieutenant, and then to major on 21 January 1862. He took part in the battles of Williamsburg and Seven Pines and in October 1862 was promoted to colonel before being captured when he fell wounded at Chancellorsville. Released in October 1863, in June of the following year, Jones secured the command of a brigade and took part in the Atlanta campaign in support of General Sherman. Later promoted to brigadier general, following the war, President Ulysses S. Grant appointed Jones postmaster of New York City. He later returned to the legal profession and remained a lawyer until his death in 1900.

Thomas Henry Kavanagh
Civilian Victoria Cross recipient 1821 – 1882
A native of Mullingar, Thomas Henry Kavanagh was a civilian in the Bengal Civil Service when on 9 November 1857, he volunteered to go through Lucknow, India in disguise in order to guide a relieving force of troops back to their beleaguered garrison. Performing this daring deed against overwhelming odds, Kavanagh succeeded in relieving the garrison. He is one of only five civilians ever to be awarded the Victoria Cross.

Brinsley MacNamara (John Weldon)
Writer 1890 – 1963
Brinsley MacNamara was born John Weldon, near Delvin, and joined the Abbey Theatre Company in 1909. As

a writer, one of his primary works was *The Valley of the Squinting Windows*, which caused great controversy upon its publication in 1918. having succeeded James Stephens (see page 192) as registrar of the National Gallery of Ireland in 1924, MacNamara wrote a second novel, *The Various Lives of Marcus Igoe* (1929) – an autobiographical examination of his life, written in the form of a dream. He also published a number of short stories, as well as many plays for the Abbey Theatre, of which he was a director for some years. His best known comedies include *The Glorious Uncertainty* and *Look at the Heffernans*. MacNamara died in Dublin in February 1963.

John McCormack
Opera and popular music singer
1884 – 1945

Tenor John McCormack was born in Athlone and was educated by the Marist Brothers and at Summerhill College, County Sligo. Considered one of the finest tenors of the twentieth century, he made his London operatic debut at Covent Garden in 1907 and toured extensively throughout the world, achieving peak popularity in the United States. During his operatic recitals McCormack invariably included some traditional Irish folk songs, which were always well received by his audiences. Having been made a count in the Papal peerage in 1928, one of the highlights of McCormack's career came four years later when he had the opportunity to sing 'Panis Angelicus' during the Eucharistic Congress in Dublin's Phoenix Park.

Thomas Power O'Connor
Journalist, nationalist and politician 1848 – 1929

Thomas Power O'Connor was educated at the College of the Immaculate Conception and at Queen's College, Galway (now University College Galway), where he studied history and modern languages and built a reputation as a powerful orator. Having entered journalism in Dublin, O'Connor later moved to London, where he was appointed a subeditor of the *Daily Telegraph* newspaper. He later became the London correspondent for the *New York Herald* and in 1880 was elected a member of parliament for Galway, representing Charles Stewart Parnell's (see page 423) Home Rule League.

From 1885 until his death in 1929, O'Connor represented the Liverpool Scotland constituency in the House of Commons. With its significant Irish population, Liverpool was the only constituency outside of Ireland that elected an Irish Nationalist Party MP. However, having provided unbroken service lasting forty-four years, O'Connor was forced to sit as an independent when the party ceased to exist following the Sinn Féin landslide elections of 1918. A founder and first editor of several newspapers and journals, such as the *Star* (1887), the *Weekly Sun* (1891) and the *Sun* (1893), O'Connor also published a number of books including *Lord Beaconsfield – A Biography* (1879) and *The Parnell Movement* (1886). A bust to his memory stands in London's Fleet Street, the inscription on it reading 'His pen could lay bare the bones of a book, or the soul of a statesman in a few vivid lines.' He died in London on 18 November 1929.

Sir Edward Pakenham
British army general 1778 – 1815

Edward Pakenham was born at Pakenham Hall, now known as Tullynally Castle. Educated at the Royal School, County Armagh, he secured a purchased commission as a lieutenant in the 92nd Foot Regiment of the British Army, at the age of sixteen and also served with the 23rd Light Dragoons against the French in Ireland. Having distinguished himself in the Peninsula War at the Battle of Salamanca in which he commanded the Third Division, Pakenham was the commanding general of British forces in the Battle of New Orleans, the last battle in the American War of Independence, fought on 8 January 1815. Pakenham, whose sister Catherine was married to the Duke of Wellington, was killed during the action. There is a statue of him in St Paul's Cathedral in London.

Thomas O'Neill Russell
Author 1828 – 1908

Born in the market town of Moate, writer Thomas O'Neill Russell was educated locally, following which he took up work as a commercial traveller for Jacobs Biscuits. A native Irish speaker, Russell made the revival of the Irish language his principle aim in life, but due to his association with Irish nationalists, he was fearful of arrest and subsequently emigrated to the United States where he spent the next thirty years as a commercial traveller while lecturing and writing about the Irish language. Upon his return to Dublin in 1895, he continued his work in reviving the Irish language, publishing a number of poems and essays. He also wrote a novel, *Dick Massey,* and was a co-founder of the Gaelic League in 1893. Russell died in Dublin on 15 June 1908.

George Wade
British army field-marshal
1673 – 1748

George Wade was born in Kilavally and joined the British army in 1690, serving in Flanders in 1692. A decade later he became a lieutenant colonel, rising through the ranks to become major general following the Battle of Saragossa in 1710. He was sent to Scotland by George I in 1724, following which, Wade recommended that roads, barracks, and bridges needed to be constructed to assist in the control of the region, and he later directed the construction of some two hundred and fifty miles of infrastructure, linking various garrisons in Scotland. He also organised a militia named 'Highland Watches' and this eventually led to the development of the present regiment in the British army known as the Black Watch. In 1742 Wade was promoted to the rank of lieutenant general, becoming a privy councillor, and the following year he was appointed a field marshal, seeing service in command of the Anglo-Austrian forces who opposed the French in the War of the Austrian Succession. In the British national anthem, 'God Save the King/Queen' he is mentioned in a verse that today, is no longer included. It goes as follows;

> *Lord grant that Marshal Wade*
> *May buy thy mighty aid,*
> *Victory bring.*
> *May he sedition hush*
> *and like a torrent rush,*
> *rebellious Scots to crush,*
> *God Save the King.*

General Sir Mark Walker
Victoria Cross recipient 1827 – 1902

Mark Walker was born in Finea, near Lough Sheelin and served as a lieutenant in the 30th Regiment of Foot of the British Army during the Crimean War. At Inkerman, Crimea on 5 November 1854, with two battalions of Russian infantry approaching, Walker jumped over a wall to face the enemy. His example encouraged his men to follow and they successfully drove back the two Russian battalions. For his valour in the face of such odds, he was awarded the Victoria Cross and he later achieved the rank of general. Walker died in Devon, England in 1902.

Wexford

Father John Murphy
1753-1798

Vinegar Hill, which overlooks the town of Enniscorthy, where rebel leader John Murphy was defeated in the 1798 rebellion.

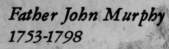

Mary Fitzgerald
1885-1960

Mary Fitzgerald Square in Johannesburg, South Africa is named after the trade unionist Mary Fitzgerald or 'Pickhandle Mary', as she was affectionately known.

Jasper O'Farrell
1817-1875

Market Street, San Francisco was designed by that city's first engineer, Jasper O'Farrell.

The Kennedys

Patrick Kennedy, great-grandfather of John F. Kennedy, left Dunganstown for America in 1848. It was there that the great Kennedy dynasty was established.

Commodore John Barry
1745-1803

The USS *Lexington*, first command of Commodore John Barry, founder of the American navy.

John Barry
'Father of the American navy'
1745 – 1803

John Barry was born in Tacumshane, near Rosslare, where his uncle captained a fishing skiff, and where Barry learned his seafaring skills. Having emigrated to Philadelphia, Pennsylvania, his first command came in 1766, plying between Philadelphia and the West Indies aboard the schooner Barbados.

Upon the outbreak of the war between the colonies and Great Britain, Barry was commissioned as a captain in the continental navy and was awarded command of the war ship *Lexington*, on which he captured the first British naval ship of the war.

His most renowned naval encounter occurred off the coast of Newfoundland, Canada on 28 May 1781 when aboard his ship, the thirty-six-gun frigate *Alliance*, Barry took on, and defeated, two British ships, the *Atlanta* and the *Trespassy*. In his final battle of the revolution, which was to be the last battle of the continental navy, Barry engaged the British frigate *Sybil* and completely destroyed her. Appointed senior captain in the Federal Navy by President George Washington on 5 June 1794, three years later Barry took command of the flagship, USS *United States* and was also promoted to commodore. He died on 12 September 1803 and in his memory, the American Congress later erected a $50,000 monument in Washington DC. A further memorial, in the form of a bronze statue, was erected in Independence Square, Philadelphia, whilst yet another statue stands to his memory in Wexford town.

Robert Brennan
Revolutionary, diplomat and author 1881 – 1964

A surveyor working for a time for Wexford County Council, Robert Brennan later became a journalist for the *Enniscorthy Echo*. Having helped organise volunteers in Wexford during the rising in 1916, Brennan was subsequently sentenced to death for his part in the rebellion. His sentence was later commuted to penal servitude for life and upon his release in 1918, he took part in the underground government until the Anglo-Irish Treaty of 1921 when he took the republican side. Appointed director of the *Irish Press* from 1930 until 1934, following which he joined the Diplomatic service, Brennan served as minister to the United States for almost a decade, before returning to Ireland where he became director of broadcasting for Radio Éireann. His autobiography, *Allegiance* was published in 1950 and he died in Dublin on 12 November 1964.

Robert Browne-Clayton
British army general and constructor
1771 – 1845

Robert Browne-Clayton was a member of a wealthy Anglo-Irish family whose principle seat was at Browne's Hill, near Carlow Town. A landowner at Carrigbyrne, Clayton was responsible for the construction of the Browne-Clayton Column, which is located on the N25 between New Ross and Wexford. Constructed in 1839, the column commemorates a victory by the British over the French in northern Egypt in 1801, but in particular the memory of Sir Ralph Abercrombie, who was Clayton's commanding officer during that campaign. It is twenty-eight metres high and is a replica of what is known as 'Pompey's Pillar', which is located at Alexandria, Egypt. Although three metres lower than the original, it is the only column of its kind with an internal staircase. Clayton's family, originally the Browne's of Carlow, were considered one of the most benevolent landowners during the Great Famine and during the Irish War of Independence, Éamon de Valera (see page 431) issued instructions that their property was to be left intact by the IRA who burned down many Anglo-Irish landowner's houses from 1920 to 1923.

Miles Byrne
1798 Rebellion leader
1780 – 1862

Often considered one of the most extraordinary figures in Irish history, at the age of eighteen Miles Byrne took part in the battles of Vinegar Hill, Enniscorthy and Arklow, as well as the last battle in County Wexford, which occurred in Ballygullen on 4 July 1798. Following the failing of that rising, Byrne led a number of the Wexford rebels to the Wicklow mountains where they waged a guerrilla struggle for Irish freedom over a number of years with Michael Dwyer (see page 419). Also involved in the Robert Emmet rebellion in 1803, he escaped to France and fought in the Napoleonic wars and had a very distinguished career, reaching the rank of lieutenant colonel and leading Napoleon's Irish Brigade. Awarded the Légion d'honneur from King Louis Philippe in 1832, following thirty-two years and some seventeen campaigns in the French army, Byrne retired in 1835. Byrne died at his home in Paris, France on 24 January 1862 and he is buried in Montmartre Cemetery, Paris.

Arthur William Conway
Mathematical physicist
1875 – 1950

Arthur William Conway was born in Main Street, Wexford and was educated at St Peter's College and University College Dublin, before going on to Corpus Christi College in Oxford, for which he won a mathematics scholarship in 1898. Appointed professor of mathematical physics at University College Dublin, where he was later elected president, Conway's research interests lay in electromagnetism, relativity and the quantum theory of elementary particles and he showed how quaternions could be used to study problems in these areas. Conway, who is perhaps best remembered for his editorship of William Rowan Hamilton's papers, died suddenly on 11 July 1950.

Martin Doyle
Victoria Cross recipient 1891 – 1940

A native of New Ross, Martin Doyle served as a company sergeant major in the 1st Battalion, the Royal Munster Fusiliers, 16th (Irish) Division, British Army during World War I. When all the officers of his company had become casualties at Reincourt, France, Doyle single-handedly rescued a party of his men who had been surrounded by the enemy. Carrying a wounded officer back to safety under heavy fire, he later assisted a tank crew, which had been attacked by an enemy machine-gun point. Capturing the machine gun and taking three prisoners, Doyle repelled a subsequent counter-attack, driving the enemy steadily backwards before once again taking prisoners. For these courageous deeds he was awarded the Victoria Cross and having survived the war, he returned to Ireland where he joined the IRA during the War of Independence. Later becoming a company sergeant in the newly formed Irish Army, which he served in until 1937, Doyle later joined Guinness's brewery where he worked as a security officer. He died in 1940 and was posthumously decorated by the Irish government for his contributions to the fight for Irish freedom.

Mary Fitzgerald ('Pickhandle Mary')
South African trade unionist
1885 – 1960

Trade unionist Mary Fitzgerald was prominent in South Africa where she became a typist for the Mine Workers Union. Recognising the terrible conditions under which the miners worked, with one in four dying from phthisis, Fitzgerald dedicated herself to their cause. It was during a strike which she led in 1911 that she earned the title, 'Pickhandle Mary'; when police dropped the pickhandles they were carrying, the strikers took them and carried them to all further protest meetings. As the country's first female trade union organiser, Fitzgerald led the miners in further strikes in 1913 and 1914 and she was also active in the suffragette movement. When women achieved the right to vote, she was the first woman ever elected to Johannesburg City Council and the famous Mary Fitzgerald Square in the centre of Johannesburg was named in her honour in 1939. She died in 1960 and is buried at Brixton Cemetery, Johannesburg.

Harry Furniss
Artist and illustrator 1854 – 1925

Having initially worked as an artist in Ireland, in 1876 Harry Furniss moved to England to work with the *Illustrated London News*, where he gained a reputation as an outstanding draughtsman. In 1884 he became a member of the staff for satirical magazine *Punch* and for the next ten years he illustrated the 'Essence of Parliament'. Renowned for drawing British prime minister William Gladstone with a large collar, even though he never wore such, Furniss was a staunch unionist and was especially harsh on Irish nationalists, often drawing crude caricatures of them. In 1894 he left *Punch* to start his own magazine, *Like Joka*, but it proved unsuccessful and he later moved to the United States where he worked in the film industry with Thomas Edison, helping to pioneer animated cartoon films. Furniss died in 1925.

John Harrison
Victoria Cross recipient 1832 – 1865

John Harrison was born in Castleborough and served as a leading seaman in the Royal Navy during the Indian Rebellion of 1857. At Lucknow, India, together with a lieutenant and a fellow seaman, Harrison volunteered to climb a tree near the wall of the Shah Nujeff Mosque in an effort to spot enemy positions and dislodge mutineers. However, with the lieutenant badly wounded and his fellow seaman killed, Harrison bravely dislodged the mutineers and was thus awarded the Victoria Cross. He died in London, England in 1865.

Bagenal Harvey
United Irishman 1762 – 1798

Bagenal Harvey was born at Bargy Castle and was educated at Trinity College, Dublin. Called to the bar in 1782, he joined the United Irishmen in 1793 and when the 1798 rising broke out in Wexford, he reluctantly accepted the position of commander-in-chief of the insurgents who were defeated in the bloody Battle of the Insurrection on 5 June. He later took refuge in a cave on the Great Saltee Island but was discovered, arrested, and court-martialed before being hanged on Wexford Bridge on 26 June 1798.

County Wexford.

Thomas Joseph Hutchinson
Physician, diplomat and writer
c. 1802 – 1885

Thomas Joseph Hutchinson was born in Stonyford and was educated at the University of Gottingen and Trinity College, Dublin. Qualifying in medicine, for a time he practiced as a surgeon at St Vincent's Hospital, Dublin and he later spent a number of years in Africa. In 1861 Hutchinson was appointed as British consul in Rosario, Argentina and during the cholera epidemic there in 1867, he and his wife established a sanatorium in their house, giving great assistance to the poor, administering free medicines and clothing. For his services, the Union Masonic Lodge of Rosario awarded a gold medal to Hutchinson, who also acted as consul for Uruguay before later being appointed consul at Callao, Peru. He recorded his experiences and investigative work in connection with the indigenous peoples of South America in *Two Years in Peru with Exploration of its Antiquities* (1873), and he retired in 1874, returning to live in Ballinescar Lodge, Curracloe, County Wexford. He later moved to Florence, Italy where he died on 23 March 1885.

William Keneally
Victoria Cross recipient 1886 – 1915

William Keneally was a British Army private in the 1st Battalion of the Lancashire Fusiliers during World War I. At Gallipoli, Turkey on 25 April 1915, he and six of his comrades, under heavy fire from hidden machine guns, cleared a beach landing for his battalion. For their actions, Keneally and his comrades were each awarded the Victoria Cross and General Sir Ian Hamilton, who was overall commander at Gallipoli, declared that 'no finer feat of bravery has ever been achieved by British soldiers.'

Patrick Kennedy
Great-grandfather of President John F. Kennedy 1823 – 1858

A member of a family steeped in Irish history, Patrick Kennedy had several uncles who had fought as pikemen in the failed rebellion of 1798. Upon the arrival of the potato famine, Kennedy was forced to emigrate from Dunganstown to the United States, but prior to his departure, he fell in love with Bridget Murphy, a cousin of his friend Patrick Barron. Undertaking the long journey across the Atlantic without her in October 1848, he arrived in Boston, Massachusetts, where Barron secured him a brewery job on Noddle's Island. Kennedy later met with his fiancée and they were married in Boston on 26 September 1849. He died of cholera in East Boston on 26 November 1858, but his wife, who was a resourceful woman, established a successful grocery and liquor store which helped pave the way for the success of their son P.J. Kennedy, who went on to establish a number of successful bars and a whiskey importing business. He became one of Boston's most successful businessmen and his only son, Joseph Patrick (Joe) Kennedy, further advanced the family business, whilst also leading a successful political career. He in turn would pass his talent onto his sons Robert, Ted and John F. Kennedy and so, from the humble beginnings in nineteenth-century Wexford, the legacy of the Kennedy family was established.

William Lamport
'The Irish Zorro'
1615 – 1659

A colourful character, William Lamport was born into a wealthy noble Catholic family and was educated by the Jesuits priests in both Dublin and London.

Reputed to have been a first-class swordsman with a deep attraction to women, both married and single, it was one of these dalliances that led to a scandal that forced Lamport to flee to Mexico, where he developed empathy for the poor slaves in that country. Living amongst them, he advocated their liberation before later becoming the leader of the fledgling Mexican independence movement. For his activities, Lamport was sentenced to ten years in prison but escaped and established a rebellion amongst the slaves who disseminated the legend of El Zorro ('night-time fox'). However, having later been found in bed with the wife of the Spanish Viceroy of Mexico, Lamport was once again sentenced to seven years imprisonment, following which he was burned to death as a heretic in 1659. The legendary Hollywood film *The Mask of Zorro* is allegedly based on his adventures.

Pierce McCan
Republican and Sinn Féin politician 1882 – 1919

Pierce McCan was born at Prospect Lodge, New Ross and was educated at the Christian Brothers School in Cashel, County Tipperary and later at Rockwell College. Having joined the Gaelic League, McCan set up a unit of the volunteers in Tipperary but he was arrested by the Royal Irish Constabulary in May 1916 and was imprisoned in Kilmainham Jail and later in Knutsford, Cheshire. Having been moved to Reading Jail, McCan was released without explanation before returning to Ireland where he was again arrested, due to the supposed 'German Plot', in 1918. This time incarcerated in Gloucester, England, whilst there, McCan was elected a member of parliament for Tipperary East but died the following year from Spanish flu, which swept through the prison.

Robert McClure
Explorer 1807 – 1873

Robert McClure was born on Main Street, Wexford and was educated at Eton and Sandhurst in England. Having joined the British Navy in 1824, he later took part in the Franklin Search Expedition on board the *Enterprise*, before engaging in a second search expedition, as commander of the *Investigator* in 1850. McClure, who achieved the distinction of completing the discovery of the North West Passage, an expedition during which he lost the *Investigator* in pack ice, was later knighted and went on to attain the rank of vice-admiral in 1873. He died on 17 October 1873. McClure Strait in Canada is named in his memory.

Fr John Murphy
1798 Rebellion leader 1753 – 1798

In 1772, Ferns born John Murphy moved to Seville, Spain, in order to study for the priesthood, a vocation forbidden in Ireland due to the persecution of Catholics under the Penal Laws. Ordained in 1779, Murphy returned to Ireland in 1785 and took up the position of parish priest of Boolavogue, County Wexford. With the clergy swearing allegiance to the British Crown and encouraging parishioners against rebellion, the mistreatment of his parishioners by the Yeomanry eventually drove Murphy to make a stand in their defence. On 27 May 1798, he led a large group of pikemen and defeated a party of government troops at Oulart, following which he took Camolin and Enniscorthy. Murphy then made camp on Vinegar Hill, but following defeat there by Crown forces, and again at Kilcumney, he retreated to Tullow where he was eventually arrested. He was executed in County Carlow on 2 July 1798.

Jasper O'Farrell
First surveyor for San Francisco 1817 – 1875

Having moved to California in 1843, Jasper O'Farrell was one of the first settlers at Sebastopol, California, where he purchased a ranch. O'Farrell was also the first to survey the new settlement, Yerbi Buena, later to be called San Francisco, and he went on to become the city's first engineer. San Francisco's famous Grand Promenade, today known as Market Street, was designed by O'Farrell, and the city's O'Farrell Street is named in his memory. He died on 16 November 1875.

Michael O'Hanrahan
Patriot and author 1877 – 1916

Michael O'Hanrahan was born in New Ross and lived for a time in Cairo, Egypt before later moving back to Dublin. An author, O'Hanrahan wrote two heroic novels, *The Swordsman of the Brigade* and *When the Normans Came*, and was also a member of the Gaelic League. He was second in command to Thomas MacDonagh (see page 372) at Jacob's factory during the Easter Rising of 1916 and following the surrender of that garrison, was taken to Kilmainhan Jail where, following court-martial, he was executed. The railway station in Wexford is named in his memory.

John Redmond
Political Leader 1856 – 1918

Nationalist politician John Redmond was born at Ballytrent House, Kilrane and was educated at Clongowes Wood College, County Kildare and at Trinity College, Dublin. A devoted follower of Charles Stewart Parnell (see page 423), he was elected a member of parliament for New Ross in 1881 and was called to the Irish bar in 1886. Later elected a member of parliament for Waterford, despite the delaying tactics of the liberals, Redmond secured the introduction of the Home Rule Bill in 1912 and saw through its acceptance in 1914, a move that granted a form of self-government to Ireland. However, due to Britain's involvement in World War I, its implementation was prevented. Redmond died on 6 March 1918 and is buried in the family vault in Wexford.

John Sinnott
Victoria Cross recipient 1829 – 1896

John Sinnott served as lance corporal in the 84th Regiment of the British Army during the Indian Mutiny. At Lucknow, India on 6 October 1857, together with a captain of his unit, Sinnott repeatedly attempted to extinguish a fire that was threatening their position. Under intense pressure from the enemy the captain was mortally wounded, but Sinnott, along with two sergeants and a private, retrieved the body before returning it back to their own lines. He later achieved the rank of sergeant and died in Clapham, London in 1896.

Charles Blacker Vignoles
Railway engineer 1793 – 1875

Orphaned at a very young age, Charles Blacker Vignoles was brought up by his grandfather, a professor of mathematics at Woolwich Royal Military Academy, and he trained in mathematics and law before qualifying as an engineer in 1814. Having seen service under the Duke of Wellington in the Peninsular wars and also in the United States, where he surveyed large areas of Florida and South Carolina, Vignoles returned to Europe in 1820. There he became involved in the construction of railways in Germany, France, Switzerland, Spain and Russia and he also undertook work in Brazil. Vignoles, who was instrumental in the development of numerous railway lines in both Britain and Ireland, was elected the first professor of civil engineering at University College London in 1841, as well as becoming a fellow of the Royal Society in 1855. Appointed the fifteenth president of the Institute of Civil Engineers, the standard form of railway line used around the world is known as the 'Vignoles Rail'. He retired in 1863 and lived in Southampton, England until his death on 17 November 1875.

Thomas Weafer
Patriot 1890 – 1916

Thomas Weafer (sometimes spelt Wafer) was born in Enniscorthy and was a captain of E Company, 2nd Battalion of the Irish Republican Army during the Easter Rising of 1916. Killed in the Hibernian Bank, Lower Abbey Street, Dublin on 27 April 1916, Weafer was trapped when the building was burned during the struggle.

His remains were consumed in the fire and to commemorate his death, a memorial plaque was unveiled on the site on Easter Sunday, 1937.

Michael James Whitty
First chief constable of Liverpool and founder of the *Liverpool Daily Post* 1795 – 1873

Having initially attended St Patrick's College in Maynooth with the intentions of becoming a priest, Michael James Whitty later decided to train as a journalist and in 1824, anonymously published two volumes of *Tales of Irish Life*, which proved a runaway success. Whitty later moved to Liverpool, England where he was appointed editor of the *Liverpool Journal*, but in 1933 he left to become superintendent of Robert Peel's new police force. Following his success in reorganising and modernising that force, he was appointed its head constable in 1836, serving until 1848 when he was forced to retire due to ill health. He subsequently returned to journalism and founded the *Liverpool Daily Post*, Britain's first penny-daily newspaper. Whitty died on 10 June 1873 and he is buried in Anfield Cemetery, Liverpool.

Wicklow

Charles Stewart Parnell
1846-1891

A statue to Charles Stewart Parnell stands on O'Connell Street, Dublin.
The inscription on it reads: 'No man has the right to fix the boundary to the march of a nation. No man has a right to say to his country thus far shalt thou go and no further. We have never attempted to fix the ne plus ultra to the progress of Ireland's nationhood and we never shall'.

Michael Dwyer
1772-1825

The memorial in Waverley Cemetery, New South Wales, Australia is dedicated to United Irishman Michael Dwyer (The Wicklow Chief).

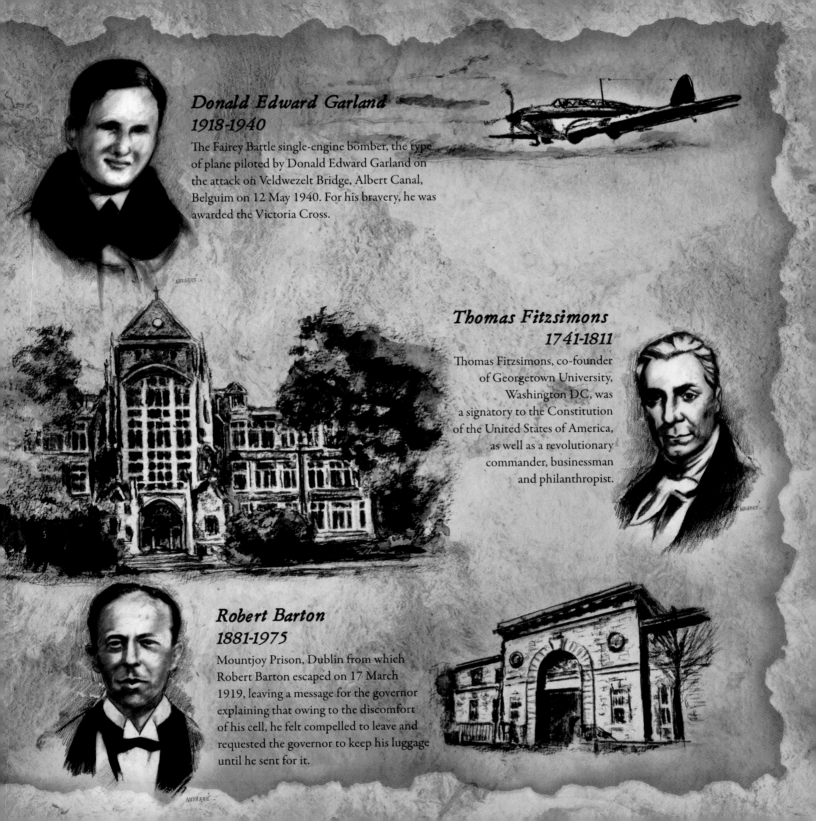

Donald Edward Garland
1918-1940

The Fairey Battle single-engine bomber, the type of plane piloted by Donald Edward Garland on the attack on Veldwezelt Bridge, Albert Canal, Belguim on 12 May 1940. For his bravery, he was awarded the Victoria Cross.

Thomas Fitzsimons
1741-1811

Thomas Fitzsimons, co-founder of Georgetown University, Washington DC, was a signatory to the Constitution of the United States of America, as well as a revolutionary commander, businessman and philanthropist.

Robert Barton
1881-1975

Mountjoy Prison, Dublin from which Robert Barton escaped on 17 March 1919, leaving a message for the governor explaining that owing to the discomfort of his cell, he felt compelled to leave and requested the governor to keep his luggage until he sent for it.

Robert Barton

Lawyer and statesman 1881 – 1975
Born into a wealthy, Protestant land-owning family, Robert Barton was educated at Rugby School and Oxford in England. An officer in the Dublin Fusiliers upon the outbreak of World War I, he was stationed in Dublin in 1916 but resigned his commission in protest at the heavy-handed British suppression of the Irish uprising and in particular, the execution of its leaders. Having joined the republican movement, Barton was arrested for sedition in 1919, but escaped from Mountjoy prison on St Patrick's Day, leaving a message for the governor stating that his escape was due to the discomfort of his cell, requesting the governor keep his luggage until he sent for it. Recaptured in 1920, he was later released under a general amnesty in July 1921. Barton was one of the Irish delegates to the Anglo-Irish Treaty negotiations, which he reluctantly signed on 6 December 1921, but he later took the side of the anti-treaty forces in the Civil War. Having served for a short period in Dáil Éireann, he died at his home in County Wicklow on 10 August 1975.

Dom Eugene Boylan

Linguist, monk and writer 1904 – 1964
Bray native Dom Eugene Boylan was educated in Dublin at O'Connell School and University College Dublin. Having also studied atomic physics in Vienna, Austria, in 1928 he was awarded a Rockefeller Scholarship before entering the Cistercian order of monks in 1933. Boylan, who spoke in excess of six languages, became known as a confessor and he also wrote several books on spiritual life, amongst them *This Tremendous Lover* (1946), which gained world acclaim. His other publications were *Difficulties in Mental Prayer* (1943), *The Spiritual Life of the Priest* (1949), and *The Priest's Way to God* (1962). He opened a house for the Cistercians at Tarrawarra, Australia in 1954 and was later appointed superior at Caldey Abbey, a monastery located on an island off the Welsh coast, where he developed a perfume industry which placed the abbey on a firm financial footing. Having lectured several times in the United States, Boylan was appointed abbot of Mount St Joseph, Rosscrea, County Tipperary in 1962. He died in January 1964.

James Byrne

Victoria Cross recipient
1822 – 1872
James Byrne was born in Newtownmountkennedy and served as a private in the 86th Regiment of the British Army during the Indian mutiny. At Jhansi, India he, along with the captain of his regiment, removed a severely wounded lieutenant from the battlefield despite being under heavy fire. During the rescue attempt, Bryne himself was wounded and for this act of bravery he received the Victoria Cross. He later became a sergeant.

George Campbell, RHA

Painter 1917 – 1979
The son of artist Gretta Bowen, George Campbell was born in Arklow. Mainly a self-taught artist, he did not take up painting until the mid-1940s, after which he held prominent exhibitions in both Belfast and Dublin. Visiting Spain in 1951,

Campbell became fond of the country's ambience, which had such a profound effect on him that he returned there on a regular basis, his paintings much influenced by its landscapes and culture. His works are represented in most major public and private collections.

Richard Crosbie
Irish aeronautic pioneer 1755 – 1800

Richard Crosbie was born in Baltinglass and was educated at Trinity College, Dublin. On 19 January 1785, he became the first Irishman to fly and in order to raise funds for his aeronautical exercise, he held an exhibition in Ranelagh Gardens, Dublin. For a small fee, Crosbie invited the public to examine both his balloon and the 'aeronautic chariot' in which he undertook his flight from Ranelagh, on the south side of the city, to Clontarf on the north. Hailed as a pioneering scientific achievement across Europe, the flight was considered a great day for aviation in Ireland.

Dennis Dempsey
Victoria Cross recipient 1826 – 1896

Dennis Dempsey was born in Bray and entered the British Army as a private in the 1st Battalion, 10th Regiment of Foot, during the Indian Mutiny. Whilst under heavy fire at Lucknow, India, Dempsey carried a powder-bag through a burning village in an effort to mine enemy positions. Although he was exposed to heavy fire, he also faced the dangerous possibility of stray sparks igniting the powder-bag that he was carrying. Regardless, Dempsey successfully carried out the feat and two days later, on 14 March 1858, in a retreat from Arrah, he transported a wounded trooper to safety. For his loyal service, he was awarded the Victoria Cross.

Anne Devlin
Confidant of Robert Emmet 1780 – 1851

Born in Rathdrum, Anne Devlin later moved to Dublin where she became a housekeeper at Butterfield House, Rathfarnham, the site where Robert Emmet (see page 165) had effectively established a revolutionary headquarters. Following the failure of his insurrection in July 1803, Emmet was highly reliant upon Devlin and as a result, she and her entire family were arrested by the authorities. Following torture and degradation that led to lifelong ill health, Devlin refused to disclose any information on Emmet or his associates and when those treacherous methods failed to yield a result, Major Sirr, head of the Dublin Castle security, attempted to bribe her, offering five hundred golden guineas and a free passage for herself and her family to any other country, plus a pension for life. Devlin scornfully rejected all of this and as a result, spent three years in prison. Upon her release, she was totally destitute but was befriended by Doctor Richard Madden (see page 177), who helped her in the final years of her life. The good doctor later had a monument erected over her grave in Glasnevin Cemetery in Dublin.

Michael Dwyer
United Irishman 1772 – 1825

Michael Dwyer was born in the Glen of Imaal and was one of the most colourful of the United Irishmen. Having fought at Vinegar Hill, Hacketstown, and at the Battle of Arklow, Dwyer retreated to his home territory of the Glen of Imaal following the failure of the rebellion. There he carried out a guerilla campaign so successfully for five and a half years that the British authorities were forced to build a special military road from Dublin to the Glen of Imaal, a distance of thirty-five miles, in order to capture Dwyer. In one incident, on 15 February 1799, an informer led a British party of one hundred troops to his hideout. In the ensuing shootout, Dwyer's party of eleven men was killed but with Sam McAllister covering his retreat, Dwyer was the only man to escape. Thereafter he continued with his guerilla campaign for another three years but on 14 December 1803, he surrendered on condition that his party were given safe passage to the United States. This was agreed upon, but the British reneged on the agreement and Dwyer was transported to Australia, where upon his release, he established a farm near Sydney. For a brief period he was appointed police chief for the area, following which he diverted his interest into selling plots of land to make a living. He died on 23 August 1825 and in 2003 the Irish government erected a statue to his memory in the Glen of Imaal. In Waverly Cemetery, New South Wales there is a very elaborate memorial, which was constructed to his memory in 1898.

Thomas Fitzsimons
Merchant and Pennsylvania statesman
1741 – 1811
In his mid-teens, Thomas Fitzsimons emigrated to the United States where he settled in Philadelphia, Pennsylvania. There, with his brother-in-law, Fitzsimons established a company trading general goods with the West Indies. He was also elected to the revolutionary government before raising and commanding a company in the United States Army in the revolutionary war. Fitzsimons, who represented Pennsylvania in the Continental Congress and the Constitutional Convention, was one of two Catholic signatories to the Constitution, the other being Daniel Carroll, and he was also a founding trustee of the Bank of North America. A trustee of the University of Pennsylvania, he helped found Georgetown University and was a generous philanthropist, giving considerable support to St Augustine's Roman Catholic Church, Philadelphia. He died in that city in 1811 and is buried in the graveyard at St Mary's Church, which is located in the present Independence National Historical Park.

Donald Edward Garland
Victoria Cross recipient
1918 – 1940
Donald Edward Garland served as a flying officer in the 12th Squadron of the Royal Air Force during World War II. On 12 May 1940, five British bombers were dispatched to demolish a strategically vital bridge over the Albert Canal in Belgium, but with the bridge heavily fortified and under the protection of German fighter aircraft and anti-aircraft positions, the attackers encountered a blaze of enemy fire. However, they succeeded in accomplishing their mission, which was attributed to Garland's coolness, as well as the resourcefulness of his navigator, Thomas Gray. The two were lost in action and for their deeds were awarded the Victoria Cross. The bridge they had attacked at Vroenhoven, today bears a monument to the memory of these brave men.

Edwin Lawrence Godkin
Author and editor 1831 – 1902
Having published *A History of Hungary* (1853), which won him the job of correspondent to the *London Daily News* during the Crimean War, in 1856 Edwin Lawrence Godkin went to the United States where he studied law and was admitted to the

New York bar. During the American Civil War he acted as correspondent for the *London Daily News* and in 1865 he founded the weekly journal the *Nation*, in New York. In 1881 Godkin became an editor with the *New York Post* and he went on to the position of editor in chief in 1883. Politically independent, he attacked the carpetbag regime of Tammany Hall and also supported home rule for Ireland, his self-assurance and integrity giving much weight to his opinion. Godkin, who later wrote *Problems of Modern Democracy* (1896) and *Unforseen Tendencies of Democracy* (1898), returned to England in 1900 and died in Devonshire on 21 May 1902.

Robert Halpin
Master of the SS *Great Eastern* cable-laying ship 1836 – 1894

Robert Halpin was born in Wicklow town and aged just ten, went to sea as a cabin boy. Just twelve years later he had graduated to the position of master of the Belfast-built steam ship the *Circassian* and in 1869 he fulfilled the same role on the SS *Great Eastern*, which launched in January 1858, and was, at the time, the largest ship in the world. As master, Halpin was responsible for laying in excess of twenty-six thousand miles of telegraphic cables from places as far apart as Brest, France to Newfoundland, Canada, Bombay, India to Aden, Yemen and the Suez Canal in Egypt. He was also responsible for the laying of cables connecting Madeira, Portugal with Brazil, and also linking Australia, New Zealand, and the Dutch East Indies. The SS *Great Eastern* was finally laid up at Milford Haven, Wales where Halpin ended his partnership with the historic vessel. The famous French author Jules Verne, who once sailed with Halpin, described him as a skilful energetic seaman and in his hometown of Tinakilly, County Wicklow, where he died in 1894, a monument stands in recognition of his great achievements as a master seafarer.

Joseph Holt
General and Irish rebel
1756 – 1826

Joseph Holt was born in Ballydonnell to a Protestant, loyalist family, but in 1797 joined the Society of the United Irishmen. Following the burning of his home, he took to the Wicklow mountains, where he formed a substantial rebel force and avoiding set-piece battles, Holt utilised his force by making quick and tactical ambushes against the loyalist military operating in County Wicklow. Having reduced loyalist influence in the county to urban strongholds, the Wexford rebel's defeat at Vinegar Hillbon 21 June 1798 saw a significant number of survivors join Holt's forces, which defeated the pursuing British cavalry at Ballyellis just over a week later. Solving the problem of a lack of gunpowder by inventing his own concoction, known as 'Holt's Mixture', he held out in the mountains for a number of years before finally arranging a negotiated surrender, allowing him to emigrate to New South Wales, Australia. He arrived there on 11 January 1800 and following some time there, Holt returned to Ireland in 1814, living the rest of his life in Dublin. However, he always regretted leaving Australia and he died on 16 May 1826.

Matthew Lyon
Political leader and pioneer
1749 – 1822

In 1765, Arklow born Matthew Lyon settled in Vermont, where he saw service during the American Revolution. In the period from 1797 to 1801, he was a vociferous Anti-Federalist member of the United States House of Representatives and was convicted under the Sedition Act for criticising President John Adams. It was following this that one of the most important elements of the United States Constitution, the First Amendment principle of free expression, was first implemented, and it resulted in Lyon being restored to the House of Representatives. His casting vote in the presidential elections saw Thomas Jefferson entering the nation's highest office, but Lyon then left politics for a number of years, concentrating instead on building an extensive business enterprise. He later returned to serve four terms as the Democratic-Republican for Kentucky where he was a strong advocate for the abolition of slavery and was appointed agent for the native Cherokee tribe. He died amongst that tribe on 1 August 1822.

Lavall Nugent
Austrian field marshal 1777 – 1862

Lavall Nugent was born at Ballinacor and joined the Austrian army as an Engineer Corps cadet in 1793. By 1805 he was a lieutenant colonel, later appointed to the general staff in 1809. As commander of Austrian troops he defeated the French in the region of Karlstadt, Germany. Nugent later went on to capture the port of Trieste, Italy and he was further involved in the defeat of the French at the battles of Reggio, Parma, and Piacenza. As a result, he was appointed lieutenant general and was also created a Knight Commander of the Bath. Later appointed field marshal of the Austrian army, he died on 21 August 1862.

John Thomond O'Brien
Army officer and entrepreneur
1786 – 1861

In 1812, Baltinglass native John Thomond O'Brien arrived in Buenos Aires, Argentina, where he opened a merchant house. Later enlisting in the Argentinean Army, he fought under General Soler in Uruguay and in 1816 served as captain of the mounted grenadiers of the Andes Army, which was established to help in the liberation of Peru, the second last stronghold of Spanish rule in South America. Having fought in the battles of Cancha Rayada and Maipú, and also in the Peru campaign, in 1821 O'Brien was promoted to colonel and awarded the 'Orden El Sol del Perú'. He later became involved in the country's mining industry and carried out many major engineering feats, including the transportation of a steam engine across the Andes, as well as digging a six hundred metre long canal, which contained nine locks, through Laycayota mountain in Peru. O'Brien, who also fostered emigration from Ireland to Argentina, in particular from the areas of Westmeath, Longford, and Offaly, was appointed special envoy of the Uruguayan Republic to Britain in 1848. Whilst returning to South America, he died in Lisbon, Portugal on 1 June 1861 and in 1938, his remains were repatriated to Argentina where a town in Bragado was named in his honour.

Peter O'Connor
Olympic gold medal winner
1874 – 1957
Sportsman Peter O'Connor was born
in Ashtown and was an accomplished
athlete, excelling in the long jump,
high jump and triple jump
events. Consistently besting
British athletes in competition, he
was invited by the British Amateur
Athletic Association to represent Britain
in the Olympic Games in 1900, but refused on
the grounds that he wished only to represent the country
of his birth. In 1901 O'Connor broke Myer Prinstein's long
jump world record with a jump of twenty-four feet, eleven
and three quarter inches, a fine performance that caused a
sensation due to the fact that it was marginally short of the
elusive twenty-five foot barrier.

In the 1906 Olympic games, O'Connor, together
with two other Irish athletes, Con Leahy and John Daly,
unsuccessfully attempted to gain entry to the Athens
Olympics under the Irish flag. Denied, they were officially
claimed by the British Olympic Council and in the ensuing
long jump competition, Prinstein gained revenge by beating
O'Connor into second place. In the flag-raising ceremony
which followed, O'Connor scaled the mast in the middle
of the arena and replaced the Union flag with an Irish flag,
which comprised a green background with a gold harp and
had 'Erin go bragh' (Ireland forever) inscribed on it. Two
days later, he went on to win the gold medal in the triple
jump. He was a founder member and first president of the
Waterford Athletics Club, as well as practicing as a solicitor
in that city. He died there on 9 November 1957.

Charles Stewart Parnell
Political leader 1846 – 1891
A member of a landowning family
with nationalist sympathies, in 1875
Charles Stewart Parnell was elected to
parliament for Meath, becoming a
member of the Home Rule Party. In
1879 Parnell was invited by Michael
Davitt (see page 305) to become the
first president of the Land League, an
organisation that reduced the restrictive
practices of landlords by organising the peasants into a
union in which to assert their rights. However, the league
was suppressed and Parnell was arrested and imprisoned
for six months, with the agitation of that organisation
eventually leading to the implementation of the Land
Act, which introduced new land reforms in 1881. Having
continuously fought for legislative independence for Ireland
by constitutional means, Parnell has been referred to as
the 'uncrowned king of Ireland'. However, his relationship
with Katherine O'Shea, a divorcee, was condemned by the
Catholic hierarchy and led to his eventual political demise.
A statue to him stands on O'Connell Street, Dublin, and
on the plinth it reads: 'No man has the right to fix the
boundary of the march of a nation. No man has a right to
say to his country thus far shalt thou go and no further. We
have never attempted to fix the ne plus ultra to the progress
of Ireland's nationhood and we never shall.'

Fanny Parnell
Patriot poet 1848 – 82
The sister of Charles Stewart Parnell,
Fanny Parnell was born in Avondale.
Having travelled to London in 1868, she
eventually immigrated to the United States
where she and her mother settled in
Bordentown, New Jersey. From 1879,
Parnell organised the Irish Famine

Relief Fund and in 1880 founded the Ladies Land League of America, in support of Michael Davitt's (see page 305) Land League in Ireland. She also wrote countless poems, most famously 'Hold the Harvest', which used the shocking imagery of murdered peasants providing compost for their descendants' crops and that evoked the heroic struggle of the Land League in Ireland. Parnell died suddenly at the age of thirty-three and whilst there were passionate requests for her body to be returned to Ireland for a large funeral, she was buried in Bordentown.

Dame Edris Stannus (Ninette de Valois)
Founder director of the royal ballet 1898 – 2001

It was Edris Stannus's passion for Irish dancing that awakened her love for ballet. Having adopted the name Ninette de Valois, feeling it was more befitting a ballet dancer, she joined the Russian Ballet in 1922. There the Blessington born performer danced as a soloist and in 1931 she founded the Sadler's Wells Ballet (now the Royal Ballet). Stannus continued as its artistic director until 1963 and she retired in 1971, having achieved her ambitions as the mother of British ballet. She was one hundred and two years old when she died.

Mary Tighe
Poet 1772 – 1810

A member of a Methodist family, Mary Tighe's father was the Reverend William Blanchford and at the age of twenty-one, the Ashford born poet married Henry Tighe, a barrister and a member of parliament who represented Inistioge, County Kilkenny. She is best remembered for her poem, 'Psyche; or, the Legend of Love', which was written in Spenserian stanza form and published privately in the United States in 1805, was extremely well received. Tighe was a very beautiful woman but she suffered an unhappy marriage and ill health. She died of tuberculosis in 1810 and was buried in the churchyard at Inistioge.

Dermot Troy
Lyric tenor 1927 – 1962

Dermot Troy was born in Tinahely and was educated at the Christian Brothers School in Synge Street, Dublin, following which he served for three years in the Royal Air Force. At the age of twenty-one, Troy took singing lessons from Professor Michael O'Higgins and appeared with many choral societies. He eventually joined the Royal Opera House in London, England, where he continued his vocal studies with Dino Borgioli. In 1957 Troy was appointed as the leading lyric tenor with the Mannheim Opera House in Germany, later being offered a three-year contract with the Hamburg State Opera, an appointment that confirmed him as one of Europe's foremost tenors. Blessed with an infectious wit, he was renowned for his modesty and sincerity, and in both looks and vocal ability he resembled fellow Irishman John McCormack (see page 404). Having suffered a heart attack in June 1961, Troy returned to Hamburg the following year, where he died aged just thirty-five.

William Woodburn
Politician and member of the United States House of Representatives 1838 – 1915

When he was eleven years of age, William Woodburn emigrated to the United States with his parents.

Settling in Maryland where he attended St Charles College, Woodburn later studied law and was admitted to the bar in 1866. Having commenced practicing law in Virginia City, Nevada, he served as district attorney of Storey County, Nevada from 1871 until 1872 and representing the republicans, he was elected to the Forty-Fourth Congress from 1875 until 1877. Later serving in the Forty-Ninth and Fiftieth Congress from 1885 until 1889, following those representations Woodburn returned to his profession in Virginia City. He died in Carson City, Nevada on 15 January 1915 and is buried in St Theresa's Cemetery.

BORN IN IRELAND, COUNTY UNKNOWN

James Edward Ignatius Masterson
Victoria Cross recipient 1862 – 1935
James Edward Ignatius Masterson was a lieutenant in the 1st Battalion, Devonshire Regiment of the British Army during the Boer War. Whilst in command of three companies of his regiment at Wagon Hill in Ladysmith, South Africa on 6 January 1900, he and his men came under very heavy fire from both the left and right flanks. Masterson subsequently decided to seek the help of the Imperial Light Horse who were positioned approximately one hundred yards away and to this end, he crossed that distance under continuous heavy fire. Whilst doing so, he was wounded in both thighs but he delivered the message before falling, exhausted to the ground. In 1911, Masterson was commissioned to major and he died in Hampshire, England on 24 December 1935.

HANDS ACROSS THE DIVIDE

Thomas Francis Meagher
1823-1867

In 1848 Thomas Francis Meagher, a twenty-five-year-old Catholic from Waterford, and William Smith O'Brien, a forty-five-year-old Protestant from Clare, travelled to Paris to observe the establishment of the new French Republic. Upon their return to Ireland, they brought with them a new Irish flag, which was patterned on the French tricolour, but in the colours of green, white and orange. During a speech in which he introduced the new flag, Meagher said that 'the white in the centre signifies a lasting truce between the orange and the green, and I trust that beneath its folds the hands of the Irish Protestant and the Irish Catholic may be clasped in generous and heroic brotherhood.'

William Smith O'Brien
1803-1864

The Orange and the Green

What are the odds if we're papes or prods?
If we're white, we're black, we're brown?
The one God above we all serve and love,
He doesn't differ as he looks down.
For while we're here,
Let's build love not fear,
And to the world let it be seen,
There is no difference now my friend,
'Tween the orange and the green.

Séamus Moran

Peace Staue, Derry City.

BORN OUTSIDE IRELAND

Erskine Hamilton Childers
Fourth president of Ireland
1905 – 1974

The son of Irish patriot Robert Erskine Childers, (see below) Erskine Hamilton Childers was born in London, England. Educated at Gresham School, Norfolk and at Trinity College, Cambridge, having worked as the manager of an American travel organisation in Paris, he was invited by Éamon de Valera (see page 431) to work for the Irish in 1932. Six years later he was elected a Fianna Fáil TD for Athlone-Longford and he went on to become minister for post and telegraphs in 1951.

Childers, who also served as minister for lands, minister for transport and power and minister for health, filled the role of Tánaiste, and he was later elected President of Ireland on 30 May 1973. The night before his execution, his father requested that his son do nothing to cause any bitterness as a result of his death, and Childers abided by this request. A very conscientious and hardworking minister, with an abiding interest in the care of the under privileged, he died suddenly in Dublin on 17 November 1974.

Robert Erskine Childers
Author and Irish nationalist
1870 – 1922

Robert Erskine Childers was born in London, England to a family who originated in Glendalough, County Wicklow. He was educated at Haileybury College, Hertfordshire, England and at Trinity College, Cambridge. Upon the outbreak of the Second Boer War in 1899, he volunteered for action and was commissioned in the British Army. Wounded whilst serving in South Africa, he was transported back to Britain and in 1903 published a novel, *The Riddle of the Sands*, which was based on his sailing experiences along the German coast. His book, which predicted the war with Germany, called for Britain to be prepared for battle and following its publication he visited the United States, where he met and married Molly Osgood.

Childers was a strong advocate for home rule for Ireland, and following his Boer War exploits he became attracted to Irish nationalism. In 1914 he and his wife smuggled German arms in their yacht to Howth, County Dublin, and these arms were later used by Irish Volunteers during the Easter Rising of 1916.

Upon the outbreak of World War I, he joined the Royal Navy as an intelligence officer, seeing active service in the North Sea and the Dardanelles. He was later awarded the Distinguished Service Order and was promoted to lieutenant commander in 1916. So angered was Childers by the violent suppression of the Easter Rising in Dublin that after the war, he moved back to Dublin to take part in the struggle against British rule in Ireland. In 1920 he published *Military Rule in Ireland*, which was an attack on British policy there, and he also served in the first Irish parliament set up by Sinn Féin. Childers filled the role of secretary general of the Irish delegation that negotiated the Anglo-Irish Treaty with the British government, but he vehemently opposed the final draft of that agreement, which eventually led to him taking the anti-treaty side in the Irish Civil War. He was later arrested by Free State forces in Glendalough, County Wicklow and was tried by a military court before being sentenced to death. Ironically, the pistol in his possession at the time of his arrest had been a gift from Michael Collins (see page 89). He was executed by firing squad at Beggar's Bush Barracks, Dublin and is buried in Glasnevin Cemetery. British prime minister Winston Churchill claimed that Childers had a malignant hatred of the land of his birth. In Ireland however, he is revered as one of its greatest patriots.

Thomas Clarke
Patriot 1857 – 1916

Thomas Clarke was born on the Isle of White where his father was a sergeant in the British Army. Following a stint in South Africa his family returned to Ireland, where they settled in Dungannon, County Tyrone. There, Clarke attended St Patrick's National School before joining the Fenians as a teenager. Later emigrating to the United States, where he became a member of Clann na nGael, Clarke also found employment as an explosive operative in a construction company and with the knowledge he gained, he was sent to London, England where it is believed he was instructed to destroy London Bridge. However, before he could carry out his task, Clarke was captured and following a trial he was sentenced to fifteen years in prison.

Having been released in 1898, Clarke married and returned to the United States where he spent seven years before travelling back to Ireland and opening a tobacconist shop on Parnell Street in Dublin. He also immersed himself in the cause for Irish independence and was one of the architects in founding the IRB military council and the foundations for the Easter Rising of 1916, during which he was stationed in the General Post Office in Dublin. A signatory to Poblacht na hÉireann (Irish Declaration of Independence), upon the surrender to the British forces, Clarke's importance to the Irish cause was recognised and he was subsequently chosen as the second leader, in addition to Patrick Pearse (see page 185), to be executed on 3 May 1916.

James Connolly
Socialist 1868 – 1916

James Connolly was born in Edinburgh, Scotland and served for a short period in the British Army, seeing service mainly in Cork, where he witnessed the bad treatment of the Irish, as well as the unjust control the landlords exerted over their tenants. It was these experiences that instilled a hatred for all landlords in Connolly, and he later returned to Edinburgh where he joined the Scottish Socialist Federation in 1889. Coming back to Ireland in 1910, Connolly joined the Irish Transport and General Workers Union and he also co-founded the Irish Labour Party and formed the Irish Citizens Army during the Lockout of 1913. In 1915 he was appointed general secretary of the Irish Transport and General Workers Union, and he later enlisted in the Irish Republican Brotherhood, selected as military commander of the republican forces in Dublin during the Easter Rising of 1916. Connolly, who was one of the seven signatories to the Proclamation of Irish Independence, was severely wounded in the General Post Office during the rising and he was subsequently court-martialed and sentenced to death. He was subsequently executed sitting in a chair, due to his extensive wounds. The circumstances of this execution enraged the Irish public and in death, Connolly and the other rebels succeeded in turning Irish support for the union with Britain on its head.

St. Patrick Cathedral in Dublin.

Éamon de Valera
Political leader and third president
of Ireland 1882 – 1975

Éamon de Valera was born in the United States of America and came to Ireland with his mother at two years of age. Educated at Bruree national school, County Limerick and Blackrock College, Dublin, he graduated with a degree in mathematics from Dublin University in 1904. De Valera, who was a fluent speaker of the Irish language, joined the Irish Volunteers, and the Irish Republican Brotherhood, and in the Easter Rising on 24 April 1916, he was in charge of the unit that occupied Boland's Mills, Grand Canal Street, Dublin. He was eventually captured and sentenced to death, but due to his American citizenship, Britain feared a consequential reaction from the United States and the death sentence was lifted.

Upon Sinn Féin's success in the 1918 general election, de Valera became president of Dáil Éireann and during the Irish War of Independence, spent most of his time as a fundraiser in the country of his birth. On the cessation of hostilities, he sent a delegation, which included Michael Collins (see page 89), to London in order to negotiate the Anglo-Irish Treaty, which resulted in the six northern counties of Ireland being partitioned and remaining under British power. In a meeting of the Dáil, the treaty was ratified by sixty-four votes to fifty-seven but de Valera refused to accept the result. His dissatisfaction, and that of his followers, led to the outbreak Irish Civil War. In 1926 de Valera founded the Fianna Fáil political party and in 1932 he established the first Irish Free State government before becoming the first taoiseach under the new Irish constitution in 1937. Following a number of periods in government in the intervening years, he was elected president of Ireland in 1959, a position he held until his retirement from public office in 1973. He died on 29 August 1975.

Phil Lynott
Thin Lizzy singer and
guitarist 1949 – 1986

Phil Lynott was born in West Bromwich, England and at the age of four, came to Dublin to live with his mother in Crumlin. Joining the band Skid Row in 1967, he later left that group and in the early 1970s formed Thin Lizzy, together with Brian Downey, Eric Bell and Eric Wrixon. For a number of years following the band experienced varying fortunes and despite maintaining an encouraging level of support within Ireland, they soon realised that if they were ever to break into the big time, they had to look beyond their native shores. In March 1975 they toured the United States with Bob Seger and Bachman-Turner Overdrive. However the behaviour of Thin Lizzy on the tour was less than professional, causing the American promoters to use no uncertain terms in sending out a warning to the group. This proved a wake-up call and upon the band's return to England, their performance at the Great British Musical Festival, on 31 December 1975, was a tremendous success.

In 1977, Thin Lizzy once again toured the United States, this time in support of legendary rock act Queen, and the tour was once again dogged by unruly behaviour. Despite these problems however, the band enojoyed substantial success. In 1980, Lynott married Caroline Crowther, daughter of British comedian Leslie Crowther. Falling into the musical gap between heavy metal and pop, the band added some Celtic flavour to its repertoire with 'Whiskey in the Jar', which was a top ten hit in 1973, and remains their best remembered record. Thin Lizzy split following their last show in Nuremburg, Germany on 4 September 1983, and having also parted from his wife and two daughters, Lynott fell further victim to the drugs that had hampered his musical career. He died tragically in London, England on 4 January 1986 and is buried in Howth parish church, Dublin, where the inscription on his headstone reads, 'Go dtuga Dia suaimhneas da anam' (may God give peace to his soul).

The best known hits of Thin Lizzy were: 'The Boys are back in Town', 'Jail Break', 'Dancing in the Moonlight', 'Rosalie', 'Wild One', and the aforementioned 'Whiskey in the Jar'. A statue to Lynott stands just off Grafton Street, Dublin.

Seán MacBride
Nobel Peace Price winner 1904 – 1988

Seán MacBride was born in Paris, France, the son of Major John MacBride and Maud Gonne. Educated at Mount St Benedict's in Gorey, County Wexford, his father was executed following the Easter Rising of 1916, after which MacBride joined the Irish Volunteers in 1919. Having taken part in the War of Independence, he was opposed to the Anglo-Irish Treaty and after being called to the bar in 1937, served as a politician for a number of years. MacBride, who was a founding member of Amnesty International, participated in many non-governmental organisations including the United Nations, the Council of Europe and Amnesty International itself, and he also wrote the constitutions of the Organisation of African Unity (OAU), and the nation of Ghana. Amongst his many awards are: the Nobel Peace Prize (1974), the American Medal of Justice (1975), the Lenin Peace Prize (1975/76) and the UNESCO Silver Medal (1980). He died in Dublin on 15 January 1988 and is buried in Glasnevin Cemetery.

Constance Markievicz
Patriot 1868 – 1927

Constance Markievicz was born Constance Gore-Booth in London. Her father was explorer and philanthropist Sir Henry Gore-Booth (see page 358), who owned a large estate in County Sligo. The most famous woman of the Irish revolutionary movement, Markievicz lived her early life in the family home in Lissadell, County Sligo and intent on becoming an artist, returned to London to study at the Slade School in 1893. Later moving on to Paris, France, where she attended the Julian School, she met her future husband, Count Casimir Dunin Markievicz, a member of a wealthy Polish family, and together the couple settled in Dublin. There in 1908, she became active in nationalist politics, joining Sinn Féin, as well as founding Fianna Éireann, a type of boy scout organisation that she trained in military drill.

Demonstrating against the visit of George V to Ireland, Markievicz was jailed for a short period before involving herself in the labour unrest of 1913 and running a soup kitchen for union workers during the Lockout. An ardent supporter of Labour leaders James Larkin and James Connolly (see page 429), she took part in the Easter Rising of 1916 as second in command to Michael Mallin in St Stephen's Green, Dublin and together they held out for a period of six days before finally surrendering to the British forces, who brought her a copy of Patrick Pearse's surrender order. Jailed, Markievicz was placed in solitary confinement where she fully expected to be executed. However, having been sentenced to death, the punishment was later commuted to life imprisonment due to her sex. She was released under the General Amnesty in 1917 and the following year was again jailed, this time in England where she became the first woman to ever be elected to the British parliament when she was nominated as a Sinn Féin candidate.

Later released, upon the formation of Dáil Éireann, Markievicz was appointed the first minister for labour and within that role she vigorously opposed the Anglo-Irish Treaty and the subsequent division of Ireland, on one occasion calling Michael Collins (see page 89) a traitor. Collins replied by calling her something that would cut Markievicz even deeper, 'English'. During the ensuing Civil War, Markievicz helped to defend Moran's Hotel, Talbot Street, and she later toured the United States, seeking funds for the republican cause. Having become a member of the Fianna Fáil party, she was elected as one of its candidates in 1927, but died that same year. Her funeral to Glasnevin Cemetery was followed by approximately three hundred thousand people.

Terence O'Neill
Prime minster of Northern Ireland
1914 – 1990

Terence O'Neill was born at 29 Ennismore Gardens, Hyde Park in London, England. His father was Captain Arthur O'Neill of Shane's Castle, Randalstown, County Antrim and he was educated at West Downs School in Winchester and at Eton College. Having served as an officer in the Irish Guards during World War II, in 1963 he succeeded Lord Brookborough in becoming the prime minister of Northern Ireland. Introducing policies that were unheard of during his predecessor's reign, O'Neill's primary aims were to end sectarianism and to bring Catholics and Protestants together in a harmonious working relationship. To this end, he invited the taoiseach of the Republic of Ireland Seán Lemass (see page 175) for talks in Belfast, which was strongly opposed by members of his own party – Ian Paisley being one of the most stringent objectors. Opposition to his reforms was such that O'Neill's friend George Forrest, a member of parliament for mid-Ulster, was pulled off the platform and kicked unconscious by fellow members of the Orange Order on the 12 July celebrations in Coagh, County Tyrone.

In 1968, faced with the Northern Ireland Civil Rights Association street demonstrations, which signalled the commencement of the troubles in Northern Ireland, O'Neill introduced a five-point reform programme covering a majority of the demands of the Northern Ireland Civil Rights Association. However, the programme did not make provisions for equal voting rights for both Catholics and Protestants, and in 1969 he called a surprise general election due to turmoil inside the Ulster Unionist Party, caused by the proposed reforms. Humiliated by near defeat to Paisley in his own constituency of Bannside some two months later, O'Neill resigned as leader of the Ulster Unionist Party and as prime minister. He once famously stated that 'if you treat Roman Catholics with due consideration and kindness, they will live like Protestants in spite of the authoritative nature of their church.'

A SHORT HISTORY OF IRELAND AND OTHER HISTORICAL EVENTS ASSOCIATED WITH THIS DICTIONARY OF BIOGRAPHY

1169 The Norman Invasion of Ireland

The Norman invasion occurred when, due to a conflict existing between Dermot MacMurrough, King of Leinster, and Tiernan O'Rourke, King of Breifne, MacMurrough invited the Normans to aid him. The Earl of Pembroke, known as Strongbow, arrived in Ireland with a force in excess of 1,500 men and having captured Waterford, he later went on to marry MacMurrough's daughter Aoife. Upon the death of MacMurrough, Strongbow became the King of Leinster. In 1177, the Norman conquest was further enhanced by the arrival of King Henry II. He having a far superior force than the native Irish comprising of knights in armour and skilled archers, further advanced the Norman conquest of Ireland. Gaelic resistance however, was never wholly eliminated, as eight centuries of Anglo-Irish conflict has since proven.

1607 The Flight of the Earls

Hugh O'Neill of Tyrone and Rory O'Donnell of Tyrconnell (Donegal) left Ireland in 1607. Up until the departure of the Earls, English Crown rule in Ireland was haphazard, with many of the original Norman conquerors siding with the Irish, becoming 'more Irish than the Irish themselves'. For a considerable period, England's rule in Ireland was limited to a small tract of land around Dublin known as the Pale, with resistance to the Crown coming principally from the Province of Ulster and the Earls O'Neill and O'Donnell. When the Protestant Queen Elizabeth took the throne in 1558, the passing of the Act of Supremacy proclaimed her Head of the Irish Church. However, the native Gaels and their allies the Old English (Norman ancestors) remained loyal to the Roman Catholic faith.

The Earl O'Neill became loyal to the Crown for a time, but his loyalty was always in doubt and was confirmed as such when he gave succour to the survivors of the Spanish Armada. In 1593 O'Neill, a skilful commander, took the offensive and secured considerable success against Crown forces at the Battle of Yellow Ford in 1598. However, his primary mistake was in 1601 when he left the safety of the virtually impregnable terrain of Tyrone and Donegal with his ally the Earl O'Donnell and marched south some three hundred miles to join a Spanish invading army. His forces were defeated and the loss led to the demise of the O'Neill and O'Donnell reign and the eventual flight of the Earls in 1607.

1610 The Plantation of Ulster

Following the flight of the Earls, the plantation of Ulster began. Having proved itself over the preceeding centuries to be the most resistant of Ireland's provinces to English invasion, Ulster was planted by English and Scottish Protestants who were given the confiscated lands of Catholic Irish landowners principally in the counties of Donegal, Tyrone, Fermanagh, Armagh and Cavan. This was the foundation of a conflict that has lasted into modern times.

1642 The Return of Owen Roe O'Neill to Ireland

A nephew of the Earl Hugh O'Neill, Owen Roe O'Neill parted with his clan as a young boy, going to Spain where he gained forty years experience in the Spanish armies. He returned to Ireland with three hundred veterans to aid an Irish rebellion, and secured a famous victory against Crown forces at the Battle of Benburb on 5 June 1646, capturing three thousand Scottish soldiers who had been led by Major General Robert Monro. Unfortunately, Owen Roe died on 6 November 1649, before he had the opportunity to test his military skills against the man dubbed the butcher of Ireland, Oliver Cromwell.

1649 Cromwell arrives in Ireland

A fanatical Protestant, Cromwell ousted Charles I from the English throne and landed in Dublin with the intention of offering, in his own words, 'no quarter to Papist rebels.' At Drogheda he ordered the death of every man in the town, proclaiming it, 'a righteous judgement of God upon these barbarous wretches.' He then turned south, killing men, women and children in Wexford and Clonmel. Catholic land owners were largely dispossessed during Cromwell's reign of terror, which resulted in the total suppression of the Irish and their religion.

1690 The Battle of the Boyne

In 1688 King James II, a Catholic, had lost his English throne to William Prince of Orange, a Dutch-speaking Protestant, and chose to strike at William through Ireland, with the aid of Louis XIV of France. The French support landed in Kinsale in March 1689 and King James, aided by the Irish army of the Earls of Tyrconnell, controlled most of Ireland. It was however, in the Protestant planted section of Ulster that resistance to James was most effective. April 1689 saw the Apprentice Boys of Derry close the city gates against his Catholic forces and survive for three months of a siege, until reinforcements arrived by sea. William of Orange landed in Carrickfergus in June 1690 with an army of 36,000 at his disposal. He marched for Dublin and on 1 July 1690, he faced the army of Jame, near Drogheda in the now famous Battle of the Boyne. James' 26,000-strong army was defeated and William of Orange entered Dublin on 6 July 1690. Then followed defeat at Aughrim, and finally the Siege of Limerick in 1691, which led again to Protestant ascendancy throughout Ireland.

1775 Grattan's Parliament

The outbreak of rebellion in the American colonies and the oratory skills of Henry Grattan secured Irish parliamentary independence, removing most of the oppressive parts of Poyning's Law, which had allowed for no act of the Irish parliament to be passed without approval by the King of England. Its removal took away constraints by the English Crown on commerce, leading to a more successful period in Irish history, whilst still retaining the Protestant supremacy. This freedom lasted until the Act of Union in 1800.

1793 Catholics Granted the Right to Vote

The Irish Parliament granted voting rights to Catholic property owners. However, as 95 percent of the property was owned by Protestants, the Act was of little advantage to Catholics. In addition, Catholics were not allowed to become MPs.

1798 The Society of United Irishmen

The United Irishmen was founded in Belfast in 1791 by Theobald Wolfe Tone Northern Presbyterians, who had suffered religious discrimination, although to a lesser degree than Catholics, took to Tone's ideals, in which he proclaimed, 'to unite Protestant, Catholic and Dissenter under the common name of Irishman in order to break the connection with England, the never failing source of all our political evils.' Tone sought the aid of the French and a substantial force in the region of 30,000 troops was dispatched but unfortunately prevented from landing near Bantry Bay in County Cork due to severe storms in 1796.

The United Irishmen had set 23 May 1798 as the date of the Rising, but the English government had successfully infiltrated the organisation and most of the leaders, including Lord Edward FitzGerald, were arrested. The counties of Antrim, Down and Wexford were the only areas where serious uprisings took place. Father Murphy and the men of Wexford, though badly equipped, fought bravely to be eventually defeated at Vinegar Hill. In Ulster, the predominantly Presbyterian forces were defeated at Antrim town and at Ballynahinch, County Down, with leaders Henry Joy McCracken and Henry Monroe eventually captured and executed. Presbyterians gave up their reasonably secure lifestyles and many sacrificed their lives in the interest of Irish freedom. Their contribution was indeed immense.

Wolfe Tone, who had gone to France, returned with a much smaller French force under General Humbert. They landed at Killala Bay on 23 August 1798 but were defeated by superior forces under the leadership of Marquis Cornwalis. Tone was captured in October aboard a French ship in Lough Swilly. He was court-martialled in Dublin and he committed suicide when he was refused a soldier's death by firing squad.

1801 The Act of Union

The Act of Union was established between Britain and Ireland on 1 January 1801. Ireland was allocated one hundred MPs in the House of Commons, London, but Catholics were still prevented from becoming MPs, and were excluded from public office.

1829 Catholic Emancipation

Daniel O'Connell, a brilliant Catholic orator and a man totally adverse to violence, formed the Catholic Association to campaign for Catholic emancipation, which was vehemently opposed by the English Crown, and in particular by King George III. It was eventually granted in 1829 by the government, which was led by the Duke of Wellington, with King George IV reluctantly signing the Act.

435

1845 The Great Famine

At this time, the potato formed the staple diet of 95 percent of Irish people. When potato blight struck and crops failed, some one million people died and another one million emigrated, mainly to America. Amongst those would be the great grandfather of the future president of America, John F. Kennedy. They sailed in what were known as coffin ships. The failure of the government in London to act decisively in respect of the famine left an enduring legacy of bitterness in Ireland.

1848 The Young Irelanders

A small, well-educated group of revolutionaries known as the Young Irelanders was founded in the midst of the great famine of 1848. Amongst them were Thomas Francis Meagher (Waterford) and William Smith O'Brien (Clare), who gave Ireland its national flag. Yet again government agents infiltrated the organisation, with most members arrested and deported to Tasmania for life. Many of them eventually escaped to America.

1858 The Fenians

Stemming from the foundation of the Irish Republican Brotherhood in Dublin in March 1858, the Fenian Brotherhood was a mainly American-based organisation and included many of the escaped Young Irelanders. Their aim was to raise funds in support of uprisings in Ireland and they also formed an escape committee which organised the escape from Freemantle Gaol in Australia, known as The Catalpa Rescue. They were also responsible for the attempted invasion of the British-ruled states of Canada, which was initially condoned by the American government but eventually suppressed.

1879 The Land League

With the spectre of yet another famine looming in Ireland and tenant farmers being evicted en masse, Michael Davitt (Mayo) founded the National Land League, with Charles Stewart Parnell (Wicklow) as its first president. Strong financial backing from America through the Fenians, now called Clan Na Gael, helped publish the evils of absentee landlords who were living in luxury and principally in London, whilst their tenants faced eviction and starvation. Based on non-violent protests, the League's action against Captain Charles Boycott in County Mayo led to the word 'boycott' entering the English language.

1911-14 Ulster says No

The greatest opposition to home rule came from the Protestants in Ulster when their new leader, Sir Edward Carson proclaimed in 1911, 'we will take over the government of Ulster if the Home Rule Bill is passed for Ireland.' In 1913 the Ulster Unionist Council announced the formation of the Ulster Volunteer Force, amounting to some 90,000 men with 35,000 rifles and ammunition secured from Germany. Outright defiance of the London government by the Ulster unionists was proclaimed. With the outbreak of World War I, all that was to change.

1914 Home Rule

William Gladstone was the first prime minister in English history to recognise the injustices that existed in respect to Ireland, stating on his appointement, 'my mission is to pacify Ireland.' He first implemented the separation of the Church of Ireland from state involvement, particularly as the Church represented no more than 15 percent of the population. In 1873, the Home Rule League was founded by, amongst others, Charles Stewart Parnell, a wealthy Protestant landowner. His obstructionist tactics in the London Parliament forced the government to attend to Irish grievances. Following much work by Gladstone, with Parnell's aid, the Home Rule Bill became law in 1914. However, it was agreed that due to the outbreak of World War I, it should not be implemented until after the war. By 1918 other events would change the course of this.

1916 The Easter Rising

On 24 April, outside the GPO in Dublin, Patrick Pearse announced the establishment of an Irish Republic. With Britain at war in Europe it was felt that in England's difficulties lay Ireland's opportunity. British forces quickly suppressed the rising, however fifteen of its leaders were tried by military courts and executed almost immediately. This would prove to be one of the greatest mistakes in British history. The Easter Rising had little support in Ireland, particularly among the some 300,000 Irishmen fighting under the British flag in Europe, of which 50,000 never returned home. The executions changed everything. There was an outcry of public revulsion at the executions, the beneficiaries of which were Sinn Féin, who in the elections of 1918 secured 73 of the 105 parliamentary seats, following which, on 21 January 1919, they set up the Assembly of Ireland, known as Dáil Éireann ireann, declaring Irish Independence.

1919-21 The War of Independence

The fight for independence was principally led by Michael Collins (Cork), who had fought in the Easter Rising and was imprisoned for some time in Wales. Collins formed an elaborate intelligence unit and a special death squad that would become the scourge of British Intelligence and British officials in Ireland. This he combined with a strategy of making the country ungovernable, forming flying columns (units comprising in the region of twenty to thirty men) throughout the country, adapting hit-and-run tactics against the police and the British military, which eventually led to a truce in July 1921, with treaty negotiations following.

The Irish delegation to treaty negotiations in London was led by Arthur Griffith and Michael Collins and following extensive discussions, Lloyd George, the British prime minister of the day, made a final offer of a twenty-six county Irish Free State, with the six northern counties containing a unionist majority remaining in union with Britain. Having added that refusal to accept such terms would result in Britain resuming hostilities in Ireland, the delegation accepted the treaty and returned to Ireland where a Dáil vote of sixty-four to fifty-seven accepted the Treaty.

1922-23 The Civil War in Ireland

De Valera refused to accept the Treaty, which resulted in a violent civil war during which Michael Collins was killed, and the pro-Treaty forces were victorious.

The Aftermath

The six northern counties known as Ulster (although Ulster comprises nine counties) with a unionist majority became a dominated statelet where Catholics and nationalists were considerably restricted in all walks of life. The policy of one man, one vote, which was the norm throughout Britain, was not introduced until the 1970s. Such restrictions forced the British Parliament in London to abolish the unionist Parliament of Northern Ireland, following an upsurge of IRA violence, and eventually led to a compromising agreement between unionists and nationalists, with the British government undertaking that Ireland will be united when a majority so desires in the six counties.

OTHER DATES IN HISTORY ASSOCIATED WITH CHARACTERS IN THIS DICTIONARY OF BIOGRAPHY

1775-83 The American Revolution (or The American War of Independence)

On 4 July 1776, a provisional government proclaimed independence of the thirteen colonies (a section of America stretching from Massachusetts to Georgia) with final victory coming at Saratoga in 1777 for the Continental army (American Army) and Yorktown in 1781, resulting in the formation of the United States of America.

1810-1824 The South Americas

Columbia, Ecuador, Peru, Venezuela, Panama and Bolivia can attribute their independence from Spain to the liberator, Simon Bolivar (1783-1830), who was born in Caracuas, Venezuala. His Aid-de-Camp was General Daniel O'Leary (Cork). The foremost battalion in Bolivia's army was the Black Rifles, led by General Arthur Sandes (Kerry). General Francis Burdett O'Connor (Cork) is credited with formulating the strategy for the final battle at Agacucho, which ended the Spanish rule in these territories. Argentina's foremost independence leader was Admiral William Browne (Mayo) whose seamanship finalised Spanish rule in Argentina. Chile saw its liberation from Spanish rule executed by Bernardo O'Higgins, the son of Ambrose O'Higgins, (Sligo), with John MacKenna (Monaghan) being acclaimed as the co-liberator of Chile. Bartholomew Hayden (Tipperary) offered his services in the liberation of Brazil from the Portuguese. Commander Bartholomew Hayden was one of the major figures in Brazil's independence from Portugal. Peter Campbell (Tipperary) the Uruguayan freedom fighter, was also the founder of the Uruguayan Navy.

1853-56 The Crimean War

The Crimean War was fought between Russia on one side and France, Britain and the Ottoman Empire (Turkey) on the other. It was mainly fought on the Crimean Peninsula in the Black Sea and Western Turkey. War, which was declared on 12 March 1854, was mainly over the authority of the Holy Land. Many Irish fought in the conflict, and were awarded a considerable number of Victoria Crosses, with Sebastopol, the capital of the Crimea, being the centre of military action.

1857-58 Indian Mutiny

The Mutiny began when Indian soldiers known as Sepoys, who were in the service of the East India Company (a massive export company who were responsible for the colonisation of India and were in effect, the English authority in India with the necessary troops to back that authority) revolted against British rule in India. The company was abolished and rule was assumed directly by the British Crown thereafter.

1861-65 The American Civil War

The Civil War commenced with the southern (slave) states declaring their secession from the Union. Hostilities began on 12 April 1861 and lasted four years, in which 620,000 men died. The Union states, under the presidency of Abraham Lincoln, were eventually victorious. In excess of 100,000 Irish troops fought in the war, mainly on the Union side, with the Irish Brigade (the Fighting 69th), led for some time by Thomas Francis Meagher (Waterford), to the fore. Some fifteen Union Generals and five Federal Generals were Irish born. The war resulted in the end of slavery in America and the formation of the United States as it is today.

1899-1902 The Second Boer War

The Second Boer War was the culmination of two centuries of conflict between the Afrikaners (Dutch settlers in South Africa) and the British. It lasted three years, with the loss of some 75,000 lives, 22,000 of which were British. Seventy-eight Victoria Crosses were awarded during the conflict, and field marshals Kitchener (Kerry) and Roberts (of Waterford ancestry), gained infamy for setting up the first concentration camps in the history of the world, in which up to 40,000 men, women and children lost their lives through starvation. It was English woman Emily Hobhouse who brought the scandal of the concentration camps to the note of the British public. Whilst there were many Irish in the British Army serving in the Boer War, the Boers were strongly supported by Irish settlers in South Africa, and the Irish Brigade, under the command of John MacBride (Mayo) saw considerable action during the conflict, which was won by the British.

1914-18 World War I

On 28 June 1914, the assassination of the heir to the Austro-Hungarian throne, Archduke Franz Ferdinand, by a Bosnian Serb sparked a chain of events that led to most of Europe becoming involved in conflict. With France, the United Kingdom, Russia and later Italy and the United States uniting against Germany and Austria-Hungary, the conflict became a global war. Over 40 million casualties, including 20 million military and civilian deaths, were the end result of this terrible war, which resulted in the drawing of the map of Europe. Germany lost its colonial possessions and the Austro-Hungarian and Ottoman empires were completely dissolved. Ireland had 300,000 troops, all volunteers, serving under the British flag and 50,000 of them never returned home.

1939-45 World War II

This was a global military conflict commencing in 1939 with the invasion of Poland by Germany. Most European countries fell into the hands of Germany reasonably quickly, with Britain putting up a dogged fight on their behalf. In this, the deadliest conflict in human history, over 70 million people, the majority of which were civilians, were killed. Whilst British defence against the might of Germany was profound, it was the German mistake of attacking Russia, as well as the entry of the United States, that finally led to victory for the allies in 1945. Here again, over 50,000 Irishmen, all volunteers, fought on the British side, and of note is Brendan Finucane (Dublin), Britain's number two fighter ace during the Battle of Britain, and with Major General Eric 'Chink' Dorman-Smith (Cavan), one of two generals responsible for breaking the back of Rommel's forces in North Africa.

INDEX

Great Irish People

MY THANKS TO THE FOLLOWING:

Professor John Alward (for historical corrections), Dublin

Adel Burke, Photographer, Dublin

James Cline, Art Collector, Limerick City

Sister Redempta Connolly, The Missionary Sisters of the Holy Rosary

Joe Delaney, Galway (contributor)

Earl Taylor, President Dorchester Historical Society, Dorchester, USA

Ed Larkin, Dublin (contributor)

Corinne Murphy, Los Angeles (contributor)

Sean O'Leary, Publicist (for assistance in compilation), Cork

Manus O'Riordan, SIPTU, Dublin

The Principle (2008) of Lagan College, Belfast

Padraig Slattery (for information on Dr Tim Mahony), Dublin

Marilyn and Gerald Shatwell (typing of complete script)

Helge Schneem Best Photos Ireland (for image contributions)

John Brady and Irish Decal Products Ltd. for county crests

Jason Moran (pre-edit)

SPECIAL DEDICATION

To my wife Vera, (née Gillespie), for her encouragement and support, and the hours spent in solitude whilst I delved the annals of history, in accomplishing this work.

www.greatirishpeople.com